ADDRESSING DIVERSITY IN LITERACY INSTRUCTION

D1424050

LITERACY RESEARCH, PRACTICE AND EVALUATION

Series Editors: Evan Ortlieb and Earl H. Cheek, Jr.

Previous Volumes:

LITERACY RESEARCH, PRACTICE
AND EVALUATION   VOLUME 8

ADDRESSING DIVERSITY IN LITERACY INSTRUCTION

BY

EVAN ORTLIEB

St. John's University, New York, NY, USA

EARL H. CHEEK, JR.

Louisiana State University, Baton Rouge, LA, USA

United Kingdom – North America – Japan
India – Malaysia – China

Emerald Publishing Limited
Howard House, Wagon Lane, Bingley BD16 1WA, UK

First edition 2018

British Library Cataloguing in Publication Data
A catalogue record for this book is available from the British Library

ISBN: 978-1-78714-049-3 (Print)
ISBN: 978-1-78714-048-6 (Online)
ISBN: 978-1-78714-908-3 (Epub)

ISSN: 2048-0458 (Series)

Printed and bound by CPI Group (UK) Ltd, Croydon, CR0 4YY

ISOQAR certified
Management System,
awarded to Emerald
for adherence to
Environmental
standard
ISO 14001:2004.

Certificate Number 1985
ISO 14001

INVESTOR IN PEOPLE

CONTENTS

FOREWORD

Addressing diversity in literacy instruction is a cornerstone to being an effective educator. Notions of diversity are ever-changing and expanding in the global contexts in which we teach. Equitable learning opportunities are created through seeing students as unique learners, primed to achieve through building on their prior knowledge, previous experiences, and ways of seeing the world. In re-envisioning diversity as an advantage in the classroom, we can position ourselves to learn from our students and view them as resources to the learning process. The global contexts that define classrooms and workplaces today demand more from teachers and as such, literacy leaders are needed more than ever.

To meet these evolving needs, this edited book showcases chapters on leveraging native languages towards English language proficiency. Moreover, other chapters provide multicultural perspectives on the sociocultural dynamics that comprise teaching English and grammar; literacy pedagogies for K-12 diverse learners are also discussed through a lens of building on students' funds of knowledge. Some chapters provide a foundation for globally connected literacy instruction inclusive of selecting and using appropriate literature that depicts the diverse world in which we live; and finally other chapters highlight how culturally relevant pedagogical frameworks can address diversity in proactive and productive ways that optimize learning opportunities for all learners.

Evan Ortlieb

EDITOR BIOGRAPHIES

Evan Ortlieb is a Professor and Coordinator of the Literacy Program in the Department of Education Specialties at St. John's University in New York City, USA. His expertise includes addressing literacy improvement, literacy teacher preparation, language diversity, and differentiated literacy instruction.

Earl H. Cheek, Jr. is the Patrick and Edwidge Olinde Endowed Professor Emeritus in the Department of Educational Theory, Policy, and Practice at Louisiana State University, USA. As a lifelong literacy leader, he has published widely across fields of content area reading, reading teacher education, diagnostic-perspective methods, and dyslexia.

LIST OF CONTRIBUTORS

Jackie Marshall Arnold	University of Dayton, Dayton, OH, USA
Sally Brown	Georgia Southern University, Statesboro, GA, USA
Sarah Catto	Spartanburg County School District Six, Spartanburg, SC, USA and Charleston County School District, Charleston, SC, USA
Earl H. Cheek, Jr.	Louisiana State University, Baton Rouge, LA, USA
Kristal Moore Clemons	Florida State University, Tallahassee, FL, USA
Debra Coffey	Kennesaw State University, Kennesaw, GA, USA
Rick Coppola	University of Illinois at Chicago, Chicago, IL, USA
Jacqueline Darvin	Queens College, Queens, NY, USA
Autumn M. Dodge	Lynchburg College, Lynchburg, VA, USA and St John's University, Queens, NY, USA
Tess Dussling	St. John's University, Queens, NY, USA
Douglas Fisher	San Diego State University, San Diego, CA, USA
Nancy Frey	San Diego State University, San Diego, CA, USA
Leslie Foley	Grand Canyon University, Phoenix, AZ, USA
Barbara Guzzetti	Arizona State University, Tempe, AZ, USA
Shea Kerkhoff	Purdue University, West Lafayette, IN, USA
Nancy Laguna Luque	Ministry of Education Language Centre, Singapore, Singapore
Emily Machado	University of Illinois at Chicago, Chicago, IL, USA

Keely Norris   North Florida Freedom Schools, Tallahassee,
                         FL, USA

Evan Ortlieb   St. John's University, Queens, NY, USA

Jodi Louise Pilgrim   University of Mary Hardin-Baylor, Belton,
                         TX, USA

Alysia D. Roehrig   Florida State University, Tallahassee, FL, USA

Mary-Kate Sableski   University of Dayton, Dayton, OH, USA

Wally Thompson   Eastern New Mexico University, Portales,
                         NM, USA

Andrea Vaughan   University of Illinois at Chicago, Chicago, IL, USA

Angela Kris Ward   University of Mary Hardin-Baylor, Belton, TX,
                         USA

Rebecca Woodard   University of Illinois at Chicago, Chicago, IL, USA

TOWARD EQUITY THROUGH OPPORTUNITIES TO LEARN LITERACY

Nancy Frey and Douglas Fisher

ABSTRACT

To identify actions, teachers and school leaders can take to ensure equity in terms of opportunities to learn literacy. We reviewed the professional literature in four major areas, including opportunity to learn (OTL), student mobility and its impact on learning, grade-level retention and its impact on equity and future success, and systems that can provide students access to complex text. We note the value of each of these four constructs (OTL, mobility, retention, and access to complex texts) in ensuring that schools become increasingly equitable such that all students develop as literate members of society. We provide classroom and school-based examples for readers to consider as they work toward equity. Far too many schools are inequitable and some students fail to develop their literate lives. We provide ideas and actions that teachers and school teams can take to ensure that diverse students have the best chance possible to learn.

Keywords: Opportunities to learn; mobility; literacy; retention; close reading

Addressing Diversity in Literacy Instruction
Literacy Research, Practice and Evaluation, Volume 8, 1–15
Copyright © 2018 by Emerald Publishing Limited
All rights of reproduction in any form reserved
ISSN: 2048-0458/doi:10.1108/S2048-045820170000008001

Issues of equity continue to plague education, despite concerted efforts to change the trajectory of student learning (Jimenez-Castellanos, 2010). Yet inequitable distributions of human and academic resources persist, and are felt most keenly within the classroom itself. Although widely acknowledged as a key to expanding the lives of children and adolescents, too many students are denied access to literacy supports that foster knowledge acquisition, critical thinking, and inquiry. Access to such supports requires examination of structures that inhibit the achievement of some students, especially those in historically low achieving schools and districts. What is necessary is a deep examination of the research on opportunities to learn as it intersects with issues of equity and literacy (Lafontaine, Baye, Vieluf, & Monseur, 2015).

Equity stands in stark contrast to equality. An equality mindset is focused on ensuring that everyone gets the same resources and experiences. But an equality mindset is predicated on the faulty assumption that students arrive at our classroom doors with similar strengths and needs. In contrast, an equity perspective begins with the knowledge that students come to us with a range of experiences and resources that must be leveraged to benefit their learning, but that might also require a redistribution of resources to accomplish this. A core value of an equity-focused classroom, school, and district is that unequal needs require unequal resources.

In this chapter, we begin with a definition of opportunity to learn (OTL) and further explore this construct across two dimensions: instructional time and degree of complexity of materials, concepts, and skills. Next, we examine the negative impact high student mobility rates and in-grade retention practices have on literacy learning, as well as the ways in which schools can ameliorate these effects. We then turn our attention to providing access to complex texts and tasks. Differential levels of OTL begin in the primary grades, as is evidenced in comparative time and curricular analyses reveal that while some children receive literacy instruction focused on critical thinking, those who are not making expected progress are relegated to discrete skills training (Allington & McGill-Franzen, 1989; Phelps, Corey, DeMonte, Harrison, & Loewenberg Ball, 2012). These detrimental effects are later evidenced in advanced course enrolment in high school, as too many historically under-taught students have been inadequately prepared to take challenging classes.

Equity in literacy education requires action. We are reminded of a slogan we have seen on T-shirts: "I don't have a solution, but I certainly admire the problem." In this chapter and throughout this book, we and other authors make recommendations for taking action to solve complex issues in literacy education as it relates to equity. Our own recommendations for remedying inequitable opportunities to learn are as follows:

1. Reverse the effects of mobility to ensure students are not losing valuable ground.
2. Channel resources for early intervention in literacy development and eliminate in-grade retention practices.
3. Provide high-quality literacy instruction that provides access to complex texts.

EQUITY AND OPPORTUNITY TO LEARN

The OTL is "the degree to which a student experiences classroom instruction, including a variety of approaches that address a range of cognitive processes, teaching practices, and grouping formats" (Heafner & Fitchett, 2015, p. 228).

Children in every classroom experience instruction differently. One differential factor in the OTL is time distribution. A case in point: a teacher devotes 20 minutes a day for independent reading. Some children in the class only need to hear "Take out your book..." and it is immediately in front of them. That child will probably use upwards of 19.5 of those minutes with eyes on text. But his classmate a few feet away is dragging himself to the bookshelf, listlessly picking a book, and flipping a few pages, then putting it back on the shelf. In the same 20-minute span, he has only had his eyes on text for 4 minutes. In this hypothetical classroom, the time allotted (20 minutes) differed in use in significant and cumulative ways (anywhere 4–19.5 minutes). Without teacher intervention, the second child will systematically experience far fewer opportunities to build reading fluency and stamina, following further behind his classmates (Stanovich, 1986).

Time considerations for English language arts (ELA) instruction are further amplified across the entire school year. A large-scale study of time allotted for ELA instruction in 112 elementary schools engaged in comprehensive school reform found that while the average number of minutes was 101, the range was anywhere from 74 to 129 minutes. The problems for schools in the lowest range were further compounded by student and teacher absences, thereby reducing the probability a student might receive ELA instruction on a given day as low as 58% (Phelps et al., 2012).

The OTL is further impacted by the relative complexity of the texts being utilized to teach. Previous studies have found that young children's contact with informational texts, while abysmal for all, was even scarcer for those living in poverty compared to their peers in high SES schools (Duke, 2000). This lack of knowledge building has a profound impact on reading comprehension, especially for those who are identified as English learners (Lesaux & Kieffer, 2010). An analysis of the 2009 Program for International Student Assessment (PISA) data from more than 70 countries found that relative access to complex texts and tasks had an impact on the 15-year-olds' learning, with the authors stating that "Students attending schools with a less privileged social intake are more exposed to impoverished OTL in reading (less demanding texts and tasks)" (LaFontaine et al., 2015, p. 8). In the US, Education Trust analyzed more than 1,500 ELA assignments given to middle school students in six schools to determine the amount of text-based and cognitively challenging work students were doing. They defined high-quality assignments across four domains: (1) aligned to grade-level standards; (2) centrality of text; (3) cognitively challenging; and (4) motivating and engaging. Their analysis revealed that only 5% of the assignments met these criteria, with 85% requiring recall and reproduction only, the lowest level of cognitive challenge (Education Trust, 2015). Similarly, an analysis of the reported practices of more than 2,000 K-12 ELA teachers found that cognitive demand in their classes and courses had changed during the first decade of this century, with significant decline within schools serving high poverty, historically marginalized groups (Polikoff & Struthers, 2013). Without time with complex texts, and associated tasks that are cognitively challenging, we cannot hope to foster the knowledge acquisition, critical thinking, and inquiry that students need to achieve their true potential.

In the remainder of this chapter, we provide evidence-based recommendations for changing the OTL in literacy that students' experience. We focus on three actions that can be address: mobility, grade-level retention, and access to complex texts.

REDUCE THE IMPACT OF MOBILITY ON STUDENTS' LITERACY LEARNING

Changing schools is harmful, and it is especially impactful, in a negative way, to students who are already at risk for school failure (Dauter & Fuller, 2016). Unfortunately, the students who change schools a lot are often those who live in poverty. Students from traditionally under-represented groups, who now represent the majority enrolment in urban schools, also move more frequently than their White, middle-class, and suburban counterparts (McDonough, 2015). And students who are homeless, the majority of whom are African-American and Latino/Hispanic students, change schools more than any other group (Cowen, 2017). Homeless students move more frequently across district and state lines than their non-homeless peers who more frequently move within the same district to new schools (Cowen, 2017).

Mehana (1997) conducted a meta-analysis of the impact of mobility on students' literacy learning and found a *negative* effect of 0.27. This is a significant impact in the world of effect sizes. Hattie (2009) has collected thousands of meta-analyses and has ranked almost 200 influences on students' learning. According to his estimates, an effect size of 0.40 is equivalent to 1 year of learning for 1 year of schooling. When all of the studies on mobility are aggregated, the impact is –0.34 – that is negative 0.34 – or the loss of nearly 1 year of learning over the course of the year (Hattie, 2009). In fact, considering Hattie's list of nearly 200 influences, mobility has the greatest negative impact on students' learning. Yet it's rarely discussed and almost never included in efforts to create equitable learning for all students. To our thinking, mobility has to be a part of every literacy improvement effort and schools and districts should include efforts to minimize the impact that mobility has on student learning in every school improvement plan. There are several things that schools can do to reduce the impact that mobility has on students' literacy learning, including the following steps.

Implement a Guaranteed and Viable Curriculum

As DuFour and Marzano (2011) noted, there are two parts to a guaranteed and viable curriculum: "The fact that it is guaranteed assures us that specific content is taught in specific courses and at specific grade levels, regardless of the teacher to whom a student is assigned. The fact that it is viable indicates that there is enough instructional time available to actually teach the content identified as important" (p. 91). We are not suggesting that schools invest in prescriptive or scripted curriculum for reading and language arts, but rather that there are reasonable and clear expectations for what students will learn and by when (e.g., Marzano, 2003). Without this, students who move schools during the year have gaps and redundancies in their educational experiences, which contribute to their lack of learning and achievement. When districts and schools implement a guaranteed and viable literacy curriculum, teachers can still innovate instructionally. They can select materials that are culturally appropriate as well as materials that introduce students to other cultures, times, places, and people. Having a guaranteed and viable curriculum ensures that all students have an equitable chance to master content.

Ensure that Receiving Teachers have Accurate Information about the Learning Profile of the New Student

There are a number of ways that school systems can make sure that teachers have immediate and accurate literacy learning information about new students that enroll (e.g., Titus, 2007). Until school records are fully digital, waiting for the students' cumulative folder is not an effective approach. Instead, some schools schedule an orientation day for new students that include screening information about literacy skills. Other schools collect information from the sending teacher immediately upon enrolment. In more sophisticated school systems, there is an electronic data summary tool that the sending teacher provides for the receiving teacher. This tool includes information about the students' current performance as well as areas of focus for the student and key concepts mastered. The key is providing the classroom teacher with actionable information so that learning time is maximized. In too many cases, teachers spend the first several weeks of a new enrollee's time learning about the student's instructional needs, wasting time that could have been spent focused on new learning. Imagine a student who has mastered 100 sight words, but whose new teacher does not know that. It could be weeks before the student is challenged to learn more. Contrast that situation with the experience of Hamza who has not yet demonstrated mastery on topic sentences in writing but who was receiving targeted instruction in this area. When he was forced to change schools, his sending teacher provided the receiving teacher detailed information, and she was able to pick up on Hamza's writing instruction immediately.

Facilitate Social Relationships

As Galton (1995) noted, when students develop close, personal friendships within the first few weeks of enrolling in a new school, the negative impact of mobility is reduced significantly. Boon (2011) has noted that providing students social support such that they could engage productively with others reduced the impact that mobility has on students' learning. It may seem beyond the scope of this book, which focuses on literacy learning, but lack of friendships and other social relationships have a powerful, but negative, impact on students' literacy learning. Teachers must facilitate social relationships with and for their students, especially those who are new to the classroom, if they want students to develop as literate citizens. As Hattie (2009) states, "Whenever there is a major transition in schools, then the key success factor is whether a child makes a friend in the first month" (p. 82). These social relationships seem to reduce the affective barriers to learning that accumulate as students move. The more often students have moved, the more likely these barriers are to exist and the greater the need is to immediately remove them. It seems so simple to say that when children and youth feel safe, secured, and cared about by peers and adults, they learn a lot more.

As we noted in the Introduction to this section, mobility is an area of need in the world of literacy for diverse learners. Too many students move and are anonymous. They do not develop friendships and other social relationships, and the lessons they experience are not tailored to their needs. In some cases, the teacher did not even know that a new student was arriving and did not have a seat, much less instructional materials, ready for that student. Imagine what that communicates to the individual who is already worried about fitting in. We can do better at addressing mobility, which will improve students' social wellbeing, and in turn their literacy learning.

ELIMINATE RETENTION AND CHANNEL RESOURCES FOR EARLY INTERVENTION

Teachers and administrators who want to deliver on the promise of equity in literacy must interrogate their grade-level retention policies. Holding students back is not an effective practice and contributes negatively to students' overall learning (Hattie, 2009; Jimerson & Kaufman, 2003). Yes, you read that correctly. The accumulated evidence indicates that repeating a grade is negatively correlated with learning. The overall effect size across subject areas of retaining students is –0.16, but in language arts the effect is –0.36 and in reading it is –0.54 (Jimerson, 2001). In other words, "failing" students and requiring that they repeat a grade does not result in improved learning, and does, in fact, harm their learning and contribute in significant ways to the drop-out problem (Foster, 1993).

In addition to the obvious psychological impact on the learner of failing and being retained, there are social influences at play that likely contribute to the negative impact. In terms of the psychological impact, students who are retained exhibit signs of stress and behavioral challenges in the years that follow their retention (Shepard & Smith, 1989). Retained students also have fewer friends (Demanet & Van Houtte, 2016). Importantly, once a teacher considers retention, that teacher reduces his or her focus on the student and instead focuses on other students who need help in the class. Further, once parents have agreed to have their child retained, they alter and lower their expectations for their child. As Holmes (1989) noted, educators would be hard-pressed to find another practice that was so unequivocally negative.

Yet the practice persists. In some states (e.g., Iowa, Florida), there is legislation demanding grade-level retention of students. The reason that we bring this to the forefront in a book about equity for diverse learners is that retention policies are not enacted in equitable, or even equal, ways. If grade-level retention were an effective practice, everyone would use it, students would learn more, and there would be few demographic differences in the application. That simply is not true. If you consider two students with the same academic achievement level, African-American and Latino/Hispanic students are four times more likely to be retained when compared to their White counterparts (Meisels & Liaw, 1993). And what data are schools using to retain the vast majority of students? Reading scores. Although some well-meaning educators suggest retention for students' social and emotional development, those same students do not score well on reading assessments. Literacy is the gatekeeper for many to progress to the next grade.

As further evidence that retention policies are not implemented in an equitable way, Warren and Saliba (2012) developed a method for determining retention rates. Overall, the average retention rate for first grade in the United States was 3.5%, or nearly one student in every classroom every year. Having said that, there are significant differences by state, with the Northern Plains having rates for first-grade retention that are essentially 0, whereas southern states have rates that exceed 5% per year. It seems that geography is one of the factors that contribute to retention.

The alternative is called social promotion and has been widely criticized, and advocates for reducing retention are told that they have low standards and expectations. There does not have to be a dichotomy between retention and social promotion. As Protheroe (2007) noted, there are a number of actions that teachers and schools can take as an alternative to retention. When students are identified as being at risk in their literacy development, additional instruction and interventions should immediately be activated. According to Hattie (2012), the effect size of response to intervention is 1.07. That's worth the effort. Retention is easy – push the problem out to a future year, despite the evidence that nothing will change for the student academically. RTI is harder because it takes a coordinated, schoolwide effort to ensure that students learn and develop. But it works. RTI involves supplemental and intensive interventions in literacy, delivered by experts who understand literacy development. It requires that students are monitored as they participate in intervention efforts and that intervention efforts are adjusted when they are not working.

In addition to RTI, the National Association of School Psychologists developed a position statement on retention (Center for Development and Learning, 2003). They do not support it. Instead, they offer the following list of recommendations as alternatives:

- Encourage parents' involvement in their children's schools and education through frequent contact with teachers.
- Adopt age-appropriate and culturally sensitive instructional strategies that accelerate progress in all classrooms.
- Emphasize the importance of early developmental programs and preschool programs to enhance language and social skills.
- Incorporate systematic assessment strategies, including continuous progress monitoring and formative evaluation, to enable ongoing modification of instructional efforts.
- Provide effective early reading programs.
- Implement effective school-based mental health programs.
- Use student support teams to assess and identify specific learning or behavior problems, design interventions to address those problems, and evaluate the efficacy of those interventions.
- Use effective behavior management and cognitive behavior modification strategies to reduce classroom behavior problems.
- Provide appropriate education services for children with educational disabilities, including collaboration between regular, remedial, and special education professionals.
- Offer extended year, extended day, and summer school programs that focus on facilitating the development of academic skills.
- Implement tutoring and mentoring programs with peer, cross-age, or adult tutors.
- Incorporate comprehensive schoolwide programs to promote the psychosocial and academic skills of all students.
- Establish full-service schools to provide a community-based vehicle for the organization and delivery of educational, social, and health services to meet the diverse needs of at-risk students.

In sum, retention is not an effective literacy intervention, and this unwise practice is being implemented in disproportionate ways such that some students are held back at higher rates. In fact, we could argue that retention in some schools, districts, and states has become institutionalized racism, in that it is supported by the social organization, and members of specific racial/ethnic groups are impacted. And it exacerbates and compounds the literacy problem as students fall further behind.

PROVIDE HIGH-QUALITY LITERACY INSTRUCTION THAT ENSURES ACCESS TO COMPLEX TEXTS

We live in southern California, a region known worldwide for its epic traffic problems. Therefore, we spend lots of time sitting on freeways, contemplating the world. A feature common to all freeways is the access ramp, which allows vehicles to reach a sufficient speed so they can safely merge with traffic flow. We think of access to complex texts similarly, with challenging texts bearing similarity to the freeway, and instructional practices as the access ramps. High-quality literacy instruction must always keep challenging texts in mind, as we use a specific set of practices to get students safely up to speed. These practices are not confined to ELA classrooms, but instead are just as effective in secondary content classrooms. Importantly, they are a cohesive system for accessing complex texts, and are not instructional approaches done infrequently and in isolation (Fisher & Frey, 2016).

Learning Intentions

Students benefit from clear learning intentions that signal the purpose for learning and their criteria for success (Hattie, 2009). It is difficult to approach a challenging text without knowing why one is doing so or for what purpose. Is the goal to learn the content, to practice a new strategy, or to engage in a debate? It begins with stating the *content purpose* ("Today we're going to read an article about how your brain works when you taste something"), the *language purpose* ("We'll read this several times, and you'll discuss it with your table"), the *social purpose* ("Remember to listen to the ideas of others so you can build on them with your comments"), and the success criteria ("You'll know you have learned this when you can explain the sequence to your shoulder partner using the diagram in the article"). These purposes are returned to throughout the lesson so that students can reorient, and at the end of the lesson, self-assess.

Teacher Modeling and Think Alouds

How we understand written texts is entirely within the mind of the reader or the writer. It is difficult for children and adolescents to make assumptions about the cognitive and meta-cognitive processes someone else is using when these are not visible to the observer. Modeling and thinking aloud about the reading comprehension processes, we are using or discarding these decisions making apparent to students. These verbalizations are planned, and not simply off-the-cuff statements. Think-aloud techniques are used to demonstrate a host of comprehension strategies such as how one monitors comprehension ("That was a complicated paragraph. I'm not sure I understood it. I'm going to go back and read it again"), or making inferences ("That statement caught my eye. The author told earlier that you don't taste with your taste buds, but with your brain. I am seeing that the signals from those cells link between the two"). Other think-aloud approaches are used to the model making connections, resolving unknown vocabulary, determining importance, and visualizing and organizing information. McClintock, Pesco, and Martin-Chang (2014) found the think-aloud approach for comprehension was especially useful for children with language impairments, as it resulted in improved ability for the student to derive literal and inferential meaning from texts. In this chapter, we demonstrated the positive impact that think alouds had on students' literacy development (Fisher, Frey, & Lapp, 2011).

Close Reading

Close reading is an instructional routine intended to foster text-based discussion and deep comprehension of complex texts, with the teacher guiding thinking rather than telling students what to think. This approach is dialogic and is anchored by text-dependent questions that cause students to reread, use evidence, and critically analyze the reading. These text-dependent questions move students through three phases of understanding. The first phase focuses on the literal-level meaning of the text through questions about the general understanding and key details (*What does the text say?*). The second phase poses structural questions about the vocabulary, word choice, organization, and author's craft (*How does the text work?*). Once student have a solid understanding of the text's literal meaning and organization, the third phase of critical and inferential analysis begins, especially by examining intention, intertextual links, and discussion of the arguments (*What does the text mean?*). Systematic movement through these phases has been shown to be effective for middle-school students who are not yet reading at expected levels (Fisher & Frey, 2014).

Scaffolding Reading with More Complex Texts

As students move out of the primary grades, their experiences with texts should reflect their evolving ability to handle more complex texts. Small group reading instruction remains of great value, but the texts themselves should change from those that scaffold the foundational skills of decoding, to those that offer more challenging content. The debate over the use of reading levels has been a contentious one, but there is agreement that reading instruction requires more than simply matching readers and text and then hoping for the best. Engagement, interest, and motivation play an important role in what children can read and comprehend, and in their ability to manage their cognitive resources. In fact, student interest appears to have a moderating effect on text difficulty and aids in the self-regulation required in reading (Fulmer, D'Mello, Strain, & Graesser, 2015). In other words, high levels of interest make it possible for students to read and comprehend more challenging texts.

Text-Based Collaborative Discussions with Peers

Peer-led reading tasks can aid students in further consolidating their understanding of text, and promote the use of self-regulated comprehension skills. One of the most robust examples is reciprocal teaching, a peer-led discussion of text (Palincsar & Brown, 1984). Four students engage in a discussion protocol of segmented portions of a text, including asking each other clarifying questions and answering them, summarizing the passage, and making predictions about what the author will tell them next, based on the information thus far. As with think alouds, the purpose is for students to verbalize the internal dialog that occurs as readers comprehend text. Students are not only teaching one another, but are also heightening their own awareness of how they learn.

Wide Reading for Pleasure and Study

We read for a number of reasons, but especially for enjoyment and to gain knowledge. Students of all ages need lots of experiences with texts that address both of these purposes. Wide reading in general builds knowledge, and fosters an understanding of other perspectives and experiences. Correlational studies have demonstrated a link between reading outside of school and performance on standardized tests (Anderson, Wilson, & Fielding, 1988). In addition to autonomous reading, students need daily experience reading on the topic of study. The effects of prior knowledge on reading comprehension have been noted in decades' worth of studies, with more recent studies demonstrating it mediating effects on conceptual understandings, the so-called "higher-order thinking" needed for deep learning (Tarchi, 2010). Knowledge acquisition through texts in turn impacts one's ability to understanding more complex texts on a similar topic.

CONCLUSION

Differential access to the OTL is not an abstract concept. OTL is enacted each day, in each classroom. These opportunities to learn have a multiplicative effect over the course of a child's academic career. The trajectories are established early and are compounded by frequent moves, in-grade retentions, and decreased access to complex texts. Inequitable access to OTL can be mitigated by taking action at the classroom, school, and district levels. At the classroom level, teachers must provide sound, research-based instruction that provides every student access to complex texts. Appropriately challenging texts with teacher- and peer-led discussion builds knowledge, fosters high-order thinking skills, and develops conceptual understandings needed as they advance in their school careers. At the school level, caring educators can mobilize their efforts to ensure that student mobility is addressed head-on and proactively. We do not need to simply accept it as an existing condition; we have the ability to influence what happens once a new student has arrived. However, we must put systems into place to do so. At the district level, educators, administrators, and related services personnel can collaborate to eliminate in-grade retention and mobilize literacy interventions, especially response to intervention efforts.

Issues of equity may seem intractable, and to be sure there are societal and fiscal factors that are outside the scope of our influence. But not being able to change *everything* doesn't give any of us the license to change *nothing*. It is time we reframe our thinking. It's not an "achievement gap that needs to be decreased." We need to increase the OTL for students who have been historically under-taught. Literacy is the gatekeeper for attainment in academics and in life. When literacy and equity are discussed in the same breath, the conversation takes a turn from admiring a problem to finding solutions. How will you start the conversation?

REFERENCES

Allington, R. L., & McGill-Franzen, A. (1989). School response to reading failure: Instruction for chapter 1 and special education students in grades two, four, and eight. *Elementary School Journal, 89,* 529–542.

Anderson, R., Wilson, P., & Fielding, L. (1988). Growth in reading and how children spend their time outside of school. *Reading Research Quarterly, 23*(3), 285–303.

Boon, H. J. (2011). School moves, coping, and achievement: Models of possible interactions. *Journal of Educational Research, 104*(1), 54–70.

Center for Development and Learning. (2003). Position statement on student grade retention and social promotion. Retrieved from http://www.cdl.org/articles/position-statement-on-student-grade-retention-and-social-promotion/

Cowen, J. M. (2016). Who are the homeless? Student mobility and achievement in Michigan 2010–2013. *Educational Researcher, 46,* 33–43.

Dauter, L., & Fuller, B. (2016). Student movement in social context. *American Educational Research Journal, 53*(1), 33–70.

Demanet, J., & Van Houtte, M. (2016). Are flunkers social outcasts? A multilevel study of grade retention effects on same-grade friendships. *American Educational Research Journal, 53*(3), 745–780.

DuFour, R., & Marzano, R. J. (2011). *Leaders of learning: How district, school, and classroom leaders improve student achievement.* Bloomington, IN: Solution Tree.

Duke, N. K. (2000). 3.6 Minutes per day: The scarcity of informational texts in first grade. *Reading Research Quarterly, 35*(2), 202–224.

Education Trust. (2015). *Checking in: Do classroom assignments reflect today's higher standards?* Washington, DC: Author.

Fisher, D., & Frey, N. (2014). Close reading as an intervention for struggling middle school readers. *Journal of Adolescent and Adult Literacy, 57*(5), 367–376.

Fisher, D., & Frey, N. (2016). Systems for teaching complex texts: A proof of concept investigation. *The Reading Teacher, 69*(4), 403–412.

Fisher, D., Frey, N., & Lapp, D. (2011). Coaching middle-level teachers to think aloud improves comprehension instruction and student reading achievement. *The Teacher Educator, 46,* 231–243.

Foster, J. E. (1993). Retaining children in grade. *Childhood Education, 70*(1), 38–43.

Fulmer, S., D'Mello, S. K., Strain, A., & Graesser, A. C. (2015). Interest-based text preference moderates the effect of text difficulty on engagement and learning. *Contemporary Educational Psychology, 41,* 98–110.

Galton, M. J. (1995). *Crisis in the primary classroom.* London: Fulton Publishers.

Hattie, J. (2009). *Visible learning: A synthesis of over 800 meta-analyses relating to achievement.* New York, NY: Routledge.

Heafner, T. T., & Fitchett, P. P. (2015). An OTL US history: What NAEP data suggest regarding the opportunity gap. *High School Journal, 98*(3), 226–249.

Holmes, C. T. (1989). Grade level retention effects: A meta-analysis of research studies. In L. A. Shepard & M. L. Smith (Eds.), *Flunking grades: Research and polices on retention* (pp. 16–33). London: Falmer Press.

Jimenez-Castellanos, O. (2010). Relationship between educational resources and school achievement: A mixed method intra-district analysis. *Urban Review, 42*(4), 351–371.

Jimerson, S. R. (2001). Meta-analysis of grade retention research: Implications for practice in the 21st century. *School Psychology Review, 30*(3), 420–437.

Jimerson, S. R., & Kaufman, A. M. (2003). Reading, writing, and retention: A primer on grade retention research. *The Reading Teacher, 56*(7), 622–635.

Lafontaine, D., Baye, A., Vieluf, S., & Monseur, C. (2015). Equity in opportunity-to-learn and achievement in reading: A secondary analysis of PISA 2009 data. *Studies in Educational Evaluation, 47*, 1–11.

Lesaux, N. K., & Kieffer, M. J. (2010). Exploring sources of reading comprehension difficulties among language minority learners and their classmates in early adolescence. *American Educational Research Journal, 47*, 596–632.

Marzano, R. J. (2003). *What works in schools: Translating research into action.* Alexandria, VA: ASCD.

McClintock, B., Pesco, D., & Martin-Chang, S. (2014). Thinking aloud: Effects on text comprehension by children with specific language impairment and their peers. *International Journal of Language & Communication Disorders, 49*(6), 637–648.

McDonough, I. (2015). Dynamics of the Black–White gap in academic achievement. *Economics of Education Review, 47*, 17–33.

Mehana, M. A. (1997). *A meta-analysis of school mobility effects on reading and math achievement in the elementary grades.* Unpublished data. The Pennsylvania State University, PA.

Meisels, S. J., & Liaw, F. (1993). Failure in grade: Do students catch up? *Journal of Educational Research, 87*, 69–77.

Palincsar, A. S., & Brown, A. L. (1984). Reciprocal teaching of comprehension-fostering and comprehension-monitoring activities. *Cognition and Instruction, 1*(2), 117–175.

Phelps, G., Corey, D., DeMonte, J., Harrison, D., & Loewenberg Ball, D. (2012). How much English language arts and mathematics instruction do students receive? Investigating variation in instructional time. *Educational Policy, 26*(5), 631–662.

Polikoff, M. S., & Struthers, K. S. (2013). Changes in the cognitive complexity of English instruction: The moderating effects of school and classroom characteristics. *Teachers College Record, 115*(8), 1–26.

Protheroe, N. (2007). Alternatives to retention in grade. *Principal, 86*(3), 30–34.

Shepard, L. A. & Smith, M. L. (1989). *Flunking grades: Research and polices on retention.* London: Falmer Press.

Stanovich, K. E. (1986). Matthew effects in reading: Some consequences of individual differences in the acquisition of literacy. *Reading Research Quarterly, 21*, 360–407.

Tarchi, C. (2010). Reading comprehension of informational texts in secondary school: A focus on direct and indirect effects of readers' prior knowledge. *Learning and Individual Differences, 20*(5), 415–420.

Titus, D. N. (2007). Strategies and resources for enhancing the achievement of mobile students. *NASSP Bulletin, 91*(1), 81–97.

Warren, J. R., & Saliba, J. (2012). First through eighth-grade retention rates for all 50 states: A new method and initial results. *Educational Researcher, 41*(8), 320–329.

MORE THAN ONE VOICE: UTILIZING STUDENTS' HOME LANGUAGES AND CULTURAL EXPERIENCES IN READING RECOVERY

Sarah Catto

ABSTRACT

To gain a better understanding of the impact of students' home languages and cultural experiences on reading and writing instruction, the instructional methods and materials that best supported these students' emerging bilingualism, and the contributions of their families in their utilization of their home languages and cultural experiences in a school setting. Mixed methods provided data on the literacy development in both home and school languages of three first-grade Latino students who were non-native English speakers enrolled in a school literacy intervention program for 12 to 20 weeks. The students' confidence and motivation within their reading and writing instruction improved greatly with the encouragement of the use of their home languages and cultural experiences. All three students showed

Addressing Diversity in Literacy Instruction
Literacy Research, Practice and Evaluation, Volume 8, 17–36
Copyright © 2018 by Emerald Publishing Limited
All rights of reproduction in any form reserved
ISSN: 2048-0458/doi:10.1108/S2048-045820170000008002

gains in speaking, reading, and writing in both their home and school lan-
guages. They made solid and useful connections between the languages and
the texts, and drew upon their cultural experiences, which strengthened
their reading and writing strategies in both languages. Involving the chil-
dren's families in lessons and in activities at school, and supporting their use
of reading and writing at home, helped build relationships among the par-
ticipants, families, and school faculty. This contributed to the beginnings of
new understandings on the part of the school's teachers and administration.
Students need to have the space to use their home languages and cultural
experiences in school, and I describe how educators in varied educational
settings can replicate the same kinds of methods, materials, and support
I offered to these students. I also describe suggested ways that teachers and
administrators could include the knowledge of emergent bilingual families
within the life of the school to further expand all students' learning and
promote social justice in the classroom setting.

Keywords: Bilingual; culturally relevant pedagogy; emergent literacy;
home language; literacy interventions; Reading Recovery

This is me, the teacher and researcher: I am a White, middle-aged, upper-middle class, female educator. When I was in school, reading and writing were my favorite subjects, and I easily excelled in them. My first language is English, and when I started learning Spanish in kindergarten, it was an option provided to my parents as an additional skill I could use in the future. I could choose whether I wanted to speak Spanish or English. I can now speak, read, and write in Spanish.

This is Antonio, one of my Reading Recovery (RR) students and one of the participants in this study: He is a 6-year-old, Latino boy in the first grade, and he is from Guatemala. Reading and writing are subjects that make him feel frustrated. His first language is Spanish. Antonio is not only expected to learn how to speak English, but he is also expected to read and write in English at the same grade-level proficiency as his English-speaking peers. Antonio became a candidate for RR, and this is where our story began.

Society is changing as ethnicities and racial groups that were once considered "minorities" are becoming the "new diverse majority" (Southern Education Foundation, 2010). The majority of teachers feel unprepared to meet the needs of this new diverse student population. A 2001 NCES survey revealed only 32% of teachers felt well prepared to address the needs of students from diverse cultural backgrounds, and only 27% felt they were adequately prepared to teach students with limited English proficiency (National Center for Education Statistics, 2001). There is a need for major changes in education in order to meet the needs of this new majority of students. One of the first steps is focusing on emergent bilingual children in primary classrooms and the connection between their native and non-native language growth and their cultural experiences as they impact their literacy lives and achievement.

In this chapter, I examine the experiences of three Latino emergent bilingual children and their RR teacher. These children received literacy instruction in English in their classrooms, while I offered RR lessons in English with the support of Spanish to increase their opportunities for growth in both languages. The support of Spanish took on a variety of forms, including reading bilingual and Spanish texts, writing in both Spanish and English, writing student-made books about their cultural experiences in both Spanish and English, and encouraging the use of Spanish in our daily conversations. I begin with a description of my study and the instructional methods and materials I used that can support students' emerging bilingualism. The impact of these methods and materials manifests in examples from the three participants: Isabel, Antonio, and Sofia. Finally, the chapter concludes with the implications the findings have for educators from all backgrounds and in all educational settings, beyond the reading intervention setting within which this study is situated.

RESEARCH DESIGN

Several theoretical concepts informed this study of effective instructional practices that support emergent bilingual students' language and literacy development within an early intervention program. Instead of limiting children to a predetermined scope and sequence of acquired abilities in school, emergent literacy research illustrated the complex relationship between learning to read, write, and talk as developing simultaneously as a result of interactions with other language users, readers, and writers (Clay, 2010). In addition, the sociocultural perspective states that curriculum content should not only authenticate students' cultural heritages, but also introduce new content in a way that is easy for a group of ethnically or culturally diverse students to understand (Gay, 2010). These kinds of culturally relevant practices support students' home languages and home knowledge while simultaneously developing literacy knowledge and skills needed for academic achievement (Compton-Lilly, 2004; García & Kleifgen, 2010; Gay, 2010; Ladson-Billings,

2009; Taylor, 1997). In a culturally relevant classroom, critical literacy perspective suggests that students should have a safe space in which to begin to question why their home culture is not privileged in the school setting, reflecting a disparity within the larger context of society. The critical literacy perspective also recognizes languages other than English and cultures other than the privileged norm as valuable literacy resources (Ruiz, 1984).

These theories fit well with my own theoretical orientation toward learning and literacy, specifically that learning is a sociocultural process; reading and writing are socially constructed, meaning-making learning tools; and culturally relevant practices support the needs of all students. These beliefs were particularly important to this study that addressed the problem of the prohibitive treatment of students' home languages and cultural experiences in schools. I believed a case study methodology provided the opportunity to pursue an in-depth analysis of these three students' experiences with their home languages and cultural experiences.

Participants

I conducted this study with three non-native English-speaking first-grade students who received literacy intervention in the form of daily RR lessons in English with the support of Spanish. Sofia, who asked questions to understand more about what she was seeing in texts and the world around her, lived with her siblings, her mother, her father, and a family friend. Sofia has lived in the United States for her entire life, but her mother, father, and older sister were born in Guatemala. Isabel, a spirited and talkative child, lived with all five of her siblings, as well as her mother. Her father still lived in Mexico, which is the family's home country. Isabel took on every challenge with a determined spirit. Antonio, who could be shy and reserved in groups, came alive with stories and a contagious laugh when he was on his own. He had one older brother who lived with him, and his parents and one younger brother who still lived in Guatemala. Antonio constantly made connections between texts and between his life experiences and texts, as if he was searching for how themes, places, and people fit together.

Sources of Data

All first-grade students completed three literacy assessments: Measures of Academic Progress (MAP) Reading, Developmental Reading Assessment (DRA) (Beaver, 2006), and AIMS Web, to determine whether they qualify for intervention services. I also administered the Oral Language Assessment Inventory, Second Edition (OLAI-2, Gentile, 2011), the Observation Survey, including the Concepts About Print assessment (Clay, 2000), and text level and Show Me tasks from the Dominie Reading and Writing Assessment Portfolio in Spanish (DeFord, 2004). In addition, I utilized several types of qualitative data to inform my instruction and gather data: a researcher's journal, transcriptions of video recordings of every lesson, informal interviews, lesson records, and student work samples.

Analysis

The analysis of interview transcripts, observations, and reflections were based on an inductive analysis by identifying patterns and themes that emerged from the data using thematic codes (Patton, 1980). Throughout the data collection, I used a priori codes, and I narrowed some of the codes to be more specific as I transcribed. After data collection, I read and re-read all of the observations, reflections, and transcripts, and then began noting the inductive codes emerging from the data. I brought all the codes together in a master list and then began to organize them, noting which codes were similar and grouping them together in a broader category. After I organized the codes into categories, I looked across all the categories to see if they represented themes or patterns in the data. I involved the participants and their parents in the analysis as we participated in member-checking sessions, sometimes over the phone and sometimes in person, examining the data and evaluating their meaning in the context of the study's purpose. After all the data were collected from the DRA (Beaver, 2006), Observation Survey (Clay, 2000), OLAI-2 (Gentile, 2011), and Dominie (DeFord, 2004), and I analyzed the progress of each student. The different assessments represented student data in varied forms, including numbered levels, numbered stages, percentages, total points, and rubric scores. I analyzed individual participants' data across different administrations and assessments, as well as across the participants.

FINDINGS

Improved Confidence and Motivation in Reading and Writing Instruction

After their weeks of instruction in RR, all three students were confident, motivated, and engaged readers and writers. However, these children did not begin their lessons as confident readers, writers, or even speakers, especially of their home language. I believe in order to see a more complete picture of these students as self-assured readers, writers, and speakers of both school and home languages, it is important to first see the uncertain and somewhat fearful children they were when we first began our lessons together. Which language are we supposed to speak? Allowed to speak? Afraid to speak, but only in certain places or with certain people? These questions seemed to be the foundation of my beginning weeks with the three participants. In my data analysis, within the first 3 weeks of our lessons, there were 29 instances of the students expressing fear in using their home language or occasions when they asked permission to use Spanish in our conversations or their reading and writing experiences.

I explained to each participant that we would use their home language, as well as English, in our conversations, reading, and writing experiences. At first, all three children reacted with surprise and caution. Even after I showed the children my limited ability in using their language, they were still unsure about the idea. Especially in those first few weeks, our building of trust was crucial to the belief that my classroom was a safe space for both of their languages and cultures.

As time progressed, the students started to show evidence of building confidence in their use of both languages in speaking, reading, and writing. In the data analysis, I coded instances of student confidence 118 times within our lessons, as compared to 31 instances of student uncertainty. While I coded 29 total instances of fear and permission around the use of their home language in September, by October, that number dropped to 0. Once given the choice, the students used Spanish confidently in their speech, reading, and writing. Their increased confidence in their home language transferred to their use and knowledge of the English language in their reading and writing.

The first instances of confidence in reading came from the students' fluency. I wrote in my field journal on October 29, 2015: "Sofia's fluency is so much better when reading familiar books in Spanish versus English. I need to record her and let her listen to herself so that she can hear how smoothly she reads." I recorded Sofia the next day and then played the video so she could hear herself reading smoothly with intonation and expression. Sofia's reaction was one of surprise, embarrassment, and eventual confidence. She exclaimed, "I sound good!" after she watched the video. She was exactly right. Her fluency improved drastically in the English texts as well as the weeks progressed. Sofia's confidence and resulting improved fluency encouraged me to record Antonio and Isabel as well. They both enjoyed listening to themselves read in both languages, and it was an effective teaching moment to hear the kind of fluent reading they could do in either language.

The students' confidence also shined in their conversations around their writing and in the process of writing their stories in either English or sometimes in Spanish. In the beginning of our lessons, I noted both Sofia and Antonio were very reluctant writers. In the first 4 weeks of lessons, Sofia appealed for assistance 27 times and Antonio did so 19 times. On April 12, 2015, Antonio flipped through his writing notebook, past some of his earlier entries of only a few words. He remarked, "That was when I did not know how (to) write. Now I know and I can write mucho (a lot)."

Gains in Speaking, Reading, and Writing in Both Languages

All three participants showed growth in speaking, reading, and writing in both languages, based on the assessment measures. It is important to note that Isabel and Sofia were in RR for the full 20 weeks of lessons. Antonio, as a second round student, started RR lessons in February and ended in May, totaling 13 weeks of lessons.

The stages of language development from the OLAI-2 (Gentile, 2011) range from Stage I to Stage III. Students in Stage I use primarily single words and phrases and understand some simple exclamations, questions, commands, and negative statements (Gentile, 2003). Students in Stage II use longer complete sentences with a few prepositional phrases and both understand and use some simple exclamations, questions, commands, and negative statements (Gentile, 2003). Finally, in the OLAI-2 (Gentile, 2011) Stage III includes using complete sentences with a variety of prepositional phrases and the understanding and use of expanded exclamations, questions, commands, and negative statements (Gentile, 2003).

All three students made gains in both measurements, Repeated Sentences and Story Retelling. At the beginning of the year, the three participants scored in Stage I for both measurements. At the end of the year, both Isabel and Antonio moved to Stage II for Repeated Sentences and Stage III for Story Retelling. Sofia moved to Stage III for Story Retelling, but remained at Stage I for Repeated Sentences. Sofia's bilateral hearing loss was identified in late May, so her ability to hear the sentences and repeat them may have been affected. However, her retelling of the stories improved drastically between the two assessment points. Her first retelling did not have the elements of a retold story. Instead, she simply stated what she saw in each picture from the story cards: "I see the girl. I see the horse. I see the leaves." For the retelling in

May, Sofia retold the story with a beginning, middle, and end, including the characters, the problem, and the solution.

I also collected achievement data using the Observation Survey (Clay, 2000). All participants' end of year scores placed them in the average or above average bands for all tasks. All three students showed strong improvements in their understanding of concepts about print, and the number of words they could write in 10 minutes (Writing Vocabulary). They also showed great progress in their ability to hear sounds and record them based on a dictated sentence (Hearing and Recording Sounds in Words). From their end of service testing until end of year testing 3 months later, both girls maintained their gains by scoring in the same or higher stanines in both reading and writing that allowed them to continue learning independently without need of one-on-one intervention services. Although Antonio received only 13 weeks of lessons, his scores placed him in the average or above-average range for all tasks.

I used Fountas and Pinnell's (2010) Benchmark Assessment System (BAS) to assess the participants' reading levels as well. The BAS is based upon the Fountas and Pinnell Text Level Gradient, which defines 10 characteristics at each level (A– Z): (1) genre/form; (2) text structure; (3) content; (4) themes and ideas; (5) language and literacy features; (6) sentence complexity; (7) vocabulary; (8) word difficulty; (9) illustrations/graphics; and (10) book and print features (Fountas & Pinnell, 2010). The assessment contains two required parts. In Part 1, the student reads aloud and discusses the text while the teacher observes and makes notes about the student's reading behavior. In Part 2, the student participates in a Comprehension Conversation with the teacher. Table 1 displays the reading levels for the three participants from the fall, mid-year, and year-end assessment points. Table 2 illustrates the reading levels for an anonymous comparison group of Spanish-speaking children who also received interventions in first grade but did not have the supports of their home language or culture in those lessons.

All three participants' beginning reading levels in the fall were below grade level for first grade. By mid-year, after 20 weeks of instruction, both

Table 1. Benchmark Assessment System Independent Reading Levels.

Student	Fall	Mid-year	Year-end
Isabel	A	G	J
Sofia	A	G	J
Antonio	A	C	I

Table 2. Benchmark Assessment System Reading Levels (Comparison Group).

Student	Fall	Mid-year	Year-end
Student 1	A	F	I
Student 2	<A	B	C
Student 3	A	D	E
Student 4	A	E	G
Student 5	A	F	G
Student 6	A	C	G
Student 7	<A	F	H
Student 8	<A	C	F
Student 9	<A	F	J
Student 10	<A	F	H
Student 11	A	F	I
Student 12	<A	E	I
Student 13	B	F	I
Student 14	B	E	I
Student 15	B	G	K
Student 16	B	E	G
Student 17	B	E	H

Isabel and Sofia were reading above the grade-level expectation for first grade (level F) at that time of the year. By the end of the year, both girls had continued their progress and were still reading above grade level (I), and this growth was happening without additional intervention services. After 12 weeks of instruction, Antonio's year-end reading level met grade-level expectations, illustrating rapid acceleration for him as well. It is interesting to note that his progress within the regular classroom setting prior to the onset of RR services documents the need for heightened intervention services (he had advanced only from levels A to C in reading in the regular classroom, with mid-year expectations being a level F in order to address his learning needs as a reader and writer).

Analyzing the comparison group's data, all 17 students' Fall reading levels were also below grade level for first grade, with six of these students below a level A at the beginning of the year, thus unable to read the lowest level book.

At the mid-year point, 41% of the comparison students were reading at the grade-level expectation for first grade (level F). Unlike Sofia and Isabel, at that mid-year point, none of the comparison group students were reading above that grade-level expectation. By the end of the year, 41% of the students were reading at grade level (level I) and only two were reading above grade-level expectations (J, K).

The Dominie Reading and Writing Assessment Portfolio (Spanish version) (DeFord, 2004) was the final achievement assessment used with the participants. Dominie (DeFord, 2004) can be administered in either English or Spanish. Since all other assessments were administered in English, I selected the Spanish version of Dominie, which provided data on the students' literacy development in their home language. The Kindergarten through Grade 3 assessments include the Show Me Book, in which students write their own names and demonstrate their knowledge of basic print conventions, such as identifying a letter and a word. Students' oral reading and comprehension are assessed as well. The phonemic awareness component of the assessment asks children to identify sounds they hear in words and match phonemes and letters. Sight words, letter knowledge, and word and sentence writing and spelling are other components of the assessment.

For the purposes of this study, I utilized the Show Me Book (El Libro Muestrame) task and the Text Reading task at the beginning and end of services. While all of the students showed progress on these tasks, they scored higher on the equivalent Observation Survey tasks in English (CAP and text level). However, all three participants improved their Spanish concepts about print stanines from below average to within the average band. On the English text level task, all three students ended the year reading on or above grade level. On the Spanish text level task, the year-end scores were equivalent to a beginning first-grade student. It is worth noting the Writing Vocabulary portion of El Libro Muestrame, in which all three students progressed from only writing their name to independently writing between 14 and 18 Spanish words.

Making Connections

Throughout my analysis, students' connections between languages, texts, and cultural experiences emerged as a dominant theme in the data. I coded students' connections between languages in 112 instances. Connections between students' lives and cultural experiences and the texts they were writing and reading emerged in 72 instances. As we started using students' home languages and cultural experiences in our conversations and reading and writing experiences, the participants made solid and useful connections between the languages, the texts, and their cultural experiences. The students applied reading and writing strategies that we practiced in the Spanish or bilingual texts to English texts and vice versa. They also made connections between their lives and texts, noticing books with characters that looked like them or writing about their cultural experiences. These connections strengthened their reading and writing strategies in both languages, and provided motivation for the students to read and write more texts.

Connections in Reading Strategies

Before our lessons began, I purchased a set of emergent level texts in Spanish from Reading books, the same publisher of some of the English texts that we used in RR. I chose this publisher's texts because of the use of strong picture cues, appropriate size of the print on the page, and the number of words on the page. When the students read the Spanish texts, I noted the miscues just as I would in an English text. I provided the prompts necessary to move them forward in their use of strategies in the text, whether they were based on visual, structure, or meaning. I started to notice that the kinds of miscues the students made in the Spanish texts were replicated in the English texts as well.

For example, in our lesson records for early October, I noted Isabel left off the plural -s ending in reading both the English and Spanish books. Therefore, I noted that I needed to focus in the strategy of looking to the end of a word in both languages (Personal Log Notes, 11-6-15 and 11-10-15). Sofia and Antonio also used their Spanish book to work on the same early kinds of reading activities I expected to see in their English text reading, including using picture cues and the initial letter of an unknown word to "get the word started" while maintaining the meaning of the text. The kinds of strategies I prompted for in the Spanish text with all three students are the same strategies I could prompt for in an English text. The more connections we could make between the kinds of strategies needed, the better. If those connections were in more than one language, it was even better for the participants. In the 137 coded instances that either I or the student mentioned a reading strategy in a Spanish text, 78% of those instances included the child attempting the same reading strategy in the English text for that lesson.

Connections in Writing Strategies

In addition to applying reading strategies in Spanish books, another strategic action involved using parts to help the participants write some unknown words. Antonio noted the similarities between two words in his story about playing with his brother in the street when he fell down.

Antonio: Mihermano y yocorrimosen la calle y yo me calli. Calli. *My brother and I run in the street and I fall.*

Sarah: Yes, what can you do to help yourself with calli?

Antonio: Say the sounds?

Sarah: You could. There's a word in your story that you've written that could help.

Antonio: (rereading his writing) Mihermano y yocorrimosen la calle … Calle. Calli.

Sarah: There you go.

Antonio: It's the same thing?

Sarah: They look and sound the same, except their endings are different. Try it.

Antonio: C. A. L. L. E?

Sarah: That's an I at the end.

Antonio: Y yo me calli. They kinda look the same. This one has I.

Sarah: You're exactly right. So sometimes if you know how to spell one word, it can help you spell another word by changing it just a little bit. It's the same when we read. (Transcription 4-25-16)

Making connections between those words in Antonio's writing was an effective way to get the new word written in the most efficient way, when he wanted to try hearing and recording the sounds instead.

Once the students were using strategies in their Spanish reading and writing work, it was not long before they started transferring the strategy work to their English reading and writing as well. For example, the same day Isabel found the parts in tortuga (tor-tu-ga), she used the same strategy in reading her English text with the word "forgetful" (for-get-ful). Sofia would make similar connections between English and Spanish as we completed the Word Work portion of her lesson a week later. We were listing words that had the -ar ending. Sofia and I used magnetic letters to build words like car, far, and star. Suddenly, she exclaimed, "Hablar has -ar too! And jugar! Y nadar!" (Transcription 12-11-15). We continued to make those words with magnetic letters as well, even though I had not planned on doing so in my lesson plans. It was a welcome adjustment to make.

As part of expanding the children's "meager knowledge of words" (Clay, 2005, p. 40), each child had a box of cards with high-frequency words. At first, these cards only had English words on them, words taken from familiar reading books, including phonetically irregular words that the child could easily learn. One day, Sofia asked if we could add Spanish words as well. Initially, we tried to write the Spanish translation on the back of each English high-frequency word. However, because of the differences between the two languages, there was not always a 1:1 match between an English high-frequency word and its Spanish counterpart. Therefore, we added the Spanish translation to the backs of some of the words, and then added separate Spanish word cards for Spanish high-frequency words as well. The connections all three students made between their languages and their texts in reading and writing reinforced the strategies that propelled them forward as strategic readers and writers.

Connections between Cultural Experiences and Texts

Along with making connections between strategic actions in reading and writing in both their home and school languages, the participants also made connections between their cultural experiences and the texts they wrote and read. For example, the students promptly noticed any texts that included Latino characters and compared those characters to themselves. In addition, the participants connected their life experiences to events in texts without any Latino characters. Furthermore, students had the choice to write about their home lives and cultural experiences during the writing portion of their lessons. The participants made connections between the texts and their own lives and cultural experiences with books that included Latino characters or families. Antonio made a statement about the book *Dennis Rides His Bike* that tells the story of two Latino boys, Elzeare and Dennis, and their experience with Dennis learning to ride a bike:

Sarah: Yesterday we read a book with Dennis and Elzeare.

Antonio: It was easy. It had people like me.

Sarah: What do you mean?

Antonio: He look like me (points to Dennis). And my big brother (points to Elzeare).

Sarah: Ah, yes they do, don't they? What do you think about that?

Antonio: I like that. You have more? ¿Otroslibros con estas personas? *Other books with these people?* (Transcription 4-19-16)

The students continued to make connections between their life experiences and the books even if those books did not include Latino characters. Isabel and I had a conversation as we previewed the book, *At the Beach*, a story where three dogs, Rosie, Bella, and their friend, Olive, search for clams at the beach. I asked Isabel if she knew what a clam was. The following exchange continued as she described watching her mother make ceviche at home:

Sarah: What does she have in it again?

Isabel: She have some … lechuga *lettuce* … Limón *lemon* … She puts cebolla *onion*. She puts the water…

Sarah: And then she puts what?

Isabel: The clam.

Sarah: She puts the clam in there? So you do know about clams.

Isabel: Yeah…

Sarah: It sounds like she was making ceviche.

Isabel: Yeah. And it had jugo de tomate *tomato juice*.

Sarah: Oh, that sounds delicious. So now that you know what clams are, let's see if the dogs find any to eat on the beach. (Transcription 2-17-15)

Previewing texts was an important part of our daily lessons when introducing a new book. Including students' cultural experiences in those conversations as well as in selecting books for lessons was essential in their understanding and connections to characters and plot events.

Approximately 10 minutes of a RR lesson are dedicated to writing a story. In our lessons, students would sometimes write about the story they read in that lesson or write about something happening in their lives. Both kinds of writing were motivating for the students at different times. If a student came to me bursting with excitement about the soccer game her father played in last night that emotion transferred to her writing about that event. I found these moments supported the students in writing in both languages, as well as capitalized on using their cultural experiences in their stories.

When we first met, Antonio shared his experience of having some of his family still living in Guatemala while his mother worked three jobs in order to make enough money to try to transport more of his family members to the United States. One day, Antonio told me he wanted to write about his experience of sending toys to his brother who still lived in Guatemala. Antonio continued to write about his experiences with having part of his family living in another country, and the challenges he faced as his mother worked so hard to provide for both her family here and her family in Guatemala. Including his cultural experiences in his writing proved to be a way for me to learn more about his family and their successes and struggles and provided an outlet for him to release his feelings about the situation as well.

Many of the students' writings about their cultural experiences came in the form of student-made books that we made together. All three students chose different topics for their books. Isabel wrote a story about her future trip to Mexico to see her grandmother. She chose to write in both Spanish and English in her book that she titled *The Story of Isabel's Trip of Mexico*. She wrote about spending time with her family in Mexico, especially her grand-mother and her cousin, Pancico. Sofia chose to write about her brother Dylan and his antics. The idea for her book was based on an English book we read the previous week, *My Big Brother*. The book was about a boy (who looked Latino) and his big brother. Sofia decided she would write a similar book about her little brother. Antonio chose to write a book about eating breakfast with his mother after she cooked a variety of Guatemalan dishes. Similar to Sofia, we had read a Spanish book, *Desayuno Con Mi Mama*, a few weeks prior and it seemed to inspire him.

Family Involvement Contributed to Students' Use of Home Languages and Experiences

Involving the participants' families in our lessons and activities at school, as well as reading and writing experiences at home, helped build relation-ships among participants, families, and school faculty. These relationships contributed to the utilization of the students' home languages and cultural experiences in school and the beginnings of new understandings on the part of Goodman teachers and administration. The ways in which I tried to involve these families included lesson visits, support of home literacy experi-ences, focus groups, and other classroom and school activities that specifi-cally focused on the Latino families and their contributions to their children's learning.

The first step I took to involve the participants' families was an invitation to observe one of their children's lessons with me. I sent home a short Spanish letter to parents asking them to choose a day and time that worked best for them to observe a 30-minute lesson. I explained they could bring younger siblings to the lesson visit to alleviate any concerns about childcare. All three participants' parents observed one lesson, and Isabel's mother brought her lit-tle sister to her lesson visit as well. I found these lesson visits helped forge my relationships with the families, as they watched their children speak, read, and write in both English and Spanish with my support. They witnessed how we read bilingual and Spanish texts, wrote in both Spanish and English, created student-made books about cultural experiences in both Spanish and English, and used Spanish in our daily conversations. The lesson visits also gave the students an opportunity to proudly show their parents what they could do in reading and writing. After each lesson visit, the parents had the opportunity to ask me any questions or make comments about what they observed. Sofia's father commented, "Estamosmuyorgullosos de ella. Y ellaestáorgullosacuandoestáen casa con suslibrosenespañol. *We are very proud of her. And she is proud when she is in the house with her Spanish books*" (Personal communication, 12-7-15). During Isabel's mother's visit, her 2-year-old sister remained directly beside Isabel, watching everything she did as she read and wrote. I asked her mother if this happened at home too, and she replied, "Yes. *Sí*. Isabel show her reading and writing. She like a teacher" (Personal communication, 1-8-16). In the same lesson, Isabel's mother reminded Isabel of a strategy that we worked on as well. Even though Isabel's mother admitted she did not know how to read and write in English, it did not prevent her from supporting her daughter in strategic reading activities. When Isabel's mother and I debriefed after the lesson, she said it felt good to share that kind of literacy experience with her daughter, something she is not as confident doing in English. She said, "Isabel come home telling me what you do when read and write. She tell me find parts and say slow. She do it in Spanish and English" (Transcription 1-8-16).

Isabel's mother paid attention to the strategies her daughter brought home from our lessons and supported her daughter in using them as well. These lesson visits enriched the relationships between me and the participants' families. Because of these visits, I felt we started to understand each other a little more, including our goals for the students and their literacy growth. As a result, the students felt even more at ease with using their home languages and cultural experiences during our lessons. The participants knew they had my support in this endeavor, as well as the support of their families.

Another part of families' involvement was their engagement in home literacy experiences with the students. Sofia constantly mentioned how she read both the Spanish and English books to her little brother, Dylan, and how her mother enjoyed reading the Spanish books with her. Sofia's brother, Dylan, was a major motivator for her reading at home in Spanish and English. She expressed excitement whenever she got a new book sent home that she thought Dylan would enjoy. Both of her parents mentioned how grateful they were to have Spanish books in the home that Sofia could read on her own, to her brother, and that they could read as well. Before her lessons with me, the family had no Spanish books in the home for Sofia to read. Similarly, Isabel's mother mentioned how much Isabel enjoyed reading the Spanish books with her little sister and brother. Although Isabel's mother stated they did have other books in Spanish in the house, she was grateful for more.

Antonio's father seemed to be the main support for Antonio in his home literacy experiences in Spanish. With working three jobs, Antonio's mother was grateful Antonio had a supportive father to help. One of their favorite activities to do together involved the magnetic letters we used in each of our lessons during Word Work time and throughout other portions of the lesson. We made a list of Spanish words Antonio wanted to make at home with his dad. The list included the names of his family members, as well as perro, gato, and color words. Another favorite activity was reading Antonio's cut up sentence every evening. After every lesson, the students had a cut up sentence from their written story from that lesson sent home. They were expected to reassemble it and glue it in their homework notebook and read it. Since some of Antonio's sentences were in Spanish or were about his cultural experiences, his father could participate in that activity with him. Antonio's father stated, "It felt good to help him. And he didn't need my help a lot. But I liked how he could read his words to me from the sentence and I felt like I was learning too" (Personal communication 2-13-16).

PRACTICAL IMPLICATIONS

This study's findings suggest implications for practice for a variety of audiences: classroom teachers, interventionists, literacy coaches, administrators, and parents of emergent bilingual children. Antonio, Isabel, Sofia, and I were from very different cultural and linguistic backgrounds. However, that did not stop me from creating the space they needed to help them use every tool at their disposal to move them forward in their reading, writing, and language skills. The support I provided through Spanish and bilingual books, student-created books in the language of their choice, and the consistent invitation to speak in the language that best fit their needs can be offered by any educator, regardless of their background or language knowledge.

Students' Home Languages and Cultural Experiences

Fear of the unknown pervades various areas of our lives. Teachers and administrators who are unfamiliar with emergent bilingual students' languages or their families' cultural experiences should open themselves to learning more about what is unfamiliar. Viewing emergent bilingual students' languages and experiences as additional helpful tools to expand their learning is an essential first step for teachers and educational leaders. Classroom teachers, even those who are unfamiliar with the students' home languages, can still provide the space for their students to use those languages. Making connections is an essential part of learning. Emergent bilingual students can make even more connections in their conversations and reading and writing experiences, if they have the support to use all of what they know in the academic setting and their first language offers a valuable resource through which to clarify meanings, extend their ability to communicate more clearly, and as a window through which to gain insight through language about language. Their first language is a rich resource; to limit their use of such a great resource is to hold them back rather than propel them forward!

Methods and Materials

The kinds of methods and materials that best supported the students in this study were processes and products embedded in continuous texts used in authentic reading and writing experiences. In fact, the more authentic the continuous text, the more engaged the students were. Authenticity was defined by these students as Spanish books, Spanish writing, texts with characters that looked like them and their families, texts written by them about important family experiences, or texts written that expanded on a book with which they felt a strong connection. These kinds of experiences were not found in a basal reader, or a set of phonics flashcards, or materials created for a one-size-fits-all curriculum. Based on the findings of this study, I advocate the use of reading continuous texts while integrating strategic problem solving within those texts (Clay, 2005). I was fortunate enough to have a large amount of texts provided by my RR teacher leader, as well as an additional stipend from my principal to purchase Spanish texts. In classrooms where this is not the case, I suggest enlisting the help of students and their families. Some of the best books I read through the duration of this study were written by Isabel, Sofia, Antonio, and their families. The ESOL teachers at the school were another resource for materials. They provided handouts with Spanish words and phrases for classroom teachers, and online resources for free, printable bilingual books for the students to take home.

Family Involvement

The involvement of the students' families in their literacy experiences contributed to their utilization of their home languages and cultural experiences in school. The connection between the parents and myself was an additional pillar of support for these students. School teachers and administrators need to explore more ways to include all families' viewpoints and opinions consistently. No Spanish-speaking family members were on the School Improvement Council, Parent Teacher Association, or Leadership Team at the time of this study. Opening the space for these families to voice their needs and opinions while including their languages and cultures in the school setting will bring about better results for emergent bilingual children and foster cross-cultural understandings across all stakeholders.

CONCLUSION

Inviting the students to utilize their home languages and cultural experiences in our time together greatly enriched our lessons and our relationships. I believe the same effect would follow other classroom teachers, interventionists, or educational leaders who care enough to open the classroom spaces for these students. These children surprised me on a regular basis with what they could do in reading and writing in both languages. However, the times when I doubted them and their abilities are when we both faltered. Whenever I let my own expectations impede their progress, I had to right the course and place my confidence in the children and the work we can do together.

Before this case study, these three children were fearful of their own language. Their identity at home and their identity at school were two disparate personalities. It seemed natural to them to forge a link between the two languages they speak and their school and home experiences. Instead of severing the ties between home and school, thereby silencing a multitude of voices and experiences, we must support children and their families in the building of these connections between learning contexts, languages, and people.

REFERENCES

Beaver, J. (2006). *Developmental reading assessment*. New York, NY: Pearson.

Clay, M. M. (2000). *Concepts about print*. Portsmouth, NH: Heinemann.

Clay, M. M. (2005). *Literacy lessons designed for individuals part one: Why? When? And how?* Portsmouth, NH: Heinemann.

Clay, M. M. (2010). *The puzzling code*. Portsmouth, NH: Heinemann.

Compton-Lilly, C. (2004). *Confronting racism, poverty, and power*. Portsmouth, NH: Heinemann.

DeFord, D. (2004). *Programa de evaluacion de lectura y escritura Dominie K-3*. New York, NY: Pearson.

García, O., & Kleifgen, J. A. (2010). *Educating emergent bilinguals: Policies, programs, and practices for English Language Learners*. New York, NY: Teachers College Press.

Fountas, I., & Pinnell, G. (2010). *Benchmark assessment system*. Portsmouth, NH: Heinemann.

Gay, G. (2010). *Culturally responsive teaching: Theory, research, and practice*. New York, NY: Teachers College Press.

Gentile, L. M. (2011). *Oral language acquisition inventory* (2nd ed). Bloomington, MN: Pearson.

Ladson-Billings, G. (2009). *The dream keepers: Successful teachers of African American children*. San Francisco, CA: Jossey-Bass.

National Center for Education Statistics (2001). *Condition of education*. Jessup, MD: US Department of Education.

Patton, M. (1980). *Qualitative evaluation methods*. New York, NY: Sage Publications.

Ruiz, R. (1984). Orientations in language planning. *The Journal for the National Association for Bilingual Education, 8*(2), 15–34.

Southern Education Foundation. (2010). *The new diverse majority report*. Atlanta, GA: Southern Education Foundation Inc.

Taylor, D. (Ed.). (1997). *Many families, many literacies: An international declaration of principles*. Portsmouth, NH: Heinemann.

TEACHING GRAMMAR WHILE VALUING LANGUAGE DIVERSITY: URBAN TEACHERS NAVIGATING LINGUISTIC IDEOLOGICAL DILEMMAS

Emily Machado, Rebecca Woodard, Andrea Vaughan and Rick Coppola

ABSTRACT

This study examines how writing teachers manage linguistic ideological dilemmas (LIDs) around grammar instruction and highlights productive strategies employed by one teacher in an instructional unit on poetry. We conducted semi-structured interviews with nine elementary and middle-school teachers to better understand how they conceptualized and enacted writing pedagogies in urban classrooms. Then, we documented the teaching practices of one teacher during a 9-week case study. We describe three LIDs expressed by the teachers we interviewed: (1) a perception of greater

Addressing Diversity in Literacy Instruction
Literacy Research, Practice and Evaluation, Volume 8, 37–53
Copyright © 2018 by Emerald Publishing Limited
All rights of reproduction in any form reserved
ISSN: 2048-0458/doi:10.1108/S2048-045820170000008003

linguistic flexibility in speech than in writing; (2) a sense that attention to grammar in feedback can enhance and/or inhibit written communication; and (3) apprehension about whether grammar instruction empowers or marginalizes linguistically minoritized students. We also highlight three productive strategies for teaching grammar while valuing linguistic diversity employed by one teacher: (1) selecting mentor texts that showcase a range of grammars; (2) modeling code-meshing practices; and (3) privileging alternative grammars while grading written work. We describe how teachers might take up pedagogical practices that support linguistic diversity, such as evaluating written assignments in more flexible ways, engaging in contrastive analysis, and teaching students to resist and rewrite existing language rules.

Keywords: Grammar; writing instruction; urban education; linguistic ideological dilemmas

Many equity-oriented writing teachers who value linguistic and cultural diversity struggle with a challenging paradox: teaching the "standard" English[1] grammar advocated in schools often contributes to the explicit or implicit marginalization of other language varieties. Even when teachers recognize that multiple equally valid grammars exist in English (e.g., African-American English; see Smitherman, 2006), that strictly forcing students to adhere to the norms of standard English can be detrimental to them (Dyson & Smitherman, 2009), and that traditional grammar instruction does not actually improve student writing (Smith, Cheville, & Hillocks, 2006), they feel pressure to teach and evaluate grammar[2] in writing. Indeed, Michael-Luna and Canagarajah (2008) argue that mastery of standard English grammar matters, particularly for multilingual students:

> Lexical and grammatical choices can demonstrate a student's way to convey meaning, index values and norms outside the discourse, or make ideologically-inscribed statements. However, in order to be "heard" in the dominant discourse, multilinguals not only need to learn the existing rules of the discursive practice they wish to be heard in, but to learn how to resist and rewrite the rules, norms or values to serve their interests by meshing the rules. (p. 59)

This chapter documents the challenges experienced by nine urban English Language Arts teachers as they sought to teach grammar in ways that valued linguistic and cultural diversity. We frame these challenges using McBee

Orzulak's (2015) construct of *linguistic ideological dilemmas* (LIDs), or the idea that "teachers who take up linguistically responsive positions that value student language variation still struggle in moments of enactment due to expectations that they serve as gatekeepers for 'standard' English(es)" (p. 176).

We describe three such LIDs: (1) a perception of greater linguistic flexibility in speech than in writing; (2) a sense that attention to grammar in feedback can enhance and/or inhibit written communication; and (3) apprehension about whether grammar instruction empowers or marginalizes linguistically minoritized students. We conclude with practical descriptions of productive strategies one of the teachers (Rick Coppola – also an author of this chapter) used during a 9-week case study in his classroom.

PRESCRIPTIVE VS. DESCRIPTIVE APPROACHES TO GRAMMAR

Although public school classrooms in the United States have become increasingly diverse (National Center for Educational Statistics, 2015), the ways that we teach grammar often remain monolithic. In fact, the most common methods for teaching grammar are decidedly *prescriptive*, meaning there is a focus on adherence to rules about how language should and should not be used. Although multiple grammars, or rule systems, exist in the English language, in schools we typically privilege "…one English grammar above all others – the one that is most typically associated with middle-class white speakers" (Woodard & Kline, 2016, p. 6). An unfortunate byproduct of this pedagogy is that children's proper use of marginalized dialects and grammars tends to be positioned as wrong and/or deficient (Dyson & Smitherman, 2009).

An alternative to this prescriptive approach is a *descriptive* one, focused on identifying patterns that reflect how individuals use language and the rules governing usage across varying contexts (Gartland & Smolkin, 2016; Razfar & Rumenapp, 2014). Promising descriptive approaches to writing and language instruction continue to gain pedagogical currency (e.g., communicative flexibility, Dyson & Smitherman, 2009; translanguaging, Michael-Luna & Canagarajah, 2008; contrastive analysis, Gartland & Smolkin, 2016). However, teachers attempting such descriptive approaches often report contradictions and dilemmas in their enactments due in large part to pervasive deficit language ideologies in society.

TEACHERS' LINGUISTIC IDEOLOGICAL DILEMMAS

Smitherman (2006), drawing from DuBois's (1903) notion of double con-sciousness, uses the term *linguistic push pull* to characterize a hesitancy toward African-American English from its own users: they both embrace and reject it. This push pull is due to our society's deeply rooted deficit ideologies about marginalized forms of English. McBee Orzulak (2015) describes:

> One aspect of deficit language ideology is the belief that if something is not "standard" English, it is not grammatical or that sloppy people use sloppy grammar. These language ideologies transfer to beliefs about people who command different languages or varie-ties of English and, therefore, reveal underlying power dynamics related to language and equity. (Lanehart, 2002, p. 180)

In her characterizations of LIDs, McBee Orzulak (2015) describes a simi-lar linguistic push pull for teachers as these deeply ingrained deficit language ideologies operate alongside contradictory "core principles of how language works that are rooted in research and agreed upon by most linguists: (1) lan-guage equity, (2) descriptive approaches to grammar, and (3) consequential language choices in classroom interactions" (p. 180). By documenting the LIDs faced by the teachers in this study, we attempt to better understand the linguistic push pull experienced by teachers, particularly when it comes to grammar instruction in writing.

METHODS

This investigation was part of a broader study examining how urban liter-acy teachers conceptualize and enact equity-oriented pedagogies in writing. First, we present findings from semi-structured interviews conducted with nine writing teachers who self-identified as enacting "culturally relevant" and "culturally sustaining" pedagogies (Ladson-Billings, 1995; Paris, 2012). Then, we share findings from a 9-week case study in one of these teachers' classrooms. While we were initially interested in many different aspects of writ-ing pedagogy, we noticed that grammar was a particularly contested area of participants' writing curricula across their interviews. In this chapter, we ask: (1) What sorts of dilemmas do teachers who value linguistic diversity face as they teach writing? and (2) How might a teacher attempt a descrip-tive approach to grammar instruction that privileges multiple linguistic varieties?

Context

Nine public elementary and middle-school teachers participated in this study (all names, except for Rick Coppola's, are pseudonyms). All participants taught in the Chicago area and were initially identified based on the recommendations of faculty members in a university-based teacher education program. Teachers were recommended based on their strengths as educators and their interests in and experiences with culturally relevant pedagogy. For additional information on participant demographics, see Table 1.

Interviews

We conducted nine semi-structured interviews over the course of five months. While interview questions addressed multiple categories (e.g., assessment and evaluation; student identity as writers), we focus in this chapter on questions regarding writing instruction and grammar, specifically (e.g., How is grammar taught or approached in the classroom? How do you teach and talk about Standard English, home language(s), and dialect? The interviews, which ranged in duration from 27 to 78 minutes, were recorded and transcribed for analysis.

We analyzed these interviews in multiple cycles, beginning with initial and descriptive coding (Saldaña, 2013) of interview transcripts. From this coding, we developed categories reflecting patterns in the data set, such as "tensions" and "curriculum." Following coding, we utilized additional analytic strategies to better understand participant dilemmas related to grammar (e.g., creating tables and data displays). We present three dilemmas related to linguistic flexibility, communication, and empowerment/marginalization.

Case Study

Following these interviews, we were invited into the classrooms of two of the teachers to conduct case studies of writing teaching and learning. In this chapter, we share findings from Rick Coppola's seventh grade classroom, documenting ways that he privileged multiple grammars in a 9-week unit on poetry. Methods of data collection included participant observation of his English language arts class ($n = 27$), semi-structured interviews with Rick ($n = 3$) and his students ($n = 16$), an end-of-unit survey of students, and the collection of artifacts and documents used or produced during instruction. Methods of data analysis included regularly writing analytic memos focused

Table 1. List of Participants (Organized by Grade Level).

Name	Gender and Racial Identity	Languages Spoken	Teaching Context	School Racial Demographics	Years Teaching
Vanessa	Female, African-American	English	1st Grade General Education	97.8% Black; 1.4% Hispanic; 0.5% White; 0.2% Asian; 0.2% other	5
Elizabeth	Female, African-American	English	1st Grade General Education	97.8% Black; 1.4% Hispanic; 0.5% White; 0.2% Asian; 0.2% other	6
Greg	Male, White	English	2nd Grade General Education	45.1% Hispanic; 27.3% Black; 18.6% Asian; 6.5% White; 2.5% other	11
Megan	Female, White	English and Spanish	2nd Grade Dual Language	83.0% Hispanic; 9.3% Black; 5.9% White; 1.2% Asian; 0.5% 2 or more races; 0.1% American Indian	14
Efrain	Male, Latino	English and Spanish	3rd Grade Dual Language	95.9% Hispanic; 2.9% Black; 0.7% White; 0.05% other; 0.01% Asian	7
Aaron	Male, African-American	English	3rd Grade General Education	98.1% Black; 1.6% White	1
Jeremy	Male, White,	English and French	7th Grade English Language Arts	68.8% White; 12.2% Black; 8.2% Hispanic; 6.3% Asian; 4.6% multiracial	6
Rick	Male, White,	English and Spanish	7th Grade English Language Arts	41.4% Black; 29.0% White; 12.9% Asian; 9.4% Hispanic; 7.3% other	11
Jamie	Female, African-American	English	8th Grade English Language Arts	97.8% Black; 1.4% Hispanic; 0.5% White; 0.2% Asian; 0.2% other	4

on the construction of themes and coding instances in interviews and field notes in which Rick talked about grammars and/or used instructional practices that supported linguistic diversity.

FINDINGS

Teachers' Linguistic Ideological Dilemmas: Findings from Interviews

In this section, we describe three LIDs expressed by the teachers we interviewed. Building on the work of McBee Orzulak (2015), we examine "...what occurs when multiple language principles and ideologies clash, yet are managed" (p. 180).

Dilemma 1: A Perception of Greater Linguistic Flexibility
in Speech Than Writing

The teachers we interviewed tended to express a dilemma around a perception of greater linguistic flexibility in speech than in writing. In other words, they felt that alternative or nonstandard grammars were more permissible in their students' talk than in their written assignments. Barton (2007) argues that written language often carries "a social priority" (p. 90) when compared to spoken language, as it is perceived as more formal, legal, and binding. For this reason, while teachers explored descriptive approaches to grammar in oral language, some tended to take more "formal" and prescriptive approaches to grammar in their instruction and assessment of writing.

We heard teachers recount descriptive approaches to grammar in discussions of oral language. For example, Megan, a second grade English/Spanish dual language teacher, discussed how she and her students examined register in their speech. She stated:

> The topic this week was formal and informal language, and we came up with ideas like, "How would you say 'Good morning, Miss Roberts,' and how would you say it if it was informal?" And they'd be like, "What's up?" And we also went into Spanish, like, "What are some things you would say in Spanish ... more academically, you'd say in school? Maybe they sound different than what you say when you talk with your friends."

In this example, Megan and her students explore the notion of multiple linguistic varieties – and their situational appropriateness – in both English and Spanish. However, when she discussed writing, Megan's approaches were decidedly more prescriptive. For example, she recounted how when her students use whiteboards to practice writing, she floats around the classroom to remind them of grammatical rules.

Similarly, Elizabeth, a first-grade teacher, described how she regularly discussed "slang" with her students in speech, but not in writing. Like Megan, Elizabeth also focused on appropriateness and language choice. She stated:

> I can use different ... forms of speech when they're talking. You know, using the slang terms that they like. I'll show them ... how they derive from the proper English, trying to get them to use the correct form as much as possible. But letting them know in certain situations, when they're at home or relaxed to use those forms of speech.

In this statement, Elizabeth brings up notions of "correctness," "slang," and propriety. While she positions standard English as proper and correct, she also acknowledges the existence of alternative linguistic forms. However, Elizabeth's approach to spoken grammar contrasts with her approach in writing. In accordance with her school's mandated curriculum, Elizabeth's written grammar instruction centers on standard English worksheets and exercises.

We also noticed that most teachers tended to *assess* students' grammar exclusively through writing rather than speech. For example, Jeremy, a seventh-grade teacher, described how he gives his students pre-tests related to grammar, assigns activities and worksheets focused on editing or identifying parts of speech, and follows up with a written post-test. He also described how students were assessed for grammar in their written essays, generally using a rubric. However, Jeremy also described how students were permitted to use alternative grammars and registers in oral language, stating, "I'm not the teacher ... who corrects [grammar in speech] ... How they speak and how they write are kind of different."

Megan, Elizabeth, and Jeremy's teaching and/or assessment practices illustrate a significant LID that some teachers in the study faced. They tended to permit the use of marginalized grammars in students' speech, which they perceived as flexible and fluid, but not in writing, which they perceived as formal and standard. However, we believe that this binary between oral and written language is a false one. Growing bodies of literature in the fields of codemeshing (Michael-Luna & Canagarajah, 2007), translanguaging (Garcia, 2009), and multiliteracies (Kalantzis & Cope, 2012) describe how twenty-first century writing is increasingly hybrid and flexible, drawing on multiple languages, grammars, and modalities. The changing nature of written language leads us to wonder how this dilemma might be reframed in terms that value all of students' grammars in both speech *and* writing.

Dilemma 2: A Sense that Primary Attention to Traditional Standard English Grammar in Feedback Could Improve and/or Inhibit Written Communication
Another dilemma expressed by some of the teachers centered on the potential power of grammar to improve and/or inhibit written communication. While these teachers felt that explicit instruction in grammatical concepts (e.g., sentence structure; parts of speech) could strengthen students' writing, they also felt that grammatical correction might keep students from expressing themselves. Some of the teachers expressed this dilemma by positioning a focus on "ideas," "communication," or "composition" against a focus on grammar.

Greg, a second-grade teacher, argued that the purpose of writing instruction is to encourage students to communicate, and described how learning traditional grammatical rules could support that communication. At the same time, however, Greg alluded to the way that grammar instruction might somehow "erase" student identity and inhibit communication, a subject that he discussed further as the interview went on. He stated:

> You want kids to realize that writing is about communicating and sending the message to someone ... You talk with colleagues, and all you hear is, "They don't know how to write a sentence, they don't know how to use a period," and ... it's this intense focus on sentence structure ... It's like, that whole idea of like giving kids back a red, marked up paper – it's just shutting them down.

Through this statement, Greg addresses the way that excessive grammatical correction might inhibit communication – in this case, by shutting down young students as they write. He wants to empower students as communicators by giving them grammatical tools, but recognizes that excessive correction could subvert that goal.

Other teachers we interviewed expressed similar dilemmas around grammar's potential to inhibit communication – with some opting not to teach grammar traditionally at all. For example, Jamie, an eighth-grade English Language Arts teacher, explicitly positioned "ideas" in opposition to "grammar." She stated:

> I value ideas, and I teach through ideas, and how to formulate ideas, but not grammar. I don't teach grammar ... because I don't want them to be in a place where I'm ignoring the bigger picture, and the bigger picture is what you're trying to say rather than how you say it.

Aaron, a third-grade teacher, similarly positioned "ideas" in opposition to grammar and spelling, describing how a focus on grammatical form might cause a student to lose his or her train of thought. He stated:

> If I stop to correct something, I lose a good thought. Even at third grade, it's hard for them to sit down and write and not worry about spelling ... I just want you to put your ideas on paper.

For these teachers, then, teaching grammar often came at the expense of communication. They expressed their pedagogical decisions to avoid explicit grammar instruction in service of building their students' communicative skills.

Nearly all of the teachers we interviewed expressed some LIDs around grammar's potential to inhibit and/or improve written communication. While some, like Greg, acknowledged that grammar instruction might be simultaneously empowering and constraining, others, like Jamie and Aaron, felt that explicit grammar instruction and correction would inhibit student communication entirely. We wonder whether reframing the nature of grammar instruction and correction might help teachers to manage this dilemma without compromising student expression. For example, Wheeler and Swords (2004) suggest that teachers might focus instruction on identifying linguistic *patterns* in a variety of grammars rather than on enforcing the *rules* of standard English. This approach empowers students to choose the patterns that best support the messages they wish to communicate, rather than on correctness.

Dilemma 3: Apprehension about Whether Standard English Grammar Instruction Empowers or Marginalizes Linguistically Minoritized Students

Finally, many teachers described experiencing apprehension about whether standard English grammar empowered or marginalized their linguistically minoritized students. While they believed that grammar instruction might give their students access to dominant codes of power (Delpit, 2006), they also worried that it might reinscribe language marginalization. Jeremy, a seventh-grade teacher, expressed this tension explicitly. He stated:

> I never want to belittle the home language. But at the same time, I don't want to do them a disservice by saying it's okay to speak this way in these settings … Unfortunately, you will be judged by the way you use grammar.

Through these statements, Jeremy expressed his apprehension about his students being "judged" for using grammars other than standard English. However, he also expresses concern that grammar instruction might "belittle" home languages, further marginalizing the languaging practices of minoritized students.

Rick, a seventh-grade teacher, expressed similar dilemmas around the potential of grammar to empower or marginalize. For example, he recounted how he has used instructional activities to empower students to speak and write in historically marginalized languages. For example, in a unit focused on Shakespeare's wordplay, he encouraged students to apply what they had learned about standard English grammar to various dialects, including language(s) of youth culture.

At the same time, Rick also recognized that grammar instruction might further marginalize "nonstandard" linguistic varieties, relegating them to contexts outside of the classroom. In fact, Rick was explicit about this tension, going so far as to say:

> It's the idea that there is a discourse of power and privilege in society ... there's a tension that we have to appropriate this language to the best of our ability in the classroom because that's what we're charged to do, right? This is a formal learning environment.

Rick's sense of conflict is clear in this statement. He feels some responsibility – a "charge" – to teach students standard English within his classroom.

The teachers we interviewed experienced real and significant LIDs related to grammar instruction. While they all valued the linguistic diversity of their students, they also tended to perceive a greater linguistic flexibility in speech than in writing, sensed that attention to traditional standard English grammar could inhibit written communication, and experienced apprehension about whether Standard English grammar instruction empowered or marginalized linguistically minoritized students.

However, as McBee Orzulak (2015) states, these dilemmas were "managed" pragmatically. Most of the teachers we interviewed worked tirelessly to explicitly value their students' languages, dialects, and grammars as they also taught grammar. In the next section, we examine one instructional unit that did just that – valued the breadth of languaging practices that students brought to their classrooms while supporting grammar instruction.

Valuing Language Diversity in the Language Arts Classroom: A Case Study

When Rick designed and implemented an instructional unit in poetry that sought to value and sustain his students' linguistic and cultural practices (see Machado, Vaughan, Coppola, & Woodard, 2017, for more on Rick's classroom), he engaged with three explicit grammar instruction practices that supported language diversity: (1) selecting mentor texts that showcased a range of grammars; (2) modeling code-meshing practices; and (3) privileging alternative grammars while grading written work. While Rick still struggled with LIDs throughout the implementation of this unit, these practices supported him in managing them in productive ways.

Selecting Mentor Texts that Showcase a Range of Grammars
Throughout the unit, Rick utilized multiple poetry mentor texts that show-cased grammars and registers being used in various ways. For example, he utilized traditional, canonical mentor texts, such as the poem *Chicago*, written by Carl Sandburg (1916). His students examined the historical language in this poem, which now feels old to many of them, discussing how Sandburg made particular linguistic choices (e.g., using the term "wanton hunger," which many students had never heard before) in order to create a portrait of his city. Engaging in historical analysis of grammars, registers, and vocabulary can support the understanding that language – and our ideas about what is "proper" – is constantly evolving.

However, Rick also utilized contemporary mentor texts that engaged with grammars other than Standard English. For example, he showed students the documentary *Louder Than a Bomb* (Siskel & Jacobs, 2010), which features four Chicagoland high-school spoken word poets. The students examined the poetry in the film, which featured the use of alternative grammatical practices. For example, one poet used code-meshing practices, weaving Yiddish and Turkish terms throughout his spoken word performance. Another presented a poem using grammatical features of African-American English, such as copula absence (Smitherman, 1997). In Rick's classroom, these spoken word poems were positioned as equally valuable as the canonical ones and their grammars were studied with the same degrees of care and attention.

Modeling Code-Meshing in Oral Language
In an interview, Rick discussed how he moves between grammars, registers, and dialects in his speech. He stated, "The way that I speak is a part of the relationships and affiliations that I have cultivated over ... my entire life." Rather than attempting to check these aspects of his life at the door of his classroom, Rick modeled oral code-meshing practices for his students, positioning code-meshing as a valuable practice. For example, Rick frequently told stories in class about his family, including his wife, who is Mexican-American, and their daughter, who is bilingual and speaks both Spanish and English. When talking about conversations with his daughter, Rick often shared things she said in Spanish, or a Spanish-English hybrid, with his class. Additionally, when Rick and his students read Shakespeare's Sonnet #73, "That Time of Year, Thou Mayest in Me Behold," Rick modeled multiple registers and grammars. He read the poem aloud in a very dramatic and formal voice, then paused and said, "So, basically, whaaa?" In this instance, a quick movement from a

formal reading of a canonized text to a more colloquial response of confusion (perhaps one shared by his students), Rick demonstrated multiple ways to respond to a poem. By switching between languages and registers, then, Rick made space for alternative grammars in his classroom.

Privileging Alternative Grammars in Written Assignments
While Rick tended to model code-meshing through oral language, he also privileged uses of alternative grammars in students' written poems. For example, at the end of the poetry unit, Rick asked his students to compose and perform a spoken word poem that reflected their cultures and/or identities. In the rubric, he created for this assignment, students were evaluated on their ability to use images, graphics, and language to "reflect one's culture and identity in the poetic form of spoken word." When students did use grammatical practices outside of Standard English (e.g., code-meshing), Rick and his student teacher praised these efforts in their narrative feedback. For example, when one student integrated Spanish phrases into his English poem, Rick's student teacher commented, "Your use of Spanish here is also incredibly moving. You are taking this language that defines who you are and where your family comes from and it brings and authenticity to the poem that really makes it personal." In this unit, then, *all* grammatical practices were celebrated through assignments and feedback that expressed value for linguistic diversity.

DISCUSSION AND IMPLICATIONS

For the teachers in this study, teaching grammar was not as simple as assigning worksheets about parts of speech or correcting their students' language on written assignments. They grappled with LIDs related to perceptions of limited linguistic flexibility in writing, the sense that attention to grammar inhibited communication, and concerns about whether grammar instruction marginalized or empowered students. Rick managed tensions like these ones in productive ways, using strategies like selecting diverse mentor texts, modeling verbal code-meshing, and privileging alternative grammars in written assignments.

In their book *Pose, Wobble, Flow: A Culturally Proactive Approach to Literacy Instruction*, Garcia and O'Donnell-Allen (2015) use a yoga metaphor to describe their framework for helping teachers to: take up culturally proactive stances or "poses" in their practice; work through the challenges, or "wobbles," that emerge in the process; and then develop strategies for working toward "flow," "that always provisional state that marks growth toward, though not once-and-for-all mastery of a given pose" (https://blogessor.word press.com/2015/10/30/how-do-you-posewobbleflow/). We find the yoga metaphor particularly poignant when considering the essence of yoga is to achieve *moksha*, the Hindu word for liberation. Consequently, we take up the Pose/ Wobble/Flow framework to describe implications for equity-oriented teachers addressing grammar in writing instruction.

Pose: Taking an Equity Stance to Writing and Grammar Instruction

What sorts of poses or intentional mindsets are necessary for equity-oriented writing teachers, particularly in relation to grammar? One promising starting point is McBee Orzulak's (2015) description of "core principles of how language works that are rooted in research and agreed upon by most linguists: (1) language equity, (2) descriptive approaches to grammar, and (3) consequential language choices in classroom interactions" (p. 180). Underlying all of these principles, we think, is an explicit commitment to resist deficit language ideology.

Wobble: Grappling with Linguistic Push Pull in Grammar Instruction

However, particularly because deficit language ideology is so pervasive in our society, it is important to make space and time for writing teachers to "wobble," or experience and critically reflect on the linguistic dilemmas and push pull they experience while teaching. For example, our team has moved from interviews and case studies to an inquiry group comprised of teachers and researchers. Over the course of a semester, we met for two hours twice a month to plan, reflect on, and document equity-oriented writing instruction. We intentionally talked together about our dilemmas and developed strategies to address them (see also Puzio, Newcomer, Pratt, McNeely, Jacobs, & Hooker, 2017).

Flow: Developing Strategies to Strengthen an Equity Stance

As teachers intentionally engage with the dilemmas inherent in teaching writing, they develop strategies to strengthen their equity poses and work toward "flow." For example, in response to the three dilemmas we documented in the findings, strategies might include:

- Supporting greater linguistic flexibility in writing and writing assessment, as we do with speech.
- Heeding Wheeler and Swords' (2004) advice to focus on "patterns" rather than "errors" to reduce the binary perception of communication vs. grammar.
- Attempting Michael-Luna and Canagarajah's (2007) advice to simultaneously teach students existing rules of the discursive practice they wish to be heard in *and also* how to resist and rewrite the rules, norms, or values to serve their interests.

Rick's case study documents some explicit strategies we observed while he was in flow, including selecting diverse mentor texts that showcase language diversity. Like Rick, we would encourage teachers to seek out alternative resources for mentor texts, including videos, websites, podcasts, and images. Rick also modeled verbal code-meshing in his classroom, drawing on languages and registers that he used in his personal life. We imagine that all teachers could draw upon the breadth of languaging practices that they use in their own lives, drawing on dialects, regionalisms, or multimodal forms of communication. Finally, Rick privileged alternative grammars in his grading during the poetry unit. While we recognize that many teachers are restricted in terms of their ability to grade in creative ways, we imagine that privileging historically marginalized grammars in even one assignment (e.g., journal or poetry writing) would go a long way in honoring all the languages that students bring to their classrooms.

CONCLUSION

This chapter contributes to the extant literature by closely examining a contested area of the literacy curriculum, acknowledging teachers' dilemmas related to enacting equity-oriented writing pedagogy, and offering some initial practical suggestions for writing teachers who value students' linguistic diversity. Our study confirms McBee Orzulak's (2015) contention that equity-oriented teachers experience linguistic push pull as they contend with deeply pervasive deficit language ideologies (see also Dyson, 2015). While an equity orientation and descriptive approach to grammar are promising stances or "poses" for entering into teaching that reimagines culturally proactive grammar instruction, we need more research and teacher-centered practices (e.g., study groups, action research groups) to understand the particular "wobbles," or kinds of linguistic push pull experienced by writing teachers. As Cindy O'Donnell says, "You gotta wobble if you ever want to flow" (Garcia & O'Donnell, 2015, p. 6).

NOTES

1. We use the term *standard English* to refer to the variety of English imbued with power and status in the US, while recognizing and emphasizing that other varieties of English are equally legitimate.

2. We will use the term *grammar* to refer to the version of grammar typically taught in schools – the rule system associated with standard English syntax and morphology. Again, we recognize and emphasize that there are multiple equally legitimate grammars, or rule-systems, governing the English language.

REFERENCES

Barton, D. (2007). *Literacy: An introduction to the ecology of written language* (2nd ed.). Malden, MA: Blackwell Pub.

Delpit, L. (2006). *Other people's children: Cultural conflict in the classroom* (2nd ed.). New York, NY: New Press.

Dyson, A. H. (2015). The search for inclusion: Deficit discourse and the erasure of childhood. *Language Arts, 92*(3), 199–207.

Dyson, A. H., & Smitherman, G. (2009). The right (write) start: African American language and the discourse of sounding right. *Teachers College Record, 111*(4), 973–998.

Garciia, O. (2009). Education, multilingualism, and translanguaging in the 21st century. In A. Mohanty, M. Panda, R. Phillipson, & T. Skutnabb-Kangas (Eds.), Multilingual education for social justice: Globalising the local (pp. 128–145). New Delhi, India: Orient Blackswan.

Garcia, A. & O'Donnell-Allen, C. (2015). *Pose, wobble, flow: A culturally proactive approach to literacy instruction.* New York, NY: Teachers College Press.

Gartland, L. B., & Smolkin, L. B. (2016). The histories and mysteries of grammar instruction. *The Reading Teacher, 69*(4), 391–399. doi:10.1002/trtr.1408

Kalantzis, M., & Cope, B. (2012). *Literacies.* VIC, Australia: Cambridge University Press.

Ladson-Billings, G. (1995). Toward a theory of culturally relevant pedagogy. *American Educational Research Journal, 32*(2), 465–491.

Machado, E., Vaughan, A., Coppola, R., & Woodard, R. (2017). "Lived life through a colored lens": Culturally sustaining poetry in an urban literacy classroom. *Language Arts, 94*(6), 367–380.

Michael-Luna, S. & Canagarajah, S. (2008). Multilingual academic literacies: Pedagogical foundations for code meshing in primary and higher education. *Journal of Applied Linguistics, 4*(1), 55–77. doi:10.1558/japl.v4i1.55

McBee Orzulak, M. J. (2015). Disinviting deficit ideologies: Beyond "that's standard," "that's racist," and "that's your mother tongue." *Research in the Teaching of English, 50*(2), 176–198.

National Center for Educational Statistics. (2015). The condition of education: English language learners. Retrieved from https://nces.ed.gov/programs/coe/indicator_cgf.asp

Paris, D. (2012). Culturally sustaining pedagogy: A needed change in stance, terminology, and practice. *Educational Researcher, 41*(3), 93–97.

Puzio, K., Newcomer, S., Pratt, K., McNeely, K., Jacobs, M., & Hooker, S. (2017). Creative failures in culturally sustaining pedagogy. *Language Arts, 94*(4), 223–233.

Razfar, A. & Rumenapp, J. C. (2014). *Applying linguistics in the classroom: A sociocultural approach.* New York, NY: Routledge.

Saldaña, J. (2013). *The coding manual for qualitative researchers* (2nd ed.). Los Angeles, CA: SAGE.

Sandburg, C. (1916). *Chicago poems.* New York, NY: Henry and Holt Company.

Siskel, J., & Jacobs, G. (Producers/Directors). (2011). *Louder than a bomb* [Motion picture]. Chicago, IL: Siskel/Jacobs Productions.

Smith, M. W., Cheville, J., & Hillocks, G. (2006). "I guess I'd better watch my English": Grammars and the teaching of the language arts. In. C. A. MacArthur, S. Graham, & J. Fitzgerald (Eds.), *Handbook of writing research* (pp. 263–274). New York, NY: Guilford.

Smitherman, G. (1997). "The chain remain the same": Communicative practices in the hip hop nation. *Journal of Black Studies, 28*(1), 3–25. doi:10.1177/002193479702800101

Smitherman, G. (2006). *Word from the mother: Language and African Americans.* New York, NY: Routledge.

Wheeler, R. S., & Swords, R. (2004). Codeswitching: Tools of language and culture transform the dialectally diverse classroom. *Language Arts, 81*(6), 470–480.

Woodard, R., & Kline, S. (2016). Lessons from sociocultural writing research for implementing the common core state standards. *The Reading Teacher, 70*(2), 207–216. doi:10.1002/trtr.1505

MULTICULTURAL ELL EDUCATORS' PERSPECTIVES OF SOCIOCULTURAL DYNAMICS IN THE ADOLESCENT CLASSROOM

Nancy Laguna Luque, Earl H. Cheek, Jr. and Evan Ortlieb

ABSTRACT

To explore middle and high school English Language Learners (ELL) teaching environments from the perspective of multicultural instructors and their understanding of ELL students' reality. This qualitative study utilized participant observation and Developmental Research Sequence (Spradley, 1980) as the systematic approach to gather and to analyze data. The study was conducted in an inner city public school district in the south of Louisiana where seven multicultural ELL specialists were located; participants included were originally from the United States, Latvia, the Philippines, Jordan, Romania, and Japan. This study shed light over the fate of most Latina/o teenagers in public middle and high schools, the appropriateness of the state's response to the literacy and human needs

Addressing Diversity in Literacy Instruction
Literacy Research, Practice and Evaluation, Volume 8, 55–72
Copyright © 2018 by Emerald Publishing Limited
All rights of reproduction in any form reserved
ISSN: 2048-0458/doi:10.1108/S2048-045820170000008004

of all students at risk of failure in the middle and high school (Latina/o and African American alike), and the status educators have in the country compared to other highly qualified professionals as perceived by the multicultural educators participating in the study. Several areas of intervention were identified and described including a strong structured program specifically designed for ELLs attending middle and high school; moreover, further research is needed to advance understanding about the relationship among literacy, shame, and students' behavior.

Keywords: ELL; Latina/o teenagers; literacy; shame; academic and social defeat; otherness

Today's educational contexts present both challenges and opportunities for teachers to hone their pedagogical proficiency with diverse learners. Many educators completed teacher education programs in a different era, removed from the current world of increasing numbers of English Language Learners (ELLs). Depending upon professional development opportunities and self-study, many teachers find themselves ill-equipped to build upon native languages and cultural connections of their student body. As such, further study is needed to explore multicultural ELL educators' worlds within those contexts of their classrooms to learn about their perspectives and instructional practices.

In one of his last interviews, French philosopher Jacques Derrida expressed his understanding of notions such as *"l'autre"* (the other), "devenir conscients" (*awareness*), and "differer" (to differ); there he exposed his ideas of self-criticism or deconstruction theory. According to Derrida (2012), Europe has always been exposed to *the other* and eclipsed by *her other* and that position had forced her to constantly question her ways through external or deconstruction criticism; in this regard, he says that "every culture is haunted by her other."[1] While in this interview Derrida elaborates his *Deconstruction* explanation personifying a whole continent (Europe), which arguably could provide an understanding on how the collective conscious and unconscious of many cultures function; his ideas of human perception of the other, awareness, and perception of human differences can be also applied to the daily experience of each individual in any given context. Similarly, T. S. Szasz (1977) further discusses the concept of *the other* as "The paradox of the social man;" he connects it to the phenomena of hatred, discrimination and social prejudice. Following Szasz and Derrida's line of thought, individually and collectively we are all constantly exposed to *the other* at multiple levels depending on the geographical and emotional proximity, which has implications for heterogeneous classrooms.

The middle and high school ELL classroom, for instance, is an interesting entity in that in a reduced area and for a certain time, a semester, or a year, many *others* (in this case immigrant children and local students at risk of failure) will interact with each other with the mediation of the instructor. The teacher might find that students have acquired some literacy skills in their native tongue, while other students may not have reached an adequate literacy proficiency to be placed in mainstream settings. Culturally speaking, all participants may not feel like they have much common ground and in turn, differences are what comes most visible. Arguably, the common ground is that "we all are outsiders, we don't know the language, we are displaced, we all have suffered some kind of social violence or abuse" (Derrida, 2012).

What becomes increasingly clear in these adolescent classrooms is that the teacher makes the difference – s/he will create a climate for all participants, hopefully one that is conducive to learning with limited risk and viewed as a place of refuge. Still, all persons in this classroom will have to overcome diverse obstacles, deconstruct or modify what they know, and build something new by constantly reflecting and taking part in purposeful revision of terms and concepts that form part of their understanding of the world and by giving place to new ones. The teacher can shift student perspectives so that diversity is seen as an advantage by choosing to explicitly address diversity first and foremost in literacy instruction.

The purpose of this study was to explore the social dynamics of awareness, deconstruction, and otherness appreciation within middle and high school settings in the public school system from the perspectives of multicultural ELL educators. We sought to reveal insight about the contexts in which ELL educators enact literacy instruction and how their teaching approaches can leverage diversity toward holistic growth and student achievement.

LITERACY ACQUISITION, AWARENESS, AND THE PARADOX OF THE SOCIAL PERSON

British neurologist Dr. Oliver Sacks in his book *Seeing Voices* (Sacks, 2000) stated that "if one is to explore the fundamental role of language, one needs to study … its failure to develop." Even though many immigrant children in the classes observed would have already developed listening and speaking abilities in their first language, once they arrive in the United States they are at odds with the contexts in which they study. Their potential to communicate and interact is often severely restricted due to cultural clashes and second language barriers. This is particularly problematic because language acquisition and literacy development that occur naturally in the process of learning new concepts in the ELL classroom facilitates deep levels of awareness development and consequently set the ground for future ethical choices (Henkin, 2005).

Getting students to think about social justice through their reading and writing is part of a multicultural education; when students are engaged in making meaning, their literacy skills develop and grow. Literacy is a vehicle that ultimately helps one understand and accept the other. Henkin (2005) further advocates for the creation of "democratic, fair, and hate-free schools that confront all forms of bullying and harassment." The present study proposes a strong connection to Henkin's (2005) teaching approach, Sacks' (2000) research about the relationship between language and thought, and Derrida's (2012) views about the perception of *the other* and self-criticism or *deconstruction*.

HUMANIZING EDUCATION AND LEVELS OF AWARENESS

Freire (1998) stated that a humanizing education is the path for students to become conscious about their presence in the world not only taking into consideration their personal needs but also the needs of others.[2] He added that illiteracy suffocates the consciousness and the expressiveness of human beings because without the ability to read and write a person's capacity to reflect and re-think their interpretation of their world will be very limited; this was also discussed above by examining Sacks' (2000) observations about the necessity of acquiring language in order to build new concepts and ideas. In other words, a person with a very limited vocabulary is unable to significantly interact with others by understanding and making self-understood, this then could throw individuals at the edge of despair because their human nature would be thus negated; as a result, accumulated frustration would translate in resentment and anger which in turn could unchain series of uncivilized behaviors; we could agree with Freire (1998) in that illiteracy is an impediment to earning full citizenship; he says that in "literate cultures illiterates can't complete the cycle in the relationship language, thought, and reality,"[3] thus, persons transitioning from one cultural context to the other will need to learn new words in order to build new thoughts and accomplish the most human necessity of communication. In doing so, they will be able to understand *the other* – this goes beyond merely grasping the meaning of disconnected words into reaching deeper layers of understanding of the mindset – the connections and the relationships among individuals, sociocultural objects, situations, events, etc. – and the rationale behind a culture patterns of social behaviors while making themselves understood.

Freire (1971) also stated that the reading of the world precedes the reading of the word, meaning that persons get awareness of their context prior to the understanding brought through the reading of the text; he uses the term *consciousness* referring to "fragmented knowledge" or the reaction to the concrete objects of the world, and the term *conscientização* referring to "critical knowledge" or the relationship between objects, facts, and the world.

SCIENCES OF COMPLEXITY AND SYSTEMIC CHANGE IN RELATION TO EDUCATION

Most scholars agree with the idea that an education model founded on the leading basics of an industrial/technology age has to be restructured taking into consideration the needs of current and future educators and students in a globalized society that is more representative of the information age than of the industrial one. They recognize that literacy challenges for educators in the middle and high school settings could stem from worlds that overlap including the student's world, the school habitat, and the complexities of the curriculum and of the pedagogy (Moje, Overby, Tysvaer, & Morris, 2008; O'Brien, Stewart, & Moje, 1995) and conclude that the school culture in the secondary school adds to the intricate world of adolescent literacy. Doll (2008) and Reigeluth (2004) also directed attention to context and connections in education; they advocated for educational systems being structured around a person's appropriate curriculum more than around students' age.

CHALLENGES IN THE FIELD

One of the greatest challenges to overcome in education in general, in academic success, and in literacy development specifically is related to poverty; poor families have limited access to books and printed materials, live in decimated neighborhoods, attend underfunded schools, and, thus, have fewer chances to succeed. Students living in school districts of 20% poverty levels or above experience even more compounded challenges because these kinds of schools receive about 29% less funding support per student than schools in more affluent areas (edbuild.org, 2015[4]); as Selcuk & Sirin (2005) found "Of all the factors examined [...] family SES at the student level is one of the strongest correlates of academic performance. At the school level, the correlations were even stronger" (p. 438). Most recent immigrants and ethnic minorities are among the poorest in the country and rank at the lowest literacy/academic attainment; furthermore, being Hispanic and/or Black is a characteristic of students found at the bottom list of underperformers, "descriptive statistics found that multiracial students who self-identify as [B]lack or Hispanic achieve lower grades than do those who self-identify as [W]hite or Asian" (Buggey, 2007, p. 153). According to edbuild.org statistics (2015) from 2006 to 2013 poor students' population across the United States increased by 60% and in school districts with poverty levels of 40% or above the number of students raised by 260%, researchers add, "These concentrated-poverty areas pose heightened risks to child well-being and opportunity." They said that schools in concentrated poverty areas "need more resources to level the playing field."

RESEARCH DESIGN

Interpretive Frameworks

This research inquiry uses the lens of social justice in that (1) the situation explored pedagogical approaches of multicultural ELL educators in the middle and high school classroom to further the understanding of literacy instruction (and its social implications) to disadvantaged minorities such as migrant, displaced, and poor populations; (2) the rigorous procedures of research and standards of evaluation and ethics respect the participants, their individual differences, and the sites where the study takes place; (3) reciprocity was provided to participants; and (4) participants and researchers are considered co-owners of the information collected (Creswell, 2007).

The current study can also be interpreted from a social constructivism perspective in that firstly, it acknowledges that the individual experiences of the participants and their interactions with others generate multiple realities; secondly, participant values are honored, and thirdly, data are obtained through methods such as observations, interviewing, and analysis of texts (2007, pp. 36–37). Furthermore, this research could be read as well from the systemic change perspective in that the researchers were probing the context in the quest for indications about ELL educators' attitudes toward concepts/ constructs of awareness, deconstruction, otherness appreciation, context, and connections. Finally, this study responds to what Spradley (1980, p. 18) calls *strategic research* in that it begins with an interest in human problems within public institutions (the school) designed for multicultural constituency.

Data Collection

The present ethnographic case study is framed within a qualitative approach to research that involves collecting data in the field, the natural setting where the participants are located, and the researcher being the fundamental instrument for data collection. The researcher collected multiple forms of data through direct observation, by interviewing participants, and using open-ended questions in questionnaires developed as new information emerged. Through the use of complex reasoning skills all along this process and focusing primarily on the participant's perspectives, their subjective view of their world, and the meanings they ascribe to their reality the researcher gleaned patterns, categories, and themes.

The participants in this research were purposefully selected multicultural ELL educators, natives from various countries (including the U.S., Philippines, Jordan, Romania, Latvia, and Japan) currently working in public middle and high school settings. Seeking to find and describe similarities and differences among these professionals' teaching practices and whether observable differences/similarities could be linked to their background they were observed in the context of daily interaction with their mixed population of ELLs and also informally interviewed during their class preparation time and/or after school hours; all observations and interviews were completed over the course of 7 weeks approximately. Ethnographic data collected were analyzed, contrasted, and compared; the analysis strategy involved identifying issues particular to the world of each participant and searching for common themes among them (Yin, 2009).

Participant Observation

The Developmental Research Sequence Method (DRS) is a systematic approach for conducting ethnographic inquiry initiated by ethnographer James Spradley (1980) in the late 1970s. As he states, both ethnographic interview and participant observation involve a succession of tasks that are better carried out following certain sequence (p. vii); the foundation of his design lies on the critical need to study meaning carefully, thus along with the DRS he affords a theory of meaning and the specific methodology for the investigation of it (p. 9).[5]

The DRS method then follows a six-stage cyclical pattern that begins by *choosing a research project* and *asking ethnographic questions*; Spradley (1980) emphasizes that question and answers must be discovered in the social situation being studied, otherwise the researcher risks obtaining distorted information by asking questions prompted through prior assumptions and outside of the cultural scene. The regard to parsimony following his method guided the researcher in the discovery of the new question to ask. Next to this was *making an ethnographic record* that included using all resources and means available to record observations; the record in this study was kept using Atlas. ti sound recording in iPad, pictures of instruments and places, and written field notes taken by the researcher. As data were gathered, their *analysis* was conducted immediately for analysis entailed the discovery of new questions; this was the twin stage of the recording one. The last stage then had to do with the *writing the final report*, which in this case was open-ended (1980, p. 34), leaving room for the researcher to pursue even more intensive analysis within this particular research agenda.

In this study, the *target place* was the multicultural ELL educator's working environment in four local public middle and three high schools. The schools were located within a perimeter of 41miles approximately[6] in a southern inner city of about 230,000 habitants where 54% of the population is black, 39% white, and 7% other.[7] The public school district consists of roughly 80 schools; ethnicity in the enrolment of around 44,400 (2014) is represented primarily by black students with 80% and the 20% remaining split between white 11% and other 9% (Latina/o, Asian, and Native Hawai'ian); gender is almost equally distributed (female 51% and male 49%). There are more than 50 languages represented among the foreign student population where Spanish speakers are the most numerous. This public school district states in its vision the desire to equip students with knowledge, skills, and values necessary to be successful; the district equally stresses the environment where students interact as caring, rigorous, and safe.

The *Actors* were the ELL instructors. In this school district, the ELL educators could be considered as itinerant teachers in two ways: (1) they do not have a classroom or a designated[8] specific area where to work with the students they serve, and (2) they are assigned to at least two schools; these instructional specialists serve then either middle or high school students or both depending on the schools they are assigned to. These ELL educators belong to various ethnic groups, have diverse nationality backgrounds, and have come to the profession through multiple academic, career, and job training experiences (all have at least a bachelor degree, teaching certification, and ELL training certification). Gender ratio is in favor of females 6 to 1 which is also representative of the profession (National Center for Education Information, 2011), the median age is 40 years old, family composition varies from single individual, to single parent, and to the traditional father, mother, and children model.

The selection of the participants included participants from various cultural and ethnic backgrounds, thus securing a representative sampling of culturally diverse teachers. Since the study intended to shed light upon how multicultural ELL educators/instructors perceive various challenges and opportunities related to their work environments, inclusive background, it was important to establish multiethnic participant representation to help detecting possible comparison and contrast facts and the connection to participants' personal history; however, equal gender participation could not be granted due to the majority of females in the field as stated before. Before proceeding with interviews and participant observation, permission from supervisors at the district level as well as IRB documentation were obtained.

Finally, the *activities* or the "streams of behaviors" and the events participants engage included the activities of ELL instructors, which could be represented in concentric circles where the greater circle is any of the spaces where the educator delivers instruction, the middle circle would be the school(s), and the smallest one – or where the educator spends less time would be the district offices and other places.

Schematic diagrams (Fig. 1) would convey a perspective of the cultural scene from a different angle.

The schematic diagram represents four main areas of the ELL specialist work: on the left below are responsibilities with the ELL office and with the school district, on the left above are assignment that ranges from one to three schools, at each of these the ELL specialist would routinely perform some or all of the typical roles and duties branching out of "errands," and on the right is represented ELL daily work duties including "push-in" model above and below are listed pulling-out instruction kinds.

In the schematic diagram (Fig. 2), following are noted unscripted duties of the ELL specialist.

ELL specialists voluntarily engage in extracurricular activities, as represented in part by Fig. 2. They are proactively learning the language of their students, and they diligently search for opportunities in the local area to establish connections between the school (ELLs) and the community.

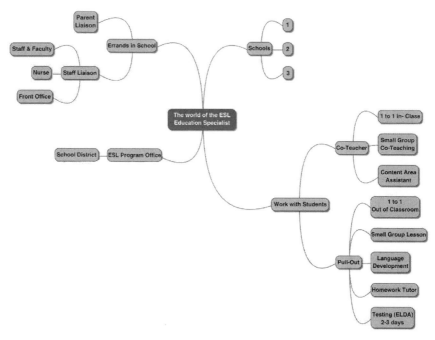

Fig. 1. The World of the ELL Specialist.

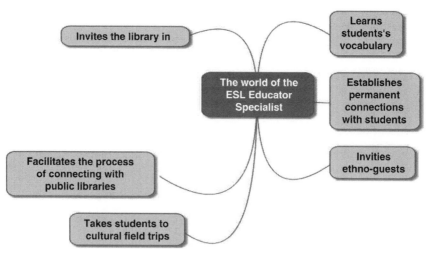

Fig. 2. Extracurricular and Outreach Activities.

BIAS AND VALIDITY

It is not easy for any kind of research to be totally free of bias; as Creswell (2007) noted "we always bring certain beliefs and philosophical assumptions to our research." He also pointed out that to avoid bias. the greatest difficulties lied in (1) becoming aware of personal assumptions, and (2) deciding whether they will be integrated into the qualitative study or not.

Great parsimony was employed regarding record keeping; the participant observer kept detailed record of both objective observations and subjective feelings, and even though the degree of personal involvement in this research was high, it has not been the intention of the researcher to gather data supporting any particular view point or philosophical perspective throughout the study.

FINDINGS

After systematic examination of all data gathered from interviews and observations, several findings emerged and implications for further research became evident as well. Before summarizing findings obtained from this investigation, it is necessary to look back at the questions that guided the research: (a) How are the approaches to literacy instruction similar or different among the multicultural ELL educators/instructors? (b) How multicultural ELL educators/instructors perceive challenges in their classroom? and (c) What are the multicultural educators'/instructors' attitudes toward concepts/constructs of deconstruction/otherness appreciation, awareness, context, and connections?

While keeping in mind the questions that steered the inquiry process three themes surfaced. It is important to notice that in the obtaining of the themes, all participants included in the study came from distinct sociocultural and ethnic backgrounds, have had diverse educational and professional experiences, interpreted in various ways their moral responsibility as educators, held different attitudes toward awareness, the other, and the context, and strongly voiced a number of challenges in their professional practice field. Yet, the themes that emerged from this exploration were extant regardless of approaches to literacy instruction, interpretation of challenges, and/or personal and career background; these themes complexly interconnected with the multicultural ELLs attitudes related to sociocultural dynamics in their teaching environment.

Furthermore, cultural themes were gathered, as Spradley (1980) suggested, from the recurrent assumptions participants have learned, used, or implied in their daily experience, thus forming complex nets of patterns. In other words, what participants believed and accepted as true and valid and the underlying interpretation principles of their rationale for action constituted the grounds where themes were identified. It is opportune then to remember that the initiator of this systematic approach to research (Participant Observation & DRS) defined cultural themes as "any principle recurrent in a number of domains, tacit or explicit, and serving as a relationship among subsystems of cultural meaning" (1980, pp. 140–141).

The three overarching themes that emerged from this investigation were (a) the reality and fate of Latina/o teenagers, (b) the State's lack of awareness regarding ELLs, and (c) the status of education and of the teaching profession in the country.

The Reality and Fate of Latina/o Teenagers

Even though ELLs population in the State come from various regions in the world and represent diverse ethnic backgrounds the Latina/o segment is the most at-risk-of-academic/social-failure. All participants agreed on that the presence of Asian and Middle Eastern students at the middle and high schools visited did not translate in difficulties for teachers, for schools enrolling them, or for the ELL program because (1) these students entered the system with adequate schooling experiences like understanding and accepting of rules, regulations, and routines proper of academic environments; (2) relating to their age and grade placement, they had normal or above-standard first language literacy and academic development; (3) they were reasonably or highly motivated to continue in school and to graduate; (4) their parents were very involved in their education and were aware of their academic progress and overall behavior; and (5) as a result of these factors combined students of Asian and of Middle Eastern origin tended to learn the language quickly or at acceptable rate, adapted to school environment, and ultimately achieved academic success. Whereas the presence of the Latina/o children in the middle and high school environment was almost always because there were few exceptions – harbingers of distress at different levels.

The reality of the majority of Latina/o students in this program is very complex. Most of these children entered the territory without resources; they fled conflict zones in the neighboring countries; they left behind very close family members, despite being so young they have risked their life crossing natural and human-made obstacles; they embarked in such an adventure with the hope to contact a relative or a friend in the United States and thus secure survival. Crossing the border and being placed with friends or relatives do not represent the end of troubles for this population of middle and high school-age children. When the joy of waking up under a friendly roof fades away, the discovery of a sour reality begins; suffering is not over, it is just of a different kind. It does not explode on their faces with a blast, rather it enters their being little by little, one unconquered obstacle after the next one, one stumbling block after the other; it is like a canker sore that devours hope and faith in society. Like the boxer struggling to stand still for one more round, many of these teenagers will take blow after blow in their fight for self-esteem, even more when education seems unattainable because the quest for dignity in their context is uncertain and it could take a lifetime.

The first difficult circumstance they face is getting enrolled in school upon taking a series of ELL assessments, even if students are explained what a placement test is they might interpret the results as a failure. Thus, entering the school system as a middle or high school displaced Latina/o teen is very problematic for at least three reasons: (1) most among these children cannot provide proper identification, medical records, or previous schooling documentation; if they happen to have some paperwork it is not translated into English; (2) not having handy what is required to enroll them in school is not only complicated for the ELL program office and for the school staff, but it is disgraceful, onerous, and frustrating for the teen and his family; and (3) finally, this enrolling process turns out to be a shocking and unfortunate circumstance because the crucial connection "parent–school system child" was not established; this could be in part due to not having a close relative fluent speaker of English that would represent both sides well, or someone else they trust to bridge the language chasm. Enduring these embarrassments makes the gap deeper, disgrace more appalling, and the prospectus of establishing an honorable and enduring connection more unlikely. Furthermore, most of these middle and high school students have not been accepted in the country "legally"; in other words, they were admitted in the territory without being granted the least of all humanitarian conditions which is asylum.

Moreover, they often realize the other children in their classes appear to have more sophisticated academic focus and goals in life. School may not have always been a priority in their development nor an integral part of their life experiences so far because when life is threatened everything else becomes secondary; in other words, survival supersedes schooling, then they have not tasted and appreciated how sweet it can be to acquire knowledge and understanding. Furthermore, to compound this situation even more, when these ELLs are placed in a language intervention class or under the protection of an ELL specialist, they become extremely aware of their hopelessness because even the most basic of basic tasks become very hard for them to perform when they are not given the time, the consistency, and the structure they need to really build a solid foundation for further knowledge; rather they are exposed to scattered and disengaged learning experiences with which are difficult to connect when they lack a solid foundation. These adolescents become keenly aware of what their fate has been so far, for they have not had: (1) ideal childhood experiences and adequate schooling that would have given them enough social and civility skills, like understanding and performing acceptable behaviors in school settings; (2) access to elementary education where they should have acquired first language literacy skills and introduction to content area fields of knowledge, and in the circumstance of students admitted to secondary schools, access to middle school education; (3) basic knowledge of social and exact sciences, and basic technology literacy skills that would help them transfer previous knowledge to middle and high school content classes; (4) parents with at least average literacy skills in first language and basic knowledge of English that would be able to follow up at home with school's assignments; (5) community-smart and community-connected parents that would be proactive finding ways to navigate the system and to be present at school, thus sparing the children further shame; and (6) parents or guardians that were not afraid of being deported at any time, thus feeling free to interact with school staff on behalf of the children hence demonstrating interest in their education.

Typically among at-risk ELLs all or most of the above are missing; these students would then have a better chance for academic and social success if upon entering the schooling system they would be granted: (1) a reasonable amount of time to make up for what they have missed so far: structured and appropriate life and learning experiences and sound literacy instruction; (2) knowledgeable teachers (highly qualified content area experts and ELL trained) that would understand the situation and provide the most adequate instruction; (3) school-based programs and materials to foster their academic and social development; (4) institutional support from their schools requesting their overall progress to be assessed in realistic ways and with adequate instruments until they reach language and content area development that could be fairly measured along with local standards; and (5) an accountability system with incentives based on language acquisition, academic, and behavior performance, and community service/involvement that would be significant in their quest for dignity.

The State's Lack of Awareness Regarding ELLs

The ELL specialists participating in the study indicated that ELLs' difficulties in the district are similar across the state and that their perceptions are confirmed when they network with colleagues. The state's lack of awareness is reflected in the: (a) minimal resources available to better fund the program (i.e., to hire enough specialists and staff that can adequately respond to the growing ELL population's needs); (b) absence of provisions for proper training in ELL instructional strategies and ELLs sociocultural awareness among the middle and high school teachers; and (c) children being placed according to age instead of socioacademic/literacy proficiency. These children are not being placed in the appropriate environment that would help them overcome various kinds of deficiencies as previously discussed; neither are provided with the resources necessary to have a fair chance at education.

ELL specialists agreed that the state needs to fund a strong structured program specifically designed for ELLs attending middle and high school. That program should have four major components: (1) a training module oriented to create a solid foundation of good habits and routines; newcomer students (foreign and local) would acquire proper study habits, understand and follow school routines, learn acceptable social behaviors, and be instructed on hygiene habits and civic manners; (2) the second module would concentrate on intensive training in different literacies ELL, first language, and cyber. Students entering with no literacy skills whatsoever would have to spend more time learning to read and write in their first language while also taking ELL; (3) the third module would focus on sociocultural involvement; children would be allowed robust exposure to artistic, scientific, sports, museums, leisure, and community service venues; and (4) the last component of such a program would offer content area classes guided by highly qualified content area teachers with ELL training, it would also include information, training, and apprenticeship opportunities for vocational and trade alternatives considering more hands-on driven students and those that were definitely not college-bound. As specialists expressed, most ELLs in the middle and high school who drop out do so because they are allowed and the environment they are in fosters frustration, shame, and anger instead of hope to overcome adversity.

The Status of Education and the Teaching Profession in the Country

All school libraries should have designated and appropriate reading-for-leisure areas, small group study cubicles, and a wealth of reading materials of all sorts readily available for the students to peruse; pre-teen/teenager ELLs must be encouraged to make use of the library (not discouraged), must be instructed on school library protocols, etiquette, and services, and they must be allowed "library-time" in their schedules. When libraries are being used as everything but a library, it could mean that: (1) the school lacks adequate physical space; and/or (2) administrators are not giving the prominence the library should have as a literacy center. Whatever the reasons for obscuring the place of the library in a learning community, it should be properly addressed.

None of the participant educators had an appropriate teaching/personal space at their work place. Participants and their students had to roam here and there in search for an available spot where to hold a short lesson. If at six schools out of seven there are not appropriate spaces for students' literacy development and study engagement and if all of educators participating do not have suitable designated spaces for instruction delivery, organization, and display of class materials, it could be a sign of unsatisfactory leadership at school, program, and district levels and/or of government's negligence to sufficiently fund school and education.

As evidenced in this study, there are crucial connections that are inadequately established, the parent–school and the parent–child's bonds seem rather fragile or inexistent in this segment of the population; thus, schools must be empowered and given the resources to properly intervene. Programs may be available at school or in the community, but the lack of access poor families have to them in terms of transportation, awareness, language barrier, or survival exigencies represent major issues for these families.

SUMMARY

Overall, this investigation concluded that the reality (academic prospectus and social fate) of middle and high school ELLs is very complex, specifically the situation of students of Latina/o origin, and intricately revealing the level of awareness the state has regarding ELLs as well as the nature of the response it gives to this population's needs through current ELL provisions. The inquiry also sheds light upon the status of education as a social institution and of the teaching profession in the country. By reviewing the data obtained from interviews and classroom observations, these findings suggest areas that require further investigation. It is from the perspectives of the multicultural ELL specialists that this investigation sheds light on possible connecting and/or modifying relationships among literacy, awareness, context, and otherness. It is also through their lens that a novel construct or series of constructs could be suggested: (1) triggers of shame among ELL pre-teens and teenagers and their incidence in dropping out of school; (2) the relationship linking literacy, pride, and behavior at the middle and high school level among ELLs; (3) the relationship linking literacy, pride, and behavior at the middle and high school level among parents of students at risk and whether it could be indicator of connection with school and involvement with child's education; (4) the relationship between immigration status and self-esteem; and (5) the relationship between parent's literacy level and parent's presence at a child's school. By uncovering these themes and bringing them to the forefront of the investigation, social awareness and attitudes toward *the other* could be better assessed in the light of social justice.

NOTES

1. Derrida (2012). Une critique extérieure ou de déconstruction [car] elle (Europe) a toujours été exposée à son autre et éclipsée par lui, elle a été obligée de se remettre en question. Chaque culture est hantée par son autre.
2. Freire (1998). p. xiii foreword. Cited by Donaldo Macedo & Ana Maria Araujo Freire.
3. Freire (1998). *Ibid.* p. 2.
4. http://viz.edbuild.org/maps/2015/student-poverty-timelapse/
5. Spradley's theory of meaning is grounded on the systematic analysis of cultural domains identified in a given social situation. He defines cultural domains as categories of meanings (p. 88) where cultural categories (or domains) include three basic elements: cover term, included terms, and semantic relationship.
6. All values in the demographic description are rounded to the closest digit.
7. https://suburbanstats.org/population
8. ESL instructors in this study appear not to have basic/acceptable working space conditions. Unlike other professionals in various fields of knowledge or expertise that are provided with adequate working spaces and tools to proficiently perform their duties.

REFERENCES

Buggey, T. (2007). A picture is worth. *Journal of Positive Behavior Interventions, 9*(3), 151–158.
Creswell, J. W. (2007). *Qualitative inquiry and research design: Choosing among five approaches.* London, UK: Sage.

Derrida, J. (2012). Interview with Richard Kerney. "La déconstruction et l'autre." *Les Temps Modernes, 669/670*, 7–29. doi:0316 K 82876

Doll, W. E. (2008), Complexity and the culture of curriculum. *Educational Philosophy and Theory, 40*, 190–212. doi:10.1111/j.1469-5812.2007.00404.x

Freire, P. (1971). *Pedagogy of the oppressed* (p. 182). New York, NY: Herder and Herder. Translated from the original Portuguese manuscript by Myra Bergman Ramos.

Freire, P. (1998). *Teachers as cultural workers*. Boulder, CO: Westview Press.

Henkin, R. (2005). *Confronting bullying: Literacy as a tool for character education*. Portsmouth, NH: Heinemann.

Moje, E. B., Overby, M., Tysvaer, N., & Morris, K. (2008). The complex world of adolescent literacy: Myths, motivations, and mysteries. *Harvard Educational Review, 78*(1), 107–154.

National Center for Education Information. (2011). *Profile of teachers in the U. S. 2011*. Washington, DC: Author.

O'Brien, D. G., Stewart, A., & Moje, E. B. (1995). Why content literacy is difficult to infuse into the secondary school: Complexities of curriculum, pedagogy, and school culture. *Reading Research Quarterly, 30*(3), 442–463.

Reigeluth, C. M. (2004). *Chaos theory*. Paper presented at the AERA Annual Meeting 2004, San Diego, CA.

Sacks, O. W. (2000). *Seeing voices*. New York, NY: Vintage Books.

Sirin, S. R. (2005). Socioeconomic status and academic achievement: A meta-analytic review of research. *Review of Educational Research, 75*(3), 417–453.

Spradley, J. P. (1980). *Participant observation*. Orlando, FL: Harcourt Brace College Publishers.

SuburbanStats.org. (2015). *Current demographics, statistics and information of every city in the U. S.* Retrieved from https://suburbanstats.org/population. Accessed on 11-12-2015.

Szasz, T. S. (1977). *The manufacture of madness*. New York, NY: Harper & Row.

Yin, R. K. (2009). *Case study research: Design and method* (4th ed.). Thousand Oaks, CA: SAGE.

SCENARIOS AND SUGGESTIONS: LITERACY INSTRUCTION FOR ENGLISH LANGUAGE LEARNERS

Tess Dussling

ABSTRACT

The purpose of this chapter is to identify specific instructional strategies to help English language learners develop literacy skills. Potential difficulties in areas of decoding, vocabulary, and fluency are explored along with suggestions to implement effective instruction. The intention of this chapter is not to be a research document, but a pragmatic guide for educators of English language learners. Through reflective practice and backed by research, I walk readers through classroom and professional development scenarios and also present ways to effectively support the emerging literacy skills of English language learners. Readers will be presented with research-based instructional methods shown to enhance crucial early literacy skills for English language learners along with practical suggestions for teachers to put research into practice in the classroom. Scenarios and research-based practices illuminate how to effectively work with English language learners. Research-based evidence is presented, showing that English language learners go through the same developmental milestones

Addressing Diversity in Literacy Instruction
Literacy Research, Practice and Evaluation, Volume 8, 73–88
Copyright © 2018 by Emerald Publishing Limited
All rights of reproduction in any form reserved
ISSN: 2048-0458/doi:10.1108/S2048-045820170000008005

as native English-speaking students, but may require some additional modifications along with explicit instruction. The chapter describes how teachers can build foundational reading skills for English language learners, something that is crucial for later academic success.

Keywords: English language learners; decoding; word study; vocabulary; fluency; cultural and linguistic diversity

Throughout the United States, growing numbers of students who are having difficulty with reading are also in the process of acquiring a new language (McCardle, Mele-McCarthy, Cutting, Leos, & D'Emilio, 2005). There is an extensive body of research documenting the academic difficulties faced by students who are learning English (e.g., Haager, 2007; Kamps et al., 2007; Klinger, Artiles, & Barletta, 2006; Leseaux, 2006), making it imperative that teachers utilize appropriate and effective instructional methods. As classrooms across the country continue to change, so too must the practices and skills of classroom teachers.

One of the greatest challenges faced by educators throughout the country is how to best instruct this growing population of students, many of whom are placed in classes with monolingual English speakers. Classroom teachers are expected to provide English language learners with intellectually demanding content while helping provide growth in the English language. To do this effectively, teachers must be able to recognize students' strengths and weaknesses in order to tailor strategies that enhance student understanding as well as growth in the English language. While there are certainly debates among policy makers, researchers, administrators, and educators about how to best instruct English language learners, it is the classroom teachers who are called on to rise to the challenge of teaching and meeting the needs of English language learners every day. It is essential that teachers of English language learners use a wide array of instructional strategies and know how to choose the most effective strategies.

This chapter is based on my personal experiences in teaching English language learners and my commitment to helping culturally and linguistically diverse learners succeed academically. I have designed this chapter to be a resource to help educators understand the needs of English language learners while providing strategies to promote reading skills. Throughout the chapter I have provided scenarios depicting English language learners I have taught in classes or conversations I have had with teachers regarding instructional methods for English language learners. It is my hope that these scenarios will help educators think about how to apply specific instructional strategies in real-world situations.

To situate the scenarios and recommendations I provide in this chapter, I begin with a short description of my experience working with English language learners. I then briefly discuss some background information as well as growth projections related to English language learners. Three main components of reading (decoding, fluency, and vocabulary) will then be addressed. Each component will include a short scenario along with practical suggestions. The chapter ends with some general suggestions for meeting the needs of culturally and linguistically diverse students.

MY EXPERIENCE WITH ENGLISH LANGUAGE LEARNERS

My career in education began at a large elementary school in southern Florida. I taught third-grade retention and all of my students were in their third year of third grade. This was because my students had not passed the reading portion of the state test. Further complicating this, all of my students were also English language learners. This certainly led me to question whether my students' below grade level test scores were due to difficulties with reading or if their low scores were due to a lack of English language proficiency. Working with these students challenged me to become a better teacher and forced me to dig deeper and find reading instructional strategies to meet their needs. Through discussions with fellow teachers, I knew that I was not alone in wanting to know more about how to effectively teach students who were learning English while learning new content. Knowing that reading is an essential skill to bridge language and culture, and being aware that children who come from homes where the primary language is not English are often at-risk for difficulty in learning to read (e.g., Duran, Roseth, & Hoffman, 2010; Ehri, Dreyer, Flugman, & Gross, 2007; Hammer, Lawrence, & Miccio, 2007; Snow, Burns, & Griffin, 1998), I wanted to explore instructional strategies to help my students develop language and succeed academically. My intention with this chapter is to share some of my experiences and insights regarding literacy instruction for young English language learners.

WHO ARE ENGLISH LANGUAGE LEARNERS?

While many students may share the label English language learner, this does not mean that they are a homogenous group. Some English language learners arrive in the United States as young children or adolescents. Others may be born in the United States. Just like native English speakers, culturally and linguistically diverse students bring a wide variety of experiences and have varying backgrounds, abilities, and needs. Knowing that children develop skills at different speeds, educators cannot expect all English language learners to learn in the same manner (Harper & de Jong, 2004). Some English language learners may come to your classroom with prior exposure to English, while others may not have been exposed to English until entering school. This is important to note because students' language learning and academic outcomes may differ depending on when they were first exposed to English (Hammer et al., 2007). Some English language learners may have prior schooling experience, while others may have experienced little to no formal schooling. While there is certainly a large range of socioeconomic status (SES) levels and parental education attainment levels among English language learners, students learning English are more likely than native English-speaking students to come from low SES homes and have parents with limited formal education (García & Jensen, 2006). I mention this because it is important for educators to keep in mind that educational achievement for all students, including culturally and linguistically diverse students, can be impacted by a variety of factors including family income, parental educational levels, and home life structure.

Throughout the United States, the number of students classified as English language learners has risen dramatically. The number of English language learners more than doubled between 1989 and 2006 – from 2 to 5.1 million (National Clearinghouse for English Language Acquisition, 2008). This dramatic growth shows no signs of stopping. Children from culturally and linguistically diverse backgrounds continue to be the fastest growing population in the United States (United States Census Bureau, 2010). While the majority of English language learners are concentrated in California, Texas, Florida, New York, Illinois, and Arizona, some of the greatest growth are in the ELL population outside of these states in places such as South Carolina and Kentucky (García, Kleifgen, & Falchi, 2008).

READING INSTRUCTION FOR
ENGLISH LANGUAGE LEARNERS

While there is agreement in the literature that English language development is related to the acquirement of literacy skills and that limited English proficiency can make the development of reading skills difficult (August & Hakuta, 1997; August & Shanahan, 2006; Francis, Rivera, Lesaux, Kieffer, & Rivera, 2006), reading instruction should not be delayed to wait for the attainment of language proficiency. Knowing that the English language has a deep orthography, resulting in longer time to learn to read English than many other languages, educators should not withhold reading instruction from students with lower language proficiency levels (Quiroga, Lemos-Britton, Mostafapour, Abbott, & Beringer, 2002). Research has consistently shown that English language learners can and do benefit from explicit reading instruction regardless of their oral language abilities (O'Connor, Bocian, Beebe-Frankenberger, & Linklater, 2010). While we must still pay attention to the oral language needs of students, it is important to note that English language learners' ability to progress in early skills, such as decoding, does not appear to be limited by their oral language proficiency (August & Shananhan, 2010; Gersten & Geva, 2003). Furthermore, research has shown that literacy development in a new language can occur even with limited oral proficiency if the student has certain basic skills developed in their native language (Genesee, Lindholm-Leary, Saunders, & Christian, 2005). It is important to note that while English language learners can learn to read in English when their oral language skills are not fully developed (Gunn, Biglan, Smolkowski, & Ary, 2000), reading instruction is more effective when it is coupled with instruction to help develop oral language skills (Gersten & Geva, 2003).

The development of literacy abilities in a new language is rather similar to literacy development in the first language (Brice & Brice, 2009; Genesee et al., 2005). Since children learning a new language go through the same developmental milestones as monolingual children (Genesee, Paradis, & Cargo, 2004), the same type of instructional sequence can be used. This means that English language learners, just like native English-speaking children, should receive systematic and explicit instruction in areas such as phonemic awareness, the alphabetic principle, irregular/high-frequency words, and fluency building. Certainly, the goals of reading include understanding and learning; however, the basic foundational building blocks must be in place first. The next sections are devoted to scenarios and suggestions for specific reading instruction activities to develop phonics and word study skills, vocabulary, and fluency with English language learners.

Phonics Instruction and Word Study Activities

In a recent professional development workshop, I heard several teachers of English language learners discussing concerns about teaching decoding skills to students with limited English proficiency. One teacher worried that since English is so irregular, teaching patterns that may not always work will simply confuse students. Another teacher jumped in and said that while English can certainly be complicated due to the irregularities, it is important for students, including English language learners, to learn the relationships between letters and sounds and that understanding this code helps students learn to read accurately and independently.

These were good points and certainly worthy of further discussion. Hearing this conversation reminded me of my experiences teaching English language learners. For example, Javier knew his short vowels, but had difficulty understanding the final "e" syllable type. This made decoding words such as *home, game,* and *life* challenging. Another type of challenge faced by my students was due to sounds in the English language that were difficult for them. Noel had extreme difficulty sounding out or spelling words with consonant digraphs and consonant blends as they were not something he heard in his native language.

Can you imagine putting together a puzzle without a picture to use as a guide? Perhaps you would start to look for pieces with a flat edge, a corner, or pieces that had similar colors. Those would be good starting points, but it would certainly be a difficult task. Learning to read in a new language without knowing systematic rules and patterns would be a similar task.

Helping English Language Learners Understand the Alphabetic Principle
Since the English language is alphabetic, knowing how to decode words is essential. The alphabetic principle is the concept that there is a systematic relationship between letters and sounds. English language learners should be explicitly taught that some letters can represent more than one sound, the same sound can be represented by different letters, and a sound can be represented by a letter or a combination of letters. To help students understand this, consider the following instructional practices:

- Explicitly teach individual sound-symbol correspondences.
- Utilize a key word for each sound (e.g., *a* says /a/ as in <u>a</u>pple, *e* says /e/ as in <u>E</u>d) (Blachman & Tangel, 2008).
- Allow students multiple opportunities to practice new sound-symbol correspondence knowledge.
- Provide explicit instruction in sounds that are not part of an English language learner's native language.
- Introduce a combination of a few consonants and a vowel so that the English language learner can build many words (e.g., /m/, /s/, /t/, /a/).
- Teach the syllable pattern types and allow for repeated practice with each syllable type.

Instruction in the Six Syllable Types

Javier had difficulty decoding words such as *hope* and *kite* because the final "e" changed the sound of the vowel. Students like Javier can benefit from instruction in the six basic syllable patterns. Understanding these patterns helps students develop accurate and fluent word identification. Blachman and Tangel (2008) introduce and incorporate these patterns in a systematic fashion to help learners. The six patterns include the following:

- Closed syllables (e.g., c<u>a</u>t and <u>i</u>t)
- Final "e" syllables (e.g., b<u>a</u>k<u>e</u> and st<u>o</u>n<u>e</u>)
- Open syllables (e.g., g<u>o</u> and sh<u>e</u>)
- Vowel team syllables (e.g., r<u>ai</u>n and m<u>ea</u>t)
- Vowel + r syllables (e.g., f<u>ar</u>m and b<u>or</u>n)
- Consonant + le syllables (e.g., thim<u>ble</u> and spar<u>kle</u>)

A great way to help a student like Javier is to make a foldable manipulative to show how the final "e" changes the sound of the other vowel. It would be easiest to start with one vowel at a time. For example, on a piece a paper you could have the words *hop, not, mop, slop,* and *ton.* Fold the paper lengthwise and write the letter *e* next to each word. This will reinforce the difference between the short vowel sound and the long vowel sound depending on whether or not the final "e" is present.

Vocabulary Instruction

I have been approached by many teachers who are confused by the types of vocabulary used by English language learners. The following snippet of conversation is not an uncommon one. "Hector seems to have a strong grasp on the English language. I hear him joking and playing with his friends at lunch and at recess. However, when it comes to completing assignments and answering academic questions, he seems to struggle. Why is this? His English seems pretty good to me."

Academic and Social Language

There is a difference between how social language develops and how academic language develops (Hawkins, 2004). Cummins (1979) coined the acronyms BICS (Basic Interpersonal Communicative Skills) and CALP (Cognitive Academic Language Proficiency) to help explain these differences in students' language abilities to teachers. This distinction helps emphasize how and why English language learners may develop casual and social language rather quickly, but have difficulty acquiring more advanced academic language.

BICS are typically acquired first when learning a language because these are the types of vocabulary words needed in social settings. This is the type of language that students may use during lunch or while playing together. Often there are many clues to help aid comprehension. English language learners may rely on body language or facial cues to understand a concept or they may have background knowledge about the topic already.

CALP refers to the more formal academic language that is needed to understand content taught in the classroom. Typically, this type of language is not part of a student's usual vocabulary and may require knowledge about topics in which they are not familiar. Granted, all children are learning new vocabulary words as they learn new content. However, English language learners have to learn many more words than their native English-speaking classmates. Research has shown that students need 3–5 years to achieve advanced English proficiency (Genesee et al., 2005) and that it typically takes 5–7 years for English language learners to develop proficiency in formal academic language (Cummins, 2000).

How Should Vocabulary Be Taught?
Teaching vocabulary to English language learners may seem like a daunting task. Keep in mind that instruction can and should be broken down into a systematic approach that allows for building off previous experiences. Effective instruction should include opportunities for explicit and implicit learning. The National Reading Panel (2000) identified five main methods of how vocabulary should be taught:

- *Explicit Instruction*: Students are explicitly given definitions or specific attributes of words that they are supposed to learn. This may include pre-teaching vocabulary before a lesson, which is helpful to English language learners because it can reduce the number of unknown concepts during a lesson. Sometimes, pre-teaching vocabulary to English language learners can simply be done by providing a label for a concept they already knew. Other times you must provide the label and explain the new concept. Clearly, the latter is more difficult.
- *Implicit Instruction*: Students are exposed to words and are expected to infer the definition. English language learners may learn words through read-alouds, oral language experiences, or from wide reading.

- *Multimedia Methods*: Students are taught vocabulary by going beyond the text. Examples include graphic organizers and feature analysis.
- *Capacity Methods*: Practice is emphasized to help students focus on the meaning of words. In order to focus on vocabulary, students must have other aspects of the reading process automatic. This may include decoding and fluency. Automaticity in those areas frees up memory space and allows the learner to focus on vocabulary.
- *Association Methods*: Learners are encouraged to make connections between unknown and known things. This may include emphasis on semantic or contextual connections.

Supporting Academic Vocabulary Learning

Snow et al. (1998) determined that students learn academic language in two ways, either from teachers or from academic text. Knowing this, it is important for teachers to support vocabulary learning by utilizing the best possible practices. Introducing key terms before a lesson, utilizing pictures with new vocabulary words, and assessing background knowledge are all ways teachers can help engage English language learners in academic language.

It is also essential for teachers to be cognizant of the types of words they choose to emphasize in a lesson. Beck, McKeown, and Kucan (2002) broke down the types of vocabulary words learned in school according to the usefulness and frequency of the words. Tier 1 words include basic vocabulary words that we come across in day-to-day conversations. These words rarely require formal instruction and do not have multiple meanings (e.g., dog, book, and pencil). Tier 2 words are considered to be high frequency and may have multiple meanings. These words lend themselves to instruction and strongly influence speaking and reading. Tier 3 words are unique to the area of study and are considered to be low frequency and context specific. These words are typically unknown to students and are only learned when a specific need arises. Beck et al. (2002) suggest that teachers focus on Tier 2 words for instruction because of their importance and utility, instructional potential, and tie to conceptual understanding.

Suggested Classroom Vocabulary Activities

The following activities require explicit instruction and are designed to help all students, including English language learners, acquire vocabulary. According to the National Reading Panel (2000), relying on a single method for vocabulary instruction will not be effective. Educators need to use a variety of methods, expose students to new words often, and create an engaging environment for vocabulary learning.

- *Semantic Map:* Students will develop definitions for concepts and words. A graphic organizer will show relationships among words (Gunning, 2016).

  1. Explain to the students that they will be learning a technique to help them learn new words.
  2. Tell the students to think about a topic they know about (e.g., mammals).
  3. Ask the students to provide words or information about the topic (e.g., has fur, some are carnivores, warm blooded).
  4. Group words and elicit names for the categories.
  5. Create the map and discuss the categories and descriptions.
  6. Students can try this type of mapping with a new concept or vocabulary word.

- *Elaborating Words:* Students will provide details to describe a word.

  1. Explain to the students that we can elaborate or add details to sentences to make them more interesting to read.
  2. Write a sentence on the board that uses a familiar word and underline the word. For example, *The* **cat** *took a nap.*
  3. Read the sentence aloud with the students.
  4. Model how you could add some more description words. For example, "I am going to think about some words that will give us more information about this cat."
  5. Add several descriptive words to the board (e.g., fluffy, white).
  6. Rewrite the sentence using the new words. For example, *The fluffy white cat took a nap.*
  7. Read the new sentence aloud with the students and talk about why this may be a better sentence to visualize the cat.
  8. Write a new sentence on the board and allow the students to try adding descriptive words on their own. Note: This activity could be modified by using pictures of objects. The pictures would enable the students to more easily visualize the objects and come up with descriptive words.

- *Academic Vocabulary Journal:* Students create pictorial and written definitions of new words (Sibold, 2011).

  1. Tell the students a new word and ask them to guess what it means.
  2. Provide a definition for the new word or concept.
  3. Students use the word in a sentence and draw a corresponding picture.

4. Students place their word alphabetically in their academic vocabulary journals. Note: The journals may also be in chart format to include ratings (e.g., never heard the word, heard the word but don't know the meaning), additional pictures, and ideas.

- *Student VOC Strategy:* Students acquire a deeper meaning of specific content vocabulary (West Virginia Department of Education, 2010).

  1. Provide a list of key words from a chapter or text the students will be reading.
  2. Students meet with partners or small groups and select one or two words which they do not know.
  3. After reading, the students discuss what they think the word might mean.
  4. Students write the sentence where the word is found in the text.
  5. Students consult an "expert" for the actual definition of the word. The "expert" may be a dictionary, glossary, website, or another resource.
  6. After learning the formal definition of the word, students choose a way to help remember the meaning of the word. This may include tasks such as drawing a picture, connecting the word to another story, or creating a song.

Fluency Instruction

Sophia knew the names and sounds of all the letters, but she struggled when it came time to reading aloud. She read slowly and would occasionally decode a word sound by sound. Often she would guess at words based on the beginning sounds. When I would correct her or help her on the word and she would come across it again in the same passage, she would often not remember it. She had little to no expression when reading and would typically ignore punctuation marks. After completing an oral reading, Sophia was not able to provide me with information from the passage. However, she was wonderful at providing detailed information about passages that had been read aloud to her. This let me know that she was able to process the information and had a grasp on some comprehension strategies. However, fluency was a big issue for her when she was the one doing the reading.

I bring up Marco here only because he presented such a different facet than Sophia. Marco was able to read a passage beautifully. However, when asked comprehension questions about the passage, he would answer most incorrectly. Similarly, when I would read a passage to him, Marco had difficulty answering any comprehension questions. This is because Marco had fairly strong decoding skills. He was a strong reader in his native language. However, he had limited vocabulary knowledge that impeded his comprehension.

In terms of reading, fluency refers to the ability to automatically and accurately read words with expression and with no noticeable effort. We can think of fluency as the bridge between word recognition and reading comprehension. While we certainly see problems with fluency in native English speakers, fluency problems appear to be more frequent with English language learners. This is likely because English language learners may have more difficulty with word meaning, which in turn impacts reading speed, fluency, and understanding. Activities focusing on fluency can be extremely beneficial for English language learners because they often can help with oral language development as well. When English language learners practice reading a text accurately and automatically, they are also taking away information about the sounds of spoken English while developing vocabulary knowledge. While there is more research on fluency instruction for native English speaker than there is for English language learners, research does suggest that English language learners can make improvements in rate and accuracy through explicit and systematic instruction (Gunn, Smolkowski, Biglan, Black, & Blair, 2005).

Accuracy, Automaticity, and Prosody
As with any type of instruction, fluency progress should be monitored and addressed through regular ongoing assessments. We typically think of accuracy as the percentage of words a student can read correctly in a text. Measuring students' accuracy helps teachers select texts at appropriate levels. The independent level is the level in which a child can read easily with few errors. When presented with a text at their independent level, a student should be able to read with fluency and expression. The instructional level is one in which the student can read about 90% of the words correctly. This text level is slightly more challenging than the independent level. The frustration level is found when a student can read less than 90% of the words correctly. Signs of difficulty are evident and there is a lack of fluency in oral reading. To quickly measure a student's reading accuracy:

- Ask the student to read aloud a short passage to you.
- Note any errors the student makes while reading (e.g., omissions, substitutions, or words you have to supply for the student). Self-corrections are not counted against a student.

- Divide the number of words the student was able to read correctly by the total number of words in the passage.
- Multiply this number by 100 to see the percentage of words read correctly.

Automaticity refers to a student's reading rate, that is, the number of words a student can read correctly in 1 minute. This can be measured in much the same way as accuracy, but a stopwatch or timer will be needed to find the number of words read in a minute.

Prosody is a defining feature of expressive reading. Prosody refers to appropriate intonation and phrasing while reading. This may include pausing at commas or periods, raising or lowering intonation to match what is happening in the text, and providing appropriate stress to particular words in a sentence. Many teachers assess prosody using a rubric. This allows teachers to evaluate how students perform in areas such as intonation and expression.

How Can Teachers Help English Language Learners Develop Fluency?
For all students, but especially for English language learners, it is important to balance fluency and comprehension. While we certainly want to help students develop faster reading rates, we do not want that to take complete precedent over expression and meaning. Practices that will benefit English language learners include

- Giving students ample opportunities to practice reading out loud. To improve fluency in English, students should be practicing with texts at their independent level that they can read multiple times.
- Allowing students to read along with a recording of the text. This practice helps English language learners learn appropriate pronunciations as well as phrasing.
- Reading with a model reader. English language learners should be given the opportunity to work with a model reader. This model may be the teacher, an assistant, or even an older student. It is important that the model reader be able to read the text accurately and automatically. The model reader can read the text out loud first and then the student can read the passage. The model reader and student can continue to practice the text, time their readings, and discuss the meaning of the text.
- Including choral reading opportunities. During choral reading, the students read a passage out loud with the teacher. Typically, the students and teacher will preview the text first. The teacher then reads the text aloud to the students while they follow along. Then the teacher and students read

the passage together. This is particularly well-suited for English language learners who may have fears reading out loud due to pronunciations or difficulties with English.

- Practicing reading a text with echo reading. During echo reading, the teacher reads part of a text and the students follow along. Then the students echo what the teacher read. Students should try to mimic the rate and expression of the teacher.

SUMMARY

Teachers can greatly influence the academic and emotional successes of English language learners. Effective teachers of English language learners utilize explicit teaching, regularly monitor students' progress, and include multiple opportunities for students to practice while supporting English language acquisition (Graves, Gersten, & Haager, 2004; Haager, Gersten, Baker, & Graves, 2003). A thriving learning environment is one that is positive, welcoming to all students, and developmentally appropriate. Teachers of English language learners can influence the success of their students by understanding the needs of the individual students, differentiating instruction, encouraging flexible grouping, using diversity as a resource, and implementing tailored strategies to enhance understanding.

The population of English language learners in the United States continues to grow and continues to be more linguistically diverse. This means that more and more teachers in all parts of the country will be working with increasing numbers of culturally and linguistically diverse students. Teachers working with diverse learners should have a collection of strategies and techniques to help meet the needs of all students. This chapter was designed to move through some real-life scenarios to provide explicit instructional strategies to help English language learners gain skills in phonics and word study, vocabulary, and fluency.

REFERENCES

August, D., & Hakuta, K. (1997). *Improving schooling for language minority children: A research agenda*. Washington, DC: National Research Council.
August, D., & Shanahan, T. (2006). *Developing literacy in second-language learners: Report of the National Literacy Panel on language-minority children and youth*. Mahwah, NJ: Lawrence Erlbaum Associates.

August, D., & Shanahan, T. (2010). Effective literacy instruction for English language learners. In M. Shatz & L. C. Wilkinson (Eds.), *Improving education for English language learners: Research-based approaches* (pp. 209–250). Sacramento, CA: California Department of Education.

Beck, I. L., McKeown, M. G., & Kucan, L. (2002). *Bringing words to life: Robust vocabulary instruction.* New York, NY: The Guilford Press.

Brice, R. G., & Brice, A. E. (2009). Investigation of phonemic awareness and phonic skills in Spanish-English bilingual and English-speaking kindergarten students. *Communication Disorders Quarterly, 30*, 208–225. doi:10.1177/1525740108327448

Blachman, B. A., & Tangel, D. M. (2008). *Road to reading: A program for preventing and remediating reading difficulties.* Baltimore, MD: Paul H. Brookes Publishing Co.

Cummins, J. (1979). *Cognitive/academic language proficiency, linguistic interdependence, the optimum age question and some other matters* (Vol. 19, pp. 121–129). Working Papers on Bilingualism. Toronto: Ontario Institute for Studies in Education.

Cummins, J. (2000). *Language, power and pedagogy: Bilingual children in the crossfire.* Tonawanda, NY: Multilingual Matters.

Duran, L. K., Roseth, C. J., & Hoffman, P. (2010). An experimental study comparing English-only and transitional bilingual education on Spanish-speaking preschoolers' early literacy development. *Early Childhood Research Quarterly, 25*, 207–217. doi:10.1016/j.ecresq.2009.10.002

Ehri, L. C., Dreyer, L. G., Flugman, B., & Gross, A. (2007). Reading Rescue: An effective tutoring intervention model for language-minority students who are struggling readers in first grade. *American Educational Research Journal, 44*, 414–448. doi:10.3102/0002831207302175

Francis, D., Rivera, M., Lesaux, M., Kieffer, M., & Rivera, H. (2006). *Practical guidelines for the education of English language learners: Research-based recommendation for instruction and academic interventions.* Portsmouth, NH: RMC Research Corporation, Center on Instruction. Retrieved from http://www.centeroninstruction.org/files/ELL1-Interventions.pdf

Garcia, E., & Jensen, B. (2006). Dual-language programs in the U.S.: An alternative to monocultural, monolingual education, *Language Magazine, 5*(6), 30–37.

García, O., Kleifgen, J. A., & Falchi, L. (2008). *From English Language Learners to Emergent Bilinguals. Equity Matters. Research Review No. 1.* New York, NY: Campaign for Educational Equity, Teachers College, Columbia University.

Genesee, F., Lindholm-Leary, K., Saunders, W., & Christian, D. (2005). English language learners in U.S. schools: An overview of research findings. *Journal of Education for Students Placed at Risk, 10*(4), 363–385. doi:10.1207/s15327671espr1004

Genesee, F., Paradis, J., & Crago, M. (2004). *Dual language development & disorders: A handbook on bilingualism and second language learning.* Baltimore, MD: Paul H. Brookes Publishing Co.

Gersten, R., & Geva, E. (2003). Teaching reading to early language learners. *Educational Leadership, 60*, 44–49.

Graves, A. W., Gersten, R., & Haager, D. (2004). Literacy instruction in multiple-language first-grade classrooms: Linking student outcomes to observed instructional practice. *Learning Disabilities Research & Practice, 19*, 262–272. doi:10.1111/j.1540-5826.2004.00111.x

Gunn, B., Biglan, A., Smolkowski, K., & Ary, D. (2000). The efficacy of supplemental instruction in decoding skills for Hispanic and non-Hispanic students in early elementary school. *Journal of Special Education, 34*, 90–103. doi:10.1177/002246690003400204

Gunn, B. Smolkowski, K., Biglan, A., Black, C., & Blair, B. (2005). Fostering the development of reading skills through supplemental instruction: Results for Hispanic and non-Hispanic students. *Journal of Special Education, 39*, 66–85. doi:10.1177/00224669050390020301

Gunning, T. G. (2016). *Creating literacy instruction for all students* (9th ed.). Boston, MA: Pearson.

Haager, D. (2007). Promises and cautions regarding using response to intervention with English language learners. *Learning Disability Quarterly, 30*, 213–218. doi:10.2307/30035565

Haager, D., Gersten, R., Baker, S., & Graves, A. (2003). The English language learner observation instrument for beginning readers. In S. Vaughn & K. L. Briggs (Eds.), *Reading in the classroom: Systems for the observation of teaching and learning* (pp. 111–114). Baltimore, MD: Brookes.

Harper, C., & de Jong, E. (2004). Misconceptions about teaching English-language learners. *Journal of Adolescent and Adult Literacy, 48*, 152–162.

Hammer, C. S., Lawrence, F. R., & Miccio, A. W. (2007). Bilingual children's language abilities and early reading outcomes in Head Start and kindergarten. *Language, Speech, and Hearing Services in Schools, 28*, 237–248. doi:10.1044/0161-1461

Hawkins, M. R. (2004). Researching English language and literacy development in schools. *Educational Researcher, 33*, 14–25. doi:10.3102/0013189X033003014

Kamps, D., Abbott, M., Greenwood, C., Arreaga-Mayer, C., Wills, H., Longstaff, J., … Walton, C. (2007). Use of evidence-based, small-group reading instruction for English language learners in elementary grades: Secondary-tier intervention. *Learning Disability Quarterly, 30*, 153–168. doi:10.2307/30035561

Klinger, J. K., Artiles, A. J., & Barletta, J. M. (2006). English Language Learners who struggle with reading: Language acquisition or LD? *Journal of Learning Disabilities, 39*, 108–128. doi:10.1177/00222194060390020101

Lesaux, N. K. (2006). Building consensus: Future directions for research on English language learners at risk for learning disabilities. *Teachers College Record, 108*, 2406–2438.

McCardle, P., Mele-McCarthy, J., Cutting, L., Leos, K., & D'Emilio, T. (2005). Learning disabilities in English language learners: Identifying the issues. *Learning Disabilities Research & Practice, 20*, 1–5. doi:10.1111/j.1540-5826.2005.00114.x

National Clearing House for English Language Acquisition. (2008). *Elementary and secondary enrollment of ELL students in U.S. 1989–1990 to 2005–2006.* Washington, DC: Author.

O'Connor, R. E., Bocian, K., Beebe-Frankenberger, M., & Linklater, D. L. (2010). Responsiveness of students with language difficulties to early intervention in reading. *The Journal of Special Education, 43*, 220–235.

Quiroga, T., Lemos-Britton, Z., Mostafapour, E., Abbott, R. D., & Beringer, V. W. (2002). Phonological awareness and beginning reading in Spanish-speaking ESL first graders. *Journal of School Psychology, 40*, 85–111. doi:10.1016/S0022-4405(01)00095-4

Report of the National Reading Panel. (2000). *Teaching children to read: An evidence-based assessment of the scientific research literature on reading and its implications for reading instruction.* Washington, DC: National Institutes of Health.

Sibold, C. (2011). Building English language learners' academic vocabulary: Strategies and tips. *Multicultural Education, 18*, 24–28.

Snow, C. E., Burns, M. S., & Griffin, P. (Eds.). (1998). *Preventing reading difficulties in young children.* Washington, DC: National Academy Press.

United States Census Bureau. (2010). *Foreign born population.* Retrieved from http://www.census.gov/population/foreign/

West Virginia Department of Education. (2010). *Student VOC Strategy.* Retrieved from https://wvde.state.wv.us/strategybank/StudentVOCStrategy.html

RAD DAD: A CHICANO MAN (RE) CONSTRUCTING MASCULINITY AND FATHERHOOD THROUGH ZINES

Barbara Guzetti and Leslie Foley

ABSTRACT

The purpose of this case study was to describe how a Chicano man, Tomas Moniz, wrote and edited zines to reconstruct stereotypical notions of masculine performance and fatherhood and formed community for grassroots action. Data were triangulated by collecting observations and photographs of the informant distributing and discussing his zine at a national zine symposium and by in situ interviews as he did so. These data were triangulated by collecting 17 issues of Tomas' zines and by a semistructured interview conducted by telephone and by informal interviews conducted by electronic mail. Screen shots were collected of Tomas' social media (his Facebook page, blog, and YouTube videos) that extended or supported his zines. These data were analyzed by thematic analysis. Member checks were conducted with the participant as a measure of trustworthiness. Results illustrated how a Chicano man wrote in atypical forms and

Addressing Diversity in Literacy Instruction
Literacy Research, Practice and Evaluation, Volume 8, 89–114
Copyright © 2018 by Emerald Publishing Limited
All rights of reproduction in any form reserved
ISSN: 2048-0458/doi:10.1108/S2048-045820170000008017

substance to reconstruct masculinity and fatherhood in an inclusive model. He wrote of being marginalized as a parent by his gender; he discussed difficult issues in the performance of masculinity and parenting; and he self-published contributions by other men (and women) that highlighted alternative ways of performing and representing masculinity. He used his zines and social media to build community for support and activism. This study contributes to the extant research that refutes gender stereotypes and presents alternative models of masculinity and literacy engagement for Latino males. Although there has been a growing interest in the status of men, there is little scholarship on Latino males, their masculinities, and their literacy practices. The absence of such scholarship has reinforced educators' stereotypical views of Latino males as hyper-masculine and nonacademic, contributing to low expectations for their academic success. This case study refutes those stereotypes and presents a model of a minority man enacting alternative representations of masculinity through literacy. Findings from this study can be used to demonstrate the functions that reading and writing can serve in an adult man's life and provide permission for minority youth to engage in literacy practices.

Keywords: Gender; writing; masculinity; Chicano/Latino men; zines

Although there has been a growing interest in the status of men, there is little scholarship on Latino men, their masculinities, and their literacy practices in everyday life (Noguera & Hurtado, 2012). The absence of such scholarship perpetuates distorted images and reinforces educators' stereotypical views of Latino males as nonacademic and violent (Bernhard et al., 2004), fueling low expectations for their academic success. These views have been advanced by the media that typically portray Latino youth as physically volatile and "all the same" (Arciniega, Anderson, Tovar-Blank, & Tracey, 2008). These traditional views of Latino masculinity have been associated with "machismo" (Opazo, 2008; Saez, Casado, & Wade, 2010), the performance of masculinity as authoritarian, sexist, emotionally restrictive, and controlling (Estrada & Arciniega, 2008; Opazo, 2008). Latino men have been characterized as heads of the family who simply protect and provide. The enactment of stereotypical notions of machismo has been associated with misogamy, violence, and recklessness, the expressions of which have led to boys' disengagement in education and their behavior problems in classrooms (Caravantes, 2006; Opazo, 2008). In the absence of alternative models of masculine performance, Latino boys take up hegemonic notions that are central to the academic struggles they face as literacy learners and perpetuate their gendered beliefs that reading and writing are females' pursuits (Martino & Kehler, 2007).

Recent evidence has shown that these patriarchal enactments of masculinity are changing and new views of masculinity for Latino men are redefining what it means to be a man (Arciniega et al., 2008). Yet, researchers have highlighted the lack of contemporary research that describes these alternative representations of masculinity (Estrada & Arciniega, 2015). Therefore, scholars have called for studies that explore cultural constructions of masculinity and how those conceptions impact Latino men's engagement in literacy (Estrada & Arciniega, 2015; Kehler, 2013).

The National Education Association (2012–2015) reported the paucity of time parents spend assisting in their children's learning. Latina mothers are less likely to read to their children than White mothers (Torres & Fergus, 2012). The National Center for Children in Poverty (http://www.nccp.org) indicated that 62% of Latino children live in low-income families as compared to 31% of White children (Jiang, Ekono, & Skinner, 2015). Latino children are least likely than other children to live in homes with a household head with a high-school diploma (Kids Count, 2014) and lack role models of adults engaging in literacy (Torres & Fergus, 2012).

Yet, there is a dearth of current research on masculinities that counter stereotypical portrayals of Latino men as hypermasculine, violent, and uninvolved with their children (Ambrose-Miller & Maiter, 2008). There is little current research illustrating minority fathers' participation in their children's education or how men can become involved as active parenting partners (Estrada & Arciniega, 2015). Researchers have yet to conduct studies that challenge negative stereotypes in popular culture of Latino males as emotionally and physically distant fathers, images that have been shown to negatively impact adolescents' self-esteem (Rivadeneyra, Ward, & Gordon, 2007) and affect their academic performance (Zoller Booth & Gerad, 2011). Studies are needed of men's literacy practices that describe Latino men's reading and writing to reconstruction masculinity.

Researchers have identified the need for and importance of investigating how cultural notions of masculinity relate to men's everyday lives, such as their literacy and fathering practices (e.g., Author, 200X; Gottzen, 2011; Ransaw, 2012). Scholars have called for studies that document Latino men's representations of masculinity by enacting social responsibility, family centeredness, and emotional connection (Estrada & Arciniega, 2015). More needs to be known about how men of all ethnicities and cultures engage in literacy and how they represent and enact alternative performances of masculinity through their literacy practices to provide important implications for motivating and supporting young men to engage in transformative literacy practices. Identifying models of how a Latino man writes against stereotypical notions of masculinity could supply alternative portrayals of what it means to be a man for today's youth. Such texts could serve as sources for deconstructing narrow views of Latino masculine identity in schools and offer new models for masculine performance.

MEN'S WRITING AND MASCULINITY

Relatively little research exists on the writing practices of men or how men engage in literacy practices to represent their masculinities (Author, 200X). Only a few studies have described how and why men write in everyday life for their own purposes or to explore their gender identities. Literacy researchers only recently described how a man composed concrete poetry (poetry that incorporates visuals) to tell his life story as a homeless person (Rogers, Winters, Perry, & LaMonde, 2015). Other investigators have described how men engage in writing to share their passion for and knowledge of a field, such as history or science (Author & Co-Authors, 201X). Scholars also recently detailed how an African-American man reconstructed masculinity through his writing (Author & Co-Author, In Press). Despite these recent efforts, gaps remain in the professional literature of studies that illustrate how men represent their lives and reconstruct masculinity through their literacy practices.

Men Writing Zines

In each of these studies described above, men wrote through the medium of zines. Zines are do-it-yourself (DIY) self-publications characterized by hybrid forms of original and appropriated text, written on myriad topics in a variety of genres. Zines can include handwritten or typed expository and narrative texts, poetry, photographs, ads, graphics, links, and sketches and are typically constructed in cut-and-paste style and collage form, copied, and sold or exchanged with other zinesters (Knobel & Lankshear, 2002). Zines are considered "cultural productions" that often represent "the intersection of lived experiences and imagined futures" (Rogers et al., 2015, p. 1) authored or edited by zinesters. Once considered an underground literacy practice (Duncombe, 1997), zines have become visible as part of the recent maker movement, promoted and crafted in public libraries' maker spaces or in after-school programs, and are being extended on zinesters' social media and Internet spaces (Author & Co-Author, 201X). Zining has been character-ized as an act of civil disobedience, a medium to effect change, and a tool for inspiring other forms of activism (Author, 200X; Harris, 2003). Zines have been created to resist against oppression (Schilt, 2003) and to deconstruct gendered performances and representations (Piepmier, 2009). Zinesters craft their zines to share common interests, represent their identities, and form community and solidarity (Duncombe, 1997; Knobel & Lankshear, 2002). Men have written perzines or personal zines (Duncombe, 1997), collections of their own prose and/or poetry, to share "the intimacies of their lives" (Duncombe 1997, p. 26). In doing so, men often critique social myths, high-light economic or social inequalities, or represent their identities in narrative autobiography (Author & Co-Author, 200X; Knobel & Lankshear, 2002).

PURPOSE

Although there have been studies of men writing to reconstruct masculin-ity (e.g., Author, 201X; Author & Co-Author, in press), there have been few inquiries into how Latino men reconstruct masculinity through their lit-eracy practices. Therefore, the purpose of this case study (Stake, 2005) was to explore how one Chicano man created zines to re-represent masculinity and refute stereotypical notions of fatherhood. The research questions were: How does a Chicano man write against gendered notions of masculinity? How does a Chicano man promote and engage in fatherhood in nonstereo-typical ways? What new models of masculinity can be constructed from this zinester's personal writings? In addressing these questions, I examined the multiple subjectivities of ethnicity, race, social class, generation, and culture that influence gender performance. By addressing these questions, I antici-pated being able to contribute to the extant literature that presents alternative gender roles and relations and identify the functions that literacy serves in a man's life that could serve as alternative models for masculine performance.

THEORETICAL FRAMEWORKS

This investigation was framed by a sociocultural theory of literacy as a social practice that focuses on how and why people engage in literacy in their everyday lives (Cope & Kalantzis, 2000; Perry, 2012; Street, 2014). This model describes literacy as more than just cognitive skills, but as a set of literacy practices in specific contexts associated with culture and power structures in society (Perry, 2012; Street, 2014). This framework acknowledges the situated nature of literacy in real social contexts and describes literacy practices as embedded in peoples' goals and cultural practices (Papen, 2016) and are associated with culture, agency, power, and identity (Perry, 2012). Literacy as a social practice posits that literacy varies within context and no single "literacy" prevails. Rather, there are multiple literacies and forms of texts, including digital, visual, auditory, and print texts (Cope & Kalantzis, 2000). This sociocultural perspective undergrounds the new literacies, those literacies that are chronologically new and constitute socially recognized ways of generating, communicating, and negotiating meaningful content (Lankshear & Knobel, 2001). A contemporary view of zining as a practice of the new literacies (Knobel & Lankshear, 2002) views zining as an act of activism to spur others to action for social and political change (Duncombe, 1997).

This study was also informed by current theories of masculinity that define masculinity as a gender-informed set of norms that regulate social behavior and personal identity (Estrada & Arciniega, 2015), shaped by and evidenced in personal interactions. Current masculinity theory posits that masculinity is a fluid identity with the aspiration of transforming stereotypical social norms and their enactments (Bean & Harper, 2007). Masculinity is socially constructed through men's personal interactions with other men and with others (Connell & Connell, 2005); through their relationships and education, and by reminders of appropriateness through social actions (Alexander, 2006; Kimmel 2002; Kimmel & Messner, 2007).

Contemporary theories of masculinity present variation in identity representation among Latino males (Torres, Solberg, Scott, & Carlstrom, 2002). A new and tenderer form of machismo has been identified, characterized as an emotionally responsive, collaborative, and flexible style of masculinity (Estrada & Arciniega, 2015; Torres, et al., 2002). Recent interpretations of machismo have included enacting values of honor, responsibility, perseverance, and courage in individual and group interactions (Arciniega et al., 2008). Contemporary Latino men have identified with values of loyalty, fairness, and justice and have expressed a compassionate and socially attuned disposition in their performance of masculinity (Abalos, 2005; Torres et al., 2002). Latino men may assume child-care responsibilities, engage in active fathering practices, and subscribe to an ideology of "familism" (Arciniega, Anderson, Tovar Blanc, & Tracey, 2008; Saenz, Mayo, Miller, & Rodriguez, 2015) that emphasizes subjugation of the self to family, honor, support, and interconnectedness (Lugo Steidel & Contreras, 2003). Scholars now recognize that machismo is a multidimensional construct that reflects wide cultural heterogeneity (Estrada & Arciniega, 2008; Wester, 2008). Researchers are working toward a more complex understanding of marginalized masculinities that challenge the myth of sameness among Latino men (Opazo, 2008; Torres et al., 2002). As a result, researchers have called for studies that present more positive interpretations of maschismo, commencing with a focus on familism as a starting point (Estrada & Arciniega, 2015; Opazo, 2008).

METHODS

The Zinester

This case study (Stake, 2005) focuses on a 46-year-old man, Tomas Moniz, because he authored or edited 27 issues of a zine, *Rad Dad*, devoted to creating community for radical parenting. Tomas also created a special Father's Day issue, two anthologies, and most recently, a magazine format of *Rad Dad.* He began this series of zines at age 35 as the father of three children. Tomas' zine has been recognized by receiving the Utne Magazine Independent Media Zine of the Year Award and the San Francisco Bay Guardian's Best Local Zine award.

Tomas' family background is racially and culturally mixed. Tomas was born to a White mother and a Latino father, but self identifies as Chicano. It is typically recognized that the terms "Hispanic," "Latino," and "Chicano" refer to those who come from or whose ancestors originate from a Latin American country, but can reflect regional and political differences in the United States. Conservative politicians tend to refer to Hispanics while liberals are more likely to use the terms Latino or Chicano (Opazo, 2008). I chose to use the terms Latino to refer to the ethnic culture in general and the term Chicano to describe Tomas due to my own and my informant's political stances and personal preferences. The mother of Tomas' three children (two daughters, ages 20 and 18 and a son, age 25) is White. Tomas and his children's mother lived together since before the time their first child was born until their children were adults or older teenagers (see Fig. 1 for a photograph of Tomas with his zines).

Tomas grew up in New Mexico, Hawaii, and California, moving around with his mother's military family because his father was incarcerated on and off for several years from the time Tomas was 3 years old. Born to

Fig. 1.

a working-class family, his education and his career allowed him to migrate to the middle class. Tomas has a Master's degree in English from UCLA and currently teaches courses in writing, literature, and basic skills in the English department at a community college in northern California where he has organized a zine library, incorporates zines into his courses, and hosts an annual zine festival for the surrounding community.

Data Collection

I met Tomas at the 2-day Portland Zine Symposium during the summer of 2013. This annual festival is one of the largest in the nation with approximately 100 zinesters and 1,000 of their readers attending to network, interact, exchange or sell their zines and participate in workshops, such as archiving zines in pubic and university libraries. I observed Tomas displaying, distributing, and discussing his zines and took field notes. I took photographs of him and his zines and conducted informal interviews with him to obtain information about his zines. I also conducted a semistructured, audio-recorded, and transcribed interview with Tomas by telephone, focusing on background and demographic information, his purpose and mission, and his history with and trajectory for his zining. Informal interviews were conducted by electronic mail to supplement information in the formal interview or to clarify or elaborate on information. These data were triangulated by collecting 17 issues of Tomas' zine, *Rad Dad,* selected from the 27 Tomas created because they showed his zines over time and were still in print, including a compilation of issues 1–10; issues 18–21; issues 23 and 24; and his Father's Day Issue.

I also examined Tomas' Internet presence and his social media that extended or promoted his zines, including his blog (http://raddadzine.blogspot.com) and his Facebook page for *Rad Dad* (https://www.facebook.com/rad-dad-zine-a-zine-on-radical-parenting-111754795510271) and took screen shots. I became his Facebook "friend" on his personal page where he posted news about issues of *Rad Dad* and announced events where he would be reading aloud excerpts from his zines. I subscribed to his YouTube channel and watched YouTube videos of Tomas reading aloud his poetry and prose from his zines (e.g., "Stories that Never End" https://www.youtube.com/watch?v=sVynErutLaI). I also examined his Internet advertisement (http://www.raddadmagazine.com) and viewed his YouTube video promoting his new magazine format (https://www.youtube.com/watch?v=l9ZRTkS940s).

Data Analysis

These data were analyzed for interpretation in both deductive and inductive ways. Data sources were analyzed deductively by examining data sources for evidence or illustrations of constructs and principles from the theoretical frameworks. The data were also analyzed inductively by thematic analysis (Patton, 1990). Data were read as soon as they were collected, reread several times, annotated with key words, and coded. Codes and subcodes were color coded for ease of comparison. Codes were grouped into larger categories and categories were compared across data sources and types. Reoccurring categories resulted in themes or propositions. Member checks were conducted as a measure of trustworthiness by returning interview transcripts and draft manuscripts to Tomas for his modifications, reactions, or additions, and his approval. Tomas approved the manuscript without any changes.

FINDINGS

Tomas' Zines' Structure and Format

Each edited issue of *Rad Dad* tended to be consistent in structure and format. The numbered issues typically contained about 45 pages folded together in 9" · 6" booklets with colorful covers (see Fig. 2]. Each began with an introduction, message, or expository piece written by Tomas. Later issues contained Tables of Contents that listed the titles and authors of the pieces. Most of these contributors were men who wrote on topics related to fathering, such as mourning a miscarriage, queer parenting, being a stepfather, a grandfather, a teen father or a single father, and parenting and active engagement. Women's voices were also represented by those who addressed parenting from their own perspectives, such as a feminist or anarchist view of

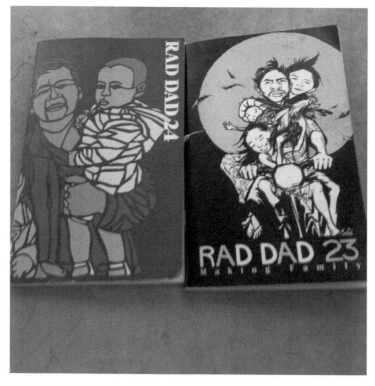

Fig. 2.

parenting, adoption, or writing of the challenges in birth mothering from prison. Issues typically contained about a dozen brief articles, including at least one by Tomas.

Some issues included special features, such as letters to the editor, book reviews, interviews (e.g., with activists and artists), and a bibliography of "Radical Books for Kids" that presented alternative gender and culture roles (e.g., *Super Cilantro Girl* by Juan Felipe Herrera and *The Paper Bag Princess* by Robert Munsch). Others contained lists of parenting resources and organizations contributors supplied, such as The Center for Successful Fathering (http://www.fathering.org) and queer parenting resources (e.g., Lesbian Dad at http://lesbiandad.net and Families Joined by Love); parenting/fatherhood blogs (e.g., Daddy Dialectic at http://daddy-dialectic.blogspot.com and Pirate Pappa at http://piratepappa.blogspot.com); and relevant groups (e.g., the Anarchist Parenting List at (http://lists.mutual.org/mailman/lst-info/a-parenting). Issues typically concluded with ordering information and Tomas' email address inviting his readers' questions, comments, and concerns.

These articles and features were typically presented in typewritten form with occasional handwritten messages, boxed or bolded text excerpts, and collages of cut-and-pasted printed texts. Photographs and other visuals typically were done in black and white. Illustrations that appeared on nearly every page included block prints, hand-drawn sketches, cartoons, comic strips, and graphics that extended the words.

Tomas' Mission and Purpose

Tomas created *Rad Dad* as "a reflective place where parents, particularly fathers, can think about their relationship to the world, their children and their families" (T. Moniz, personal communication, February 27, 2015). Urban Dictionary (www.urbandictonary.com) defines a "rad dad" as a father who spends quality time with his children. Tomas described a *Rad Dad* as "an action, not a label; it is what we aspire to be, not what we are" (T. Moniz, personal communication, February 27, 2015). He was inspired by the messages of empowerment in the feminist zines he read in his undergraduate women's studies class and by the Chicana writer and feminist activist, Cherrie Moraga, who challenged him to "write what I am afraid to" (Issue 8, p. 185). Tomas constructed his zines to stay connected to people and to issues that were important to him and as "a way to grow as a male ally" as he struggled to incorporate feminism, environmentalism, and activism into his parenting. Noticing that there was no equivalent of *Hip Mama* (http://hipmamazine.com), "the original alterative parenting zine" written for mothers and inspired by *The Future Generation*, a zine by China Martens on parenting and anarchism, Tomas created *Rad Dad* as a prototype "for fathers to explore parenting that isn't based in sexist, outdated gender biases" (Issue 1, p. 8), a space where fathers "can be honest and open about the pressures they face in their daily lives" (Issue 1, p. 8). Tomas sees sharing experiences through zining as "intimate"; "a way to be vulnerable"; "a way to have a voice"; and as "a way to learn about culture through the stories zinesters share" (T. Moniz, personal communication, February 27, 2015).

Tomas classifies *Rad Dad* as both personal and political. He primarily writes for other fathers, but aims to create an egalitarian society through his zines that would have implications for others, as well. The zine allows Tomas and other fathers to challenge themselves "to combat patriarchy, to question gender roles, and to see privilege" (Issue 9, page 28), particularly White male privilege. Tomas considers the appeal of *Rad Dad* to be its compelling storytelling with its diversity of stories that lend insight into little-known topics, such as being a queer or transgender father, intended to promote understanding of and compassion for the societal and personal issues that impact fathering while reconstructing masculine performance in doing so. Tomas solicits and publishes pieces from radical, feminist, and antiauthoritarian parents of all gender identities, sexual orientations, ages, ethnicities, and cultures to assist in recognizing how the myths of traditional fatherhood and gender roles are perpetuated in society; how they might be evidenced in his own and others' views and actions; and how stereotypical views of parenting are transmitted by the media. Tomas hoped these stories would lend insight into the complexities of fathering and raise awareness of how fatherhood has been prostituted as a marketing ploy.

THEMES IN TOMAS' ZINES

Reconstructing Masculinity through Literacy

Tomas' literacy practices represent alternative performances of masculinity as manifested in the form and content of his writing. Tomas' writing chiefly consisted of autobiographical narratives or personal reflections and memoir, genres atypical for men's writing (Ball, 2009; Barrette, 2014). Tomas wrote in memoirs by recalling his experiences reconnecting with Chicanismo, an ideology of cultural affirmation for social and political change (Garcia, 1997) as influenced by the feminist Chicana scholar, Gloria Anzaldua (T. Moniz, personal communication, August 8, 2016). He reminisced about reuniting with his father who was incarcerated in "la pinta" (Mexican slang for prison) for most of Tomas' teenage years. He reflected on how his father ascribed racial identity and transmitted subtle notions of the performance of race to him:

> The first time my father saw me, arms cubby and legs fat like little sausages, he poked at me and said, This one's a Chiconky. It was just like my father to mash two thing together into a new thing: Chicano. Honkey. Years later, he'd ask me like a dare, What's the brown part of you. When angry he growl, That's the white part of you. When high or desperate or lonely he'd whisper, I love every part of you. (Father's Day Issue, p. 23)

These reflections represented life stories. Tomas considered storytelling to be a popular means to convey a message and "compelling to anything we believe in" (T. Moniz, personal communication, February 27, 2015). He recalled in Issue 19 how he came to the realization of the power of stories and storytelling when his daughter asked him for money to purchase a zine after hearing zinesters' stories read aloud at the Zine Mecca in San Francisco's Mission district. Tomas highlighted the importance of storytelling as a persuasive medium in Issue Three:

> Our strongest weapons are our stories, the stories we tell our children, the ones we whisper to each other in beds of our own making, the myths that fill our imaginations, shared among conspirators at bars or over camp sites or sitting in jail cells. It is those weapons we must employ over and over to create the world we want. (p. 53)

Tomas told many stories in his zines, ranging from poignant to humorous, stories that illustrated a principle of or lesson about radical parenting. He wrote of how after his partner gave birth, he reflected on the time when his mother informed him of his family's dissolution, deciding then that he would not allow that experience to shape the future, and coming to the realization that "making family is not something that just happens. It's a choice that takes intention, dedication, and perseverance" (Issue 23, p. 7). In the same issue, Tomas conveyed the tale of how his son eventually left for New York City, moved back, and now reconnects weekly with Tomas as Tomas attempts to "close the distance between us" and broach difficult subjects, like their family breaking up when his children's mother moved out, and the way their family used to be and the way it had become. Tomas told this story to illustrate that, "family is the stories we tell to give ourselves roots, to make connections, to foster new possibilities" as families "continue to grow and change" (p. 8). Tomas observed, "I write stories to make sense of it all" (Issue 23, p. 6), and to be critical and reflective.

Tomas also published his own poems and quoted others' poetry in his zines. In Tomas' poem, "My Father's Name," he reflected on his dying father while his untitled poem questioned when fathers should be forgiven. He quoted lines by Walt Whitman, alluding to the comfort of community and a poem by Jimmy Baca, a Chicano writer, promising his child he would never leave illustrated "that loving spirit of fathering ... at the core of radial parenting" (Issue 1, p. 25).

The topics Tomas took up of deconstructing patriarchy and challenging stereotypical gender roles reconstructed traditional notions of masculinity. Tomas wrote of relearning gender, finding that there were few role models for him in a society that "disempowers men to break from the prescribed role of the male parent, the role that supports patriarchy, capitalism, hierarchy and authoritarianism" (Issue 2, p. 30). He lamented that women often colluded in the process of marginalizing men as he related his own experiences of being viewed as a "bumbling father," being told he was incompetent by mothers and female babysitters – that he was holding his baby incorrectly or had not dressed his child properly – or by women would not speak with him at parks and playgrounds. He reported the constant reproaches, snide looks, and unsolicited advice he received from mothers and grandmothers when he was in public with his infant son. In response, Tomas rebelled against ascribed gender roles by questioning how women were enabled to speak about parenting "because some how they are better with kids, more sensitive, more nurturing because they are women" (p. 30). He discovered the limited ways men are allowed to speak of fatherhood in terms of "being proud, happy, and supportive" (p. 30) and acknowledged only for their expertise on discipline. He reflected on how difficult it was to get other men to write about their parenting ideas, fears, and experiences due to these societal constraints and men's feelings of shame, being silenced, and not knowledgeable enough to contribute.

Tomas continued to question gender-specific roles by calling for women to become equal partners in society, as well as equal partners in parenting. He asked men "to work diligently for equal access and rights for women in the world outside parenting" (Issue 7, p. 157). He discussed with other men ways to challenge accomplish this, such as Dads offering to watch their children as often as they could do so to enable their children's mothers to stay connected to their lives outside of parenting. He recalled his own mother's struggles as a single mother on welfare, continuing her education despite raising children alone. Tomas conceded there was nothing wrong with women being primary caregivers if it was a choice and not a default. He urged men to reconsider what it meant to be successful.

In his writings like these, Tomas wrote missives of emotionality, providing texts that refute the notion that men cannot be emotionally expressive (Kimmel, Hearn, & Connell, 2004). He confessed to his fears about the daunting task of creating a zine about radical parenting issues – that people would consider him narcissistic and think he was claiming to be a "rad dad" himself. He relayed his worries that there were too many important issues about patriarchy, race, and class to do justice to these topics in his zine. He conveyed his anxiety about "how to walk the line between male privilege and parenting" (Issue 9, p. 238). He expressed trepidation about projecting male appropriation of parenting by performing occasional childcare tasks and paying narcissistic homages of self-satisfaction while mothers did the housecleaning and errands. Tomas asked fathers to hug and kiss their boys, as well as their girls. He called on fathers to model forgiveness, love, and engagement give permission to their children to show sadness.

Tomas chronicled stories of the times he felt angry, including when his partner confronted him about his "anger issue" and the way he "butted heads" with his son for losing a key or for throwing his teenage paraphernalia on the ground at the front door. He admits to experiencing terror in moments like these, recalling his own father's searing anger that could appear so suddenly and his alarm at recognizing that trait in himself. His zine was a space for him to reflect on how it sadden him to remember how often he got frustrated at his son for some transgression and had his anger "taint the rest of the day or evening or sadly, the next three days and evenings" (Issue 24, p. 5). Parenting has taught Tomas to realize how to make amends, to apologize, and to "remember that being upset about one thing does not mean I should globalize the issue making me angry about everything" (Issue 24, p. 5).

Tomas also wrote of his emotions about men's and boys' personal relationships with other males. In doing so, he lamented the loss of his friendship with a man who became involved with a woman, pondering how expected it was to be "dumped" for this reason and how most men minimize their relationships with other men, avoiding deep emotional relationships between them. Tomas noted that being buddies or experiencing camaraderie among men was not the same as being vulnerable and intimate. He observed his 16-year-old son with his friends "acting big and talking shit," but also saw him standing up for a boy who could not skate and walking away from a challenge without shame. Reminiscing about how he as a boy had exhibited those same behaviors, realizing that had fewer friends now than he did in college and that most of his friends were ones he had made back then. Tomas questioned:

> Why is it so difficult for men to be intimate with each other, why is it so hard to not have something between us – money, jobs, women, egos? I think there is something in patriarchy itself, in society itself that fears men becoming emotionally connected with other men. I mean if we put our beers and our balls and our bragging aside and began talking, began breaking down the shit we've been taught to fear – ourselves and our feelings and our anger and our power – we might see that we have a lot to offer each other, a lot to share and to show. I wonder how our priorities would change if we could be emotionally invested in caring for the well-being of other men. (Issue 6, p. 14)

Performing Fatherhood as Radical Fathering

Tomas wrote of fatherhood as "radical fathering" and the struggles, challenges, failures, and rewards he experienced in fathering in alternative ways. He characterized a father as "a warrior, synonymous with dedicated" and "analogous to activist, environmentalist, feminist, gangsta, and anarchist" (Issue 7, p. 156). For Tomas, fathering meant being an agent for change in attitudes toward and limitations placed on men in their parenting. Being an anarchist in his fathering to him implied "being transparent and equitable" with the world around him rather than fathering by "coercion, fear or domination" (T. Moniz, personal communication, July 29, 2016). Tomas cautioned that when boys see men enacting fatherhood as stoic and aloof disciplinarians they internalize gendered messages about the performance of masculinity. He called for reclaiming fatherhood by "questioning the social stereotypes of fathering that so long have been used to justify gender specific parental roles" (Issue 24, p. 156) and for fathers to speak up for other fathers. He wrote of the silence among men about fathering, their nervousness about making mistakes, and their anxiety about fathering in ways they had not been fathered.

Tomas wrote of the struggles he experienced in fathering, such as "the difficulties in supporting your children when their decisions run counter to your own" (Issue 4, p. 89). He wrote of his fears that his youngest daughter, influenced by mainstream popular culture and her light-colored skin, identified as White despite his other children seeing themselves as racially mixed and regardless of how he had worked to be critical of Whiteness. Tomas wrote of his efforts to help her see and talk about "how ethnicity is connected to power, privilege, and class" (Issue 4, p. 88), by explaining his own challenges in being biracial, by reading his zines to his children, and by taking his daughters to zine festivals and to meetings and events in the radical community where issues of identity politics were discussed. Eventually, he rationalized his daughter's choice of racial identity:

> Ethnicity is persuasive in our society as the silence around it. I hate the privilege of Whiteness to act as if race is passE, that when someone brings up ethnicity they are playing the "race" card. That is the ultimate in racial privilege. But, I can't really have this conversation with my eight-year-old daughter when she asks me," Why is it boys get into trouble in school more than girls, especially the black boys?" Do I launch into a diatribe against teachers who privilege certain learning styles or enter the classroom predisposed to see young boys of color as problems? She has learned her lessons of ethnicity well from me and from this racist culture we live in. If you claim a color or are seen by your color you get noticed, usually in bad ways. Why shouldn't she choose to blend?

In addition to his struggles like this one, Tomas wrote of the challenges he experienced in radical fathering, including awkward moments that resulted from his efforts to expose his children to different ways of performing gender. He wrote of sharing queer zines with his daughter who while reading one asked an awkward question about sexuality in a public place where all present seemed to fall silent waiting for his response. He relayed his experience in taking his daughter to an anarchist café where she noticed a person with an androgynous appearance displaying contradictory gender cues, prompting her to ask Tomas if that person was a boy or a girl, eventually answering her own question by asking if it had to be one or the other, and inventing her own gender category of a "bgirl."

Tomas also reflected on his perceived failures in fathering, such as the irony of being informed by his son's high-school counselor that his son was failing with Fs in every class on the same day he was asked to speak about *Rad Dad* at the Hip Mama's Mother's Day event. He reported that his son had missed over 100 days of a semester, was on probation with Juvenile court, had failed drug tests, and was eventually sentenced to Juvenile Hall for a weekend. Tomas wrote of his realization of "the power and pain of parenting" as he saw his son hurt, deal with disappointment in the world or in him, and distance himself from his family. Tomas acknowledged that although he tried to model other options for the performance of masculinity as did his brothers and his cousin, his son saw his grandfather and his uncle in jail and his friends choosing to experiment with drugs and violence. Tomas reflected:

> Moments like these aren't talked about in books or zines; there are no answers found by doing readings in front of other people or participating in Mother's Day Extravaganzas.

In fact, all that stuff just seem silly. Instead, what you discover in those moments is your capacity to love unconditionally, to forgive and forget, to be gentle, to put things in perspective. But it is not easy; it's ugly and hard, and it hurts. (Issue 10, p. 242)

These are the rewards of fathering that Tomas inscribes in his zine – self-discovery and lessons learned – especially that fathering requires "love, respect, patience, trust, and kindness" (Issue 1, p. 24). He wrote of his insights, particularly that fathering is collaboration with others because it cannot be accomplished in isolation. He analogized parenting to writing as being "a lot like revision; you gotta come back to things again and again; you rephrase, rethink, at times regret, but you're always willing to return and reconsider" (Issue 9, p. 287). Tomas reflected on his emotional growth in this "revision" process, displaying empathy when his daughter spilled her potato chips and he helped her pick them up rather than becoming angry. He recalled letting go of the distancing role of adulthood by continuing to play ball with his son and not allowing the pressure to cook dinner end their moment of joy in togetherness or racing down the street circling his arms because it made his kids laugh, reminding himself that he had "license to celebrate and play," allowing parenting to liberate rather than constrain gender performance.

In many of his issues, Tomas wrote of his appreciation for and acknowledgement of his children as individuals who had much to teach him. In his article in Issue Six, "Where My Boys At: What I Learned from My Son about Being a Man" Tomas praised his son for being open, caring, and sensitive to his friends, qualities that Tomas hoped to learn from his son's example, and thanking him for being who he is today. In his "Letter to Teenagers" in Issue 23, Tomas acknowledged that young people are often right in their priorities, commenting that friends are more important than part-time jobs, homework, or the family potluck, and to be there for them in their times of need. He gave credit to teens for their instincts and aspirations, encouraging the possibilities they imagined in trying to create a life worth living.

For Tomas, radical fathering represented inclusive fathering. In answer to those who fear parenting because of their apprehension that fatherhood or motherhood will sedate or settle them, Tomas responded that parenting can radicalize a person, describing his own realization of the need to stand up for all children who are hungry, abused, intimidated, bullied, or violated. He observed that "family is nebulous, shifting, and consensual… family is the stories we tell to give ourselves roots, to make connections, to foster new possibilities" (Issue 23, p. 8). For Tomas, the epitome of fathering is caring for all children. He reflected that all men father the children in their lives by their interactions and examples whether they are prepared or intended to father.

BUILDING COMMUNITY FOR
SUPPORT AND ACTIVISM

Tomas defined zining as "storytelling to build community," charactering his zine as "outreach for community" (T. Moniz, personal communication, February 27, 2015). He expressed his need for a community of other radical parents to raise awareness of instances where his own beliefs or behaviors reflected stereotypical and traditional fathering. Tomas considered zines to be "absolutely worthless without community" (Issue 19, p. 42). For Tomas, forming community was best accomplished by soliciting diverse and complex perspectives that could support and inform. Tomas' calls for community were stimulated by the shortcomings of popular-culture media that reduced fathering to a trend with movies like *Daddy Daycare* and *Daddy Day Camp,* presenting fathers as loving, but not primary-caregiver material; by films that reinforced stereotypes of fathers as "reformed womanizers" or "bumbling fools"; and by action-adventure movies that limited fathers' roles to stereotypical protectors/patriarchs. In an article in Issue Seven titled, "Who's Your Daddy? Fathering in Pop Culture," Tomas wrote of his dismay at books with promising titles on fathering, like *Punk Rock Dad, AlternaDad,* and *Dadititude: How a Real Man Became a Real Dad,* discovering that they were written by White, middle-class men with wives at home, finding they failed to mention race or social-class differences. Missing were the stories of men of various ethnicities, cultures, and backgrounds attempting to parent.

In writing stories to address these gaps, Tomas attempted to "find a new language, one that is mine yet communal" (Issue 8, p. 185), one that reflected the voices of the powerless and the poor and honored their stories. In doing so, Tomas followed the teachings of Ursula Le Guin, an American author and advocate for anarchism to listen to other voices than the ones of those in power. To address this directive, Tomas solicited and published stories of what it is like to be a step-parent, a transgender parent, a queer parent, or a queer ally parent, issues not taken up by the commercial press. He extended his supportive community to include his own children as he read aloud issues of his zine to them for their feedback and approval and published their contributions in his issues, including a bibliography of alternative children's books complied by his youngest daughter; "A Letter to Adults" authored by his teenage daughter; and reviews of his zine by each of his three children printed on the back cover of the compendium of Issues 1–10.

Tomas' Facebook presence extended his zine' focus on creating radical community in multitextual ways by sharing videos and stories, including

"How to Parent on Night Like This" by Carvell Wallace, a Black father in Oakland, California, home with his children during the announcement of the Grand Jury's verdict for Darren Wilson, the police officer not convicted for shooting an 18-year-old Black boy in Ferguson, Missouri (http://themanifeststation.net/2014/11/25/how-to-parent-on-a-night-like-this); an article by Karen Grigsby Bates on Project Fatherhood, fathers helping other fathers in the Watts area of Los Angeles (http://www.npr.org/sections/codeswitch/2015/06/21/415542992/project-fatherhood-in-a-struggling-neighborhood-dads-are-helping-dads); "Confessions of a Latino Dad" by Julio Ricardo Varela who failed in his attempt to inscribe ethnic identity to his children before they had a chance to explore identity for themselves (http://latinousa.org/2015/09/24/confessions-of-a-latino-dad/); and a photograph of a father holding his young son with a sign, "Black and Brown Boys Matter." These stories and visuals each extended the theme of social and political action for radical parenting in contemporary society. (See Fig. 3: Tomas' Facebook Page).

Fig. 3.

To solicit contributions, Tomas posted writing prompts in his zines and on his blog, such as "how do we counter the mainstream narrative around gender race and class?" and "how do we stay connected to our communities once we become a parent (or how do we not lose people once we become parents)?" In his zines, he called for stories that deal with fathering from a "feminist, authoritarian, radical bent" to solicit readers' "essays, rants, collaborations, interviews or birth stories" (Issue 20, p. 4). On his blog, Tomas requested stories from "mothers, fathers, grandparents, caregivers, allies, friends, activists, teens and kids…who understand the revolution begins at home." (See Fig. 4: Tomas' Blog). He called for contributions from people of all genders, particularly writers of color, and the queer and transgendered who desire to write about their relationships to children, families and community. Tomas' promoted and advertised these contributions by creating postcards and flyers and by his blog where issues can be ordered.

Tomas' efforts to advance *Rad Dad* community also included in-person events. He traveled on speaking tours of Northern California, the Pacific Northwest, and the East coast where he read aloud excerpts from his zines in parks, bookstores, community spaces, comic art shops, band venues, and infoshops, places that archive anarchist and feminist work.

Fig. 4.

Fig. 5.

(See Fig. 5: Tomas performing a reading of his zines). To promote his zine, he has attended zine festivals in six cities across the USA, sharing others' experiences with parenting issues, like talking with teenagers about drugs, stories that comforted him.

To become "more sustainable, collaborative, and inclusive" in building community, Tomas has experimented with varying formats of *Rad Dad*. He created two anthologies centered on specific themes, the first of which focused on representations of fatherhood in mainstream media. The second book, *Rad Families*, presents stories of adoption, parenting special-needs children, and alternative family structures. To advance community through editorial boards and guest editors, Tomas transitioned his zine to a magazine, publishing three issues that took up lifespan topics, including getting pregnant, sending kids to school, and empty nesting. In announcing the end of his *Rad Dad* series on Dia de Los Muertos, a Mexican holiday to honor and celebrate losses and remembrances, Tomas blogged: "*Rad Dad* was never meant to be just a book, a zine or a magazine; it was a plea, a promise, a confrontation, a commitment, an action.' For Tomas, revolution for social justice and social change "begins with the families we choose to create" by sharing their stories of vulnerability, error, and insight.

SIGNIFICANCE/IMPLICATIONS

Findings from this investigation offer new understandings of and models for men's performances of masculinity. Tomas' writings provide evidence that men can challenge patriarchal performance and hegemonic elements of masculinity portrayed in the media. This study contributes to the growing body of literature providing counter evidence that Latino men are emotionally distant and uninvolved fathers (e.g., Ambrose Miller & Maiter, 2008). Findings contribute to contemporary research that showcases disruption of the dominant discourse of the Latino male as hyper-masculine, misogynistic, and violent (Opazo, 2008).

This study presents options to the limiting ways boys are taught to engage in literacy practices that reify traditional notions of masculinity (Kehler, 2013) by offering alternative constructions of men's writing in both substance and style. Tomas' case illustrates the functions that literacy can serve in a man's life. Providing boys with zines written by males who are not professional writers, but engage in writing for their own purposes can demonstrate how literacy can give voice to the unheard. Everyday texts of zines can assist in providing cultural relevance to young men's lives. Honoring zines as legitimate literacy practices may inspire others to create alternative texts (Brozo, 2013) and can serve as safe spaces to interrogate stereotypical constructions of masculinity (Kehler, 2013, p. 127). This study also provides an impetus for additional investigations that further explore the intersections of race, culture, social class, and gender that influence literacy development and practice, particularly for Latino men. Additional studies are needed that identify inclusive constructions of masculinity and culturally relevant literacy practices that can provide alternative models for today's diverse youth.

REFERENCES

Abalos, D. T. (2005). Transforming the personal, political, historical and sacred faces of the Latino male. *The Journal of Men' Studies, 15*, 1–167.

Alexander, B. K. (2006). *Performing black masculinity: Race, culture and queer identity.* Lanham, MD: Alta Mira.

Ambrose-Miller, W., & Maiter, S. (2008). Fatherhood and culture: Moving beyond stereotypical understandings. *Journal of Ethnic & Cultural Diversity in Social Work, 17*(3), 279–300.

Arciniega, G. M., Anderson, Tovar-Blank, & Tracey, T. (2008). Toward a fuller conception of machismo: Development of a traditional machismo and caballerismo scale. *Journal of Counseling Psychology, 55*(1), 19–33.

Author, (200X).

Author & Co-Author, (201X).

Author & Co-Author, In Press.

Ball, P. (2009). Computer program detects author gender. *Nature, 18.* Available: http://www. nature.com/news/2003/030714/full/news030714-13.html

Barrette, E. (2004, May). Do men and women really write differently? *The Internet Review of Science Fiction, 1*(5). Available: http://www.irosf.com/q/zine/article/10049

Bean, T. W., & Harper, H. (2007). Reading men differently: Alternative portrayals of masculinity in contemporary young adult fiction. *Reading Psychology, 28*(2), 11–30.

Bean, T. & Ransaw, T. (2013). Masculinity and portrayals of African American boys in young adult literature. In B. Guzzetti & T. Bean, (Eds.). *Adolescent literacies and the gendered self: (Re) constructing identities through multimodal literacy practice*s, (pp. 22–30). New York, NY: Routledge.

Bernhard, Frerie, Buchanan, Arenes, Vera, & Dana, (2004). Social theories for researching men and masculinities. In M. S. Kimmel, J. Hearn, & R. W. Connell (Eds.), *Handbook of Studies on Men and Masculinities*, (pp. 1–34). Thousand Oaks, CA: Sage.

Brozo, W. (2013). Outside interests and literate practices as contexts for increasing engagement and critical reading for adolescent boys. In B. Guzzetti & T. Bean, (Eds.). *Adolescent literacies and the gendered self: (Re) constructing identities through multimodal literacy practices*, (pp. 3–12). New York, NY: Routledge.

Caravantes, E. (2006). *Clipping their own wings: The incompatibility between Latino culture and American education.* Falls Village, CT: Hamilton Books.

Connell, R. W., & Connell, R. (2005). *Masculinities.* Oakland, CA: University of California Press.

Cope, B. & Kalantzis, M. (2000). *Multiliteracies: Literacy learning and the design of social futures.* New York, NY: Routledge.

Duncombe, S. (1997). *Notes from underground: Zines and the politics of alternative culture.* Portland, OR: Microcosm Publishing.

Estrada, F. & Arciniega, G. M. (2015). Positive masculinity among Latino men and the direct and indirect effects on well-being. *Journal of Multicultural Counseling and Development, 43*(3), 191–205.

Garcia, I. M. (1997). *Chicanoismo.* Tucson, AZ: University of Arizona Press.

Gottzen, L. (2011). Involved fatherhood? Exploring the educational work of middle class men. Gender and Education, *23*(5), 619–634. Available: http://dx.doi.org/10.1080/09540253.2010.527829

Harris, A. (2003). gURL scenes and grrrl zines: The regulation and resistance of girls in late modernity. *Feminist Review, 75*(1), 38–56.

Jiang, Y., Ekono, M., & Skinner, C. (2015). *Basic facts about low-income children: Children under 18 years.* New York: National Center for Children in Poverty. ERIC Document Reproduction Service, ED 598496. Available: http://files.eric.ed.gov/fulltext/ED558496.pdf

Kehler, M. (2013). Who will "save the boys"? (Re) examining a panic for underachieving boys. In B. Guzzetti & T. Bean (Eds.), *Adolescent literacies and the gendered self: (Re) constructing identities through multimodal literacy practices*, (pp. 121–130). New York, NY: Routledge.

Kimmel, M. (2002). Global masculinities: Restoration and resistance. In Pease, B., & Pringle, K. (Eds.) *A man's world? Changing men's practices in a globalized world, vol. 4*, (pp. 21–37). London, UK: Zed Books.

Kimmel, M., & Messner, M. (Eds.), (2007). *Men's lives* (9th ed.). London, UK: Pearson.

Kimmel, M. S., Hearn, J., & Connell, R. W. (Eds.), (2004). *Handbook of studies on men and masculinities*. Thousand Oaks, CA: Sage Publications.

Knobel, M., & Lankshear, C. (2002). Cut, paste, publish: The production and consumption of zines. In D. E. Alvermann (Ed.) *Adolescents and literacies in a digital world*. New York, NY: Peter Lang.

Lankshear, C., & Knobel, M. (2011). *New literacies: Everyday practices and social learning*. New York, NY: McGraw-Hill.

Lugo Stiedel, A. G., & Contreras, J. M. (2003). A new familism scale for use with Latino populations. *Hispanic Journal of Behavioral Sciences, 25*(3), 312–330.

Martino, W., & Kehler, M. (2007). Gender based literacy reform: A question of challenging or recuperating gender binaries. *Canadian Journal of Education, 30*(3), 406–431.

Noguera, P., & Hurtado, A. (2012). The status and experience of Latino males from multidisciplinary perspectives. In P. Noguera, A. Hurtado, & E. Fergus (Eds.) *Invisible no more: Understanding the disenfranchisement of Latino men and boys*, (pp. 1–16). New York, NY: Routledge.

Opazo, R. M. (2008). *Latino youth and machismo: Working toward a more complex understanding of marginalized masculinities*. Unpublished Master's thesis, Toronto, Ontario, Canada, Ryerson University.

Papen, U. (2016). *Literacy and education: Policy, practice and public opinion*. New York: Routledge.

Patton, M. (1990). *Qualitative evaluation and research methods* (2nd ed.). Newbury Park, CA: Sage.

Piepmeier, A. (2009). *Girl zines: Making media, doing feminism*. New York: NYU Press.

Perry, K. (2012). What is literacy: A critical overview of sociocultural perspectives. *Journal of Language & Literacy Education, 8*(1), 50–71. Available: http://jolle.coe.uga.edu/wp-content/uploads/2012/06/What-is-Literacy_KPerry.pdf

Ransaw, T. (2012). *A father's hands: African American fathering involvement and the educational outcomes of their children*. Doctoral dissertation, Las Vegas, Nevada: University of Nevada, Las Vegas, UNLV Theses/Dissertations/Professional Papers/Capstones. Available: http://digitalscholarship.unlv.edu/cgi/viewcontent.cgi?article=2613&context=thesesdissertations

Rivadeneyra, L., Ward, M., & Gordon, M. (2007). Distorted reflections: Media exposure and Latino adolescents' conceptions of self. *Media Psychology, 2*, 261–290.

Rogers, T., Winters, K. L., Perry, M., & LaMonde, M. (2015). *Shouting from the street: Youth, homelessness and zining practices*. New York, NY: Routledge.

Saez, P. A., Casado, A., & Wade, J. C. (2010). Factors influencing masculinity ideology among Latino men. *The Journal of Men's Studies, 7*(2), 116–128.

Stake, E. (2005). Qualitative case studies. In N. K. Denzin & Y. S. Lincoln (Eds.) *The Sage Handbook of Qualitative Research*, 3rd ed. Thousand Oaks, CA: Sage.

Street, B. V. (2014). *Social literacies: Critical approaches to literacy in development, ethnography and education*. New York: Routledge.

Torres, M. & Fergus, E. (2012). Social mobility and complex status of Latino males: Education, employment and incarceration patterns from 2000–2009, (pp. 16–40). In P. Noguera, A. Hurtado & E. Fergus (Eds.). *Invisible no more: Understanding the disenfranchisement of Latino men and boys*. New York: Routledge.

Torres, J. B., Solberg, V. S., & Carlstrom, A. H. (2002). The myth of sameness among Latino men and their machismo. *American Journal of Orthopsychiatry*, *72*(2), 163–181.

Zoller Booth, M., & Gerard, J. M. (2011). *Self-esteem and academic achievement: A comparative study of adolescent students in England and the United States*. Bethesda, MD: National Center for Biotechnology information. Available: http://www.ncbi.nlm.nih.gov/pmc/articles/PMC3779915/

A QUALITATIVE INQUIRY EXPANDING NOVICE TEACHERS' DEFINITIONS OF STUDENT DIVERSITY TO INCLUDE ECONOMIC DISPARITIES AND LIFESTYLE DIFFERENCES

Jacqueline Darvin

ABSTRACT

To examine whether or not exposing novice teachers in a graduate literacy education diversity course to particular texts and activities focused on economic diversity and lifestyle differences among students makes them more likely to positively respond to these lesser understood forms of diversity in their own teaching and if so, in what ways. The research design was qualitative and included written reflections from the teacher–participants at the beginning, middle, and end of the semester, and videotaping and transcribing activities and post-activity discussions. Ethnographic observations and notes were made by the primary investigator. The theoretical frameworks

Addressing Diversity in Literacy Instruction
Literacy Research, Practice and Evaluation, Volume 8, 115–133
Copyright © 2018 by Emerald Publishing Limited
All rights of reproduction in any form reserved
ISSN: 2048-0458/doi:10.1108/S2048-045820170000008006

that were foundational to the study were critical literacy and teaching for social justice. The findings of this qualitative study indicate that exposing teachers to texts, discussions, and activities that educate them on economic diversity and lifestyle differences among students makes them more likely to positively respond to these forms of diversity in their own teaching. Specific examples of how participants did this are provided. This study contributes to the literature on diversity in literacy instruction by providing concrete, research-based suggestions for how both teacher educators and K-12 teachers can expand their definitions of student diversity to include economic disparities and lifestyle differences among students. It includes recommended texts and activities for both teacher educators and K-12 teachers to address less typical forms of diversity, with a focus on economic diversity and lifestyle differences.

Keywords: Student diversity; lifestyle differences; economic disparities; critical literacy

In my first year teaching English in New York City, I had 159 students: 18 were in foster care, 26 were homeless and living in shelters, 16 had at least one parent that was incarcerated, 28 were being raised by their grandparents or other guardians, and all lived in poverty and received free lunch. I had nine students who gave birth during the school year. I took a required diversity course in my undergrad teacher ed program, but we never addressed these kinds of student diversity. Sure, we talked about English language learners (ELLs) and meeting the needs of special education students, but nothing prepared me for dealing with the incredibly diverse families and lifestyles that I encountered last year. I felt so helpless and had so much to learn. I was really unprepared, and I know now that I made a lot of mistakes.

The preceding excerpt was taken from a beginning-of-the-semester reflection that was written by a student in a graduate literacy education course at Queens College of the City University of New York. This student was a participant in a qualitative study that had several overarching goals and purposes, one of which was to examine whether or not exposing novice teachers in a diversity course to particular texts and activities that focused on economic diversity and lifestyle differences among students would make them more likely to positively respond to these lesser understood forms of diversity in their own teaching and if so, in what ways. This teacher's lament is representative of so many teachers that take required diversity courses in their teacher education programs, yet still feel unprepared to meet the needs of the students they encounter in their first few years of teaching.

This is due, in part, to the fact that the definition of what constitutes student diversity in American classrooms is rapidly expanding. Although many teachers receive preparation in how to address culturally and linguistically diverse students in their classrooms, far fewer receive training on how to address other, less-spoken-about forms of student diversity, including the vast economic disparities and lifestyle differences that exist in our classrooms today, several of which are mentioned in the quotation above. In the context of this study, economic diversity refers to differences in students' socioeconomic conditions that impact factors such as their access to educational resources and parental involvement in their education, and lifestyle differences refer to where and with whom students reside and how their daily living conditions impact their literacy learning.

INTRODUCTION: CONTEXT OF THE RESEARCH

For 10 years, I have been teaching a graduate course titled "Literacy Education for Diverse Learners." On the first day of class, I always ask my students, who are novice practicing teachers, to respond in writing to the following question: "When you think of the word *diversity*, what kinds of student differences come to mind? Please list as many as you can." In asking this question to over 200 teachers in the New York metropolitan area, I have never had one teacher specifically list "economic" or "lifestyle" differences. The most common responses are: learning style, intellectual ability, culture, language, gender, sexual orientation, color, nationality, and religion. Why is this? We have to wonder if teacher education programs are doing the best jobs possible when it comes to educating teacher candidates about the many forms of diversity among American students.

The second question to which students are asked to answer is, "What are some of the ways that literacy educators can accommodate diversity in their teaching?" Again, the responses are quite telling with regard to our teacher preparation programs and the content of our required diversity courses in education. The most common replies are: celebrating students' cultural differences, providing students with texts that depict diverse characters, allowing

ELL students to use their first languages in class, engaging in bilingual team teaching, modifying lessons for special education students and ELLS, and allowing students to adhere to their cultural and religious values and practices.

Not one teacher has ever answered this question with any of the following responses: engaging students in activities and discussions that promote ongoing critical thinking and critical literacy, giving students greater choice in their reading and writing, helping students attain needed educational resources, actively involving students in heterogeneous discussion groups, involving students in critically reflecting on their own lives and futures, designing more inclusive student projects that expand students' views of what constitutes an American family, assisting students in learning how to advocate for themselves, and making positive changes in their communities, and so forth. It is important that beginning teachers are able to provide practical classroom applications as responses to this question because developing more inclusive classroom practices is the primary goal of exposing teachers to diversity coursework. Therefore, the remainder of this chapter describes a qualitative study that yields suggestions for how both teacher educators and K-12 teachers can expand their definitions of student diversity to include economic diversity and lifestyle differences among students. It includes recommended texts and strategies for both teacher educators and K-12 teachers to address less-discussed forms of student diversity, with focus on economic diversity and lifestyle differences.

RESEARCH DESIGN AND THEORETICAL FRAMEWORK

This inquiry is part of a larger qualitative research study conducted at Queens College, using 26 graduate students of literacy education as participants. At the time of the study, the students were all practicing teachers in their first 5 years of teaching in New York City or Long Island. The qualitative research design included written reflections from the students at the beginning, middle, and end of the semester and videotaping and transcribing activities and post-activity discussions that were conducted in class. Extensive ethnographic observations and notes were made by the primary investigator (PI).

The primary theoretical lens for this research is a critical literacy framework (Apple, 2014; Freire & Macedo, 1987, 2013; Gee, 2014; Janks, 2013; Janks, Ferreira, Granville, & Newfield, 2013; Rogers, 2013; Vasquez, 2013) that seeks to inspire teacher educators, K-12 teachers, and K-12 students to use powerful literacy, critical dialog, and empowering pedagogical practices to expand upon their definitions and understandings of student diversity and in doing so, ultimately improve literacy education for all learners. The conceptual framework supporting this research is the idea that when teacher educators (professors) expose their students, who are also practicing teachers themselves, to pedagogical strategies that promote critical thinking and expand upon narrow definitions of diversity, those teachers will then have the increased desire, knowledge, and resources to do the same with their own students. Specific examples of how this "ripple effect" occurred in the present study are provided in the following sections.

Closely related to the vast body of work on critical literacy is a movement in education of teaching for social justice (Adams, Bell, & Griffin, 2007; Bell, 2010; Christensen, 2000; Kumashiro, 2009; Shor, 2012; Winn, 2011). Teaching for social justice involves attempting to right social wrongs and teaching in ways that reveal social injustices and inequalities to students, inviting them to problem solve and create solutions to help alleviate these injustices. Teaching for social justice is closely related to critical literacy because as students of any age critically dialog about their beliefs, it is a natural progression for them to take greater interest in the social issues that surround them and want to correct injustices. The following examples from the study demonstrate that the teacher–participants used the pedagogical practices they learned in their graduate diversity course to then engage their own students in class activities and discussions around real-life issues occurring in their diverse schools and communities.

Read and Revisit: Situated Performances on Supporting
Homeless Students

One form of student diversity that is rarely discussed in education courses is where and with whom students reside and how their daily living conditions impact their literacy learning. One of the pedagogical strategies used with the participants in this research study was having them engage in what are termed situated performances around the theme of supporting homeless students. According to Finders and Rose (1999):

> Situated performances are role-taking activities with the following characteristics: (1) learners actively participate by assuming specific subject positions (as opposed to merely observing others' actions or imagining their own actions); (2) the social, cultural, institutional and interpersonal contexts for the actions and situational constrains are fore-grounded; and (3) the performed actions, motives, and circumstances are subjected to critical reflection and revision. (p. 208)

Situated performances involve students not only acting and engaging in role-play but also participating in critical reflection and revision of their performed actions and dialog. Situated performances differ from traditional role-plays because participants are asked to reflect on their actions and aspects of their communication and are also required to identify and discuss the cultural, political, institutional, social, and contexts of their actions (Darvin, 2015). Fischer and Vander Laan (2002) note that in educational contexts "role-playing has a special power in that it allows students to place themselves in a vulnerable social position without any real threat or danger to themselves ... they are able to discuss the causes, the pros and cons, and even the dangers and the advantages of lifestyles unlike their own" (p. 25).

Cultural and Political Vignettes (CPVs)

In the present study, the teachers were given what is referred to as a Cultural and Political Vignette (Darvin, 2015, p. 3) on supporting homeless students and asked to create situated performances based on the situation provided. The PI coined the term "Cultural and Political Vignettes (CPVs)" and has published extensively on their use in both teacher education contexts and K-12 settings (Darvin, 2009, 2010, 2011a, 2011b, 2011c, 2011d, 2015, 2017). The definition of a CPV is as follows:

> CPVs are potential cultural and/or political situations, real or imagined, that are presented to students so that they can practice the complex decision-making skills that they need in today's diverse classrooms, schools, and communities. They invite students to dialogue, problem-pose and problem-solve around controversial issues that they need to evaluate critically and view through multiple perspectives or lenses. CPVs can be used as part of pre-reading, or during reading and post-reading and writing activities. They are designed to aid students in both developing their own viewpoints on critical, contentious issues, and actively listening to and critiquing those of others. (Darvin, 2015, p.3)

The following CPV on supporting homeless students was assigned to the participants in the study, and they were asked to create situated performances of it in groups:

> Sally, a student in your first period class, is often late. She rarely has her homework completed, although her class work is quite good. Sally often looks disheveled and tired and sometimes even acts defiantly toward the teachers and other students. She has frequent emotional outbursts and as a result, she does not have many friends. She is new to the school and when you try and check her records, your school is unable to locate them. She tells you that her family moves around a lot, and later you hear from a school counselor

that Sally and her family are homeless and living in a motel nearby. What can you do to help Sally, your homeless student, to be more successful in her literacy learning?

The directions that were given to the teacher–participants with the CPV above read:

> Please create two short situated performances related to the above situation with your role-play groups. The first should depict pitfalls the teacher should avoid, and the second should show things that the teacher can say/do to try and improve this situation. All members of the group must have speaking roles in at least one of the two performances. Your group should discuss the CPV first and then write brief scripts for these role-plays before performing them for the class.

The first time that the participants responded to the aforementioned CPV, they had little prior knowledge on best practices for educating homeless students and supporting their literacy learning. Of the 26 teachers enrolled in the course, only 2 had homeless students in their classes at the time of the study (to their knowledge), and both indicated in their beginning-of-the-semester reflections that they had received no prior training on working with this population. Not surprisingly, the teachers were at a bit of a loss as to how to respond to the CPV in the form of a situated performance. In the situated performances, the participants who played the roles of the teachers did a wonderful job depicting the pitfalls that the teacher should avoid in the first performance, but were far less confident in the second performance, which were intended to show things that the teacher can try and say/do to improve the situation.

The following brief excerpt was taken from one of the group's second CPV performances:

TEACHER: Okay students; please take out your homework. Sally, where is your work?

SALLY (homeless student): I don't have it, Miss.

TEACHER: Why not?

DAN (another student): Because she's a loser!

TEACHER: Dan, knock it off. That's not funny. Why not, Sally?

SALLY: I just don't. I don't have a computer, and my mom couldn't take me to the library. It's too noisy where I live, and my three brothers and sisters won't stop bothering me.

TEACHER: Okay, Sally. It's not an excuse, but I understand. I have a large, noisy family too. Please come to detention with me today at lunchtime and get caught up.

SALLY: Okay, Miss. I will.

When the participants from this group were asked to explain why they believed their second CPV performance demonstrated things that the teacher said/did to improve the situation, one group member responded that by telling Sally to come to detention to finish her incomplete homework. The teacher was being cognizant of Sally's homeless status and allowing her to make up the missed work. One of the other group members added that doing this would give the teacher some one-on-one time with Sally that she could use to get her caught up and also to perhaps connect with Sally on a personal level. Finally, a third group member added that the teacher showed empathy in her response to Sally by saying that her family was noisy too, and that the teacher did not negatively single Sally out in any way in front of her peers. Although these responses are reasonable explanations for why the participants believed that the teacher in the second CPV performance was saying/doing things that might improve Sally's situation as a homeless student, this example illustrates that the teachers' knowledge about serving as an advocate for and educating homeless students was in its infancy.

Read: Exposing Participants to Texts and Discussions on Educating the Homeless

The next part of the study involved exposing the teachers to carefully selected texts that would promote critical dialog on supporting homeless students and might make them more knowledgeable about how to advocate for homeless students and educate them more successfully. One of the texts that the participants were asked to read and discuss was *Rachel and Her Children: Homeless Families in America* (1988), written by Jonathan Kozol. Although this text is nearly 30 years old, it is sadly just as relevant today as it was when it was written. In addition to this book, participants read "Emerging Faces of Homelessness: Young Children, Their Families, and Schooling," a chapter written by Thoennes in *Other Kinds of Families: Embracing Diversity in Schools* (2009), edited by Turner-Vorbeck & Marsh. The teachers also read two journal articles, "Meeting the Educational Needs of Homeless Children" (Rafferty, 1997/1998) and "Residential Instability and the McKinney-Vento Homeless Children and Education Program" (Cunningham, Harwood, & Hall, 2010).

In addition to reading and discussing the texts at length in class, the participants examined some primary source documents and U.S. policies related to homelessness and education. These included the McKinney-Vento Act, a federal legislation that requires schools to appoint a liaison to communicate with homeless families, publicize the rights of homeless parents at schools, oversee district programs for identifying and enrolling homeless students, and ensure that homeless children are given opportunities to achieve the same academic state standards as other children (Berliner, 2002; Thoennes, 2009). They studied Five Principles for Educators in Teaching the Homeless, which include not stigmatizing them, making schools safe havens, considering the needs of the whole child, including physical health, mental health, and nutritional needs, actively working with parents and guardians to develop goals and programs, and collaborating with community members and developing networks (Berliner, 2002).

The participants read poetry that was written by homeless youth and for extra credit, 12 of the teachers engaged in a voluntary field experience and attended an art exhibit that featured paintings and drawings that were made by homeless youth in New York City. The participants actively and critically reflected on several questions and issues with regard to educating homeless youth, including: comparing and contrasting the image that society depicts the typical homeless person in America with the actual demographics and statistics regarding who is really homeless in America, discussing the various economic and societal reasons for the recent increase in homelessness in America (mortgage crisis, unemployment, etc.), evaluating the legislation that currently advocates for the educational rights of homeless students, and brainstorming the specific ways in which teachers and schools can help homeless students. At the conclusion of the unit, the participants were asked to do what the PI terms a Read and Revisit and respond to their pre-reading CPV situated performance task a second time, as a post-reading task.

Revisit: Readdressing the CPV Situated Performances on Supporting Homeless Students

The intention of the Read and Revisit Stage is for students and teachers to reflect upon what impact, if any, reading course texts has had on their thinking, responses, and future actions, as revealed through revisiting a previously addressed CPV. It is an excellent way for you to assess whether or not the texts read and studied in class have influenced the students' thinking about culturally or politically charged issues… (Darvin, 2015, p. 98)

When participants were asked to revisit the original CPV, the revised situated performances clearly indicated that their sensitivity and knowledge had increased exponentially. The following excerpt was taken from one of the group's Read and Revisit CPV performances:

TEACHER: Sally, please take out the portfolio that I gave you and go type up your homework responses for today on the class computer.

SALLY: Okay, Miss. I will.

TEACHING ASSISTANT (talking quietly to the teacher): Why are you letting Sally use your computer? And wasn't that homework meant to be done at home?

TEACHER: Sally is homeless and does not have a quiet place to complete her schoolwork. Her family does not have a computer, and she does not even have a desk to do her work. I am trying to get her a laptop with some federal grant money through the school that she can borrow. In the meantime, I let her use my class computer and gave her a clipboard with a pen attached to act as a portable desk for now. I'm having her keep all of her work in a portfolio, in case she transfers to another school again and needs to show her new teachers samples of her work.

T.A.: Oh, okay. I understand. That also might help explain what happened in the cafeteria the other day. One of the other students accused Sally of stealing her food, and it almost caused a fight. Maybe she did that because she is hungry.

TEACHER: Yes, that may be the reason. She receives free lunch, but I am looking into her receiving free breakfast as well. I noticed that she wears the same clothes a lot, and the other girls make fun of her. I'm going to mention it at the faculty meeting and see if we can establish some clothing supplies right here at school for students in need. I have a lot of clothing that I can donate, and I am sure other teachers, parents, and community members can too.

T.A.: That's a great idea. I'm sure people would donate if they knew the clothes were going to a good cause. I'm going to check on Sally now and see how she's doing.

As one can see from the preceding excerpt, which is representative of all of the Read and Revisit situated performances documented in the study, the teachers' sensitivity to the homeless student Sally, as well as their abilities to advocate on her behalf more effectively were increased as a result of reading the texts, dialoging about them extensively in class, critically reflecting on them, writing about them, and revisiting the CPV through a lens of increased prior knowledge. When the participants from this group were asked to explain why they believed their Read and Revisit performance demonstrated things that the teacher said/did to improve the situation, they gave in-depth responses that demonstrated their newly acquired knowledge regarding educating homeless students, including the teacher providing Sally with needed resources, such as the portfolio and clip board, since she had no work space in the hotel/shelter where she was living, seeking to obtain Sally a laptop with federal grant money allotted to the school district via the McKinney-Vento Act, trying to get her additional meals so that she would not remain hungry and steal food, starting a community clothing drive and clothing repository, and considering Sally's needs as a whole child, including her physical and mental health and nutritional needs.

More impressive than this change in the teachers' thinking; however, was the "action" phase of the research,the hallmark of pedagogical strategies that promote critical literacy, and teaching for social justice. This qualitative inquiry sought to uncover whether or not exposing novice teachers in a graduate diversity course to particular kinds of texts and activities focused on economic diversity and lifestyle differences among students would make them more likely to positively respond to these lesser understood forms of diversity in their own teaching. Since the premise was that it would, the study carefully documented the specific ways in which the teachers' practices and curriculum were directly impacted by their exposure to the CPV activities. The following section describes one way that a participant from this performance group, who was a teacher of Social Studies, chose to integrate situated performance activities on the theme of homelessness in America into his own twelfth grade participation in Government class. He did this to raise awareness in his community and to experiment with the situated performance strategy that he learned in his diversity course. He indicated in his end-of-the-semester reflection that he felt that as a teacher of Social Studies, he had a responsibility to share his new knowledge about the homeless with his own students and community.

Investigating Homelessness in America: Twelfth Grade CPV Unit

As the beginning of the unit, the students examined U.S. government policies toward homelessness, beginning with the first task force on homelessness that was created in 1983. They researched the formation of various homeless advocacy groups, including the National Coalition for the Homeless, the National Housing Institute, and the Welfare Center. Students read, analyzed, and discussed primary source documents, including the Stewart B. McKinney Act of 1987 and the more recent McKinney-Vento Homeless Education Assistance Improvements Act in the No Child Left Behind Act of 2001–2002. The students were shocked by the demographic statistics regarding homelessness in America and the disparity between what came to their minds when they first thought of homelessness and the true faces of homelessness in America today (Darvin, 2015, p. 86).

The students, in the tradition of critical literacy theory and practice (Apple, 2014; Freire & Macedo, 1987; 2013; Gee, 2014; Janks, 2013; Janks et al., 2013; Rogers, 2013; Vasquez, 2013), developed their own inquiry questions based on their preliminary research:

- What are the stereotypes regarding the homeless in America today as compared to the realities?
- How has homelessness changed from the past until now?
- Why do some people actually choose homelessness as a life style, even when they are presented with other options?
- Why do homeless people stay in cold cities like New York and how do they survive the brutal winters?
- Why do homeless people seem invisible to many people who see them every day and how and why does this invisibility develop in American society?
- How can we help increase awareness about homelessness in our community and help our local homeless people? (Darvin, 2015, p. 86)

The teacher also incorporated several literary texts, including excerpts from *Rachel and Her Children: Homelessness in America (1988)*, one of the texts that the teacher had read in his graduate diversity class, and *The Soloist: A Lost Dream, An Unlikely Friendship and the Redemptive Power of Music* (Lopez, 2010). The second text is a portrait of Nathaniel Ayers, a mentally ill cello prodigy who chose homelessness as a way of life. This book is based on a true story of a relationship between Steve Lopez, a Los Angeles reporter and Ayers, a homeless musical genius. The students also watched the 2009 film version of *The Soloist*, staring Jamie Foxx and Robert Downey, Jr. Other supplemental texts from which excerpts were read included *Open Our Eyes: Seeing the Invisible People of Homelessness* (Hendricks, 2010), *Living at the Edge of the World: How I survived in the Tunnels of Grand Central Station* (Bolnick & Bolnick, 2001), and *The Mole People: Life in the Tunnels beneath New York City* (Toth, 1995).

For the CPV situated performances in this unit, the teacher asked the students to encapsulate the most important things that they learned while researching answers to their inquiry questions. The instructions that the students were given for their situated performances were also specific to their groups' particular inquiry questions:

Please create a skit that does one of the following:

- *Group/Inquiry Question #1*. Compares and contrasts the stereotypes that many have regarding homeless people in America with the realities of homelessness we learned about in our research.

- *Group/Inquiry Question #2.* Compares and contrasts homelessness in a past era (i.e., the 1980s, the 1990s) with homelessness in America today.
- *Group/Inquiry Question #3.* Compares and contrasts someone being homeless voluntarily with someone being homeless due to circumstances outside of his or her control.
- *Group/Inquiry Question #4.* Presents some of the reasons why homeless people choose to remain in certain places and shows some of the ways in which they survive (i.e., shelters, tunnels, food banks).
- *Group/Inquiry Question #5.* Presents possibilities as to why homeless people seem invisible to many people who see them every day and how and why this invisibility develops in American society.
- *Group/Inquiry Question #6.* Presents ways in which we can increase awareness about homelessness in our community (Darvin, 2015, p. 87).

The students were told to incorporate information from the texts into their situated performances. The last group's situated performance, Group/Inquiry Question #6, even became the basis for a follow-up community service project. Five interested students, with the leadership of the teacher, established a tutoring program to help homeless students living in their community. The seniors from the Participation in Government class tutored ten students in grades 1–10 who were living in motels serving as homeless shelters in the community in reading, writing, and mathematics, and also served as mentors for the younger, displaced youth. At the conclusion of the school year, these seniors were presented with awards at graduation for their exemplary service to the community (Darvin, 2015, p. 93).

CPV activities on supporting homeless students that were first presented to the teacher in his graduate diversity course later provided a springboard for his own secondary students to achieve the ultimate critical literacy goal of acquiring knowledge through literacy and applying it to help solve a real social dilemma in their local community. Proponents of critical literacy (Apple, 2014; Freire, 1970; Freire & Macedo, 2013; Gee, 2014; Janks, 2013; Janks et al., 2013; Rogers, 2013; Vasquez, 2013) have long-lamented that the most important yet typically overlooked part of developing critical literacy skills in students involves them actually *doing* positive things in their communities as a result of the transformations that occur from engaging in problem-posing and dialoguing about these problems in school (Darvin, 2015, p. 93). In this example from the study, the action component of critical literacy and teaching for social justice was fully realized, and one can readily see how one participant positively responded to understanding lesser-understood forms of diversity in his own teaching.

Increasing Teachers' Understanding of Student Economic Diversity

Another example of a CPV that was presented to the teacher–participants in the study centered on the theme of understanding and being more sensitive to studenteconomic diversity. It read:

> A boy in your class named Jay is often absent and does not hand in his assignments. He refuses to complete any worksheets or answer the assigned questions from the textbook, causing him to be in danger of failing your class. You have tried contacting his parents several times, but have been unable to reach them by phone or email. When you confront the student about his excessive absences and missed work, he appears indifferent. When you push him a bit harder, he becomes oppositional and defiant. He tells you that he's not learning anything at this stupid school anyway and might as well just drop out now and get a job at the factory where his father and older brother work. What would you do?

The teachers responded to the preceding CPV in writing and then had an extensive class discussion about the various actions they might take in this situation (i.e., contacting a guidance counselor, failing the child, asking the child to attend extra help, etc.). Afterwards, they were assigned a class text; Patrick Finn's book *Literacy with an Attitude: Educating Working Class Children in Their Own Self-Interest* (2009). This book goes into great detail about the socioeconomic differences between working class, middle class, and affluent schools and the different ways in which teachers, students, parents, and administrators from these socioeconomic groups and schools typically communicate and why. Additional texts that were included in this unit were excerpts from *Savage Inequalities* (Kozol, 1991), and three articles; "Lifelines for Poor Children" (Heckman, 2013), "Poor Teaching for Poor Children in the Name of Reform" (Kohn, 2011), and "The Pedagogy of Poverty Versus Good Teaching" (Haberman, 2010). The teachers engaged in continued discussions about the texts, role-played various situations inspired by the texts in the form of situated performances, and responded to questions about techniques for educating working class, middle class, and affluent students verbally and in writing. They read excerpts from the foundational work of Jean Anyon (1997), John Ogbu (1991), Paul Willis (1977), and Shirley Brice Heath (1986), all of whom wrote about the relationships between social class and school knowledge.

At the conclusion of the economic diversity unit, the participants were asked to Read and Revisit their original written responses to the CPV and decide if after reading and discussing the texts on socioeconomic differences, they wanted to change their responses or leave them the same. They wrote detailed reflections about their original responses and how reading and discussing the assigned course texts influenced their responses. They were asked to use evidence from the texts, in the form of citations, to support their decisions to either keep their original responses the same or to change them and explain why. This Read and Revisit activity served as an eye-opener for many teacher–participants that had not previously considered the vast differences in the socioeconomics of their students'lives and how these differences can impact students' access to educational resources, communication styles of parents, etc.

The participants reported in their end-of-the-semester reflections that the Read and Revisit activity showed them the direct influences of the course texts on their thinking and subsequent actions in their own classrooms. Participants described actions that they began taking as a result of participating in this Read and Revisit CPV activity in their graduate diversity/literacy course. These actions ranged from small ones, such as making themselves more accessible to working-class parents by holding parent–teacher conferences outside of their schools' regularly scheduled days and times to bigger, more expansive actions, such as changing their pedagogical approaches for working with working class and middle-class students to encompass those teaching strategies that are typically reserved for affluent and elite schools and learners.

FINDINGS AND IMPLICATIONS

The findings of this qualitative inquiry indicate that exposing novice teachers in a diversity course to particular texts and activities that focused on economic diversity and lifestyle differences among students did, in fact, make them more likely to positively respond to these lesser understood forms of diversity in their own teaching in a variety of ways, large and small.The participants were asked to consider the full range of lifestyle differences and economic diversity among their students and to become more sensitive to their students' needs and more knowledgeable about how to provide them with more effective, differentiated instruction. The teachers were asked to discuss and write about how teachers might address the varying needs of wealthy, middle class, and low-income students in the same classroom and had to contemplate the many ways in which access to educational resources, communication styles, and other societal factors influence their students' educational experiences, challenges, and successes in ways that they had not taken into account previously. An implication that results from these findings is that the selection of texts that are thought-provoking and can be viewed from multiple perspectives is essential in stimulating thoughtful discussion in teacher education programs and promoting critical literacy and teaching for social justice.

With that being said, the texts were selected for use in this study by combining earlier classic, foundational works to which the majority of new teachers have never been exposed (i.e., Freire, Brice Heath, Anyon) with more recent articles or excerpts from books that expand on those earlier works and/or provide more current applications of the foundational works. Edited volumes, such as *The Skin that We Speak* and *Other Kinds of Families* were also used because in these collections, each chapter addresses a different aspect of diversity. Therefore, these kinds of texts expose teachers to several prominent literacy scholars' ideas. Finally, it is important to note that unlike novice secondary teachers, who are often constrained in their text selection and must deal with issues of administrative and parental censorship, professors of teacher education often have the luxury of using whatever texts they want, under the umbrella of academic freedom. The secondary teachers' selection processes of controversial texts are, therefore, very different. They have to consider issues, such as obtaining administrative and parental consent, collaborating with guidance counselors or school psychologists, and offering alternative text selections for students that may not want to read particular texts or whose parents do not grant them permission (Darvin, 2015, pp. 31–32).

In addition to the previously described, detailed examples involving supporting homeless students and becoming more responsive to economic disparities among students, similar Read and Revisit units and situated performances were implemented in the course that centered around the themes of more-actively supporting students that are in foster care or adopted, better preparing teachers to work with students reared by gay and lesbian parents, and teachers working more effectively with students whose parents are incarcerated or addicted to drugs and alcohol. At the present time, two new units are being developed; one on supporting secondary students who are pregnant or teen parents and a second on working more effectively with transgendered youth. These are yet more student lifestyle differences for which very few secondary teachers are properly prepared in teacher preparation programs.

In summation, the participants in the present study believed, as indicated in their end-of-the-semester reflections, that exposure to texts, class discussions, and activities that educated them on student lifestyle differences and economic diversity made them more likely to respond to these variations positively in their own teaching. The findings of this small qualitative study indicate that there is a pressing need, both in teacher education and K-12 schooling, to increase opportunities for students of all ages to be exposed to texts and pedagogical practices that expand their definitions of student diversity, increase their critical literacy skills, and compel them to act in ways that promote social justice in their schools and communities.

CONCLUSION

In her end-of-the-semester reflection, the student whose writing appears as the opening of this chapter wrote:

> At the end of this course, I feel like I have a much better understanding of the diverse student needs and challenges at my school. I definitely don't have all of the answers, but at least I have some understanding of the lives and lifestyles of my students and how I can make a difference in helping to improve their literacy skills. As an English teacher, I can expose them to texts that get them to think critically about societal issues that impact their lives. I can also help support them in trying to make positive changes in their community. The Read and Revisit and situated performance strategies are ones that I will use with my own students next year. I already use CPVs now as a Do Now, to get the students thinking and writing about topics we are studying from multiple perspectives. In the end, I'm really grateful to know more about my students and believe that knowing more about them will make me an even better teacher than I was last year.

In conclusion, teacher preparation programs should be informed by studies encouraging teacher educators to employ pedagogical strategies aimed at increasing the level of preparedness of novice teachers with regard to student diversity. These same pedagogical practices can then be adopted by K-12 teachers to help them promote critical literacy and teaching for social justice. We are living in an age where lifestyle differences and economic diversity among students are just as important and impactful on their literacy learning as their cultural and linguistic differences. Teacher preparation programs, particularly diversity courses and curriculum, should be modified and expanded to reflect these notable societal changes.

REFERENCES

Adams, M., Bell, L. A., & Griffin, P. (Eds.). (2007). *Teaching for diversity and social justice*. New York, NY: Routledge.

Anyon, J. (1997). *Ghetto schooling: A political economy of urban educational reform*. New York, NY: Teachers College Press.

Apple, M. W. (2014).*Official knowledge: Democratic education in a conservative age*. New York, NY: Routledge.

Bell, L. A. (2010). *Storytelling for social justice: Connecting narrative and the arts in antiracist teaching*. New York, NY: Routledge.

Berliner, B. A. (2002). Helping homeless students keep up. *Education Digest, 68*(1), 49.

Bolnick, J. P., & Bolnick, S., T. (2001). *Living at the edge of the world: How I survived in the tunnels of Grand Central Station*. New York, NY: St. Martin's Griffin.

Brice Heath, S. (1986). *Ways with words*. Cambridge, UK: Cambridge University Press.

Christensen, L. (2000). *Reading, writing and rising up: Teaching about social justice and the power of the written word*. Milwaukee, WI: Rethinking Schools.

Cunningham, M., Harwood, R., & Hall, S. (2010). Residential instability and the McKinney-Vento homeless children and education program: What we know, plus gaps in research. Washington, DC: Urban Institute (NJ1).

Darvin, J. (2009). Cultural and political vignettes in the English classroom: Problem-posing, problem-solving, and the imagination. *English Journal, 92*(2), 55–60.

Darvin, J. (2010). Using cultural and political vignettes to explore justice issues in teacher education courses. In C. Rhodes & L. Wolf (Eds.), *Social justice and education: Navigating stormy waters* (pp. 109–122). East Rockaway, NY: Cummings & Hathaway Publishers.

Darvin, J. (2011a) I don't feel comfortable reading those books in my classroom: A qualitative study of the impact of cultural and political vignettes in a teacher education course. *The Teacher Educator, 46*(4), 274–298.

Darvin, J. (2011b). I would rather feel uncomfortable in an education class than at the school where I teach: Cultural and political vignettes as a pedagogical approach in teacher education. In A. Cohan & A. Honigsfeld (Eds.), *Breaking the mold of pre-service and in-service teacher education* (pp. 15–23). Lantham, MD: R & L Education.

Darvin, J. (2011c). Situated performances in a graduate teacher education course: An inquiry into the impact of cultural and political vignettes (CPVs). *Teachers and Teaching: Theory and Practice, 17*(3), 345–364.

Darvin, J. (2011d). Teaching critical literacy using cultural and political vignettes. *Critical Education, 2*(6). Retrieved from http://m1.cust.educ.ubc.ca/journal/index.php/criticaled/article/view/155

Darvin, J. (2015). *Teaching the tough issues: Problem solving from multiple perspectives in middle & high school humanities classes*. New York, NY: Teachers College Press.

Darvin, J. (2017). Critical conversations with children's literature: How cultural and political vignettes (CPVs) support young readers. *Literacy, 51*(3), 131–137.

Freire, P. (1970). *Pedagogy of the oppressed*. New York, NY: The Continuum Publishing Company.

Freire, P., & Macedo, D. (1987). *Literacy: Reading the word and the world*. New York, NY: Routledge.

Freire, P., & Macedo, D. (2013). *Literacy: Reading the word and the world*. New York, NY: Routledge.

Finders, M., & Rose, S. (1999). If I were the teacher: Situated performances as pedagogical tools for teacher preparation. *English Education, 31*(3), 205–222.

Finn, P. J. (2009). *Literacy with an attitude: Educating working-class children in their own self-interest* (2nd ed.). Albany, NY: SUNY Press.

Fischer, J., & Vander Laan, S. (2002). Improving approaches to multicultural education: Teaching empathy through role-playing. *Multicultural Education, 9*(4), 25–26.

Gee, J. P. (2014). *Social linguistics and literacies: Ideology in discourses*. New York, NY: Rutledge.

Haberman, M. (2010). The pedagogy of poverty versus good teaching. *Phi Delta Kappan, 92*(2), 81–87.

Heckman, J. J. (2013, September 15). Lifelines for poor children. *The New York Times*, accessed at: https://opinionator.blogs.nytimes.com/2013/09/14/lifelines-for-poor-children.

Hendricks, K. D. (2010). *Open our eyes: Seeing the invisible people of homelessness*. Seattle, WA: CreateSpace Independent Publishing Platform.

Janks, H. (2013). Critical literacy in teaching and research. *Education Inquiry, 4*(2), 225–242.

Janks, H., Dixon, K., Ferreira, A., Granville, S., & Newfield, D. (2013). *Doing critical literacy: Texts and activities for students and teachers*. New York, NY: Routledge.

Kohn, A. (2011). Poor teaching for poor children. *Education Week*. Retrieved from http://www. alfiekohn.org/teaching/edweek/poor.htm

Kozol, J. (1988). *Rachel and her children: Homeless families in America*. New York, NY: Ballentine Books.

Kozol, J. (1991). *Savage inequalities: Children in America's schools*. New York, NY: HarperCollins Publishers.

Kumashiro, K. K. (2009). *Against common sense: Teaching and learning toward social justice*. New York, NY: Taylor & Francis.

Lopez, S. (2010). *The soloist: A lost dream, an unlikely friendship and the redemptive power of music*. New York, NY: Berkley Trade.

Ogbu, J. U. (1991). Cultural diversity and school experience. In C. E. Walsh (Ed.), *Literacy as praxis: Culture, language, and pedagogy* (pp. 25–50). Norwood, NJ: Ablex Publishing Corporation.

Rafferty, Y. (1998). Meeting the educational needs of homeless children. *Educational Leadership, 55*(4), 48–52.

Rogers, R. (2013). Cultivating diversity through critical literacy in teacher education. In C. Kosnik, J. Roswell, P. Williamson, R. Simon, & C. Beck (Eds.), *Literacy teacher educators* (pp. 7–19). Rotterdam, The Netherlands: SensePublishers.

Shor, I. (2012). *Empowering education: Critical teaching for social change*. Chicago, IL: University of Chicago Press.

Thoennes, T. (2009). Emerging faces of homelessness: Young children, their families, and schooling. In T. Turner-Vorbeck & M. M. Marsh (Eds.), *Other kinds of families: Embracing diversity in schools* (pp. 162–175). New York, NY: Teachers College Press.

Toth, J. (1995). *The mole people: Living in the tunnels beneath New York City*. Chicago, IL: Chicago Review Press.

Vasquez, V. (2013). Living and learning critical literacy in the university classroom. In C. Kosnik, J. Roswell, P. Williamson, R. Simon, & C. Beck (Eds.), *Literacy teacher educators* (pp. 79–92). Rotterdam, The Netherlands: SensePublishers.

Willis, P. E. (1977). *Learning to labor: How working class kids get working class jobs*. Westmead, England: Saxon House.

Winn, M. T. (2011). *Girl time: Literacy, justice, and the school-to-prison pipeline: Teaching for social justice*. New York, NY: Teachers College Press.

READING TOWARD EQUITY: CREATING LGBTQ+ INCLUSIVE CLASSROOMS THROUGH LITERARY AND LITERACY PRACTICES

Autumn M. Dodge

ABSTRACT

The goal of this chapter is to address the importance of helping teachers develop an understanding of LGBTQ+ issues and ways to create inclusive classrooms for LGBTQ+ students with particular attention to how LGBTQ+ identities/experiences can be valued and visible through literary and literacy practices. The issues addressed in this chapter are grounded in queer theory and intersectionality, which provide a space for challenging heteronormative environments in many schools as well as acknowledging the complex intersectionality of diverse identities. This framework is unpacked so readers can see how it supports instructional practices. Theory and literature inform discussion of the move in the literacy profession toward LGBTQ+ -inclusive mindsets and pedagogies. They further inform practical

Addressing Diversity in Literacy Instruction
Literacy Research, Practice and Evaluation, Volume 8, 135–154
Copyright © 2018 by Emerald Publishing Limited
All rights of reproduction in any form reserved
ISSN: 2048-0458/doi:10.1108/S2048-045820170000008007

implications and examples provided by the author. A major issue of our time is LGBTQ+ inclusion in schools and the role of teachers in implementing literacy practices that address the needs of LGBTQ+ students and making visible their diverse identities. For the field of literacy, this is evidenced in the revision of Standard 4 Diversity and Equity in the International Literacy Association's (ILA) Standards for the Preparation of Literacy Professionals 2017 (Standards 2017). ILA Standards 2017, which will be released in 2018, require programs preparing literacy professionals to develop candidates' knowledge of queer theory and literacy practices inclusive of diverse students, with diversity including sexual orientation, gender identity, and gender expression. Further, ILA Standards 2017 acknowledge intersectionality across forms of diversity and that a rich understanding of diversity improves the quality of teaching and learning within and across classrooms, schools, and communities. This chapter expands on these topics and offers foundational content and resources to help literacy teacher educators, candidates in literacy programs, and other stakeholders to answer this call for building a literacy field that is welcoming, inclusive, and equity-oriented. Developing the knowledge base about LGBTQ+ issues, including theoretical foundations, social justice teaching mindsets, and concrete pedagogical literacy practices that build inclusive classrooms, can be an accessible, meaningful, and fruitful endeavor that will enrich literacy education programs and the learning communities in which literacy professionals work. Teacher educators and teachers can utilize book choices, approaches to classroom discussion and assignments, and school initiatives to build a learning environment that values LGBTQ+ students' identities and experiences and disrupts heteronormativity in the curriculum. Multiple examples of how this can be done are offered. Understanding intersectionality also helps teacher educators and teachers see how forms of diversity are not silos. Individuals' identities are comprised of various aspects. The topics discussed in this chapter center on LGBTQ+ issues but are applicable beyond just this scope.

Keywords: LGBTQ+; diversity; literacy; literature; teachers; teacher educators; intersectionality; queer theory

For decades, diversity was addressed through conceptual and pedagogical notions of multiculturalism and multicultural education (e.g., Nieto, 2000). Multiculturalism and multicultural education situated diversity almost exclusively in the context of race, ethnicity, and language (e.g., Nieto, 2000). While the goals and efforts of early multicultural education should be lauded, multicultural education often resulted in teaching and learning *about* the 'other' (Levine-Raskey, 2000) as opposed to learning about how the complex factors involved in issues of diversity, inequity, access to schooling, interrogating issues of power, and more affect diverse learners in school environments. Early notions of culturally relevant teaching (Ladson-Billings, 1995) took steps to push beyond the limiting aspects of early constructs in multicultural education. Teachers who embrace culturally relevant teaching must interrogate current pedagogical, instructional, and curricular norms to determine changes that can be made to be inclusive of and build on the strengths of diverse learners. Moll, Neff, Amanti, and Gonzales (1992) coined the phrase "funds of knowledge" and advocated for teachers who actively seek to learn about the practices, families, and communities of their diverse learners and incorporate their funds of knowledge into the classroom.

These efforts have continued to be pursued by researchers, teacher educators, and teachers forwarding social justice and social justice pedagogy as an important focus of teaching (e.g., Nieto, 2000). However, again, the majority of attention in this area has been on advocacy for students from diverse racial, ethnic, and linguistic backgrounds. Other forms of diversity such as sexual orientation, gender expression, and gender identity are often relegated to "school hallways … or dreaded and embarrassed silences" (Vavrus, 2009, p. 383).

While LGBTQ+ identities (*acronym discussed below*), experiences, and inequity issues have recently been more visible in our social, political, and educational sphere, these issues are still fraught with controversy and discomfort for many in and outside schools. Legislation protecting the rights of LGBTQ+ students have been put in place and taken away. Administrators, teachers, students, and other stakeholders receive mixed messages about the role of schools in advocating for the rights of and embracing their LGBTQ+ students. Thus, the most common response to diversity in sexual orientation, gender expression, and gender identity in schools is silence.

This silence is dangerous – often literally – to LGBTQ+ students though. Research shows that teacher education programs rarely address LGBTQ+ issues or how to integrate LGBTQ+ issues or texts in curricula (Kissen, 2002). Programs for promoting safe schools also often don't directly address harassment, violence, and slurs against LGBTQ+ students, and teachers may not know or be comfortable about how to address discrimination against LGBTQ+ students in their communities (Au et al., 2014). Research shows that LGBTQ+ students face pervasive and disproportionate rates of harassment and violence at schools (Bochenek & Brown, 2001; Kissen, 2002; see GLSEN surveys 1998–2009) and that these experiences have serious repercussions, such as depression, dropping out of school, homelessness, and suicide (Bochenek & Brown, 2001; Kissen, 2002; MAP, 2011; Schneider & Owens, 2002; Uken, 2013).

Silence also effectively means invisibility. Silence makes invisible the identities and experiences of LGTBQ+ students and, therefore, privileges heterosexuality. Heteronormativity can be described as "an overarching system for organizing and regulating sexuality, whereby certain ways of acting, thinking and feeling about sex are privileged over others" (Cameron & Kulick, 2006, p. 9). Heteronormativity thus privileges one story – the heterosexual or "straight" story. Famed author, cultural critic, and activist Chimamanda Ngozi Adichie (2009) has described "the danger of a single story." She explained, "Many stories matter. Stories have been used to dispossess and to malign, but stories can also be used to empower and to humanize. Stories can break the dignity of a people, but stories can also repair that broken dignity" (17:13).

THE ROLE OF TEXTS AND THE ROLE OF LITERACY PROFESSIONALS

One way that individuals, including students, see and hear stories is through literature and other texts. The books students read can be both "windows" and "mirrors" (Bishop, 1990a). Bishop (1990b) explains:

> When children cannot find themselves reflected in the books they read, or when the images they see are distorted, negative, or laughable, they learn a powerful lesson about how they are devalued in the society of which they are a part. (p. 557)

For LGBTQ+ students, however, texts are most often *windows* – they look into books and see the stories, experiences, and identities of those who are not like them. Less often do they look into books and find *mirrors* – books where they see characters who resemble them and embody a shared story. Tschida, Ryan, and Ticknor (2014) state that, "When readers are able to find themselves in a text, they are therefore validated; their experiences are not so unique or strange as to never be spoken or experienced by others. This inclusion, in turn, connects readers even more strongly to the larger world of books" (p. 29).

A FIELD THAT EMBRACES LGBTQ+ IDENTITIES

The move toward creating inclusive literacy classrooms for LGBTQ+ students begins with a field that embraces diversity in sexual orientation, gender identity, and gender expression. The International Literacy Association's (ILA) Standards for the Preparation of Literacy Professionals 2017 (Standards 2017) evidence significant revision from Standards 2010 and represent our field joining the ranks of organizations such as the National Council of Teachers of English (NCTE, 2007) in including sexual orientation, gender identity, and gender expression as forms of diversity that must be valued and addressed in classrooms. The 2017 Standard 4 Diversity and Equity (previously Standard 4 Diversity in 2010) provides guidance for specialized literacy professionals to build the foundational knowledge, professional dispositions and reflective practices, pedagogies, and advocacy mindsets that will support their LGBTQ+ students. This guidance includes building foundational knowledge of queer theory and intersectionality, developing reflective practices to interrogate one's own privileges and biases, developing pedagogical instructional practices that are relevant and reflect all forms of diversity, and advocating for equity in classrooms, schools, and communities.

As literacy teacher educators and literacy teachers, we have a responsibility to create learning environments where many stories and identities matter, where many stories are incorporated in our literacy instruction, and where those many stories are reflected in the texts we choose for our students to read. We need to explicitly address the connections between literacy and LGBTQ+ identities and stories. Bringing in the stories of LGBTQ+ students and disrupting the heteronormativity of schooling is not an easy task, but it is one that teachers who believe in social equity must take on (Giroux, 2001). Clark and Blackburn (2009) argue, "English language arts classrooms can be significant sites for combating homophobia and heterosexism in schools, and that reading LGBT-themed literature is one of the best ways to do that work" (p. 25).

In this chapter, I first lay out a framework of queer theory and intersectionality for understanding how LGBTQ+ issues are situated in a social justice model of education and how LGBTQ+ issues can be taken up by literacy professionals through the texts we choose and the discussions we facilitate around those texts. Second, I introduce multiple approaches to addressing LGBTQ+ issues through text choices and discussion, including concrete examples drawn from current work of scholars and teachers addressing LGBTQ+ inclusive literacy practices. Third, I discuss ideas for preparing teachers for creating LGBTQ+ inclusive literacy classrooms, including initial conversations about LGBTQ+ issues and resources for instruction. Finally, I return to emphasize the important role of teachers in creating inclusive schools and classrooms for *all* diverse students and return to intersectionality as an important lens for disrupting single stories.

THEORY AND LITERATURE

Social justice advocacy for LGBTQ+ students is grounded most broadly in notions of critical pedagogy (Freire, 1970). Work in social justice can be attributed to the work of Paulo Freire (1970) in his work with adult literacy learners in Brazil. Freire helped them use literacy as a tool for pushing back against oppression. Calls for using literacy as a space for disrupting heteronormativity in schools and making inclusive spaces for LGBTQ+ students harken back to the notion of literacy as power and the close link between literacy and identity. Advocates in higher education and teachers doing work in the field often refer to work to disrupt heteronormative schooling environments as *queering the curriculum.*

While the term *queer* has a history as a pejorative term and still has mixed associations for members both in and outside the LGBTQ+ community, the term *queer* has "been actively under reconstruction and has been infused with new meanings and applications" (Meyer, 2007, p. 15). At the most basic, *to queer* is *to make strange.* To make strange is to disrupt and question norms, to liberate and make visible silenced identities, and to reimagine socially engrained binaries and organizing structures. As Meyer (2007) explains, queer theory:

> questions taken-for-granted assumptions about relationships, identity, gender, and sexual orientation. It seeks to explode rigid normalizing categories into possibilities that exist beyond the binaries of man/woman, masculine/feminine, student/teacher, and gay/straight. Queer theory offers educators a lens through which educators can transform their praxis so as to explore and celebrate the tensions and new understandings created by teaching new ways of seeing the world. (p. 15)

Queer is also taken on by some individuals as an identity, thus the recent inclusion in the LGBT*Q*+ acronym. This acronym has evolved from LGB to the trans-inclusive LGBT to the queer-and-beyond inclusive LGBTQ+. There are iterations that stretch to LGBTQIAPK (Lesbian, Gay, Bisexual, Transgender, Queer, Intersexual, Asexual, Pansexual and Polygamous, and Kinkiness). However, because LGBTQ+ is widely considered inclusive (+), and for sake of brevity, I will use LGBTQ+.

Meyer's explanation of queer theory and its role in education situates education as a space for upturning taken-for-granted assumptions and for clearing spaces for reimagining who we are and what schools do. Teachers who use queer theory as a means to understand how to make changes to create LGBTQ+ inclusive classrooms need to interrogate the ways that current existing curriculum, pedagogy, and texts support and reproduce heterosexual stories and silence others. Meyers (2007) suggests that teachers can use queer theory to question how their teaching practices might reinforce gendered practices, how their teaching practices may support heteronormativity, and how they present culturally specific information in their classrooms (p. 28). Queer theory and queer readings or considerations of books can help teachers "look at the work the [book] does to limit, shape, make possible, one kind of world or another" (Davies, 2003, p. xx) and then promote discussions that explode limiting, silencing worlds. Engaging in reading books and talking about books in these ways can help students see how society – and therefore ourselves – construct rigid meanings and identities surrounding gender and sexuality and "thus begin to imagine alternative ways of thinking and living" (Sullivan, 2003, p. 51).

Intersectionality

Intersectionality has emerged from critiques and rejections of approaches to diversity that limit and simplify, which have been described through the terms *unitary approach* and *multiple approach* (Blackburn & Smith, 2010; Hancock, 2007; Kumashiro, 2001). A unitary approach to addressing diversity focuses on a single type of difference and situates those who fit into that type of diversity as a monolithic group (Blackburn & Smith, 2010). For example, a unitary approach might be focusing solely on racial diversity when discussing a topic or analyzing a text. A multiple approach to addressing diversity examines multiple types of diversity but situates types of diversity as parallel and thus does not allow for types of diversity that exist across categories (Blackburn & Smith, 2010). For example, a multiple approach might discuss an issue or text with a focus on race and sexuality but not address how these types of diversity are situated in our social and political climate or about the intersecting and diverging experiences of LGBTQ+ persons of color. Both unitary and multiple approaches "provoke[s] competition among groups of focus" (Blackburn & Smith, 2010, p. 630). In contrast, *intersectionality* aims to explore multiple categories of difference, examine the relationship within and among them, and think about how both individual and social institutions shape notions of diversity and personal identity (see Hancock, 2007, for a more in-depth discussion). Just as absence of discussions of LGBTQ+ individuals and experiences results in a "single story," a discussion or notion of the LGBTQ+ individual or experience as monolithic silences the ways that the LGBTQ+ experience intersects with categories such as race, ethnicity, socioeconomic status, language, nationality, (dis)ability, cognitive ability, and religion, and results in what Purdie-Vaughns and Eibach (2008) call *intersectional invisibility*. For example, the LGBTQ+ story most prominent in our society is that of the American, WASP, gay, white, adult male. Less often do we explore the story of the Iranian, Muslim, lesbian, teen (like Sahar in *If You Could Be Mine*). Intersectionality as a lens for discussing diversity and choosing and using texts to address issues of diversity allows for us to look at all situations, texts, and even discussions of diversity and ask *who is being left out?* and ***why** are they being left out?*

EXPLORING LGBTQ+ INCLUSIVE LITERACY PRACTICES

If we understand the foundations and goals for developing LGBTQ+ inclusive literacy practices, the next step is guiding teachers in developing and engaging in these practices. Jill Hermann-Wilmarth and Caitlin Ryan have contributed much to the field of literacy in their application of queer theory to literary and literacy practices that create LGBTQ+ inclusive classrooms. The example literacy practices in this section are framed by Hermann-Wilmarth and Ryan's (2015) three broad approaches to creating LGBTQ+ inclusive classrooms through text choices and pedagogies: (1) including/contextualizing LGBT texts; (2) reading "straight" books through a queer lens; and (3) queering LGBT-inclusive texts.

Including/Contextualizing LGBTQ+ Texts

Maybe just one of the clearest ways to include and contextualize LGBTQ+ texts is to integrate them into existing curriculum, requiring discussion, and contextualizing them by pairing them with other texts and content through creating "Linked Text Sets" (Elish-Piper, Wold, & Schwingendorf, 2014). Dodge and Crutcher (2015) developed linked text sets (LTS) pairing both fiction and nonfiction books including or centered on LGBTQ+ experiences and identities with books suggested in the Common Core State Standards Appendix B for classroom instruction (National Governors Association Center for Best Practices & Council of Chief State School Officers, 2010). My colleague and I offered two units – one for ELA and one for History/Social Studies – framed through LTS along with discussion questions, and assignments. We also showed how an LGBTQ+ LTS approach can be aligned with the kinds of close reading and higher-level thinking that the CCSS urge teachers to address. In the ELA example, our LTS included the classic tale of love and adversity that is a staple in ELA classrooms – Shakespeare's *Romeo and Juliet*. We also chose other texts from the CCSS Appendix B that could be read through a lens of love and adversity: "A Poem of Changgan" by Li Po and *A Doll's House* by Henrik Isben. We chose the award-winning text *If You Could Be Mine* by Sarah Farizan about two young women in love in the country of Iran where their love is unsafe. Table 1 below shows potential for discussion between *two* books from this LTS.

In our other example, we developed a LTS for a unit on World War II. Additions to commonly taught texts like *Anne Frank: The Diary of a Young Girl* and Elie Wiesel's *The Book Thief* were Ken Setterington's *Branded by the Pink Triangle* and Lutz Van Dijk's *Damned Strong Love: The True Story of Willi G. and Stefan K.* The nonfiction *Branded by the Pink Triangle* introduces the rarely taught history of gay and lesbian persons persecuted by the Nazis. *Damned Strong Love* tells the true story of Willi and Stefan, two gay soldiers on opposing sides who fought to save their love. This unit aims to show the shared and unique experiences of persecution, horror, and love in a time of despair during one of the most important events in our history. Our two examples show concrete ways to integrate LGBTQ+ texts in meaningful ways in middle and high school classrooms.

Table 1. Sample Graphic Organizer to Think about Themes across Forms of Love (Components Drawn from Dodge & Crutcher, 2015, p. 99).

Text	Context	Characters and Experiences	Themes	Discussion Questions
Romeo and Juliet	Verona, Italy (c. 1600); arranged marriages	There is a blood feud between the Capulets and Montegues. Lady Capulet wants Juliet to marry Paris.	Young love can be tragic.	How does the historical and geographic context of these two stories relate to the forbidden nature of the characters' love?
If You Could Be Mine	Tehran, Iran (contemporary); arranged marriages	Sahar is in love with Nasir, but because they are both female, their love is illegal and punishable by death.	Young love can be tragic. Our interests and love must sometimes be suppressed for the better.	What factors influenced the characters' decisions? What factors influence love and relationships today?

Reading "Straight" Books through a Queer Lens

While adding books with LGBTQ+ characters to the classroom library and/ or integrating them into instruction is a positive, progressive step for teachers, some states and schools have prohibited the inclusion of such books or even the use of the word *gay* in schools (Ryan & Hermann-Wilmarth, 2013). Reading "straight" books through a queer lens is one way that teachers can still address the silences surrounding LGBTQ+ issues without using books with LGBTQ+ characters. Even when LGBTQ+ books are used in the classroom, reading straight books through a queer lens is still an important way to disrupt taken for granted norms and associations surrounding binaries of sexuality and gender.

Reading straight books through a queer lens can be done with texts already present in elementary classrooms. An excellent example is seen in Ryan and Hermann-Wilmarth's (2013) queer analysis of Kate DiCamillo's (2003) *The Tale of Despereaux: Being the Story of a Mouse, a Princess, Some Soup, and a Spool of Thread,* which is the tale of a mouse who is born different from other mice, much to the dismay of his family and mouse community. Despite stigma and persecution, Despereaux will not change who he is despite the hardships it brings. While the text is at the grades 2–5 level, it can be used for all grade levels. Table 2 captures key elements in Ryan and Hermann-Wilmarth's queer reading of the award-winning children's book *The Tale of Despereaux*, in which they use the concept of "deviant" to show how aspects of Despereaux are considered strange and negative by those around him. In their queer reading of *Despereaux*, Ryan and Hermann-Wilmarth point to several aspects of Despereaux that are considered deviant: his body, his activities, and his love. In Table 2, I summarize Ryan and Hermann-Wilmarth's descriptions of Despereaux's deviant aspects and how they result in a queer read of Despereaux.

There are multiple overarching takeaways from a queer read of *The Tale of Despereaux*. As Ryan and Hermann-Wilmarth (2013) explain, "Despereaux gives a queer voice to the feelings, meanings, and desire behind his choices" and "Despereaux calls into question traditional and taken-for-granted notions of love, bodies, and desire" (p. 162).

The Tale of Despereaux could easily be integrated into Dodge and Crutcher's (2015) LTS that centers on the theme of love and adversity; the questions posed in relation to *Romeo and Juliet* and *If You Could Be Mine* apply for *The Tale of Despereaux*. Further questions might be: *Do our bodies dictate whom we love? What differences are accepted by families and communities and which are not? Why are some differences considered okay and others not?*

Table 2. Components of Ryan and Hermann-Wilmarth's Queer Reading of *Despereaux* (see pp. 159–162).

Aspect of Despereaux	Description of Despereaux's aspects	Queer read of Despereaux's aspects
Despereaux's "deviant" body (see p. 160)	Despereaux is born not looking like other mice. Upon birth, he has a small body, huge ears, eyes open wide (when they should be closed at birth). His family and community see Despereaux's physical differences as problems and talk disparagingly about him. As he grows up, Despereaux continues to be different. His body doesn't grow, he doesn't like the things mice are supposed to like.	Despereaux is unlike the other mice –he is queer or strange. Desperaux is aware of his queer status and embraces his differences.
Despereaux's "deviant" activities (see pp. 160–161)	Desperaux's interests are different than other mice. He is interested in the arts. His family says, "There's something wrong with him." In the middle of scurrying, he stops to look at the colors in a stained-glass window. Instead of following instructions for nibbling on paper, he wants to read the words.	Despereaux's interests bring him solace in a mouse community that marginalizes him, but these interests serve to further ostracize him.
Despereaux's "deviant" love (see pp. 161–162)	Desperaux's interests differ so much from his fellow mice that he spends time with humans who also share his love for the arts. Then his transgression is worst of all – falling in love with a human princess. Despereaux's is a forbidden love. This is made concrete when Despereaux is separated from his community for the forbidden act of touching – the princess touches the top of his head. Desperaux is put on trial for letting a human touch him which is breaking the rules of being a mouse. His own father ultimately banishes him to a dungeon.	Despereaux stands up for what he did – experiencing pleasure and love when behaving in a way not accepted by his mouse community. His love costs him his family and his freedom.

The Tale of Despereaux could also be paired with texts to talk about characters who don't fit into their families for other reasons such as adopted children (Ryan & Hermann-Wilmarth, 2013, p. 162).

Queering LGBTQ+ Inclusive Texts

Another approach is doing a queer reading of an LGBTQ+ inclusive text. The example I share here is a queer reading of Christine Baldacchino's (2014) *Morris Micklewhite and the Tangerine Dress*, a book for Pre-K-2.

Morris Micklewhite is a young boy who likes dress-up time at school because he gets to try on dresses and shoes. His favorite dress is a long flowing tangerine dress and a pair of shoes with heels that click when he walks. The other kids in his class make fun of Morris. He stays home from school, citing a stomachache, stays in bed, and doesn't want to go back to school. His mom encourages him to be himself and he returns confident in his tangerine dress, where the other kids newly like him and play in his spaceship. In Table 3, I follow the format of Table 2 for *The Tale of Despereaux* and target particular "queer" aspects of Morris, descriptions of these queer aspects, and how they result in a queer reading of *Morris Micklewhite and the Tangerine Dress*.

Table 3. A Queer Reading of Christine Baldacchino's (2014) *Morris Micklewhite and the Tangerine Dress.*

Queer Aspect of Morris	Description of Morris' Queer Aspects	Queer Read of Morris' Queer Aspects
Morris' activities	Morris likes dress-up time in school. He likes wearing a tangerine dress. He likes the color and the sounds it makes, "swish swish." Morris likes dress-up time in school. He likes trying on all the shoes, especially ones that go "click-clack."	LGBTQ+ experiences do not necessarily include gender nonconforming clothing. Kids who dress up aren't LGBTQ+.
Morris' body – nails	Morris likes his mom to paint his nails. The girls chase him and make fun of his nails.	LGBTQ+ experiences are not defined by physical adornment
Morris' deviant, dangerous body	The boys in his class tell Morris that because he looks and dresses like a girl that he will turn them into girls. They don't want Morris to sit with them or play in their spaceship.	The LGBTQ+ body is not magical and LGBTQ+ bodies are not any more contagious than non-LGBTQ+ bodies Gender nonconforming behaviors are as contagious as anything else in a peer group
Morris' social self	Morris's stays home from school, sad because of the things the boys and girls say. Morris' mother supports him and encourages him to be himself. She prompts him to feel good, and he eventually does. Morris goes back to school self-confident and his classmates accept him.	Discrimination and bullying of gender nonconforming and LGBTQ+ persons isn't remedied by self-confidence or defiance. Parents play an incredibly important role in the emotional health of all kids, including LGBTQ+ kids.

A queer reading of queer texts differs only in how the critical questioning of LGBTQ+ representation is applied. Both approaches to queer reading prompt consideration of complexity and intersectionality in human existence. That said, all three of these approaches can be taken on in a variety of formats and represent important ways to develop LGBTQ+ inclusive classrooms.

Preparing Future Literacy Teachers to Create LGBTQ+ Inclusive Classrooms

Conversations with Teachers

While standards advocating for LGBTQ+ students are a starting point, they do not guarantee that future teachers are being equipped to meet the needs of their LGBTQ+ students. Indeed, Smolkin and Young (2011) note that "despite NCATE standards that include sexual orientation in types of discrimination teachers must understand, nearly half of America's teachers may not receive any information on sexual orientation and/or LGBT families during their preservice training. If they do so, such information is typically found in foundations classes" (p. 218).

Smolkin and Young (2011) also point to research that suggests that preservice teachers' attitudes may be changed through university coursework and opportunities to use children's literature to engage with LGBTQ+ pedagogies (p. 218). Therefore, perhaps the most important initial step for this work with future teachers is engaging conversations and exploring LGBTQ+ inclusive texts, teaching materials, and pedagogies. While these conversations can initially be intimidating or discomforting for teachers, they are crucial. There are multiple challenges associated with these beginning conversations but they are certainly not insurmountable.

While including LGBTQ+ texts is an important approach to creating LGBTQ+ inclusive literacy practices, there are caveats to be considered. Critiques are that

> focusing on the sexual identities of LGBTQ people, as so often LGBT-themed texts do, typically comes at the expense of attending to intersecting identities. Sexual identities cannot be effectively separated from the race, class, gender, and other identities embodied by people since no one is solely sexual. Sexuality cannot be understood well in isolation from other identity markers. (Blackburn & Smith, 2010, p. 633)

This concern is taken up by considering intersectionality. Indeed, Blackburn and Smith (2010) suggest that for teachers who do not find "LGBT inclusivity to be a viable option, we encourage them to consider taking on the concepts of heteronormativity and intersectionality as alternatives" (p. 633). Blackburn and Smith (2010) note that intersectional approaches can focus on who is being left out and why (Kumashiro, 2001).

Envisioning Classrooms

Every teacher wants to make a difference in the lives of students and wants their classroom to be a happy and welcoming space. In his work with future teachers, Hall (2006) starts with preservice teachers' visions of their classrooms and future teaching as an entry point into conversations about creating LGBTQ+ inclusive classrooms. Hall explains:

> [I] ask students to describe how they want their prospective classrooms to look and feel. Initially, they hesitate, but then their responses start to flow … clean, colorful, bright, safe, spacious, welcoming, intellectual, nurturing, respectful, sensitive, caring, humorous, understanding, encouraging, fun, and fair. Next, I present them with several real-life situations that they may encounter in the day-to-day classroom. We examine each scenario, brainstorming various strategies for handling them. (p. 149)

In what follows, Hall (2006) discusses how he helps his preservice teachers unpack their responses to the scenarios and whether their ideas and "recommendations are consistent with or contrary to their description of the ideal classroom" (p. 150). He notes that scenarios where students often disagree are in relation to a scenario of dealing with a gay teen being teased. Hall helps students work through what are most often contradictions between the actions they would take and their stated beliefs about themselves as educators.

Discomfort and Uncertainty

Such discussion provides openings for teachers to talk about discomfort they have talking about LGBTQ+ issues, of fear they have of talking about issues due to school, or family pushback. In my own work with preservice and inservice teachers, and in the literature, there are several common issues teachers grapple with.

First, teachers often are skeptical about the topic of sexuality in the classroom, especially in the younger grades. Because of heteronormativity in broader culture and in schools, it is important to understand that everything is sexed and gendered, from the arrangement of classrooms to the activity arrangements to the content. In *Queering Elementary Education*, Bickmore

(1999) argues that schools censor information about gender and sexual orientation, and that teachers and administrators were unprepared to address related questions when they came up. Cahill and Theilheimer (1999) discuss the heterosexism and reification of heterosexuality in early grades and Letts (1999) discusses how heteronormativity is replicated in elementary science courses.

A second common topic is fear of pushback from parents or administrators. For instance, Thein (2013) found resistance to teaching LGBTQ+ issues and literature in the following common responses by K-12 teachers: Appropriateness (*I would, but it's not my job*), Displaced Negative Stance (*I would, but others will protest*), Force of Facts (*I would but the fact is ...*), Reversal (*I would, but it will cause more harm than good*), Fairness (*I would but it's not fair to everyone*), and Ability/Preparedness (*I would, but I don't know how*). In some cases, teachers have legitimate fear of being fired for discussing LGBTQ+ issues or even saying the word "gay" (Larrabee & Moorehead, 2010; Ryan & Hermann-Wilmarth, 2003; see also Alabama, Arizona, Louisiana, Mississippi, Oklahoma, South Carolina, Texas, and Utah, http://www.glsen.org/learn/policy/issues/nopromohomo). Larrabee and Moorehead (2010) suggest teachers "seek out allies in... schools and districts to gain a better understanding of what changes could be implemented to create a more inclusive campus climate" (p. 48). The Southern Poverty Law Center's Teaching Tolerance's website offers a list of "Common Roadblocks" teachers encounter and offers commentary to help teachers dissect these issues (Teaching Tolerance, 2017a).

Resources for Instruction

For teachers who are taking on the task of creating LGBTQ+ inclusive classrooms, instructional support can do much to assuage uncertainty. Two core instructional starting points for addressing LGBTQ+ issues and making classrooms inclusive for LGBTQ+ students through text choices are (1) choosing literature and (2) developing teaching strategies, lesson plans, and approaches to discussion.

Choosing Texts

Award-winning LGBTQ+ book lists are a great starting point. Multiple award-winning book lists are easily accessible online that include books for K-12 students. Notable LGBTQ+ award-winning book lists include the

Rainbow Book List, the Stonewall Book Awards from the American Library Association's Gay, Lesbian, Bisexual, and Transgender Round Table (2017), and the Lambda Literary Awards. The Rainbow Book List is an especially helpful tool for teachers. The Rainbow Book List (http://glbtrt.ala.org/rainbowbooks/rainbow-books-lists) offers a bibliography of books with LGBTQ+ content for readers' birth through age 18. Books are by multiple publishers, appear on other awards lists, and are evaluated by committee members. Notably, the organization aims to "aid as a collection development or reader's advisory tool for librarians serving children and young adults" (Rainbow Book List, 2017). Other notable resources are the Stonewall Book Awards (http://www.ala.org/glbtrt/award/stonewall/honored) and the Lambda Literary Awards Book List (http://www.lambdaliterary.org/29th-annual-lambda-literary-award-finalists-61452-2/). By consulting these lists, teachers can learn about the topics and contents of the books and suggested grade levels.

Curricular and Instructional Resources

Beyond locating book titles, teachers may want further support for using literacy to advocate for LGBTQ+ students. The Southern Poverty Law Center's Teaching Tolerance website is an incredible repository of information and instructional resources for teachers who want to be advocates for social justice and diversity. Teachers who familiarize themselves with the site can find resources for professional development modules and webinars, tools for choosing books, ready-made lesson plans, and more.

Teaching Tolerance has also developed its own Social Justice Standards supported by an Anti-bias Framework (Teaching Tolerance, 2017b). They explain:

> The Teaching Tolerance Anti-Bias Framework is a set of 20 anchor standards and 80 grade-level outcomes organized into four domains – Identity, Diversity, Justice and Action – that reflect the desired impact of successful anti-bias and multicultural education on student personal and social development. The standards provide a common language and organizational structure: Teachers can use them to guide curriculum development, and administrators can use them to make schools more just, equitable and safe. (Teaching Tolerance, 2017c, para. 1) *The full Anti-bias Framework requires free registration with the site.*

Teaching Tolerance also offers "Perspectives for a Diverse America," which is a "literacy-based curriculum that marries anti-bias social content with the rigor of the Common Core State Standards" (Teaching Tolerance, 2017d).

This provides teachers with essential questions, text choices, and activities to guide discussion. These are all connected to the Anti-Bias Framework.

A strength of the Teaching Tolerance website is that it addresses *all* forms of diversity and acknowledges and harnesses the intersectionality across forms of diversity. An example of a lesson for grades 9–12 that exemplifies intersectionality across race and sexual orientation is "Bayard Rustin: The Fight for Civil and Gay Rights" (Teaching Tolerance, 2017e). The goals of the lesson explicitly include developing awareness of "how individuals have the ability to simultaneously advocate for multiple causes, even if those causes conflict or overlap." Other goals include helping students "analyze the connection between civil rights and gay rights" and "understand the similarities and differences between racism and heterosexism." The lesson also breaks down key vocabulary, offers a graphic organizer, and links the lesson to the CCSS (Teaching Tolerance, 2017e).

CONCLUSION

As teachers, we have an enormous influence on the world that students encounter when they walk through the doors of their schools and classrooms every day. The cornerstone of teaching and learning is the texts that we choose and that our students read. Books can be a window looking into the lives of others or a mirror where we see affirmation of our own lives and identities. As students read and learn, they should encounter books that offer them both windows *and* mirrors. We all need to learn about others and also see our own lives and identities valued and represented in the world. As teachers, we can make choices and develop instruction that provides all our students windows *and* mirrors. And through choosing texts that represent LGBTQ+ students' lives and identities, we can create inclusive classrooms that disrupt the single story of heteronormativity. Disrupting the single story is not limited to addressing LGBTQ+ diversity. Diversity is intersectional and individuals have overlapping and unique stories. As teachers, we can take steps to make diversity, advocacy, and social justice cornerstones of our literacy curriculum.

REFERENCES

Adichie, C. N. (2009). The danger of a single story [Video]. *TEDGlobal*. Retrieved from www.ted.com/talks/ chimamanda_adichie_the_danger_of_a_single_story

Au, W., Bigelow, B., Christensen, L., Gym, H., Levine, D., Karp, S., ... Watson, D. (2014). Editorial: Queering schools. *Rethinking Schools*, *28*(3), 5–7.

Bochenek, M. A., & Brown, A. W. (2001). Hatred in the hallways: Violence against lesbian, gay, bisexual and transgender students. Human Rights Watch. Retrieved from www.hrw.org/reports/2001/uslgbt.

Bickmore, K. (1999). 'Why discuss sexuality in elementary school?' In W. J. Letts and J. T. Sears (Eds.), *Queering elementary education: Advancing the dialogue about sexualities and schooling* (pp. 15–26). Lanham, MD: Rowman & Littlefield.

Bishop, R. S. (1990a). Mirrors, windows, and sliding glass doors. *Perspectives*, *6*(3), ix–xi.

Bishop, R. S. (1990b). Walk tall in the world: African American literature for today's children. *The Journal of Negro Education*, *59*(4), 556–565.

Blackburn, M. V., & Smith, J. M. (2010). Moving beyond the inclusion of LGBT-themed literature in English language arts classrooms: Interrogating heteronormativity and exploring intersectionality. *Journal of Adolescent & Adult Literacy*, *53*(8), 625–634.

Cahill, B. J., & Theilheimer, R. (1999). "Stonewall in the Housekeeping Area: Gay and Lesbian Issues in the Early Childhood Classroom." In W. J. Letts and J. T. Sears (Eds.), *Queering elementary education: Advancing the dialogue about sexualities and schooling* (pp. 39–48). Lanham, MD: Rowman & Littlefield.

Cameron, D., & Kulick, D. (2006). General introduction. In D. Cameron & D. Kulick (Eds.), *The language and sexuality reader* (pp. 1–12). New York, NY: Routledge.

Clark, C. T., & Blackburn, M. V. (2009). Reading LGBT-themed literature with young people: What's possible? *English Journal*, *98*(4), 25–32.

Dodge, A. M., & Crutcher, P. A. (2015). Inclusive classrooms for LGBTQ students: Using Linked Text Sets to challenge the hegemonic "single story." *Journal of Adolescent & Adult Literacy*, *59*(1), 95–105.

Elish-Piper, L., Wold, L. S., & Schwingendorf, K. (2014). Scaffolding high school students' reading of complex texts using linked text sets. *Journal of Adolescent & Adult Literacy*, *57*(7), 565–574.

Freire, P. (1970). *Pedagogy of the oppressed*. New York, NY: Herder & Herder.

Gay, Lesbian, Bisexual, and Transgender Round Table (2017). *Stonewall Book Awards*. Retrieved from http://www.ala.org/glbtrt/award/stonewall/honored.

Gay, Lesbian, Straight Education Network (GLSEN) (2017). *GLSEN's national school climate survey: Lesbian, gay, bisexual and transgender students and their experiences in school*. Retrieved from http://glsen.org/research or http://glsen.org/learn/research/nscs-archive

Giroux, H. (2001). *Theory and resistance in education*. Westport, CT: Bergin & Garvey.

Hall, H. R. (2006). Teach to reach: Addressing lesbian, gay, bisexual, and transgender youth issues in the classroom. *The New Educator*, *2*(2), 149–157.

Hancock, A. (2007). When multiplication doesn't equal quick addition: Examining intersectionality as a research paradigm. *Perspectives on Politics*, *5*(1), 63–79.

Hermann-Wilmarth, J. M., & Ryan, C. L. (2013). Interrupting the single story: LGBT issues in the language arts classroom. *Language Arts*, *90*(3), 226–231.

Hermann-Wilmarth, J. M. & Ryan, C. L. (2015).Doing what you can: Considering ways to address LGBT topics in language arts curricula. *Language Arts*, *92*(6), 436–443.

Kissen, R. M. (2002). *Getting ready for Benjamin: Preparing teachers for sexual diversity in the classroom*. Lanham, MD: Rowman & Littlefield.

Kumashiro, K. K. (2001). Queer students of color and antiracist, antiheterosexist education: Paradoxes of identity and activism. In K. K. Kumashiro (Ed.), *Troubling intersections of race and sexuality* (pp. 1–26). New York, NY: Rowman & Littlefield.

Ladson-Billings, G. (1995). Toward a theory of culturally relevant pedagogy. *American Educational Research Journal, 32*(3), 465–491.

Larrabee, T. G., & Morehead, P. (2010). Broadening views of social justice and teacher leadership: Addressing LGB issues in teacher education. *Issues in Teacher Education, 19*(2), 37–52.

Letts, W. J. (1999). How to make "boys" and "girls" in the classroom: The heteronormative nature of elementary-school science. In W. J. Letts and J. T. Sears (Eds.), *Queering elementary education: Advancing the dialogue about sexualities and schooling* (pp. 97–110). Lanham, MD: Rowman & Littlefield.

Levine-Rasky, C. (2000). Framing whiteness: Working through the tensions in introducing whiteness to educators. *Race Ethnicity and Education, 3*(3), 271–292.

MAP. (2011). Talking about suicide & LGBT populations. Retrieved from http://www.lgbtmap.org/effective-messaging/talking-about-suicide-and-lgbt-populations.

Meyer, E. J. (2007). "But I'm not gay": What straight teachers need to know about queer theory. In N. M. Rodriguez & W. F. Pinar (Eds.), *Queering straight teachers: Discourse and identity in education* (pp. 15–32). New York, NY: Peter Lang Inc.

Moll, L. C., Amanti, C., Neff, D., & Gonzalez, N. (1992). Funds of knowledge for teaching: Using a qualitative approach to connect homes and classrooms. *Theory into Practice, 31*(2), 132–141.

National Council of Teachers of English. (2007). *Resolution on strengthening teacher knowledge of lesbian, gay, bisexual, and transgender (LGBT) issues [Position statement]*. Urbana, IL: Author. Retrieved from http://www.ncte.org/positions/statements/ teacherknowledgelgbt

National Governors Association Center for Best Practices & Council of Chief State School Officers. (2010). *Common Core State Standards for English language arts and literacy in history/social studies, science, and technical subjects: Appendix B: Text exemplars and sample performance tasks*. Washington, DC: Authors.

Nieto, S. (2000). Placing equity front and center some thoughts on transforming teacher education for a new century. *Journal of Teacher Education, 51*(3), 180–187.

Purdie-Vaughns, V., & Richard P. E. (2008). "Intersectional invisibility: The distinctive advantages and disadvantages of multiple subordinate-group identities." *Sex Roles, 59*(5–6), 377–391.

Schneider, M. E., & Owens, R. E. (2000). Concern for lesbian, gay, and bisexual kids: The benefits for all children. *Education and Urban Society, 32*(3), 349–367.

Smolkin, G. B., & Young, C. A. (2011). Missing mirrors, missing windows: Children's literature textbooks and LGBT topics. *Language Arts, 88*(3), 217–225.

Sullivan, N. (2003). *A critical introduction to queer theory*. New York, NY: New York University Press.

Rainbow Book List. (2017). Retrieved from http://www.glbtrt.ala.org/rainbowbooks/rainbow-books-lists

Ryan, C. L., & Hermann-Wilmarth, J. M. (2013). Already on the shelf: Queer readings of award-winning children's literature. *Journal of Literacy Research, 45*(2), 142–172.

Teaching Tolerance. (2017a). *Common roadblocks*. Southern Poverty Law Center. Retrieved from http://www.tolerance.org/supplement/common-roadblocks

Teaching Tolerance. (2017b). *Anti-bias framework*. Retrieved from http://perspectives.tolerance.org/node/419

Teaching Tolerance. (2017c). *Teaching tolerance's social justice standards*. Retrieved from http://www.tolerance.org/seminar/teaching-tolerance-s-social-justice-standards

Teaching Tolerance. (2017d). *Perspectives for a diverse America*. Retrieved from http://www.perspectives.tolerance.org/

Teaching Tolerance. (2017e). *Bayard Rustin: The fight for civil and gay rights*. Retrieved from
    http://www.tolerance.org/lesson/bayard-rustin-fight-civil-and-gay-rights
Thein, A. M. (2013). Language arts teachers' resistance to teaching LGBT literature and issues.
    Language Arts, 9(3), 169–180.
Tschida, C. M., Ryan, C. L., & Ticknor, A. S. (2014). Building on windows and mirrors:
    Encouraging the disruption of "single stories" through children's literature. *Journal of
    Children's Literature, 40*(1), 28–39.
Uken, C. (2013). *LBGT youth at increased risk for suicide*. Retrieved from http://helenair.com/
    news/state-and-regional/lgbt-youth-at-increased-risk-for-suicide/article_e27bfa34-8482-
    11e2-aa5f-0019bb2963f4.html
Vavrus, M. (2009). Sexuality, schooling, and teacher identity formation: A critical pedagogy for
    teacher education. *Teaching and Teacher Education, 25*(3), 383–390.

LITERATURE CITED

Baldacchino, C. (2014). *Morris Micklewhite and the tangerine dress*. Toronto, Ontario, Canada:
    Groundwood Books.
DiCamillo, K. (2003). *The tale of Despereaux*. Cambridge, MA: Candlewick Press.
Farizan, S. (2013). *If you could be mine*. Chapel Hill, NC: Algonquin.
Frank, A. (1952). *Anne Frank: The diary of a young girl* (B. M. Mooyaart-Doubleday, Trans.).
    Garden City, NY: Doubleday.
Isben, H. (2008). *A doll's house*. Redford, VA: Wilder. (Original work published 1879).
Po, L. (1964). A poem of Changgan. In *The jade mountain: A Chinese anthology, being three
    hundred poems of the T'ang Dynasty, 618-906* (pp. 47–48; W. Bynner, Trans.). Garden City,
    NY: Anchor Books. (Original work published 1929).
Shakespeare, W. (2007). *Romeo & Juliet* (S. Weller, Ed.). New York, NY: Dover. (Original work
    published 1599).
Setterington, K. (2013). *Branded by the pink triangle*. Toronto, ON: Candada: Second Story.
Van Dijk, L. (1995). *Damned strong love: The true story of Willi G. and Stefan K.* (E. D. Crawford,
    Trans.). New York, NY: Henry Holt.

ACCENTUATING SOCIAL AND CULTURAL CONNECTIONS TO REVITALIZE LITERACY ACHIEVEMENT

Wally Thompson and Debra Coffey

ABSTRACT

This project was designed to study situated literacies, using New Literacy Studies *(NLS) in a community school and included five distinct, progressive phases. This chapter reports on the* Preparatory Phase. *We led in-service sessions to share insights for student-centered instruction from a constructivist perspective with faculty members whose experience with literacy instruction had primarily been reflective of the skills-based paradigm. The focus of the first phase was to prepare the teachers to employ literature circles to revitalize literacy instruction and achievement. During this first year of this longitudinal study, teachers began gradually introducing constructivist methodologies into their literacy instruction and discussing them with us in the in-service sessions. All aspects of this project emphasized synergistic collaboration, featuring community building and collaborative sessions with teachers. Literature circles with high-interest*

Addressing Diversity in Literacy Instruction
Literacy Research, Practice and Evaluation, Volume 8, 155–170
Copyright © 2018 by Emerald Publishing Limited
All rights of reproduction in any form reserved
ISSN: 2048-0458/doi:10.1108/S2048-045820170000008008

literature by indigenous authors enhanced the learning activities and mini-lessons prepared teachers and their students for this exploration. In-service sessions laid the foundation for the project, and these sessions provided opportunities for ongoing collaboration. As we invited teachers and administrators to participate in constructivist pedagogical approaches featuring literature circles, we emphasized collaborative discussions to determine the most beneficial books, materials, and pedagogical strategies for students. Teachers and students experienced the power of synergistic collaboration as they explored engaging literature and shared their schema in meaningful discourse. This experience revitalized literacy achievement as students became more engaged in learning, and teachers noted the impact of their enthusiasm for learning. Students and teachers have experienced the power of synergistic collaboration while reading and writing during literature circles. Connecting culture and literacy with the power of synergistic collaboration invariably increased the learners' engagement with and enjoyment of reading, writing, speaking and listening. This research-based design can serve as a template for incorporating cultural heritage into literacy education for all who educate indigenous students.

Keywords: Culture; native language; literacy; meaningful discourse; literature circles

Native Americans have enjoyed oral traditions over the centuries. When parents told stories around the dinner table, their children learned about significant aspects of their culture. Our project connected modern Native Americans with these oral traditions by focusing on all aspects of literacy during literature circles rather than limiting educational experiences to reading and writing. Discussions in literature circles provided students with opportunities to connect with each other and the texts they read. Insights into literature increased as students discussed what they read and listened to each other during group sessions rather than just reading and writing for typical assignments. This gave the books personal and cultural significance as they shared what they learned.

Experiences of this nature helped students to gain insights that bridged the old and new perspectives. As students developed proficiency with all aspects of language, they were more equipped to transcend age-old stereotypes and launch into creative endeavors. This proficiency equipped them for successful achievement in and beyond their communities. It also gave them opportunities to learn in culturally relevant ways that made the educational experience personally satisfying.

PURPOSE OF THE STUDY

As researchers in the field of literacy acquisition, it is important for us to learn how children in various situations acquire literacy skills. *Situated literacy,* also known as *New Literacy Studies*, posits that the learners' environment and cultural connections to the literacy activity are important elements of communication because of the social nature of literacy (Street, 2003).

Phase 1
- Preparatory Mini-lessons in Teacher In-service Sessions
- Introduction to Literature Circles in Teacher In-service Sessions
- Exploration of Roles and Questions for Discussion
- Open-ended Discussions, Focusing on Literacy Strategies

Phase 2
- Literature Circles with Books by Indigenous Authors
- Mini-lessons Featuring the Six Traits of Writing
- Penpal Letters Highlighting Insights from Reading
- Discussions Emphasizing Cultural Heritage

Phase 3
- Literature Circles with Books by Indigenous Authors
- Penpal Letters Featuring Insights from Reading
- Original Stories about Navajo Culture
- Writing Workshop Sessions and Peer Tutoring

Phase 4
- Literature Circles with Expository Texts and Poetry
- Original Stories about Navajo Culture
- Writing Workshop Sessions and Peer Tutoring
- School and Community Author Celebration

Phase 5
- Literature Circles with Expository Texts and Poetry
- Penpal Letters Highlighting Insights from Reading
- Readers Theater with Poetry Featuring Science and Culture
- School and Community Cultural Heritage Celebration

All phases feature community building and collaborative in-service sessions with teachers. Mini-lessons prepare students for the literature circles and enhance the learning activities.

To study this concept, we used *New Literacy Studies* (NLS) in a Navajo school to revitalize literacy instruction and achievement.

As discussions with the school principal initiated this project, he revealed that typical language instruction in the school followed a "skills-based approach." We proposed a two-month project, and he suggested extending it to three years to give the teachers and students opportunities to experience the more constructivist approach. This suggestion led to in-service sessions to share insights for student-centered instruction from a constructivist perspective with faculty members in the school, emphasizing ways to employ literature circles to facilitate proficiency with literacy.

REVIEW OF THE LITERATURE

This project synergized constructivism, situated literacy, and the precepts of Invitational Education to promote enthusiasm for reading and revitalize literacy achievement in a Navajo community school.

Situated Literacy

Street (2003) emphasized the ways connections among language, social, and cultural realities contribute to the power of literature circles to increase the comprehension of children from ethnic minorities. He stated that "[w]hat has come to be known as 'New Literacy Studies' (NLS)... represents a new tradition in considering the nature of literacy, focusing not so much on acquisition of skills,... but rather on what it means to think of literacy as a social practice" (p. 77).

Although Street spoke of situated literacy as something new, it can be considered a reification of Vygotsky's sociocultural constructivism as it relates to literacy. Vygotsky (1978) explained that through the process of internalization, we are all products of hundreds, if not thousands of years of social and cultural traditions. Using the illustration of the first grasping, then pointing baby (p. 56), he explicated the concept that we learn everything twice; "*[a]n interpersonal process is transformed into an intrapersonal one.* Every function in the child's cultural development appears twice" [italics original] (p. 57). To understand this, it can be helpful to view it from a *schema formation* perspective. As the child experiences something externally, it is internalized, and in the process, becomes a part of that which is the composite of the child's total life experiences, which will then be involved in interpreting and understanding all future experiences, his or her schema.

To explain this, Gee (2001) stated that a language, any language, is not a single thing, but is tailored to every social and cultural setting. The way in which words are arranged in a sentence, the vocabulary, and the subtle differences of meaning vary from setting to setting, from group to group, and are reflective of the culturally constructed literacy-schema. Gee referred to unique languages as "social languages, specifically Discourses (with a capital D)" (p. 714).

Discourses can be seen as communities of shared schema. It may not be obvious, but there is a *Navajo English,* and this is the language we encourage for literature circle discussions. Gee (2005) explained Discourses as "ways with words, deeds, and interactions, thoughts and feelings, objects and tools, times, and places that allow us to enact and recognize different socially situated identities" (p. 35). Each person belongs to many Discourses, but by connecting to the situatedness of the literature circle project, the students have the opportunity to strengthen their connection to their *Navajo Discourse.* Simi and Matusitz (2015) posited "that attachment to Native American culture has made a positive difference in reversing academic struggles among Native Americans" (p. 91).

Collaborative Learning

We selected a collaborative learning process to activate and employ the dynamics of situated literacy. Roschelle and Teasley (1995) defined collaboration as "a coordinated, synchronous activity that is the result of a continued attempt to construct and maintain a shared conception of a problem" (p. 70). In other words, people work together to address a problem. Vygotsky (1978) advocated students learning together through sociocultural education with protégés. Leont'ev (1979) stated, "that humans' mental processes (their higher psychological functions) acquire a structure necessarily tied to the socio-historically formed means and methods transmitted to them by others in the process of cooperative labor and social interaction" (p. 55).

Simi and Matusitz (2015) stated that unlike their professors who process information linearly:

Native Americans use circular communication and prefer receiving graphic, perceptual and spatial material...they take signals from their surroundings; they need a visible foundation and member body. Such people also integrate their social network to the learning process and necessitate advising and support through group work. (p. 100)

Invitational Education

The perspectives promoted in situational literacy and collaborative learning align well with the fundamental beliefs of Invitational Theory and Practice, which affirm individuals as valuable, capable, and responsible. Optimism is emphasized in this approach while recognizing individual power along with the responsibility to empower others by creating intentionally inviting places, policies, programs, and processes (Purkey, 2006; Purkey & Novak, 2008; Schmidt, 2004, 2007).

THEORETICAL FOUNDATIONS

Reading is a dialogic activity; the author transmits and the reader receives. This is explained by Rosenblatt's (1978) Transactional Theory of Literacy. Certo, Moxley, Reffitt, and Miller (2010) extended this explanation by saying that "[t]he specific event of *reading a text*, situated in a particular time or environment, involves transactions drawing on past and present experiences as well as the interests of the reader" [italics original] (p. 244). Demény (2012) concurred that it is the transaction of the reader's experience with the text that generates meaning. Certo et al. (2010) then related this to *literature circles*. If transactions between the unique experiences of one reader, or the reader's schema, and the author are the genesis of constructed meaning, the wider and the more extensive the experiences involved in group transacting will produce broader, more diverse, and richer meaning. Therefore, literature circles offer the opportunity for a greater experience with the text as readers gain access to each other's schema through discussion.

DESIGN OF THE STUDY

This project emphasized synergistic collaboration. Instead of following the traditional approach of developing the elements of communication in isolation, they were developed in collaboration with each other, synergistically. P. David Pearson (2012) stated, "reading and writing are synergistic processes – what we learn in the one benefits the other" (p. 101), and therein is the power of synergistic collaboration. Combining the strengthening aspect of connecting culture to literacy with the power of synergistic collaboration invariably increases the learners' literacy skills, their literacy efficacy, and therefore, their engagement with and enjoyment of reading, writing, speaking, and listening. Roberts and Billings (2008) stated, "There is no question that reading, writing, speaking, and listening are interconnected skills that develop synergistically" (p. 2).

Community Building

All activities pursuant to achieving the objectives of (1) identifying the dynamics of situated literacy, (2) learning ways and means of implementing the principles of situated literacy to increase the student engagement in reading, and thereby (3) increasing both their comprehension and love of reading, were conducted at a Navajo school near the "Four Corners" area. Many steps have been taken to ensure the maximum level of involvement from both the professional community and the Navajo citizens of the local communities. In planning this project, meetings were first held with the principal and a teacher at the Navajo school. Later, the first principal's successor and the entire faculty of the Navajo school participated in every aspect of planning the research project. To further ensure the involvement and approval of the community, the project was presented to a meeting of the Community School Board.

This Navajo school is supported by three *Chapters*, structured communities that are part of the Navajo Nation's social and political organization. This project was presented during a Chapter meeting at each of these Chapters, and the details of this project were explained. Chapter approval of the project led to an opportunity to attend a meeting of the Northern Navajo Agency, one of six *Agencies* spread over three of the four states represented in the Four Corners area. The project was presented to the assembled leaders of the Northern Chapters of the Navajo Nation. Then a motion to Support the project was made, seconded, and a Resolution of Support was approved.

The final step was to attend the Navajo Nation Research Review Board meeting and present the project personally. The Review Board wanted to know how this research would benefit the Navajo people. This more student-centered approach to literacy instruction interlaces reading and writing with speaking and listening, and therefore, is more in touch with the Navajo's oral tradition than previous, more traditional methods.

Additionally, because these literature circles employed literature written by Navajo and other Indigenous American authors, they provided the opportunity to strengthen the children's connection to their heritage culture and enhance their self-esteem. Enriching the students' *Navajo pride* is a real benefit to the Navajo Nation. Research has shown that when students connect to the material being taught, and the manner in which it is taught, that is, situated literacy, reading comprehension increases (Nystrand, 2006), and this greatly improves the students' success in life's later enterprises. When this study is disseminated, it will serve as a template for incorporating cultural heritage into literacy education for all who educate both Navajo and other indigenous students.

Procedures for the Project

All aspects of the project featured community building and collaborative sessions with teachers. Mini-lessons were conducted to prepare teachers to share insights for exploration of literature with their students. Then teachers used literature circles with high-interest literature by indigenous authors to give students specific opportunities to explore their cultural heritage.

Literature Circles

Harvey Daniels (2002), one of the pioneers of book clubs for kids, described traditional literature circles as "a cooperative learning, student led-experience for students around a common text" (p. 100). Reading and writing are means of communicating, and as such they are activities between people; they are inherently social and will provide the format for administering literacy instruction in a dynamically situated and collaborated way. Literature circles can demonstrate the value of interaction, and discussions help teachers and students to value interaction (Heineke, 2014; Lenters, 2014; Lindfors, 1999; Townsend & Pace, 2005).

When we asked about the most beneficial approach for in-service sessions, the teachers requested a demonstration of literature circles. This project began with an in-service session emphasizing a Native American story and an initial mini-lesson featuring the format for literature circles. The teachers selected roles for the session and shared their insights in literature circles. We started with role sheets and shared insights for questioning strategies to gradually promote more open-ended, authentic discussions. A teacher later mentioned that the story we chose was one of her favorite stories. During this session, the teachers began choosing books by indigenous authors for literature circles in their own classrooms.

Mini-lessons consistently prepared students for the literature circles and enhanced learning activities throughout the project. In-service sessions provided opportunities for ongoing communication as we discussed experiences and the impact of literature circles in the classroom.

FINDINGS

As we invited teachers and administrators to participate in a constructivist pedagogical approach, featuring literature circles, we emphasized collaborative discussions to determine the most beneficial books, materials, and pedagogical strategies for students. Our approach aligned with the precepts of Invitational Education.

Invitational Education (IE) is designed to create a welcoming environment that prepares students to become effective members of society (Purkey & Novak, 2008). This overarching goal impacts the domains and the elements of IE. The domains of IE are (1) people, (2) places, (3) policies, (4) programs, and (5) processes. The elements of IE are (1) care, (2) trust, (3) respect, (4) optimism, and (5) intentionality. These domains and elements align with each other and the findings of this study. The findings of this study demonstrated the impact of that alignment.

Elements and Domains of IE

Conveying Care

As we began the Navajo project, one of our main goals was to convey the ways we care and seek to promote the success of the Navajo Nation. As we began in-service sessions, we conveyed our hopes for the project, our fascination with Navajo culture, and our deep desire to enhance literacy achievement through constructivistic pedagogy. Our authentic care and concern aligned with the emphasis on an inviting stance that encourages shared opportunities through IE (Purkey & Novak, 2008). Tomlinson (2015) discussed ways to demonstrate care by nurturing culture and conveying the importance of cultural heritage while caring *for* and *about* everyone in a program. When we were finalizing book orders for the Navajo project via email, a teacher said, "Thank you for caring for our students."

As we have conveyed the ways we care for and about teachers and students, we have given teachers opportunities to experience literature circles, and they have conveyed these insights and procedures for literature circles to their students. During our discussions, teachers have spontaneously expressed enthusiasm when they have noted the ways their students really care about the stories they are reading. As certain students take responsibility for exploring the significance of vocabulary words, they genuinely want to know what the words mean, and their interest in the books goes beyond the level of a typical assignment.

Building Trust
We were actively involved in community building as we visited Navajo Chapter Houses to present our project and shared literature circles during in-service sessions with teachers. As we have built a trusting relationship with the Navajo Chapters and the school, we have learned more about the community and their sacred mountains. Certain places have great significance to the Navajo, and students have explored the significance of certain places during literature circles.

During our in-service sessions, teachers have spontaneously shared experiences with literature circles and comments made by students. Spontaneous leadership has emerged during literature circles, and this has led to discussions of cultural heritage and family experiences. Our emphasis on building trust consistently aligned with the emphasis in IE on the importance of building trust in the places we teach or visit.

Showing Respect
We conveyed great respect during each aspect of the project as we established constructivist policies, which encouraged freedom of expression rather than a prescriptive approach. As we have nurtured a respectful atmosphere, teachers have shared their experiences. A teacher discussed significant interaction between students and parents in relation to discussions of books and said, "That never would have happened without literature circles."

Demonstrating Optimism
We promoted optimism as we used a positive stance with the programs we developed. A teacher became so enthusiastic about the literature circles in her classroom that she began preparing unsolicited video tapes using her iPad to capture what they were learning. She initially read stories to her class. Then they read independently. When she realized that some students were pretending to read, she slowed down the process to make sure they were really reading. She also used careful scaffolding to make sure students completed their book reports according to the rubric for an authentic learning experience.

Designing with Intentionality
We planned in-service sessions with intentionality, using a positive approach that encouraged success. As we have designed sessions with intentionality,

the teachers' enthusiasm has increased. We have seen the general engagement of the teachers increase from about 25% to about 75% as they have become more involved in the process. One teacher noted that students discovered that the word "wow" originated with the Powhatan Tribe in Virginia. Other teachers noted their students' attention to certain words. A teacher noted that one group of students discussed freedom in their literature circles. Then they asked an adult if we are really free in America. She said, "Yes, to an extent…" The students acknowledged her careful wording and discussed it. Our intentionality, which aligned with IE, has resulted in literature discussions that reflect purposeful and intentional exploration of vocabulary words and concepts.

The Six Elements for Diversity and the Impact of Our Project

Schmidt (2007) discussed applications for IE with diverse populations. He proposed six elements (Es) of diversity "by which researchers and practitioners can assess relationships and organizations in terms of accepting, embracing, and celebrating diversity." Schmidt listed these six Es as "enlistment, encouragement, equity, enjoyment, empowerment, and expectation" (p. 17).

Enlistment

Schmidt defined enlistment as "gaining the cooperation and support of people for moving an organization (or a relation-ship) toward common goals (2007, p. 18)." Enlistment involves a series of invitations to promote this cooperation and support in the community. Our period of enlistment was comprised of a series of meetings, beginning with the initial meeting with the school principal and a teacher in the Navajo school. This meeting laid the foundation for significant results, changed the direction of the project from a research emphasis to a more student-centered approach, and led to the opportunity to conduct in-service sessions with teachers.

Encouragement

Schmidt (2007) emphasized that the ways encouragement literally builds courage, self-esteem, and self-confidence. Throughout in-service sessions, we presented ideas for literature circles and effective pedagogy as we encouraged teachers to try these approaches in their own classrooms. Teachers were encouraged to adapt ideas to their own classrooms and use them in the ways which would be most beneficial for their classes. Our approach aligned with Schmidt's (2002) "Encouraging Stance," which incorporates "the qualities of optimism, respect, and trust into intentionally helpful relationships" (pp. 56–61).

Expectation

Schmidt noted, "When working with diverse populations, we will be successful to the degree that our expectations limit or expand the relationships we form" (p. 18). Throughout our in-service sessions, we maintained high expectations, and teachers made comments illustrating the ways they were personalizing this project. When we received approval from the Navajo National Internal Review Board, they stated, "Welcome to the family, and we have high expectations for this research."

Equity

Equity "refers to behaviors and treatment of people that create conditions of fairness, justice, and nondiscrimination (Schmidt, 2007, p. 17). A sense of equity in a community promotes "a deep and abiding relationship with participative democracy... an educative way of life in that it allows people to gain understanding and develop a more fulfilling character as a result of being meaningful constructors of a social order" (Novak, 2002, p. 152). As we have conducted in-service sessions, we have promoted equity throughout our discussions. This was a natural result of our respect for each teacher and our desire to contribute positively to the school and community.

Enjoyment

William Purkey (2006), one of the founders of IE, promoted enjoyment in his extensive writings and speeches. He encouraged us to "Give more attention to life's small pleasures and wonder" (pp. 99–100).

We promoted enjoyment of literature as we built deeper relationships during our sessions. When we asked the teachers what we could do that would be most beneficial during our in-service sessions, we were pleased when they requested a demonstration of literature circles. During in-service sessions, we saw teachers' enjoyment of literature increase as they participated in literature circles. This progression was most evident during a literature circle in which teachers began to tease each other while they shared ideas. This session provided insights into their thinking and deepened the bond of our learning community.

Empowerment

Schmidt (2007) stated, "The verb empower means to give people a sense of power and authority over the decisions they face. It includes notions of self-confidence and self-efficacy that connect with self (p. 19)." During our pivotal in-service session, a literature circle discussion empowered teachers to more fully see the benefits of literature circles for exploration of literature and the bonding potential of these discussions. This session demonstrated the ways literature circles take classroom experiences into the social realm of interaction beyond typical assignments.

PRACTICAL IMPLICATIONS

Throughout our project, we have noted the power of synergistic collaboration during literature circles. We initially selected a collaborative learning process to activate and employ the dynamics of situated literacy. As noted from the beginning of the project: if transactions between the unique experiences of one *reader*, or the reader's schema, and the *author* are the genesis of constructed meaning, *wider* and more extensive experiences involved in *group* transacting will produce broader, more diverse, and richer meaning. Through our experiences in this project, we have seen the ways that literature circles offer this opportunity for a greater experience with the text as readers discuss insights and gain access to each other's schema. Thus, literature circles, emphasizing situated literacy, have promoted a reification of Vygotsky's sociocultural constructivism as it relates to literacy.

We have seen the ways that connecting culture and literacy with the power of synergistic collaboration increases the learners' literacy skills, literacy efficacy, and therefore, their engagement *with* and *enjoyment of* reading, writing, speaking, and listening. These experiences have demonstrated the power of discussion as a means of providing access to schema, and we look forward to more extensive opportunities to explore Discourse, or communities of shared schema, in literature circles (Gee, 2005).

Now that the *Preparatory Phase* has been completed, we will have the opportunity, under the direction of the Navajo Nation Human Subjects Committee, to gather and analyze data to ascertain the extent to which this project is successful. Then we will collaborate with teachers to explore the ways students may strengthen their connection to their *Navajo Discourse* as they exchange ideas in literature circles using their *Navajo English* and connect to the situatedness of the literature circle project.

The Impact of Literature Circles

The impact of literature circles has demonstrated the importance of sustaining this constructivist approach and exploring additional ways of promoting constructivist methods in the Navajo school. As we have built a community of active learners who sincerely care about exploration of literature, we have often considered the importance of the initial principal's wise suggestion to continue this project over three years rather than two months. To actualize this plan, we have the enthusiastic support of the Navajo Nation, and we have planned specific phases to scaffold constructivist pedagogy in order to sustain the impact of literature circles for maximum student learning.

Future Plans

As we continue to collaborate with the teachers, *Phase 2* of our project will continue our emphasis on literature circles with books by indigenous authors. Mini-lessons will highlight the author's role and feature the Six Traits of Writing. We will also introduce penpal letters to give students opportunities to share their insights from reading with students in other classes. Discussions throughout this process will feature Navajo cultural heritage.

Phase 3 will highlight books by indigenous authors as students begin to think of themselves as authors and write their own original stories about Navajo culture. Writing workshops and peer tutoring will help students to fine-tune their writing as they use the Six Traits of Writing and explore the writing process with each other.

Phase 4 will feature ongoing collaboration in literature circles with expository texts and poetry by Brod Bagert. Students will read expository poetry emphasizing science concepts as well as poetry about Native Americans, which Brod Bagert has written especially for the students and teachers in the Navajo school. Students will continue to exchange penpal letters with insights from their reading, and they will finalize their original stories about Navajo culture. This will lead to a school and community author celebration.

Phase 5 will emphasize sustainability, and we will reflect on key ideas with teachers. During this phase, students will continue to read expository texts and poetry during literature circles. Then they will exchange penpal letters and share what they have learned during Readers Theater. We will analyze the penpal letters and the discourse of students in literature circles. As we meet with teachers, we will analyze the impact of the literature circle project and discuss ways the Navajo students can continue to strengthen their connection to their *Navajo Discourse.* We will collaborate with teachers to design an opportunity for students to celebrate what they have learned about their cultural heritage with the community.

As the findings of this research are disseminated, this research-based design has the potential to serve as a template for incorporating cultural heritage into literacy education and extending opportunities for all who educate Navajo and other indigenous students.

CONCLUSION

Evenings around ceremonial fires have traditionally been times of great celebration in Native American culture. We are collaborating with teachers in a Navajo school to make the reading process a celebration. As discussions in literature circles provide students with opportunities to connect with each other and the texts they read, we are hoping that these texts will continue to capture their imaginations as they share insights from literature. As students continue listen to each other, share ideas with penpals, and write their own stories about their culture rather than just reading and writing for typical assignments, we hope these projects will help them to think deeply about the insights they glean and become lifelong readers who prioritize reading.

REFERENCES

Certo, J., Moxley, K., Reffitt, K., & Miller, J. A. (2010). I learned how to talk about a book: Children's perceptions of literature circles across grade and ability levels. *Literacy Research and Instruction, 49*, 243–263.

Daniels, H. (2002). *Literature circles: Voice and choice in book clubs and reading groups.* Portland, ME: Stenhouse Publishers.

Demény, P. (2012). Developing written text production competence using the Reader-Response Method. *Acta Didactica Napocensia, 5*(3), 53–60.

Gee, J. P. (2001). Reading as situated language: A sociocognitive perspective. *Journal of Adolescent and Adult Literacy, 44*(8), 714–725.

Gee, J. P. (2005). *An introduction to discourse analysis: Theory and method* (2nd ed.). New York: Routledge.

Heineke, A. A. (2014). Dialoging about English Learners: Preparing teachers through culturally relevant literature circles. *Action in Teacher Education, 36*(2), 117–140. doi:10.1080/01626620.2014.898600

Lenters, K. (2014). Just doing our jobs: A case study of literacy-in-action in a fifth grade literature circle. *Language & Literacy: A Canadian Educational E-Journal, 16*(1), 53–70.

Leont'ev, A. N. (1979). The problem of activity. In J. V. Wertsch (Ed.), *The concept of activity in Soviet psychology* (pp. 37–71). Armonk, NY: M. E. Sharpe.

Lindfors, J. W. (1999). *Children's inquiry: Using language to make sense of the world.* New York: Teachers College Press.

Novak, J. M. (2002). *Inviting educational leadership: Fulfilling potential and applying an ethical perspective to the educational process.* London: Pearson.

Nystrand, M. (2006). Research on the role of classroom discourse as it affects reading comprehension. *Research in the Teaching of English, 40*(4), 392–412.

Pearson, P. D. (2012). Point of view: Life in the radical middle. In R. F. Flippo (Ed.), *Reading researchers in search of common ground: The expert study revisited* (2nd ed., pp. 99–106). New York: Routledge.

Purkey, W. W. (2006). *Teaching class clowns (and what they can teach us).* Thousand Oaks, CA: Corwin.

Purkey, W. W., & Novak, J. M. (2008). *Fundamentals of invitational education.* Kennesaw, GA: The International Alliance for Invitational Education.

Roberts, T., & Billings, L. (2008). Thinking is literacy, literacy thinking. *Educational Leadership, 65*(5), 32–36.

Roschelle, J., & Teasley, S. D. (1995). The construction of shared knowledge in collaborative problem solving. In C. E. O'Malley (Ed.), *Computer-supported collaborative learning* (pp. 69–197). Berlin: Springer-Verlag.

Rosenblatt, L. M. (1978). *The reader, the text, the poem: The transactional theory of the literary work.* Carbondale, IL: Southern Illinois University Press.

Schmidt, J. J. (2002). *Intentional helping: A philosophy for proficient caring relationships.* Upper Saddle River, NJ: Prentice Hall.

Schmidt, J. J. (2004). Diversity and invitational theory and practice. *Journal of Invitational Theory & Practice, 10*, 27–46.

Schmidt, J. J. (2007). Elements of diversity in Invitational practice and research. *Journal of Invitational Theory & Practice, 13*, 6–23.

Simi, D., & Matusitz, J. (2015). Native American students in U.S. higher education: A look from attachment theory. *Interchange, 47*, 91–108.

Street, B. (2003). What's "new" in new literacy studies? Critical approaches to literacy in theory and practice. *Current Issues in Comparative Education, 5*(2), 77–91.

Tomlinson, C. A. (2015). The caring teacher's manifesto. *Educational Leadership, 72*(6), 89–90.

Townsend, J. S. & Pace, B. G. (2005). The many faces of Gertrude: Opening and closing possibilities in classroom talk. *Journal of Adolescent & Adult Literacy, 48*, 594–605.

Vygotsky, L. S. (1978). *Mind in society: The development of higher psychological processes.* Cambridge, MA: Harvard University Press.

BUILDING ON EMERGENT BILINGUALS' FUNDS OF KNOWLEDGE USING DIGITAL TOOLS FOR LITERACY

Sally Brown

ABSTRACT

To explore the funds of knowledge that six emergent bilingual students build upon as they produce multimodal texts, how the practices surrounding these events are mediated, and the role of student agency within an ethnographic social semiotics framework. Ethnographic methods were used to document this yearlong study that included videotaping small group interactions, writing field notes, conducting interviews, and collecting multimodal work samples. The researcher served as a participant observer in a third-grade classroom where she met with students two days per week to interact with mulitmodal poetry. The findings reveal the media-rich popular culture and home digital practices students bring with them to school and the ways in which these resources were utilized for designing multimodal poetry. Several essential factors are discussed including funds of knowledge, role of play and creativity, nonlinear writing structures, and agentive

Addressing Diversity in Literacy Instruction
Literacy Research, Practice and Evaluation, Volume 8, 171–192
Copyright © 2018 by Emerald Publishing Limited
All rights of reproduction in any form reserved
ISSN: 2048-0458/doi:10.1108/S2048-045820170000008018

design decisions. Multimodal text making requires a revamping of class-room literacy instruction that embraces multiple modes especially noting the importance of images, central role of experiential learning, and space for student choice thus empowering them as learners.

Keywords: Multimodal writing; emergent bilinguals; early literacy; new literacies; diversity

Beast Boy, Rosalina, and Rosabelle (all emergent bilinguals) along with two English domi-nant peers are gathered together for a guided tour of a concrete poetry book called Splish Splash (Graham, 1994). Each of them is holding a copy of the paper-based book and exam-ining the poem "Oceans." I ask the students to tell me what they notice about the design of the poem and accompanying images. The conversation moves to the words "Now I'm all in" which are written in blue font and situated underneath some wavy lines. Rosabelle remarks, "I think it, it means that you go under the water. Because it is blue and last in the poem, plus that's what you do at the ocean," as she attempts to decode and comprehend this poem. Sunny responds, "The ocean is light blue. All the stuff kinda like the ocean is, like the beach. Yea, it's like Rosabelle is saying." As the researcher, I remain quiet. Sunny adds, "See the sun is going down. Like back of the water." Rosalina blurts, "PLOP!" as she reads the word. Beast Boy smiles and says, "It in all big letters, capital letters. And even an exclamation mark." After a few quiet moments of close observation, Beast Boy continues but this time with a cultural connection, "I went to the beach with my cousin. He and my dad went all over. There were some waves so big that it knock him down. We had good time at the beach and I remember it a lot and I like to go back some more." Bowser responds, "One time my cousin put me on his back and we went all the way down there to the water [at the beach] and there was a big wave and the big wave got me." Laughter fills the space and Rosabelle tells her account of a beach story, "I went to the beach too and I was under the water and there was a big big wave and they [family] was calling me and I didn't hear and I went all the way out in the ocean." (Brown, field notes, October 1, 2014)

This literacy event occurred at the beginning of a yearlong multimodal poetry investigation focused on emergent bilingual students' literacy experiences in an elementary classroom. The initial engagement began by reading a pleth-ora of concrete poetry, moved to digital interpretations of professionally authored poems, and finally involved students designing and composing their own moving poetry to be published on YouTube. It was a case where students were given opportunities to move beyond the "basics" and became agentive text designers through the use of cultural and digital resources (Dyson, 2013). The social practices and digital related processes were explored as students assumed roles that led to final semiotic productions of moving poetry (Kress, 2010). These experiences featured in this chapter move us closer toward understanding a contemporary way of being literate in the world (Husbye & Zanden, 2015).

In addition to the students in the above vignette, Wonder Woman, Rabby, and Jolisa (all names are student-chosen pseudonyms) comprise the six emergent bilinguals who take us on their journey with multimodal literacy. Many researchers express the need for more studies detailing the experiences of young learners with multimodal texts and in particular emergent bilinguals (Moses, 2015; Zapata & Van Horn, 2017). This project capitalizes on the learners' home and school experiences as resources. "As children transport representational resources between school and home, they make the most of familiar and newly discovered forms in their shaping of meaning (Mavers, 2011, p. 5)." The study provides insight into important questions: (1) What are the funds of knowledge that these emergent bilinguals bring from home and build upon as they interact with and produce multimodal texts in the classroom, (2) What does the design process look like for these students as they use multiple modes to make meaning, and (3) How is agency a part of these literacy events?

THE EXCHANGE OF INFORMATION

Funds of Knowledge

As students develop communicative competencies within their culture, they draw upon complex linguistic resources and the literacy practices surrounding their lives (D'Warte, 2014). Within home environments, much literacy learning occurs and is embedded in the funds of knowledge available in households (Gonzaléz, Moll, & Amanti, 2005). This knowledge assumes multiple forms and is dependent on family members and their areas of expertise. For example, a mother may share her knowledge of gardening with her daughter who learns to read and write from working with seed packets.

The funds of knowledge that students are exposed to is rapidly changing as the digital world evolves, allowing students quick access to immense amounts of information. Many parents, at all socioeconomic levels, utilize smartphones, tablets, computers, and highly technical television sets in the home (Guernsey, 2014). This results in the development of new skills, strategies, and shared practices for literacy that are driven by home-based experiences with digital tools and interactions with the family members who engage with technologies.

Learning Beyond the Linguistic

Routinely, language users are engrossed in learning through multiple modes within sociocultural contexts. While this includes traditional types of practices like reading and writing, it also expands to incorporate the decoding of images, downloading and inserting pictures, posting to a website, and visiting sites like YouTube (Rowsell & Walsh, 2011). In other words, learning is about acting semiotically in the world (Bjorkvall & Engblom, 2010). Interactions within a digital environment offer access to new literacies and experiences that require students to mix and remix existing media (Flewitt, 2011). For example, the types and kinds of popular culture students interact with online reflects much of what happens in the media and is promoted by for profit corporations.

Companies such as Disney and Cartoon Network Studios are at the forefront of children's everyday lives. As a result, students develop expertise or funds of knowledge on these topics; therefore, this knowledge, along with the digital literacy practices they used while obtaining it, follows students to school (Marsh, 2013). Dyson (2003) refers to the intertextual nature of these interactions between home, school, and media as "familiar frames of reference (p. 15)" that students employ to navigate the school curriculum, language expectations within classrooms, and use of available tools.

In order to communicate within the 21st-century world, the use of multi-literacies must be emphasized in order to move us beyond a monocultural, monolingual world where reading is defined only by decoding and writing as encoding using paper-based systems (Kalantzis & Cope, 2008). Building on multilingualism is as important as acknowledging the role of multiple modes in literacy development (Durán, 2017). Further, Zapata and Van Horn (2017) request that we rethink the emphasis that we place on standard English and open spaces for new definitions of what it means to be a multimodal writer or a designer. They recommend allowing students to move beyond materials and processes and toward "becoming and improvising" (p. 310). "From this perspective students become active designers when they combine available multiple modes in collaborative ways to create meaning texts" (New London Group, 1996). Text construction is embedded in social practices that deeply involve new perspectives and ways of sharing information throughout the world (Miller, 2010).

Sign Making

Social semiotics is one field that offers insight into this notion of students as designers and manipulators of available cultural and mode (signs) affordances. Given that meaning exists in more than just language, it is essential to look closely at students being active communicators through the choices they make regarding text construction, their interests, and the social relationships that unfold as a result of the process (Kress, 2010). Students, as sign makers, are influenced by available modes and resources for meaning-making. Kinetics, the movement of words, as well as the color, size, directionality, and type of font have the potential to be used to represent meaning and are all part of the design process. Images, culturally based resources, offer different potential to learners because each individual interprets and understands an element in a unique way that is tied to their background experiences (Kress & van Leeuwen, 2006).

The multimodal composing process does not assume a linear direction. Rather, it is nonlinear in nature, and therefore, students must be afforded opportunities to work within this alternative framework (Holzwarth & Maurer, 2001). As Ranker (2008) indicates the functions of digital tools make new semiotic resources available, and this requires rethinking the ways in which students compose. In his classroom case study, he noted the need for unique opportunities for students to make meaning. This includes adapting to multiple pathways for composing, designing, and producing texts as mediated by dialogic spaces. Flexibility is fundamental along with, "fostering, collaborating, and build[ing] upon children's lived experiences outside of the classroom (Husbye & Zanden, 2015, p. 110)."

Communication Channels

An essential aspect to learning that cannot be overlooked is the social nature of the context in which it is embodied and enacted. In classrooms, this often takes the form of shared events where students collaborate and interact as a means to advance their learning and build upon existing skills. When Bauer, Presiado, and Colomer (2017) investigated writing partnerships with emergent bilinguals, they found buddy pairs offered students opportunities to become writing leaders and develop their own expertise as a writer. As a result, students became more agentive in their actions, which allowed them to draw upon a broader base of resources.

In addition to the immediate physical, social environment, we must also consider virtual environments given rapid changing technological advances that keep the world moving. For young text designers creating multimodal productions, this may take the form of an audience that exists outside of the classroom. Reflecting about the importance of audience for young composers is essential, and as Durán (2017) suggests, audience impacts design choice and language use. Having an authentic audience triggers students to carefully consider the impact of their design decisions like weaving in the use of color with other modes to influence interpretation of the production. Similarly, Holzwarth and Maurer (2001) add to this idea in their study of film making with two students where they established the value of audience and feedback in motivating the construction and presentation of digital texts to others.

REORIENTING TO MULTIMODAL LITERACY EXPERIENCES

The poetry productions in this project used moving images and words to balance a composition of available modes. Close observations of this process (both social and digital practices) help us understand emergent bilinguals as text designers. In order to provide students with an understanding of the genre of poetry as an initial step, repeated readings of a large sample of poems written by diverse authors like Francisco Alarcon and Julia Durango were explored. Students were immediately drawn to images, color, shapes of words, and the words themselves. Through small group conversations, students talked about the power of the signs and their personal experiences added to their transaction with the poem (Rosenblatt, 1978).

Exploring Affordances

Upon reading numerous paper-based poetry books, students chose their favorite poems to remix based on their interpretations and transactions with the text (Bezemer & Mavers, 2011). As a way to introduce students to kinetic typography, the students watched videos of moving poetry in order to understand the medium and discuss the ways it added new layers of meaning to the poetry. The transformation work began as students drew from the author's original words which were static. As designers, students added dynamic elements causing words to move and change colors for a new aesthetic experience (Strehovec, 2004).

Becoming Text Designers

Ultimately, students were ready to become independent text designers and crafted their kinetic poetry which was posted on YouTube. This encompassed an initial decision about a topic which is where the emergent bilinguals began drawing from their funds of knowledge that included cultural resources like family experiences as well as media-based expertise. Learners built their own repertoires of resources for expressing meaning.

Once a topic was identified, students began composing not on paper as in traditional writer's workshop, but on a Chromebook or laptop. Instead, they opened Google Slides and immediately began writing the title of their poems followed by additional slides that were combined into a moving video. All design decisions were made by the students and included modes such as color, space, and images from Google searches (limited by the school district's filter), directionality of text, transitions between slides, movement of text/ images along with types of movement, size of text/images, backgrounds, timing of slides/movement, and narration. The final step was posting the productions on YouTube for audience purposes.

CAPTURING STUDENT PERSPECTIVES

My role as researcher was one of participant observer (Spradley, 1980) where I served as a facilitator for a small group instruction that usually led with a mini-lesson about reading poetry, writing craft, revising, or the demonstration of a digital tool. The emergent bilinguals were not all in one small group. Rather, the teacher had these students embedded in various groups based on reading levels, mixed with their English-only peers. The groups were flexible and changed at various times throughout the year.

The participants were third grade, nine-year-old emergent bilinguals ranging in English proficiency from newcomer level one 'entering' (just entering a U.S. English-only school with first attempts at learning English) to proficient or level six "reaching" (able to engage in sustained discussions and comprehend at a deep level) as indicated by scores on the Assessing Comprehension and Communication in English State to State for English Language Learners (ACCESS) (WIDA, 2017). These participants were part of a larger study that comprised all of the students in the third grade classroom.

The term "emergent bilinguals" is used throughout this chapter to refer to students who are in the process learning an additional or new language in order to frame their language learning as a resource and not a deficit (García & Kleifgen, 2010). The home languages spoken included Spanish and Arabic, and students ranged in reading levels as measured by the Scholastic Reading Inventory (SRI) from Lexile level 0 (beginning reader that is unable to achieve any score by reading English passages) to 896 (grade five equivalent).

Looking Closely at the Data

To carefully capture the perspective and experiences of the emergent bilinguals, an ethnographic approach was applied with a focus on situated literacy practices (Green & Bloome, 2004). Each literacy event was videotaped, photographed, and documented through field notes and reflective memos (Fetterman, 2010) as I met with students two days per week for the school year. Selected interactions were transcribed using NVivo10. Thirteen student-authored poems were produced by the emergent bilinguals and then analyzed. Moreover, at the end of the project students participated in semistructured interviews to offer insight into their experiences and design choices (Seidman, 2012).

Grounded theory was applied to the data as an initial layer of analysis for determining what was emerging from all of the data collected (Glaser & Strauss, 1967). The data went through multiple rounds of reading that led to the development of codes that began to illuminate the relationships among the data (Charmaz, 2014). As part of this process, overlapping of codes developed and therefore, required the refinement of codes and the construction of categories; some codes were eliminated and others condensed. Through multiple iterations of this practice, themes came to the surface that began to paint a portrait of these students as text designers as influenced by cultural and social factors (Barton & Hamilton, 1998). These results directed the selection of transcripts for a closer analysis where multimodal discourse analysis was applied to determine the wwrole various modes played in the meaning-making process (Baldry & Thibault, 2006).

The multimodal transcripts were embedded with images from the videos and photographs taken during the production process along with detailed descriptions of student behavior and movement to add to the transcribed language that already existed within the transcripts (Bezemer & Mavers, 2011). Comparing the visual images and the language assisted in the discovery of the ways multiple modes contributed to the learning process and how students physically scaffolded one another using digital tools. This process allowed for an analysis of literacy events within the social context of learning. Finally, the student productions were examined in regard to the ways students chose resources to make meaning (Kalantzis & Cope, 2012).

Table 1. Emergent Bilinguals' Funds of Knowledge – Out-of-School Semiotic Resources.

	Themes	Categories	Subcategories	Examples	Modes
Material Resources	Media-based	Popular culture	Books Cartoons Movies Dolls Toys	*Magic Tree House* *Ben 10 Omniverse* *Frozen* *Little Mermaid* Legos	Linguistic, Image, Kinetic, Gesture, Gaze, Sound Multimodal Interplay (mixture of modes)
		Technology	Smartphone Smart TV Tablets/Laptops Video Games DVD Players	Apps for Games Netflix Websites/YouTube Minecraft Movies	Linguistic, Image, Kinetic, Gesture, Gaze, Sound Multimodal Interplay (mixture of modes)
Interactions and Experiences	Family-based	Digital practices	Interacting with Parent's Smartphone Using Smart TV Exploring with Tablets/Laptops	Texting, playing games, scrolling up and down, conducting Google searches, watching YouTube videos, taking pictures, sending photos via messenger, cropping and editing photos, downloading apps, using emojis, visiting websites, decoding images	Linguistic, Image, Kinetic, Gesture, Gaze, Sound Multimodal Interplay (mixture of modes)
		Language and literacy practices	Family Outings Watching TV Reading Writing Parents as Writers	Oral discussions in multiple languages, learning new vocabulary, reading together, writing to family members, consulting parents for writing ideas, playing Grand Theft Auto	Linguistic, Image, Kinetic, Gesture, Gaze, Sound Multimodal Interplay (mixture of modes)
	Peer-based	Digital practices	Multiplayer Online Video Gaming Using Smartphones	Accessing the Internet; connecting with the selected peer group virtually, sending and receiving texts, earning coins/jewels as rewards	Linguistic, Image, Kinetic, Gesture, Gaze, Sound Multimodal Interplay (mixture of modes)
		Language and literacy practices	Multiplayer Online Video Games	Talking to peers online through headsets, applying gaming strategies, negotiating, collaborating, making decisions, following directions, multi-tasking	Linguistic, Image, Kinetic, Gesture, Gaze, Sound Multimodal Interplay (mixture of modes)

Source: Brown, 2017.

FINDINGS

Extracting from the Known

All of the emergent bilinguals brought indispensable, multimodal resources with them to the classroom (See Table 1) and continually tapped these sources during the project. These funds of knowledge fell into two themes: material resources and interactions and experiences. The material resources were media-based and encompassed both popular culture things found in their homes as well as available technology-based devices (e.g., video games, tablets, and smartphones). Even though these students attended a Title I public school, there was an abundance of material riches that they engaged with on daily basis.

In addition, a wealth of knowledge and expertise took the form of interactions and experiences that were either family- or peer-based outside of school. The students gained skills and strategies from scaffolding that occurred through both face-to-face and virtual connections. These consisted of both digital and language literacy practices always connecting to the available material resources.

Frozen

In the case of Jolisa (newcomer), she based her first poem on the Disney movie *Frozen*. Even though her experiences were limited with the English language, which was the only language of instruction in the classroom, she immediately went to work designing a *Frozen* poem based on her understanding of the story, characters, and princesses in general. She saw the movie in both Spanish and English and had several dolls from the movie at home. It was not the materials alone that provided Jolisa with expertise about *Frozen*, but the interactions that occurred utilizing the materials (Marsh, 2013).

Jolisa already knew how to conduct a Google image search, so when she was given a Chromebook open to Google Slides, she opened a new tab and searched using the term "frozen." Numerous images appeared and Jolisa scrolled through the list until she located the perfect one for her cover. Jolisa double clicked her chosen image and instantly inserted into the first slide. She then added her name and the title which she knew how to spell in English. This was followed by a second slide image search where Jolisa kept looking until she found animated images. She did not have the English words to say, "No static images." Instead, she would just indicate, "Not that one. Not that one...," as she clicked on static images. This changed once she found moving *Frozen* images or animated images. Her face exploded with delight, and her poem continued by utilizing a new resource for meaning-making.

The actual poem was written in free verse and capitalized on the English words she already knew. She consulted Rosalina for assistance with words like "beautiful" which was negotiated through dialogue in Spanish. Within her poem, it was evident that Jolisa's work was mediated by her knowledge of *Frozen*, interactions with material resources (including technology), and a mixture of two languages both helping her to construct this poem in English.

Mother as Resource

Another example of the power of familial resources for school-based literacy learning came in the form of Wonder Woman's mother who is from Egypt and speaks Arabic (Durán, 2017). After completing her first poem, "All about Purple and Red," Wonder Woman struggled to identify a new topic. During small group instruction, she stared at her computer and talked to her peers but still could not decide on an idea. Then, Wonder Woman had a thought "I know I will ask my mom. She's written stories before and she knows about stuff. She can help me decide." She went home that evening and recalled the following conversation with her mom in Arabic.

> She tells me it should come from my heart. She tells me in Arabic not English. Not other people's hearts. The poem has to be my vision. Not other people's vision. And you want to have, you need a little bit of encouragement, from people like family members. She told me to go with what my own heart said and my heart said Egypt.

During the following week, Wonder Woman designed a poem called "All About Egypt." Wonder Woman explained that she knew about Egypt because that was her mother's birth country and where she lived for most of her life before coming to the United States. She began with Google searches for images and commented, "Pictures will inspire me to write. They'll help me see what's in my heart." A significant amount of time was spent decoding images (looking closely at the messages hidden). She decided to use a background of a photograph taken in the city of Cairo where the Egyptian flag flew high above the tops of buildings and a large number of people were gathered below.

The Egyptian flag became the backdrop for some additional slides as it represented Wonder Woman's culture, language, and the value of her as a human being. She utilized colors from the flag in her composition – red, white, and black as well as a map of the country. In this example, Wonder Woman drew from interactions with her mother, love and knowledge of Egypt, and Internet images that captured her intended message. Here, Wonder Woman transformed traditional types of resources by remixing them with digital tools, and the result was a culturally relevant moving poem (Kalantzis & Cope, 2008; Holzwarth & Maurer, 2001).

Home Resources for School-Based Text Designing and Production

Even though we have made advances against a deficit view of emergent bilinguals, there are still a large number of educators who are unable to take advantage of the splendid stores of knowledge, skills, and strategies that these students transport to classrooms on a daily basis. Sometimes, there is no acknowledgement of the digital practices that children learn at home through independent interactions and engaging with family members and friends. As evident in Table 1, these students grasped a plethora of digital practices that they learned at home. These skills easily transferred to the poetry project allowing many of the emergent bilinguals to surpass their English-only peers in terms of using technology for the design and production process.

Designing an Alien Poem

Beast Boy was an emergent bilingual who was advanced in his English basic interpersonal communication skills and working to develop his academic discourse. The designing of "Aliens" began as Beast Boy decided on a topic that he was knowledgeable in and was interested in pursuing. He loved aliens of all kinds – cartoon, movie, and what he thought were "real" aliens. He relied on existing digital practices (learned at home) to guide his work in the classroom. Additionally, he developed new skills through peer-to-peer interactions that included language and literacy practices as well as the use of specific technology functions.

The design process began as Beast Boy pulled the Chromebook close and meticulously made design decisions assuming the role of agentive learner for each slide (New London Group, 1996). He chose to use images on each section of his poem, thus fore fronting the role of the visual in his production. This took the form of cartoon-based and movie photographs; he also considered color (backgrounds and font) and the ways these mixed to contribute to an overall product (Kress, 2010). For example, his title was written in green font, and according to Beast Boy, "It is green because you know aliens

Table 2. Multimodal Transcript – Beast Boy Designing "Aliens."

Line #	Speaker	Language	Gestures/Body Movement/Kinetic	Related Images
197	Beast Boy	[Talking to self.] Hey, I need a alien picture. I go to Google. Yeah, like this. [Types: Ben 10 Alien] *The tab for searching Google images was already open when he received the Chromebook.	Clicked on the 'insert image' icon in Google Slides. Typed into Google search bar using one finger at a time.	
198	Beast Boy	Wow, look at them all. So many aliens to pick from. Hey, look at this Rosalina!	Scrolled up and down to look at long list of images. Using the arrow keys.	
199	Rosalina	What? I can't see over there. You need help or what?	Seated across from Beast Boy.	
200	Beast Boy	I got all of them aliens. Which one to get for my poem? Got any ideas?	Continued scrolling through images.	
201	Rosalina	Let me see. Yeah, yeah, I like this one. [Large, purple alien from Ben 10 Omniverse.]	Moved to look at Beast Boy's screen. Returned to seat.	
202	Beast Boy	Yeah, yeah, that be the one. I going to make it big on my page so everyone sees it. He's scary when Ben change into him. Look at his arms.	Enlarged image by clicking on it. Uploaded image to Google Slides.	
203	Rosabelle	Why you making your poem about aliens? They're nasty.		

Table 2. (*Continued*)

Line #	Speaker	Language	Gestures/Body Movement/Kinetic	Related Images
204	Beast Boy	You know. Don't you watch Ben 10 Omniverse on Cartoon Network? They are cool aliens but creepy too. [Typed: Aliens live in space.] [Reads words to self.] Aliens live in space.	Began typing words. Deleted image of alien. Completed typing first line in his poem. Went back to images and re-uploaded the same alien image. First poem line is in black Ariel font size 36.	
205	Rosabelle	Well, I don't know about that. Mines about mermaids cuz I love mermaids. You know like Little Mermaid on TV.		
206	Rosalina	Me too. I might make a poem later about mermaids.		
207	Beast Boy	[Talking to self.] That be better. Like that. Now for some red. I need red here. Reds going to be cool. It make him powerful and scary. I want them [viewers/peers] to be scared.	Made image a bit larger by dragging the corner. Clicked to add background color.	

are green. It represents them." This indicated he was taking into account his topic, knowledge of aliens, and even the audience that would eventually view his poem on YouTube.

Beginning with slide two, Beast Boy searched for alien images and sought help from Rosalina about the best possible fit for his poem. The multimodal transcript (Table 2) detailed the literacy event where Beast Boy engaged in some independent learning and actions and consulted Rosalina and Rosabelle. Each student co-contributed to the composition and allowed one another to assume different roles or identities where their expertise was valued (Bauer et al., 2017). The gesture/movement/kinetics column of the transcript concentrated on the digital practices that Beast Boy mastered and benefited from while designing individual slides. In other words, his digital funds of knowledge were advancing his school-based literacies.

As highlighted in the transcript, Beast Boy took the image of the alien and moved it through a transduction process (moving a resource from one mode to another) which intertwined multiple modes in order to achieve a cohesive and coherent text in the end (Kress, 2010). He utilized the mode of movement to make the image appear and disappear in the final production. Beast Boy worked to manage still images, spatial organization, and timing that resulted in a complex composition (Moss, 2003). Thus, Beast Boy's decisions commanded a particular view of his poetry and reflected him as a learner (Kress, 2010). Throughout the text-making experience, Beast Boy continually negotiated with the available resources (human, material, and digital) and guided the process so that the outcome was the result of his agentive moves as a designer and offered a unique aesthetic experience for the viewer (Kuby & Vaughn, 2015; Strehovec, 2004; Rosenblatt, 1978). He was a semiotic worker within a global world and enacted multiple literate and digital identities (Bjorkvall & Engblom, 2010; Vasudevan, Schultz, & Bateman, 2010).

Agentive and Empowered Emergent Bilinguals

Assuming the role of decision maker and thinking independently in the knowledge-building process were agentive practices for the emergent bilinguals. Given the multimodal context of the project, student agency involved semiotic work where choices were made regarding the remaking of available resources and materials (Kenner & Kress, 2003). Taking control of design decisions was a complex process that entailed numerous evaluations on the part of each student which resulted in a variety of meaning-making potentials.

Advanced Knowledge

Agency and a sense of empowerment were evident in several ways during the overall production process for the emergent bilinguals including talk with peers, actions, choice of modes, and idea decisions. In particular, Rabby was representative of the types of agency that occurred during the entire production process as he learned to negotiate departures from traditional notions of literacy and opened doors to an advancing, multimodal world (Vasudevan et al., 2010). In this sense, students maximized the possibilities of communication and thought intensely about the audience (Hamel, 2017). Rabby's experiences in the area of agency and empowerment illustrated a concept called "embodied knowledges" (Kenner & Kress, 2003). In other words, Rabby developed new kinds of knowledge that were based on interacting with the multimodal design process. Additional modes became available to him, and he integrated them into his cognitive understanding of composing a meaningful text. Using particular sign combinations provided novel, embodied knowledges that Rabby controlled and used to his advantage as a text designer. Knowing when to combine and/or switch modes afforded him the opportunity to augment his viewpoint.

The poetic text that he constructed, titled "Boom Cannon Level 11," was based on an Android app called Boom Beach. It taught his audience about weapons such as cannons, mines, and shock launchers. Rabby began this project feeling a bit uncomfortable with technology because he did not have access to digital devices or the Internet at home. He stated, "I'm not like a person who likes to use computers, like any computers, but this one [Chromebook being used for the project] let's me type what's in my minds and search the pictures I need." Because Rabby was unsure of how to begin his poem given his inexperience with technology, Ghost agreed to serve as a technology expert for him.

The two boys worked on Rabby's computer where they opened a tab for a Google search for his cover image and typed the words Boom Beach. When a rich array of images appeared, Rabby filled with excitement. He blurted, "You know what's on this computer? Boom Beach stuff. It's on my computer." Then, he learned that these images could be captured and used in his poetry production. This seemed to increase his level of engagement, and he was intent on selecting only images that matched those from the actual game. He was not interested in drawing his own pictures or using photographs of real cannons. This is when it was evident that his feelings about technology changed, and he took more control of his learning.

Being Agentive

From this point forward, Rabby became an active author of his own poem and continually made agentive moves as he acted strategically within the design process. He sought to understand the available tools by asking multiple questions to inform his decision making. In one case, Rabby asked, "Is there a way for me to have sound effects for the mines?" Although he was not aware of any resources for this special effect, he understood that the computer had many unknown capabilities. In the end, Rabby navigated sound clips found on Google but did not find just the right one for his poem, so his design decision was to record himself making the exploding mine sounds that were eventually inserted on the appropriate slide. These literacy events offered a space for Rabby to experiment with multiple ways to represent meaning and to be creative and imaginative with the ways he remixed resources.

LITERACY LESSONS LEARNED FROM EMERGENT BILINGUALS

The emergent bilinguals' knowledge, expertise, interactions, and design decisions enacted through the social practices of meaning-making teach us several important lessons about multimodal communication (Dyson, 2013; 2003). First, the power of not assigning topics or restricting the choice of students in regards to composing was of the utmost importance. Jolisa was a prime example of valuing the unfolding of funds of knowledge that students brought to the classroom. She was placed in this English only classroom being a Spanish dominant language user, yet when provided with an open-ended opportunity to design a multimodal poem, she did not refuse or disengage. Instead, Jolisa embraced this experience and drew upon her knowledge of the movie *Frozen*. From this, she was able to craft a lovely poem, using available resources including herself, peers, and digital tools. Her text was triggered by her media experiences with Disney, which became the catalyst for her poem (Gauntlett, 2015). This would not have been possible if Jolisa was given scripted prompts crafted by the teacher.

Second, there was no need to abandon traditional literacy practices. Rather, the multimodal design process required the emergent bilinguals to merge new and old literacies throughout the process. In order to learn about the genre of poetry, the students spent time reading paper-based books and discussing their ideas (which was all very traditional). Later, there was a move to taking an idea in one's head and transforming it into a video. This consisted of a complex series of decisions, interactions, and moves to capture a re-mix of words with other available modes. This process was nonlinear in nature which was very different from many approaches to poetry writing (Husbye & Zanden, 2015; Moss, 2003). An illustration of this was when Beast Boy made changes to his poem in the moment. There was no set instructional time for drafting followed by revising and editing. As an alternative, he selected images prior to writing words on slide one. He continued designing slides two through six, and while in this process he noticed that he needed to return to slide five and add the word "ugly." Some slides were complete and others were incomplete before moving on to the next one. There was no lock, step structure to his design process. Students functioned as complex, meaning-makers and applied a, nonlinear process to the creation of their texts (Husbye & Zanden, 2015).

Another factor that impacted the students was the role of play in the text-making and designing processes. The emergent bilinguals had varying levels of experience with digital devices, but none of them used a program such as Google Slides; therefore, there was some uncertainty about the affordances of this program as mediated through a Chromebook. As a result, students needed time to play with the digital tools in order to experiment with semiotic potential of each mode for the desired achievement within the poem (Bjorkvall & Engblom, 2010; Kress, 2010; Moss, 2003).

Play also involved the use of the imagination and creativity (Hamel, 2017; Kuby & Vaughn, 2015). Once students like Rabby understood the tools, they still needed time to manipulate text, objects, sounds, etc., in novel ways. This experimentation was the only way students labored through the unlimited options available and visualized how the modes and content would come together for the final production process when converting the poem to a video. Kuby and Vaughn (2015) referred to this process as, "a multimodal visionary (p. 433)."

Play, creativity, and use of imagination were also avenues for developing agency or control over design choices. Jolisa's search for animated clip art was an example of how imagination guided an inquiry about the availability of such items and her insistence in choosing the moving clip for her poem. Locating the first animated clip was unintentional as Jolisa accidently discovered this resource but later was insistent about its use. In this case, creativity involved an innovative contribution (animated clip) that made a visible difference in her text making (Gauntlett, 2015). Educators should be mindful about setting up spaces for play and creativity that not only build from a discovery perspective but also are driven by teacher demonstrations or explicit investigations. For example, a student like Rabby may never discover the voice or sound component on his own. He may need some guidance in order to locate and understand this tool. Then, he can move forward playing with the tool, learning about its assets, and finally using it to capture what he imagines.

MOVING TOWARDS CHANGE

Van Sluys and Rao (2012) reminds us to, "not wait for perfect policy or central office mandates, but begin imagining the possibilities, trying out possible practices, and reflecting on the impacts and potentials for particular learners in particular spaces (p. 288)." Instead, we must jump in, get busy transforming outdated practices, cultivate the innovative, and allow for the unexpected to rise. Literacy practices of the twenty-first century are living, dynamic practices that require educators to push some criteria to the backdrop and forefront other aspects that align with lived experiences and reflect the media-driven popular culture of contemporary childhoods (Hamel, 2017; Zapata & Van Horn, 2017).

Part of this transformation of pedagogy requires valuing visual and other modes and no longer relying solely on written and spoken language. This can be particularly important for emergent bilinguals who are learning English as an additional language in English-only classrooms (Moses, 2015). As Ranker (2008) states, "multimedia composing environments offer a rich intertextual landscape and unique ways of making meanings (p. 196)." Transacting within multiple modes allows all students to showcase their growth as learners and as a result, these enacted identities enhance how students see themselves and how others view them.

In addition, the importance of discovery or play cannot be overstated. Other than hands-on, open-ended learning opportunities, there is no way for students to learn about and understand the available semiotic resources. Experimental learning should arise from children's real-world experiences and not be stifled by linear structures and/or one-size-fits-all curricula. This requires flexibility on the part of the educator and respect for agentive students (Dyson, 2013; Holzwarth & Maurer, 2001). Spontaneity and improvisation can be assets for both the students and their teacher as unintentional designs reveal themselves. Zapata and Van Horn (2017) say it quite eloquently, "the infinite openings and inquiries that are possible when teachers and students alike envision and live out multimodal composition as a material process of emergence and emotion, of doing and being who they are in their everyday worlds (p. 312)." I hope that the emergent bilinguals featured in this chapter open your eyes to what is possible when we rethink classroom literacy instruction.

REFERENCES

Baldry, A., & Thibault, P. (2006). *Multimodal transcription and text analysis*. Oakville, CT: Equinox.

Barton, D., & Hamilton, M. (1998). *Local literacies: Reading and writing in one community*. New York: Routledge.

Bauer, E., Presiado, V., & Colomer, S. (2017). Writing through partnership: Fostering translanguaging in children who are emergent bilinguals. *Journal of Literacy Research*, *49*(1), 10–37.

Bezemer, J., & Mavers, D. (2011). Multimodal transcription as academic practice: A social semiotic perspective. *International Journal of Social Research Methodology*, *14*(3), 191–206.

Bjorkvall, A., & Engblom, C. (2010). Young children's exploration of semiotic resources during unofficial computer activities in the classroom. *Journal of Early Childhood Literacy*, *10*(3), 271–293.

Charmaz, K. (2014). *Constructing grounded theory* (2nd ed.). Thousand Oaks, CA: SAGE.

Durán, L. (2017). Audience and young bilingual writers: Building on strengths. *Journal of Literacy Research*, *49*(1), 92–114.

D'warte, J. (2014). Exploring linguistic repertoires: Multiple language use and multimodal literacy activity in five classrooms. *Australian Journal of Language and Literacy*, *37*(1), 21–30.

Dyson, A. (2003). *The brothers and sisters learn to write: Popular literacies in childhood and school cultures*. New York: Teachers College Press.

Dyson, A. (2013). *Rewriting the basics: Literacy learning in children's cultures*. New York: Teachers College Press.

Fetterman, D. (2010). *Ethnography: Step-by-step* (3rd ed.). Los Angeles, CA: Sage.

Flewitt, R. (2011). Bringing ethnography to a multimodal investigation of early literacy in the digital age. *Qualitative Research*, *11*(3), 293–310.

García, O., & Kleifgen, J. (2010). *Educating emergent bilinguals: Policies, programs, and practices for English language learners*. New York: Teachers College Press.

Gauntlett, D. (2015). *Making media studies: The creativity turn in media and communication studies*. New York: Peter Lang.

Glaser, B., & Strauss, A. (1967). *The discovery of grounded theory*. Hawthorne, NY: Aldine de Gruyter.

González, N., Moll, L., & Amanti, C. (2005). Introduction: Theorizing practices. In N. González, L. Moll & C. Amanti (Eds.), *Funds of knowledge: Theorizing practices in households, communities and classrooms* (pp. 89–111). Mahwah: Lawrence Erlbaum Associates.

Green, J., & Bloome, D. (2004). Ethnography and ethnographers of and in education: A situated per-spective. In J. Flood, S. Heath, & D. Lapp. (Eds.), *Handbook of research on teaching literacy through the communicative and visual arts* (pp. 181–202). New York: Macmillan Publishers.

Guernsey, L. (2014). *Envisioning a digital age architecture for early education.* New America Education Policy Program. Washington, DC. Retrieved from https://www.newamerica.org/education-policy/policy-papers/envisioning-a-digital-age-architecture-for-early-education/

Hamel, F. (2017). *Choice and agency in the writing workshop: Developing engaged writers, grades 4–6.* New York: Teachers College Press.

Holzwarth, P., & Maurer, B. (2001). Aesthetic creativity, reflexivity and the play with meaning: A video culture case study. *Journal of Educational Media, 26*(3), 185–202.

Husbye, N., & Zanden, S. (2015). Composing film: Multimodality and production in elementary classrooms. *Theory into Practice, 54*(2), 109–116.

Kalantzis, M., & Cope, B. (2008). Language education and multiliteracies. In S. May and N. Hornberger (Eds.). *Encyclopedia of language and education* (pp. 195–211). New York: Springer.

Kalantzis, M., & Cope, B. (2012). *Literacies.* New York: Cambridge University Press.

Kenner, C. & Kress, G. (2003). The multisemiotic resources of biliterate children. *Journal of Early Childhood Literacy, 3*(2), 179–202.

Kress, G. (2010). *Multimodality: A social semiotic approach to contemporary communication.* New York: Routledge.

Kress, G., & van Leeuwen, T. (2006). *Reading images: The grammar of visual design* (2nd ed.). New York: Routledge.

Kuby, C., & Vaughn, M. (2015). Young children's identities becoming: Exploring agency in the creation of multimodal literacies. *Journal of Early Childhood Literacy, 15*(4), 433–472.

Marsh, J. (2013). Early childhood literacy and popular culture. In J. Larson and J. Marsh (Eds.), *The sage handbook of early childhood literacy* (2nd ed., pp. 207–222). Thousand Oaks, CA: SAGE.

Mavers, D. (2011). *Children's drawing and writing: The remarkable in the unremarkable.* New York: Routledge.

Miller, K. (2010). A review of the "digital turn" in the New Literacy studies. *Review of Educational Research, 80*(2), 246–271.

Moses, L. (2015). The role(s) of image for young bilinguals reading multimodal informational texts. *Language and Literacy, 17*(3), 82–99.

Moss, G. (2003). Putting the text back into practice: Junior-age non-fiction as objects of design. In C. Jewitt & G. Kress (Eds.), *Multimodal literacy* (pp. 73–87). New York: Peter Lang Publishing.

New London Group. (1996). A pedagogy of multiliteracies: Designing social futures. *Harvard Educational Review, 66*(1), 60–92.

Ranker, J. (2008). Composing across multiple media: A case study of digital video production in a fifth grade classroom. *Written Communication, 25*(2), 196–234.

Rosenblatt, L. (1978). *The reader the text the poem: The transactional theory of the literary work.* Carbondale, IL: Southern Illinois University Press.

Rowsell, J., & Walsh, M. (2011). Rethinking literacy education in new times: Multimodality, multiliteracies, & new literacies. *Brock Education Journal, 21*(1), 53–62.

Seidman, I. (2012). *Interviewing as qualitative research: A guide for researchers in education and the social sciences* (4th ed.). New York: Teachers College Press.

Spradley, J. (1980). *Participant observation.* New York: Harcourt Brace.

Strehovec, J. (2004). The software word: Digital poetry as new media-based language art. *Digital Creativity, 15*(3), 143–158.

Van Sluys, K. & Rao, A. (2012). Supporting multilingual learners: Practical theory and theoreti-cal practices. *Theory into Practice, 51*(4), 281–289.

Vasudevan, L., Schultz, K., & Bateman, J. (2010). Rethinking composing in a digital age: Authoring literate identities through multimodal storytelling. *Written Communication, 27*(4), 442–468.

WIDA. (2017). *Spring 2017 interpretive guide for score report: Kindergarten-grade 12*. Retrieved from file:///C:/Users/te01100/Downloads/WIDA%20ACCESS%20interpretive%20guide%20scores%202017%20(1).pdf

Zapata, A., & Van Horn, S. (2017). "Because I'm smooth": Material intra-action and text productions among young Latino picture book makers. *Research in the Teaching of English, 51*(5), 290–315.

CHILDREN'S LITERATURE CITED

Graham (1994). *Splishsplash.* New York: Houghton Mifflin.

TEACHING FOR GLOBAL READINESS: A MODEL FOR LOCALLY SITUATED A GLOBALLY CONNECTED LITERACY INSTRUCTION

Shea Kerkhoff

ABSTRACT

Today's students are being called to graduate global ready. The term global ready encompasses the multiple literacies as well as the global citizenship needed in the 21st century to participate, collaborate, and work in a globally interconnected society. This chapter introduces a model for teaching for global readiness. A sequential exploratory mixed methods design was employed to operationalize and validate a teaching for global readiness model. The first phase was a qualitative exploration with 24 expert global education teachers. The second phase was a quantitative analysis using factor analysis and model fit statistics to determine if the findings of the qualitative phase were generalizable to a larger population. Based on the results, the Teaching for Global Readiness Model consists of four dimensions:

Addressing Diversity in Literacy Instruction
Literacy Research, Practice and Evaluation, Volume 8, 193–205
Copyright © 2018 by Emerald Publishing Limited
All rights of reproduction in any form reserved
ISSN: 2048-0458/doi:10.1108/S2048-045820170000008009

Situated practice, integrated global learning, critical literacy instruction, and transactional cross-cultural experiences. The chapter describes an array of literacy instruction teacher practices that promote global readiness knowledge, skills, and dispositions and points to the importance of locally situated but globally connected literacy instruction.

Keywords: Multiliteracies; global citizenship; global readiness; K-12 literacy instruction

Today's world is increasingly interrelated and interconnected (Friedman, 2006). In addition to global interconnectedness, increased global migration has led to more diversity in schools around the world (Suarez-Orozco, 2001). The effects of a quickly changing society are manifested in the field of literacy education today. Literacy researchers have called for students to develop new literacies, new competencies, and new ways of thinking to be ready for college, career, and civic life in this globally interconnected society.

Some have criticized U.S. schools for a lack of global education in the curriculum (Friedman, 2006; Hayward & Siaya, 2001). Global education aims to prepare students for public and private life in an interconnected global society (Dagenais, 2003). What our students need in order to communicate and interact in today's globally interconnected, information society is both multiliteracies and global citizenship (Manfra & Spires, 2013). Together, multiliteracies and global citizenship form the construct *global readiness* (Kerkhoff, 2017). A *global ready graduate* is a socially responsible global citizen with the multiliteracies necessary in the twenty-first century to participate, collaborate, and work in a global society.

Teaching for global readiness is not for world language teachers or for social studies teachers alone; literacy teachers have the potential to promote students' global readiness as well (West, 2010). The problem is that literacy teachers may not be trained in teaching students for global readiness (Cushner, 2012; Parkhouse, Glazier, Tichnor-Wagner, & Montana Cain, 2015; Rapoport, 2010). Internationalizing pre-service teacher education is an emerging field in the research (Cushner, 2012), but does not address the teachers that are already in the classroom nor the translation to K-12 classrooms. The research that has been conducted on in-service teachers shows that even if teachers believe in global ready teaching, they may not be practicing it in the classroom. Two reasons cited by Rapoport (2010) are that teachers perceive they do not have time or report that they do not know how. Recently, two groups have operationalized global ready teaching, LearnNC and Partnership for 21st Century Skills. However, there is not a body of literature that supports or refutes their claims. In addition, there are related concepts, such as the Intercultural Development Inventory (Hammer, Bennett, & Wiseman, 2003) and the Cross Cultural Adaptability Inventory (Kelley & Myers, 1992), but these constructs are not about teaching. This construct validation project was intended to fill the gap. Good teaching should be grounded in theory and research; therefore, this chapter introduces a theoretically grounded and empirically tested model for teaching for global readiness.

APPLYING RELEVANT THEORIES

The relevant educational theories that ground the Teaching for Global Readiness Model come from two streams of literature: global citizenship education and literacy education. Specifically, the supporting theories are cosmopolitanism (Hansen, 2010; Wahlström, 2014) and multiliteracies (New London Group, 1996; Cope & Kalantzis, 2015). Multiliteracies encompasses the "social turn" (Gee, 1999) and the "digital turn" (Mills, 2010) in literacy education. In 2010, Hull and Stornaiuolo (2010) called for a "cosmopolitan turn" in literacy education. Together multiliteracies and cosmopolitanism adopt these three "turns" in literacy education. Furthermore, theorists created both theories (i.e., multiliteracies and cosmopolitanism) in response to globalization, which is the impetus of this study.

Cosmopolitanism

Cosmopolitan is an ancient Greek word that translates to *citizen of the world*. This citizenship does not displace local or national allegiances; it adds global allegiance (Rizvi, 2008; Wahlström, 2014). While the word is not new, what is new is that information and communication along with transportation technologies make global connections faster and more frequent than ever before (Cope & Kalantzis, 2015). The likelihood of intercultural dialogue and transactions of perspectives across cultures is heightened. In educational cosmopolitanism theory, people across the world are described as united in a global community sharing universal values while at the same time recognizing and respecting differences (Hansen, 2010; Rizvi, 2008). The theory also acknowledges the diversity within a culture and encourages dialogue around similarities and differences as part of learning (Wahlström, 2014). Cosmopolitanism is an optimistic theory that sees how progress can bring desired changes while at the same time respecting tradition and not encouraging change for change sake. In this way, teachers and students are open to the new while looking reflectively and loyally to the old (Hansen, 2010).

Multiliteracies

The second theory that serves as the foundation for the Teaching for Global Readiness Model is pedagogy of multiliteracies (Cope & Kalantzis, 2015; New London Group, 1996). This pedagogy aligns with the changing ideas of identity, culture, and citizenship in the twenty-first century. Pedagogy of multiliteracies was conceptualized by a group of prominent literacy scholars who met in New London to discuss the current state and the future of literacy pedagogy. Their collective analysis was that the workplace now valued multiskilled workers, public and private life included interaction with more diverse others, and information and communication technologies produced a variety of multimodal texts. They agreed that a monolingual, monocultural literacy pedagogy should not be taught anymore and coined the term "multiliteracies" to account for the plurality of text types and discourses that could be taught to students with differences in culture, language, gender, (New London Group, 1996, p. 63) and ability (Cope & Kalantzis, 2015). Multiliteracies comprise traditional and new literacies, as well as multimodal, multilingual, and multicultural literacies. In pedagogy of multiliteracies theory, practitioners situate learning in a relevant way, utilize overt instruction to demystify discourses, teach critical literacy, and facilitate knowledge construction so that students are transformed through learning (New London Group, 1996).

METHODS

To design an empirically valid model, I utilized a two-phase mixed methods study. Mixed methods allow for the strengths of both qualitative, namely participant voices, and quantitative, namely generalizability (DeCuir-Gunby, 2008). Fig. 1 displays the sequence of the two phases. The first phase of the study was a qualitative exploration of what expert teachers believed it meant to prepare their students to participate, collaborate, and work in a global society. Teachers' voices were important to capture, for me, because one goal of my research was to empower teachers. I believed and continue to believe, as Eisner (1991) did, that the voices of teachers are powerful, are missing, and are needed in educational research. This belief led me to choose to interview current K-12 classroom teachers in addition to global education research-ers who are professional teacher educators. Criteria for inclusion in the pur-poseful sample included at least three years K-12 teaching experience and global education professional training. Participants were recruited through *4 the World*, an international education organization that provides profes-sional development to teachers; a state Department of Public Instruction Global Ready Designation Committee; and the New Literacies and Global Learning College of Education master's degree program at a Southeastern U.S. university that contextualized learning in a global society. Participants were chosen to represent a maximum variation in ethnicity, grade-level taught, and subject taught. Data was collected until saturation was reached. In all, I conducted 24 expert teacher semistructured interviews and transcribed all audio recordings. The interview transcripts were analyzed using Braun and Clarke's (2006) iterative thematic analysis process.

The second phase was a quantitative analysis to determine if the findings of the qualitative phase were generalizable to a larger population. From the initial exploration, the qualitative findings were used to develop a quantita-tive survey. Key quotes identified from the interviews became potential sur-vey items (Creswell & Clark, 2011). The survey was developed in Qualtrics and sent to 22 education experts to review the quality and relevance of the items. After this review, I conducted cognitive interviews (Willis, 2005) with six members of the target population, K-12 teachers. In the cognitive inter-views, the teachers took the survey in front of me and told me what they thought each question was asking and if the response options were adequate enough to represent their answers. This process resulted in a 39-item teaching for global readiness survey with Likert scale response options.

The survey was sent to 3,433 K-12 teachers who were part of the VIF International network. VIF International (now called Participate) is an organization that provides professional development on global teaching and learning within the U.S. While some teachers had been a part of the VIF International network for years and received a number of global edu-cation professional development sessions, others were new to the network and had not yet begun. The network also included teachers who voluntarily

Fig. 1. Exploratory Sequential Mixed Methods Design Diagram.

registered and teachers who were registered by their district offices as part of a mandated program. Therefore, the network contained variance in levels of experience and interest thus providing the variance around the statistics that would be needed for analysis (Comrey & Lee, 1992; Hinkin, 1998). In all, 630 K-12 teachers in the U.S. responded. The survey respondents were split randomly into two groups. The first sample was analyzed using exploratory factor analysis with orthogonal rotation, which resulted in four factors being extracted and 30 items retained. The proposed four-factor model from the exploratory factor analysis was then tested with the second sample using confirmatory factor analysis and model fit statistics. The resulting model as shown in Fig. 2 was a good fit to the data according to Hu and Bentler's (1999) widely accepted criteria (^{2}(143) 246.909, ^{2}/df = 1.73, CFI = 0.960, TLI = 0.953, SRMR = 0.061, RMSEA = 0.051). Cronbach's revealed good reliability with the overall reliability for the model at 0.88. Over 0.70 is generally considered adequate (Comrey & Lee, 1992; Nunnally, 1978).

The quantitative analysis resulted in an empirically valid Teaching for Global Readiness Model with 19 items loading on four dimensions: *situated practice, integrated global learning, critical literacy instruction*, and *transactional cross-cultural experiences*. In other words, teaching for global readiness is situated, integrated, critical, and transactional, which will be described in greater detail in the next section.

TEACHING FOR GLOBAL READINESS MODEL

Teaching for global readiness should include all four dimensions but not necessarily at the same time. Fig. 3 displays the four dimensions of the model across the second row and the corresponding teaching practices for each dimension below. This section will describe each of the four dimensions of the model.

The first dimension is *situated practice*. Situated practice is concerned with the context of the people, place, and time of learning. Teaching for global readiness embraces *glocalization*, meaning that instruction is locally situated and globally connected. For example, middle school students in a rural farming community in the Midwest U.S. examined how agriculture could reduce world hunger. Students in one collaborative group connected their knowledge of raising poultry with a solution for increasing protein in children's diets in Peru by raising money to purchase a flock of egg-laying chickens for a

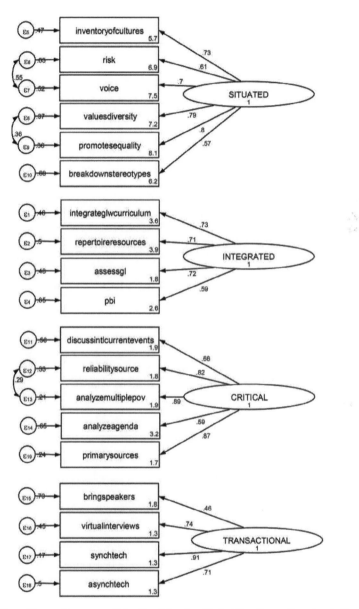

Fig. 2. Four-Factor Structure of the Teaching for Global Readiness Construct. *Source*: Kerkhoff (2017).

Fig. 3.   Teaching for Global Readiness Model. *Source*: Adapted from Kerkhoff (2017).

Peruvian family. Situated practice is a sociocultural pedagogy that is relevant and responsive to students as social and cultural beings. In the example from the middle school, the teachers shared authority with students as students choose the country to study and worked collaboratively with peers to construct knowledge. The following list comprises practices that teachers can enact in order to contextualize instruction in a multicultural way:

- Teachers take inventory of the cultures (languages, nationalities, ethnicities, religions, etc.) represented by their students;
- Teachers cultivate a classroom environment that values diversity;
- Teachers cultivate a classroom environment that promotes equality;
- Teachers provide a space that allows learners to take risks;
- Teachers provide a space that allows students a voice; and
- Teachers attempt to break down students' stereotypes.

The second dimension is *integrated global learning*. Integrated global learning requires explicit instruction on global readiness. Specifically, teachers include global topics in existing curriculum structures and intentionally scaffold global learning. For example, a high school English teacher in the Southeast U.S. integrated global learning with an inquiry project on an existing curricular topic, coming-of-age stories. She partnered with a school in China, and students worked in international teams to complete an analysis of coming-of-age literature. She set academic content goals for the project but she also set global learning goals, such as students would learn how the teenage experience in China is similar to and different from U.S. culture. She scaffolded by frontloading academic vocabulary needed for the collaboration, having conversations with the students about how to best approach political subjects with people from other countries, and by formative assessment throughout the inquiry project. Formative assessments included checking in with students after they designed their inquiry questions and after they found their resources to establish that their question was of social significance to both cultures and their sources were from both countries. This teacher connected cultural awareness and global issues with the standard course of study so that students were explicitly and actively learning how global issues were relevant to the content. The following lists teaching practices for integrating global learning:

- Teachers integrate global learning with the existing curriculum;
- Teachers seek out resources related to global education;

- Teachers facilitate inquiry-based lessons about the world (e.g., research projects, project-based learning, exploratory learning, discovery learning); and
- Teachers assess students' global learning.

The third dimension is *critical literacy instruction*. Critical literacy approaches reading, writing, speaking, listening, viewing, visually representing, inquiring, thinking, and acting from a critical frame. Students are taught to question the credibility of claims and assess bias in texts they read and view. They learn to construct their own claims by reading primary sources and sources from multiple perspectives, including international media. In addition, students learn to apply critical literacy knowledge, skills, and dispositions to society and themselves by questioning the status quo and their own ideological assumptions. Students enact critical literacy as they "read the word and the world" (Freire & Macedo, 1987, p. i) and design new social futures (New London Group, 1996). The following outlines desired student outcomes resulting from critical literacy instruction:

- Students engage in discussions about international current events;
- Students analyze the reliability of sources;
- Students analyze content from multiple perspectives;
- Students analyze the agenda behind media messages; and
- Students construct claims based on primary sources.

The fourth dimension is *transactional cross-cultural experiences*. Transactional experience involves transactions, or exchanges, between people. In these learning experiences, students interact with others in an exchange of information and ideas in a way that requires receptive language (e.g., listening and reading) as well as expressive language (e.g., speaking and writing) so that there is give and take from both parties. These learning experiences are based on equality of perspectives, where partners in other countries are viewed as resources to protect against U.S.-centric or U.S.-superiority thinking.

International travel is a highly regarded form of global education, but travel alone is not sufficient. To promote global readiness, students need opportunities to interact with locals and to critically reflect on their encounters. Rest assured, travel is not the only way to teach for global readiness. K-12 teachers can take advantage of international resources in their home communities for field trips, such as visiting places of worship, ethnic restaurants, and museum exhibitions from other countries. Teachers can also harness the affordances of technology to bring experts and peers from other countries into the classroom virtually for question and answer sessions or collaboration on projects. The following lists how K-12 teachers have created transactional cross-cultural experiences for their students without leaving the classroom:

- Teachers bring in speakers from different backgrounds so that students can listen to different perspectives;
- Teachers utilize technology for virtual interviews (one-on-one, whole class, etc.) about global issues (with subject-matter experts, international partners, cultural community leaders, etc.);
- Students utilize synchronous technology (e.g., Skype, GoogleHangout, WeChat, FaceTime) for international collaborations; and
- Students utilize asynchronous technology (e.g., Google Drive, Quip, email, blogs) for international collaborations.

CONCLUSION

Today's students are being called to graduate global ready. The term *global ready* encompasses the multiple literacies as well as the global citizenship needed in the 21st century in order to communicate and collaborate cross-culturally. The four dimensions of the Teaching for Global Readiness Model (i.e., situated practice, integrated global learning, critical literacy instruction, and transactional experiences) were created based on master teachers' explanations of how they teach for global readiness in their K-12 classrooms. Every item in each of the four dimensions is a consensus of these 24 classroom teachers' practices. The teachers explained that they integrate global learning and situate their instruction so that it is relevant to the students in their class. The model points to the importance of being locally situated but globally connected. In other words, the model supports the importance of cultivating a community of learners inside the classroom and facilitating experiences where students interact with diverse others both inside and outside the classroom. However, teachers explained that situated and integrated is not enough. They believed that teaching for global readiness must be critical and transactional as well. That is to say, the model highlights the importance of critical pedagogy and global partnerships established in equality that promote the values of reflexivity, perspective-taking, and equity. Together, the four dimensions embrace the multiple cultures in the classroom and broaden students' understanding of cultures new to students.

The model contributes to the field of literacy education by providing an array of teacher practices that promote global readiness literacy skills and cosmopolitan dispositions. Through the validation of the operational and conceptual definition of teaching for global readiness, the model provides common language and a conceptual framework on which to make instructional tools and programs. The survey (see Kerkhoff, 2017) provides a free tool to use in professional development at the individual teacher level to increase awareness of teaching practices that promote global readiness and at the institutional level for pre- and posttesting for program evaluation. The model can inform education researchers, teacher educators, policy-makers, administrators, and teachers, hopefully leading to global readiness for all graduates.

REFERENCES

Braun, V., & Clarke, V. (2006). Using thematic analysis in psychology. *Qualitative Research in Psychology, 3*(2), 77–101.

Comrey, A. L., & Lee, H. B. (1992). *A first course in factor analysis* (2nd ed.). Hillsdale, NJ: Lawrence Erlbaum.

Cope, B., & Kalantzis, M. (2015). *Pedagogy of multiliteracies: Learning by design.* New York: Palgrave Macmillan.

Creswell, J., & Clark, V. L. P. (2011). *Designing and conducting mixed methods research.* (2nd ed.). Thousand Oaks, CA: SAGE.

Cushner, K. (2012). Intercultural competence for teaching and learning. In B. Shaklee & S. Baily (Eds.), *A framework for internationalizing teacher education* (pp. 41–59). Lanham, MD: Rowman Littlefield.

Dagenais, D. (2003). Accessing imagined communities through multilingualism and immersion education. *Journal of Language, Identity, and Education, 2*(4), 269–283.

DeCuir-Gunby, J. T. (2008). Designing mixed methods research in the social sciences: A racial identity scale development example. In J. Osborne (Ed.), *Best practices in quantitative methods* (pp. 125–136). Thousand Oaks, CA: SAGE.

Eisner, E. W. (1991). What really counts in schools? *Educational Leadership, 48*(5), 10–17.

Freire, P., & Macedo, D. (1987). *Literacy: Reading the word and the world.* Westport, CT: Bergin & Garvey.

Friedman, T. L. (2006). *The world is flat [updated and expanded]: A brief history of the twenty-first century.* New York: Farrar, Strauss and Giroux.

Gee, J. P. (1999). The future of the social turn: Social minds and the new capitalism. *Research on Language & Social Interaction, 32*(1–2), 61–68.

Hammer, M. R., Bennett, M. J., & Wiseman, R. (2003). Measuring intercultural sensitivity: The intercultural development inventory. *International Journal of Intercultural Relations, 27*(4), 421–443.

Hansen, D. T. (2010). Cosmopolitanism and education: View from the ground. *Teachers College Record, 112,* 1–30.

Hayward, F. M., & Siaya, L. M. (2001). *Public experience, attitudes, and knowledge: A report on two national surveys about international education*. Washington, DC: ACE.

Hinkin, T. R. (1998). A brief tutorial on the development of measures for use in survey questionnaires. *Organizational Research Methods, 1*(1), 104–121.

Hu, L. T., & Bentler, P. M. (1999). Cut-off criteria for fit indexes in covariance structure analysis: Conventional criteria versus new alternatives. *Structural Equation Modeling, 6*, 1–55.

Hull, G. A., & Stornaiuolo, A. (2010), Literate arts in a global world: Reframing social networking as cosmopolitan practice. *Journal of Adolescent & Adult Literacy, 54*, 85–97.

Kelley, C., & Meyers, J. (1992). *Cross-cultural adaptability inventory* (CCAI). Yarmouth, ME: Intercultural Press.

Kerkhoff, S. N. (2017). Designing global futures: A mixed methods study to develop and validate the teaching for global readiness scale. *Teaching and Teacher Education, 65*, 91–106. Retrieved from http://dx.doi.org/10.1016/j.tate.2017.03.011

Manfra, M. M., & Spires, H. A. (2013). Creative synthesis and TPACK: Supporting teachers through a technology and inquiry-rich graduate degree program. *Contemporary Issues in Technology and Teacher Education, 13*(4), 386–418.

Mills, K. A. (2010). A review of the "digital turn" in the new literacy studies. *Review of Educational Research, 80*(2), 246–271.

New London Group. (1996). A pedagogy of multiliteracies: Designing social futures. *Harvard Educational Review, 66*(1), 60–92.

Nunnally, J. C. (1978). *Psychometric theory*. New York: McGraw-Hill.

Parkhouse, H., Glazier, J., Tichnor-Wagner, A., & Montana Cain, J. (2015). From local to global: Making the leap in teacher education. *International Journal of Global Education, 4*(2), 10–29.

Rapoport, A. (2010). We cannot teach what we don't know: Indiana teachers talk about global citizenship education. *Education, Citizenship and Social Justice, 5*(3), 179–190.

Rizvi, F. (2008). Epistemic virtues and cosmopolitan learning. *The Australian Educational Researcher, 35*(1), 17–35.

Suarez-Orozco, M. M. (2001). Globalization, immigration, and education: The research agenda. *Harvard Educational Review, 71*(3), 345–365.

Wahlström, N. (2014). Toward a conceptual framework for understanding cosmopolitanism on the ground. *Curriculum Inquiry, 44*(1), 113–132.

West, C. (2010). Borderless via technology. *International Educator, 19*(2), 24–33.

Willis, G. B. (2005). *Cognitive interviewing: A tool for improving questionnaire design*. Thousand Oaks, CA: SAGE.

UTILIZING A RUBRIC TO IDENTIFY DIVERSITY IN CHILDREN'S LITERATURE

Jackie Marshall Arnold and Mary-Kate Sableski

ABSTRACT

To describe the development of a rubric for identifying diversity in children's literature to inform literature selection for classroom instruction. Drawing on research literature and data collection reporting the need for increased awareness of the use of diverse children's literature in elementary and middle school classrooms, we designed and field-tested a rubric for use in identifying diversity in children's literature. Using constant comparative methods to identify themes in the data, we continually refined the categories in a rubric designed to guide the selection of diverse children's literature. Content analysis of children's literature for diverse elements informed the development of the rubric categories. The results of this study produced a field-tested rubric that can be utilized by classroom teachers and researchers to guide their literature selections with the goal of representing increased diversity. Findings demonstrated that a rubric with four clearly defined categories was more user-friendly to classroom teachers, and that applying the rubric when discussing children's literature led to conversation

Addressing Diversity in Literacy Instruction
Literacy Research, Practice and Evaluation, Volume 8, 207–228
Copyright © 2018 by Emerald Publishing Limited
All rights of reproduction in any form reserved
ISSN: 2048-0458/doi:10.1108/S2048-045820170000008010

and collaboration among colleagues. This study demonstrated that the rubric can be applied to literature selections with classroom teachers and can be used to stimulate conversation about diversity in children's literature as it applies to the classroom context. This chapter's rubric provides a useful tool for classroom teachers. Teachers can use this tool to assist them in selecting diverse children's literature for their classrooms. Administrators and literacy coaches can use this rubric as a way to stimulate conversation surrounding diverse children's literature.

Keywords: Diversity; children's literature; preservice teachers; in-service teachers

I taught Alexis for two years. For her it was third and fourth grade, and for me it was teaching years 1 and 2. There is no surprise who learned more. Alexis was an extremely bright girl and an avid reader. The way she raced through books reminded me of myself in third grade, and I wanted to share my own eight-year-old literary passion, The Baby-Sitters Club. One day during summer vacation, my grandma bought me two paper bags full of Baby-Sitters Club books at a yard sale, and I spent the next two years reading them over and over until I could recite verbatim the emotional stories of Boy-Crazy Stacey *(Martin, 1987) or* Mary Anne Saves the Day *(Martin, 1987). I was a little sad to pass these paper bags on to Alexis, but mostly I was imagining inspiring a whole new generation of Baby-Sitters Club fanatics.*

The day after she took one home, I raced up to her in the morning, eager to hear her rave and dying to reminisce. "Oh," she said, "It was okay. I didn't get very far yet." It was like she was trying to break my heart. "Okay?" I repeated. "Just okay? What about Claudia's funky outfits and Kristy's hilarious jokes?" "Oh yeah, they're okay. I like Jessie the best."

That was when it hit me. Claudia and Kristy had nothing to do with Alexis. They were middle class, white girls in suburban neighborhoods. Alexis was African American and lived with her single mom in an area so poor and with so many challenges. Alexis, unsurprisingly, identified with Jessie, who was the only African American character. Jessie's life, however, was just like all of the other girls, and she was rarely the focus of the books. Personally, I had always loved reading books, but I completely took for granted that I had spent my whole life reading a lot of books about people a lot like me.

This story illustrates the complexities teachers face as they select and utilize literature in their classrooms, especially while the majority of current classroom teachers are Caucasian. Diversity has been an important topic in pedagogical discussions of the utilization of children's literature in classrooms for decades (Larrick, 1965). In current contexts, diversity in children's literature is being articulated as a way to reconsider the availability of books of diversity and to carefully evaluate the books we choose to include in our classrooms as representative of the diversity in our society (Boyd, Causey, & Galda, 2015). Best practice instruction incorporates quality diverse children's literature, widening all students' views on the world.

Though research has clearly demonstrated and called for the seamless use of diverse children's literature, there still exists a paucity of that diverse literature in today's classrooms (Cooperative Children's Book Center, 2015). Knowing that classrooms are composed of increasing numbers of diverse students, it is essential that teachers understand the importance of selecting high-quality diverse literature and use it as an integral component to their instruction. Ample research exists surrounding the ways in which preservice and in-service teachers come to understand the need for diverse literature in classrooms (DeNicolo & Franquiz, 2006), but there is a need for research that documents the purposeful identification and utilization of this diverse literature within instructional practices.

BACKGROUND OF THE PROBLEM

Diversity in children's literature is a discussion occurring at the national and international level among scholars of children's literature (Johnson, Mathis, & Short, 2016). Short (2015) identified that less than 10% of children's books written in 2015 incorporated diversity. The Cooperative Children's Book Center maintains statistics on the number of books published by and about diverse groups, and these statistics consistently indicate a disparity in the number of books by or about diverse groups as compared to the number of books published in a given year. Teachers need the dispositions and knowledge to locate diverse literature, include it in their classroom libraries, and *intentionally* use it within their instructional practices. While today's classrooms incorporate significant numbers of diverse students, we know the gap between the classroom context and the literature shared is significant and problematic. Though research exists documenting and practicing teachers' understanding of the importance of this topic (DeNicolo & Franquiz, 2006; Iwai, 2013), little exists that identifies how diverse literature is actually utilized in instruction. Thus, it is critical to identify the ways in which quality diverse literature is being utilized in classrooms and encourage additional integration across classroom contexts.

For decades, children's literature scholars (Koss, Martinez, & Johnson, 2016; Smith-D'Arezzo, 2003; Yokota, 1993) have identified the critical need for all students to see themselves accurately represented in the stories that they read. Scholars have called for literature that provides "mirrors and windows" (Bishop, 1990) and assists students in knowing more than their own "single story" (Tschida, Ryan, & Ticknor, 2014). Yet, despite decades of identified need and a current national campaign pleading for the need, we still find our bookshelves and classrooms lacking high-quality diverse literature.

Significant research has identified that the majority of teachers in the United States are Caucasian even in settings that are particularly diverse. Research illustrates this dichotomy and the need to help teachers (both preservice and in-service) incorporate diverse literature. Morton, Sierra, Grant, and Glese (2008) utilized diverse literature in their instruction to help candidates preparing to teach to consider the complexity of their diverse classrooms, challenge their beliefs about diverse issues, and increase their awareness of diversity in general. Iwai (2012) conducted research illustrating that by scaffolding students' exploration of multicultural literature across a semester, students developed positive attitudes about using diverse literature. Gibson (2012) demonstrated that having her preservice teachers read multicultural literature influenced their abilities to consider multiple perspectives and the importance of culturally relevant teaching.

These studies and others provide a strong case for the need to support preservice and practicing teachers understanding of the importance of using diverse literature, but little exists to help them knowledgeably select that literature. Brinson (2012) conducted research which documented that although teachers may know they "should" include diverse literature, they potentially have very limited experiences reading and identifying high-quality diverse literature. Brinson (2012) asked 113 preservice and in-service teachers to identify two children's books from the following categories: African-American, Anglo-American, Asian-American, Latino-American, Native-American, and multicultural characters. While 61% of participants could identify two books that represented Anglo-Americans, only 53% could identify two books with African-American characters, and only 34% could identify two books with Asian-American characters. When identifying Latino-American, Native-American, and Multicultural Characters only 24% to 28% of participants could name two books with characters in these categories.

Multiple studies (Koss, Martinez, & Johnson, 2016; Smith-D'Arezzo, 2003; Yokota, 1993) state that though our society continues to deepen in its representation of diversity, our classroom libraries and our utilization of diverse children's literature do not reflect this representation. With research clearly documenting an understanding of the importance of utilizing diverse literature, an essential question remains unanswered. How can we support and guide preservice and in-service teachers beyond the understanding that the presence of diverse literature is important, into the application and utilization of this literature in instruction? This chapter will describe the development of a rubric to help guide these choices and inform the use of diverse literature in the classroom.

METHODS

Our goal as two children's literature professors at a Midwestern private university is to develop and field test a rubric to categorize children's literature according to the types of diversity, and to use this rubric in selecting and identifying diverse children's literature in classroom instruction. Previous classroom observations that we conducted demonstrated wide variations in the use of children's literature across elementary and middle school classrooms, and particular disparity in the selection and use of diverse children's literature in these classrooms. In specific, our hypothesis was that diverse children's literature is challenging to find in elementary and middle school classrooms. Further, we supposed that when diverse children's literature is present in classrooms, it is often simply present and not purposefully applied as an integral component to classroom instruction.

Building on the work of Duke (2000), who found that teachers devoted an average of only 3.6 minutes per day to nonfiction literature in classrooms, we hypothesize that a similar scenario occurs with diverse literature. We started to examine this critical problem by investigating what children's literature is utilized in classrooms that represent diversity (i.e., multicultural, gender, and ability), and what percentage of texts utilized in classroom instruction can be categorized as diverse. For the purposes of this chapter, we define diversity as any representation beyond the dominant culture of race, gender, or ability.

Our data collection and analysis revealed that before examining authentic uses of diverse literature in classrooms, we needed a tool to evaluate the literature in use. A review of existing tools demonstrated that we needed to develop a reliable and valid tool that we could apply in subsequent phases of our study and that teachers could use to identify and select diverse literature for their classrooms. The rubric development portion of this multi-phase research study, including identification and field-testing of the rubric categories, is the focus of this chapter.

In the pilot phase of the study, we followed an emergent process to identify classrooms for analysis. We visited three early and middle childhood classrooms jointly to participate in shared observations and collect observational data concerning the literature in use. We analyzed each data set to inform the selection of the next classroom to visit. Participants were purposefully selected for these classroom observations. We selected classrooms representing a range of community settings and degree to which children's literature was used as a part of daily classroom instruction. Our goal was to observe classrooms in urban, suburban, and private school contexts. Additionally, our goal was to observe teachers using children's literature daily in their instruction in order to be able to identify literature that would be considered diverse. Participants were not informed of the specific goal to analyze diverse children's literature until after the survey data was collected to ensure authentic responses.

Our classroom observations documented the literature the teachers read with their students, but our analysis of the data demonstrated a need for a systematic process to identify the books according to the range of diversity represented. We identified the need for a tool to categorize the diversity observed in the books the teachers utilized with their students. As this next section will detail, our process was iterative, as we reviewed books, developed categories, field-tested the categories, and applied the categories to a new round of books to continually test and refine the emerging categories (Strauss & Corbin, 1998).

RUBRIC DEVELOPMENT

The current rubric evolved from a recursive, iterative process in which we developed categories, field tested these categories with books and teachers, and revised the categories based on the results. The following section will describe this process of rubric development and refinement before discussing each of the current rubric categories in depth.

Following the initial classroom observations identifying the need for a tool, our first step in the rubric development involved gathering 30 recently published books, randomly selected by a librarian colleague who provided us with the 30 most recently added books to her collection. We read the books separately from each other, physically placing them on the floor from "most diverse" to "least diverse." This process quickly revealed the nuances inherent in this process, as a book's placement on the line was influenced by our own responses to the literature, and by the discussions we had with each other regarding the diversity we observed in the books. Sorting this way quickly proved to be unwieldy as books piled up at the ends and in the middle, and we struggled to capture the nuances of the books and our responses to them.

As we stood back and looked at the physical continuum line on the floor, we saw five major groupings of books. Thus, we assigned books to five categories, from "incidental diversity," in which a background character represented diversity but was not a part of the text, to books intentionally written to teach and represent diversity. This continuum ranged from a "one" at the lowest level of diversity represented, to a "five" at the highest level of diversity in the texts (Fig. 1).

As the questions surrounding diversity in books grew more and more complex, we identified the need for a level of interrater reliability concerning the continuum and how to apply it to books. We asked a graduate assistant in our department to apply the continuum to the list of books, then compared her ratings with ours. Her input helped us to further refine our categories and address the questions regarding what makes a book diverse.

These conversations led to a revision of the categories and format of the continuum. Four next step involved carefully creating and defining categories from the continuum into a rubric for evaluating diversity in books. Rather than placing books along a continuum, the categories helped us to identify the characteristics of books at each point, capturing the nuances and differences of the diversity in the books. For example, we came across books which did not represent any diversity at all, such as *Our Tree Named Steve* (Zweibel, 2005) which was given a "0," creating a new category we did not previously account for in the initial continuum. Books with a "0" became those with no diverse elements represented in the characters or with animals as the main characters representing no diversity.

Additionally, in our original five-point continuum, categories two, three, and four all contained similar characteristics. The five categories grew out of our original conception of a continuum line with multiple points along the line, but we discovered in applying the categories to the books that these

Fig. 1. Continuum of diversity in books. *Source*: Arnold and Sableski, 2017.

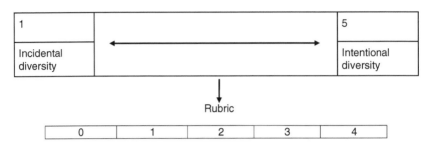

Fig. 2.   Revision and Reduction of Categories. *Source*: Arnold and Sableski, 2017.

middle categories were far too similar. Based on this constant comparative approach to the application of the categories, we chose to revise the content in the middle categories, changing our original numbering from a 1–5 scale to a 0–4 rubric. Fig. 2 represents this revision and reduction of the continuum categories into a rubric tool at this stage in the analysis.

CONTINUUM

With these newly developed categories, we proceeded to test the rubric in the field. We invited four classroom teacher participants to keep track of the books they read in their classrooms across four weeks of time. Each teacher maintained a document to keep track of the books they read each day in their classrooms.

Using these titles, we again refined our rubric categories. We found similar challenges using the 0–4–point rubric as with the previous continuum version due to the various types of diversity present in the books. The definition of "diversity" can be largely dependent on the stance of the reader, including background and purpose. One of the four teacher participants, for example, completed a "Christmas around the World" study with her class, so her book list included quite a few books focused on Christmas celebrations in different cultures. We immediately assigned books such as *Tree of Cranes* (Say, 2009) a score of 3 due to the diversity clearly represented in the text. However, when the book *The Night before Christmas* (Moore, 2011) came up in the list, we found ourselves wrestling with a seemingly nondiverse book because of the purpose for which it was used in the unit. This led to influential conversations with each other and with colleagues regarding what made a book diverse – is it the content or the purpose? If this book, which was the traditional representation of the story, were read to a group of African-American students in an urban setting, would it then be considered "diverse" since it represents the nondominant culture in that particular setting? Our conversations meandered through these challenging questions as we applied the categories of the rubric to more and more books. Table 1 summarizes the books we reviewed based on the classroom teachers' submissions.

Inter-rater reliability was accomplished in this process as we first categorized books individually, then shared these ratings with each other. We discussed any books we disagreed about initially, until we arrived at a consensus concerning the rubric category in which it belonged. Member checks further confirmed the descriptions of the books. After we categorized the books and developed initial rubric categories from this process, we shared the rubric with the teacher participants and asked them to categorize the books from the list they provided to us. We reviewed the rubric categories the teachers identified for the books, and again discussed any that were different from our original identification, changing selections or revising the rubric categories based on these conversations. Further, we asked two graduate assistants to read the books and assign them a rubric category, adding to the data for each book concerning the category to which it belonged. We aimed to not only identify rubric categories for the specific books, but to clearly define our rubric categories through this process. The conversations we had with each other, with the teacher participants, and with the graduate assistants, informed the refinement of the category descriptions and classification, based on the feedback from the iterative scoring process and member checking with the teacher participants.

We continued content analysis with field-testing in a local public library. Our librarian colleague pulled one hundred new picture book titles for us to have ready for our review with the rubric. As a group of three (the two authors and our graduate student) we independently scored the 100 books according to our 0 to 4 rubric. After we had worked through our scoring of

Table 1. Books Read in Classrooms by Teachers.

Total number of books			302
Number 4 Ratings	37	12%	Example: *Fish in a Tree* (Hunt, 2015)
Number 3 Ratings	49	16%	Example: *Monster* (Myers, 2004)
Number 2 Ratings	24	8%	Example: *The Legend of Old Befana (dePaola, 1980)*
Number 1 Ratings	32	11%	Example: *Indian in the Cupboard* (Banks, 1980)
Number 0 Ratings	160	53%	Example: *Tales of Fourth Grade Nothing* (Blume, 2002)

the titles we had a group discussion of our determinations. Books that we disagreed on were placed in their own independent pile. Once that pile had been identified, we went through each one to discuss our thoughts and differences in the score selection. Through this conversation, we recognized that our category 2 and category 3 examples were highly similar in terms of the diversity represented. Consequently, we adjusted the rubric to a 0 to 3 scale to make the distinctions more readily apparent. Table 2 illustrates the similarities of ratings in categories 2 and 3.

With the rubric categories developed, we purposefully selected 14 classrooms from the student teaching placements of the undergraduate students in our methods courses. We selected six Early Childhood, three Middle Childhood, and five Intervention Specialist student teaching placements. Each of these licensure sets were purposefully selected for variation in urban and suburban school settings (see Fig. 3). We obtained permission from the undergraduate student teachers and the cooperating teachers for their participation in this research study. Participants were not informed about the specific goal of analyzing diverse children's literature to ensure authentic selections of utilized literature. Student teachers documented the children's literature read in their classrooms using a weekly Google survey, and these data were analyzed for the rubric categories of the books.

The student teachers reported a total of 45 books read across their observations in the classroom. After we received the list of books from each student teacher, we chose to apply the rubric to the books ourselves, rather than asking the student teachers to apply the rubric. The student teachers did not receive any training on the rubric, and thus would not be reliable sources to apply the rubric to the books. As our purpose in this phase of data collection centered on refining the rubric categories to make them most applicable to books teachers use in classrooms, utilizing raters familiar with the rubric was

Table 2.   Reduction of Rubric Categories.

Total number of books vs. number of ratings	77	270	
Number 4 Ratings	33	12.2%	Example: *A Morning with Grandpa* (Liu, 2016)
Number 3 Ratings	13	4.8%	Example: *I Wonder: Celebrating Daddies Doin' Work* (Richards, 2016)*
Number 2 Ratings	17	6.3%	Example: *Cricket Song* (Hunter, 2016)
Number 1 Ratings	78	28.9%	Example: *Have You Seen Elephant?* (Barrow, 2016)
Number 0 Ratings	129	47.8%	Example: *Are We There Yet?* (Santat, 2016)

Source: Arnold and Sableski, 2017.

Setting: Urban v Suburban

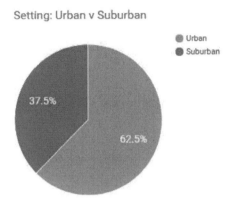

Fig. 3.   Student Teacher Participants. *Source*: Arnold and Sableski, 2017.

a critical component to the evaluation of the books. We (the two research-ers and the graduate assistant involved in the study) collectively discussed the books and came to consensus on the rubric categories they should be assigned.

When we applied the rubric to the books, we reported no rankings of "3," the most complex level of diversity, to any of the books. The highest percent-age of books read in the classrooms received a ranking of "0," indicating no observable diversity present in the books. The preliminary results these data point to in terms of the number of books of diversity not being read in classroom contexts will be discussed later in the chapter and is also the focus of the next phases of data collection and analysis for this study. In regards to the refinement of the rubric categories, these data provided us with insight in regards to the distinctions in each of the rubric categories. The collapsing of our previous level 2 and 3 categories into one level 2 category resulted in a greater level of difference in the rankings assigned across the four categories. Not only did this data provide us with a window into the results the rubric might reveal when applied in classroom contexts, it also provided us with confirmation that the more limited scale of the revised rubric more effectively identified the range of diversity present in books.

Building on this data set, we also wanted to understand how others would apply the revised categories. We continued field-testing the rubric at a "read-in" event, to which we invited undergraduates and area teachers to read recently published books, using the rubric to analyze the diversity in the books. We led a brief discussion at the beginning of the event, providing context to the rubric and explanation of the categories. We also explained

Table 3.   Books Read in Classrooms by Student Teachers.

Total number of books vs. number of ratings	45	45	
Number 3 Ratings	0	0%	
Number 2 Ratings	2	4.4%	Example: *Have You Filled a Bucket Today* (McCloud, 2006)
Number 1 Ratings	15	33.3%	Example: *The Recess Queen* (O'Neill, 2002)
Number 0 Ratings	28	62.2%	Example: *No, David* (Shannon, 1998)

that we wanted the participants to apply the rubric to the books they read throughout the event.

Participants kept track of the books they read and assigned them a rubric category, and we collected these tally sheets at the end of the event. These data were analyzed through counting the rubric responses and calculating percentages of books ranked at the various rubric categories. This analysis further informed the development of the rubric categories, as our categories one and two received equal numbers of rankings. Though we previously collapsed these middle rubric categories from three (categories 1, 2, 3 in the previous rubric) to two (categories 1 and 2 in the revised rubric), these responses indicated a continued clustering of responses around the middle rubric categories. We chose not to collapse the rubric categories any further because as the descriptions of each category will demonstrate in the next section, these middle categories describe critical nuances in the diversity of the texts. Continued field-testing is warranted; however, our initial analysis of the equal numbers across levels 1 and 2 is that this points to the types of texts available to teachers in classrooms, rather than a confusion over the meaning of the categories. The example texts listed with each category demonstrate the distinct differences in the categories. *Excellent Ed* by Stacy McAnulty (2016) is an animal text with no human categories to represent diversity, while *One Word from Sophia* by Jim Averbeck (2015) is a picture book with diverse characters present in the book, but not central to the story. These data also informed our understanding of how and if teachers select diverse children's literature, which will be discussed later in this chapter.

Throughout all phases of the study, data analysis recursively influenced further refinement of the rubric categories, reflecting the constant comparative process of our data analysis. We aimed to have a well-developed rubric to impact the amount of diverse literature that is utilized as an integral component to classroom instruction. In the following section, we will discuss each

Table 4. Read-in Rubric Ratings.

Total number of books vs. number of ratings	224	768	
Number 3 Ratings	248	32.3%	Example: *Freedom Over Me* (Bryan, 2016)
Number 2 Ratings	167	21.7%	Example: *One Word from Sophia* (Averbeck, 2015)
Number 1 Ratings	167	21.7%	Example: *Excellent Ed* (McAnulty, 2016)
Number 0 Ratings	186	24.2%	Example: *Grumpy Pants* (Messer, 2016)

of the current rubric categories in detail. These categories arose out of the field-testing we completed with the rubric, resulting in the refinement of the categories from five to the current four rubric categories.

RUBRIC CATEGORIES

As the previous section illustrated, our rubric developed over time and through a constant comparative process. Through this process, four categories emerged that we will now discuss with exemplars for each. See Table 5 for the developed rubric.

We developed the rubric to incorporate a category, descriptive characteristics, a nonfiction example, and a fiction example to help users identify the continuum that builds in the rubric as well as anchor texts that could help clarify the difference between ratings. Throughout this process, we continue to debate the "category" for each book. Many books could go across different categories based on the viewer's set of experiences, understanding of the book, and most importantly personal lens in which he or she reads the text. However, our developed rubric attempts to bring attention to how diversity is or is not represented in any given text.

A book that obtains a category of 0 is a book in which no diversity is represented at all. Books in this category may incorporate animals as the main characters. The book would not contain characters who represent diversity. An example of children's nonfiction literature from this category might be *The Iridescence of Birds: A Book about Henri Matisse* (MacLachlan, 2014). This nonfiction piece is a representation of the life and work of the artist Henri Matisse and could be utilized for multiple instructive and enjoyment purposes. However, there is no diversity represented in the text or in the illustrations. Another example can be found in *Sam and Dave Dig a*

Table 5. Rubric.

Rating	0	1	2	3
Characteristics	There is no diversity represented at all. Books in this category often have animals as the main characters, or contain only characters who are from the dominant culture.	In this category, diverse characters may be present but are highly limited in scope and incidental. Diverse characters may be present in the background but are not main or supporting characters. There is no mention of the diverse nature of the characters nor do they "stand out" or have any role other than to be present in the text.	A book rated at a two would have diversity as part of the story or part of the central theme. However, the distinction of a level two book is that the book could stand on its own without consideration of the diversity context. The book has cultural overtones that lend themselves to the story.	Books in this category intentionally and explicitly display a theme of diversity. The author's goal is to provide information or background experiences about diversity. These books cannot be read without considering the theme of diversity throughout the text.
Nonfiction Example	*The Iridescence of Birds: A Book about Henri Matisse* (MacLachlan, 2014)	*Too Hot, Too Cold* (Arnold, 2013)	*Viva Frida* (Morales, 2014) *Drowned City: Hurricane Katrina and New Orleans* (Brown, 2015)	*The Price of Freedom* (Fradin & Fradin, 2013)
Fiction Example	*Our Tree Named Steve* (Zweibel, 2007)	*One Word from Sophia* (Averbeck, 2015)	*The Rough Faced Girl* (Marin, 1998); *This is the Rope* (Woodson, 2013)	*Last Stop on Market Street* (de la Pena, 2015)

Source: Arnold and Sableski, 2017.

Hole (Barnett, 2014). Again, this Caldecott Honor award-winning book, is another example of a high-quality piece of literature that does not necessarily represent diversity.

The category of 1 in our rubric incorporates books that have diverse characters that may be present but are highly limited in scope and may be considered more incidental than central to the story. Diverse characters may be present in the background but are not main or supporting characters. In a category 2 book, there is little mention or representation of any diverse nature of the characters nor do they "stand out" or have any role other than to be present in the text. For example, in the nonfiction book *Too Hot, Too Cold* (Arnold, 2013), there are minimal characters that represent diversity in the background of the illustrations, but they have no real inclusion in the text. A fiction example for this category resides in the Harry Potter series (Rowling, 1999–2009). All of the main characters in the Harry Potter series are depicted as Caucasian characters, with only one or two characters "in the background" representing any diversity.

As we move along the rubric continuum, a book in category 2 would now have diverse characters as part of the central theme of the book. The diverse character might not be a main or supporting character, but is an important element to the story and/or illustrations.

However, the distinction of a level two book is that the book could stand on its own without consideration of the diversity context. A category 2 book tends to have cultural overtones that lend themselves to the story. For example, we placed *Drowned City: Hurricane Katrina and New Orleans* (Brown, 2015) as a category 2 example nonfiction text as it is about how Hurricane Katrina affected the city and people of New Orleans. Diversity is present in the illustrations and in the themes present in the text regarding the ways in which the hurricane differentially affected people of the city. As we discussed this book with colleagues, there were multiple debates about the intent of the diversity in this book. However, after reading and discussing the book several times, we decided that the primary intent of the book was not to communicate a message of diversity, thus it was placed in category 2.

Finally, a category 3 book intentionally and explicitly display a theme of diversity. The author's goal is to provide information or background experiences about diversity. These books cannot be read without considering the theme of diversity throughout the text. For example, *Because They Marched: The People's Campaign for Voting Rights That Changed America* (Freedman, 2015) intentionally communicates information about an event in history directly related to diversity. Therefore, it was placed at the farthest end of the spectrum with books that were "most diverse" in their characters, illustrations, or themes. Additionally, *Last Stop on Market Street* (de la Peña, 2015) is another example of a book that could be placed in the category 3. Throughout the illustrations and text, this book exemplifies a diverse culture and a diverse story meant to share a universal theme of appreciation and respect.

DISCUSSION

The rubric shared in this chapter is the result of multiple rounds of data collection and analysis to refine the categories to reflect the diversity present in children's literature. The creation of this rubric grew out of our observations of classroom instruction and the lack of diverse literature. Throughout this process, we wrestled with the challenging task of capturing the nuanced presence of diversity in children's literature. However, this rubric holds promise when applied to classroom contexts as a method of identifying and selecting books of diversity to use meaningfully in classroom instruction.

Our field-testing of the rubric in classroom contexts revealed intriguing trends in classroom literature selections that warrant further study. First, reader stance influences the perceived diversity in some texts. Our rubric identified categories at opposite ends of the spectrum that are readily apparent to readers, including a "0," with no diversity present, to a "3," in which diversity is an integral component to the text. The categories in the middle, however, present increased opportunities for nuance and interpretation. We engaged in multiple debates and lively discussions concerning books in which the diversity was not as readily identifiable, and much of the varied responses came from a difference in reader stance. Each and every one of us reads a book with our own individual lens and understanding of diversity. Throughout our work developing, field testing and using this rubric we kept in mind the impact of our lens as Caucasian, middle class women on this work. Our own experiences, as well as our data collection process, demonstrated the influence of reader stance on the perceived diversity of a text.

Another nuanced component that influences the application of the rubric to books includes definitions of diversity. Similar to reader stance, the definition of diversity can be influenced by multiple factors outside the book. For example, when evaluating books with input from multiple perspectives, we found individual experiences and contexts influenced what some saw as diversity and what others did not. For example, one of the books read by a teacher was a Patricia Polacco (1998) story, *Thank You, Mr. Falker*. Our team held a lengthy discussion about this text as though it depicts predominantly Caucasian characters, the main character is struggling to learn to read. Some readers may utilize their background knowledge and experiences to infer that the main character may have dyslexia and thus be seen as a character with a diverse learning context. Others may see it "simply" as a story about a young girl challenged by learning to read.

Current award winners in children's literature represent across diverse populations, including African-Americans, LGBTQ, people with disabilities, Mexican-Americans, as examples. We wrestled with the differences between identifying a text as "multicultural" versus "diverse." Our goal is to identify diverse books, rather than multicultural books, as diversity implies a range of representation in differing ways and forms. We aim to identify books that represent people beyond the dominant, majority culture, but not limited to minority or racially diverse cultures alone. This goal is in line with the primary objective of the larger study of which the rubric development is one component of a broader goal which aims to identify how teachers select and intentionally utilize books in their classrooms that provide both windows and mirrors (Bishop, 1990) for their students to see within and beyond themselves in the books they read. Defining diversity beyond multiculturalism is in line with the categories included in our rubric, based on field-testing and participant input.

The purpose of the text also influences the rubric category a book is assigned and is an important consideration when applying the rubric to classroom contexts. In our field-testing, we came across the situation in which a classroom teacher selected multicultural texts to use in a study of world cultures at Christmas time, and this purpose influenced the reader perceptions of how diverse the texts were in this context. Our rubric does not include consideration of context and purpose in the evaluation of books, as it is intended to be used to evaluate the diversity within the books themselves, and not within the context in which they are read. We do not see the rubric as a tool to only categorize books for the sake of categorization; rather, we hope that it will become a tool to inspire discussion and conversation regarding what constitutes diversity in books and the role this plays in classrooms. Given this goal, the role of purpose in evaluating diversity becomes an important consideration within the discussion of applying the rubric categories to books.

Our rubric also does not include a consideration of whether or not the books are of quality, in terms of the literary elements and integration of illustrations with the text. Books are assigned categories based on the observed diversity in the text, not based on literary merit. Thus, caution should be applied when teachers select books for classroom use that they are of both relatively high literary merit, as well as representative of a wide range of diversity. During our time in classrooms, we notice a mixture of high quality, recently published books, along with books with older publication dates and of weaker quality. As teachers work to select books of diversity to use in their classrooms, they will need to balance these choices from the selections available to them in libraries and from book publishers. The representation of diversity in published books is an identified concern in the field (CCBC, 2015), with movements such as *We Need Diverse Books* advocating for greater availability of high quality, diverse texts from publishers. As teachers work to select books of both quality and diversity for use in their classrooms, this rubric can be one source of consideration for the books they use in their instruction.

Following the research of Duke (2000) in which she identified the lack and utilization of nonfiction texts in primary classrooms, we started this journey to see what texts were seen and utilized in classrooms. However, we quickly identified our need for a tool to support a grounded identification of diverse texts. Though we realized we did not physically "see it," we knew we needed a tool to help "name it." Through this process and the development of the rubric, we hope to help teachers move along their own continuum of consciously seeing it to heuristically incorporating it.

In sum, the rubric shared in this chapter is intended to facilitate conversation with colleagues regarding diverse literature and its use in classroom instruction. The stance of the reader, the purpose of the text in the classroom, the definition of diversity at work, and considerations of quality will all come together to influence the "rating" a book receives from a rubric user. We emphasize that the category assigned to a book is less important than the conversations that occur around these issues in consideration of how and why the book might be used in the classroom.

LIMITATIONS AND POSSIBILITIES

This rubric presents a multitude of possibilities for classroom teachers to re-consider the availability and use of books of diversity in their classroom instruction. With these possibilities, however, come several limitations to its application in classrooms. In addition, the factors lend themselves to several steps for future research.

This chapter discussed the nuances inherent in the discussion of diversity in children's literature. The categories in the rubric are not firm and rigid, but are influenced by the multiple factors discussed previously, such as reader stance and purpose of the book. The rubric categories, therefore, are not intended to be generalized across settings or even from user to user. Colleagues in the same school would very likely assign different ratings to the same book, which facilitates conversations about the reasons for the rating and what this means for classroom instruction. Thus, although the limited generalizability of the rubric categories is an identified limitation of the study, it also leads to multiple possibilities in the conversations it inspires.

This inherent nuance leads to the need for increased field-testing of the rubric to better understand its application in classroom contexts. The rubric changed significantly from our first conceptions of it as a continuum from 1 to 5, to the current 0, 1, 2, 3 rubric as it stands in this chapter. Our understanding of how diversity is both viewed in books, and how this translates into classroom applications of children's literature was significantly influenced by the contributions of the classroom teacher and student teacher participants who supplied book titles and applied the rubric to these titles. We plan to increase our field-testing of the rubric, inviting the responses of an increased number of participants across settings to achieve a "crowd-sourced" evaluation of the rubric categories. This will increase the validity of the rubric and its reliability across contexts.

Finally, we began this study with the goal of understanding how teachers used diverse literature in their classroom instruction, and we maintain that goal now that we have a rubric we can use in our observations. The rubric is not a tool to evaluate and categorize books, but a tool to understand diversity in children's literature and consider its use in instructional contexts. Further, our goal is not to survey classroom libraries for the availability of diverse books, but to offer insights into how the diverse books are or are not being used within instruction. If this rubric does not get applied into classroom contexts with practicing teachers, it will be limited in its scope and possibilities. Our next steps involve application of the rubric into classroom contexts to understand how diverse literature is used in classrooms, and to impact the book selections of classroom teachers seeking to include books representing diverse groups in their classroom libraries and instructional contexts.

CONCLUSION

The vignette shared at the beginning of this chapter illustrates the need for the rubric to guide the selection choices of teachers as they consider literature for use in their classrooms. Though we do not see this rubric as an evaluative tool for diverse children's literature, it is intended as an impetus for conversation and collaboration around the use of diverse literature. Teachers balance multiple factors as they select literature for instruction, and the rubric places diversity as a central consideration to reflect the multiple perspectives present in both classrooms and in the larger communities of which students are a part beyond their classroom doors. Our teacher from the vignette can theoretically use the rubric to guide the recommendations she provides to her students, pushing them beyond the books of her childhood and helping them to find books in which they can see themselves, as well as see beyond themselves to the diversity they will encounter throughout their lives.

REFERENCES

Bishop, R. S. (1990). Mirrors, windows, and sliding glass doors. *Perspectives*, *6*(3), ix–xi.

Boyd, F. B., Causey, L. L., & Galda, L. (2015). Culturally diverse literature. *The Reading Teacher*, *68*(5), 378–387.

Brinson, S. (2012). Knowledge of multicultural literature among early childhood educators. *Multicultural Education*, *19*(2), 30–33.

Cooperative Children's Book Center. (2015). Children's books by and about people of color and First/Native nations published in the United States. Retrieved from https://ccbc.education.wisc.edu/books/pcstats.asp

DeNicolo, C. P., & Franquiz, M. E. (2006). "Do I have to say it?": Critical encounters with multicultural children's literature. *Language Arts*, *84*(2), 157–170.

Duke, N. K. (2000). 3.6 minutes per day: The scarcity of informational texts in first grade. *Reading Research Quarterly*, *35*(2), 202–224

Gibson, K. (2012). Influences on diversity in teacher education: Using literature to promote multiple perspectives and cultural relevance. *International Journal for the Scholarship of Teaching and Learning*, *6*(1), 1–14.

Iwai, Y. (2013). Multicultural children's literature and teacher candidates' awareness and attitudes toward cultural diversity. *International Electronic Journal of Elementary Education*, *5*(2), 185.

Larrick, N. (1965). The all-white world of children's books. *Saturday Review*, *48*(11), 63–65.

Johnson, H., Mathis, J., & Short, K. (2016). *Reframing perspective: Critical content analysis of children's and young adult literature*. New York, NY: Routledge.

Koss, M. D., Martinez, M., & Johnson, N. J. (2016). Meeting characters in Caldecotts: What does this mean for today's readers? *The Reading Teacher*, *70*(1), 19–28.

Morton, J. K., Siera, M., Grant, K. L., & Giese, B. (2008). Confronting dispositions towards diversity through children's literature. *Southeastern Teacher Education Journal*, *1*(1), 67–76.

Short, K. (2015). *A curriculum that is intercultural*. Paper presented at the Annual Meeting of the National Council of Teachers of English, Minneapolis, MN.

Smith-D'Arezzo, W. M. (2003). Diversity in children's literature: Not just a black and white issue. *Children's Literature in Education*, *34*(1), 75–94.

Strauss, A., & Corbin, J. (1998). Basics of qualitative research: Procedures and techniques for developing grounded theory. Thousand Oaks, CA: Sage.

Tschida, C. M., Ryan, C. L., & Ticknor, A. S. (2014). Building on windows and mirrors: Encouraging the disruption of "single stories" through children's literature. *Journal of Children's Literature, 40*(1), 28–39.

Yokota, J. (1993). Issues in selecting multicultural children's literature. *Language Arts, 70*(3), 156–167.

CHILDREN'S LITERATURE CITED

Arnold, C. (2013). *Too hot? Too cold?: Keeping body temperature just right.* Watertown, MA: Charlesbridge.

Averbeck, J., & Ismail, Y. (2015). *One word from Sophia.* New York: Atheneum Books for Young Readers.

Banks, L. R. (1981). *The Indian in the cupboard.* New York: Doubleday.

Barnett, M., & Klassen, J. (2014). *Sam & Dave dig a hole.* Somerville, MA: Candlewick Press.

Barrow, D. (2016). *Have you seen elephant?* Wellington, New Zealand: Gecko Press.

Blume, J. (2002). *Tales of a fourth grade nothing.* New York: Dutton Children's Books.

Brown, D. (2015). *Drowned city: Hurricane Katrina and New Orleans.* Boston: Houghton. Mifflin Harcourt.

Bryan, A. (2016). *Freedom over me: Eleven slaves, their lives and dreams brought to life.* New York: Atheneum Books for Young Readers.

de la Peña, M. (2015). *Last stop on market street.* New York: G.P. Putnam's Sons.

DePaola, T. (1980). *The legend of old Befana: An Italian Christmas story.* New York: Harcourt Brace Jovanich.

Fradin, J. B., & Fradin, D. B. (2013). *The price of freedom: How one town stood up to slavery.* New York: Walker Books for Young Readers.

Freedman, R. (2014). *Because they marched: The people's campaign for voting rights that changed America.* New York: Holiday House.

Hunt, L. M. (2015). *Fish in a tree.* New York: Nancy Paulsen Books, Penguin Group.

Hunter, A. (2016). *Cricket song.* New York: Houghton Mifflin Harcourt.

Liu, S. (2016). *A morning with grandpa.* New York: Lee & Low Books Inc.

MacLachlan, P., & Hooper, H. (2014). *The iridescence of birds: A book about Henri Matisse.* New York: Roaring Brook Press.

Martin, A. (1987). *Boy-crazy Stacey.* New York: Scholastic, Inc.

Martin, A. (1987). *Mary Anne saves the day.* New York: Scholastic, Inc.

Martin, R. (1998). *The rough-faced girl.* St. Louis, MO: Turtleback Books.

McAnulty, S. (2016). *Excellent ed.* New York: Random House Children's Books.

McCloud, C. (2012). *Have you filled a bucket today? A guide to daily happiness for kids.* Northville, MI: Ferne Press.

Messer, C. (2016). *Grumpy pants.* Chicago, IL: Albert Whitman & Company.

Moore, C. C. (2011). *The night before Christmas.* New York, NY: HarperCollins Publishers.

Morales, Y. (2014). *Viva frida!* New York: Roaring Brook Press.

O'Neill, A. (2002). *The recess queen.* New York: Scholastic.

Polacco, P. (1998). *Thank you, Mr. Falker.* New York: Philomel Books.

Richards, D. (2016). *I wonder: Celebrating daddies doin' work*. New York: Feiwel and Friends.

Rowling, J. K. (1999–2009). *Harry Potter* series. New York: Scholastic, Inc.

Santat, D. (2016). *Are we there yet?* Boston: Little, Brown and Company.

Say, A. (2009). *Tree of cranes*. Boston, MA: Houghton Mifflin Harcourt.

Shannon, D. (1998). *No, David!*. New York: Blue Sky Press.

Sims, G. A. (2015). *Monster: A graphic novel*. New York: Harper Collins Publisher.

Woodson, J. (2013). *This is the rope: A story from the Great Migration*. New York: Nancy Paulsen Books.

Zweibel, A., & Catrow, D. (2005). *Our tree named Steve*. New York: G.P. Putnam's Sons.

ADDRESSING DIVERSITY THROUGH THE UNIVERSAL DESIGN FOR LEARNING LENS

Jodi Louise Pilgrim and Angela Kris Ward

ABSTRACT

The purpose of this chapter is to describe the Universal Design for Learning (UDL) framework and explore ways UDL decreases potential barriers for diverse students while increasing opportunities to learn. The sociocultural theory of Lev Vygotsky (1978) serves as a theoretical framework for UDL. Vygotsky (1978) placed much emphasis on the role of the social interaction in the development of cognition stating, "Every function in the child's cultural development appears twice: first, on the social level, and later, on the individual level" (Vygotsky, 1978, p. 57). Additionally, he focused considerable attention on language and private speech. The ability to express oneself in any environment, particularly the classroom, is critical to intellectual development. Another pivotal concept is that of the Zone of Proximal Development (ZPD), which reflects the point between what a child has previously learned and can complete independently and that which they cannot do, even with supports. Our intent was to use student examples, or case studies, of typical diversity in the

Addressing Diversity in Literacy Instruction
Literacy Research, Practice and Evaluation, Volume 8, 229–249
Copyright © 2018 by Emerald Publishing Limited
All rights of reproduction in any form reserved
ISSN: 2048-0458/doi:10.1108/S2048-045820170000008011

classroom, to demonstrate the application of UDL principles. Specifically, we provide ways planning for representation of material, expression of material, and engagement in material, which can benefit all learners. The case study examples demonstrate ways effective planning can benefit learners in many areas. The case studies presented in this chapter reflect a small portion of the diverse population in classrooms across the nation. Yet the case studies demonstrate ways planning can incorporate students "in the margin" while at the same time benefitting all students in the classroom. Addressing diversity through the UDL lens helps teachers accommodate individual differences through intentional instructional design, while at the same time providing resources for all students in the classroom.

Keywords: Universal Design for Learning; curriculum planning; representation; expression; engagement

Classrooms are increasingly diverse, presenting a host of challenges and opportunities for educators. A challenge for educators is to provide learning opportunities in the general-education curriculum that are inclusive and effective for all students (Ralabate, 2011). Universal Design for Learning (UDL) leads contemporary efforts to create universal access to educational curricula for *all* students, including those with learning challenges. *Universal* implies the intentional integration of teaching and learning that meets the needs of different kinds of learners (Rose & Meyer, 2006). Regardless of behavior, learning style, background, culture, gender, physical difficulties, or cognitive diversity, all students deserve quality instruction. UDL is achieved when teachers present information through various formats, provide instruction, and assessments that work for diverse learners, and encourage motivation and engagement with content.

Even if you are not familiar with the term "UDL," you have probably seen its principles in action. For example, building accessibility, such as elevator and escalators, reflects Universal Design. Public streets and stoplights reflect intentional design for the deaf, blinds, and disabled. Digital information, especially online coursework, reflects UDL, as careful consideration should be given to how content is presented to all learners, with and without disabilities. Many university professors and students may recognize this effort to improve learning management systems for online courses as "Quality Matters," a process used to examine the quality of online courses. The Quality Matters (QM) standards incorporate the principles of UDL (Frey, Kearns, & King, 2012). UDL is an increasingly hot topic, with a presence in the Every

Students Succeeds Act (2015) and in the newly revised National Educational Technology Plan (2016). A variety of materials, especially technology tools, enables teachers to support learners in new and exciting ways. This chapter describes the UDL framework and how it decreases potential barriers to reading and learning while increasing opportunities to learn (Ralabate, 2011). Our goal is to help educators understand UDL so they may design instruction that meets the needs of all learners.

UNIVERSAL DESIGN FOR LEARNING

Creating an inclusive environment for learners should be a priority for classroom instruction. "Unfortunately, the typical curriculum – usually centered on printed materials – is designed for a homogeneous group of students" (Ralabate, 2011, para 4). This curriculum design lacks flexibility and places the burden on learners to adapt to curricula. In addition, this design requires that educators create modified materials adapted to the needs of each student. How can educators provide learning opportunities in the general-education curriculum that are inclusive and effective for *all* students? UDL improves this difficult situation by placing the burden of change on the curriculum itself (Higher Education Opportunity Act of 2008). The UDL model promotes effective design and a flexible, responsive curriculum, where there are options for how information is presented, how students demonstrate knowledge and skills, and how students engage in learning. The application of UDL affords opportunities for all students to access, participate in, and progress in the general-education curriculum by reducing barriers to instruction (Ralabate, 2011).

UDL Origin

The philosophy of UDL evolved from architectural design. The term "universal design" was coined by Ron Mace at the Center for Universal Design at North Carolina State University (Center for Applied Special Technology [CAST], 2011; Rose & Meyer, 2002). Mace and his colleagues defined universal design (UD) as "the design of products and environments to be usable by all people, to the greatest extent possible, without the need for adaptation or specialized design" (Center for Universal Design, 1997, para 1). The Americans with Disabilities Act (1990), UD gained popularity with architects and designers working to make public buildings and city streets accessible to all.

In recent years, the UD philosophy has entered the field of education. The UD philosophy inspired the founders of the CAST to collaborate with schools to adapt print-based curricula (Rose & Meyer, 2002). Where the goal of UD is the removal of barriers from the physical environment, the goal of UDL is the elimination of barriers from the learning environment. CAST applied the concept of UD to a framework for curriculum reform in education to provide flexibility in curriculum so that the diversity of learners found in today's schools would have access and opportunity to learning that would meet individual needs (Rose & Meyer, 2002). CAST realized the focus need not be on the problems of the students, but the problems with the curriculum (Meyer, Rose, & Gordon, 2014). Therefore, Meyer et al. (2014) defined curriculum as the "learning goals, the means of assessment, the teaching methods, and the materials" (p. 3) and promoted a UDL framework to improve classroom instruction.

UDL Policy

Prior to the conception of UDL, legislation began to address ways to support all learners. For example, in 1973, the implementation of Section 504 of the Americans with Disabilities Law, as well as P.L 94-142 (which later became known as the Individuals with Disabilities Act, IDEA, and reauthorized in 2004), required that children with disabilities gain access to the "least restrictive environment." To the maximum extent appropriate, children with disabilities should be educated in the general education classroom. In order to accomplish this task, the use of supplementary aids and services is appropriate including technology that utilizes print to voice, voice to print, enlarged print, color-coded print and/or background, and numerous other strategies that would allow the child to gain access to the general curriculum and the least restrictive environment. These supplementary aids and services provide greater access to the general curriculum for all students and later became principles of UDL.

No Child Left Behind (NCLB), passed into law in 2001, ensured "all children have a fair, equal, and significant opportunity to obtain a high-quality" education. (20 U.S.C. § 6301). NCLB reflected general education law while IDEA reflected special education law, both laws sharing goals regarding high expectations for students and teachers with the implied expectation that opportunities are present for students to meet standards. UDL design recognizes the needs of individual students and provides a means to an end. Referenced numerous times throughout the new Every Student Succeeds Act

(ESSA) bill (2015), ESSA legislation encourages states to design assessments using UDL principles, to award grants to local education agencies who use UDL, and to adopt technology that aligns with UDL.

UDL Framework

The sociocultural theory of Lev Vygotsky (1978) serves as a theoretical framework for UDL. Vygotsky (1978) placed much emphasis on the role of the social interaction in the development of cognition stating, "Every function in the child's cultural development appears twice: first, on the social level, and later, on the individual level" (Vygotsky, 1978, p. 57). Additionally, he focused considerable attention on language. The ability to express oneself in any environment, particularly the classroom, is critical to intellectual development. Another pivotal concept is that of the Zone of Proximal Development (ZPD). ZPD represents the area of learning where scaffolding of new information is provided. Scaffolding involves interaction between a learner and another person more knowledgeable who can support the learning process by providing necessary assistance until the child can complete the task independently. UDL utilizes a similar framework, building on the foundations of scaffolded learning.

UDL provides scaffolds for learners during the planning stage of instruction, when selecting materials, and using appropriate assessments. "UDL represents a shift in how we look at learner differences. It emphasizes the need for curriculum that can adapt to student needs rather than require adaptation from the learners" (Coyne, Ganley, Hall, Meo, Murray, & Gornan, 2007, p. 2). Through UDL, teachers maximize student engagement and opportunities for learning by intentionally planning lessons and assessing learning to meet the needs of all students (Coyne, Pisha, Dalton, Zeph, & Smith, 2013). Teachers who use UDL principles consider children in the margins when they plan resulting in learning for all children.

An inclusive education requires consideration of all components of learning. The UDL framework addresses the recognition, strategic, and affective network of learning in the brain and provides principles for effective utilization. The recognition network is referred to as the *what* of instruction and aligns with the first UDL principle, Multiple Means of Representation, where instructors identify and plan various ways to represent material, recognizing the need for the learners in the margins as they plan. The strategic network reflects the *how* of learning, which aligns with UDL principle two, multiple means of engagement, where instructors provide options for action and expression. Consider the learner who has low muscle tone and struggles writing, though cognitively is capable of producing standard expectations. Traditionally, the instructor may determine to reduce the amount of written work required of the learner. However, using UDL principles, the instructor would offer an alternative method for action and expression. The affective network of learning includes the *why* of learning and aligns with UDL principle three, Multiple Means of Engagement, where instructors plan lessons that engage learners (Smith, Polloway, Patton, & Dowdy, 2012). Engagement may occur when the learner has a means to maintain self-control, can self-monitor, or attaches meaning to the lesson. Instructors meet the learning needs of all students by offering multiple methods of instruction, allowing for alternative ways to demonstrate learning, and engaging students in the process. As a result, all learners, including those in the margins, have the greatest opportunity for success.

UDL and Technology Tools

Where technology exists, technology tools alleviate barriers to learning by allowing "alternatives to 'one-size-fits-all' academic materials that used only one fixed medium – print" (Ralabate, 2011, para. 8). Technology has the potential to be a game changer for students who rarely experience success in school due to print barriers. Research related to UDL has focused on the integration of technology and instruction to create customized experiences, which scaffold learning for students with diverse needs (Coyne et al., 2013). Increased technology in schools enables educators and students to manipulate text and media through assistive technologies for flexible instructional options (Ralabate, 2011). Therefore, technology plays an important role in UDL. For example, technology tools enable teachers to enlarge, simplify, highlight, translate, convert (speech to text, text to speech), or summarize text. Most technology applications included in this chapter are available at no cost.

THE APPLICATION OF UDL PRINCIPLES

UDL is not a set or packaged curriculum. It is an "educational process that weaves itself throughout a school" (Samuels, 2016, para. 12). Supporters of UDL believe the process has enormous potential for learners with diverse needs because it eliminates or reduces barriers to academic success. To eliminate

Table 1. UDL Principles for Planning and Application.

UDL Principle	Explanation	Application	Examples
Representation (The *What* of Learning)	Learners differ in the ways they perceive and comprehend information, so teachers apply *representation* in design by consulting a variety of ways to reach all learners.	– Present information using different modalities (vision, hearing, touch) – Format instruction to allow adjustments by the user (i.e., ability to enlarge print, amplify sound)	ebooks Listen to audio Text to speech Multimedia glossary Language translation tools Google Doc (speech to text option) Newsela
Expression (The *How* of Learning)	Learners differ in the ways they best demonstrate knowledge and understanding, so teachers apply *expression* by allowing options and choice for all learners.	– Provide opportunities for assignments to be completed using various formats, tools, and modes of communication (visual, auditory, etc.)	Pencil, stylus, mouse Choice of tools – writing, e-book, podcast Support tools – spell-checkers, speech to text (Dragon Dictation)
Engagement (The *Why* of learning)	Learners differ in ways in which they can be motivated to learn, so teachers apply *engagement* by considering neurology, culture, personal relevance, collaborative preferences, and background knowledge.	– Provide an external learning environment that provides options and supports various learners. – Encourage intrinsic motivation by addressing self-regulation.	Real-world, authentic tasks Flexible grouping Collaboration via Google Drive Games, simulations, interactives Experiments Community Projects Arts

Source: Jodi Pilgrim, 2017.

barriers, UDL applies the three learning networks previously described (recognition network, strategic network, and affective network). Table 1 presents examples of options for these UDL principles.

ESSA (2015) calls for states to create plans for comprehensive literacy instruction and to incorporate UDL principles in those plans. This section of the chapter includes case study examples of diverse students and ways intentional design for learning impacts literacy instruction. Four case studies are presented: an English Learner, a learner with autism, a student with a significant cognitive disability, and a learner with dyslexia. Each case study will use the UDL framework to provide ways teachers may provide multiple means of representation, multiple means of expression, and multiple means of engagement. Teachers must realize that planning to address the needs of the learners in the margins by providing multiple means of representation, expression, and engagement does not mean they will plan multiple lessons. The UDL model is a framework for teachers to be intentional about how to teach all students. When needs are addressed prior to instruction, minor adjustments can be planned so all students can learn.

Case 1: Maria

Maria is a third grader who has been in the United States for about one year. The language spoken at home is Spanish. She is a beginning English Learner in all areas of language proficiency – speaking, listening, reading, and writing. Maria is a social child and enjoys engaging with her peers. She especially enjoys recess and PE. The principles of UDL presented highlight ways a teacher can intentionally design instruction to encompass students like Maria who lack language proficiency but need grade-level instruction in order to learn content.

Multiple Means of Representation

The learning goals of English Learners (ELs) extend beyond that of content knowledge. Maria is a beginning language learner in the areas of speaking, listening, reading, and writing; therefore, she needs scaffolding in these areas. There are many ways to represent information in the classroom to meet the needs of all students. Maria and others may struggle with print barriers. Efforts to remove this barrier may include strategies that make daily language accessible in the classroom as well as instructional strategies Maria can use to access language.

As we consider making language accessible in the classroom, imagine a regular classroom with additional features to make learning accessible for all learners. Many technology tools enhance a teacher's ability to support language learners as they struggle with print and vocabulary. For example, a typical second-grade classroom includes a word wall, where students can access sight words and other vocabulary words they have encountered. The word wall may be made more accessible through the use of QR codes with auditory features. Websites like vocaroo.com enable teachers to create QR codes for the word that can be scanned to produce the pronunciation of the word and even the definition if desired. Many teachers label classrooms for ELs. Labeling the classroom could include a bar code with additional information for learners with barriers to print. Providing students with access to tools such as language translators may enhance the ELs' daily experience in school. Further instructional enhancement may occur with Jordan's teacher uses QR codes next to test questions so Maria can listen to a question as many times as needed.

Maria's reading proficiency is below grade level (beginning). Maria would benefit from leveled reading that aligns with the third-grade curriculum. Resources like Newslela (Newsela.com) enable teachers to find appropriate nonfiction texts to use with a classroom of diverse learners (Arabo, Budd, Garrison, & Pacheco, 2017). Newsela is an educational website focused on building student-reading comprehension by providing high-quality news articles for elementary and secondary students. The site, used by more than six million students across the U.S., offers both a free version and a paid version (Arabo et al., 2017). The free version includes current news articles, historical documents and texts, and student assessment features. The use of Newsela as a way to *represent* information for all learners is that it reflects adaptive text, with each article accessible at five Lexile (reading) levels. The original article has the highest Lexile level, and revised versions of the article are available for different grade levels, using a Lexile conversion chart available on the Newsela website. Other features of Newsela include annotation tools and articles translated into Spanish.

Many ELs rely on visual scaffolds to help them gain meaning from the environment or from text (TEA, 2015). When applying the principles of UDL, teachers may intentionally design instruction to include visual scaffolds for *all* of their students. An example of visual scaffolds may include the use of images during instruction. The use of video to support content may help provide a context and background knowledge for Maria and the other students. For instance, prior to a lesson on the ocean, a teacher may show students a video of the ocean and ocean life. This practice provides background knowledge as well as necessary vocabulary knowledge. Another alternative would be the use of virtual reality (VR) tools to share an underwater experience. The use of visuals with vocabulary instruction, especially content vocabulary would be beneficial. The teacher may use hyperlinks with a digital list of vocabulary words so students can click on a hyperlink to receive additional images/information related to the word. Another vocabulary tool that helps students visualize words is visuwords.com. This interactive website provides definitional information in the form of a graphic organizer. Students enter words in the search box, which generates a visual. The website produces additional information when the student selects the word. Visuals include vocabulary connection and enhance knowledge about word relationships as students click and drags "nodes" to help clarify connections (visuwords.com).

Multiple Means of Expression

Teachers support diverse strategic networks by providing flexible models of skilled performance and opportunities to practice with supports (Coyne et al., 2007). "Offering multiple means of action and expression enables them to demonstrate most effectively what they have learned" (p. 3). Instruction may include techniques and materials that vary expression and engage students in practice. Maria lacks oral language proficiency and will benefit from opportunities to express herself through her primary language. The use of recording devices that translate the spoken languages are becoming more common. These types of devices would enable Maria to share knowledge in her primary language and then listen to the English version of the same information. Maria may also benefit from the use of a translation dictionary (or Google translate), which she can use as needed. The use of illustrations to depict knowledge may be necessary at times. Other ways to share the *How* of learning may include exposure to graphic organizers to help Maria visually organize information.

Cooperative learning strategies may benefit Maria as well as other students. The think-pair-share strategy enables Maria to work with her peers to solve problems or answer questions. The strategy allows students to think individually about a topic, to pair up with a classmate to compare ideas, and to share ideas with the entire class. Discussion with a partner engages students through participation and promotes understanding of material (Reading Rockets, 2017). Cooperative learning strategies provide students with ways to *express* their knowledge in a risk-free environment.

Multiple Means of Engagement

Teachers support diverse affective networks through multiple means of engagement. "Motivation, meaning-making, and emotional involvement originate in the affective networks" (Coyne et al., 2007). Students have little choice in what they learn in school (Coyne et al., 2007), but teachers can design activities in a way that includes choice and challenge. Opportunities for Maria to practice language in fun ways are important. Due to limited English proficiency, sight word practice may be helpful for Maria. Sight word practice may be made more fun for all students if the teacher utilizes tools like tablets, which provide fun practice of sight words or decodable stories in fun and engaging ways. For example, many apps provide sight word practice with a game-like experience. Examples include Play Sight Words or Sight Word Bingo (https://itunes.apple.com/us/app/sight-words-bingo/id634113828?mt=8). Another app which may benefit ELs as well as other students include Vocabulary PCS, which provides picture communication symbols available on flashcards along with auditory capacity or rainbow sentences to provide images and auditory assistance during sentence creation. Many students, including ELs struggle with idioms in the English language. Kidioms (https://itunes.apple.com/us/app/kidioms/id475844040?mt=8) is an app with provides sample phrases combined with graphics to help students understand common phrases. Through choice and engagement, teachers impact all students by promoting participation and active learning.

Case 2: Joe

Joe is a seventh-grade boy with autism, who participates in a general education classroom. Joe receives inclusion support for the first 30 minutes of his content courses. Joe performs just below grade level academically. Socially, he engages in several odd behaviors and has communication difficulties that distract him from completing his work and further disrupt the teacher's instruction. For example, he verbalizes his intent, but he gets off-topic in class by talking about subjects that are of interest to him. This is typical of autism, which is characterized by repetitive behaviors, verbal and nonverbal communication challenges, and deficits in social interactions (Raymond, 2012).

Multiple Means of Representation

Children with autism lack nonverbal communication skills and consequently may miss many of the details given during classroom instruction (Raymond, 2012). Providing a child with autism a visual representation of the material benefits his/her understanding. To provide multiple means of representation for Joe, the teachers could offer several options. Preteaching would be a valuable representation of new material for Joe. Sending home a copy of the upcoming vocabulary and key points would allow Joe to work with his resource teacher or parents to become familiar with the material prior to instruction. This strategy could be as simple as a list of words or as complex as words with definitions and examples. During lecture, the teacher could provide notes for Joe. In Joe's case, the notes would only need to have an outline of the content with keywords provided. Other students would benefit from keywords, definitions, and pictorial representations of the concepts on the notes page. A final means of representation could occur following instruction. Many students with autism learn best when seeing and hearing the material. Allowing Joe to view videos of the concept online would reinforce the concepts he learned during lecture and would fill in learning gaps he missed due to his autism.

Multiple Means of Expression

Children with autism demonstrate various differences in communication skills (Raymond, 2012). Some children have verbal language capabilities but lack the reciprocity skills necessary to engage in conversation. Other children have no verbal skills and fail to compensate using nonverbal communication. Joe exhibits excellent verbal skills, but he tends to use an inappropriate amount of time in class talking about topics of interest to him. Typical of children with autism, writing is a challenge due to deficits in proprioceptive awareness (Raymond, 2012). Joe is able to write a few paragraphs; however, he holds the pencil so tightly that he fatigues quickly and causes pain to himself. Rather than reducing the amount of work Joe is required to do as a means of modification, allowing a different form of expression would be preferred so as not to squelch Joe's full potential. Since Joe uses verbal communication, assignments that would typically be written could be spoken into a recording device to allow Joe to demonstrate his knowledge. There are many applications such as Dragon Dictation that have speech to text capabilities, which allow students to speak the assignment into the device and then print or email the final product. This strategy is successful with assignments where the content knowledge is being assessed as opposed to the child's ability to write.

Multiple Means of Engagement

Engaging students with autism is sometimes challenging and may result in what appears as the student being defiant. In fact, the student may lack the self-regulation skills necessary to remain on task and focused. Joe is a student who engages in verbalizations that are off-topic and distract him from fully engaging in the lesson. It is necessary to teach Joe self-monitoring skills in order to regulate his attention to task. One way to teach self-monitoring is to give Joe a timer set to vibrate at a given interval along with a chart on which to indicate his attention level. In Joe's case, he regularly vocalizes, so his chart would have the question, "Am I making noise?" written at the top. There would be 15 blocks below the question. At every vibration, Joe would refer to the chart and indicate in a box "yes" or "no" to the question written at the top. He would reset the timer and continue this pattern for 30 minutes until all the boxes are filled. This practice requires Joe to pay attention to the behavior that is distracting him. Research indicates when the student pays attention to the behavior, the awareness can result in greater self-monitoring and self-regulation (Raymond, 2012).

Case 3: Intellectual Disability

Mary is in a first-grade general education classroom and has Down syndrome with an intellectual disability. At the beginning of kindergarten, Mary was nearly at grade level. As she has progressed through first grade, it has become apparent that Mary is struggling in all content areas and is experiencing behavioral challenges. Mary does not learn reading skills using phonics like typically developing children. She memorizes words, which requires a different mode of instruction. In math, Mary understands the concept of addition but struggles with subtraction. She knows all of the two dimensional shapes required of a first grader and can count to 40, which is lower than expected of her age and grade. Mary's greatest challenge is communicating her knowledge. She knows how to say many words, but her sentences are incomplete and often difficult to understand. She not only uses sign language at home with her mom but also has an augmentative communication device that is used on a limited basis. Mary's Individualized Education Plan (IEP) states she is to receive accommodations including oral administration of tests, preferential seating, and extended time for completion of assignments. Mary regularly works with the resource teacher to finish her classwork.

Multiple Means of Representation

Mary has difficulty transitioning between activities and instructional tasks. Therefore, Mary's teacher could scaffold her awareness of time by providing a visual schedule for transitions. A visual schedule can be in any format but simply shows the student the plan for the day. Mary's would have pictures with words underneath that state each activity she will complete throughout the day. An example is provided in Fig. 1.

The example in Fig. 1 hangs on the wall. The procedure for implementation varies, but in this case, the student is given a token and instructed to "check your schedule." The student would drop the token in the cup at the bottom of the schedule. The incomplete tasks are located on the left side of

Fig. 1. Visual Schedule.

the schedule and a row of velcro is on the right side. When the student checks the schedule, he moves the top card from the left side to the right, then completes the task. The process of moving the card from one side to the other is a visual acknowledgment of the task to be completed. Visual schedules can be smaller, on the student's desk, written, or used with technology. A visual schedule is a means to represent the tasks the student will complete throughout the day and minimize frustration and anxiety. Another way to offer multiple means of representation is to provide a picture or a video representation of the text being taught. Mary likely needs multiple views of material to aid comprehension. Having the text available through video, ereader, websites, or a recording of the teacher that Mary can access as often as necessary will provide greater opportunity for her to be successful.

Multiple Means of Action and Expression
Mary's intellectual disability has limited her expression of knowledge as well as her communication level. Assistive technology in the form of an

augmentative communication device will allow Mary to express her knowledge of the new material. Mary uses sign language to express her wants and needs, but the children and the teacher in the classroom cannot understand her. Therefore, Mary's communication skills may present a barrier to learning. An augmentative communication device can be programed with task-specific words as well as general phrases that can be used in a variety of settings. In addition, alternative expression may include alternative activities that would demonstrate learning. For example, if the teacher expects students to write answers in a short answer format, Mary's responses may be in the form of circling the correct answer from an array of three pictures.

Multiple Means of Engagement
Mary is in the general education classroom and by nature is very friendly. Unfortunately, Mary is very small for her age and her peers tend to treat her like a baby rather than an equal peer. Not only does her size impact her inclusion in the classroom, her inability to communicate further distances her from her classmates. The augmentative communication device mentioned in the multiple means of action and expression section above also serves to engage Mary in her classroom. The communication device will provide a way for Mary to be independent and not rely on an adult to speak for her. Mary will be able to actively participate in her class rather than be a spectator. Membership in the peer group requires interaction without the dependence on another person to be the voice. Independence is the first step toward engagement. The second step is teaching Mary to self-monitor and stay on track with the requirements of the teacher. Breaking tasks into small, discrete steps with picture representations will provide a visual that Mary can follow and check off as she completes each step. Independent navigation of the classroom as well as independent completion of tasks increase self-esteem and elevate engagement.

Case 4: Jordan

Jordan is a third grader with dyslexia. She makes good grades and catches on to new concepts, but she struggles with accurate and fluent reading. Decoding unknown words is difficult. In addition, spelling is a weakness for Jordan. She does not like to read aloud, and she rarely finishes in-class assignments and test on time. Spelling is a significant issue for Jordan, which has caused her to dislike writing. She receives accommodations that allow extended time on assignments. Jordan excels in music and enjoys choir and singing.

Multiple Means of Representation

Dyslexia is the most common cause of reading, writing, and spelling difficulties (TSRHC, 2014). The Texas Education Agency (TEA) defines dyslexia as a "disorder of constitutional origin manifested by a difficulty in learning to read, write, or spell, despite conventional instruction, adequate intelligence, and sociocultural opportunity" (TEA, 2014, p. 8). In order to prevent reading and writing skills from becoming a barrier to learning for this large population of learners, teachers should become acquainted with assistive technology tools that enable students to access text more effectively. For example, many text to speech tools help struggling readers by providing ways for students to listen to the text while they follow along. Most tablets provide speech to text options. In other words, this option offers students to generate text through their voices instead of thought typing/writing. One benefit of this technology tool is that students with weak fluency skills have access to content. In the case that students in the classroom need occasional help deciding words, tools like Dictionary.com can be used for students to determine pronunciation. They work when the student types in the word and taps the audio icon to hear the pronunciation.

Tools like the Livescribe Smartpen enable older students to record lectures while students take notes (Ryan, 2015). Content may be presented in many ways, in order to reach all students in the classroom. For students where print may be a barrier to learning, *representing* information in various ways benefits diversity.

Multiple Means of Expression

Traditional forms of expression, such as writing a report, may be challenging for students with spelling deficiencies. Students with dyslexia often resist writing activities. Technology tools provide ways for students to experience success in writing activities. For example, Dragon Dictation enables Jordan to dictate her story orally. The transcribed story can then be edited by the student. Dragon dictation is available as a free app on phones and tablets. Other tools, like Dictionary.com, are also available as apps, enable students to determine correct spellings of words through speech to text capabilities. Google Docs allow speech to text capabilities as well. Google Docs also provide the ability for the teacher and the student to work on a document together in real time.

Apps like Story Kit provide a way for students to write their stories and then record them for extra reading practice. The alternative mode of storytelling enables students to share their story in both a written and oral format, with the use of pictures to aid in the storytelling. Apps that provide an interactive whiteboard, like ShowMe or Educreation, enable students to demonstrate learning across the disciplines, using varied means of expression.

Multiple Means of Engagement

Jordan lacks fluent reading skills; therefore, fluency instruction is necessary so that she can learn to read faster, with more ease. Engaging students with dyslexia may be challenging, as reading is difficult, and they may resist reading and writing activities (TSRHC, 2014). Therefore, teachers must engage students in reading for fun. Sharing quality children's literature instills the value of lifelong reading. Reading aloud to children instills a love of literature, models fluency, and exposes students to new vocabulary (Vacca, Vacca, Gove, Burkey, Lenhart, & McKeon, 2012). Student choice in fluency practice is also beneficial. Some students may enjoy practicing with poetry, while others may enjoy reading books at the independent level, which are easy for them to read fluently. Allowing students to listen to their oral readings can be motivating, especially when teachers use technology tools like Voki.com. Voki.com provides a platform where students create an avatar and have the avatar "speak."

According to Rasinki (2012), the learning goal of fluency instruction is for students to read accurately, quickly, expressively, with good phrasing, and with good comprehension. In order to support diverse recognition networks when teaching fluency, teachers must provide multiple examples of fluent reading (Coyne et al., 2007). Modeling fluent reading is critical and can take many forms, from whole class read alouds of literature, to guided reading, to the use of technology to provide visual and audio support. Choral reading promotes reading fluency, self-confidence, vocabulary knowledge, and motivation (Vacca, et al., 2012). Choral reading of text, especially of poetry, provides an opportunity for the teacher to intentionally model prosody, or reading with expression. Choral reading involves reading aloud in unison with a whole class or group of students (Ortlieb, Young, & Majors, 2016; Vacca et al., 2012). With echo reading, a similar strategy, a teacher reads a line (modeling fluency) and the students repeat the line.

Traditionally, audio-assisted reading, where students follow along in their books as they listen to an audio-recording of a fluent reader, has been used for multisensory learning (Vacca et al., 2012). The recording enables the learner to hear the prosodic features of language modeled, with the idea that students will then practice reading the same material, using expression. According to Reading Rockets (2015), audio-assisted reading helps build fluent phrasing and expression, sight word recognition, tone and pace, and comprehension. Audio-assisted reading has advanced with increased technology capabilities. Instead of a tone signaling the turn of a page, audio-assisted reading now incorporates digital formats, where words appear on a screen for the reader to follow. Karaoke websites, where students listen to favorite songs while following along with the lyrics (Pilgrim, 2015), utilize a type of audio-assisted reading. Fluency practice with music may be a great way to engage students like Jordan, who enjoy music. With the advancements in tablet technology and accompanying apps (applications), karaoke-style sing-alongs are available free of charge. For example, the Sing! Karaoke App by Smule is a free app available through Apple (https://itunes.apple.com/us/app/sing!-karaoke-by-smule/id509993510?mt=8). Although the reader hears a tune instead of the prosodic features of oral reading, the learner gains exposure to words and text that may not have been read without the motivation of music (Pilgrim, 2015). "Print put to music also allows children to build on past experiences, which in turn invites them to participate in reading and singing at the same time" (Woodall & Ziembroski, 2012, para. 7). Jordan enjoys music and is likely to benefit from fluency practice in this environment.

IMPLICATIONS FOR TEACHERS

Growing diversity in today's classrooms increases the need for teachers to design instruction to maximize learning for all students. Learner differences extend beyond the traditional ideas of inherent strengths and weaknesses of the students. The interaction between the learner and the educational curriculum must be considered (Meyer & Rose, 2005). In other words, in looking for ways to include all learners in high-quality education, educators and researchers should examine ways in which the curriculum presents barriers and supports to academic achievement by diverse learners and how the curriculum can be developed to include all learners from the outset.

The case studies presented here reflect a small portion of the diverse population in classrooms across the nation. Yet the case studies demonstrate ways planning can incorporate students "in the margin" while at the same time benefitting all students in the classroom. Addressing diversity through the UDL lens helps teachers accommodate individual differences through intentional instructional design, while at the same time, providing resources for all students in the classroom. We recommend teachers share technology tools with all students in order to maximize learning. For example, the speech to text tools discussed in the case students may also benefit the child that broke a hand and cannot write. The QR codes may benefit a student in need of modifications but may also benefit a child who wishes to display an auditory message on a science fair project. Technology tools are not a requirement of UDL but enhance learning for all. When classroom design includes students in the margins – the child with physical limitations, verbal inabilities, reading challenges, visual struggles – then all children in the classroom gain access to the curriculum, including those without disabilities who may struggle with a new concept. The UDL framework supports classroom instruction for all learners, regardless of behavior, learning style, background, culture, gender, physical difficulties, or cognitive diversity. All students deserve quality instruction.

REFERENCES

Americans with Disabilities Act of 1990, as amended with ADA Amendments Act of 2008. (n.d.). Retrieved from http://www.ada.gov/pubs/adastatute08htm

Arabo, M., Budd, J. S., Garrison, S., & Pacheco, T. (2017). *The right tool for the job: Improving reading and writing in the classroom*. Washington, DC: Thomas B. Fordham Institute.

Bergin, C. C., & Bergin, D. A. (2012). *Child and adolescent development in your classroom (What's new in education)*. Belmont, CA: Wadsworth Publishing.

CAST. (2011). Cast timeline. Retrieved http://www.cast.org/about/timeline.html#.Vs3d7UBRqrY

CAST. (2015). About universal design for learning. Retrieved from http://www.cast.org/our-work/about-udl.html#.VT_d5NJVhBd

Center for Universal Design. (1997). *The principles of universal design*. Retrieved from https://www.ncsu.edu/ncsu/design/cud/about_ud/udprinciplestext.htm

Common Core State Standards Initiative. (2010). Common core state standards for English language arts and literacy in history, social studies, science, and technical subjects, Washington, DC: Author.

Coyne, P., Ganley, P., Hall, T, Meo, G., Murray, E., & Gordon, D. (2007). Applying universal design for learning in the classroom. In D. H. Rose, & A. Meyer (Eds.). *A practical reader in universal design for learning* (pp. 1–13). Cambridge, MA: Harvard Education Press.

Coyne, P., Pisha, B., Dalton, B., Zeph, L. A., & Smith, N. C. (2013). Literacy by design: A universal design for learning approach for students with significant intellectual disabilities. *Remedial and Special Education 33*(3), 162–172.

Every Student Succeeds Act. (2015). Pub. L. 114–195. *Stat. 1177* (2015).

Fautsch-Patridge, T., McMaster, K. L., & Hupp, S. C. (2011). Are current reading research findings applicable to students with intellectual disabilities? In S. J. Samuels, & A. E. Farstrup (Eds.), *What research has to say about reading instruction* (pp. 215–235). Newark, DE: International Reading Association.

Florian, L. (2012). Preparing teachers to work in inclusive classrooms: Key lessons for the professional development of teacher educators from Scotland's inclusive practice project. *Journal of Teacher Education, 63*(4), 275–285.

Frey, B. A., Kearns, L. R., & King, D. K. (2012). Quality Matters: Template for an accessibility policy for online courses. Retrieved from https://www.qualitymatters.org/sites/default/files/research-docs-pdfs/QM-Accessibility-Policy.pdf

Gordan, D., Gravel, J. W., & Schifter, L. A., (Eds.). (2009). *A policy reading in universal design for learning*. Cambridge, MA: Harvard Education Press.

Guthrie, J. T. & Wigfield, A. (2000). Engagement and motivation in reading. *Handbook of reading research, 3*, 403–422.

Lipson, M. Y., & Wixson, K. K. (1997). Assessment and instruction of reading and writing disability: An interactive approach (2nd ed.). Fort Worth, TX: Harcourt Brace.

Meo, G. (2008). Curriculum planning for all learners: Applying universal design for learning (UDL) to a high school reading comprehension program. *Preventing School Failure, 52*(2), 21–30. doi:10.3200/PSFL.52.2.21-30

Meyer, A., & Rose, D. H. (2005). The future is in the margins: The role of technology and disability in educational reform. In D. H. Rose, A. Meyer, & C. Hitchcock (Eds.), *The universally designed classroom: Accessible curriculum and digital technologies* (pp. 13–35). Cambridge, MA: Harvard Education Press.

Meyer, A., Rose, D. H., & Gordon, D. (2014). *Universal design for learning: Theory and practice*. Wakefield, MA: CAST Professional Publishing.

Nguyen, N. N., Leytham, P., Whitby, P. S., & Gelfer, J. I. (2015). Reading comprehension and autism in the primary general education classroom. *The Reading Teacher, 69*(1), 71–76.

No Child Left Behind Act. (2001). Pub. L. No. 107–110, 115. *Stat., 1425*(2002).

Ortlieb, E., Young, C., & Majors, Y. (2016). Never too old: A how-to guide for developing adult readers' oral reading skills. *Journal of Adolescent and Adult Literacy, 60*(2), 213–216. DOI: 10.1002/jaal.568

Paris, S. G., Wasik, B. A., & Turner, J. C. (1991). *The development of strategic readers*. In R. Barr, M.L. Kamil, P. Mosenthal, & P.D. Pearson (Eds.), Handbook of reading research (Vol. 2, pp. 609–640). White Plains, NY: Longman.

Pilgrim, J. (2015). Hitting the right "note": Using music to promote fluency skills for dyslexic students. *English in Texas, 45*(1), 15–20.

Ralabate, P. K. (2011, August 30). Universal design for learning: Meeting the needs of all students. *The ASHA Leader*. Retrieved from http://www.readingrockets.org/article/universal-design-learning-meeting-needs-all-students.

Rasinski, T. (2012). Why fluency should be hot. *The Reading Teacher, 65*(8), 516–522.

Raymond, E. B. (2012). *Learners with mild disabilities: A characteristics approach*. Upper Saddle River, NJ. Pearson Education.

Reading Rockets (2015). Elkonin boxes. Retrieved from http://www.readingrockets.org/strategies/elkonin_boxes

Reading Rockets (2017). Think-pair-share. Retrieved from http://www.readingrockets.org/strategies/think-pair-share

Rose, D. H., & Meyer, A. (2002). *Teaching every student in the digital age: Universal design for learning*. Alexandria, VA: Association for Supervision and Curriculum Development.

Rose, D. H., & Meyer, A. (Eds.). (2006). *A practical reader in universal design for learning*. Cambridge, MA: Harvard Education Press.

Ryan, M. (2015). Software & assistive technology. Dyslexia help. Retrieved from http://dyslexiahelp.umich.edu/tools/software-assistive-technology

Samuels, C. A. (2016). ESSA spotlights strategy to reach diverse learners. *Education Week*. Retrieved from http://www.edweek.org/ew/articles/2016/02/24/essa-spotlights-strategy-to-reach-diverse-learners.html

Smith, T. E., Polloway, E. A., Patton, J. R., & Dowdy, C. A. (2012). *Teaching students with special needs in inclusive settings*. Upper Saddle River, NJ. Pearson Education.

Texas Education Agency. (2014). The dyslexia handbook: Procedures concerning dyslexia and related disorders. Retrieved fromhttp://www.decodingdyslexiatx.org/wp-content/uploads/2014/05/TEA_DyslexiaHandbook_2014-DRAFT-5-12-14.pdf

Texas Education Agency. (2015). Preparation manual English as a second language supplemental. Retrieved from http://cms.texes-ets.org/files/5814/5881/8962/154_esl_supplmntl.pdfTEA

Texas Scottish Rite Hospital for Children (2014). Dyslexia defined. Retrieved from http://www.tsrhc.org/TSRHC/media/Media-Library-Files/PDF/Dyslexia-Defined-2015-links_3.pdf

The Higher Education Opportunity Act (Public Law 110-315).

Vacca, J. L., Vacca, R.T., Gove, M.K., Burkey, L.C. Lenhart, L.A., & McKeon, C.A. (2012). *Reading and Learning to Read* (8th ed.). New York: Pearson.

Vygotsky, L. S. (1978). *Mind in society: The development of higher psychological processes*. Cambridge, MA: Harvard University Press.

Woodall, L., & Ziembroski, B. (2012). Promoting literacy through music. Retrieved from http://www.songsforteaching.com/lb/literacymusic.htm

THE FIERCE URGENCY OF NOW: CDF FREEDOM SCHOOLS AND CULTURALLY RELEVANT PEDAGOGY

Alysia D. Roehrig, Kristal Moore Clemons
and Keely Norris

ABSTRACT

We explore how K-8 student scholars experience culturally relevant texts provided during Freedom Schools summer camps, discuss ways Freedom Schools can be a vehicle for youth to become advocates for social change, and consider opportunities created by Freedom Schools for community engagement and partnerships. Mixed methods were used to investigate the experiences of 38 scholars at two different Freedom Schools sites (one rural and one mid-sized urban) in the southeastern U.S. The majority of scholars identified as African American and lived in low-income households. Primary data sources included scholar surveys and reading assessments, camp observations, and interviews with scholars, as well as our own personal reflections as the Research Director (Alysia Roehrig) and Co-Executive Directors (Kristal M. Clemons and Keely Norris) for the

Addressing Diversity in Literacy Instruction
Literacy Research, Practice and Evaluation, Volume 8, 251–269
Copyright © 2018 by Emerald Publishing Limited
All rights of reproduction in any form reserved
ISSN: 2048-0458/doi:10.1108/S2048-045820170000008013

sites. We triangulated descriptive statistics from surveys with qualitative data, primarily from interviews, which we analyzed using open coding and axial coding to develop themes (Strauss & Corbin, 1998). The majority of scholars, who participated in the 2016 North Florida Freedom Schools, reported being able to identify with specific characters and situations in the books included in the culturally relevant reading summer program, and they expressed positive thoughts and feelings about the books. Most scholars (74%) maintained or gained in instructional reading levels and did not experience summer learning loss. Children's confidence that they could act prosocially also increased significantly during the summer camps, which children characterized as different from regular school. Freedom Schools can offer a valuable forum for diverse community members to learn about one another, focus on their strengths, and become agents for social change. We provide suggestions for how other communities can implement the Freedom Schools model.

Keywords: Culturally relevant reading instruction; reading attitudes; social action; community engagement; Freedom Schools

Dr. Martin Luther King, Jr. reminded a divided nation we are stronger when we work together to improve our conditions. He called this the "fierce urgency of now" at the historic March on Washington. For every child in America whose access to a quality education is in jeopardy, there is an urgency of now. Freedom Schools provide a unique educational opportunity to celebrate the rich history of the Civil Rights Movement and the passions of children traditionally considered at risk for school failure in our communities. An anti-deficit framework allowed us to structure our investigation of Freedom Schools in what Harper (2010) calls an "instead of fashion" (p. 68). Instead of seeking to understand, for example, why some high-poverty African American students are placed at greater risk for dropping out of school than white students, we wanted to study the successes high-poverty black students have as readers and social activists.

WHY FREEDOM SCHOOLS NOW?

The Children's Defense Fund (CDF) Freedom Schools movement developed out of the 1964 Mississippi Freedom Summer Project, which served thousands of young children and adults in over 40 Freedom Schools created to help combat voter suppression and encourage youth to engage in the civil rights movement (Clemons, 2014). "With little money and few supplies, the Freedom Schools set out to empower African Americans in Mississippi to become active citizens and change agents in their respective communities" (Clemons, p. 141), using a "curriculum focused on the philosophy of the Civil Rights Movement, reading, writing, arithmetic, and African American history" (Clemons, Price, & Clemons, 2017, p. 856). The idea was "to supplement what children were not getting in their traditional public schools and mobilize voter registration" (Clemons et al., 2017, p. 857).

We still have a need for liberatory education, even 50 years after the 1964 Mississippi Freedom Schools. A cradle-to-prison pipeline has developed for children of color who live in economically disenfranchised communities (Clemons et al., 2017). CDF pointed out how deteriorating schools along with the juvenile justice system and prison industrial complex have resulted in the disproportionate incarceration of people of color (The State of America's Children, 2008). In part, to help develop young activists who could make social change through grassroots and community organizing methods, the Freedom Schools movement was reborn by CDF in 1992. Marian Wright Edelman and the CDF's Black Community Crusade for Children also sought to use Freedom Schools to enhance intergenerational collaboration between Civil Rights Era activists and the younger generations (Clemons et al., 2017).

Contemporary CDF Freedom Schools are typically six-week summer enrichment programs offered free of cost to families of school-aged children. At Freedom Schools, students are called "scholars" to inspire them to focus on their educational and civic endeavors. The ratio between scholars and servant leaders must be no more than ten students to one teacher. The staff is usually composed of diverse local stakeholders, including college students who serve as teachers or Servant Leader Interns (SLIs) (Clemons et al., 2017). The purposeful selection of college interns works as a pre-collegiate program effort to support students in preparing for college. The CDF believes in modeling and wants the college interns to help scholars begin to think about various college majors and career opportunities. The staff also are required to participate in a weeklong national training at Alex Haley's Farm in Clinton, Tennessee and the University of Tennessee Knoxville in Knoxville, Tennessee, where they learn how to implement the Integrated Reading Curriculum properly. In addition, at national training, SLIs:

> meet other SLIs from across the nation and recognize that they are indeed part of a movement where every student who is participating will be reading the same book, singing the

same songs and participating in the same social action in their respective city. (Clemons et al., 2017, p. 857)

A typical day at CDF Freedom Schools starts at eight o'clock in the morning with campus arrival. Scholars are welcomed by cheering SLIs as parents and guardians usher their children into the building. The scholars enjoy a nutritious breakfast with their classmates and Servant Leader Interns. They typically talk about the fun day ahead and get ready for the morning activities. Following breakfast, scholars engage in *Harambee!*, which is a Kiswhahili word that means "let's pull together." Harambee is rooted in an Afrocentric pedagogical tradition that invokes musical improvisation and call and response. It can be described as a morning pep rally aimed at positively motivating the scholars for the learning ahead. Harambee includes a guest/community reading, motivational song, cheers and chants, recognitions, moment of silence, meditation, and announcements. It is sharing time where children and staff come together to celebrate themselves and each other. The inclusion of a guest/community reader works to help students meet a variety of adult community stakeholders who are invested in their future. Immediately following Harambee, scholars transition to their classroom for the Integrated Reading Curriculum.

CDF developed the culturally relevant, Integrated Reading Curriculum or IRC, which is now implemented by SLIs during mornings at almost 200 Freedom Schools summer camps across the U.S. annually. It is based on books written by African American, Latino/a, and Caribbean authors on subjects addressing social action via weekly thematic units focused on making a difference in self (week 1), family (week 2), community (week 3), country (week 4), world (week 5), and with hope, education, and action (week 6). At CDF Freedom Schools, scholars are separated not by individual grades but into four levels. Level I includes grades K–2, Level II includes grades 3–5, Level III includes grades 6–8, and Level IV includes grades 9–12. At the end of camp, student scholars, receive a set of these books for their personal libraries. Books read in the Summer 2016 curriculum included *Grandpa, Is Everything Black Bad?* by Sandy Lynne Holman (Level II, self), *Freedom Summer* by Deborah Wiles (Level I, country), *Confessions of a Former Bully* by Trudy Ludwig (Level 3, with hope, education, and action), among others (see Appendix for complete list).

Scholars of culturally relevant pedagogy (e.g., Gay, 2000; Ladson-Billings, 1998; Lee, 1995) have demonstrated the importance of appealing to students' worldviews, values, cultural orientations, and experiences in order to affect greater educational outcomes (Clemons et al., 2017). Nevertheless,

Ladson-Billings (2014) encountered teachers who communicated strong beliefs in their students' academic efficacy, though "they rarely pushed students to consider critical perspectives on policies and practices that may have a direct impact on their lives and communities" (p. 78). In her many observations of teachers she perceived, "there was no discussion on issues such as school choice, school closing, rising incarceration rates, gun laws, or even everyday school climate questions like whether students should wear uniforms (which typically sparks spirited debate)" (Ladson-Billings, 2014, p. 78).

Unlike the heavy focus on testing in many contemporary public schools, the emphasis in Freedom Schools is on children experiencing success and on providing opportunities to make literacy meaningful and relevant to their lives, by relating to the books and putting ideas into action. This approach follows Ladson-Billings' (1995) work on effective teaching for African American students. With culturally relevant teaching: "(a) Students must experience academic success; (b) students must develop and/or maintain cultural competence; and (c) students must develop a critical consciousness through which they challenge the status quo of the current social order" (Ladson-Billings, 1995, p. 160). Student scholars at Freedom Schools also take part in a variety of afternoon activities facilitated by parents, volunteers, university faculty and students, and other community organizations.

The mission of our nonprofit North Florida Freedom Schools (NFFS), aligned with that of CDF, "is to ensure every child has a *Healthy Start*, a *Head Start*, a *Fair Start*, a *Safe Start*, and a *Moral Start* and successful passage to adulthood with the help of caring families and communities" (CDF, 2017, "Our Mission"). NFFS strives to reach low-income, primarily African American students, during free 6-week summer day camps that are intended to support the empowerment of local children to make a difference in their world through a social action project, while also celebrating and reinforcing positive attitudes and efficacy for reading.

METHODS

Mixed methods were used to investigate the experiences of scholars at two different Freedom Schools sites (one rural and one mid-sized urban) in the North Florida region, in and around Tallahassee, Florida. Tallahassee is a mid-sized, capitol city with two state universities, Florida Agricultural and Mechanical University (FAMU, an HBCU, i.e., one of the Historically Black Colleges and Universities) and Florida State University (FSU, a Primarily

White Institution or PWI), which partnered to help organize our local Freedom Schools. The urban center of Tallahassee, with FAMU to the south and FSU just to the north, strikingly mirrors the racial segregation in the community, which was identified in 2015 as the most economically segregated city in the nation (Florida & Mellander, 2015). Of the 100 total K-8 scholars (of whom 95% identified as African American and 98% were eligible for free or reduced priced lunch) enrolled at the camps, we conducted interviews with or had at least two time points of reading or survey data from 38 scholars (who had parental consent to participate in research). While males and females were evenly represented at the camps, females are slightly overrepresented (approximately 60%) in the data presented here.

Primary data sources included scholar surveys and reading assessments, camp observations, and interviews with scholars and facilitators, as well as our own personal reflections as the Research Director (Alysia Roehrig) and Co-Executive Directors (Kristal M. Clemons and Keely Norris) for the sites. Descriptive statistics from surveys were triangulated with qualitative results, primarily from interviews, which we analyzed using open coding and axial coding to develop themes (Strauss & Corbin, 1998). We administered two surveys to scholars during the first and last weeks of camp. The 20-item Elementary Reading Attitudes Survey (ERAS; McKenna & Kear, 1990) assesses changes in attitudes about recreational and academic reading (e.g., "How do you feel about spending free time reading?" [recreational], "How do you feel about learning from a book?" [academic]) rated on a 4 point scale (1 = "Don't like it!" to 4 = "Love it!"). We developed another 12-item survey to assess efficacy for prosocial behaviors aligned with the IRC themes (e.g., "I can be a good friend," "I can be respectful of others," "I can make a difference in other people's lives") using a 100% certainty scale. The surveys have acceptable levels of internal consistency (s = .75 − .85). Reading level data came from pre- and posttest administrations of the Basic Reading Inventory (BRI; Johns, 2012), an informal reading inventory assessing instructional reading levels.

FINDINGS

Based on data from the 2016 North Florida Freedom Schools summer camps, we first explore K–8 children's experiences with a culturally relevant reading curriculum and their experiences with the various culturally relevant texts from CDF's IRC. Next, we discuss Freedom Schools as a critical thinking and social activism vehicle for youth to become advocates for social change.

Finally, we consider the opportunities created by having CDF Freedom Schools in communities to integrate the experiences and insights of parents, teachers, College of Education faculty and students, and volunteers from community organizations.

"Reading Books Is Really Cool!": Connecting with
Culturally Relevant Texts

One of the goals in Freedom Schools is to position reading as empowering, relevant, accessible, and even fun for scholars. A core belief that guides CDF Freedom Schools is that "literacy is essential to personal empowerment and civic responsibility" (CDF, 2017, "Core Beliefs"). Most scholars enthusiastically (with the exception of a handful of middle school/level III scholars) participated in the energizing cheers and chants during morning Harambee, to get them geared up for Integrated Reading Curriculum. The majority of cheers and chants celebrate reading and books, with lines such as, "See a book, grab a book, read a book, hey!" and "There's no school like Freedom School! Reading books is really cool!" This led us to ask, how do young scholars actually connect (or not) with the books provided during Freedom Schools IRC? In the following sections, we describe the ways scholars found IRC books relevant, enjoyable and understandable, as well as how SLIs may help sustain positive attitudes about reading.

High-Achieving Readers
Though low-income, ethnic and racial minorities are often characterized in the literature as "at risk" for school failure, the large majority of scholars in our camps (84%; 32 of 38 scholars with pre-BRI data and consent to participate in research) were reading at (16%) or above (68%) grade level during the first week of camp. During the last week of camp, 83% (29 of 35) of scholars were reading at (11.5%) or above (71.5%) grade level. Of the scholars participating in research, 74% (25 of 34) maintained or gained at least one grade level in reading on the BRI by the end of Freedom Schools. These results suggest our Freedom Schools met one of CDF's goals, which is to prevent summer learning loss. Even more importantly, we believe, the following interview and survey results reveal that the reading opportunities allowed many scholars to flourish.

Positive Attitudes About Reading and Books

The scholars, who had consent to participate in research and completed at least one survey, also began Freedom Schools with relatively positive attitudes about both recreational ($M_{pre} = 2.75$, $SD = .649$, $n = 43$) and academic ($M_{pre} = 2.67$, $SD = .681$, $n = 43$) reading. (Note, 3 indicates "I like it" and 2 indicates a "ho hum" attitude about reading activities like "How do you feel about spending free time reading?" [recreational] and "How do you feel about learning from a book?" [academic]). Scholars ended the camp with descriptively more positive attitudes about both recreational ($M_{post} = 2.81$, $SD = .588$, $n = 52$) and academic ($M_{post} = 2.81$, $SD = .660$, $n = 52$) reading, though the average gains for the 36 scholars with no missing data were not significant.

When interviewed, the majority of scholars also expressed positive thoughts and feelings about the books read and some relayed they enjoyed reading even more after participating in Freedom Schools. One Level II scholar said he liked reading more "because they made it fun and we all take turns reading." However, most had an existing passion for reading. For example, a Level I scholar said she liked to read, "Because it's my favorite... it's my favorite thing because... when I read I just see, I use my imagination, and pretend, like I was in it." Along those lines, a Level II scholar said, "Because it can, it can enhance my mind!" On the other hand, scholars, who indicated they did not enjoy reading in general and had low confidence in their reading ability ($n = 4$) reported negative thoughts and feelings about IRC books, explaining that the books were sometimes too hard or too long. A few other scholars reported mixed feelings. For example, though a Level II and a Level III scholar both said they liked reading, they added that they really did not like reading aloud, which is a common practice in IRC. The Level III scholar said, "I enjoy it but not reading out loud. I hate that. I read a whole lot more better, like, in my mind and stuff. Like whenever I mess up in front of everybody. I don't like that."

Many interviewed scholars (18 of 31) also reported being able to identify with specific characters and situations in the IRC books. The way students related took a variety of forms, which ranged from identifying with a character's health problems or rough childhood to excitement to create their own menu because they love cooking and want to be a chef. One of the Level II scholars said he could relate to *Tamika and the Wisdom Rings* because "somebody in my family [also] got shot and died" and to *The Harvest Hope* because "me and my uncle...garden too and we get paid." Another Level II scholar reported relating to Tamika, "Because she, she is brave and like she likes to help people out and stuff like that... I like to help people out sometimes." A Level III scholar explained clearly how the books supported perspective taking as well as perseverance, particularly with regards to a favorite book, *We Beat the Street*: "I can kind of relate to it because like, stuff, like people go through, they still end up successful, but like I had, I didn't go through what they went through, but still I think we all go through something difficult to like get to success." Even the youngest scholars reported making important meaning from texts, like *Freedom Summer*: "I just, now I know that it wasn't fair to black people that they had to go to the back door." Thus, we found the diverse IRC texts to serve effectively as both mirrors and windows (Tschida, Ryan, & Ticknor, 2014):

> The concept of a book acting as a mirror implies that readers see something of themselves in the text. Such a book reflects back to readers portions of their identities, cultures, or experiences. When readers are able to find themselves in a text, they are therefore validated; their experiences are not so unique or strange as to never be spoken or experienced by others. This inclusion, in turn, connects readers even more strongly to the larger world of books. The reality for many readers, however, is that they do not see reflections of themselves in children's literature... To view worlds that are not their own, books must also act as windows, allowing for a vicarious experience to supersede the limits of the readers' own lives and identities and spend time observing those of others...readers need books that show them their place in our multicultural world and teach them about the connections between all humans. (p. 29)

Role of SLIs

How do such human connections link to reading achievement for our scholars? All scholars described positive feelings or thoughts about their SLIs, regardless of whether their SLI was the same race/ethnicity as themselves. (Approximately half of our SLIs were African American like the majority of scholars, and the other SLIs were Hispanic or white.) Moreover, we found that scholars who demonstrated reading level gains cited the time SLIs spent laughing with them, reading to them, and giving them patient, individual attention as strong factors of Freedom Schools. For example, one Level III scholar said of his SLI, "He's nice and funny. And we're like gonna do the play and he makes us laugh and stuff ... He lets [us] take turns reading, he lets us pick the activities we wanna do."

"Something Inside So Strong": Knowing You Can Make a Difference

In addition to a focus on empowerment through reading, Freedom Schools provide a critical thinking and social activism vehicle for student scholars to become advocates for social change. Each morning at Freedom Schools,

Harambee includes singing the motivational song, "Something Inside So Strong," which was written by Labi Siffre after he saw video of black youth being shot by a white soldier in South Africa (Mathur, 1989). The purpose of singing the song is to make explicit scholars' intrinsic value even though others may treat them poorly. A foundation to encourage scholars to follow their passions and become community advocates can be found in the IRC's six week-long units, beginning with making a difference in (1) oneself, (2) one's family, (3) one's community, (4) the country, (5) the world, and (6) ending with "Hope, Education and Action." These themes align with daily IRC activities meant to support scholars in finding and using their voices. As one Level II scholar explained, he liked "writing activities, drawing activities, and um talking about activities [because] you can talk and communicate to others," which he said helped his learning. The curriculum also acted as a forum for scholars to find ways to serve others and build their community.

Inspired to Serve

The themes of the IRC align with the larger social action project, which CDF identified as voter education for 2016, a presidential election year. Participants at every Freedom Schools camp collaborate on the identified social action project and participate in the National Day of Social Action to bring their community's attention to important social issues. Scholars were clearly inspired by the social action focus of Freedom Schools. At one of our sites, the scholars discussed with SLIs how they could address the hunger needs of their peers. We offered free breakfast, lunch, and snacks via the Federal Summer Feeding Program and donations, and it was clear to us that many children greatly valued the opportunity to eat at Freedom Schools. Indeed, scholars often mentioned food as a favorite aspect of Freedom Schools. The Scholars at our urban location brainstormed ways they could create discrete food backpacks for children to take home on weekends. They did not have enough time to garner the support needed to implement the service before the end of the camp, but the children's compassion and drive to make a difference for others was inspiring.

Building Community

The "making a difference" themes in IRC effectively address many prosocial behaviors such as friendship, advocating for others, and respecting others and their differences. The majority of interviewed scholars (22 of 31) described getting along well with some or most classmates, and the culture of Freedom Schools seemed to shape the quality of their relationships. For example, one Level III scholar said of his peers, "In the very beginning it was kind of rough... [Now] it's pretty much good. We're all getting along and, um, they know now that we all know each other's strengths now, I guess." Similarly, a Level III scholar said of her peers, "They don't really judge people." This interview finding triangulated with the significant gain found in scholars' confidence that they could act prosocially, $t(33) = 2.474$, $p = .019$. On average, during the first week of camp, scholars reported that they were 79% ($SD = 13.539$) confident that they could act prosocially. During the last week of camp, they reported, on average, being 84% confident ($SD = 15.070$). Three of the younger (Levels I and II) boys with large gains on the Prosocial Efficacy Survey described liking their Freedom Schools peers for the following reasons:

- "They're caring, they help me when I have problems... And they just help me whenever I need help."
- "Because, hmm, we work together."
- "Because they're like nice kids and we get to play and we're nice to each other and act like family."

These findings are clearly aligned with the core beliefs of CDF Freedom Schools regarding culture and community: "Culture and community conditions influence child learning," and "Appreciation and knowledge of one's culture engenders self-worth and the ability to live in community with others" (CDF, 2017, "Core Beliefs").

"Let Me Put Some Freedom In It": Reimagining How We Do School

"Let me put some freedom in it" is a quote from an inspirational Harambee chant that highlights how Freedom Schools differ from traditional schools (Clemons et al., 2017). Not only are civil rights emphasized in the curriculum, but the camps are organized to support and celebrate scholars' successes. The goal is to provide scholars with more equitable opportunities that can help change the status quo.

Serving the Whole Child

We approached the organization of our Freedom Schools sites from the perspective of community schools, which offer wrap around services to children and their families. We provided group counseling services via college-aged School of Social Work interns. Local companies, church members, and university students and faculty organized other activities (e.g., fitness, healthy habits, number talks, writing and art workshops, STEM club, music production, dance). Scholars also were offered clothes if they came in unwashed ones, and staff picked them up in a church van if they couldn't walk or their parents couldn't bring them.

To participate in Freedom Schools, families did not have to bear the burden of tuition, lunch, or fees for supplies, but they did have to commit sending one adult family member to the bi-weekly parent meetings held in the evenings during camp. This is because one of the core beliefs guiding CDF Freedom Schools is that "parents are crucial partners in children's learning and need supports to become better parents" (CDF, 2017, "Core Beliefs"). Parent meetings provided a venue for parents to learn about their scholars' Freedom Schools experiences and a forum to discuss community concerns as well as access to workshops on healthy habits. The health habits workshops created a dialogue among parents about ensuring access to healthy, affordable foods, increasing physical activities, and empowering parents and caregivers to make good choices for their families. The workshops also covered the importance of mental health counseling. Mental health counseling professionals from a local agency were on hand if any family needed intervention strategies or support as it related to stress management, grief, or disabilities.

The Freedom School Way

Beyond the community schools orientation, Freedom Schools are characterized by the way they create close knit, caring communities in their camps. This is the "Freedom School way," which is characterized by mutual respect and caring, choice, and self-discipline. We often overheard SLIs talking about and reminding their scholars of the Freedom Schools way when they did not follow the classroom management agreements each class of 10 scholars developed together. And SLIs worked closely with one another and their site coordinator too, forming supportive professional learning communities (PLCs; DuFour, 2004). During their daily afternoon debriefs, SLIs discussed successes and challenges of the day, with a focus on identifying ways to better support one another and their scholars. These findings are aligned with the core CDF Freedom Schools beliefs that

- "effective teaching requires planning, creativity, and implementation, with reflection and processing, [and]

- classroom discipline and management are integral parts of instructional practice" (CDF, 2017, "Core Beliefs").

Freedom Schools offer a different way of doing school than many students experience in traditional schools the rest of the year. In interviews, scholars often expressed what they liked about Freedom Schools in terms of how participating in Freedom Schools differs from regular school. For example, one Level III scholar said what she liked about her SLIs was "that they love teaching us. Because I never got the attention that these teachers give me here… They got the same personality that I got. Like fun and determined to do anything." Another Level III scholar said of his SLI, "He was fun I guess… Wasn't like normal teachers… And he doesn't really force us to do anything." The scholars also found the activities and books at Freedom Schools to be different from previous experiences as well. One Level II scholar characterized the books as "interesting and different than the usual ones I read."

CONCLUSION

Our findings suggest that Freedom Schools can offer a valuable forum for diverse community members to learn about one another, focus on their strengths, and become advocates for social change. We conclude by providing, for others who would like to implement Freedom Schools in their communities, some practical suggestions based on what we have learned from our experience and research with Freedom Schools.

In summer 2016, we helped to organize the very first Freedom Schools camp in Tallahassee, which served 50 scholars. We also organized a camp serving 50 scholars in Quincy, Florida. As we write this chapter, we are helping to organize two camps that will serve 130 scholars from the low-income, south side of Tallahassee in summer 2017, as well as another 35 in rural, Gretna, Florida. Recruiting the scholars to enroll has been the easy part, as families welcomed an affordable, high-quality summer experience for their children, and Freedom Schools cost only a $25 registration fee. There were many on our waiting list that we could not accommodate. To make NFFS's inaugural camps in 2016 a reality, we first had to raise over $40,000, as well as recruit scores of interns and volunteers. How did we accomplish this? We did not do it alone, but with the strong support and engagement of people throughout the community. Students, alumni, and faculty from both FAMU and FSU as well as residents and community organizations from both sides of town seemed eager to contribute to something that would address the historic divides in our region of the South.

Racial tensions have been running high across the U.S. over the last couple of years, so your community might be as supportive as ours was to find a productive way to address the divides by founding new Freedom Schools. Alternatively, you may have Freedom Schools in your community already, as there were almost 200 sites across the U.S. in 2016. The majority of CDF's Freedom Schools partnerships are with public schools, churches, and/or other community organization. However, only a handful of Freedom Schools are part of active collaborations with university partners. We represent a collaboration between both university and community partners, and we work closely with multiple businesses, churches, as well as public schools. These multiple perspectives have informed the following implementation suggestions:

1. Partner with at Least One Local College or University

FAMU and FSU faculty, alumni, and students collaborated to establish and run the NFFS camps. We also joined forces with many other local partners mentioned above, but the advantage of partnering with a university is that it provides a large, eager, and diverse pool of potential collaborators. One of the main sources of SLI applicants are current undergraduates or recent graduates, particularly education majors. We have also found the universities' reach, through social media, to faculty, staff, and alumni and current students to be invaluable for recruiting SLIs and volunteers, not to mention for raising money for the curriculum, books, supplies, and SLI training. Moreover, social media campaigns by the universities about our efforts have been picked up by local news outlets, which further expands our source of volunteers and donors.

In addition, the faculty at both universities provided support for afternoon programming, grant writing, research, and program evaluation. Faculty organized afternoon programming staffed by undergraduate and graduate student volunteers, many of whom receive supervised internship credits for their efforts, making them a reliable source of free labor. Research grants helped pay for programming costs and incentives for children and parents. Faculty also organized data collection for program evaluation and other research initiatives carried out by undergraduates and graduate students, who often received individual study credits for assisting with research. Thus, Freedom Schools provided not only K–8 scholars but also college students with a rich venue for learning.

2. Brag about Freedom Schools to Whomever Will Listen

A valuable long-term impact that findings from program evaluation and research can have is on the credibility of the Freedom Schools, which should help to attract more donors and serve more children. As previously mentioned, we also have had great success with raising needed funds to implement Freedom Schools by sharing about the program and its effectiveness though social media, news outlets, and churches. Another way to brag about your Freedom Schools is to invite folks to visit! Every morning, Harambee includes a read-aloud guest. Not only is it important to expose the scholars to diverse guests from all walks of life, but to share with the wider community the enthusiasm of young scholars passionate about reading and social action. So invite potential volunteers and donors to participate in Harambee, read aloud, and tell the scholars about their careers and passion for reading. Don't forget to take and post lots of videos to social media or to invite the community to attend the finale on the last day of camp that showcases all the scholars' accomplishments.

3. Find Diverse Partners from Throughout the Community

Closely related to our first two tips, we have found that having diverse partners from throughout the community is key to establishing a sustainable Freedom Schools initiative. One invaluable partner who found us through the media is AmeriCorps VISTA; they provide matching grants that best SLIs' stipends as well as provide a tuition waiver or student loan forgiveness. This means less money for us to raise and a more attractive package to recruit talented college-aged applicants for SLI positions. Moreover, having multiple churches and local businesses providing money, time, supplies, and talent equals more stability. In fact, we had too much interest and had trouble fitting in all the activities people offered to provide to scholars in the afternoons! With many options comes the benefit of having resources available in coming years, even as the ability of individual organizations to provide support may fluctuate from year to year.

4. Believe in and Love the Scholars

Last but not least, the core beliefs that guide CDF Freedom Schools include the following principles, which are supported by the research on the positive effects of high expectations and caring (cf. Roehrig, Turner, Arrastia, Christesen, McElhaney, & Jakiel, 2012): "All children are capable of learning and achieving at high standards," and "Learning communities that offer a sense of safety, love, caring, and personal power are needed for transformative education" (CDF, 2017, "Core Beliefs"). The CDF Freedom Schools provide a model of schooling that offers support and praise upon the first encounter with the students. It is a model of schooling that does not wait for the scholars to demonstrate mastery of any content before they are praised; rather it praises students first, establishing a foundation of positive self-efficacy where students know they are loved. The CDF Freedom Schools see intelligence as the unique balance between knowledge of self, family, community, country and world alongside a commitment to social action. Thus, we emphasize self-care with our staff, who can wear themselves out during the intensive summer. And, above all, we encourage our staff and other key stakeholders to constantly remind the scholars they are smart and loved.

IMPLICATIONS

The growing Freedom Schools movement represents one promising method for focusing on and harnessing the strengths of communities to help encourage children, who are often considered "at-risk," to follow their passions and become advocates for themselves and their communities. We have found that incorporating powerful tools such as culturally relevant pedagogy – in contexts that do not just recreate the existing societal hierarchies that lead to inequality – to be effective and rewarding. Thus, we strongly encourage professional educators and community members to find ways to work together to level the playing field for the next generation of scholars who want to make a difference.

ACKNOWLEDGMENTS

We are ever grateful to and inspired by our dedicated NFFS scholars, families, staff, and research team. This work is dedicated to you.

REFERENCES

Children's Defense Fund. (2017). *CDF Freedom Schools Program*. Retrieved from http://www.childrensdefense.org/programs/freedomschools/

Clemons, K. M. (2014). I've got to do something for my people: Black women teachers of the 1964 Mississippi Freedom Schools. *Western Journal of Black Studies, 38*(3), 141–154.

Clemons, K. A. (2014). I'm hip: A musical exploration of rap music's creative guise. In B. Kopano & T. L. Brown (Eds.), *Soul thieves: White America's appropriation of African American popular culture* (pp. 51–60). New York: Palgrave Macmillan.

Clemons, K. M., Price, P. G., & Clemons, K. A. (2017). "Hold up, wait a minute, let me put some freedom in it": Hip-hop-based education and the Freedom School experience. In W. T. Pink & G. Noblit (Eds.), *Second international handbook of urban education* (pp. 853–873). New York: Springer.

DuFour, R. (2004). What is a "professional learning community"? *Educational Leadership, 61*(8), 6–11.

Florida, R., & Mellander, C. (2015). *Segregated city: The geography of economic segregation in America's metros.* Toronto, Canada: Martin Prosperity Institute. Retrieved from http://martinprosperity.org/media/Segregated%20City.pdf

Gay, G. (2000). *Culturally responsive teaching: Theory, research, and practice.* New York, NY: Teachers College Record.

Harper, S. R. (2010). An anti-deficit achievement framework for research on students of color in STEM. In S. R. Harper & C. B. Newman (Eds.), *Students of color in STEM: Engineering a new research agenda. New Directions for Institutional Research* (pp. 63–74). San Francisco, CA: Jossey-Bass.

Johns, J. (2012). *Basic Reading Inventory* (11th ed.). Dubuque, IA: Kendall Hunt Publishing Company.

Ladson-Billings, G. (1995). But that's just good teaching! The case for culturally relevant pedagogy. *Theory into Practice, 34*(3), 159–165. doi: 10.1080/00405849509543675

Ladson-Billings, G. (1998). Just what is critical race theory and what's it doing in a nice field like education? *International Journal of Qualitative Studies in Education, 11*, 7–24.

Ladson-Billings, G. (2014). Culturally relevant pedagogy 2.0: A.k.a. the Remix. *Harvard Educational Review, 84*, 74–84.

Lee, C. D. (1995). A culturally based cognitive apprenticeship: Teaching African American high school students' skills in literary interpretation. *Reading Research Quarterly, 30*, 608–630.

Mathur, P. (1989, August). So strong. *Spin, 5*, 32.

McKenna, M., & Kear, D. (1990). Measuring attitude toward reading: A new tool for teachers. *Reading Teacher, 43*, 626–639. doi: 10.1598/rt.43.8.3

Roehrig, A. D., Turner, J. E., Arrastia, M., Christesen, E., McElhaney, S., & Jakiel, L. (2012). Effective teachers and teaching: Characteristics and practices related to student outcomes. In T. Urdan, S. Graham, M. Royer, & M. Zeidner (Eds.), *Educational psychology handbook, Volume 2: Individual differences, cultural variations, and contextual factors in educational psychology* (pp. 501–527). Washington DC: American Psychological Association.

Strauss, A., & Corbin, J. (1998). *Basics of qualitative research* (2nd ed.). Thousand Oaks: SAGE.

Tschida, C. M., Ryan, C. L., & Ticknor, A. S. (2014). Building on windows and mirrors: Encouraging the disruption of "single stories" through children's literature. *Journal of Children's Literature, 40*, 28–39. Retrieved from http://www.childrensliteratureassembly.org/docs/JCL-40-1-Article_Tschida.pdf

The State of America's Children. (2008). Retrieved from http://www.childrensdefense.org/library/data/cradle-prison-pipeline-report-2007-full-highres.html

APPENDIX: IRC TEXTS BY WEEKLY "I CAN MAKE A DIFFERENCE" THEME AND LEVEL IN 2016V

Weekly Theme	Level	Book Title	Author
Week One: Self	I (grades K–2)	Mr. George Baker	Amy Hest
		Just Because I Am: A Child's Book of Affirmations	Lauren Murphy Payne
			Victoria Sperrow
		Wilma Rudolph	Douglas Wood
		Miss Little's Gift	Labon Carrick Hill
		Dave the Potter	
	II (grades 3–5)	Grandpa, Is Everything Black Bad?	Sandy Lynne Holman
		Miss Little's Gift	Douglas Wood
		Light in the Darkness: A Story of How Slaves Learned in Secret	Lesa Cline-Ransome
			Lizzy Rockwell
		Good Enough to Eat	
	III (grades 6–8)	Out of My Mind	Sharon M. Draper
Week Two: Family	I (grades K–2)	¡Si, Se Puede! Yes We Can!: Janitor Strike in L.A.	Diana Cohn
			Susan Kuklin
		How My Family Lives in America	Maribeth Boelts
		Those Shoes	Kathleen D. Lindsey
		Sweet Potato Pie	Linda Jacobs Altman
		Amelia's Road	
	II (grades 3–5)	Always My Grandpa: A Story for Children About Alzheimer's Disease	Linda Scacco
			Karie Smith Milway
		The Good Garden	Karen Lynn Williams
		Circles of Hope	Jeanie Franz Ransom
		What Really Happened to Humpty?	
	III (grades 6–8)	The Road to Paris	Nikki Grimes
Week Three: Community	I (grades K–2)	The Storyteller's Candle	Lucia Gonzalez
		Miss Tizzy	Libba Moore Gray
		Have You Filled A Bucket Today?	Carol McLoud
		Crossing Bok Chitto: A Choctaw Tale of Friendship & Freedom	Tim Tingle
			Eve Bunting
		Smokey Night	
	II (grades 3–5)	Tamika and the Wisdom Rings	Camille Yarbrough
	III (grades 6–8)	We Beat the Street.' How a Friendship Pact Led to Success	Drs. Sampson Davis, George Jenkins, & Rameck Hunt with Sharon M. Draper

Weekly Theme	Level	Book Title	Author
Week Four: Country	I (grades K–2)	*Freedom Summer*	Deborah Wiles
		Biblioburro: A True Story of Colombia	Jeanette Winter
		Elizabeth Leads the Way: Elizabeth Cody Stanton and the Right to Vote	George Littlechild
			Michael S. Bandy &
		Granddaddy's Turn: A Journey to the Ballot Box	Eric Stein
			David Adler
		A Picture Book of Thurgood Marshall	
	II (grades 3–5)	*Moses: When Harriet Tubman Led Her People to Freedom*	Carole Boston Weatherford
		Tucky Jo and Little Heart	Patricia Polacco
		Lillian's Right to Vote	Jonah Winter
		Crossing Bok Chitto: A Choctaw Tale of Friendship & Freedom	Tim Tingle
	III (grades 6–8)	*The Watson Go to Birmingham, 1963*	Christopher Paul Curtis
Week Five: World	I (grades K–2)	*The Day Gogo Went to Vote*	Elinor Batezat Sisula
		Mama Miti	
		Donna JoNapoli	Emily Pearson
		Ordinary Mary's Extraordinary Deed	Mem Fox
		Whoever You Are	Lynne Barasch
		Knockin' On Wood: Starring Peg Leg Bates	
	II (grades 3–5)	*Kid Caramel, Private Investigator: The Case of the Missing Ankh*	Dwayne J. Ferguson
			Lesa Cline-Ransome
		Young Pele: Soccer's First Star	Paula Yoo
		Twenty-two Cents: Muhammad Yunus and the Village Bank	
	III (grades 6–8)	*You Don't Even Know Me: Stories and Poems about Boys*	Sharon G. Flake
Week Six: With Hope, Education, and Action	I (grades K–2)	*A Picture Book of Cesar Chavez*	David Adler
		Freedom's School	Lesa Cline-Ransom
		Keep Your Ear on the Ball	Genevieve Petrillo
		One Hen: How One Loan Made a Difference	Kacie Smith Milway
	II (grades 3–5)	*Harvesting Hope: The Story of Cesar Chavez*	Kathleen Krull
			Suzanne Slade
		Climbing Lincoln's Steps: The African American Journey	Jeanette Winter
			Vaunda Micheaux Nelson
		Malala, a Brave Girl from Pakistan/ Iqbal, a Brave Boy from Pakistan: Two Stories of Bravery	
		The Book Itch: Freedom, Truth & Harlem's Greatest Bookstore	
	III (grades 6–8)	*Confessions of a Former Bully*	Trudy Ludwig

INDEX

Ethical and Social Perspectives on Situational Crime Prevention

Edited by

ANDREW VON HIRSCH
DAVID GARLAND
ALISON WAKEFIELD

·HART·
PUBLISHING

OXFORD – PORTLAND, OREGON
2000

Hart Publishing
Oxford and Portland, Oregon

Published in North America (US and Canada) by
Hart Publishing
c/o International Specialized Book Services
5804 NE Hassalo Street
Portland, Oregon
97213-3644
USA

Distributed in Netherlands, Belgium and Luxembourg by
Intersentia, Churchillaan 108
B2900 Schoten
Antwerpen
Belgium

Hart Publishing is a specialist legal publisher based in Oxford, England.
To order further copies of this book or to request a list of other publications
please write to:

Hart Publishing,
Salters Boatyard, Folly Bridge, Abingdon Rd,
Oxford, OX1 4LB
Telephone: +44 (0)1865 245533 Fax: +44 (0) 1865 794882
email: mail@hartpub.co.uk
WEBSITE: http//:www.hartpub.co.uk

British Library Cataloguing in Publication Data
Data Available

ISBN 1 84113-171-7 (hardback)

Typeset by John Saunders Design & Production
Printed in Great Britain by
Biddles Ltd., www.biddles.co.uk

Preface

'Situational crime prevention' refers to crime prevention strategies that aim at reducing criminal opportunities in the routines of everyday life. Methods of situational crime prevention (SCP) include 'hardening' potential targets, improving natural surveillance, controlling access to property, and deflecting offenders from settings in which crimes might occur. This approach, pioneered by Ronald V. Clarke and others in the late 1970s and 80s, has now become an important area of criminal-justice research and policy. To get a sense of SCP's influence, one needs merely to stroll down the streets of an English city, and witness the extent to which CCTV cameras, steering wheels locks and burglar alarms have become standard features of our urban environment.

While there has been extensive discussion and research on situational crime prevention in recent years, much of it has focused on SCP's more technical aspects: criminologists have been concerned to ask 'does SCP work?', 'does it merely displace crime to other locales?' and 'do its assumptions match what we know about prospective offenders and victims?' There has been much less discussion of how to *situate* this approach and of how it relates to the policy predicaments and strategies of crime prevention that characterise contemporary society. SCP also raises a variety of ethical questions – concerning, for example, its potential impact on the freedom of people to go about their everyday business. It seems to us that the time has come for addressing these issues, and for legal scholars, philosophers and sociologists to join criminologists in assessing SCP's social and ethical aspects.

This volume, in its various essays, addresses two kinds of questions. The *first* concerns the ethics of situational crime prevention. To what extent do SCP strategies unduly constrain people's liberty of movement? Will such strategies involve increased scrutiny of people's everyday activities, and what problems are involved in such scrutiny? Can ethical principles be developed that would help distinguish acceptable from unacceptable forms of intervention? The *second* kind of question concerns SCP's position in criminological discourse and in the contemporary culture of crime control. To what extent does SCP represent a shift in thinking about the nature of crime, and about the prospects and strategies for dealing with it? Does the emergence of SCP reflect a fundamental change in our expectations concerning crime prevention in a modern society? To the extent SCP treats crime as a 'normal' risk to be managed, or looks beyond the state apparatus to the organisations and institutions of civil society, what are the social and political implications of doing so?

Insofar as the ethics and social aspects of situational crime prevention have been addressed at all, the discussion has tended to be couched in sweeping terms. Sceptics argue that SCP leads to a fortress or a 'Panopticon' society, that it is manipulative and amoral in its management of conduct, that it involves a cynical view of people's motivations, and so on. Defenders of SCP suggest that its strategies are generally benign, that they are less intrusive than punishment; and that problematic applications (such as the sale of CCTV tapes for public entertainment purposes) can readily be dealt with. The essays in this volume will suggest that the relevant issues are actually more complex, and more interesting. It is only certain types of SCP strategies, not all, that potentially interfere with such important rights as privacy and freedom of movement. How and to what extent they do so varies with the particulars of the practices involved. Certain SCP strategies may inhibit social trust, or may erode citizens' attachment to values of law abidingness; others may do the contrary. In discussing the ethics and the social aspects of situational crime prevention, it is essential to address and analyse *which* SCP strategies, *which* ethical values, and *which* social norms and practices are involved. The essays in this volume embark upon this task, and suggest the value of that undertaking.

The thinking reflected in this book was stimulated by two colloquia held in Cambridge, in January 1997 and October 1999. We are most grateful to those who took part in these meetings – presenters and commentators alike. Their insights and arguments made the colloquia immensely enjoyable and have contributed greatly to the analyses that appear in this volume. A list of those present at the meetings is set forth at the end of this book.

We wish to thank Joy Anderson and Jenny Lewis for their painstaking work in preparing the manuscript for submission.

During the preparation of this book, there has been established at the Institute of Criminology in Cambridge a new Centre for Penal Theory and Penal Ethics, to deal with ethical and jurisprudential issues in criminal law and policy. Thinking about the Centre's aims and activities has been influenced considerably by the present undertaking. For this reason, and in virtue of the themes addressed in the volume, the Board of the Centre believes it most appropriate that the work appears as the Centre's first publication.

A.v.H., Cambridge
D.G., New York
A.W., Cambridge

Contents

Notes on Contributors

Ronald V. Clarke is University Professor at the School of Criminal Justice, Rutgers University. He is a former Head of the Home Office Research and Planning Unit where he played a significant part in the development of situational crime prevention and in the launching of the British Crime Survey. He is Editor of *Crime Prevention Studies* and the author of numerous books and articles.

Adam Crawford is Professor of Criminology and Deputy Director of the Centre for Criminal Justice Studies, Law Department, University of Leeds. He is author of *The Local Governance of Crime* (Oxford University Press, 1997), *Crime Prevention and Community Safety* (Longman, 1998) and co-editor of *Integrating a Victim Perspective Within Criminal Justice* (Ashgate, 2000). He has published various chapters and journal articles on restorative justice, crime prevention and the inter-agency approach. He has worked for the New Zealand Ministry of Justice and the Northern Ireland Office concerning matters of community safety. He is currently part of a Home Office funded team evaluating the pilots of reforms introduced by the Youth Justice and Criminal Evidence Act 1999.

Antony Duff is Professor of Philosophy at the University of Stirling where he has taught since 1970, and has written widely on issues in the philosophy of law. His two most recent books are *Criminal Attempts* (Oxford University Press, 1997) and *Punishment, Communication and Community* (Oxford University Press N.Y., 2000).

David Garland, F.R.S.E., is Professor of Law and Sociology at New York University. He was previously Professor of Penology in the Centre for Law and Society, University of Edinburgh. He is the author of a number of works in the sociology of punishment and the history of criminology and is Editor-in-Chief of *Punishment and Society: The International Journal of Penology*. His most recent book, *The Culture of Control*, is soon to be published by Oxford University Press.

Tim Hope is Professor and Head of the Department of Criminology, Keele University. His research and publications lie in the related fields of crime prevention, community safety, crime victimisation and programme evaluation. He was formerly a Principal Research Officer at the Home Office responsible for crime prevention research. He has recently edited *Perspectives on Crime Reduction* (Ashgate, 2000) and *Crime, Risk and Insecurity* (with Richard Sparks, in press).

John Kleinig, Director of the Institute for Criminal Justice Ethics and Editor of the journal *Criminal Justice Ethics*, is Professor of Philosophy in the Department of Law and Police Science, John Jay College of Criminal Justice, and in the Ph.D. Programs in Philosophy and Criminal Justice, The Graduate Center, City University of New York. His books include *Punishment and Desert* (Martinus Nijhoff, 1973), *Paternalism* (Manchester University Press, 1983), and *The Ethics of Policing* (Cambridge University Press, 1996). He is currently writing a book on loyalty.

Sandra Marshall has taught philosophy at the University of Stirling since 1969; she is currently Dean of the Faculty of Arts. She has published articles on a range of issues in social and legal philosophy, including recently 'Criminalization and Sharing Wrongs' (*Canadian Journal of Law and Jurpisrudence*, 1998) and 'Body Shopping: The Case of Prostitution' (*Journal of Applied Philosophy*, 1999). She is President of the UK Association for Legal and Social Philosophy.

Joanna Shapland is Professor of Criminal Justice and Director of the Institute for the Study of the Legal Profession at the University of Sheffield. She has written extensively about victimisation and policing (for example, *Policing by the Public*, Routledge, 1988), as well as carrying out evaluations of crime prevention projects and an audit of criminal justice in Milton Keynes. Her recent interests in crime prevention have focused on business and crime, including work on industrial estates, shopping centres, violence against staff and a review of retail crime prevention.

Clifford Shearing is Professor of Criminology and Sociology at the University of Toronto and Professor in the School of Government at the University of the Western Cape. He is interested in developments in governance and has used policing as a vehicle for exploring them. At present his primary research focus is on innovative forms of policing and dispute resolution in poor communities.

David J. Smith is Professor of Criminology at the University of Edinburgh. He has carried out inter-disciplinary research in a variety of fields, including inequality (especially related to ethnic and religious groups), policing, crime trends, criminal process, child and adolescent development, and school effectiveness. Among his books are *Racial Disadvantage in Britain* (Penguin, 1977), *Police and People in London* (Policy Studies Institute, 4 vols., 1983), *The School Effect* (Policy Studies Institute, 1989), *Racial Justice at Work* (Policy Studies Institute, 1989), *Inequality in Northern Ireland* (Oxford University

Press, 1991), *Democracy and Policing* (Policy Studies Institute, 1994), and (with Sir Michael Rutter) *Psychosocial Disorders in Young People: Time Trends and Their Causes* (Wiley, 1995). With Lesley McAra, he directs the Edinburgh Study of Youth Transitions and Crime, a longitudinal study of 4,300 young people in the City of Edinburgh.

Richard Sparks is Professor of Criminology, Keele University. His principal research interests are in public responses to crime and in penal politics, particularly imprisonment. His recent books include *Prisons and the Problem of Order* (Oxford University Press, 1996, with A. E. Bottoms and W. Hay), *Crime and Social Change in Middle England* (Routledge, 2000, with E. Girling and I. Loader), and *Crime, Risk and Insecurity* (edited with Tim Hope, in press).

Andrew von Hirsch, LL.D., is Honorary Professor of Penal Theory and Penal Law and Fellow of Fitzwilliam College, University of Cambridge. He is also Director of the Centre for Penal Theory and Penal Ethics at the Institute of Criminology, Cambridge. His books include *Doing Justice* (Hill and Wang, 1976); *Past or Future Crimes* (Manchester University Press, 1986); *Censure and Sanctions* (Oxford University Press, 1993); and (with Andrew Ashworth) *Principled Sentencing* (Hart Publishing, 1998). He is currently writing on a variety of issues concerning ethical aspects of criminal justice policies.

Alison Wakefield is a doctoral researcher at the Institute of Criminology, University of Cambridge and a member of Churchill College. *Exclusion: Who Needs It?* (NFER, 1997) and *Talking Back: Pupil Views on Disaffection* (NFER, 1996), both with co-authors Kay Kinder and Anne Wilkin, are among her publications. Her current doctoral research is titled *The Private Policing of Public Space*, and she is also writing about criminal record checks by employers.

1

Ideas, Institutions and Situational Crime Prevention

David Garland[*]

IDEAS AND INSTITUTIONS

Situational crime prevention (SCP) is a set of recipes for steering and channelling behaviour in ways that reduce the occurrence of criminal events. Its project is to use situational stimuli to guide conduct towards lawful outcomes, preferably in ways that are unobtrusive and invisible to those whose conduct is affected. Institutions, as Mary Douglas (1986) has shown, work in similar ways. Their institutional routines and practices, their distinctive ways of organizing the flow of social life, have the usually unnoticed consequence of channelling the thinking and acting of those caught up in them. The effect of embedded institutional arrangements (such as the criminal justice system) is to gently guide our thought and action in predetermined directions, shaping how we think about problems (such as crime) and how we routinely respond to them (e.g. by processing and punishing individual criminals).

What interests me most about the recent rise to prominence of situational crime prevention is its apparent success in breaking free of some of the institutionalized patterns of criminological thought and action that have prevailed for most of the 20th century. Without wishing to overstate the matter, or to attribute too much importance to this otherwise rather modest development, I want to suggest that situational crime prevention marks a break with the institutional epistemology that has characterised criminological thought and action for most of the modern period. Understanding the nature of that 'epistemological break' (to give an absurdly grandiose but actually quite accurate name to the event in question) and explaining how it came about, will be the purpose of this paper.

The striking thing about the premises and propositions of situational crime prevention is how very simple, how very mundane, how very straightforward they appear once they have been explicitly articulated. As an account of how

* The author is grateful to the Filomen D'Agastino and Max E. Greenberg Research Fund for its support during the writing of this chapter, and to the participants at the Cambridge SCP conference of January 1997 for their insights, comments and corrections.

crime events occur, and as a practical means for reducing the occurrence of these events, SCP has all the seeming obviousness and simplicity of common sense. Indeed, the commonsensical character of their diagnoses and prescriptions clearly appeals to the chief proponents of SCP – who take pains to stress that their insights derive not from fancy theorising or a close reading of criminological literature but simply from attending to the practical world and observing how it works. They like to think that the truth claims of SCP should be apparent to anyone, so long as they can shake themselves free of the legacy of criminological theory and see the world for what it is.[1] SCP thus presents itself as a layperson's criminology; as an empirical account of crime and a pragmatic account of what to do about it. And insofar as it entails an account of offenders and the processes that motivate their offending – that is to say, a criminological theory in the conventional sense of the phrase – SCP offers an account that seems equally simple and straightforward. Offenders are, for the most part, deemed to be normal, mundane individuals who give in to temptation as and when criminal opportunities arise. The common sense wisdom of age-old aphorisms tells us all we need to know: 'Opportunity makes the thief' (Felson and Clarke, 1999).

THE STRANGE DISAPPEARANCE OF
SITUATIONAL PREVENTION

The first question to pose might therefore be, where has SCP been up until now? Why has this way of thinking and acting not been much more prominent in the history of criminology and governmental crime control? How do we explain the fact that until recently, the criminological ideas and crime prevention recipes that constitute the 'SCP' approach have hardly featured in the lecture courses and textbooks of criminology, were seldom mentioned in policy statements of governments, and had no significant place in the practices of criminal justice? (A first clue to answering these questions is contained in the very language that we use to pose them. That we routinely refer to our apparatus of crime control as a 'criminal justice' system is significant. It indicates that our standard institutionalised response to crime gives priority to case-processing and the punishment of offenders, and uses the threat of such processing and punishment – general deterrence – as its primary prevention technique.)

So, we have something of a paradox. Once it has made its way onto the agenda, and has been stated forcefully and repeatedly by well-placed proponents, SCP takes on the appearance of an obvious and commonsensical approach. But somehow or other, it has managed to be largely absent from the mainstream commonsense of criminology for most of the discipline's history. We need to emphasize this absence, and insist on its significance because our

[1] See my discussion of Marcus Felson's *Crime and Everyday Life* in Chapter 12 of this volume.

historical memory will soon be altered by present day concerns. Now that SCP has been developed and elaborated, now that it has achieved a measure of status and recognition in the world of criminology, it is increasingly able to summon up a respectable criminological lineage, pointing to people like Cyril Burt, Leslie Wilkins, Scott Briar and Irving Piliavin, and David Matza as its forerunners (see Clarke, 1997: Introduction). And as the textbooks come to be rewritten, these earlier criminologists will no doubt be represented as the harbingers of the current interest in situations, temptations and the blocking of opportunities, in much the same way that Cesare Beccaria has come to be viewed as a 'rational choice criminologist'. But for anyone who has lived through this period, and who knows how these earlier criminologists were read and understood, it is clear that their relation to SCP is a retrospective creation. This is a line of antecedents that has only now become visible, as we read criminology's history in the light of our present concerns.

Yet if we go further back to two centuries ago, there was real and explicit interest in situational prevention strategies. What can explain the virtual disappearance of the ideas and concerns that were so prominent in the crime-control writings of Patrick Colquhoun and others like him at the end of the 18th century – notably in his *Treatise on the Police of the Metropolis* first published in 1795? As I argued in an earlier article (Garland, 1996), the common sense of the late 18th century is remarkably close to the assumptions of SCP. Here are some of the propositions (phrased in our idiom, not his) that Colquhoun set forth with every expectation that they would strike his 18th century readers as obvious:

(a) Crime, especially property crime, is a matter of temptation and opportunity, not a matter of special dispositions. Criminal conduct is widely distributed, not a peculiarity of particular individuals.

(b) Wealth and abundance bring crime in their wake. Modern capitalism sets wealth free to circulate and, in consequence, produces new temptations and occasions for crime.

(c) The poor are always with us. So are criminals. Our efforts to control crime should focus upon reducing the occasions and opportunities for crime events rather than trying to change criminal dispositions.

(d) 'Policing' or 'prevention' is a matter of improving security, hardening targets, reducing the exposure of potential victims. The task is to address what Colquhoun called the 'ten thousand different ways' in which the newly mobile property of a modern commercial society is 'exposed to depredation'.

(e) Policing is the task and responsibility not of 'the state', nor of a single specialist agency, but of everyone with an interest in preserving private property and personal security.

By the beginning of the 20th century, this older common sense had been largely expunged from criminology. By that time our modern, specialized, differentiated response to crime had already been established in the form of the criminal justice state and the state agencies that had taken shape during the 19th century – the police, prosecution and the prison – had made the response to crime primarily a matter of pursuing, prosecuting and punishing individual offenders. Crime control had come to be institutionalised as 'criminal justice' – the sanctioning of individual offenders, one by one, in a reactive response to completed crimes – together with the generalized prevention through deterrence that this was supposed to entail.

If we look at the criminological writings of the late 19th and early 20th centuries, we find that Colquhoun's ideas of 100 years before had all but disappeared. In the influential writings of Lombroso or Ferri or Garofalo, Colquhoun's assumptions are reversed, or else reinterpreted in a new framework of thought. In this new, 'positive' science of criminology, crime has been reconceptualized as 'criminality' and criminality is chiefly a characteristic of individuals. Criminal *events* cease to have much significance in themselves and become, instead, symptomatic manifestations of underlying criminal dispositions. And in terms of its intellectual interests and practical priorities, criminology has come to focus upon the peculiarities of the criminal type and the means necessary to correct or contain him. The discipline had little time to be distracted by the circumstances in which 'occasional criminals' – who were not truly 'criminal' at all – came to break the law.

In this new criminological framework, the progress of modern civilization and economic growth were no longer assumed to be causes of crime. On the contrary; they were taken to be means of ameliorating criminality and making criminal dispositions less widespread. Garofalo remarks: 'It is impossible to believe that progress in civilization contributes to the increase of crime...its effect is quite the opposite' (Garofalo, 1914: 174). The Gladstone Report (1895) takes the same view when it argues that social reform and the growth of wealth will dissolve the chief causes of crime and further reduce the crime rate. And when Cesare Lombroso addresses the notion that increased 'wealth' might cause increased crime, he takes this to be a proposition about affluent individuals and their characters, not a proposition about wealthy societies and the opportunities they generate: 'Rapidly acquired wealth, which is not balanced by high character...is harmful rather than helpful' (Lombroso, 1911: 132). Or again, 'wealth is a source of degeneration' (Lombroso, 1911: 134).

The idea of *opportunity* enters the argument only as an outlet for a criminality that is already established and must be expressed: 'The born criminal finds...more opportunities for crime in wealth than in poverty' (Lombroso, 1911:135).

By the start of the 20th century, the idea of crime prevention had shifted to become what we now term *social* prevention rather than the *situational* prevention advocated by Colquhoun. In this new way of thinking, crime control is to be achieved not through 'a correct police' and the widespread use of situational measures, but through social improvement and individual reform, through generalised social security and remedial social work intervention. The proper target of preventive action has become the (social, psychological and biological) processes bearing upon the formation of criminal character, not the situational dynamics that produce particular criminal events.

A partial and interesting exception to this is to be found in the writings of Enrico Ferri, the most sociological and the most radical member of the positivist school of criminology. Ferri's analysis begins with a critique of the penal response to crime. Rather in the manner of the Home Office in the 1980s, he emphasizes the limitations of a crime control policy that focuses upon the individual offender: 'Punishment, far from being the convenient panacea which it seems to classical criminal legislators, and the public, has but a very limited power to control crime' (Ferri, 1917: 242). Ferri proposed instead a series of 'penal substitutes' – economic, political and moral measures that would prevent crime rather than punish it. Legislative action was to reach right down 'to the slightest details of existence' in order to guide 'human activity...into non-criminal ways'. Ferri's long and detailed list of preventative proposals contains several measures that we would today characterize as 'situational crime prevention'. He proposes the substitution of metal coinage for paper money to prevent counterfeiting; personal letters of credit rather than cash payments; the presence of a concierge at the entrance of apartment buildings; safety chains on doors; 'mechanisms against thieves such as safes, safety locks and alarm systems' and even the use of Roentgen Rays by customs officials to examine baggage and prevent smuggling (Ferri, 1917: 267).

But Ferri's argument is above all an argument for social reform and social engineering. His 'situational measures' are minor items on a political laundry list that is dedicated to more profound change. Here is his argument for what he calls 'social hygiene':

> The legislator...should realize that social reforms have much more power to prevent the overflow of crime than penal codes. His task is to maintain the health of the social body. He should, therefore, imitate the physician who preserves the health of individuals, and as little as possible and only in extreme cases, within the limits of strict necessity, have recourse to the violent methods of surgery. He should have but very limited confidence in the problematical value of remedies and should rely upon the safe and continuous services of hygiene (1917:279).

And here is his view of the place of punishment: 'The purely and stupidly repressive function [should] be transformed into a clinic, by which society will be preserved from the disease of crime as from any other physical or mental disease' (1917:286). Ferri was arguing, in effect, that crime was a social disease that presented itself as an individual pathology. Its treatment called for deep-rooted measures of social reform and continuous social hygiene. Situational measures occupied a relatively minor role in this radically social policy.

As it turned out, Ferri's radical proposals – and his situational measures –

were largely marginalised in the historical process whereby criminological ideas came to be translated into law and practice. As I have argued elsewhere (Garland, 1985), the silencing of these aspects of Ferri's radical programme came about not just as a result of political selection and compromise, but also because the criminal justice system, once established, quickly became the primary vehicle for crime control policies. Given the monopolizing tendencies of these institutions, a policy that could not be implemented as an aspect of responding to crime complaints and processing cases had little prospect of being put into practice. The established institutions acted as a grid that filtered out incompatible or disruptive proposals, denying them the legal, organisational and budgetary support that they required to succeed.

The emergence of the criminal justice state, and of the new 'positivistic' science of criminology thus tended to diminish the perceived relevance and utility of the kinds of measures that Colquhoun took to be central to crime control. So although situational measures remained present in the armoury of crime control – particularly in the low-level, order maintenance work of the professional police – at the level of policy and research they quickly became a subordinate, marginal element that attracted little institutional support. A good example of this is the 1949 *Memorandum on Juvenile Delinquency* (Home Office and Ministry of Education, 1949) in which situational measures are mentioned, only to be characterized as superficial, insufficiently constructive, incapable of tackling the 'real' problem: 'To some extent, juvenile delinquency can be combated by the practical device of removing...the temptations to wrongdoing; but as a permanent solution something more constructive is required'. Even as late as 1975, in a Report that fully recognizes the limits of traditional criminal justice measures and that acknowledges the apparent failure of the rehabilitative ideal, the Scottish Council on Crime adopts this same mildly dismissive approach:

> In this Memorandum, we discuss how society might raise the height of its defensive barricades to prevent crime – how to reduce opportunities for theft, how to reduce the availability of weapons for use in crimes of violence, etc. Measures such as these, necessary though they are, provide no long-term solutions to most crime problems, *they do nothing to tackle the problem of crime where it has its roots, namely in the individual, the family and the community.* (Scottish Council on Crime, 1975:89. My emphasis.)

To tackle a problem *at its roots* is to prevent it reappearing; to adopt an effective, thoroughgoing, radical strategy. By comparison, situational measures are viewed as merely cosmetic, superficial, doing nothing to address the *real* problem. The Report – by a Council that numbered Nigel Walker among its members – continues:

> Some of the measures which we suggest...might be expected to produce results in the shorter term; the measures concerned are largely those which would make it more difficult or less rewarding for a person to commit a crime. Such measures do

nothing however to reduce the inclination or tendency within the individual to commit crime (p.98)

Somehow it has become obvious that the *crime* problem is a *criminality* problem. In the 200 years between Patrick Colquhoun and his fellow Scottish expatriate Nigel Walker, it somehow became natural for criminologists to assume that the problem of crime is a problem of criminal *individuals*, not of criminal *events*, and that effective action must focus its energies upon the former and not the latter. The strangeness of that 'common sense' has only now become apparent in the wake of SCP's deliberate challenge to it.

My suggestion is that SCP tended to drop out of sight during the two centuries following Colquhoun because a framework of thought and action became established that had the effect of marginalising these ideas. The criminal justice state, and later the penal-welfare version of the criminal justice state, operated in ways that routinely downplayed the significance of 'situational' ideas and prescriptions. The new agencies, which increasingly monopolized society's organized response to crime, directed attention to criminal individuals and the problem of criminality, aiming to transform them by penal measures or else by individual and social reform. Today we still experience the astonishing tenacity of that 'way of seeing', however much we strive to think outside its terms. How ever many times we tell ourselves and our students not to confuse crime control with the sanctioning of offenders we repeatedly find ourselves slipping back into the habits of thought that the established institutions impose upon us. There is such a thing as institutionalised forgetting, and criminological discourse shows all the signs of this when it effortlessly slips from the problem of controlling crime to the solution of sanctioning offenders.

For most of the 20th century, in summary, situational measures and ideas have remained present in the field of criminological thought, but have been accorded a low status and priority.[2] The state's institutions were structured in ways that made this style of thinking largely irrelevant. The key policies and practices of the criminal justice state turned away from managing situations and reducing opportunities to the pursuit and reform of individual offenders and their criminality. The institutional environment selected for other kinds of criminology, favouring above all the criminologies of disposition and deprivation that became central in the middle decades of the 20th century. These were criminologies that fitted better with the institutional epistemology of crime control in the 20th century and with the social and legal rationalities that underlay crime control and criminal justice (Garland, forthcoming). And once criminology became firmly established in the universities in the 1960s and 1970s, academic pressures and disciplinary commitments tended to pull

---

[2] These ideas would occasionally surface – as in the Cornish Report (1960) – only to drop from sight again without any appreciable practical effect. See Laycock and Heal (1989).

criminologists still further away from the kinds of mundane practical reasoning about crime that SCP embodied.

I should stress that I am certainly not suggesting that no one made use of SCP ideas and the preventive practices associated with them. Police forces deployed foot patrols and gave advice about locks and bolts; they supervised soccer games, industrial disputes and demonstrations where disorder was likely. Security firms sold alarm systems and private security. Insurance companies required preventive devices and a measure of care. And many commercial firms, private citizens and residential communities engaged in avoidance behaviour and routine precautions. But SCP was not an important aspect of the teaching and research of criminologists nor did it feature prominently in official crime control policy. And this was so because it did not fit with the social and legal rationalities that have increasingly dominated crime control policy over the course of the last two centuries.

THE RE-EMERGENCE OF SITUATIONAL PREVENTION

If SCP was, until recently, quite marginal to the criminological enterprise, it becomes necessary to ask: 'What explains the re-emergence of SCP in the last two decades?' One ought not to exaggerate its influence, of course. As a criminological approach and as a policy framework, it exists as one theme among many others, and its proponents are often dismayed (and perhaps a little puzzled) that they have not been yet more influential. But clearly over the past two decades SCP has become more prominent and more influential than it has been at any time in the last 200 years. It is now a standard feature in lecture courses that twenty years ago gave no place to it whatsoever. Criminological textbooks – the most slow-changing and conservative of academic institutions – now devote substantial sections to this approach. In graduate schools of criminology, whole courses are now devoted to it. More importantly, SCP has increasingly formed a central theme of the research programme of the British Home Office and has, since the early 1980s, attained an established place in official policy. There is nowadays a rapidly expanding crime prevention infrastructure – much enhanced by the Crime and Disorder Act of 1998 – of agencies, organizations, committees, and careers in which SCP features very prominently (see Crawford, 1997).

One important part of any explanation of how SCP re-emerged in criminological theory and practice will be a story about the (re)discovery and development of these ideas by particular individuals, most notably Ronald V. Clarke and a number of co-workers such as Derick Cornish, Paul Ekblom, Kevin Heal, Mike Hough, Gloria Laycock, Pat Mayhew, Ken Pease, Barry Poyner, Nick Tilley and later Marcus Felson. Indeed, we have already been told some of this story in a series of retrospective accounts of the formation of the SCP research programme and the ideas that underlie it (Cornish and Clarke, 1983;

Clarke, 1995; 1997). Clarke's background in psychology; his interest in Walter Mischel's work and its insistence that situational causation has primacy over dispositional accounts; the impasse reached by Home Office research in the mid-1970s following the largely negative findings about the effectiveness of rehabilitation and of the police; the influence of James Q. Wilson's argument for a criminological approach that would be directly useful for government; Clarke's research on absconding from Approved Schools and its finding that immediate environment seemed to explain more than inherent dispositions (Clarke and Martin, 1971) – these are the biographical and intellectual events that gradually resulted in the development first of an 'opportunity model', then a 'choice model', and eventually of the SCP framework in its fully elaborated form.

But the SCP framework did not develop in theoretical isolation. It emerged as one of a cluster of cognate theories and ways of thinking that has developed over the last three decades and which includes rational choice theory, routine activity theory, criminal lifestyle analysis, crime as opportunity, the economic analysis of crime – a whole new genre that I have elsewhere termed 'the new criminologies of everyday life' (Garland, 1996). These new developments derived support from a variety of sources, among them the economic analyses of Gary Becker (Becker, 1968); Oscar Newman's theory of 'defensive space' (Newman, 1972); Jane Jacobs' analysis of 'natural crime prevention' (Jacobs, 1961); C.R. Jefferey's *Crime Prevention Through Environmental Design* (1977); Goldstein's problem-oriented policing (Goldstein, 1979); and James Q. Wilson's influential critique of academic criminology, causal analysis and social solutions (Wilson, 1975).

Nor did the SCP framework develop in isolation from policy and governmental considerations. This was not a set of ideas that first developed academic respectability and then slowly spread into the world of practice. On the contrary, it was a set of ideas which was developed for official use, despite resistance from academic criminologists and from Home Office mandarins who had long been committed to a welfarist approach. It was an idea that had found its time – and more to the point, had found a favourable institutional climate – after being exiled for the best part of two centuries. What explains the new favour that SCP has found in the 1980s and since? Why is it now being positively selected by its institutional environment after such a long history of marginalisation?

The 'accident' of its location was obviously important. The person most closely associated with the development of SCP – Ronald V. Clarke – happens to have been located in the Home Office's (Criminological) Research and Planning Unit (HORPU), advising government officials on crime policy, evaluating current policies and casting around for a more effective approach to crime control at a time when crime rates were rising rapidly and the existing policies were increasingly discredited. Eventually he became Head of the Unit and was able to implement a new research agenda, organised in part around

SCP conceptions. If Clarke had emigrated to the USA in 1974 instead of 1984, one wonders whether SCP would have taken off in Britain in quite the way it did.

On the other hand, perhaps it was not so much the location that was 'accidental': perhaps the accident was Dr Clarke. Perhaps a particular configuration of institutional pressures, problems, commitments and constraints had made the Home Office Research and Planning Unit an institutional niche in which SCP was sooner or later liable to develop. As Cornish and Clarke (1983) describe it, the previous research agenda and policy approach had run adrift on a sea of negative research evidence. The 'nothing works' context of the late 1970s and early 1980s had severely undermined the established approach of the Home Office and the criminal justice agencies that it oversaw. This effect was reinforced by the more general critique of 'welfarist' and 'social' solutions to crime and other problems that was increasingly prominent from the mid-1970s onwards. Implementation failure was beginning to look like theory failure. The promise of a research-driven policy on crime, which formed the fundamental *raison d'être* of HORPU, was evidently not being fulfilled. Its former head, John Croft, talked publicly about the failure of criminology (Croft, 1978). In such a conjuncture, a new framework of thought and action comes to be desirable, providing it can meet the institutional needs of the organization, and does not disturb the powerful interests that form the organization's immediate environment. SCP and its associated ideas and techniques fitted the bill – if not perfectly then at least tolerably well. It offered a new direction for research and action: a direction with inherent appeal for pragmatic, empirical researchers whose bottom line was to develop politically acceptable policies that could work and could be shown to work. Unlike social programmes of crime prevention that typically had to cut through a tangle of other social pathologies before they could begin to impact upon criminal behaviour, SCP could be directly targeted upon crime events. It was quite separate from welfare benefits and community work, and so could avoid attracting the political criticism that it provided benefits to the undeserving. It could be delivered in the form of small-scale demonstration projects that were eminently practical and were not prohibitively expensive. In political terms it avoided the inflammatory political connotations that had come to be associated both with welfare and with penal programmes. And most importantly, its proposed interventions were attractively short-term in their impact, promising to produce immediate practical results that could be evaluated and, if successful, generalised.

By the mid-1980s, SCP had come to have a definite appeal for a Conservative government that had tried (and failed) to reduce crime rates and which was beginning to become acutely aware of the limits (and the costs) of conventional criminal justice measures. Ronald Clarke likes to insist that SCP found official favour for the simple and singular reason that 'it works' where other policies have failed, and regularly points to evaluation research and displacement studies that give support to this view. But the political appeal of SCP was no doubt enhanced by a number of other features that have little to do with crime-prevention effectiveness. The fact that SCP uses a language of economic reasoning (risk and reward; opportunity; demand and supply; rational choice, etc.) that is usually associated with the market, rather than the social reasoning associated with the welfare state; its focus upon the victim rather than the offender; its insistence that crime is everyone's responsibility and not solely the state's business; its promise of short-term, low-cost interventions rather than large-scale social programmes – all of these undoubtedly increased the resonance of the approach for the post-welfarist, neo-liberal governments of the 1980s and 1990s. Similar considerations of pragmatism, short-term results, policy-related research agendas and governmental rather than scientific priorities had earlier shaped the criminological research agendas of the Home Office and of the Cambridge Institute of Criminology in the 1950s and 1960s (Home Office, 1959; Radzinowicz, 1988; and Garland, 1997). Our account of the re-emergence of situational crime prevention should be phrased not in terms of a lone criminologist coming up with a new theory but instead of a productive convergence of individuals, ideas and institutions that occurred in a uniquely receptive social and political conjuncture.

SCP AND THE NEW CULTURE OF CRIME CONTROL

A more general answer to the question: 'Why does SCP prosper now when it failed to prosper before?' would have to do with the fracturing of the institutional framework of the criminal justice state and the erosion of the particular epistemology that it sponsored. I have told that story elsewhere (see Garland, 1996) so I will not go into detail here, but two considerations seem worth mentioning: (a) The fact that high rates of crime and of victimization became, in this period, a normal social fact – a fact of life that was widely acknowledged as such, and to which behaviour was increasingly adapted; (b) The fact that criminal justice agencies, and eventually politicians and policy-makers, began to recognize the limits of criminal justice as a means of governing crime.

From the 1960s onwards, self-report studies, victim surveys, and interviews with convicted offenders, have all provided evidence of the generality of deviance and the normality of crime (see Gabor, 1994; Hirschi and Gottfredson, 1994). The force of this evidence was significant above and beyond its character as criminological data because it constituted evidence about crime that was not produced by the routines of the criminal justice system agencies and did not reproduce their way of seeing the world. Evidence of this kind worked to break the theoretical link between crime and individual personality; to undo the conflation of crime and criminality; and of course, to show very clearly the limited grip that criminal justice had on the phenomenon of crime.

Over the same period it became increasingly apparent that the historical experience of the post-war decades, especially the 1950s and 1960s, had undermined the assumption that economic growth and social reform would eventually reduce crime rates. Crime rates rose steeply during the period of the long boom. Full employment, higher standards of living, education and welfare for the poor were generally accompanied by more, not less, criminal conduct. In the 1960s, British criminology – including the criminology of the two main political parties (see Labour Party, 1964; Conservative Party, 1966) – shifted from an emphasis upon deprivation to new theories of 'relative deprivation' and 'strain theories' in an attempt to explain this, relying particularly upon the arguments of Merton and Cohen about the effects of raised expectations in producing consequent frustration. Patrick Colquhoun's equation between goods in circulation and temptations to crime thus became an increasingly plausible one again. Late 20th century consumer capitalism clearly generated a plenitude of opportunities for crime, and the social and cultural trends that began in the 1960s were widely viewed as relaxing some of the traditional inhibitions upon law-breaking and illegal acquisition. In this context, the utility of restricting criminal opportunities became more and more self-evident.

The normality of crime and the generality of deviance – particularly once they acquired the status of acknowledged social facts – have had major consequences for the day-to-day lives of individuals and businesses, and major costs to the taxpayer. The focal concern of official crime control until recently had been the criminality of individual delinquents. Penal-welfarism tended to downplay the significance of occasional and minor offending unless it was clearly linked to an underlying pathology. And in the 1960s and 70s, the police and prosecution agencies had tended to filter minor crime out of the system to curtail soaring costs and case-loads. A consequence of this pattern was an increasing fear of crime and a sense that minor, everyday criminality such as theft from cars, shoplifting, vandalism and disorderly behaviour were becoming widespread because of a relative immunity to official action.

Over a short period of time, no more than a single generation, large numbers of people have been obliged to change their learned habits of daily life, adopting new and more defensive precautions as a matter of routine, engaging in new forms of avoidance behaviour, all of which tend to increase levels of crime consciousness and the kinds of fears, distrustfulness and resentments typically associated with this sensibility. One consequence of these concerns has been the increased popularity of 'law and order' policies and a more punitive approach to convicted offenders. The appeal of 'quality of life' and 'zero tolerance' policing owes much to this new experience, as does the remarkable growth of the private security industry. But it is also within this cultural and criminological context that we should understand the emergence of the SCP framework, which also addressed these mundane, generalized, 'normal' forms of crime and did so in ways that were inexpensive and could become the responsibility of individual citizens, communities and businesses.

In criminological research, the generality of deviance in the midst of affluent consumer society has tended to shift the focus of inquiry away from criminal motivation towards questions of social control and self-control. In criminal and social policy, the same conditions have tended to displace social reforms and emphasize social controls. SCP rises to prominence in 'administrative criminology' at the same time that the social control theories of Hirschi (and later Hirschi and Gottfredson) become the dominant ones in academic criminology.

What are the wider cultural conditions that make SCP a possible and desirable approach to crime after such a long period of marginality? One might have to do with the re-emergence of private sector policing and security (see Shearing and Stenning, 1987; Johnson, 1992; Jones and Newburn, 1998). In the post-war period, businesses and commercial concerns as well as individual citizens adapted to the high crime environment by making their own security arrangements alongside those provided by the state. What one might term an 'economic' rationality of crime control grew up in this sector – concerned with costs, risks, harm reduction, reducing opportunities and rewards, minimizing exposure, insuring against major loss, and displacing criminal behaviour away from this particular victim. This economic rationality is now, belatedly, being taken up and emulated by government. What was once a 'private sector' mentality is now being reproduced by public agencies and government departments – in this field as in so many others.[3]

Another feature of SCP that has been attractive to policy-makers is that it addresses its prescriptions for action beyond the criminal justice state agencies to the actors and agencies of civil society (Garland, 1996). It reconfigures crime control policy as a partnership between the state and the private sector, the state and its citizens, rather than as a professional state monopoly. It is oriented towards self-starting, non-state solutions; to activating citizens and communities; to encouraging private individuals and organizations to take responsibility for crime control. One can see how this fits well with the political climate of the 1980s and 90s. However, one can also see the difficulties of implementation that this produces. SCP implies the generalization of crime control to meet the generality of crime. It seeks to dedifferentiate a social function that for 200 years has been increasingly differentiated, specialized, and professionalized. This is a major undertaking that will require very extensive changes in incentives, motivations and habits.

SCP may also be aligning itself with the dominant current of public opinion by adopting a 'victim-centered' perspective in contrast to the 'offender-centered' perspective of most post-war criminology. It responds practically and immediately to the public's demand for increased security. It also allows a form of local or even individual action that can be undertaken directly by

---

[3] And of course, SCP now feeds back into the private sector, advising, exhorting and organising preventive action on the part of commercial concerns and private householders.

those fearful of crime. Instead of the indirect and long-term promises of social engineering it offers the immediate returns of 'situational engineering'. Instead of extending compassion, help and support to offenders, it offers protection to the public. And of course it is by no means incompatible with punishments for those whom it fails to deter or prevent. In a political context in which the goals of social inclusion and social solidarity no longer dominate, it offers a more immediate form of security to potential victims, albeit one that is increasingly commercialized and may involve fortification, restricted access and social exclusion.

It seems clear enough, however, that SCP has no fixed ideological meaning or determinate political affiliations. It is quite conceivable that its crime prevention techniques could be provided at public expense to those in most need of them, such as repeat victims living in council housing schemes, or groups who are otherwise vulnerable to victimization, such as women and ethnic minorities. By the same token, a commitment to SCP could certainly help to further the development of a mixed economy of crime control wherein private security and measures of exclusion play a much larger role than they currently do, and where the state further reduces its commitment to the social provision of security. In terms of its practical uses, SCP is as much at home in 'Fortress LA' (Davis, 1990) as it is on the Kirkholt housing estate (Pease, 1991). But if SCP's specific political affiliations are loose and shifting, it has strong elective affinities with the generalized culture of control that has grown up in late modernity (Garland, forthcoming). And it will become increasingly attractive to governments of all stripes as they move further away from the grand projects of social engineering that once defined our modernity and seek instead to create order through embedded mechanisms of situational control.

REFERENCES

Clarke, R.V. (1995) 'Situational crime prevention', in M. Tonry and D. Farrington (eds.), *Building a Safer Society: Crime and Justice* 19: 91-150, Chicago: University of Chicago Press.

—— (1997) *Situational Crime Prevention: Successful Case Studies* (2nd ed.), Albany, NY: Harrow and Heston.

—— and Martin, D. N. (1971) *Absconding from Approved Schools*, Home Office Research Study No. 12, London: Home Office.

Colquhoun, P. (1796) *Treatise on the Police of the Metropolis*, (2nd ed.), (orig published 1795), London: H. Fry for C. Dilly.

Conservative Party (1966) *Crime Knows No Boundaries*, London: Conservative Party Office.

Cornish, D. and Clarke, R. (1983) *Crime Control in Britain: A Review of Policy Research*, Albany NY: State University of New York Press.

Crawford, A. (1997) *The Local Governance of Crime*, Oxford: Oxford University Press.

Croft, J. (1978) *Research in Criminal Justice*, Home Office Research Study No 44, London: Home Office.

Davis, M. (1990) *City of Quartz: Excavating the Future in Los Angeles*, London: Vintage.

Douglas, M. (1986) *How Institutions Think*, Syracuse, NY: Syracuse University Press.

Felson, M. and Clarke, R. (1999) *Opportunity Makes the Thief: Practical Theory for Crime Prevention*, Police Research Papers No. 98, London: Home Office.

Ferri, E. (1917) *Criminal Sociology*, London: Heinemann.

Gabor, T. (1994) *Everybody Does It: Crime by the Public*, Toronto: University of Toronto Press.

Garafalo, C. (1914) *Criminology*, London: Heinemann.

Garland, D. (1985) *Punishment and Welfare*, Aldershot: Gower.

—— (1996) 'Limits of the sovereign state: strategies of crime control in contemporary societies'. *British Journal of Criminology* 36: 445–471.

—— (1997) 'Of crime and criminals: the development of criminology in Britain' in M.Maguire et al. (eds.), *The Oxford Handbook of Criminology* (2nd ed.), 11–56 Oxford: Oxford University Press.

—— (2000, forthcoming) *The Culture of Control: Crime and Social Order in Late Modernity*, Oxford: Oxford University Press.

Gladstone, H. (1895) *The Report of the Departmental Committee on Prisons*, Parliamentary Papers LVII, London: HMSO.

Goldstein, H. (1979) 'Improving policing: a problem-oriented approach', *Crime and Delinquency* 25: 236–258.

Hirschi T. and Gotfredson, M. (1994) *The Generality of Deviance*, New Brunswick, NJ: Transaction.

Home Office and Ministry of Education (1949) *Memorandum on Juvenile Delinquency*, London: HMSO.

—— (1959) *Penal Practice in a Changing Society*, London: HMSO

—— (1965) *Report of the Committee on the Prevention and Detection of Crime* (The Cornish Committee), London: HMSO.

Jacobs, J. (1961) *The Death and Life of Great American Cities*, New York: Random House.

Jeffery, C. R. (1977) *Crime Prevention Though Environmental Design* (2nd ed.), Beverly Hills, CA: Sage.

Johnson, L. (1992) *The Rebirth of Private Policing*, London: Routledge.

Jones, T. and Newburn, T. (1998) *Private Security and Public Policing*, Oxford: Oxford University Press.

Labour Party (1964) *Crime: A Challenge to Us All* (The Longford Report), London: Labour Party.

Laycock, G. and Heal, K. (1989) 'Crime prevention: the British experience' in D.J. Evans and D.T. Herbert (eds.), *The Geography of Crime*, London: Routledge.

Lombroso, C. (1911) *Crime: Its Causes and Its Remedies*, London: Heinemann.

Newman, O. (1972) *Defensible Space: Crime Prevention Through Environmental Design* (2nd ed.), New York: Macmillan.

Pease. K. (1991) 'The Kirkholt project: preventing burglary on a British housing estate' *Security Journal* 2: 73–77.

Radzinowicz, L. (1988) *The Cambridge Institute of Criminology: Its Background and Scope*, London: HMSO.

Scottish Council on Crime (1975) *Crime and the Prevention of Crime*, Edinburgh: Scottish Home and Health Department.

Selznick P., (1992) *The Moral Commonwealth*, Berkeley, CA: University of California Press.

Shearing C. & Stenning P. (eds.) (1987) *Private Policing*, New York: Sage.

Wilson, J. Q. (1975) *Thinking About Crime*, New York, Vintage.

2

Benefits, Burdens and Responsibilities: Some Ethical Dimensions of Situational Crime Prevention

R A Duff and S E Marshall[1]

In 1997, Felson and Clarke found no previously published 'extensive ideological or ethical critique of the ethics of situational crime prevention' (1997: 199). What we offer here is not such an 'extensive . . . critique', but a prolegomenon to it – an initial exploration of some of the general ethical issues raised by various types of situational crime prevention (hereafter, SCP) measures.

SCP involves 'the management, design, or manipulation of the immediate environment . . . so as to reduce the opportunities for crime and increase its risks as perceived by a wide range of offenders' (Clarke, 1983: 225), or so as to 'reduc[e] the rewards of crime' (Clarke, 1995: 92). However, there are morally significant differences between the groups on which SCP measures impact, and between the ways in which such measures will prevent crime:[2] between, for instance, 'target hardening' measures (such as fitting steering locks on cars) which make it harder for would-be offenders to succeed in their crimes, 'access control' measures (such as road closures to keep cruising 'johns' out of red light districts) which exclude potential offenders from places where they might offend, and measures to 'deflect offenders' (such as the provision of graffiti boards, or alternative venues for teenage cruising) which offer potential offenders alternative, non-criminal ways of achieving their aims; or between measures that impact only on actual or intending criminals, measures that impact on potential victims of crime, measures that impact on those identified as 'potential' offenders, and measures that impact similarly on everyone.

The ethical significance of these differences will emerge in what follows.

---

[1] We are grateful to participants in the two Cambridge SCP conferences, and especially to Anthony Bottoms and Andrew von Hirsch, for helpful comments; we apologise to anyone whose comments we have used (or garbled) without due acknowledgement.

[2] Here and later we draw on the classification and illustrations of SCP measures provided by Clarke (1995: 109–19).

Section 1 deals with some general points about the structure and scope of a discussion of 'the ethics of SCP'; section 2 raises some issues about the allocation of the costs and benefits of SCP; and section 3 focuses on questions about the tones in which, and the force with which, SCP measures are urged on those who are to undertake them. But we should emphasise that our aim is to raise relevant questions, rather than to offer confident answers to them; and that, in order to make those questions clear, we focus on a limited range of simple examples of SCP.[3]

THE STRUCTURE AND SCOPE OF AN 'ETHICS OF SCP'

In this section we discuss the kind of normative perspective that should structure an 'ethics of SCP', and the aspects of SCP measures which require ethical attention.

Structures of Ethical Thought

Two familiar modes of ethical thought might be applied to SCP, but we will suggest a third possibility.

We might, first, take a strictly consequentialist perspective: we identify the goods which SCP measures can bring, and the harms or costs that they incur; and we then try to determine which SCP measures are cost-effective means to those goods. Such a perspective need not be crudely utilitarian, taking 'happiness' as the only good: it could adopt a morally rich account of the relevant goods and harms – for instance one that includes such familiar liberal values as freedom, autonomy and privacy as goods, and their loss or infringement as harms.[4] Thus our account of the benefits of SCP could include the protection of those liberal goods, which crime typically infringes; and our account of its costs could include both the material costs involved in implementing SCP measures, and the ways in which they impinge upon people's freedom, autonomy or privacy.

However, if our perspective is strictly consequentialist, we must see such goods and such costs aggregatively: our aim must be to maximise the extent to which such goods are enjoyed, and to minimise the extent to which such costs or harms are suffered. One implication of this is that we must be willing, in principle, to accept measures which deprive some of such goods in order to increase the extent to which others can enjoy them – to infringe the autonomy or freedom of some, for instance, in order to protect that of others (by preventing crimes which themselves infringe freedom and autonomy). This

---

[3] As should become clear, however, these questions are not peculiar to *situational* crime prevention; versions of them are raised by any 'crime prevention' strategy.

[4] Compare Braithwaite and Pettit (1990), on 'dominion' as a central good which a system of criminal law should serve.

generates the familiar kind of objection to any purely consequentialist perspective: that it allows individuals to be sacrificed to a larger social good. The objections offered in this volume by von Hirsch (2000) to some kinds of CCTV surveillance, and by von Hirsch and Shearing (2000) to some modes of exclusion from public spaces, are of this type: what raises moral doubts about the practices these authors criticise is not the question of whether a calculus of relevant costs and benefits would favour them, but the question of whether they do justice to the individuals whose privacy or freedom of movement they infringe.[5]

Implicit in such objections is a view of freedom, autonomy and privacy not just as *goods* which we must *maximise*, but as *rights* which we must *respect* – and which can 'trump' the maximising claims of larger social goods (see R. Dworkin, 1978). This then points us towards a second familiar model of ethical thought: side-constrained consequentialism.[6] On this view SCP measures, like any social policy, must be justified as efficient means to a consequential good: but such consequentialist efficiency is not a complete justification, since our pursuit of those goods is also subject to the constraints set by certain *non*-consequentialist values; SCP measures are justified only if they are also consistent with those constraints. We might then, with strict consequentialists, posit the reduction of crime as the 'general justifying aim' of SCP; but add (as strict consequentialists would not) that the pursuit of that aim is constrained by the non-consequentialist requirement that SCP measures must not violate citizens' rights to freedom, autonomy or privacy, even when such violations might efficiently reduce crime.[7]

This is perhaps the most common perspective on the ethics of SCP: we must ask not only which SCP measures efficiently reduce crime, but also whether those measures are consistent with the rights (or other non-consequentialist values) that should constrain our pursuit of the goal of crime reduction.

There is, however, another kind of ethical perspective, with a different logical structure: one which denies the sharp distinction between 'ends' and 'means' common to the first two perspectives (see Duff, 1996: 8-9, 45-54).

Both strict and side-constrained consequentialists specify the 'ends' that SCP measures are to achieve in a way that leaves open the question of what 'means' we may use to achieve them. 'Crime prevention', as a specification of the end, means simply that crimes that would otherwise have been committed are not committed: the question of what means we should use to that end is then answered, for strict consequentialists, by working out which measures

---

[5] We leave aside here the question of whether or how such a calculus could be carried out, were it to include such values as freedom, autonomy and privacy.

[6] On side-constraints, see Nozick (1974: 28–9); Braithwaite and Pettit (1990: 26–36).

[7] Compare Hart (1968), on the consequentialist 'general justifying aim' of punishment, and the non-consequentialist side-constraints to which our pursuit of that aim is subject. Different side-constrained accounts will of course posit different normative constraints, and will differ on whether such constraints are absolute or defeasible.

will be efficient means to that end; or, for side-constrained consequentialists, by discerning which efficient measures are consistent with the appropriate side-constraints. Those constraints are, however, independent of the end: measures which violate important rights might efficiently prevent crime, but are ruled out because they flout that independent constraint. Analogously, if my end is simply to bring it about that someone acts as she should (that she pays a debt, for instance, or refrains from lying), this leaves open the question of what means I should use to achieve that end: I might simply look for cost-effective means; or I might recognise certain side-constraints which, for instance, forbid me to achieve that end by bullying or deceiving her.

The third perspective denies that we can always specify the end in a way that leaves the question of means thus open: what the side-constrained consequentialist sees as independent constraints should rather enter into our understanding of the end itself. If I bring someone to pay her debts only by bullying or deceiving her, the result is not that I achieve a proper end, but by improper means: I have not achieved a proper end at all. For the end that I should be pursuing, if I am to treat her (as we should treat each other) as a responsible moral agent, is not simply that she pays her debt, but that she does so *as* a responsible moral agent, because she sees that and why she should do so; and *that* end cannot be achieved by deception or by bullying. The demand that we respect others as responsible moral agents does not merely set constraints on the means we may use, but helps determine the ends we should pursue in our dealings with others. Those ends themselves then set limits on the means by which they can be pursued: what is wrong with bullying or deceiving her is not that these possibly effective means to my end are nonetheless improper, but that they are not possible ways of achieving my proper end.

What has this to do with SCP? It suggests that we should look more carefully not just at the efficiency of SCP measures as means to a presupposed end, or at their consistency with whatever non-consequentialist values constrain our pursuit of that end, but at the very ends which such measures should be designed to serve, in particular at whether we should take the end to be simply 'crime prevention'. Just as what matters in the moral case is not just that the person pays her debt, but how and why she comes to do so, in the case of crime what matters is not just that crime is 'prevented' (that people do not commit crimes they would otherwise have committed), but how and why they come not to commit them. This point clearly bears on criminal punishment, since it suggests a new objection to purely deterrent or incapacitative modes of punishment: that whilst they can prevent crime, they are not means to the ends that the criminal law *should* serve, since they are not ways of persuading citizens, as responsible moral agents, to refrain from crime because they see it to be wrong.[8] It also bears on SCP.

Consider, for instance, a shopping mall which excluded those under the age

---

[8] See Duff (2000: Chs. 1.2–3, 2.4, 3.1–3).

of 21, or the unemployed. Such a policy might efficiently reduce crime in the mall; and side-constrained consequentialists who objected that it infringed the rights of those who were excluded might agree that at least it brought about the legitimate good of reducing crime – and of increasing shoppers' security and convenience. But this is just what we should question. For assuming that the mall is or should be a public space, providing public goods,[9] to exclude these people from the mall is to exclude them from access to goods (to secure, convenient shopping and to the mall's other benefits) in which they should as citizens be able to share; and this is also to transform those goods from public goods, accessible to all citizens, into private goods from which some citizens are excluded. Now SCP measures which aim to prevent crime in public spaces should, surely, aim at the *public* good of freedom from crime and the threat of crime: but such an exclusionary policy does not then achieve, or even aim to achieve, an appropriate end or good. It is *intrinsically* inappropriate to the proper end of securing the *public* good of crime prevention, since it prevents crime only by transforming, and distorting, that public good into a private good.

Much more needs to be said about which ends are legitimate in public and social policy, and which means are or are not intrinsically appropriate to them, but our aim here has simply been to introduce this third kind of normative perspective, and to indicate the difference it can make to our understanding of the ethical dimensions of SCP. It requires us to attend carefully to 'ends' as well as to 'means', and to the intrinsic as well as to the contingent, instrumental relationships between 'ends' and 'means'.

Impacts and Meanings

Discussions of 'the ethics of SCP' often (rightly) focus on the *impacts* of such measures: the benefits they bring by reducing crime; the burdens they impose in material costs, in limiting freedom or in infringing privacy. We should also attend, however, to their *meanings*: to the attitudes, the conceptions of citizens and their mutual relationships, that they manifest. Two examples will illustrate this point.

The first concerns trust. It is commonplace that civil society depends on our ability to trust each other not to attack or harm us in various ways. That trust is very far from complete or unconditional; we take various precautions to protect ourselves against the possible malice or indifference of others, especially strangers. But some level of general trust of others, of our fellow citizens, helps distinguish civil society from Hobbes's state of nature.[10] SCP

---

[9] We realise that this assumption needs explanation, which we cannot provide here, but see von Hirsch and Shearing (2000). Similar points would apply to a neighbourhood which turned itself into a 'gated community' – which turned what had been public roads into private roads.

[10] See Kleinig (2000); also Dimock (1997) for an (over-) ambitious attempt to ground criminal law and punishment in the need to maintain trust.

measures typically manifest a lack or loss of trust: they are (seen as) necessary because we do not trust people not to commit the crimes that they aim to prevent. So, apart from empirical questions about the need for, the likely efficiency of, and the possibly damaging further effects of, such measures, we must ask about the moral propriety of the attitudes that they thus manifest.

Suppose that I take to locking my wallet away when I leave my office with colleagues or students in it, to make sure that they don't steal from me. Apart from questions about whether such a measure is cost-effective, we might question the attitude it displays: we might say that I *insult* my colleagues and students by taking such mistrustful precautions – even if I conceal what I am doing from them; or that such manifested lack of trust impoverishes or vitiates my relationship with them. Similarly, if an employer introduces a policy of searching employees as they leave work, we should question not just the cost-effectiveness of this measure,[11] but the attitude it displays towards her employees, and the conception it implies of their role in the enterprise in which she and they are engaged.

Bottoms suggests that we should see at least some kinds of SCP measure as manifesting not a *loss*, but a *shift*, of trust, away from personal trust towards trust in 'abstract systems'.[12] Set in their proper context, such measures need not then be 'insulting', especially if they are imposed on everyone without discrimination – as when everyone entering a prison, even the governor, must be searched (see at n. 20 below). Now we agree that the meaning both of trust and of any SCP measure depends on the larger context of social structures, relationships and expectations in which they are set: what counts as, or is required by, trust between friends is different from what counts as or is required by trust between colleagues, or between citizens who may be strangers; and what any SCP measure says about or to those upon whom it is to be imposed is likewise context-specific. However, we can still note that a shift towards trust in 'abstract systems' is also a loss of trust in people; and that the ethical significance of SCP measures depends on their meaning as well as on their impact.

The second example concerns inclusion and exclusion, in relation to fellow-citizenship. Consider again a policy of excluding certain groups from a shopping mall; or a housing estate whose streets used to be a public space open to all, which is turned into a private estate that admits only residents and 'legitimate' visitors. 'Public' space is space to which all citizens have access, in which they can coexist and interact: to exclude some groups from such space (as from a mall) is to refuse to treat them as fellow citizens; it manifests a view of them as a 'them' who have no proper share in the goods that 'we' enjoy. Similarly, to turn what was a public space into a private space is to distinguish

---

[11] In both examples, the measure's long-term cost-effectiveness will depend in part on its effect on the attitudes and future behaviour of those affected by it.

[12] In his comments on an earlier draft of this paper: on such different forms of trust, see Crawford (2000).

a narrower 'we', whose space it is, from a 'them' with whom we are no longer willing to share this space as fellow citizens. Thus what raises moral questions about such measures is not merely their consequential impact on those who are excluded, but their meaning: their manifestation of an exclusionary attitude, denying a central aspect of fellow-citizenship, towards those who are excluded.[13]

In this section, we have suggested that an inquiry into 'the ethics of SCP' should attend not only to the cost-effectiveness of SCP measures, and to their consistency with independent moral side-constraints, but also to their intrinsic appropriateness to the ends that they should be designed to serve, and to their meanings. This is not to suggest that cost-effectiveness and consistency with side-constraints are not important (they clearly are), or that attention to these further dimensions of SCP will show all SCP measures to be morally dubious (it clearly will not): but it is to suggest that these are important ethical dimensions of SCP.

WHO PAYS, WHO BENEFITS?

Any cost-effective SCP measure brings some benefits (such as a reduction in crime and in the fear of crime, an increase in security and the sense of security), and imposes some costs (such as the material resources required to implement it, the degree of inconvenience it creates, and its possible deleterious impact on such interests as freedom, autonomy or privacy). We must therefore ask who gains, or should gain, the benefits, and who bears, or should bear, the costs.

Potential Victims and Would-be Offenders

Consider a simple example of target hardening: locking one's house when one goes out. The direct benefits of this measure accrue to those who undertake it – lower risks of burglary, and increased security in their homes and possessions.[14] The direct costs are of two kinds. First, there is the modest cost of buying and fitting the lock (if one doesn't yet have a lock), and the modest burden involved in using it – remembering to lock the door and take one's keys, etc.: this cost falls on the potential victims whom the measure protects. (Such measures might, for most of us, be now so routine that they do not seem burdensome:[15] but they impose a burden, as one who begins to take such

---

[13] But see Bottoms (1990: 11–12), for examples of crime-preventive measures which could be seen as manifesting and fostering – rather than denying – an idea of community.

[14] We ignore here the possible wider 'diffusion' of such benefits: see Pease (1991); Clarke (1995: 129–32).

[15] See Home Office (1993: 16), on making crime prevention 'part of the routine day-to-day practice and culture of all agencies and individuals'; quoted by Garland (1996: 454).

precautions for the first time finds.) Second, there is the cost which falls on those who would burgle the house if they could – would-be burglars who try to break in, and cannot; intending or opportunistic burglars who realise the house is locked, and abandon or never form the intention to burgle it. These people also 'pay' for the benefits that this measure provides: their criminal efforts or intentions are frustrated, or their opportunities are limited.

This provides one simple, and seemingly ethically unproblematic, model for 'Who pays and who benefits'. The costs are borne partly by the potential victims of crime, who also gain the benefits, and partly by those who would commit the crimes. As to the former, it seems *prima facie* acceptable that those who will benefit from such measures should pay for them. As for the latter, we surely do not *wrong* would-be offenders, or *violate* their freedom or autonomy, by taking target-hardening measures whose *only* impact on them is to make it harder or impossible for them to succeed in carrying through their criminal enterprises. Such measures manifest a lack of trust; and we might regret the lack, or impossibility, of such trust between fellow citizens (or its loss, if we believe in a past golden age in which 'no one locked their doors'). But that lack of trust is not focused on *particular* individuals or groups; nor does it utterly undermine the possibility of seeing others as our fellow citizens (contrast a case in which members of a family, or a group of cohabiting friends, take to locking their rooms within the shared home).

We have said that target-hardening measures impose 'costs' on the would-be criminals whose crimes they frustrate. This is indeed both how the would-be criminals would see such measures, and how they would figure in many standard calculi of costs and benefits: we must then weigh these costs, along with others, against the benefits in a justificatory calculus. We would in fact want to argue, however, that we should not count these as 'costs' at all: to call them 'costs' implies that they involve the loss of something of *value*, but there is nothing valuable in the opportunity to commit a criminal wrong.[16] We need not pursue this argument here, however: all we need point out is that even if they are 'costs' which should figure in the normative appraisal of such measures, they are not such as to cast doubt on either their cost-effectiveness or their justice.

Locking one's house is a simple example of SCP: we can see why it is ethically simple by contrasting it with other examples, which raise more difficult questions about who pays and who benefits.

Displacement and Differential Protection

Basic house locks are cheap; the protection they provide is available to almost everyone (but not to the homeless, or to some who live in ill-protected rented

[16] Compare the argument that freedom and autonomy, as values, are not enhanced simply by increasing the range of a person's opportunities, if those new opportunities are to pursue what is bad rather than what is valuable: see Raz (1986: chs. 14–15); G. Dworkin (1988: ch. 5).

accommodation or in squats). It is also, of course, rather inadequate protection: even unskilled burglars are not frustrated by mere locked doors. More adequate kinds of target-hardening are available: more complicated locks, double glazing and the like. We can also introduce measures which make targets less attractive by visibly increasing the risk of detection for those who would attack them: burglar alarms and patrols by security guards are obvious examples. Suppose then that such measures are provided (if at all) only privately by the potential victims, rather than publicly by central or local government: provided either by individuals for themselves, or by voluntary groups which form themselves to provide such protection for their members.

Such measures are more costly than basic house locks, and are thus not readily available to (almost) everyone: some can afford them, others cannot. We then face the phenomena of displacement and of differential protection.

Displacement involves shifting crimes from one set of potential victims to others: would-be burglars turn their attention from well-protected houses to others which are less protected; my increased protection is bought at the cost of your increased risk. Differential protection is, by contrast, simply a matter of some being better protected than others: it can, of course, lead to displacement, if those who would have burgled me burgle you instead; but even if it does not, those who lack the more sophisticated kinds of protection are less well protected and more at risk of burglary than are those who have them.[17]

Now differential protection is ethically unproblematic when (as with basic house locks) the protection is relatively unburdensome and available to all: the fact that you don't bother to lock your house casts no doubt on the propriety of my locking my house. It becomes more problematic when the protection is not thus cheaply available to all: not because the fact that you cannot afford to protect your house makes it morally dubious for me to protect mine, but because it requires us to ask whether such protection should be a private, or a public, matter. How far should it be for each of us (either individually, or through voluntary association with others) to provide such protection for ourselves; how far should it be for us collectively, as a community, to provide such protection for all members of the community?[18] We will not try to answer this question here, but would simply note one further point which implies a strong presumption in favour of the collective provision of at least a certain level of equal protection for all citizens.

On one reading of the notoriously problematic idea that crimes are 'public', rather than merely 'private', wrongs, their 'public' character consists in their being wrongs in which the political community as a whole should share: wrongs that should be seen not merely as 'his' or 'her' wrong, but as 'ours'

---

[17] This assumes that there is no very tight correlation between being able to afford such protection and having possessions which will tempt burglars.

[18] Such provision can take different forms, involving both collective and individual responsibilities: resources might, for instance, be provided by the community, whilst it is up to individuals to draw on them.

collectively (see Marshall and Duff, 1998). An implication of this conception of crimes is that they involve wrongs against which the political community must seek to protect its members: it should not be left to individuals to protect themselves as best they can; they should all have a claim to an equal level of collective protection. This does not tell us what levels or kinds of protection should be provided collectively: but it argues against any general presumption that it should be for potential victims to protect themselves against crime.

Displacement raises further problems. If I protect my house against floods in such a way that any flood will be diverted into your house, ethical doubts surely arise. I might quell them by arguing that you could protect yourself as easily as I can protect myself – so that it is up to you to do so, and your fault if you do not: but that, we have seen, is not always the case. With SCP measures, I might also argue that the displacement is not my responsibility, but that of the criminals who then commit their crimes elsewhere. That argument is plausible if, but only if, such protection is properly a private matter: I, who protect myself, could then argue that I do not *intend* that those onto whom crime is foreseeably displaced should be victimised; and that I am not responsible for that foreseen outcome. But if such protection should rather be a public or collective matter, however, it is harder to displace the responsibility along with the crime: for to say that it should be a collective matter is to say not just that protection should be provided, or ensured, by governmental agencies, but also that we should collectively look out for each other; and if I share in such a collective responsibility, it is hard to deny that I am responsible (in part) for the crime displacement which I realise will flow from my individual protective measures.

Both differential protection and displacement take on a different ethical character if the protection is provided collectively rather than privately. If it is provided by central or local government bodies, we need to ask what, if anything, could justify providing some citizens with greater protection than others, or displacing crime from some citizens onto others. Here again we want to raise such questions rather than to answer them – but also to warn against the temptation to accept too readily an aggregative consequentialist perspective on them. On such a view protection should be focused where it will do most good, i.e. produce the greatest overall reduction in the relevant type of crime at the lowest cost; displacement is acceptable, as a side-effect of such protection, so long as there is a net reduction in crime and its costs. Such considerations are, of course, relevant – but so too are considerations of equality (of the 'equality of concern and respect' that a liberal state owes its citizens) and of justice, which might conflict with such consequentialist concerns. Furthermore, once we ask whether it is just, as well as efficient, to provide differential protection or to displace crime, we must look at such crime-preventive measures in the context of larger issues of social justice: we cannot divorce crime-preventive justice, any more than we can divorce penal justice, from social or political justice.

Burdening Potential Victims

We have talked so far of SCP measures which might be financially costly, and so beyond the individual means of many potential victims, but which are not otherwise very burdensome for those whom they protect. Sophisticated locks and burglar alarms can be a nuisance; patrolling security guards might raise worries about intrusive surveillance: but such measures typically protect, rather than hinder, the ordinary lives and activities of those protected by them.[19]

In other cases, such as the screening of airline passengers and their baggage, protective measures are more burdensome. Such measures burden *everyone* indiscriminately: everyone travelling by air is subject to rigorous scrutiny; everyone using an area with CCTV cameras is subject to that surveillance. Such measures can be justified by the claim that the burdens they impose on all are a price worth paying for the protective benefits they bring to all (and in this context 'all' should be read as 'all collectively' rather than as 'each individually'): which is to say in part that though their immediate aim is to detect *offenders* (and thus also to warn off potential offenders), they can be seen as treating all those subject to them as potential *victims* who are to be protected. We must still ask whether such measures are justified – whether the benefit is worth the burden; whether the measures violate rights which should be respected. However, the point we want to emphasise here is that the acceptability of such measures also depends on their non-discriminating character, as imposing similar burdens on *everyone*, qua potential victims of crime:[20] for we want to contrast them with measures which raise moral doubts precisely because they impose special burdens on *some* potential victims.

Suppose, for instance, that women are advised not to walk alone in certain areas at night, or not to wear certain kinds of 'provocative' clothes in certain places; or that black men are advised not to visit certain pubs which are known to be frequented by racists. Much depends on the source from which, and the tones in which, that advice is offered (see s. 3 below), but our concern here is with cases in which the advice implies that it is up to the potential victims (that it is their responsibility) to take such self-protective precautions for themselves.

We have here a kind of activity – walking freely around a city, wearing what clothes one likes (within the constraints of decency), visiting what pubs

[19] We cannot discuss here the relevance of the nuisance that such measures can create for others: for a simple instance, consider the nuisance caused by malfunctioning burglar alarms.

[20] Measures like passenger screening can be discriminatory if focused on those judged to be potential offenders; on this kind of issue, see the following subsection. Even supposedly non-discriminatory measures can also in fact impose very discriminatory burdens: cash-less shopping impacts more severely on those who cannot get credit or debit cards, and removing public telephones from places used by drug dealers (see Clarke, 1995: 112) on those who do not have their own telephones.

one chooses – which is 'normal' or 'ordinary' for many citizens: a kind of activity in which many citizens in fact engage (it is *statistically* normal or ordinary), and which is rightly seen as a proper part of our social lives (it is *normatively* normal or ordinary). To say to women, or to black men, that they should not engage, or should not engage so freely and unrestrictedly, in such activities is then to say that they should partly exclude themselves from this aspect of the normal ordinary life of citizens. The aim of such advised self-exclusion might be to protect them – those who are burdened by this measure are those who benefit from it as potential victims protected by it; and such advice need not imply that if a potential victim who does not take these precautions is attacked, their failure mitigates the attacker's guilt – though it can all too easily lead to the thought that one who does not take such precautions 'provokes' the attack and must share responsibility for it. But this kind of SCP measure is nonetheless exclusionary: for it imposes the burden of self-exclusion from an aspect of normal life on a particular group of potential victims; it says to them that they cannot expect the kind of public or collective protection in going about their normal lives that others can expect – that any citizen should be able to expect.[21]

This should raise further doubt about any idea that the cost of SCP measures can always properly fall on those who are protected by them. The doubt is not now that those who cannot afford such measures will be unfairly disadvantaged, but that some such measures impose burdens on particular groups of potential victims which are unreasonable in that they exclude such groups from, or limit their participation in, 'normal' or 'ordinary' activities;[22] and thus, by implication, partially exclude them from the kind of collective protection against crime that all citizens should be able to expect.

Actual, Would-be and Potential Offenders

The impact of simple target-hardening measures like locking one's house is focused only on actual or would-be offenders – on those who try or intend to commit the relevant crimes; and that impact consists solely in making it harder or impossible for them to commit such crimes. Other kinds of SCP measures, however, are focused on *potential*, rather than actual or would-be, offenders, and have a larger impact than this.

Suppose that the owners of a shopping mall aim to reduce thefts in the mall by excluding those who can be identified as potential thieves.[23] Such a

[21] Does it matter that the groups on whom such advice is urged also suffer other kinds of unjust discrimination? Compare the advice that might be urged on those who are obviously English not to go into Scottish pubs whose clientele are prone to violent anglophobia.

[22] Since the notion of 'normal' or 'ordinary' activities is partly normative, there may be controversy about which kinds of activity should count as 'normal' and 'ordinary'; we cannot pursue this issue here.

[23] We are still assuming (see n. 9 above) that shopping malls should be seen as 'public' spaces. We are also concerned only with measures aimed at preventing *crime*: another issue which we

measure does not just make it hard or impossible for *would-be* thieves, who have already formed and are acting on the intention to steal, to succeed in stealing: it deprives *potential* thieves, who have as yet formed no such intention, of opportunities to form or act on such intentions; and it also deprives them of other opportunities and goods by excluding them from the benefits of the mall. The question then is whether such a measure can ever be justified, which is to ask whether we can specify criteria for identifying 'potential offenders' such that those who satisfy the criteria can justifiably be excluded from public spaces for crime-preventive reasons.

One question about any such criteria of potential criminality will concern their empirical reliability: how accurately do they identify those, and only those, who would commit relevant crimes if admitted to the mall; how large will be the proportion of 'false positives' – of those who are identified as 'potential offenders' but who would not have committed such crimes if admitted to the mall?[24] Our concern, however, is with the intrinsic moral legitimacy of such criteria rather than with their empirical reliability: with whether they provide the right *kind* of ground for such crime-preventive exclusions from public spaces.

The possible criteria of potential criminality are of two kinds. The first kind concerns the person's own prior and relevant criminal conduct – that she has in the past committed crimes of the relevant kind. The second kind concerns the possession of other characteristics, whether behavioural or non-behavioural, which are supposedly correlated with the commission of the relevant kind of crime: that this person engages in disruptive or 'suspicious' behaviour, that he is a young, unemployed male, that he is dressed like a tramp or a gypsy – and that there is a correlation between the possession of these characteristics and the commission of the relevant kinds of crime (for without such a correlation there could be no crime-preventive rationale for excluding those with such characteristics). We'll deal with the second kind of criterion first.

No such criteria, we suggest, can provide legitimate grounds for exclusion: for exclusions based on such criteria fail to treat, or to trust, those excluded as responsible fellow citizens.[25] To treat someone as a responsible fellow citizen is to treat her as someone who can determine her own conduct in the light of her own values, and as someone whom we should trust not to commit crimes unless and until she gives us good reason to qualify or suspend that trust. But to exclude someone from public space on the grounds of his possession of

cannot pursue here is that of whether and how far exclusions can properly be used to prevent offensive or annoying, but non-criminal, behaviour. Finally, we are concerned only with permanent, or at least long-term, exclusions – not with temporary, very brief exclusions; see Wakefield (2000), and von Hirsch and Shearing (2000).

[24] Compare von Hirsch (1986: Ch. 9) and Tonry (1998: 132–4), on 'false positives' in the context of policies of selective incapacitation aimed at high-rate offenders.

[25] For a more detailed explication of this line of argument in the context of selective incapacitation, see Duff (1998: 151–6).

some non-criminal characteristics is to treat him as if his behaviour is determined by those characteristics ('he is young, male and unemployed, so of course he'll try to steal'), or as if the possession of those characteristics itself makes him untrustworthy: it is thus to deny him the respect and the trust due to him as a fellow citizen. The *effect* of such a policy is to exclude him from what should be public goods, to which he should have the same access as other citizens; its *meaning* is to insult him, by denying him the trust that is accorded to other citizens.

What then of the first kind of criterion for exclusion, based on the person's own relevant criminal conduct? This seems a more appropriate kind of criterion, since we can now say that those excluded have defined themselves as untrustworthy by their own criminal conduct, and have thus brought their exclusion on themselves. A drunken driver cannot complain at being temporarily disqualified from driving; and a persistent drunken driver cannot complain if that disqualification is made permanent: she has shown by her own conduct that she cannot be trusted (that she is unfit) to engage in the normal activity of driving, and her disqualification is appropriate both as a punishment for her crimes, and as a way of protecting others against the danger that she has shown herself to present to them. Analogously, one could then argue, one who steals from shops or shoppers in the mall can justly be excluded temporarily, whilst one who persistently steals can justly be excluded permanently: he has shown by his own criminal conduct that he cannot be trusted to engage in this normal activity; his exclusion is justified both as a punishment for his crimes, and as a means of preventing the future crimes that he would predictably (given the pattern of his past conduct) commit if he could.[26]

Even here, however, there are serious questions to be asked: questions about proof (that the person to be excluded has been *convicted* of the relevant crime(s) is clearly sufficient, and we suggest should also be necessary, as proof that he committed them); questions about who should decide on the fact and the length of the exclusion (should this be a matter for the mall-owner, for instance, or only for the court that convicted the person?); and questions about the length of exclusion that could be justified – in particular whether *permanent* exclusion could ever be justified. We cannot pursue these questions here, but we suggest that while temporary exclusions can be readily justified in the way sketched above, and while permanent exclusion could *in principle* be justified for sufficiently persistent and serious offenders (so long as this does not deprive them completely of access to significant public goods), the requirement that such exclusions be justified by reference to the person's own past criminal conduct subjects them to demands of due process and proportionality which will radically constrain their use.[27]

[26] On 'civil disqualifications' resulting from criminal convictions, see von Hirsch and Wasik (1997); for this line of argument, see also Duff (1998: 157–9).

[27] We would thus go further than von Hirsch ands Shearing (2000) in that we allow – at least in principle – permanent exclusions, but with appropriate safeguards.

In this section we have discussed various questions about how the costs (and benefits) of SCP measures should be distributed; we now turn, finally, to some questions about the way in which such measures may be urged on or recommended to those who are to undertake them.

ADVICE, RESPONSIBILITY AND OBLIGATION

For the sake of brevity, we shall focus here on SCP measures which individuals are to undertake for themselves, to protect themselves, but similar questions arise about measures to be taken by other kinds of agent or to protect other people. Recommendations of such measures might constitute simply *advice*; or ascriptions of *responsibility*; or ascriptions of *obligation*.

Advice – Informal and Formal

Car owners are advised to lock their cars, or to fit anti-theft devices; lone women are advised to avoid certain streets at night; and computer owners are advised to take precautions against hackers. What such advice means or implies depends on the context in which it is offered, on who offers it, in what tones, and on what follows from a failure to take it.

Suppose it is offered informally, by a friend, as a matter of simple prudence: given the existing inadequacy of other kinds of (collectively provided) protection against such crimes (a lack which the adviser is not committed to approving), the advisee would do well to take such precautions for herself. Such advice, as thus offered, is consistent with the thought that the potential victim should not have to take such precautions; and whilst the adviser might think it imprudent not to take them, she might sometimes rather admire someone who refused to follow the advice on the grounds that citizens should not have to take such precautions against each other.

Suppose instead that the advice is offered formally, by some official agency (by a crime prevention officer; through a government publicity campaign). It is then more likely, if not inevitable, that it will imply an ascription of responsibility: that it will say, or be reasonably heard as saying, that potential victims have a responsibility to play such a role in protecting themselves against crime. The message now is not: 'Since others won't protect you, you had better protect yourself', but: 'You should not expect us [the community in whose name the official speaks] to protect you to that extent; you are responsible for protecting yourself'.

Such ascriptions of self-protective responsibility are, of course, sometimes justified, but they raise again the question of what kinds of self-protective burden potential victims should be expected to bear (see text at pp. 27–28 above). We must also consider the force, and the implications, of such ascriptions.

Responsibilities and their Implications

If I fail to fulfil a responsibility, I may be criticised as irresponsible. Such criticism naturally also qualifies the sympathy I can expect if I am harmed or wronged as a result of my failure: if I am attacked, or my car is stolen, I still deserve sympathy for the wrongful harm I suffer; but that sympathy is qualified by the thought that I irresponsibly failed to take precautions which would have protected me. One question, then, is when is it appropriate to respond in this way to victims who did not take precautions that they were advised to take?

Failures to fulfil self-protective responsibilities can also have further implications. One concerns the allocation of responsibility for the wrong or harm which the person then suffers, and the victim's rights to compensation. In civil cases, the idea of 'contributory negligence' can play a significant role: if I suffer harm as a result of another's culpable conduct, but had myself failed to take precautions which would have averted or reduced that harm, I am held part-responsible for the harm, and must bear part of the cost of repairing it (the damages to be paid by the other party are reduced). Now responsibility which is shared is not *necessarily* diminished for each of those amongst whom it is shared: if two people join in committing a murder, the responsibility for it is shared, but each is fully responsible, and culpable, for it. Thus whilst someone who is victimised as a result of her failure to fulfil her self-protective responsibilities (because she failed to take precautions which it was her responsibility to take) must be judged part-responsible for her own victimisation, it does not necessarily follow that her assailant is less responsible or culpable. But ascriptions of self-protective responsibilities do open the way to such further judgements of 'contributory negligence' (judgements which have played a notorious role in some rape cases); we must ask when, if ever, such responses to victims of crime are appropriate.

To make this question more concrete, we could ask, first, whether and when it is proper that the amount of compensation a victim can claim from a criminal injuries compensation scheme, or from the offender through a compensation order, or through an insurance policy, should be reduced by the fact that he failed to take certain protective precautions; and second, whether and when it is proper that he should be able to expect less help from the community (most obviously from the police), either in protecting him or in detecting and prosecuting his assailant, if he fails to take such precautions. We will not try to answer these questions: our point is only that they are implicit in the question of what kinds of responsibility citizens should have to protect themselves against crime.

Responsibilities and Obligations

Responsibilities can easily be formalised or strengthened into obligations: in particular, in the context of SCP, into legal obligations. Such obligations might be imposed on governmental or private bodies, but they can also be imposed on individuals: so a legal requirement that all cars on the road be fitted with steering locks (see Clarke, 1995: 128-9) imposes an obligation not just on manufacturers to fit such locks on new cars, but on individuals to fit such locks on older cars that they already own.

The difference between responsibilities and obligations, as we use these notions here, is that failure to fulfil a responsibility can make me liable to criticism, and to the loss of kinds of sympathy, help and compensation to which I would otherwise have been entitled if I suffer harm as a result; whilst failure to discharge an obligation also lays me open to the possibility of being subject to some kind of civil or criminal sanction for that failure.

Such legal obligations to take crime-preventive precautions are most familiar, and most easily justified, when they aim to protect *others*, not just the agent. This is true, for instance, of the requirement on car-makers to fit anti-theft devices; and of requirements concerning the secure keeping of firearms – whose primary aim is, presumably, to protect not owners against the theft of their firearms, but others against the criminal use to which such firearms might be put if stolen. A requirement on car owners to fit anti-theft devices *might* also be thus justified: what justifies requiring me to fit a steering lock to my car is not that it protects *me* against the theft of *my* car, but that it is a contribution I should make to a general practice which protects car *owners* against theft, and others against the crimes that are committed by the use of stolen cars. We should ask, however, whether it can ever be right to impose legal *obligations* on citizens to take purely *self*-protective precautions.

One other possibility is worth noting. If self-protective precautions are made a matter of responsibility, or of obligation, for potential victims, it is still true that those who fail to take the precautions and are then victimised have been the victims of crime. However, one could instead so define the crime that it is not committed if the 'victim' failed to take the specified precautions: for instance, so to define 'auto theft' that it is committed only by taking a *locked* car without the owner's consent; or to declare that in law an owner 'consents' to her property being taken if she does not protect it in specified ways.[28] We do not suggest that this is a proper way to make potential victims part-responsible for their own protection, but we should ask whether it is ever legitimate, or if it is not legitimate, why it is not.

---

[28] Compare the hacking provisions in German and Norwegian criminal law, which proscribe hacking only when the victim's computer is protected by a security device; see Wasik (1990: 80–81).

CONCLUDING REMARKS

This paper has no neat conclusions. Its aim has not been to determine which particular kinds of SCP measure are, or are not, ethically acceptable; nor to lay down the principles by which SCP measures should be guided and judged. Its aim has rather been to offer a prolegomenon to a discussion of 'the ethics of SCP', by raising some of the questions that should be asked about SCP policies, by sketching the kind of perspective from which those questions should be asked, and by indicating some of the values by which answers to them should be informed.

REFERENCES

Bottoms, A.E. (1990) 'Crime prevention facing the 1990s', *Policing and Society* 1: 3–22.

Braithwaite, J. and Pettit, P. (1990) *Not Just Deserts*, Oxford: Oxford University Press.

Clarke, R.V. (1983) 'Situational crime prevention: its theoretical basis and practical scope', in M. Tonry and N. Morris (eds.), *Crime and Justice: An Annual Review of Research*, 4: 225–56, Chicago: Chicago University Press.

_____ (1995) 'Situational crime prevention', in M. Tonry and D Farrington (eds.), *Building a Safer Society: Strategic Approaches to Crime Prevention. Crime and Justice: A Review of Research*, 19: 91–150, Chicago: Chicago University Press.

Crawford, A. (2000) 'Situational crime prevention, urban governance and trust relations', this volume.

Dimock, S. (1997) 'Retributivism and trust', *Law and Philosophy* 16: 37–62.

Duff, R.A. (1996) 'Penal communications: recent work in the philosophy of punishment', in M. Tonry (ed.), *Crime and Justice: An Annual Review of Research*, 20: 1-97, Chicago: Chicago University Press.

_____ (1998) 'Dangerousness and citizenship', in A.J. Ashworth and M. Wasik (eds.), *Fundamentals of Sentencing Theory*, 141–63, Oxford: Oxford University Press.

_____ (2000) *Punishment, Communication and Community*, New York: Oxford University Press.

Dworkin, G. (1988) *The Theory and Practice of Autonomy*, Cambridge: Cambridge University Press.

Dworkin, R. (1978) *Taking Rights Seriously*, London: Duckworth.

Felson, M. and Clarke, R.V. (1997) 'The ethics of situational crime prevention', in G. Newman, R.V. Clarke, and S.G. Shoham (eds.), *Rational Choice and Situational Crime Prevention*, 197–218, Aldershot: Ashgate.

Garland, D. (1996) 'The limits of the sovereign state: strategies of crime control in contemporary society', *British Journal of Criminology* 36: 445–471.

Hart, H.L.A. (1968) *Punishment and Responsibility*, Oxford: Oxford University Press.

Home Office (1993) *A Practical Guide to Crime Prevention for Local Partnerships*, London: Home Office.

Kleinig, J. (2000) 'The burdens of situational crime prevention: an ethical commentary', this volume.

Marshall, S.E. and Duff, R.A. (1998) 'Criminalisation and sharing wrongs', *Canadian Journal of Law and Jurisprudence* 11: 7–22.

Nozick, R. (1974) *Anarchy, State, and Utopia*, Oxford: Blackwell.

Pease, K. (1991) 'The Kirkholt project: preventing burglary on a British public housing estate', *Security Journal* 2: 73–7.

Raz, J. (1986) *The Morality of Freedom*, Oxford: Oxford University Press.

Tonry, M. (1998) 'Selective incapacitation: the debate over its ethics', in A. von Hirsch and A.J. Ashworth (eds.), *Principled Sentencing*, (2nd ed.), 128–37, Oxford: Hart Publishing.

von Hirsch, A. (1986) *Past or Future Crimes*, Manchester: Manchester University Press.

_____ and Wasik, M. (1997) 'Civil disqualifications attending conviction', *Cambridge Law Journal* 56: 599–626.

_____ (2000) 'The ethics of public television surveillance', this volume.

_____ and Shearing, C. (2000) 'Exclusion from public space', this volume.

Wakefield, A. (2000) 'Situational crime prevention in mass private property', this volume.

Wasik, M. (1990) *Crime and the Computer*, Oxford: Oxford University Press.

3

The Burdens of Situational Crime Prevention: An Ethical Commentary

John Kleinig

"Potential victims have ethical responsibilities to
reduce the risk of crime."
(Felson and Clarke, 1997: 210)

INTRODUCTION

The purpose of this essay[1] is to draw attention to some *tendencies* in
theorising about situational crime prevention (SCP), tendencies that are
probably associated with attempts to legitimise and elevate SCP, but which, I
believe, lead it to overreach its capabilities. I speak of tendencies, because in
each case I think that SCP theorists also advance a more modest agenda.
Further, this more modest agenda may help to explain the frustration that
such theorists feel at the apparent lack of enthusiasm for their position. First I
shall draw attention to the way in which SCP, in distinguishing itself from
traditional criminological theory, could foster an unpalatable *social* vision. I
suggest that SCP, to the extent that it distances itself from (what it characterises as) traditional criminological theorising, tends also to encourage an
unpalatable *moral* vision. I look then at the theory behind cost allocations for
crime prevention. This is applied to SCP theorising about responsibility for
crime prevention. I next address the issues of opportunity, temptation, and
fault, before making some concluding observations.

Although I characterise much of my discussion as a consideration of SCP, it
needs to be remembered that SCP does not itself constitute a unitary set of
practices or techniques. Target hardening is very different from access control;
formal surveillance is very different from the removal of inducements; rule
setting is very different from the deflection of potential offenders; and so on.
Not every SCP measure is likely to be susceptible to the critical concerns I
raise. For present purposes, it is sufficient that some of them, or the proliferation of some of them, and their incorporation into a general theory of crime

[1] For critical comments and helpful suggestions, I want to thank participants at the conference
at which this paper was presented, and in particular Ron Clarke, Sandra Marshall, and Andrew
von Hirsch.

prevention, trigger these concerns, for they do not seem to have been directly addressed by proponents of SCP.

SITUATIONAL CRIME PREVENTION'S SOCIAL VISION

A little ideal theorising

My concerns about the social assumptions that inform SCP are most easily brought out if I provide a crude schematic account of the kind of social world in which I think we would all like to live. At its heart, it would be a world in which we could trust our fellows to do the right thing by us – a world in which they would not prey upon us, a world in which our vulnerabilities would not be taken advantage of, a world in which, even if others were tempted to wrong us in some way, they would generally possess the moral fortitude to resist such temptation. It would be a world in which we could go about our lives, separately and with others, in the confidence that their regard for us, like our own regard for ourselves, was rooted in the notion of human lives as autonomous, guided by a conception of the good in which the autonomy of other lives was likewise acknowledged.

No doubt, for a world like this to exist, certain other conditions – economic, physical, and social – would also need to exist, and even if we could specify these conditions, the world so described would still be vulnerable to bad choices, lapses, and self-deception. It is, of course, an oversimplified world, one characterised by face-to-face interpersonal relations. The world that we live in is much more complex, since it is also criss-crossed by a multitude of formal and informal institutions, and these too, in a fuller sketch of my idealised world, would need to be trustworthy. But I stick for present purposes with the simplified version, since even the trustworthiness of institutions requires the trustworthiness of a significant number of those who 'populate' or 'administer' them.

With the dubious – and temporary – exception of the Garden of Eden, the world has never come close to the idealised sketch I have outlined, and there is little chance that it will. Nevertheless, there is something to this social ideal that we strive for not simply aspirationally but concretely, in the sense that fallings short are seen not simply as regrettable but also as unacceptable. That is, even though we do not expect complete success, we generally believe that we should do what we can to make our world one in which interpersonal trust is significantly implicated in our social relations. Interpersonal trust – a recognition *inter alia* that others will have competent regard for our good in their dealings with us – is important not only to our freedom but also to the quality of our social dealings with others. Let me be clear, though: this is not an argument for massive assaults on, or zero tolerance for, the sources of social distrust. Such a strategy would be self-defeating. I have in mind something much more piecemeal and constructive, far more in keeping with the liberal pluralism that underlies my idealised schema.[2]

Most of us inhabit a social world that is vastly different from the one I have attempted to sketch. Not only do we lock our houses, but we fit them with special locks, often with alarm systems and, if we are urban apartment dwellers, there are probably security cameras and personnel watching over or out for us. We have become chary of walking home or using public transport at night. Security, once a relatively minor consideration for many of us as we went about our lives, has now become a major and expensive preoccupation. We are confronted with threats to our security, and require an array of complex strategies for shoring it up.

Although the idealised world I described is a distant and, I believe, unattainable hope, I think most of us are aware that some social environments have been – and are – closer to realising its central values than others. Some of us grew up in urban or suburban environments in which our doors could be left unlocked, the bicycle could be left unchained, we could play in the street without fear of abduction, and so on. It was not by any means a perfect social world, it was local or regional rather than universal, and may well have been achieved at an unacceptable cost to the autonomy and well-being of others socially remote from us. Nevertheless, it was an environment characterised by a greater degree of social trust than the one that many of us currently inhabit, and provides us with some reason to work for its recovery or at least for a more egalitarian analogue within today's less trustful environments.

In pointing to the eroded social trust that characterises a great deal of contemporary urban life, I am not suggesting that suspicion has replaced trust as the coinage of our interpersonal dealings. Were that to be so, we would suffer from a paralysis of initiative and creative activity. Along with an increase in suspiciousness there has been a substantial depersonalisation of our social trust. We have increasingly placed our trust in institutions, strategies, and mechanisms, and these now mediate our relations with others and help to secure us against the hazards and vagaries of social life. To that extent they secure space for us that is sufficient to enable us to be what we want to be and do what we want to do. And they may even offer a site or opportunity for renewed interpersonal trust. Nevertheless, as I shall soon suggest, this has not been a completely satisfactory social bargain. We have been left short-changed. Even though the somewhat idealised world I characterised will remain well beyond our reach, we have good reason not to settle for depersonalised trust, but to foster as much interpersonal trust as we can.[3]

---

[2] It might be asked what level of crime I would be prepared to tolerate. I think the question can only be answered procedurally and programmatically. We must tolerate whatever level of crime cannot be diminished without incurring unacceptable social/moral costs.

[3] For an extended discussion of this issue, see Adam Crawford (2000) in this volume, and the references therein.

The response of traditional criminologists

By focusing particularly, though not exclusively, on the dispositions that lead to criminality, traditional criminological theorists – at least in the view of major SCP proponents (e.g. Clarke, 1995: 94–95) – have sought to provide an understanding of why it is that some are moved to prey on others, and thereby to undermine interpersonal and social trust. Traditional explanations have variously focused on the inner dynamics of criminality or on a range of external influences that reputedly generate such anti-social dispositions and behaviour. By seeking proximate explanations of criminality in dispositional factors, traditional criminology has usually presented itself – like diagnostics in medicine – as an adjunct of well-being. Through an understanding of the sources of criminality, we hope to devise ways of reducing its social presence and thus of creating or restoring social trust.

SCP theory professes to be less ambitious in its goals, though it presents itself as more efficient in combating crime. It is less ambitious in that it takes the breakdown, absence, or depersonalisation of social trust as a given. If anything, it increases the depersonalisation. It is sceptical of attempts to change dispositions ('human nature'), seeing only failure or very limited success in past attempts to achieve such change. Instead, it seeks to foster (through informal and formal means) environmental changes that are designed to make criminal activity more difficult and less attractive. And this, its proponents believe, it does acceptably and efficiently.

Partnership, not rivalry

To the extent that SCP sees itself as "ethically superior" to, and thus seeks to replace, traditional criminological approaches to criminality (Felson and Clarke, 1997: 199), and to the extent that SCP accepts as given such criminal dispositions as are currently found in society, seeing poor returns for any attempt to change them, SCP has the potential to become socially divisive, fragmented, and/or erosive. Instead of seeking to sustain or recover significant interpersonal and social trust by grasping and tackling – better, perhaps, than much traditional criminological theory does – the social and/or other sources of criminality, such an approach would seek merely to prevent those sources from finding opportunities for expression. It is a nostrum for our social ills that addresses symptoms rather than diseases. In focusing on preventive measures without regard to the quality of interpersonal trust, it distances many of those who can be trusted.[4] In some respects it would "prisonise" society by replicating – on a large scale – a fundamental principle of prison organisation: structure the environment so that violations are designed out,

---

[4] The point is not, perhaps, that we put our trust in systems rather than people, but that our trust in people is mediated by systems. It is "thinned" rather than replaced.

deterred, or made less attractive. Prisons are built around the absence or territorialisation of interpersonal trust, and those who advocate SCP as the pre-eminent strategy for our crime problems foster a view of social life in which broad-based interpersonal trust is tribalised or reduced to gullibility or irresponsibility: "the best policy is to regard most strangers and even neighbors with a moderate dose of benign suspicion" (Felson, 1998: 43). Instead, much of what remains of our trust will reside in locks and alarms, CCTV, environmental design, and regulation, rather than in some conception of others as trustworthy.

The mistake here is one of dichotomisation. To the extent that we detach the kinds of strategies that SCP theorists advocate from the larger social purpose of addressing the dispositional sources of crime (and the factors feeding those dispositional sources), we divorce ourselves from much of what makes social life intrinsically (as against instrumentally) worthwhile. Much of the intrinsic value of social life resides precisely in the quality of the interpersonal associations we are able to enjoy. If SCP is to be at all acceptable as a strategy for our social ills, it must not construct itself as "a radically different approach to crime control" (Felson and Clarke, 1997: 197), a substitute for traditional criminological concerns, but at best as an adjunct or complement to such approaches and concerns.

SITUATIONAL CRIME PREVENTION'S MORAL VISION

In Plato's *Republic* (359d–360a; 612b), Glaucon argues that most people, if subjected to the Gyges' Ring Test,[5] would act immorally if not criminally should opportunity arise: our conformity with moral and legal standards is largely a function of external factors such as lack of opportunity, likelihood of getting caught, and access to facilitators. Socrates, countering Glaucon, says that a truly moral (or just) person would act well even were he wearing the ring. Something like the Glauconian view of human beings informs much SCP theorising. There is an unchallenged presumption that humans are essentially self-interested and, even though we may recognise the benefits of community life, the intrinsic value of community life and the interests of others have a tenuous grip on our decision making. We are kept in check not by acknowledging such value or by our respect for others' rights, but rather by the absence of, the deflecting of, or discouragements to, self-serving temptation.

This is, of course, a fairly cynical view of human nature and of social and moral bonds. It might be a bit easier to take were it a view about some rather than about most or all of us. But Felson and Clarke seem to see it as a general characterisation. "Human weaknesses are widespread and everyone falls prey to temptation to commit crime on occasion. The dichotomy between criminals

---

[5] Reputedly, Gyges' ring would make its wearer invisible.

and others [is] false" (Felson and Clarke, 1997: 216). "Nobody is exempt from the temptation to commit crime since human weaknesses are widespread, not confined to any one segment of the population" (ibid.: 200).

It may well be that we are all subject to temptation. But that does not mean that most of us are likely to succumb to the temptations that we experience, or are deterred from doing so only because of the difficulty of succeeding or the social consequences of being caught. The temptations, once reflected upon, are recognised as violative of the legitimate interests of others, and we do not take them further. Generally speaking, we do not need to design out occasions for temptation. For ourselves, perhaps, and others, what we need to design in is better socialisation, that is, a recognition of the rights of others and what is rightfully theirs. Felson and Clarke take it for granted that we aren't going to succeed in the latter, and therefore they settle for something less. Not just something less, but a whole lot less, an essentially calculative and self-interested view of the moral life.[6]

The picture of humans that is conveyed is that of essentially self-interested people – some perhaps more self-interested than others, all of us inclined to advance our personal interests, some of us more willing than others to curb our self-interest by reference to the rights of others, but many of us kept in check only by certain external constraints – the difficulty of succeeding in violating others' rights, the (felt) likelihood of our getting caught and not profiting, and so on. Were Gyges' ring available to us, we would be busily at work violating others for self-interested reasons.

That this view of human nature – and morality – infects SCP is further suggested by Felson and Clarke's discussion of the diffusion of benefits that SCP can produce. At one point they claim that "if one person's efforts against crime serve in this way to reduce the risk for neighbors, self-interest and altruism become bound together" (Felson and Clarke, 1997: 202). Not so, any more than in the trickle-down theory of capitalism. Altruism is not constituted by the mere benefiting of others, and certainly not by the accidental benefiting of others in seeking to benefit oneself. Altruism involves the intentional benefiting of others for their own sake. The only self-interest that can be involved in altruism is the interest one has in benefiting others for their own sake.

Perhaps they could argue that by designing out opportunity and temptation they will also restructure dispositions so that they will not remain self-interested. And sometimes they seem to move in this direction (Clarke, 1995: 122, 140). Others have suggested as much.[7] But to the extent that they move in this

---

[6] It might be argued that one of the attractions of SCP is that it sees crime as something of which we are all capable. Indeed we are. But the SCP version of human nature tends to be overly calculative in its explanation of why some of us do and others of us don't succumb to criminal temptation.

[7] John Elster, for example, has suggested that the disutility involved in satisfying a preference may make its otherwise desirable object less attractive (1983: 109–40; *cf.* Sunstein, 1986: 1146–50).

direction, what they consider to be relatively intractable will be acknowledged as not so intractable after all. In effect they will be arguing that though other well-tried techniques (those sponsored by traditional criminology) will fail to alter dispositions, their own are likely to be more effective. In that case, their theory becomes somewhat more consistent – in its goals, at least – with traditional criminological strategies.

ALLOCATING COSTS FOR CRIME PREVENTION

Having given an account of the sort of social world in which I think we would all like to live, let me now offer an equally schematic and crude theoretical picture of the social world which we now inhabit and which, I believe, is intended to take us in the direction of securing or ensuring as much as we reasonably can of the idealised social world I outlined. Its basic assumptions are probably not greatly different from those that inform Felson and Clarke's liberal democratic commitments and yet, because those authors fail to articulate and develop those assumptions, I think they are left without a rationale for allocating the burdens of SCP. I will address the latter contention below.

There are many alternative (and sometimes competing) ways of providing the kind of social ordering that I am suggesting here, but to cut short a very long debate I begin at a point that will be fairly recognisable and also recognisably related to some of the assumptions underlying the idealised picture with which I started. My account begins with a characterisation of individual human beings – at least those "in the maturity of their faculties" (Mill, 1869: Ch. 1) – as rational agents ("progressive beings"), both capable of and (by virtue of that characterisation) normatively entitled to choose for themselves the direction their lives should take, given their specific abilities, the resources available to them, and their acknowledgment that others are similarly entitled. On this account of human entitlements, it is understood that social freedom and recognition of the kind I have outlined are unlikely to occur spontaneously but must be created, fostered, and secured by a variety of social institutions, some formal and others informal.

As this story of institutionalisation unfolds, it usually incorporates some form of social contract theory. It posits a recognition by rational choosers of the reasonableness of their collective acceptance of political authority, whereby laws are established to provide a uniform basis for social conduct, a judiciary is instituted to ensure that such societal rules are fairly applied, and some mechanism for their effective operation is put in place (Locke, 1690: Ch. 9). This collective recognition of, and commitment to, a rule of law, its impartial administration and effective enforcement, is intended both to express (to the extent possible) and to help achieve the idealised social picture with which I started.

With respect to something like crime prevention, this account acknowledges that if left to individuals the task of crime prevention would be excessively burdensome[8] and therefore its proponents delegate to some form of broadly political structure a significant responsibility for ensuring that crimes are not committed, or, if committed, are then prosecuted and punished. Although individuals are not exempted from a continuing responsibility for minimising the likelihood of legal breaches, nevertheless crime prevention, no less than criminal prosecution and punishment, is understood to be a central function of some larger collectivity or political authority.[9]

How much responsibility for crime prevention should be ensured through some larger or centralised mechanism and how much should fall to individuals?[10] At this point the theoretical story tends to proceed in two broadly different directions (with variants in between). One fork of the story is usually characterised as libertarian, the other as communitarian. The characterisations are themselves complex and susceptible to many subtle variations, but I am going to ignore the subtleties in order to bring out two different ways in which the burdens of crime prevention may be allocated among the various institutions and individuals that comprise our society.

At bottom, the two broad traditions often differ significantly over the initial account they give of the human beings who accept some collective oversight, and hence differ about the prerogatives of the structure that such beings would accept.

Libertarian responsibility

The libertarian account takes our primary obligation to others to be that of non-interference (or non-aggression). An individual should be left to go about his/her life as he/she chooses as long as, and just as long as, in going about it, certain central concerns of others are not invaded. Exactly what those significant concerns are or should be is a bit unclear (or at least contested), though libertarians tend to draw them narrowly, focusing in particular on life, liberty, and property. (And these, too, tend to be interpreted narrowly rather than expansively.)

[8] In speaking of the "burdens" or "costs" of SCP, I have in mind not only economic but also social and normative burdens – costs to freedom as well as costs in resources. These, of course, are not totally unconnected.

[9] It is not an accident that modern policing – going back to Peel in 1829 – formally cast itself in terms of crime prevention: "It should be understood, at the outset, that the principal object to be attained is the Prevention of Crime" (Metropolitan Police, 1829: pt. I). *Ceteris paribus*, it is better to prevent crime than to mop up after it.

[10] The distinction here is a bit fuzzy, because collective or centralised mechanisms can be used to require that individuals bear a burden of crime prevention responsibility: those individuals who do not do enough might be fined or denied certain forms of compensation. What I have in mind is a distinction that refers to the allocation of costs: there will be varying degrees of sharing among broader collectivities and the individual.

Although this position tends to favour minimal government, the crime preventive role that it gives to government is central.[11] The function of government *just is* to secure fundamental interests against encroachment by others, and that is where governmental efforts should be directed. Placing the burden on innocents to ensure that their securable interests are not violated forgets the point of the contract and represents a serious dereliction of contractual responsibility. On this view, SCP – to the extent that it involves a burdening of individuals with the task of securing their own rights – would require an unacceptable shifting of (direct) responsibility from government to individuals. Not that the government should prevent crime at any cost: if the centralised prevention of crime will interfere significantly with the securable interests of innocent individuals, then it should stay out of providing it. Libertarians want as little government as they can get away with, but what they minimally expect is security.

One of the main challenges confronting the libertarian allocation of responsibility for crime prevention lies in its apparent failure to appreciate the extent to which individual life, and the securable interests of individuals, are products of, and dependent on, a relatively richly textured social life. This constitutes a failure to appreciate the extent to which the satisfaction of individual interests is a function of various forms of social coordination. There are deeper bonds of attraction and association that inform our relationships, and that pre-exist the language of contract, bonds that will themselves play a significant role in crime prevention. As I will later suggest, the intimate bonds of social life make a major contribution to SCP. If anything, the language of contract is erected upon the preexisting bonds of friendship, familial and tribal ties, social tradition, and so on, and it is through the fostering of these that crime prevention efforts will succeed. We do not start as libertarian individuals; nor, except in a substantially non-libertarian world, do we find our satisfaction in being such individuals.

Communitarian responsibility

The communitarian account begins from the view that libertarian individualism fails to recognise a continuing obligation we have to ensure that our social world remains unwelcoming of crime. A social world governed solely by (what are generally assumed to be) libertarian values would be harsh and undignifyingly divisive. Although it would not necessarily eschew the intimacy of noncontractual associations, it would make them inherently unstable and would fragment them to a point that would derogate from many of the satisfactions of human life (if not for all, then for many).[12]

[11] I am, of course, leaving out of the account those libertarians who see even minimal government as unacceptable, and think that all security arrangements – along with other governmental functions – should be privatised. That is another story, whose telling and criticism was imaginatively attempted by Nozick (1974).

[12] Ayn Rand's (1957) *Atlas Shrugged* is an attempt to characterise positively a world of that kind. *Res ipsa loquitur.*

Communitarian approaches reject what they see as the atomistic assumptions underlying libertarian individualism, and argue instead that the conception of autonomous personhood that underlies the libertarian position is essentially communal: it is communally or socially produced and sustained. We do not enter this world ready-made, but as people who are quite radically dependent on the nurture of others. Nor do we become what we are as the product of some natural maturation, as a tree might develop its full potential given only an adequate supply of nutrients, light, and water. Our coming to be what we are is substantially a function of our immersion in a social environment through which we interactively learn – in part through some form of directed program – the knowledge, habits, and understandings that are characteristic of an autonomous human life. Our individual projects, moreover, frequently involve the informal cooperation of others. Communities, and our close involvement with them, then, are the condition for our (continued) flourishing as autonomous beings.

Not every community of course is equally congenial to our well-being. Some communities will tend to suffocate their members even as they sustain them. Even so, the communitarian understanding is that there are forms of community – essentially diverse and richly textured communities – that need to be fostered and sustained if humans are to be able to live good lives. These communities will not be constituted solely by contractualised associations, even though 'contract' may figure in their public ideology.

Unlike the libertarian position, which recognises only duties of non-interference, or obligations that have been contractually entered into, the communitarian position recognises interpersonal duties of mutual assistance and aid along with those accorded to governmental and other authority. The task of central and corporate authorities is not simply to provide whatever assistance might be built into the 'formal articles of association' that reasonable people would draw up for themselves. By virtue of their communal embeddedness there remains an ongoing obligation of people to sustain the conditions of their association. Included among such obligations will not only be the obligation to assist the needy, but also an obligation to secure an environment in which violations of legitimate interests – one's own and others' – are minimised.

The communitarian approach, therefore, is likely to support a stronger ongoing individual obligation to engage in (situational) crime prevention than the libertarian one. It will, however, see the primary fulfilment of that obligation in the socialisation of each new generation into a respect for the securable interests of others, a care for others that will manifest itself in a recognition of their destiny as choosers of their own ways of life, recognising that we flourish best in a social environment which not merely tolerates but sustains a wide range of options. Crime prevention will first and foremost be a responsibility of socialisation – though not just the socialisation produced by families, but its communal expressions in schools and other nurturing social institutions.

Second, beyond the socialising role that groups and institutions will have in crime prevention, there will be a situational responsibility. That is, associations and their members – be they members of families, businesses, or community organisations – will be expected, as part of their communal or civic responsibility, to seek to ensure environmental conditions that will minimise opportunities for crime, consistent with the flourishing of their members.

Third, the communitarian approach, like the libertarian approach, will recognise that this will not be sufficient. It is a non-ideal world, and communitarians will recognise the need for some form of centralised protection against anti-social behaviour. There will be a need for law enforcement organisations of various kinds to deter crime and secure the prosecution of criminals. Like the libertarian position, the communitarian one will view crime prevention as an important function of political authority, albeit one that takes on and to some degree takes over a pre-existing responsibility of individuals and natural associations.[13]

Although the communitarian approach is likely to ascribe to its members a much greater responsibility for SCP than the libertarian one, it will not see this as a detached individual responsibility but as a communitarian one. It will, in other words, not unfairly burden its individual members, but seek to spread the costs. If the burdens of SCP are likely to be too great for individuals to be reasonably asked to bear – because too disruptive or too costly – the burdens will be assigned to organisations or collectivities that are better placed and more suited to bear them or to more centralised agencies such as municipal, state, or national government. Sometimes there may be some form of coordination between individuals, organisations, and government agencies: individuals might be expected to lock their cars in shopping mall parking areas, the managements of shopping malls might be expected to design and maintain their parking areas in such a way that crime is deterred, and this may be reinforced by occasional police patrols or by holding shopping mall managements responsible for failures of reasonable supervision.

ALLOCATING BURDENS IN SITUATIONAL CRIME PREVENTION

No doubt the foregoing sketches need a lot of filling in and refinement, but I think they indicate two lacunae in the account of SCP provided by Felson and Clarke.

The first is their fairly bland appeal to a 'liberal democratic' society, one that does not take adequate account of the spectrum of viewpoints that is indicated by the somewhat stylised alternatives I have been discussing. Failing

---

[13] By stating the communitarian position in this way, I am suggesting that something like individual SCP logically precedes civil society, and that civil authority not only assumes the burden of SCP but also reinforces it: it encourages a sense of civic responsibility that complements its own responsibility.

to attend to that spectrum (except, perhaps, as a foil for various ideological challenges to their position), they fail to recognise that very different constructions of individual responsibility for SCP will be suggested by different accounts of an appropriately liberal society. The kind of civic responsibility that they claim the members of a liberal society should observe cannot therefore be taken for granted.

I have suggested my own general sympathy for an account of liberal society in which some individual responsibility for SCP is borne. But the second gap in Felson and Clarke's account is to be found in their failure to indicate the extent to which individuals ought to be burdened with the costs of SCP. Should it be shared through taxes for greater law enforcement presence, or higher prices on goods so that their security can be enhanced, or through specific behavioural requirements imposed by law? Or through some combination, and, if so, what combination? Felson and Clarke need to show why individuals should be asked to bear a burden of (situational) crime prevention, and they need some criteria to enable the burdens of performance to be allocated among individuals, organisations, and more centralised agencies.

Distributing burdens

Reading Felson and Clarke's articles, one is bombarded with a plethora of practical suggestions about SCP, but without a clear procedure for determining whether (and if so to what extent) the costs in any particular case should be placed on individuals, or should rather be made the responsibility of manufacturers, businesses, or that of a central agency. They refer approvingly, for example, to a German requirement that citizens install column locks by a certain date, noting only what they call a "minor expenditure and inconvenience" (Felson and Clarke, 1997: 208), and suggest that for the carelessness of leaving keys in a car, it might not be unreasonable to fine a person (*ibid*.: 211). Here, individuals are not merely held to some degree responsible for SCP (perhaps by having claims diminished in the case of car theft), but are subject to penalties if they do not conform. Why should this be so? We need an account of the responsibilities for SCP that shows not only why and when individuals have such a responsibility, but also indicates what a reasonable burden might be.

From time to time, there is a suggestion of an underlying efficiency criterion: responsibility will be allocated in a way likely to be most effective in reducing crime. But if this is so, questions of distributive justice will need to be addressed: is it fair to place the greatest burden on those who are best positioned to prevent crime? And it then becomes necessary to determine what will be fair in matters such as this.

The lack of an adequately articulated theoretical reference point is shown by Felson and Clarke's table, "Degrees of responsibility for car theft and its prevention" (*ibid*.: 212). The person who is "least responsible" for his/her car theft is the person who keeps an eye on the vehicle after parking it – a demanding and, in most cases, impractical suggestion.[14] Leaving that aside, the person next least responsible is the person who locks his/her car. At first blush, this does not seem unreasonable: most cars have locks, and it requires minimal effort to use the locking mechanism. But – as already noted above – in the body of their discussion, Felson and Clarke seem willing to hold car owners to a rather higher standard. Requiring that a column lock be installed is considerably more demanding, and I suspect that they would not be averse to similar requirements, such as the (purchase and) use of Clubs. Why should individuals be made to bear the costs of security and not manufacturers?[15]

Ideologically skewed distributions

Yet another factor may also be of relevance, particularly if our contractualised understanding of civil society is moderated by some recognition that social ordering is to some extent conflictual. That is, compromising the idealised view that we are all equally represented actors in social decision making, we might consider our social order to be tilted in the favour of a dominant class (of "haves") who, operating under the banner of democratic decision making, are able, in a way familiar to us in cases in which different parties have unequal bargaining power, to impose social solutions (on 'have nots') that reflect partisan or class interests. Shifting the burden of SCP to individuals may be construed as a 'societal' response to crime that addresses symptoms and not diseases. Perhaps it diverts attention from alternative 'solutions' to crime that would be thought too costly for those with social power. If there is any substance to an account of this kind, there is a strong likelihood that the individuals who are most likely to be burdened with responsibility for SCP will be those who are least able to carry this burden.[16]

The likelihood and longevity of benefits

As long as we focus on the successes of SCP there is a certain intuitive plausibility to the idea that individuals should be expected to be responsible for taking measures that may help to prevent crime. But, as Clarke acknowledges, not every SCP measure succeeds (Clarke, 1995: 119–22). It is not just that there

[14] To some extent the same may be said about parking in safer/riskier places. In urban areas one parks where one is able, not usually where one wants to. Or – albeit often at considerable cost – one may park in a private parking lot.

[15] Of course, manufacturers will, to some extent, pass on these costs. But they are likely to be considerably lower than those that would otherwise have to be borne by individuals. In fairness to Ron Clarke, however, I should note that in the conference discussion he was strongly supportive of systemic SCP rather than expecting the burden to be placed on individuals. What is still lacking is some ethically satisfactory method of allocating costs.

[16] This suggestion is reinforced if it is the case – as it is often claimed to be – that the victims (as well as the perpetrators) of crime are more likely to be drawn from the ranks of the disempowered.

will always be a percentage of victims even if a particular SCP measure generally lowers the incidence of a particular kind of crime, but that some SCP measures have turned out to have only limited effectiveness. Individuals and others have been burdened with costs but with little or no societal – let alone individual – return. We should be very careful about shifting burdens to individuals in cases in which the probability of their benefiting is uncertain.

Account should also be taken of a 'leapfrogging' factor. Over time, the strategies available to criminal opportunists as well as so-called career criminals are likely to change. The lock that bars a thief this month may not be an adequate disincentive next month. The steering wheel bar that provides me with security in May may no longer serve me in September. Burdening me with the purchase of a steering wheel bar that may protect me for only a short period of time is, at best, questionable protection. Of course, as Felson and Clarke (1997) argue, the leapfrogging need not be endless and, even if it is, the number of crimes is likely to diminish. Nevertheless, the burdening of individuals to ensure that such (potentially temporary) measures are adopted is troubling. There ought to be ways in which such burdens – insofar as they have to be borne – can be shared more broadly.

Evolving legal responses

There is an interesting evolution in the thinking of courts about the relative SCP responsibilities of various parties.[17] In a 1962 New Jersey case, a milkman who sued a public housing authority after being mugged in an elevator was told that he had no case. The landlord of the housing project was under no obligation to perform a task "that must be left with the duly constituted police forces. The job is theirs to prevent crime and to go wherever need be to that end. [T]he duty to provide police protection is and should remain the duty of government and not the owner of the housing project."[18] The court did, however, allow that a landlord might be held liable if an intruder gained entrance to the premises as a result of the landlord's "carelessness."[19]

[17] Here I draw heavily on Scheid (1997).

[18] *Goldberg* v. *Housing Authority*, 10 A.L.R.3d 595, at 607-08, 186 A.2d 291 (NJ, 1962). But note also the recent Minnesota case of *Sulik* v. *Total Petroleum, Inc.*, 847 F.Supp. 747 (1994), cited by Scheid. In the course of arguing that "the prevention of crime is a governmental function that should not be shifted to the private sector," the court argued:

> It appears to this Court that the duty sought to be imposed by plaintiff is essentially to provide police protection, a duty traditionally vested in the government. The Court cannot gainsay the truth that we live in difficult times. If they ever were, the Twin Cities are no longer islands of respite from violent crime. These facts, however, do not undo the law of tort or reimpose the late-medieval need for private armies. Our municipalities are guarded by community police departments. Under the circumstances presented by this case, the law does not impose on a business owner/merchant the duty of employing protection beyond that provided by the community itself (at 751, 752).

[19] *Goldberg*, at 604. See further, *Ramsay* v. *Morrissette*, 252 A.2d 509 (D.C., 1969).

In 1970, however – in *Kline* v. *1500 Massachusetts Ave. Apartment Corp.*–
the courts began placing a more positive duty on the owners of premises.[20] In
1959, when the complainant in this case first moved into the apartment
complex, there was a 24-hour doorman, an employee at the front desk, and
two garage attendants. By mid-1966, however, there was no longer a doorman,
the front desk was frequently unattended, and the garage was frequently
unguarded and unlocked. Despite tenant requests, based on recurring crimes,
the landlord failed to restore services. After she had been seriously injured and
robbed in the common hallway outside her apartment, Sarah Kline sued the
apartment corporation. The D.C. Court of Appeals accepted her complaint,
finding that a duty of the landlord to provide protection in common areas
under his control had been breached, because the landlord had exclusive power
to take preventive action and had reason to expect crimes such as that of which
she was a victim to occur. Although the reasoning of courts that followed *Kline*
often relied on the implied warranty of habitability and other aspects of
residential contracts, a more expansive tort rationale has come to prevail.[21]

Although judges do not generally lay bare their deeper reasoning, one of the
things that is surely at work in the changing allocations of legal responsibility is
an evolving recognition concerning the burdens/costs that individuals can be
fairly expected to bear in regard to the maintenance of their safety and security.
There appears to be a growing belief that there are good reasons for seeking to
share that responsibility more broadly – if not by deployment of the agents of
political authority (police officers), then with landlords, businesses, and
manufacturers who in various ways profit from the presence or custom of
potential victims.

In sum, we can suggest several considerations that bear on the issue of
allocation: (1) civil society is founded on the recognition that for many –
perhaps most – people, their flourishing is jeopardised if there is not some
political authority to assume responsibility for securing various social conditions, including crime prevention; (2) a central purpose of the social contract is
to share the burden of crime prevention – to ensure, as far as possible, that
individuals will generally have maximal opportunity to flourish. To the extent
that they have to devote their individual resources to crime prevention, they

---

[20] *Kline* v. *1500 Massachusetts Ave. Apartment Corp.*, 439 F.2d 477 (D.C., 1970):

> [I]n the fight against crime, the police are not expected to do it all; every segment of society
> has obligations to aid in law enforcement and to minimise the opportunities for crime (at
> 484).

Scheid notes that public attention on the issue was focused by the 1974 attack on Connie Francis
in a Howard Johnson Motor Lodge: *Garzilli* v. *Howard Johnson's Motor Lodges, Inc.*, 419
F.Supp. 1210 (E.D.N.Y., 1976).

[21] Scheid cites Merrill (1985). A tort liability rationale enables the responsibility for crime
prevention to be extended to other premises. See *Erickson* v. *Curtis Invest. Co.* 447 N.W.2d 165
(Minn., 1989), in which Ms Erickson was sexually assaulted in her car in a parking building
whose management was deemed not to have taken sufficient precautions to ensure the security of
its clientele.

will be disabled from devoting their resources to making use of social opportunities and realising their individual and joint projects;[22] (3) where private
institutions intend to profit from the presence of individual citizens, they
should – where feasible – accept a significant part of the burden of SCP. Once
again, this will have the effect of spreading the burden, since the costs are
likely to be borne by all clients (and perhaps others via insurance, etc.)[23]; and
(4) although individual citizens certainly have a duty not to foment crime, they
should be expected to bear the costs of crime prevention only where these are
not too burdensome and cannot be efficiently borne by collectivities or some
centralised political authority.

RESPONSIBILITY AND TEMPTATION

Beyond the issue of cost-bearing there are further questions about what is
involved in coming to have responsibility for crime that is committed. There
are several issues that need further consideration by SCP theorists.

Models of responsibility

More than one model of responsibility of criminal actors is discernible in
Felson and Clarke's (1997) discussion of SCP. The first, an *accordion* model,
sees responsibility for crime as something that may be extended without
diminution. If one person commits crime *A* and two people commit crime *B*
which is substantively the same, the involvement of the additional actor does
not *ipso facto* diminish the full responsibility that each actor has for *B*. The
point may be extended to the responsibility of crime victims. If *X* negligently
provides *Y* with an opportunity for crime, *X*'s responsibility for failure to take
precautions does not diminish *Y*'s responsibility for the crime.

For the most part, Felson and Clarke work with this model. They write that
"the potential victim's responsibilities to society do not erase those of the
potential thief" (Felson and Clarke 1997: 211), and that "the offender's

[22] In considering the ethical problems of SCP, Felson and Clarke (1997) focus on the objection
that SCP shifts crime from the rich to the poor (because the rich can afford prevention measures
that are beyond the financial capability of the poor). My point is a related but somewhat different
one: SCP (particularly if it is institutionally demanded) may disproportionately burden the poor.
It is one thing to ask that motor vehicle manufacturers build in steering locks – for then the
burden is spread more thinly – it is another to require that individual vehicle owners fit them.
Felson and Clarke do advert to the former option, and for the same reasons that I mention, but
there is little attempt to sort out what should be the responsibility of manufacturers, and what
should be required of individuals.

[23] A point acknowledged by Felson and Clarke (1997: 213). Scheid (1997: 173) cites a number
of additional considerations that weigh in favour of businesses accepting a significant responsibility for crime prevention: business proprietors are usually in a better position to secure a police
presence, are usually more aware of the potential for crime on their premises, and are usually
better placed to take crime prevention measures (alarms, CCTV, etc.) or to provide security
personnel.

criminal responsibility is in no way diminished by the bad judgment of the victim" (*ibid.*) On this view the fact that the victim failed to take adequate or reasonable precautions against victimisation should provide little comfort or relief for the victimiser.

Sometimes, however, they slip into what might be seen as a *hydraulic* model of responsibility. There is just so much responsibility to go around, and as the potential victim's responsibility increases, the actor's responsibility decreases. Near the beginning of their article, for example, they assert that "situational prevention introduces discrete managerial and environmental change to make criminal action more difficult and risky, less rewarding and less excusable" (*ibid.*:197). And later: "With situational prevention, invitations to crime are fewer and hence it is more difficult for those who do offend to escape responsibility" (*ibid.*: 212). The suggestion here is that failure to take SCP measures shifts part of the responsibility from the perpetrator to the victim. It is a strategically attractive suggestion, because it provides their position with something like a *moral* incentive for individual SCP: those who fail to take reasonable preventive precautions will have themselves partially to blame for what befalls them, and, moreover, will diminish the responsibility of those who have victimised them.

Although this appears to be something of an unspoken belief of Felson and Clarke, they seem reluctant to press it too explicitly. This is not, perhaps, surprising, since it does not comport with traditional moral or legal notions of responsibility. Nevertheless, it has a clear advocate in Alon Harel (1994), and it is instructive to consider his arguments for it.

Harel's starting point is the tort/contract principle of comparative fault, expanded to cover not only comparative fault but also contributory negligence (Harel, 1994: 1193). Moral symmetry requires that just as the victim in a tortious suit may find that his/her compensatory claim is diminished or even completely undermined by virtue of what he/she contributed to the harm suffered, so too should a perpetrator's liability to punishment be diminished or removed by a victim's "contribution" to the circumstances under which the crime occurred. It is Harel's belief that traces of this can already be observed in the criminal law of provocation, but he believes that it warrants more general acceptance in criminal law.[24]

Two considerations inform this extension – efficiency and fairness – both fundamental to law's *raison d'être*, and each is capable of grounding the incorporation of victim-related data in the determination of criminal responsibility.[25]

---

[24] Harel's argument is in fact more ambitious than this, since he wishes to claim that the principle is already latent in a good deal of criminal law, though his case for this – no less than his argument for its underpinning the law of provocation – strikes me as tendentious.

[25] Significantly, Harel concedes that the practicality of his claims will be determined in part by wider socio-political factors such as the reasonable capacity of crime victims to take precautions against victimisation. The disabled and poor might, therefore, claim exemption from the expectations of a comparative fault principle.

The social purpose of criminal sanctions is to guarantee the efficient production of protection and its fair distribution among potential victims (ibid.: 1182). Efficiency considerations would lead one to believe that the amount of criminal conduct would be lessened, and the social costs of providing protection from it would be minimised, were potential victims given an incentive either to be less careless or alternatively to take preventive precautions. The theory here is that potential criminals will have an incentive to avoid cautious potential victims and to pick instead on careless victims, and that otherwise careless victims will now have an incentive to be more careful. The incentive might be either to lessen the punishment of offenders [26] or to penalise victims.[27]

The argument from fairness begins from the premise that protection is not a pure public good. It is a limited resource that can be differentially provided and should therefore be fairly distributed. To the extent that vulnerability is a function of voluntary choice,[28] it is fairly distributed where the same amount of resources is expended on each individual.[29] This is fair because careless victims increase the costs of protection and unfairly divert resources to their own case.

Although Harel believes that both efficiency and fairness arguments point in the same direction, they differ in their demandingness: efficiency requires optimal precautions, whereas fairness requires only that precautions be reasonable. The latter should take priority – otherwise the more vulnerable will find themselves subject to unreasonable constraints. A woman who walks on the street at night will be seen as less justified in doing so than a man.

Whatever the attractions of Harel's position – and it does have some, at least in cases of grossly careless, reckless, or provocative behaviour – it also suffers from several deficiencies. For one thing, it fails to confront the public/private distinction to the extent that it operates in dividing criminal law from tort and contract law. The criminal violates a public norm in victimising another; the tortfeasor or violator of contract violates a private duty. If a criminal's punishment is lessened or the criminal is more likely to be acquitted if the victim has been careless, the offence is treated as though it were the violation of a private norm rather than of a publicly-upheld standard of conduct. For another, it is not clear why the careless need to be given a greater incentive for taking precautions than that which arises from the fact that they

[26] This of course assumes that offenders will have reason to believe that the probability of their getting caught is high enough to be affected by the alternative penalty structure.

[27] Other efficiency-based arguments might also be posited: those who pick on the cautious might be subject to increased penalties, and those whose victimisation results from their own "carelessness" might find their cases pursued less earnestly or find greater prosecutorial leniency displayed. On the counterintuitiveness of the economic perspective, see Seidman (1984: 340).

[28] Harel claims, however, that where increased vulnerability has great social value (e.g., social workers in ghettoised communities), an exception should be made.

[29] This is distinguished from and defended against a distributive model that would provide equal protection (rather than resources) for each individual. Only where vulnerability is not voluntary would equal protection be justified on grounds of fairness.

are more likely to be victimised. People do not generally want to become victims. Affecting the *compensation* for which they are eligible is not likely to add significantly to the incentive they have to avoid victimisation. And with regard to fairness, although it may be fair for burdens to be shifted in the direction of victims in tort cases, in criminal cases the issue is not about the fair allocation of burdens.[30] Mitigating the punishment of offenders does not shift its burden to victims, and Harel provides no reason for seeing the victim's fault as rendering the offender less blameworthy.

Situations arise, no doubt, in which one person's acts diminish another person's criminal responsibility, but they are not likely to be instanced in most of the cases that SCP theorists have in mind – in which mere 'opportunities' for crime are provided or created. There is no badgering, inviting, or provoking. Harel's thesis does not provide support for the hydraulic model of criminal responsibility.

Opportunity and temptation

SCP rhetoric is replete with talk of 'opportunities for' and 'temptations to' crime. But what is it to provide an opportunity? And is the mere provision of an opportunity a responsibility-incurring act? To what extent are temptations created as against experienced? Does the fact that X is tempted to steal my watch impose a responsibility on me to diminish the likelihood of X's acting to take it, or do I acquire a responsibility only if I do something to tempt X? Is my mere having of a watch (about which X knows) sufficient to generate a SCP responsibility on my part?

Talk of 'providing an opportunity' for someone is vague at best. At bottom, the most that is implied is the failure to erect certain barriers with respect to that person. Even that may suggest too active an involvement: the very fact of my existence provides an opportunity for crime that would not otherwise have existed. Whether even the active provision of an opportunity also constitutes an omission (a failure) is a further question. Unless the provision can be shown to violate a negative duty, no omission will be involved.

Felson and Clarke frequently give opportunity provision a much more intentional cast, as though it involves responsibility in the event that a crime is committed. They speak of opportunities as 'extremely enticing,' of their 'creating temptation' or 'inducing' or 'inviting' crime (Felson and Clarke, 1997: 212, 214, 216). They speak of various services, products and modes of operation as 'spawning opportunities for a vast range of crimes' (ibid.: 197), of certain of our actions as 'assisting' our neighbour's children in becoming burglars (ibid.: 210). This kind of language needs to be used with great care. For the most part we now reject the view that the woman who frequents a bar

---

[30] Here I distance myself from a theory of punishment first advanced by Herbert Morris (1968), but developed at length by others. See the detailed and critical discussion in Duff (1986: Ch.8).

or wears a tight dress or walks alone at night is 'asking for trouble,' but SCP theorists tend to gravitate in that direction in seeking to advance their position.

If I close but fail to lock my car door, does that create an 'opportunity'? What if it is the door of my apartment? Someone must first 'try' the handle to find out that it is unlocked. What if it is the back door of my house that I fail to lock? In the latter case, someone has to trespass in order to discover that that is the case. At what point – if at all in these cases – does the 'opportunity' manifest a failure in civic (and moral?) responsibility?

What about 'tempting *X* to do *A*'? The phrase suggests some positive act on *Y*'s part that induces *X* to do *A*. It is traditionally believed that the serpent tempted Eve, and that Eve tempted Adam; but did God tempt Adam and Eve by putting an attractive tree in the Garden? Was it insufficient to forbid the eating of its fruit? Ought God to have fenced it in (or banned serpents)?

Felson and Clarke seem to require something less than a positive inducement for the creation of a temptation. My owning a Mercedes Benz will be enough to constitute a temptation for someone to break in and steal its Blaupunkt. My owning a car favoured by joyriders will constitute a temptation. Likewise my owning some fancy electronic equipment or valuable paintings or jewellery will constitute temptation for some. Does this impose on me a heightened responsibility to ensure that they are not stolen?

Perhaps we are misled here by passive and active senses of 'tempt.' From the fact that my possession of something constitutes a temptation for *X*, it does not follow that in having it I tempt *X*. But if *X* is tempted by my having a particular brand of car, does that mean I have some civic responsibility for securing it if I am not to tempt him? We might argue that a woman who flirts with a man tempts him, but if he is tempted simply by the fact that she is an attractive woman, does she have some responsibility to make herself less attractive or less vulnerable?

Felson and Clarke do not seem to have worked through these issues on their way to ascribing responsibility to the sources of 'opportunity' and 'temptation.'

Tempting opportunities and dispositions

Felson and Clarke write: "In our view, it is ethically more defensible to arrange society so that people are not readily tempted into crime, than to allow temptations to abound and then to visit punishment on those who fall" (Felson and Clarke, 1997: 215).[31] Whether temptations abound seems to be a

---

[31] *Cf*.: "Waiting for people to commit crime, trying to apprehend them and then denying them freedom for a long time – these steps are far more intrusive against civil liberties than any situational measure of which we are aware" (Felson and Clarke, 1997: 210). Are they right about this? Maybe there is less 'suffering' overall if we engineer society in the way that they suggest. But it is not only the totality but also the distribution of burdens that is at issue. It might be argued that burdening potential victims beyond a certain point with crime prevention responsibility is also unfair. One can make more sense of such claims only if one accepts the hydraulic model of responsibility that I have criticised.

function of dispositions as much as of opportunities, and perhaps the focus should be on the traditional criminological concern with the former as much as on the SCP concern with the latter. I see the sidewalk tables laden with their wares. An 'opportunity' for theft, no doubt, but I am not tempted. No one whispered in my ear that I could get away with taking something, and I had no inclination to take what was not mine to take. Or I am tempted, but think better of it: these things are not mine to take. Better that we attempt to develop a society of people who recognise the legitimate rights of others than that – in our failure to do that – we must constantly seek to diminish 'opportunities'— if not this one then that one – and with that imperative our freedom to live fulfilling social lives. If Glaucon is right, perhaps it is vain to hope for more. But if Glaucon is right, it is also a sorry day for human society.

CONCLUSION

It has not been my intention to claim that SCP should be rejected. As a cluster of strategies it has many merits and reflects an ongoing responsibility that we all have to create and maintain a world that is safe for, and conducive to, diverse forms of human flourishing. What I have argued against is the tendency of its advocates to set it against, rather than alongside, more traditional strategies of crime prevention. It should complement rather than supplant the longstanding concern to create a social environment in which public norms are accepted as authoritative and weighty rather than weakly supported barriers to victimising conduct. If proponents for SCP can accept that more modest role for their theory, they might be able to accept that the considerable use of SCP techniques already evident in our social life do not represent their half-hearted acceptance but a fuller recognition of their real but limited place.

REFERENCES

Clarke, R.V. (1995) 'Situational Crime Prevention', in M. Tonry and D. Farrington (eds.), *Building a Safer Society. Crime and Justice: A Review of Research* 19: 91–150, Chicago: University of Chicago Press.

Crawford, A. (2000) 'Situational crime prevention, urban governance and trust relations', this volume.

Duff, R.A. (1986) *Trials and Punishments*, Cambridge: Cambridge University Press.

Elster, J. (1983) *Sour Grapes: Studies in the Subversion of Rationality*, Cambridge: Cambridge University Press.

Felson, M. (1998) *Crime and Everyday Life*, (2nd. ed.), Thousand Oaks, CA: Pine Forge Press.

—— and Clarke, R.V. (1997) 'The ethics of situational crime prevention', in G. Newman, R.V. Clarke, and S.G. Shoham (eds.), *Rational Choice and Situational Crime Prevention: Theoretical Foundations*, 197–217, Aldershot: Ashgate.

Harel, A. (1994) 'Efficiency and fairness in criminal law', *California Law Review* 84: 1181–1229.

Locke, J. (1690; 1924) *Second Treatise Of Civil Government*, London: J.M. Dent.

Merrill, I.W. (1985) 'Landlord liability for crimes committed by third parties against tenants on the premises', *Vanderbilt Law Review* 38: 431-60.

Metropolitan Police (1829; 1836) *Instructions, Orders, &c. &c.* London: HMSO.

Mill, J.S. (1869; 1965) *On Liberty*, D Spitz (ed.), New York: W.W. Norton.

Morris, H. (1968) 'Persons and punishment', *Monist* 52:475-501.

Nozick, R. (1974) *Anarchy, State, and Utopia*, Oxford: Blackwell.

Plato (1955) *The Republic*, H.D.P. Lee (trans. and intro.), Harmondsworth: Penguin.

Rand, A. (1957) *Atlas Shrugged*, New York: Random House.

Scheid, D.E. (1997) 'Business entities and the state: Who should provide security from crime?', *Public Affairs Quarterly* 11: 163–82.

Seidman, L.M. (1984) 'Soldiers, martyrs, and criminals: Utilitarian theory and the problem of crime control", *Yale Law Journal* 94: 315–49.

Sunstein, C.R. (1986) 'Legal interference with private preferences', *University of Chicago Law Review* 53: 1129–74.

4

The Ethics of Public Television Surveillance

Andrew von Hirsch[1]

INTRODUCTION

CCTV as a Surveillance Strategy

Ronald Clarke (1995: 113-14) describes surveillance as an important technique of situational crime prevention. Its functions are to deter potential offenders from offending because their activities are on view; and to facilitate detection in the event they do offend. The use of closed circuit television cameras (CCTV) is one method of surveillance, but there are others – including, for example, requiring employees to observe customers as part of their regular routines, or using special personnel such as watchmen.

CCTV surveillance has a wide ambit of scrutiny, because the cameras record the activities of anyone present in the location. This involves a substantial number of affected persons, including a majority of non-violators. A person cannot avoid having his or her activities observed and recorded by complying with a specified set of criminal prohibitions.

CCTV is now in extensive use in privately-owned shopping malls and similar facilities. In the UK in recent years, television surveillance is also being employed in public spaces such as downtown streets and shopping plazas. An example is the extensive scheme of television surveillance in the downtown streets and shopping areas of the City of Cambridge.

Types of Surveillance

Situational crime prevention refers, roughly, to strategies designed to reduce opportunities for offending within a given physical environment. A place is to be protected from crime by making it more difficult, or less profitable, to offend there. Television surveillance can perform this function, by making it

[1] I am grateful to the participants of the two Cambridge SCP conferences, in January 1997 and October 1999, for their valuable comments – and particularly to Paul Roberts, Michael Tonry, and Alison Wakefield. Thanks are also due to Beatrice Silva-Tarouca, Amanda Matravers, and Meena Bhamra for their suggestions and assistance with the research.

harder to offend with impunity in the space involved. Given this general function, there are three different types of surveillance which merit consideration:

- *Filmed Camera Sweeps.* A camera automatically sweeps a specified area, and records images of the activities of those present. The film provides a permanent record of those activities.
- *Filmed Surveillance with Focusing Capabilities.* This is a technique used, for example, in many downtown areas and shopping malls. The cameras are directed from a manned control booth, and can be trained upon, follow and record the movements of particular persons. More detailed scrutiny may be possible, through the use of zoom capabilities.
- *Audio Capability.* Surveillance could include overhearing and recording persons' conversations in public space. Because of cost and technical problems, this technique now is seldom in use, but it could become so in future.

In addition to these methods, public television surveillance can be used for various purposes that go beyond situational crime prevention. One such purpose is that of tracking suspects through an extended geographical area. The technology now exists to follow someone's whereabouts from place to place, through linked television cameras that are designed to respond to certain images or patterns. Such techniques, while raising formidable ethical problems of their own, do not involve situational crime prevention, strictly speaking: their aim is to track criminal suspects, rather than to protect a particular physical location against crime.

Regulatory Schemes to Date

In Great Britain, efforts on a national level to regulate CCTV surveillance have been virtually non-existent. No legislation exists on the subject. The House of Lords' Select Committee on Science and Technology (1998) recommended that the use of CCTV be regulated, but did not specify in what manner. The Government since 1998 has had under consideration a proposal to bar the use of CCTV tapes for public entertainment,[2] but no draft has been circulated, and the proposal is not expected to address other uses.

On a local level, regulatory efforts are uneven. Some municipalities operating their own systems of CCTV surveillance, such as Cambridge, have adopted relatively detailed codes of practice;[3] other municipalities have more

---

[2] The then Home Office Minister, Alun Michael, announced on February 2, 1998 that such a proposal was under consideration.

[3] See Cambridge City Council (1998). Some of the salient features of Cambridge's regulatory scheme will be discussed below.

limited regulatory schemes or voluntary codes of practice.[4] The private sector sometimes follows guidelines set up by an industry body, the CCTV Association, but as a rule subjects itself to little restraint.

Constitutional civil liberties law, such as that based on the European Convention on Human Rights, has not yet yielded much in the way of specific limitations regarding the use of public television surveillance. David Feldman (1997) has argued that Article 8 of the Convention, guaranteeing 'respect for [a person's] private . . . life', should be interpreted as calling for regulation of CCTV surveillance. This, however, would mean that the content of such regulation would have to be spelled out.

Topic of this Essay

Developing a regulatory scheme for public television surveillance requires consideration of when, and for what purposes, such surveillance may be deemed legitimate, and when not. Conceptualising CCTV surveillance and its proper uses and limits requires one to address two major issues. The first is that of *surveillance and privacy interests*. To what extent are there legitimate expectations of privacy or anonymity in public spaces, and how much does CCTV impinge on such interests? The second is *the legitimising role of crime prevention*. To what extent does crime prevention legitimise impinging on any interests of privacy or anonymity in public space? This essay addresses each of these issues in turn.

The essay does not rest its arguments on existing law (such as it is), nor on current constitutional civil liberties doctrines. It is believed, rather, that regulating public television surveillance adequately requires a coherent ethical conception concerning CCTV surveillance's proper use and limits. The aim of this article is to sketch such a conception.

To make the analysis easier, the essay focuses on CCTV in public spaces such as streets, publicly-owned shopping areas, parks, and transit facilities. In Britain, as just noted, this kind of surveillance is becoming common. I then address briefly some questions involved in surveillance in 'mass private space' such as shopping malls.

PRIVACY INTERESTS IN PUBLIC SPACE

The Expectation of Anonymity in Public Space

Public television surveillance involves scrutinising ordinary people's comings and goings in open, publicly-accessible space. In such spaces, ordinary people expect to remain anonymous – to be able to go about without being identified,

---

[4] See Thames Valley Police (1998), which has only cursory references to privacy, and no provisions regulating access to CCTV tapes by police personnel.

and without having their activities subjected to special or prolonged scrutiny.

When abroad in this fashion, a person may expect to be exposed to *casual* scrutiny: if I decide to walk in the park, I cannot object to others seeing me and taking perfunctory notice of my activities. Moreover, if I act in certain ways that attract attention (such as screaming or disrobing), I properly may become the object of closer attention.

If I do not thus call attention to myself, however, scrutiny of more than a casual character would seem to offend reasonable expectations of being able to remain anonymous. If I walk in the park and talk with a friend, others might properly take brief notice of us or overhear snatches of our conversation. But various kinds of closer observation would seem inappropriate, such as walking closely behind us to listen into our conversation, trying to join in, or videotaping or audio-taping us. Such scrutiny would seem inappropriate, even if our activities were not of a particularly intimate or sensitive nature. If my friend and I chatter about the weather and the football scores on our walk, we still would assume that we are entitled not to be followed, or to have our conversation listened to.

What Underlying Privacy Interests?

With regard to this expectation of being able to remain anonymous, what rights or liberties are involved? In certain circumstances, various traditional political freedoms may be affected. Surveillance in public spaces may, for example, have a 'chilling effect' on freedom of speech or assembly. The extent to which this is so, however, depends on the character of the behaviour being scrutinised. Filming the participants in a political demonstration may discourage the free expression of political views, but not necessarily filming persons strolling in shopping streets or parks.

Intimacy Concerns. An important privacy-related interest concerns the protection from scrutiny of *intimate* activities.[5] Intimacy is involved, for example, in various activities within the home, such as sexual, familial and personal relations. It is this concern with protection of the intimate sphere that helps account for the limitations imposed on police searches or seizures of the home.[6]

But does the interest in protecting intimacy extend to the public domain? To some extent, it does. Public television surveillance can touch upon people's interests in intimacy, in a variety of ways. Examples are:

- Audio recording of conversations conducted in public. People often discuss intimate, personal matters when walking in a public place out of earshot of others; indeed, this may be a preferable method, when the office or home is unsuitable or inconvenient.

---

[5] See essays on intimacy collected in Schoeman (1984); see also Inness (1992).

[6] See Ashworth, 1998: 57, 136.

- Use of manned cameras with 'zoom' capabilities to undertake detailed scrutiny of certain persons' physical characteristics. Young women are usually the targets, but others may be affected as well (for example, persons with physical disabilities, etc.)

The foregoing, however, involves only certain uses of surveillance. It does not appear that CCTV surveillance in public spaces *generally* intrudes upon privacy interests that are related to intimacy.

Privacy and Control over Presentation of Self. A broader notion of privacy, capable of applying beyond the intimate aspects of life, concerns protecting a person's ability to affect how he presents himself to the world. The conventions of privacy, in this view, are an important way of keeping under a modicum of control whose expectations a person needs to respond to, and whose curiosity he or she needs to satisfy.[7] The reason, for example, that I should not have to account to my employer about my life outside the office is not just that some of these might involve personally sensitive aspects of my life; it is, rather, that I should be allowed to perform my professional functions at the office without having to respond to or be concerned about my employer's preferences and attitudes regarding the remaining aspects of my life. A tolerable existence is one in which not all one's activities, even of a quite routine nature, are everyone else's business.

Privacy, in this conception, may be seen as affording differing kinds of protections to different, concentric circles of activity. The narrowest circle concerns the person's inner and intimate life, where there should be a broad entitlement to resist demands for disclosure of any kind: his intimate life is something he should be able to keep to himself or reveal only to chosen others. Within the next concentric circle of social and working life, the disclosure that may reasonably be demanded should be germane to specified aspects of the business at hand: my employer is entitled to know when I wish to take my holiday and for how long, but not what my planned activities will be when I am away from work. Here, however, determining what information should and should not be protected from disclosure is a difficult issue to resolve, both theoretically and practically, because this second circle concerns relationships with chosen working and social associates who have certain legitimate matters to transact with the person involved.

It should be evident that there also is a third concentric circle which should have its own protections against disclosure – namely, that relating to activities in public. It is in public that a person has the least control over whom he will encounter, and such other persons may have different (and possibly uncongenial) commitments, values and attitudes. It thus becomes critically important for the person to be able to limit the extent to which he may be called upon to respond to the expectations, or even to satisfy the curiosity, of such unchosen

[7] This general conception of privacy is drawn from Thomas Nagel (1998); Alan Ryan (1983); David Feldman (1994); and Ferdinand Schoeman (1992).

others. The entitlement of non-disclosure is more straightforward in this third circle, because it concerns *strangers* – those with whom the person has not undertaken dealings of any kind.

Privacy and Anonymity in Public Space

The notion of this third circle of privacy, applicable to public spaces and activities, provides support for the everyday conventions concerning anonymity in public places.[8] Thus:

- The convention that there should be only *casual* and *momentary* scrutiny means the person can go about his or her business with little reference to the expectations of other observers. If an eccentric academic colleague likes to compose his lectures by walking in the park and reciting them under his breath, others might briefly notice the odd person who talks to himself. But he need not be particularly concerned about the attitudes of others who might find such behaviour silly or irritating. The same convention, on the other hand, allows others with such different attitudes to go about their own business. Those passers-by who dislike eccentric behaviour may simply give the person a brief (perhaps disapproving) glance, look away, and go on.
- The observability of the casual observer is also important. If one walks in a downtown street or public park, one can see whether others are present who might observe or overhear; and thus temporarily alter one's behaviour if one wishes. If our academic is a bit more conventional, he may recite his lecture to himself only when he is out of close sight and hearing of others. He need not worry about the hidden observer watching and, perhaps, laughing at his expense.
- Closer scrutiny by others may occur, however, when the person calls attention to himself by manifestly aberrant behaviour (say, by shouting out his lecture). Others need not have to pretend disinterest, when the behaviour strongly would impinge on an ordinary person's attention.

None of this has anything to do with the intimate or otherwise sensitive character of the activities involved. The anonymity conventions of public space should leave free from intensive scrutiny even the most innocuous forms of activity. Our mumbling academic should be protected from such scrutiny, even if he is speaking not of his love life but of this month's trade statistics.

Why CCTV Surveillance Intrudes on Anonymity Interests

CCTV surveillance, I submit, infringes these anonymity conventions, and thus intrudes on privacy in the sense just referred to. It does so in the following respects. Firstly, the scrutiny is not casual or momentary, but focuses more

---

[8] For an alternative rationale for such anonymity conventions, based on notions of autonomy, see Roberts (2000).

closely on the activities in public of particular individuals. This is readily apparent for CCTV surveillance of the more concentrated kinds – such as that involving zooming-in on particular individuals. But it is true also for the commonplace CCTV surveillance that sweeps and records activity in a given area automatically – since the tapes may then be reviewed to examine more closely the activities of a particular person. It is not just apparent criminal behaviour that may thus be subject to scrutiny, but *any* behaviour that is recorded and that happens to interest those in possession of the tapes. The behaviour involved does not need to be of the kind that ordinarily would call attention to itself.

Second, the observer may be unobservable. Often, the presence of CCTV is unannounced, and the cameras are concealed. But even if the cameras are unconcealed, the fact that they are mechanical, positioned above people's line of vision, and blend in with other features of the physical environment makes them easily overlooked. A camera is likely to be ignored in a way that a police officer present is not. And even if the presence of the cameras is discernible, the identity of those reviewing the film is not. It is like conducting one's activities in a space with a one-way mirror: while one may know that someone is watching behind the mirror, one does not necessarily know who they are or what they are looking for.

Having such targeted, and unobservable, surveillance is troublesome, even if the person is engaged in perfectly innocuous activities. Our mumbling academic may be deeply humiliated if a tape of his walk is aired for public entertainment, or shown to neighbours or potential employers. And the intrusion on privacy persists, even if the viewers are limited to law enforcement personnel. Perhaps, in the latter instance, that intrusion can be justified by overriding interests in law enforcement (see discussion next). But a group of uninvited strangers still are poring over activities which the person could reasonably have expected to be free from scrutiny.

CRIME PREVENTION'S LEGITIMISING ROLE

Let us suppose, as has just been argued, that public television surveillance does infringe anonymity expectations that have their basis in important privacy interests. The question remains whether surveillance can nevertheless be supported on crime prevention grounds.

What Crime-Preventive Effects?

CCTV is said to be a useful instrument of crime prevention. It serves, assertedly, to deter potential offenders from committing crimes, and to aid in detecting crimes already committed. There is evidence that the use of CCTV, in certain settings and for certain kinds of crime, is accompanied by decreases in crime rates, or increases in clear-up rates. The extent of those associations, however, is quite variable; the causal links involved far from clear; and the extent to which crime has been 'displaced' to other areas also difficult to assess (for a review of the evidence, see Skinns, 1999; Phillips, 1999).

For present purposes, however, such issues of effectiveness need not be resolved. Our question concerns the ethics of CCTV surveillance *if it were shown to be effective.* Thus for the sake of the argument I shall be assuming that CCTV can have significant crime-preventive effects; and then ask whether and to what extent such effects would justify its use, notwithstanding the intrusions on privacy and anonymity involved.

To What Extent Do 'Rights' Constrain Crime-Prevention Aims?

In order to address the possible legitimising role of crime prevention, it may be useful to consider briefly the logic of this role generally. Why should crime prevention ever be reason for restricting various rights or liberties?

Here, we should begin with the Harm Principle. That principle holds that state-imposed restrictions on freedom of action may be warranted *prima facie*, for the purpose of preventing harm to other persons. An actor's options of acting as he chooses may be restricted in order to prevent him from hurting other persons – because such injurious conduct would restrict or threaten to restrict the choices and interests of those injured (see Feinberg, 1984).

This harm-based justification for state intervention, however, may be superceded or narrowed in scope when that intervention would intrude on certain rights – that is, certain interests warranting a special degree of protection.[9] The state ordinarily should not, for example, be entitled to restrict free speech even where that might eventually involve some risks of harm. The reason is that a person's interest in being able to express his or her views is deemed to have a sufficiently high degree of importance to restrain the pursuit of ordinary societal objectives, including crime-preventive ones (see, for example, Schauer, 1982: 141-45).

The standard account of this kind of reasoning is Ronald Dworkin's 'rights as trumps' thesis: that the function of rights is to override or 'trump' ordinary societal objectives (Dworkin, 1977: Ch. 7). To say that I have a right to do X implies that I should remain entitled to do X even if preventing me from doing it would provide societal benefits or prevent possible injury. Speaking of 'trumps', however, may be somewhat confusing because it suggests an absolute and either-or character: that when a right is involved, it overrides virtually any societal objective;[10] and that when it is not, societal concerns may be pursued with no ulterior constraints.

---

[9] For discussion of a right as a specially protected interest, see Dworkin, 1977, Ch. 7.

[10] Dworkin does concede, however, that certain extraordinarily urgent social purposes, of an 'order of magnitude' in importance beyond ordinary social costs and benefits, may be the basis for intruding upon (at least some) rights; see Dworkin, 1977: ch 7.

The role of 'rights' in limiting crime-preventive interventions is actually more complex, and should depend on the nature of the protected interests involved. Certain interests, such as that in not being tortured, are of such importance that they should *never* be infringed for crime prevention aims: suspects should not be mistreated in order to obtain confessions, no matter how heinous the crime or urgent the need to forestall future offending (see Murphy, 1980). Other specially protected interests, however, do not appear to have quite so high a degree of importance – so that certain crime-preventive justifications for intruding may be permissible, at least to a limited extent. An example concerns freedom of speech. Generally, criminal legislation should not restrict free speech, but an exception may be made in situations of 'clear and present danger', where the speech involves immediate risks of seriously harmful consequences (see Schauer, 1982: 141–45). The idea here is that speech, while it should be deemed a specially protected interest, has a somewhat lower ranking of importance than (say) the interest in not being tortured; so that intrusions are permitted for the most immediate and urgent crime-preventative purposes.

With respect to interests in privacy in public spaces, therefore, there are two kinds of questions that need to be asked, in deciding the appropriate scope of crime-preventative interventions. First, *what degree of priority should be given to such privacy interests?* That degree of priority might vary, depending upon which underlying rationale for privacy is involved: concerns about intimacy, for example, might be given a somewhat higher priority than concerns about anonymity. Second, *how urgent are the crime prevention objectives involved?* Preventing immediate criminal harms, for example, might be treated as having a higher degree of urgency than identifying persons who merely *might* offend in future.

The Model of Searches or Private Premises – What Relevance?

It may be helpful, at this juncture, to consider a model that exists already – that governing searches of private premises. According to this model, a person's home may be entered, upon a showing of reasonable grounds for suspicion that he or she has been criminally involved.[11] This doctrine thus gives crime prevention significant scope: where grounds for suspicion exist, the privacy of the person's home may be breached to obtain additional evidence of crime. However, the doctrine limits the potential extent of such privacy invasions, by barring them where proper grounds for suspicion have not yet been established. The police may not enter someone's home or tap his or her telephone on a hunch, or conduct a sweep search of dwellings in a neighbourhood in the hope of uncovering evidence of possible crimes. This restriction is designed to protect the privacy of apparently uninvolved third parties.

[11] Ashworth, 1998: 122–23.

This model cannot, however, directly be extended to cover CCTV surveillance. Searches of private premises can be targeted to a particular suspect; it is possible to assemble other evidence to support reasonable grounds for suspicion, before invading the privacy of the suspect's home. Public television surveillance, however, is not limited to particular targets: it sweeps whole areas, and draws within its ambit all persons present. If I enter a surveyed area, my behaviour will be recorded even if I have done nothing to attract suspicion; and if the police review the tapes in order to uncover evidence of crimes, they will observe my behaviour, and not just the suspicious behaviour of suspected perpetrators. A major forensic use of CCTV, moreover, is precisely to help identify suspects, not just that of developing further incriminating evidence against already-identified suspects.

Notwithstanding its lack of direct applicability, the search model may have some broader relevance in principle. What it suggests is that privacy interests should limit the *manner* in which criminal investigations are pursued, but not necessarily rule out such investigations entirely. In that sense, privacy is treated as a right or specially protected interest that has an intermediate protective role. Its 'trumping' effect is not so strong as the right against torture (which should bar torture-based investigations entirely) or the right of free-speech (which should permit prosecutions only when immediate and serious risk of criminal harm is involved). However, privacy should retain a significant protective effect in limiting how surveillance is carried out. The question then becomes, how can such intermediate-level protection be provided?

WHAT LIMITATIONS ON CCTV SURVEILLANCE?

With the foregoing general framework in mind concerning interests in anonymity in public spaces and the possible legitimising role of crime-prevention, it is time to consider how this analysis might help resolve questions of regulating CCTV surveillance. What kinds of limitations on CCTV surveillance might be imposed, in order to protect anonymity? I can offer no confident answers to this question but can, on the basis of the preceding discussion, suggest a mode of analysis. This analysis will address various aspects of privacy and anonymity affected by CCTV, and propose possible ways of dealing with them.

The Unobservable Observer Problem: A Bar on Covert Surveillance

One way in which CCTV surveillance can infringe the entitlement to privacy and anonymity in public space is through covert observation. The conventions on anonymity in public space, as noted earlier (p. 64), call not only for no more than casual but also for *observable* observation. When going about in a public street or park, one should at least be able to see who is watching. This enables the person, to the extent that he is sensitive to the reactions of others, to adjust his behaviour when others are present. Our mumbling academic can, if he wishes not to appear foolish, stop reciting his lecture under his breath when passers-by approach. Hidden observation is problematic for two reasons: first, it takes the person unawares: he may think that he is free from scrutiny when he is not. Second, it can exercise a chilling effect: once people become aware of a practice of covert surveillance, they may feel under constraint when they go about in public. To say potential offenders ought to feel constrained about committing crimes in public is no answer to these objections, for the surveillance extends beyond criminal suspects to anyone present under the cameras' gaze.

To deal in part with this problem, CCTV coverage should not be covert. Surveillance cameras should be visible, and areas under observation should be required to have signs indicating that CCTV is in use. The Code of Practice for Cambridge's CCTV scheme already contains such a requirement.[12] The person thus will at least be able to know when he is being watched.

Protection against Intimacy Intrusions: Audio Surveillance, etc.

Privacy interests that are related to intimacy, I have suggested (pp. 62–63), are not generally affected by CCTV surveillance, but they are so in certain contexts – such as audio surveillance and certain kinds of detailed physical scrutiny of those viewed. On the analysis of privacy sketched earlier (pp.63–64), intimacy concerns the 'first circle' of privacy interests, and relates to matters of particular sensitivity that should have broad protections against non-consensual disclosure. If intimacy is given this degree of protection, then there should be special safeguards, including a prohibition of surveillance with audio capabilities (which the Cambridge scheme already has adopted[13]). There should also be safeguards against misuse of surveillance capable of detailed physical scrutiny of persons, such as that potentially involved in staffed surveillance cameras with zoom capabilities.

Use of CCTV Tapes for Law Enforcement – What Limitations?

In terms of impact on anonymity in public spaces, what counts most is not the operation of the cameras but the uses that are made of the resulting tapes. It is through re-running and reviewing the tapes that a particular person's activities can be focused upon, and subjected to prolonged and repeated scrutiny. To

[12] Cambridge City Council (1998). The Code of Practice, in para. 1.3, provides: '[A]ll cameras are sited so that they are clearly visible . . . Publicity will be given to the system by clear signing within the area . . . . This will ensure . . . that the public are clearly aware when they are in the monitored area.'

[13] Cambridge City Council, 1998. The Code of Practice, para. 1.3, provides that 'the System will not record sound in public places.'

what extent, then, should CCTV tapes be accessible for law enforcement purposes? There are three options to consider, in order of increasing permissiveness. (1) The tapes could be reviewable only to assist in the detection or prosecution of a suspected offence at a location and time for which a complaint has been received. (2) The tapes could be used also to identify possible violations in certain restricted settings in which risks of offending are higher than in immediately surrounding areas, and the potential for scrutiny of uninvolved third parties is reduced. (3) The tapes could be used for law enforcement purposes generally, without the foregoing limitations. I shall argue in favour of the first and possibly the second option, and against the third.

(i) A problem with CCTV surveillance at present is that often it may be used, and its recordings reviewed by law enforcement personnel, anywhere in public space, without the need to point to ulterior grounds for suspicion. Conventional 'probable cause' requirements will not work, for reasons explained earlier (p. 68). But it may be desirable to impose somewhat analogous restrictions, designed to limit the ambit of scrutiny tapes to places and times where there already exists reason for suspecting that a crime may have been committed.

This could be accomplished by permitting CCTV cameras to operate anywhere in public space, but restricting access to and review of the resulting tapes by law enforcement personnel to locations and times for which a complaint concerning commission of a crime has been received. If a robbery or a break-in has been reported at time x and place y, the tapes for that location and approximate time could be reviewed to help determine whether the crime occurred and who the perpetrators may be. The City of Cambridge's Code of Practice has adopted such a limitation. The Code provides that camera recordings are not to be used to monitor the progress of persons through public space, and monitoring may occur only where there is reasonable cause to believe that an offence has been committed. The police thus are required to specify the time and location of a particular incident and ask the municipal authorities for permission to view the appropriate recording.[14]

This limitation would preclude 'fishing expeditions' – browsing through tapes for an extended time and broad area, in the expectation of spotting someone committing a crime. Such a practice would have lower law enforcement priority, in any event. Ruling it out would also significantly reduce the extent of intrusions into anonymity interests in public space. A person could wander at will in public streets and parks, without fear of his activities being scrutinised; this could occur only if he happens to be present at a time and place at which a crime has been reported. Where that occurs, his activities

[14] See Cambridge City Council (1998). Code of Practice, para. 1.2: 'Cameras will not be used to monitor the progress of individuals in the ordinary course of lawful business. . .'; 'Individuals will only be monitored if there is reasonable cause to suspect that an offence has been committed' (para. 1.2).

would be subject to scrutiny even if he were only an innocent bystander; but the spatial and temporal limitations much restrict the ambit of the scrutiny.

(ii) What of the second option, of permitting also the monitoring of high risk locations? It would seem reasonable to allow continuous monitoring of places such as cashpoints, in view of the apparent greater risks of crimes being committed in such places. Risk, however, is not the only relevant factor here; two other factors seem important. The first is the restricted geographical location involved: if narrowly circumscribed places such as cashpoints are subjected to more extensive scrutiny, ordinary persons retain a scope for moving anonymously elsewhere. The second factor relates to something referred to by Antony Duff and Sandra Marshall (2000) in their article in this volume: the degree to which the persons burdened by the intervention are also its beneficiary. Ordinarily, the persons who are present and being observed at cashpoints are those drawing money, not mere bystanders; and those persons are specially at risk of being robbed of the money they withdraw. This is not a case of monitoring the public activities of one group in order to protect another group from victimisation. Our friend the mumbling academic thus would continue to be free to traverse public spaces without fear of close scrutiny. The police, in monitoring tapes, will see his image only if he goes to a cashpoint to withdraw money, when he himself has special interest in being protected. Continuous monitoring of tapes should thus be authorised, only where both of the factors just mentioned are present.

(iii) Restricting monitoring in the manner just suggested – to times/places for which suspected criminal activity has been reported, and possibly to specified high risk locations – would have two kind of advantages. The first is that the law enforcement grounds for intruding upon anonymity would be stronger. It is, for example, a more urgent matter for the police to be able to review CCTV tapes at places where they have grounds for suspicion that a crime has been committed, than to be allowed to trawl through tapes of wider areas in order to uncover new crimes. The second is that the impact on anonymity interests is reduced. If tapes may be reviewed only in the restricted situations just discussed, there is considerable remaining scope for anonymity in public. If, however, the police are entitled to review tapes without restrictions, then we need fear always being watched whenever we enter public space.

A Ban on Collateral Non-Crime-Preventive Uses

Because CCTV surveillance of public spaces is now so little regulated in many local jurisdictions, data ostensibly obtained for crime prevention may be used for ulterior purposes. This includes making CCTV tapes available to parties in private disputes – for example, to private firms seeking evidence of employee absenteeism, or to detective agencies for use in matrimonial proceedings. It also includes dispositions for entertainment use. It is not only possible criminal behaviour that could thus be the object of scrutiny, but also a variety of non-criminal conduct involved in potential civil disputes (e.g. being seen with a person of the opposite sex not one's spouse); and even, in the case of entertainment use, entirely legitimate conduct.

It is a truism that if the purported justification for a potential intrusion into privacy is crime prevention, then the use at issue should be crime preventive and not one serving ulterior aims. This point is clearest with regard to tapes' disposition for entertainment purposes. If CCTV stands in need of justification in virtue of its intrusion into privacy/anonymity interests, and if the claimed basis of the intrusion is the prevention of crime, that creates no warrant whatever for selling tapes for use in commercial TV programmes.

Surveillance tapes therefore should be accessible only for the *criminal justice* uses just discussed, not ulterior purposes. Uses that should be ruled out include, most obviously, making the tapes available for public entertainment. Excluded also should be the turning over of tapes to parties in private disputes: for example, in eviction proceedings, proceedings to discharge truant employees, or matrimonial proceedings. Not only are such uses unsupported by a purported crime prevention justification; but they seem less warranted in their own right. Where the cause-of-action in private disputes is not also a criminal offence (as it is not in most contract, employment discharge, tenant eviction, and matrimonial disputes), the public interest involved appears to be less urgent, thus suggesting a weaker case for overriding citizens' interests in anonymity in public space. Cambridge's Code of Practice has such limitations on dispositions to private parties: CCTV materials may be released only 'in connection with law enforcement processes'.[15]

A bar on such collateral, non-law-enforcement uses of the tapes is warranted for a reason that goes beyond the lower priority that such uses have as grounds for overriding privacy and anonymity concerns. It is also warranted because, by extending permissible audience for the tapes, privacy interests themselves become more seriously compromised. Those interests, according to the previous discussion (pp. 63–64), relate to keeping under a modicum of control whose curiosity we need to satisfy and whose expectations we need to respond to. If only law enforcement personnel are entitled to inspect the tapes, and only for evidence of criminal activity, then one has less reason for concern about their possible expectations concerning other kinds of conduct. If, however, the tapes can be made available to others – to employers, colleagues, possible litigants, and perhaps the public at large, then not only can larger numbers of persons view one's conduct, but their possible expectations and interests may have a much wider scope. In going about in public, one then needs not only to avoid conduct that gives rise to legitimate suspicion of criminal activity, but also to think twice about conduct that an employer might disapprove of, a disaffected spouse might wish to utilise in a matrimonial proceeding, or a bored TV viewer might find funny or ridiculous.

---

[15] Cambridge City Council (1998), Code of Practice, para. 6.1 and 6.2.

Limiting disposition of CCTV materials to crime-prevention uses also raises the question of what kind of crime prevention should be involved. According to standard criminalisation doctrine, conduct should be criminalised if it either involves harm (or risk of harm) to others, or certain forms of grave offence (see Feinberg, 1984; Feinberg, 1985; von Hirsch, 2000b). Recently, however, a variety of exclusion strategies are developing, designed to keep out from public places persons who are deemed socially undesirable, or are thought to represent risks of offending in future.[16] These strategies may involve exclusion orders backed by criminal sanctions. In another essay in this volume, Clifford Shearing and I (von Hirsch and Shearing, 2000) describe some of these strategies, suggest why they may involve inappropriate restriction of people's freedom of movement in public space, and recommend limitations on their use. If such limitations are not adopted, however, then the question arises whether CCTV tapes should be admissible in criminal prosecutions based on such exclusion orders. I would suggest not, because the harm to be prevented is more contingent: we are speaking not of actual commission of acts doing or risking harm but rather, of keeping persons out of public places who merely *might* do harm in future. The contingent character of the harm weakens the case for compromising privacy and anonymity concerns.

CCTV SURVEILLANCE IN MASS PRIVATE SPACE

The present essay addresses the use of CCTV surveillance in *public* space. CCTV surveillance, however, also is in extensive use in mass private space. There, as Alison Wakefield (2000) indicates in her essay in this volume, the surveillance has broad uses, including uncovering evidence of actual crimes such as shoplifting; identifying undesired (criminal or non-criminal) conduct, whose perpetrators can then be expelled; or spotting 'blacklisted' individuals whose previous conduct provides supposed grounds for exclusion.

Mass public private space constitutes facilities that are owned by private organisations, but offer themselves as being generally available for public use

---

[16] Under the Anti-Social Behaviour Order provisions of the Crime and Disorder Act 1998, a local or police can obtain a court order against persons who engage in 'anti-social conduct' that causes or is likely to cause 'harassment, alarm or distress' in one or more other persons. A court order may issue against such a person, directing him to cease from engaging in the conduct involved, or from *any other* conduct described in the order – so that the order may include an exclusion directive. The order is to run at least two years, and violation of it may attract criminal penalties of up to five years' imprisonment. The legislation thus permits someone to be excluded from specified public or semi-public space, on the basis of non-criminal conduct that is deemed 'anti-social'. Once imposed, however, the exclusion need no longer be conduct-dependent: the person may be barred from re-entering the space, even were he to desist from the kind of conduct that initially triggered the order. These provisions have recently been used to ban two disruptive boys for a period of two years from the centre of a small city, Weston-super-Mare (*Times*, 17.ii.00). For a critique of this legislation, see Ashworth, Gardner et al. (1998); White (1999).

without restriction of specific purpose. Often, the facilities involved resemble in their physical layout and uses traditional public spaces: a large downtown shopping mall may operate in many respects like a traditional shopping street.

English law now treats mass private space much like purely private property; American law has important qualifications of that approach, relating for example to racial discrimination: whereas a purely private organisation (such as a small social club) may discriminate, a privately owned facility that is generally open and available to the public may not do so (Gray and Gray, 1999). The situations we are discussing are somewhat harder to deal with: whereas racial classifications are manifestly suspect, the ethical considerations involved in public television surveillance are of a more complex character (as we have seen), and a purported law enforcement justification is involved. Nevertheless, the public character of the space and its uses would appear to warrant regulation comparable to that appropriate for publicly-owned space with similar functions. Underlying this view is the notion of property as constituted by a bundle of rights held by the property-owner: some of these may be restricted while preserving others (Gray, 1991). The owner of mass public space thus should be entitled to operate and seek to make a profit on it much like other private investment. But if the facility's use is comparable to that of public space, there should be restrictions on practices that infringe the privacy of its users comparable to those that should be applicable to public spaces.

Extending the foregoing analysis concerning CCTV to mass private space would necessitate criteria for determining when privately-owned property should qualify as mass public space. The problem here is that the uses involved represent a spectrum – at one end of which is a small atrium operated by a few shops or restaurants for the enjoyment of their customers; and at the other are general-use mall facilities which may even involve the incorporation of formerly public downtown areas. It would need to be decided where on this spectrum use becomes sufficiently public so that the principles applicable to the public forum should apply. But in any event, large, multi-purpose shopping malls, to which members of the public are invited without regard to performing any particular activity, should qualify as having a 'public' use (see von Hirsch and Shearing, 2000).

In public areas, one can establish a principle that CCTV tapes should be available only for specified law enforcement purposes such as detection and providing court evidence; and that it should not be supplied to ulterior private uses (see pp. 71–72). A shopping mall, however, is itself a corporate enterprise and its security personnel are the enterprise's employees. It thus would be necessary to decide to what extent a mall may use CCTV tapes – supposedly obtained in the interests of crime prevention – in order to admonish, discipline or fire lazy or inefficient employees. The problem is, of course, that it is not only those employees whose activities are being filmed, but other visitors to the site who have no employment link to the corporation.

Questions of enforcing restrictions on surveillance will need to be addressed. Difficult as the problems of enforcing restrictions on public law-enforcement authorities are, securing compliance from private firms operating malls and similar facilities is a still more formidable task. It would be necessary to develop mechanisms for monitoring compliance. (Would it be helpful, for example, to establish publicly-appointed monitoring groups or a local or regional *ombudsman* for the purpose?) It also would be necessary to specify what steps should be taken against those who infringe the applicable restrictions. Addressing questions such as these would call for further reflection and analysis.

Until appropriate limitations on surveillance in such mass private spaces are adopted, there will need to be limits on information-sharing between public authorities and the security operations of private malls. As Wakefield (2000) points out, it now has become customary for large, privately-owned malls to exchange data with public authorities operating CCTV schemes. Security operations in malls do have significant crime prevention functions. But such private organisations today may use surveillance information for all sorts of other purposes – including the disciplining of erring employees, and the exclusion from the mall of persons who are deemed 'undesirable' for a variety of reasons. Were free interchange allowed, then CCTV tapes from a downtown street site, showing a person engaged in eccentric or erratic behaviour, could be used by the mall to exclude the person from its space. The appropriate remedy would be to bar facilities from obtaining CCTV tapes from public facilities, unless the mall is willing to subscribe to specified restrictions on the disposition of such materials.

REFERENCES

Ashworth, A. (1998) *The Criminal Process,* (2nd ed.), Oxford: Oxford University Press.
—— , Gardner, J., Morgan, R., Smith, A.T.H., von Hirsch, A. and Wasik, M. (1998) 'Neighbouring on the oppressive: The Government's "Anti-social behaviour order" proposals,' *Criminal Justice* 16(1): 7-14.
Cambridge City Council (1998) *Guaranteeing Public Confidence: A Code of Practice for the Cambridge CCTV Scheme,* Cambridge: Cambridge City Council, December 1998.
Clarke, R.V. (1995) 'Situational Crime Prevention', in M. Tonry and D. Farrington, (eds.), *Building a Safer Society. Strategic Approaches to Crime Prevention. Crime and Justice: A Review of Research* 19: 91–150, Chicago: University of Chicago Press.
Duff, R.A. and Marshall, S. (2000) 'Benefits, burdens and responsibilities: some ethical dimensions of situational crime prevention', this volume.
Dworkin, R. (1977) *Taking Rights Seriously,* Cambridge, Mass.: Harvard University Press.
—— (1996) *Freedom's Law,* Oxford: Oxford University Press.

Feldman, D. (1994) 'Secrecy, dignity, or autonomy? – views of privacy as a civil liberty' in M. Freeman (ed.), *Current Legal Problems*, 47:41–71, Oxford: Oxford University Press.

—— (1997) 'Privacy-related rights and their social value', in P. Birks (ed.), *Privacy and Loyalty*, Oxford: Oxford University Press.

Gray, K. (1991) 'Property in thin air', *Cambridge Law Journal* 50: 252–307.

—— and Gray, S.F. (1999) 'Civil rights, civil wrongs, and quasi-public space', *European Human Rights Law Review* [1999]: 1-59.

House of Lords (1998) Select Committee on Science and Technology, *Digital Images as Evidence*, HL Paper 64, London: The Stationery Office.

Inness, J. (1992) *Privacy, Intimacy and Isolation*, Oxford: Oxford University Press.

Murphy, J. (1980) 'Cruel and Unusual Punishments', in J. Murphy, (1980) *Retribution, Justice, Therapy*, 223–249, Dordrecht: D. Riedel.

Nagel, T. (1998) 'Concealment and exposure,' *Philosophy and Public Affairs* 27: 3–30.

Phillips, C. (1999) 'A review of CCTV evaluations: crime reduction effects and attitudes toward its use' in K. Painter and N. Tilley (eds.), *Surveillance: Lighting, CCTV and Crime Prevention*, Monsey, N.Y.: Criminal Justice Press.

Roberts, P. (2000) 'Privacy, autonomy and criminal justice rights' in P. Alldridge and L. Brants (eds.), *Personal Autonomy: The Private Sphere and Criminal Law*, Oxford: Hart Publishing.

Ryan, A. (1983) 'Private selves and public parts', in S.I. Benn and G.F. Gaus (eds.), *Public and Private in Social Life*, New York: St. Martin's Press.

Schauer, F. (1982) *Free Speech: A Philosophical Inquiry*, Cambridge: Cambridge University Press.

Schoeman, F. (ed.) (1984) *Philosophical Dimensions of Privacy: An Anthology*, Cambridge: Cambridge University Press.

—— (1992) *Privacy and Social Freedom*, Cambridge: Cambridge University Press.

Skinns, D. (1998) 'Crime reduction, diffusion and displacement: evaluating the effectiveness of CCTV', in C. Norris, J. Moran and G. Armstrong (eds.), *Surveillance, Closed Circuit Television and Social Control*, Aldershot: Ashgate Publishing Ltd.

Thames Valley Police (1998) *Closed Circuit Television in the Thames Valley: Model Codes of Practice*.

von Hirsch, A. (2000) 'The offence principle in criminal law: affront to sensibility or wrongdoing?' *King's College Law Journal* 11: 78–89.

—— and Shearing, C. (2000) 'Exclusion from public space', this volume.

Wakefield, A. (2000) 'Situational crime prevention in mass private property', this volume.

5

Exclusion from Public Space

Andrew von Hirsch and Clifford Shearing[1]

EXCLUSION AS A SITUATIONAL
CRIME-PREVENTION STRATEGY

Exclusion Strategies

Ronald Clarke (1995) characterises 'access control' as an important technique of situational crime prevention (SCP), aimed at reducing criminal opportunities. This refers to 'measures intended to exclude potential offenders from places such as offices, factories, and apartment buildings.' (*ibid*.: 110). One type of access control consists simply of making access less easy. Clarke cites a road-closure scheme for a former red-light district in North London, aimed at discouraging potential customers from soliciting sexual favours of local women from their cars. The scheme did not prohibit anyone from entering the district, but merely made access less simple by putting up impediments to automobile travel. Another type of access control, however, involves true exclusion: the person is barred entirely from entering the area, and faces sanctions of some kind if he enters. It is this latter kind of strategy which most plainly raises questions of freedom of movement, and it is this strategy which our essay addresses.

Exclusion is now being used extensively in privately-owned spaces that have public functions, such as shopping malls. In her chapter in this volume, Alison Wakefield (2000) describes the use of exclusion in three such facilities. Recent legislation permits exclusion strategies to be extended further, to publicly owned spaces. Notable in this regard is the Anti-Social Behaviour Order (ASBO) legislation, passed as part of the Crime and Disorder Act 1998 (discussed below).

Exclusion may be invoked on a variety of grounds. One is exclusion at will: certain persons are simply denied entry, for no stated reason. English law now permits the private owner of a shopping mall to keep undesired entrants out,

[1] The authors are indebted to the participants of the two Cambridge SCP conferences, of January 1997 and October 1999, for their comments on earlier versions of this paper. Special thanks are also due to Kevin Gray, John Gardner, Michael Tonry, Antony Duff, Alison Wakefield, ATH Smith, and Ivan Hare for their suggestions; and to Amanda Matravers and Meena Bhamra for their assistance with the research.

without reasons having to be provided. Another is exclusion of 'nuisances' who commit or are deemed likely to commit petty annoyances that are not criminal in character, such as begging. Robert Ellickson (1996) recommends the zoning of such persons out of large areas of urban space. While we touch on these practices to provide perspective for our discussion, we shall concentrate on access control as a *crime prevention* strategy. This includes (1) 'profiling' – the exclusion of persons who are believed to represent a risk of future criminality; and (2) exclusion of persons who have been found to have committed crimes, and who therefore are deemed to be 'bad risks'.

Harmful, disruptive, or grossly offensive behaviour in public spaces has long been proscribed by the criminal law. The criminal law, however, operates through the volition of its intended audience: the potential offender is warned against violations, and needs to be motivated to comply. To be so motivated, the potential offender must be aware of the penalty, must fear it sufficiently to desist, or else feel morally obligated to observe the prohibition (see more fully, von Hirsch, Bottoms, et al., 1999: 4-9). If a violation occurs, that must be proved beyond reasonable doubt. The resulting sanction must bear a degree of proportionality to the seriousness of the crime – so that minor offending ordinarily may not draw substantial penalties.[2] After the penalty is imposed and is served, the person is permitted to return to the space involved.

Exclusion seems a simpler and more effective strategy. It *forecloses* harmful or disruptive behaviour: the person is just kept out. There will be no need to induce the person to behave properly while present, since he no longer can be there. Exclusion also is easier to administer. True, the person still needs to be induced to comply with the exclusion directive. But this is no longer a matter of having to observe and prove actual criminal misbehaviour. If the barred individual is merely found present, that suffices to have him penalised.

Exclusion seems capable of dealing more easily with the recidivism problem. The offender no longer just serves a proportionate penalty (usually brief, in cases of public order offences); he now may be excluded for a long period, or even permanently. The ASBO legislation, for example, contemplates that anti-social behaviour orders (which may involve exclusion) would operate for a minimum of two years.[3]

---

[2] The Criminal Justice Act 1991, in §§2 and 6, imposes such a requirement of proportionality. For the uncertain implementation of these requirements by English courts, however, see Ashworth and von Hirsch (1997).

[3] Under the Anti-Social Behaviour Order provisions of the Crime and Disorder Act 1998, a local or police authority can obtain a court order against persons who engage in "anti-social conduct" that causes or is likely to cause "harassment, alarm or distress" in one or more other persons. A court order may issue against such a person, directing him to cease from engaging in the conduct involved, or from *any other* conduct described in the order – so that the order may include an exclusion directive. The order is to run at least two years, and violation of it may attract criminal penalties of up to five years' imprisonment. The legislation thus permits someone to be excluded from specified public or semi-public space, on the basis of non-criminal conduct that is deemed "antisocial". Once imposed, however, the exclusion need no longer be conduct-

In this essay, we examine the ethical issues that arise with respect to such exclusion strategies. Attractive as exclusion might seem as a device for preventing crime, we shall suggest that its use in areas having public use entails serious losses of personal liberty. We concentrate our attention on the normative issues. Devising remedial steps to protect public access, especially for privately-owned spaces having public uses, raises also complex issues of property law and issues of practical implementation. We leave these latter issues for further exploration.

Changing Understandings of Public and Private Space

Before proceeding with our analysis, it may be worth commenting briefly on some changes that appear to be taking place in prevailing understandings of public and private spaces, and of their functions. Public space has traditionally been conceived of as a space of freedom, in which people are entitled to move about at will. So long as their behaviour does not violate specified conduct regulations (principally sent forth in the criminal law), they are at liberty to proceed as they please. These spaces are 'public' in the sense that they are supposed to be available to any member of the public; such persons, it is assumed, need not be required to account for their presence in such spaces to anyone. Private spaces offer another kind of personal freedom to their owners: a wide ambit of choice not only regarding their own behaviour, but also regarding who may and may not enter and share the space. Owners thus are entitled to exclude others from these spaces and have government back this up through coercive means. All citizens thus are seen as having a right to share in public space; and those who have the means to obtain ownership of private spaces may also regulate the use of their own spaces. Within liberal democratic societies, this distinction between public and private space has been thought to be essential to liberty. Any development that undermines this distinction, and the freedoms it provides for, thus appears to threaten liberty. But these are precisely the kinds of developments that are happening today, and it is this threat and the appropriate response to it that is our focus.

It is worth noting that the organisation of space into the public and private spheres that we take for granted today is a comparatively recent invention. Public space arose as the sovereignty of monarchs; as kingdoms developed, so did the concept of the King's Peace. While this peace initially applied primarily to the royal domains (for example, royal estates and forests) it gradually came to include the King's highways and other spaces. Gradually the King's Peace swallowed up the peaces of more local sovereignties. The result was the emergence of what we now recognise as a public physical

dependent: the person may be barred from re-entering the space, even were he to desist from the kind of conduct that initially triggered the order. These provisions have recently been used to ban two disruptive adolescent boys for a period of years from the centre of a small city (*Times*, 17.ii.00). For a critique of this legislation, see Ashworth, Gardner et al. (1998); White (1999).

domain, along with a public peace guaranteed by governments. This public domain came to constitute the network of locations (roads, parks, public squares, and the like) that we now recognise as public spaces. As this happened the common areas that existed within 'private domains' (for example feudal manors and corporate spaces such as those of the Dutch and British East India Companies and the Hudson's Bay Company) became public space, and new private spaces emerged in contrast to them. As space became 'public' and 'private', the older common spaces faded away. Unlike the earlier common spaces, which were only 'common' to a local community, public spaces became available to all citizens of an emerging state.

We are now, however, beginning to witness the emergence of new forms of collective space that bear some resemblance to the 'common' spaces which public space had swallowed up. Those new collective spaces, like their forebears before the development of public space, are common to some but not common to all; they include many persons but they also exclude some others – and it is through these exclusions that they put in question the inclusive nature of the public domain. Some of these new realms are contractual spaces, in the sense that they establish collectivities on the basis of explicit contracts.

These new forms of collective space are blurring the public-private distinction. These spaces, while 'public' in the sense that they are common places in which daily life is carried out in the public view, may at the same time be private in the sense that they are legally private property. The consequence of this has been that rules that define the rights of property owners – rules that had developed when both well-defined private and public spaces existed – are being applied to the regulation of these new common areas. This is eroding public space as we have come to know it, namely as spaces which people are entitled to frequent simply because they are citizens. In the new emerging 'common' spaces – in the form of malls, industrial parks, recreational domains, residential communities and the like – property owners under existing law have broad entitlements to exclude undesired entrants, and to do so with the backing of state authorities. As these new quasi-public domains swallow up public spaces, liberty of movement is impeded. It is now not difficult to find throughout America and Western Europe areas that once had vibrant public spaces but are now organised primarily and sometimes exclusively around malls, industrial and office complexes, and even gated communities. Simultaneously, even public spaces operated by public authorities – parks or downtown areas, for example – are beginning to adopt restrictions on entry, making them also common to many but not to all.

It may well be that current trends concerning ownership and organisation of common spaces are difficult or impossible to reverse. This, however, does not mean that we must be quiescent while the freedoms we value are eroded. The task facing us is that of rethinking our regulatory framework in ways that recognise these new styles of ownership and management, while at the same time preserving important values and liberties. What is required, in particular, is development of a normative framework that will give adequate recognition to rights of free access in the newly-emerging common spaces and in the spaces still in possession of public authorities.

LIBERTY AND THE PUBLIC-SPACE/PRIVATE-SPACE DISTINCTION

The foregoing sketch has suggested that there may be important liberty-preserving functions in having private property with restricted access but also public space with free access. Let us examine these functions more fully.

The Public/Private-Space Distinction

The landlord's power to exclude has been central to the conception of private property; indeed, Kevin Gray (1991) has persuasively argued that it is that power which principally defines private real property as such. Characteristically, permission to enter may be denied by the owner for any reason, and previously permitted entry may be revoked for any reason. While the space is thus deemed private, exclusion may be enforced by *state* action, via the trespass laws.[4] Where exclusion is permissible, it may be *permanent*: no time-limit is necessarily involved.

In public spaces, however, the widest liberty of movement has been assumed to exist. A person should be able freely to come and go, without need to justify his presence. Order is maintained through the public order provisions of the criminal law. The disruptive individual may thus be arrested, and undergo the applicable punishment. But permanent or long-term exclusion has not ordinarily been assumed to be an option: once the disruptive individual has completed his punishment, he may return to the same space.[5]

Granted, there have been a variety of official and unofficial exceptions to this understanding of public space. The police could invoke vagrancy laws, or newer variants thereof, to expel undesired entrants. Such measures, however, were considered suspect – and indeed, certain kinds of vagrancy statutes have been ruled unconstitutional in the US.[6]

---

[4] Whereas trespass itself is a crime under German law (German Criminal Code §123), it is not so under English law. In England, however, a trespasser who remains on private land after having been asked to leave by the owner may be deemed to have committed a breach of the peace if he resists the owner's efforts to expel him.

[5] The disruptive individual may be escorted away from a public place at which he is being disruptive, as part of the police's arrest and enforcement powers. But this involves only temporary exclusion, to 'defuse' the disruptive incident.

[6] *Papachristou v. Jacksonville*, 405 U.S.156 (1972) (striking down a broadly worded vagrancy statute); *Chicago v. Morales*, 119 S.Ct. 1849 (1999) (striking down a statute authorising police officers to order to disperse persons 'reasonably believed to be . . . criminal street gang member[s] loitering in a public place').

Function of the Distinction in Preserving Liberty

Maintaining an exclusion power in private but not public spaces has certain important liberty-preserving functions. In private space, the exclusion power creates an expanded ambit of personal choice. It permits the owner to decide with whom (if anyone) he wishes to share his space, and for what purposes and activities. There is no need to share the space with others who are unknown to him, or whose manner or interests are not congenial. The saying that 'A man's home is his castle' has this kernel of truth: at home, one can be at home, to do what one likes and be with whom one likes.[7]

In public space, by contrast, the absence of an exclusion power assures free entry and movement. This assures everyone of access to the common facilities and the social goods that such spaces provide: the public park is a place which we *all* should be able to enjoy. The public space provides also a 'corridor' function: it permits movement from one private space to another. If I am barred from public thoroughfares, I cannot visit my friends in other places, even if they invite me.

On this understanding of public space, order is maintained primarily through the operation of the criminal law. This law operates *through the volition of the subject*. Prohibitions are stated in advance, with prescribed penalties. It is up to the person to decide whether to comply or to risk the legal consequences. This serves interests in liberty in several important respects:

- It treats the addressees of the prohibition as self-governing persons. The sanction deals with them as rational moral agents, in that it conveys blame for the conduct which an agent might consider, and creates a disincentive to make the temptation to offend easier to resist.[8]
- It ensures that the addressees of the prohibition have access to the space, so long as they choose to comply. The person himself thus is in control of his ability to secure entry. There is no prior restraint.
- In case of a violation, the person may be subjected to a criminal sanction. That sanction may contain exclusionary elements: in case of a serious violation, he may be imprisoned – which sharply curtails his movements and access; for intermediate violations, he may be placed on probation, and the probationary order may limit his entry to places which are deemed likely to give rise to offending. But criminal sanctions should be subject to proportionality requirements, based on the seriousness of the offence.[9] Thus sooner or later, such restrictions must end.

[7] Naturally, private space has this liberty-preserving function only if ownership of property is distributed with some degree of equity. The right to one's own home has little value to those forced to live on the streets. Jeremy Waldron (1988) makes this point: that any liberty-based justification of private property presupposes that everyone has some minimal assurance of being able to have it.

[8] For more on this conception of punishment and why it is respectful of persons' agency, see von Hirsch (1993: ch. 2).

[9] *Ibid.*; Ashworth, (1995: chs 4, 9, 10); Criminal Justice Act 1991, §§ 2, 6.

- After the completion of the punishment, the person has the right to return to the public space in question. He has renewed freedom to use and enjoy the space – and any further loss of access would depend on a subsequent choice on his part to offend again. His initial disruptive conduct thus would not result in permanent exclusion.

Why Is Freedom of Access to Public Spaces Important?

While it is commonly believed that citizens have a broad entitlement to move freely in public space within their own country, this has received surprisingly little attention in law and legal scholarship. Constitutional provisions and doctrines concerning free movement, to the extent these exist, have been focused on movement across national borders. Free movement *within* state boundaries has been offered less protection.[10] Statutory or common-law guarantees of free movement in public space are also scant, in Britain[11] and many other Western countries. And purported rights of free movement have not received the kind of attention from legal philosophers as have other kinds of rights, such as those of privacy, speech and assembly.

A number of reasons may be offered, nevertheless, for considering free movement in public space to be an important interest for denizens of a free society, and one that should be accorded a special degree of protection.

When we think of liberty of movement in the present context, we should bear in mind that it is freedom of *access* that is at issue: that is, the freedom to enter places at which a person wishes to be present. Loss of the freedom to travel to Slough may not seem much of a deprivation, if one has no desire to visit that city. But exclusion sanctions do not just affect such hypothetical destinations; they preclude entry into public or semi-public spaces to which the person *does* wish to gain access.

One reason why freedom to enter such spaces is important is to make use of the social resources available there. If a person cannot enter common spaces in his area, he may be barred from access to important goods and services, and also may be excluded from the variegated aspects of social life that take place at such locations. Depending on what remaining space is available to him, this may entail loss of access to places at which to purchase food or other necessities, or to purchase non-essential goods that nevertheless are important to an adequate quality of life; to recreational facilities, and (particularly for young persons) to opportunities for social interaction. A dramatic illustration may be

---

[10] The Fourth Protocol to the European Convention on Human Rights, in its Article 2, provides that everyone lawfully within the territory of a signatory shall have 'the right of liberty of movement'. However, the right is made subject to broadly worded exceptions, including that for the maintenance of *ordre public*. Moreover, the right may be restricted 'in particular areas' if warranted by the public interest. Britain has not subscribed to this Protocol.

[11] See Feldman (2000).

drawn from the facts of *Rawlins*[12], decided by the Court of Appeal in 1995. The shopping mall involved in the case occupied the greater part of the former downtown shopping area of the city of Wellingborough, and serves as the city's principal shopping and congregating space. Those excluded were unemployed youths who had not been found guilty of any offence, but were deemed nuisances by the mall owner. Exclusion meant that the youths involved were barred from the locality's primary shopping and recreational area.

Other, less consequentialist arguments support also this interest in free access. One such consideration relates to personal liberty. Freedom requires place: to be free to do something, one needs a place at which to do it.[13] A person has, as noted, a wide ambit of choice within the confines of his own property. But most persons' properties (usually, consisting just of their dwelling-places) offer only limited geographical space and few facilities, and some people (the young, the homeless) lack any spaces of their own at all. This makes public space all the more important as the *locus* of free choice.

In public space, a person's options are ordinarily constrained to a modest degree by prohibitions of the criminal law. Such prohibitions, however, generally leave a wide residual ambit for free choice. The person still may freely enter and leave the space without prior permission, and still would be free to perform any activities that do not impinge on other persons' liberties through their harmful or offensive character.

If restrictions on access are imposed, however, liberty is drastically curtailed. When access is denied, the person is debarred from *all* options at that place. If access is made to depend on discretionary permission to enter, then liberty is also lost: he might be able to enter and to engage in various activities – but he is no longer *free* to do so, as permission to enter or remain may be withdrawn at any time.

Denial of access to a particular place, it might be objected, still leaves the person free to engage in his preferred activities elsewhere. The person who is barred from entering Shopping Mall X may still go to other malls in the area, to shop or window-shop on downtown streets, or to meet friends in the local public park. Sometimes, however, Shopping Mall X may be the only place in the area with adequate shopping, recreational, or congregating facilities, (as seems to have been the case in Wellingborough). And, more fundamentally, if exclusion from public and semi-public spaces is permissible, then access can be denied at those other locations also. Suppose, for example, that Shopping Mall X may keep out persons with previous criminal histories. The facility may then share its information with comparable facilities in the area (indeed, such information-sharing is becoming increasingly common; see Wakefield,

---

[12] CIN Properties Ltd. v. Rawlins (1995) 2 E.G.LR.130. For discussion of the case, see Gray and Gray (1999).
[13] Waldron, 1993: Ch. 13.

2000); and those facilities may use the same information to bar the person. The ASBO legislation,[14] for example, authorises exclusion not just in the specific location where the supposed anti-social conduct occurred, but from the entire local government or police district – or, under certain conditions, from neighbouring districts.

The interest in being able to move about freely in public space may also rest also on ideas of membership in a free community. To move about unhindered in public spaces seems a basic entitlement of community membership: that if it is one's own country, then one should be able to go about in it and to observe and enjoy what its public spaces have to offer. To be restricted in one's movements, in this view, imposes something like the status of second-class citizenship (see Duff and Marshall, 2000). This view would need fleshing out – and depends, ultimately, on political theory.[15]

Where do these arguments about the importance of the interest in free movement lead? They suggest that that free movement is an interest of a very considerable degree of practical and moral importance. If it has that importance, then the sanctions used to enforce public order in public space should be ones which help preserve such an interest. Our argument in this paper is that sanctions addressed to persons' volition can be made to comport reasonably well with liberty of movement, but that exclusion sanctions – especially those of certain kinds, to be discussed below – may not.

SEMI-PUBLIC SPACES: THE STATUS OF MASS PRIVATE PROPERTY

In the foregoing discussion, we have treated spaces such as shopping malls as 'semi-public' areas, to which a right of access should exist. This raises the question of the moral and legal status of such places.

In the 1995 *Rawlins* case, the Court of Appeal held that the owner of a shopping mall may exclude persons from entering for any reason.[16] This was so despite the fact that the facility clearly constituted semi-public space to which members of the public were invited without restriction of purpose. The claimed legal basis of the exclusion was a landowner's unrestricted entitlement to exclude others at will.

---

[14] See n 3, above.

[15] A fleshed-out account would need to furnish a fuller rationale of why free movement is a central feature of full membership in a community. It would also need to confront who should qualify for membership. Citizens and legal residents only? Visitors?

[16] See n 11, above. The American cases prohibit mall owners from barring visitors on racially-discriminating grounds (see Gray and Gray, 1999), and the coming into force of the Human Right's Act may lead English courts to adopt similar prohibitions. The Rawlins doctrine of exclusion at will has now been questioned in a concurring opinion by Lord Justice Sedley in *Porter v. Commissioner of Police*, decided by the Court of Appeal on 20 October 1999.

A full analysis of the defects of this decision is ably developed by Gray and Gray (1999). Briefly stated, the mall performs the functions of public space – namely, of a downtown shopping area. Exclusion means serious loss of access to important social goods and services, including shopping, employment, and recreational opportunities. What is more fundamentally objectionable here is that the exclusion sanction – which can serve to *enhance* liberty in functionally private spaces – is being used to *restrict* liberty of movement and access to social goods in functionally public space. The exclusionary regime of private space is being extended to swallow up the inclusive regime of public space. The Grays' suggested solution is to recognise that such 'mass private space' is functionally public; and that in public space, the power to exclude should be limited by public interest concerns. Such concerns, they suggest, can be safeguarded by a requirement that exclusions be subject to a 'reasonableness' test. Exclusions at will, for no stated reason, clearly would not satisfy such a test, and should be impermissible.

Such semi-public spaces should be distinguished from privately-owned space that is offered for public admission, but only for particular uses. Instances are shops and restaurants. All are invited to enter, but only for the stated purpose. A person thus may enter the shop to 'browse', but not for too long. In a restaurant, the person must order food; he may not sit at the table just to take notes on his newest research project. Semi-public space, for present purposes of analysis, constitutes space to which the general public is admitted without reference to specific uses. Shopping malls thus qualify, because members of the public are invited to come there without regard to performing any particular activity. While it is hoped visitors will shop there, they are encouraged to wander about the place or meet friends – in hopes that such casual presence and exposure to goods on display might encourage them to shop.

The extent of the public character of such privately-owned retailing spaces actually represents a spectrum. At one end of the spectrum lie facilities that are primarily designed for specified uses: say, a small atrium in front of a few shops, meant for the convenience of customers but not for general use. At the other end, is the large shopping mall which contains numerous retail outlets, restaurants, recreational facilities, and parking spaces – and which is meant for general public use. Where, along this spectrum, privately-owned property comes to have sufficient general public uses to qualify as 'semi-public' is a matter that would call for further analysis. For present purposes, however, it suffices that we treat as public in character those spaces that clearly are designed for general public use, such as a large downtown shopping mall replacing a traditional shopping area.

It might be objected that restricting an owners' power to exclude would be unfair, because it could adversely affect the profitability of the enterprise. If a mall is not permitted to expel undesired entrants, it might be less able to attract more respectable paying customers, and thus sustain financial losses. Certain kinds of businesses, however, offer essentially public services; and when they do, they may legitimately be regulated to ensure that the service is made fully available to members of the public and not just to preferred segments thereof. If a group of entrepreneurs purchase and operate a formerly state-owned railway or airline, or if they invest in a newly-organised bus line, they are permitted to profit from those activities; but they will be required to assure that all members of the public can have access. The possible effect of such requirements on the profitability of the enterprise is one of the business risks to consider, when deciding whether to invest in such an enterprise. Our argument is, essentially, that a large privately-owned mall that invites the public to enter without specification of purpose is likewise offering a public service, and thus may be called upon to ensure that all members of the public have proper access.

MINOR (NON-CRIMINAL) NUISANCE AS GROUNDS FOR EXCLUSION

If unlimited powers of exclusion should not be permissible in public or semi-public spaces, as has just been suggested, what, if any, should proper grounds for exclusion be? A possible exclusion ground is the prevention of minor (but non-criminal) nuisance conduct. Let us consider this briefly.

A variety of measures have been undertaken or proposed, that would permit the exclusion of persons from public space (even that which is publicly owned) for conduct that is not criminal but nevertheless is deemed obnoxious. Robert Ellickson (1996) proposes a zoning scheme whereby 'chronic street nuisances' could be zoned out of most of a city's downtown space. He defines a chronic street nuisance as a person who, without necessarily infringing the criminal law, "persistently act[s] in a public space in a manner that violates prevailing community standards of behavior, to the significant cumulative annoyance of persons of ordinary sensibility who use the same spaces" (*ibid.*, 1185). An example he gives is persistent acts of polite begging. He suggests a strict-liability test: no intention to annoy would be required. The aim of his proposal would be to bar such persons from most areas of a city, in order to make those areas more attractive for ordinary persons.

It is far from clear whether 'obnoxious' conduct, so broadly defined, constitutes a legitimate basis for coercive state intervention at all. Mere 'significant annoyance' would not be a sufficient intrusion to satisfy the Harm Principle.[17] It is also doubtful that it could satisfy a reasonably formulated Offence Principle.[18] The Ellickson proposal, for example, relies on the sensibilities of

[17] The Harm Principle holds that harm to others – involving a setback of interests of such persons – is a legitimate *prima facie* grounds for prohibiting conduct; for a fuller discussion of the principle, see Feinberg, 1984.

[18] The Offence Principle holds that offensiveness to others may, under specified circumstances, be *prima facie* grounds for prohibiting conduct. For formulations of the Offence Principle, see Feinberg 1985; or, for a somewhat different perspective that emphasises the normative reasons underlying claims of offensiveness, von Hirsch (2000b).

ordinary persons, without regard to how intrusive into the actor's life the measures to protect those sensibilities would be, or to whether there are any persuasive normative reasons why such sensibilities should be spared.

In any event, this kind of exclusion cannot be defended as a *situational crime prevention* strategy. A crime prevention rationale for exclusions assumes that it is *crime* that is to be forestalled. Here, however, the exclusions are based on behavioural standards that are considerably more stringent than the criminal law's public order rules; they are meant to maintain a higher level of public decorum. To the extent that is so, crime prevention cannot sustain such exclusion practices.[19]

The Ellickson proposal, at least, is conduct-based: the city is to be zoned so as to preclude in most of its public space certain kinds of 'obnoxious' conduct, and persons who engage in such behaviour may be punished. After completion of their (presumably rather modest) punishments, however, such people could presumably return to the space, provided they then desist. The recently-enacted ASBO (Anti-Social Behaviour Order) legislation takes matters a step further – to bar even this possibility of return. A single act of 'anti-social' conduct may result in the person being banned for a lengthy period from a specified area.[20]

LONG-TERM EXCLUSIONS FOR CRIME PREVENTION

Let us turn, then, to our primary topic of exclusions designed to promote *crime prevention*. Here, there are two kinds of strategies which strike us as being of a questionable character: profiling exclusions, and those based on prior offending. In both cases, we are speaking of exclusions that are permanent or of substantial duration.

Profile-Based Exclusions

One of these suspect strategies is *profile-based* exclusions. The idea here is to bar from entry certain persons whose characteristics are deemed indicative of a heightened risk of criminal offending. It is not present unacceptable behav-

---

[19] Ellickson (1996: 1171) does invoke crime prevention in support of his scheme by citing the Wilson/Kelling thesis that non-criminal incivilities, when permitted to become frequent in a neighbourhood, will lead to the locality's decay and eventually to higher crime rates (Wilson and Kelling, 1982). But empirical support for this latter thesis is far from unequivocal (Taylor, 1997). And it involves the further problem of 'remote harms': the persons targeted by the measure are not committing crimes at all, and their conduct is merely said to have effects on the area's environment that may prompt *others* to commit crimes. This raises questions of whether it is fair to hold those committing mere incivilities responsible for others' eventual criminal choices. See more fully, on 'remote harms', von Hirsch (1996).

[20] See n 3, above.

iour that is the concern here, but *potential* for future criminal offending. These profile-based exclusions may be of two types:

- Profile-based exclusions may dispense with any prohibited conduct, and base the exclusion simply on the excludees' having certain characteristics associated with higher risks of criminal offending. An example is airlines' former practice, before the present metal-detecting devices were installed, of barring from flights certain individuals who fitted the profiles of potential hijackers.
- Profile-based exclusions may adopt conduct-related requirements that function actually as pre-emptive exclusions: persons considered bad risks are kept away by prohibiting conduct that is deemed to typify them. For example, groups of male teenagers, or persons dressed in a certain manner, are kept out of a shopping mall because their presence is thought to bode risks of potential disruption or theft.

Profiling of these two kinds differs from the exclusion strategy discussed earlier (pp. 87–88), in that its aim is to prevent *criminal* conduct. The profile is used as grounds for exclusion, because of its utility in predicting subsequent criminal behaviour. Thus persons are not being barred from public or semi-public space *merely* because they have certain characteristics or engage in possibly irritating but harmless conduct; rather, the claim is that persons who have those characteristics or engage in such conduct are more likely than others to commit crimes in future; and are being kept out in order to prevent such crimes from occurring. Profiling is thus a genuine *situational crime prevention* strategy.

It should not suffice, of course, merely to claim that possessing a given profile or having given behaviour-patterns is predictive of the person's propensity for criminal behaviour; this would need to be supported by empirical evidence[21]. But *if* evidence of this link to subsequent crime can be established, should this kind of exclusion be permissible?

We think not. The persons thus profiled substantially lose access to public spaces which formerly were accessible to all. The exclusion may substantially restrict their access to publicly-available resources and services, and involves a drastic curtailment of their liberty of movement and access to public space. The profiling criteria relied upon are problematic because they bypass the actor's agency: the person is being kept out of public or semi-public space, without regard to any choice on his part to engage in harmful or seriously offensive conduct. Indeed, profiling represents an extreme version of bypassing volition: the person is excluded before he has any chance to show whether he is willing to behave properly. What counts is not his actual

---

[21] The evidence in question would need to show the profile is predictive of criminal conduct in the near future on the part of the persons to be excluded. Valid evidence of this kind might be obtainable, albeit with a great deal of 'overprediction' – that is, with most of the persons fitting the profile not engaging in the predicted conduct.

criminal choices, but his membership in a class of persons considered to represent higher risks.

This bypassing-of-the-agency objection holds most obviously for 'pure' profiling strategies, where the exclusion is based on the person's having certain characteristics that are deemed predictive of future misconduct. The person loses his freedom of access to public or semi-public spaces, without *any* opportunity whatever to demonstrate that he would have conducted himself properly were he permitted access. The person is being treated not as an agent capable of choice, but much as a dangerous animal, which may not be brought into a public places (even on a leash) because it is the sort of creature that is known to bite.

The objection holds also, however, for profiling exclusions based on current conduct of a non-criminal nature, as in the example of excluding groups of male teenagers. True, there is a choice involved here: for example, the teenagers must choose to congregate, in order to trigger the exclusion. Because of that conduct requirement, volition is not wholly foreclosed: if the teenager wishes access, he can have it by going in alone. The difficulty remains, however, that there is here no requirement of *wrongful* choice: there is nothing illegal, or even morally questionable, for a young man to go about with his friends. The absence of wrongfulness means that the person has no independent normative inducement to refrain from the conduct involved. Unless the person gives up something he would otherwise be entitled to do, his moral agency is still bypassed: he is being excluded not because of any wrongful choice he has made, but because he is (or more accurately, people who resemble him are) deemed more likely to engage in such choice in future; and the exclusion is meant precisely to preclude that choice.

Exclusion Based on Previous Criminal Offending

This is probably the most common type of exclusion. Many shopping malls do not operate with profiles, but use exclusions against persons found already to have engaged in illegal acts (see Wakefield, 2000, in this volume). The Anti-Social Behaviour Order[22] may also be employed in this fashion: against disruptive neighbours whose conduct does violate criminal statutes prohibiting assault, threatening conduct or disruption. What the ASBO then permits, however, is imposing a long-term exclusion order on the person, once he has been found to have engaged in such behaviour.

A threshhold objection relates to the possible unfairness of the procedure for determining that a criminal violation has occurred. A mall operator may simply decide *ex parte* that a criminal violation has taken place, with no opportunity granted for the suspect to have his case heard impartially, or to

---

[22] This measure is described briefly in n 3, above.

present a defence. Or with the ASBO, a neighbour who engages in violence or illegal threats is not convicted of this conduct; rather, he is simply found to have engaged in 'anti-social' behaviour under the much looser standard of conduct and lower proof requirements that the ASBO legislation permits.

Suppose, however, that a criminal conviction were properly obtained against the person, and it is desired to exclude him from the space thereafter. What objection can there be to that? This way of proceeding *seems* to be a volition-based sanction. The person must have made a culpable choice to offend, before he can be excluded. Should he have wished access, he could have refrained from criminal offending.

A crucial difficulty remains, however: it lies in the permanence of the exclusion. Unlike punishment, the response is not 'over' when a proportionate sanction has been carried out. Once found to have committed the proscribed conduct, the person may not return – or may not return for a lengthy period – to the space involved. So this sanction still involves the bypassing of the person's agency because he loses the crucial 'second bite' which the criminal law permits: he is denied the opportunity of re-entering the space after completion of his punishment, even if he were subsequently willing to comply. Since so many people, especially young persons, have at one or another time been found to have committed petty thefts or lesser acts of disruption,[23] a very substantial class could thus be denied the freedom to utilise public spaces.

It might be asserted that the exclusion is not meant to be a punishment but rather a reasonable 'civil' response to the misuse of public space. If viewed as a civil response however, the pre-emptive character of the sanction becomes all the more apparent. Persons are being denied access to public or semi-public space on grounds of risk of future offending; and the prior criminal conviction serves merely as evidence of the risk involved. By denying the person the opportunity of returning, the sanction still bypasses the will: the person, once identified as a risk through previous conduct, no longer has the option of returning to the public space provided he subsequently is willing to comply with legal requirements.[24]

---

[23] According to 1987 Home Office statistics, it is estimated that 34% of males born in 1953, and 8% of women born that year, were convicted of a standard list offence before age 40 (Home Office, 1997: 199-200).

[24] Von Hirsch and Wasik (1997) have defended a limited use of civil disqualifications from professions – to bar from further practice, for example, a solicitor convicted of dishonest dealings with clients. These situations involve, however, established professions with entry qualifications, services having a fiduciary character, and a clientele that is vulnerable to abuses of trust. In the situations of which we are speaking here, no such factors are present. Access to public space is not a matter for which one needs or should need special qualifications – indeed, it should be available to all. No special vulnerabilities or interests of a fiduciary character are involved: the user of public or semi-public space does not entrust his interests to other users, in the manner that a patient or client entrusts his interest to his or her doctor or solicitor.

Exclusion of Convicted Persons – Any Exceptions?

Might there, however, be exceptional cases where permanent or long-term exclusions should be permissible? A possible exception involves cases where the environment is especially 'sensitive' to certain kinds of misconduct, involving potential harm of an unusually grave character in the circumstances. If a person starts fighting in a park, that involves the normal risks of assaultive conduct; but if he starts fighting on an airplane or joins in a riot in a crowded stadium, that creates the risk of a crash or a stampede in which many lives may be lost or endangered.

How would permitting such an exception comport with our basic thesis, that access to public space is an interest of fundamental importance, and thus requires special protection? This raises the question of the extent to which 'rights' constrain the pursuit of crime prevention claims – a matter discussed more fully in another essay in this volume (von Hirsch 2000a). To treat access to public or semi-public space as a 'right' or interest worthy of special protection involves giving it a degree of priority over the pursuit of ordinary social aims including those of crime prevention. One may give the interest in public access such priority under ordinary circumstances, and yet accede to the pursuit of crime preventive objectives when these are of unusual urgency. It is thus arguable that in the specially sensitive environments just referred to, where disruptive conduct can lead to seriously harmful results, that such a degree of urgency is established. We think, however, that this type of exception should be drawn narrowly.

BRIEF, CONDUCT-RELATED EXCLUSIONS

The reservations we have just outlined concerning permanent or long-term exclusions still leave open the possibility of *brief* exclusions based on current behaviour. A person who misconducts himself is kept out or invited to leave, while he is engaging in the behaviour. This approach leaves volition intact, since the person can enter the facility by deciding not to misbehave; and if he does offend, he may be removed for the particular occasion but is not subsequently barred from returning.

The intervention may involve denial of admission: the conspicuously inebriated individual is prevented from entering the public park or mall. Additionally, it may involve expulsion: the rowdy youngster is escorted out of the facility and told not to return until he has calmed down. These are common practices in mass private spaces such as malls (see Wakefield, 2000). In public facilities such as streets or parks, the police may exercise a similar function: the drunk is escorted home. On the basis of the preceding argumentation, such strategies seem less problematic, because bypassing-of-agency is less clearly involved. The person has no business engaging in his current misconduct. Once barred from entry or expelled, he still may re-enter at a later time, provided he then avoids that kind of behaviour. His liberty of access to public space has not been permanently curtailed.

In public streets or parks, the expulsion function has traditionally been performed by the police: the officer informs the person that he had best leave, if he does not wish to be arrested. But even such public facilities are, to varying degrees, turning this function over to private security – which may lack full arrest powers. In semi-public spaces such as malls, this function is left chiefly to private security personnel, who have more limited arrest powers than the police.[25] Given the fact that police enforcement and prosecution are costly and relatively scarce resources, it does not seem practical to insist that only the police may expel.

Extending the expulsion power beyond criminal justice agencies, however, raises another problem: that of the evidentiary standards for establishing that a criminal violation has actually occurred, that would support the decision to expel. When the police are involved, this ordinarily is less of a problem: the officer directs the person to leave, and warns him that if he does not comply he will be arrested for the misconduct he is committing. Should the individual wish to contest the latter claim, he may challenge the officer to perform the arrest – in which event the question of whether the misconduct has occurred will be decided in court.

Once private security personnel lacking arrest powers are involved, however, this procedure ceases to be available. The security agent makes his own determination, on the spot, that criminal misbehaviour is occurring; there ordinarily is no independent forum for determining whether the individual has actually misconducted himself. If the problem is primarily one of establishing fairly that a criminal violation occurred, however, ingenuity may offer some possible procedures or remedies. One possibility (although one of limited practical effectiveness) is to provide a wrongly-expelled individual with a cause of action in tort. Another would be that if the person refuses to leave, the police are called in and he is charged with disorderly conduct, then conviction would require a demonstration that he was conducting himself improperly (and not merely remaining present) when he was asked to leave. There may be other possibilities, but some procedure is needed for establishing fairly (even after the fact) that a violation has actually taken place.

---

[25] Private security have ordinary citizens' arrest powers, that relate to indictable offences committed in their presence; and also the somewhat expanded arrest powers of property owners, that relate to other crimes committed in their presence on their property. This includes the ability to hold a suspect until arrival of the police or a deputised person. However, private security seldom have the full arrest powers of the police.

WHAT LEGAL CHANGES ARE NEEDED?

How much change in existing law would be required to implement the suggestions we have made in this essay? The extent of such changes would depend, of course, on the state of law of the particular jurisdiction involved. In England, the required changes would be quite extensive. Current law treats the owners of mass private spaces like private landlords, entitled to expel at will (see p. 85). Suitable limitations on the expulsion power would have to be imposed – for example, to restrict profiling exclusions, and long-term exclusions imposed on the formerly convicted (see pp. 88–92). Indeed, changes in England's law relating to public property may also be required – as publicly-owned land is now treated in significant respects like private land, with substantial powers to exclude persons other than those present for specified purposes.[26] We thus leave this topic for those more versed in land law and public law than ourselves to consider.

CONCLUSIONS

In the foregoing pages, we have sketched a conceptual framework regarding when it should be permissible, in the interests of crime prevention, to exclude persons from public and semi-public spaces. Our analysis has been designed to preserve the liberties and freedoms associated with and made possible by conceptions of a public spatial domain. We recognise this to be a somewhat cautious way of argument, in that it seeks to retain – and extend to mass private space – freedoms and entitlements that traditionally have been associated (at least in theory) with that public domain.

Perhaps this strategy will ultimately prove to be too limiting, because it retains the values associated with existing conceptions of space, and tries to apply them to rapidly changing forms of space ownership and management. It thus views the newer forms of collective space, and the collective life they express and make possible, through an established normative lens. A more radical approach could be to take advantage of the new possibilities made available by these newer spatial forms to rethink the normative framework itself. This is not something that we feel equipped to undertake at present, although we recognise it as a possibility. Doing so would require novel ways of thinking that might leave currently-conceived distinctions between public and private spaces behind, rather than trying to adapt these conceptions to the newer forms of collective space. Possibly, we might stop thinking of the new emerging spaces as either quasi-public or quasi-private and develop new spatial categorisations and a new normative framework appropriate to them –

[26] Feldman (2000).

this, after all, is how the public/private framework emerged in the first place. Were this possibility realised, our proposals might subsequently look like transitional developments in the rethinking of how liberty should be maintained in common spaces. But any such reconceptualisation should maintain and emphasise certain values – those of liberty, and of wide access by members of the public to common goods and spaces.

REFERENCES

Ashworth, A. (1995) *Sentencing and Criminal Justice,* (2nd. ed.) London: Butterworths.

——, Gardner, J., Morgan, R., Smith, A.T.H., von Hirsch, A. and Wasik, M. (1998) 'Neighbouring on the oppressive: the government's "anti-social behaviour order" proposals', *Criminal Justice* 16(1): 7–14.

—— and von Hirsch, A. (1997) 'Recognising elephants: the problem of the custody threshold', *Criminal Law Review [1997]*: 187–200.

Clarke, R.V. (1995) 'Situational Crime Prevention', in M. Tonry, and D. Farrington (eds.), *Building a Safer Society. Crime and Justice: A Review of Research* 19: 91–150, Chicago: University of Chicago Press.

Duff, R.A., and Marshall, S. (2000) 'Benefits, burdens and responsibilities: some ethical dimensions of situational crime prevention', this volume.

Ellickson, R.C. (1996) 'Controlling chronic misconduct in city spaces: of panhandlers, skid rows, and public space zoning', *Yale Law Review* 105:1165–1248.

Feldman, D. (2000) 'Property and public protest' in F. Meisel and P. Cook (eds.), *Property and Protection*, Oxford: Hart Publishing.

Feinberg, J. (1984) *Harm to Others*, New York: Oxford University Press.

—— (1985) *Offense to Others*, New York: Oxford University Press.

Gray, K. (1991) 'Property in thin air', *Cambridge Law Journal* 50: 252–307.

—— and Gray, S.F. (1999) 'Civil rights, civil wrongs, and quasi-public space' *European Human Rights Law Review [1999]*: 1–59.

Home Office (1998) *Criminal Statistics, England and Wales 1997*, Cm 4162, London: Stationery Office.

Taylor, R.B. (1997) 'Crime, grime, and responses to crime', in S.P. Lab (ed.), *Crime Prevention at a Crossroads*, Cincinnati, Ohio: Anderson.

von Hirsch, A. (1993) *Censure and Sanctions*, Oxford: Oxford University Press.

—— (1996) 'Extending the harm principle: "remote" harms and fair imputation,' in A. Simester and A.T.H. Smith (eds.), *Harm and Culpability*, 259–276, Oxford: Oxford University Press.

—— (2000a) 'The ethics of public television surveillance', this volume.

—— (2000b) 'The offence principle in criminal law: Affront to sensibility or wrong-doing?' *King's College Law Journal* 11: 78–89.

——, Bottoms, A.E., Burney, E., Wikström, P-O. (1999) *Criminal Deterrence and Sentence Severity*, Oxford: Hart Publishing.

—— and Wasik, M. (1997) 'Civil disqualifications attending conviction: a suggested conceptual framework' *Cambridge Law Journal* 56: 599–626.

Wakefield, A. (2000) 'Situational crime prevention in mass private property', this volume.

Waldron, J. (1988) *The Right to Private Property*, Oxford: Oxford University Press.
—— (1993) *Liberal Rights: Collected Papers 1981–1991*, Cambridge: Cambridge University Press.
White, R. (1999) 'Anti-social behaviour orders under section 1 of the Crime and Disorder Act 1998', *European Law Review Human Rights Survey* 24: 55–62.
Wilson, J.Q. and Kelling, G. (1982) 'Broken windows: the police and community safety', *Atlantic Monthly (March 1982)*.

6

Situational Prevention, Criminology, and Social Values

Ronald V. Clarke

INTRODUCTION

Advocates of situational crime prevention have claimed that the systematic reduction of opportunities for crime would lead to substantial reductions in a society's crime rate. Critics have responded that this claim gives too little importance to the social and psychological determinants of criminal motivation. Unless motivation is also reduced, they argue, the removal of opportunities will simply result in crime being redistributed, not reduced.

In buttressing their position, advocates of situational prevention have helped to develop theories portraying crime as the outcome of an interaction between motivation and opportunity. Perhaps the three most important of these theories, which David Garland (1996) has described as 'the new criminologies of everyday life', are the routine activities approach, crime pattern theory and the rational choice perspective. These are complementary theories but each has a slightly different focus (Felson and Clarke, 1998). Routine activities theory deals with the ways that opportunities arise (and decline) in society. Sociologists would describe it as a 'macro' theory because it seeks to explain broad social trends. Pattern theory deals with the ways that offenders encounter or seek out opportunities for crime. Because it considers offenders in the context of the neighbourhoods where they live, it provides explanations at the 'meso' level. The rational choice perspective provides accounts of the various situational influences – motives, desires, emotions, justifications – that result in offenders deciding to take advantage of particular criminal opportunities. Because it focuses on the immediate setting for crime, it could be called a 'micro' theory.

Taken together, these theories show how crime is generated by the interaction of motivational and situational variables. They explain how opportunities for crime draw people into criminal conduct just as much as criminal dispositions lead people to seek out crime opportunities. This helps in making the case that reducing opportunities is as important as reducing criminal motivation. At the same time, advocates of situational prevention have been engaged in applying opportunity-reduction on the ground. More than 100 documented examples of successful situational prevention now exist[1]. Early applications were focused on opportunistic property offences, but situational prevention has been used more recently in preventing a much wider range of offences, including street prostitution, drunken brawling, obscene phone calling, domestic violence and various forms of commercial robbery (Clarke, 1997). In these evaluations of situational prevention, displacement effects have been found to be much less common than often assumed. No evidence of displacement was found in 22 out of 55 situational prevention projects recently examined in a review for the Dutch Ministry of Justice, and only partial displacement was found in the remainder (Hesseling, 1994).

The methodology of many of the evaluations can be criticised, but taken together they suggest that situational prevention can be effective across a broad range of crimes at both a societal and local level. In addition, many studies are discovering that the benefits of situational crime prevention have diffused so that there was not only a reduction in crimes targeted by the measures, but crime supposedly outside the direct reach of the measures (Clarke and Weisburd, 1994). For example, when CCTV cameras were installed on the top deck of three buses in one city, vandalism was reduced not just on those buses, but on the entire fleet (Poyner, 1988). In another example, improved lighting of the streets in one housing estate not only reduced crime in that estate but also in an adjoining one (Painter and Farrington, 1997). It seems that offenders respond to reduced opportunities in a variety of ways, sometimes by shifting their attention elsewhere, but often by reducing their offending as a result of a real or perceived increase in the risks or effort entailed.

As a result of these developments, situational prevention has now gained a place in the crime control policies of many countries, but it is still viewed with little enthusiasm by most criminologists. Some of them continue to question its effectiveness[2], but more now concentrate on its supposed detrimental social consequences, and on its 'conservative' values and politics (O'Malley, 1997; O'Malley and Sutton, 1997; Crawford, 1998; Hughes, 1998). This paper focuses on these more recent lines of criticism. It argues that the harmful consequences of situational prevention can often be anticipated, and with care can also be avoided or ameliorated. As for the criticism of values, it argues that this reflects the preferences of most criminologists for social reform over

---

[1] Clarke (1997) and Sherman et al. (1997) provide overlapping reference sources to these case studies.

[2] Despite this record of success, important questions about the effectiveness of situational crime remain to be answered. For instance, little has been written about implementation difficulties and about why some measures fail. Nor is much known about how long measures retain their effectiveness before offenders find ways round them. Further, it is not clear how situational prevention can be used to reduce some important categories of crime such as sexual assaults, hate crimes, organised crime and corporate crime. Most important, it is not yet clear whether the piecemeal elimination of specific kinds of opportunities for crime can make a substantial enough impact on the overall level of crime in society to justify an increased government investment in the approach.

opportunity reduction; they need to be persuaded, however, that opportunity reduction equally demands their attention.

HARMFUL SOCIAL CONSEQUENCES

The potential harms of situational prevention are difficult to discuss in the space of a single paper, for reasons that include the following:

1. Situational prevention has come to mean different things. In particular, it now has both a broad and a narrow meaning. In its broad meaning, it encompasses any attempt to manipulate the environment to reduce opportunities for crime. In its narrow meaning, it refers to a specific problem solving approach, developed by criminologists, which is the subject of an extensive technical and theoretical literature (Clarke, 1995; 1997). The present chapter is focused on this narrower definition, whereas many other chapters in this book deal with situational prevention defined more broadly. As explained below, the narrower form has more built-in ethical safeguards.

2. Even when narrowly defined, situational prevention encompasses many different techniques to reduce opportunity. In the latest classification, 16 of these techniques are identified under the four general headings of increasing the difficulty of crime, increasing the risks, reducing the rewards and removing excuses (see Table 1). Each of these techniques varies in its potential drawbacks. For instance, 'access control', one technique for increasing the difficulty of crime, has more 'exclusionary' costs than, say, 'target hardening', another such technique. Moreover, specific applications of a particular technique may be more problematic than others are. For instance, improved lighting and 'neighbourhood watch' are both means of improving natural surveillance (one of the ways to increase the risks of crime), but the latter carries more ethical risks because it may encourage vigilantism.

3. Both private and public agencies engage in situational prevention projects. Those undertaken by private agencies may have more injurious consequences than those undertaken by government, because the latter must take a much broader range of interests into account.

4. Harm can be considered from an individual or community perspective as well as an overall societal perspective. Depending on which perspective is adopted, there will be differing assessments of harm[3].

In addition, there seems to be no generally accepted classification of the possible harmful consequences of crime policies to guide the discussion of the ethics of situational crime prevention. Felson and Clarke (1997) have proposed

[3] As noted by Joanna Shapland in her commentary at the Cambridge conference, this paper adopts a 'top down, government' perspective.

Table 1. Situational crime prevention: examples of the main approaches

INCREASING PERCEIVED EFFORT	REDUCING ANTICIPATED REWARDS
1. Target hardening • Strengthened coin boxes in telephone kiosks • Steering column locks on cars • Anti-robbery screens in banks	9. Target removal • Removable car radios • Women's refuges • Phonecards to eliminate cash in public pay phones
2. Controlling access • Fencing around car parks • Entry phones • Concierges	10. Property identification • Property marking • Vehicle licensing • Cattle branding
3. Deflecting offenders from targets • Segregating rival soccer fans • Pub location • Closing streets to stop cruising for prostitutes	11. Reducing temptation • Gender-neutral phone listings • Off-street parking • Rapid repair of vandalism
4. Controlling crime facilitators • Photographs on credit cards • Toughened glasses in pubs • Passwords for mobile phones	12. Denying benefits • Ink merchandise tags • Graffiti cleaning • Disabling stolen mobile phones
INCREASING PERCEIVED RISKS	REMOVING EXCUSES
5. Screening entrances and exits • Automatic ticket gates at stations • Baggage screening at airports • Merchandise tags in shops	13. Setting rules • Customs declaration • Harassment codes • Hotel registration
6. Formal surveillance • Speed cameras • Burglar alarms • City guards	14. Alerting conscience • Roadside speedometers • 'Shoplifting is stealing' signs • 'Idiots drink and drive' signs
7. Surveillance by employees • Locate pay phones where employees can see • Park attendants • CCTV systems	15. Controlling disinhibitors • Laws controlling drinking age • V-chips in TVs to block violent programmes • Breathalyzers in pubs
8. Natural surveillance • 'Defensible space' designs • Improved street lighting • 'Cocoon' neighbourhood watch	16. Encouraging compliance • Easy library checkout to discourage book theft • Public lavatories • Litter bins

Source: Adapted from Ekblom (1998)

that three general principles deriving from the ethical standards of a liberal democracy should govern crime prevention policy: it should provide crime prevention equally to all social strata, it should show respect for individual rights, and it should share responsibility for crime prevention with all sections of society. However, it is too early to say whether these principles will be accepted as an adequate framework for discussing the ethical questions raised by situational prevention. While they inform the discussion below they do not govern its structure. Rather, the discussion is focused on some specific claims about the harmful results of situational prevention. In each case, it will be argued that ways to avoid the harms can be found and that the criticisms often take no account of the countervailing benefits of situational prevention.

1. Displacement resulting from situational prevention can lead to crime becoming worse.

This is not simply the criticism, which is incorrect, that situational prevention achieves little net benefit as a result of displacement. Rather, it is that displacement can sometimes result in an escalation of harm so that more serious crimes replace less harmful varieties[4]. For instance, when token booths in the NYC subway system were target hardened, some thieves attacked them by pouring petrol under the doorway and threatening to set the booth alight (Dwyer, 1991). The subway authorities quickly installed fire extinguishers in booths to counter this threat.

In fact, the idea of escalation does not comport with the circumstances of many forms of crime. For example, it seems unlikely that if casual shoplifting were made more difficult, those denied this opportunity would feel compelled to find some other way of getting the goods – such as grabbing the shopping baskets from pensioners. Even so, those implementing situational prevention must be prepared to respond if the threat of escalation becomes a reality (as in the case of the petrol attacks on token booths). This is a recognised part of situational prevention's action-research methodology, which requires an examination of actual outcomes after the implementation of opportunity-reducing measures.

Another version of the increased harm hypothesis is that situational prevention can result in crime being displaced from the rich to the poor. Thus the rich man's burglar alarm may displace burglary to his poorer neighbour. The possibility of this kind of displacement should be considered whenever governments conduct publicity campaigns to get people to safeguard their

---

[4] It is equally true, as Barr and Pease (1990) have argued, that even if displacement were complete – in the sense that equally many, though different crimes, occurred after the measures than before – this might still result in a net benefit for society. The new crimes might be less serious than the old (what might be called de-escalation) and crimes may be diverted from repeat victims to be shared more equally among the members of a particular community.

property. In fact, there are few documented examples of crime being displaced from the rich to poor, though, for a time, vehicle-tracking devices to prevent car theft carried this risk. These devices are expensive and would not be worth fitting to most cars. They also require a receiver to be installed on police cars to pick up the signals from stolen vehicles. As a result, police attention could become concentrated on stolen cars fitted with tracking devices at the expense of those without the devices. Consequently, many municipalities in America now make it a condition of police cooperation that cars fitted with the tracking device do not use decals to advertise this fact. Thieves therefore do not know which cars have the devices and which do not, which may help to produce a more general deterrent effect. Indeed, a recent econometric evaluation of the use of these devices in the Northeastern United States suggests that they have helped to bring down overall levels of a car theft in the communities concerned (Ayres and Levitt, 1998). If so, poorer car owners would have collected 'free rider' benefits from the preventive efforts of more wealthy owners. Felson and Clarke (1997) have argued that similar benefits may diffuse to poorer communities as the result of more effective crime prevention in more wealthy neighbouring communities.

2. Situational crime prevention reinforces a harsh, uncaring fortress society, of which gated communities are the most recent manifestation.

When first introduced, situational prevention, especially in its 'target hardening' varieties, fed fears about the imminence of a fortress society in which citizens terrified of crime locked themselves in their homes, shunned their neighbours, and emerged only for work and other essential business. The result, it was feared, would be a growing alienation of the population and the gradual destruction of community life. In fact, much situational prevention practice has had exactly the opposite objective of strengthening community ties and reinforcing social controls, by enabling people to keep an eye on the neighbourhood around their homes. Essentially, this is the purpose of the 'defensible space' designs that Oscar Newman (1972) proposed for public housing estates in the early 1970s.

Nevertheless, the criticism has lingered on, though in different forms over the years. Currently, it is focused on the 'gated community', where access is restricted to those residing there on the assumption that much crime is the result of offenders cruising in neighbourhoods, looking for crime opportunities. Access is controlled by walled or fenced perimeters, by gates and by barriers. In many cases, the residents of these communities are seeking protection from crime, but they are also hoping to avoid traffic, litter and other incivilities of modern life. The number of these communities has increased rapidly in America in the past fifteen years. A recent estimate puts the numbers of American families now living in some form of gated community at about 2.5 million (Blakely and Snyder, 1998).

It is not clear whether the ethical considerations surrounding gated communities are much more troublesome than those relating to restricted entry into apartment blocks, many of which house just as many residents. Nor is it clear how these considerations differ from those concerning walled country estates belonging to the very wealthy. Some of the criticism of gated communities certainly assumes that they are only for the rich. In fact, many of these neighbourhoods recently built in the United States, perhaps most of them, are intended for middle-income residents (Blakely and Snyder, 1998). Gated communities also have their analogues in poorer parts of the city where residents have demanded that street barriers be installed to keep drug dealers and criminals out of their neighbourhoods. Some inner city public housing estates in America have also in effect been turned into gated communities.

No careful study has been made of whether gated communities do protect wealthy and middle-income people from crime. They might do so if the community is located in a high crime area and if security is tight. However, many of the new gated communities do not fulfill these conditions. They are being built in the outer suburbs where crime is already low. Where they began with manned gates, many quickly give these up because of the expense. On the other hand, several studies in poorer neighbourhoods have shown that street barriers can be effective in reducing crime. For example, Matthew's (1986, 1993) work in London suburbs has shown that street closures have been an important component of the successful efforts to reduce street prostitution. Lasley (1998) has recently shown that street barriers installed in an impoverished area in Los Angeles reduced a variety of crimes including homicide committed in drive-by shootings by gang members.

As so often turns out, the truth about gated communities is more complex than portrayed by the critics. Gated communities are not merely for the rich and may not be widely resented by the poor. They do not simply consist of walled residential neighbourhoods with guarded entrances. Barriers to entering can often be more symbolic than real, and may inconvenience rather than prohibit entry. If their development has been encouraged at all by situational prevention, this is in poorer rather than in wealthier neighbourhoods. It is in these poorer neighbourhoods that their benefits may be most obvious and direct. They may strengthen community bonds rather than weaken them, and they might enhance rather than impede informal controls. Because they might help to reduce fear, they may even reduce the perceived need for other, more harmful forms of self-protection such as purchasing guns. In any ethical assessment of gated communities, however, these and their other possible benefits need to be balanced against their possible harms in limiting public access and freedom of movement (see von Hirsch and Shearing, 2000).

3. **The use of situational crime prevention results in the exclusion of so-called 'undesirables' (vagrants, the homeless, minorities and unemployed young people) from public places such as shopping malls, parks and entertainment facilities.**

The use of technology or police and security guards to control access always carries the danger of exclusion, even when exclusion is disavowed as an objective. In fact, this danger is smaller in situational prevention projects than in some of the newer forms of policing. This is because situational prevention (at least as defined in the narrow sense of this paper) seeks to use access control in a more closely targeted manner. Rather than being used to restrict access to public facilities such as shopping malls or downtown districts, it is used to keep people out of private facilities, such as office blocks or factories, who have no business to conduct there. It would tend to focus less on specific groups of 'undesirables' because situational prevention assumes that any stranger might exploit opportunities for crime in these facilities. Where the purpose is to exclude perceived 'troublemakers' from public and semi-public spaces such as downtown districts and shopping malls, it is more likely to be served by 'order-maintenance' policing undertaken by public police forces, or private policing undertaken by security companies. While these forms of policing might fall under a broader interpretation of situational prevention, they are not encompassed within the narrower focus of this paper.

'Deflecting offenders', another of the situational prevention techniques listed in Table 1, also carries some exclusionary potential since its purpose is to keep likely offenders away from suitable targets. For example, the coordination of last buses with pub closing times, an example of deflecting offenders, is designed to get late night drinkers out of the city centre before they get into trouble. Another example would be closing off cut-throughs and alleyways near high schools to prevent pupils from vandalising cars or stealing items left in back gardens on their way to and from school. As these examples again show, however, the use of this situational technique is targeted to particular problems and settings and is less likely to involve a general attempted exclusion of 'undesirables'.

4. **CCTV surveillance of public space, speed cameras, and Caller-ID are just three recent examples of the threat to civil liberties posed by many situational crime prevention measures.**

Any new technology used in law enforcement and crime prevention poses possible new threats to civil liberties. CCTV raises the spectre of being spied upon as we go about our daily business. Speed cameras can give the authorities information about where we drive and when. Caller-ID can remove our anonymity when making casual enquiries over the phone or can reveal where we are calling from when we wish to keep this private.

These threats need to be exposed, subjected to critical evaluation, and resisted where they might result in harmful intrusions on freedom. Unfortunately, in their zeal to be the guardians of liberty, the critics of new technology often fail to ask questions about the reality of the threat and about the possibility of it being averted (other than by banning the technology). If some infringements of liberty seem unavoidable, they often fail to consider whether these costs are outweighed by the benefits of crime reduction.

In fact, ideals of freedom and suspicions of technology combine to make it unlikely that situational prevention will result in significant infringements of individual liberties. Rather, the danger is that valuable technologies will not be used, or their introduction delayed, by unrealistic fears about their effects. Several examples of this can be cited:

- New technology making it impossible for anyone but the owner to fire a handgun is being resisted by the gun lobby in America.
- Towns and cities throughout America are resisting the introduction of CCTV in downtown areas and other public places, despite some positive evidence from Britain and elsewhere of its preventative effects (Brown, 1996; Painter and Tilley, 1999). Fears of CCTV are fuelled by stories of the inappropriate use of cameras by security officers to entertain themselves by inspecting passing women or by the inappropriate sale of video footage. These stories less frequently discuss the limitations commonly established on the deployment of CCTV or ways of supervising operators and protecting tapes to reduce the dangers of inappropriate use (for fuller discussion of possible safeguards on use of CCTV, see von Hirsch, 2000).
- The New Jersey State Senate has banned speed cameras on the grounds that these will result in impersonal policing or in raised insurance costs (resulting from the accumulation on driving licences of 'points' for speeding).
- Despite its value in deterring obscene and other unwanted calls, the introduction of Caller-ID in many states in America has been accompanied by the requirement that callers can selectively block the display of their numbers on Caller-ID devices. This puts a premium on the privacy of the caller – which was made possible only by the development of automatic telephone exchanges – at the expense of those called.

The democratic process that produces these outcomes can in time also lead to their reversal. Open discussion about the threats posed by preventive technology may lead to its greater acceptance. In some cases, such discussion may also result in modifications to the technology that lessen its harms without impeding its effectiveness. For example, in the latest technological twist, Caller-ID devices are now being marketed which reject all calls from blocked numbers. This restores some of Caller-ID's preventive benefits and gives more privacy to those called. As a further example, it does not seem unlikely that, as a result of the extensive public discussion of gun controls, the

United States will soon accept significant restrictions on the numbers and the kinds of lethal weapons in private hands.

5. Situational crime prevention leads to a regimentation of society and achieves its results by requiring law-abiding people to endure irksome and inconvenient precautions.

Many situational prevention measures are entirely unobtrusive or can even improve the quality of life. Most people are unaware of the steering column locks on their cars, while 'defensible space' ideas have helped rid public housing of tower-block designs. In some cases, however, situational prevention does result in greater regimentation and inconvenience. It can certainly be irksome to undergo the security checks now required when checking-in for airline flights. It is also inconvenient to use a PIN with one's bankcard and to remember the PIN or keep its record secret. It is particularly galling that these costs paid by everyone are due to the criminal conduct of a minority. On the other hand, baggage screening and other measures introduced in the 1970s have made terrorist bombings of airliners very rare and have largely eliminated hijackings. Similarly, without PINs, bankcards would quickly become unusable, and the conveniences of carrying around less cash and of obtaining money at any time of the day or night would be forfeited.

People generally accept the need for security, but in some cases they are subjected to inconvenience or annoyance without any compensatory benefits. Other people's car alarms sounding at night is an example of this. Nobody should have to endure this kind of cost (see Duff and Marshall, 2000). In fact, car alarms have been banned in some cities and they could be replaced by alarms that rouse only the vehicle owner. Another example of unwarranted inconvenience is provided by the procedures to prevent fraud imposed on people by insurance companies or by government bureaucracies collecting taxes and dispensing benefits. In the world of commerce, competition will help ensure that irksome and unnecessary precautions will quickly be eliminated. In state-run or public enterprises lacking competition, other avenues exist for procuring change in tiresome regulations and requirements, including elected representatives, the press, complaint lines, ombudsmen and other devices of a democratic state. The process of change may take longer, but the problem of bureaucratic roadblocks and delays is not unique to crime prevention. At worst, a higher price will be paid for security, for longer than needed, but there is no reason to be saddled with unnecessary regimentation forever.

6. Situational crime prevention promotes 'victim blaming'.

It is indefensible to blame rape on short skirts and other 'sexually provocative' conduct. Nonetheless, there is a place for giving people information about behaviours that put them at risk of crime. Hence, the popularity of guides to good crime prevention practice. For example, tourists often ask whether it is safe to use the local taxis or to walk in the streets at night. It is also useful for car owners to know, as the British Crime Survey has shown, that if they put their cars away overnight in their garages and do not leave them on the driveway, they can reduce by twenty-fold their risks of vehicle crime (Clarke and Mayhew, 1998). They can then decide whether the reduced risk is worth the effort of putting the car away.

In general, if people decide to take a known or easily knowable risk, they must bear some of the responsibility for the consequences. Where risks are taken in blatant disregard of the consequences for others, responsibility can shade into blame, as in the case of shopkeepers who refuse to alter practices – such as displays to encourage impulse purchases – that they know increase the risks of theft. Despite this, they may continue to expect the police and the courts to deal firmly with any shoplifters. Blaming and shaming them may be a way of getting these merchants to change.

Other business victims deserving their share of blame include insurance companies which skimp procedures in checking claims and thus make it easier for policy holders to commit fraud, the costs of which can be passed on through increased premiums. Some managers of rental apartment complexes fail to establish codes of conduct and consequently increase the risks of crime, not merely to their own property and persons, but to that of their other tenants (Clarke and Bichler-Robertson, 1998). Some pubs create conditions that lead to drunken fights by failing to serve alcohol in a responsible manner or by employing aggressive bouncers (Homel et al., 1997). And some convenience store owners save money, but raise their risks of robbery, by employing inexperienced and young clerks to staff their stores at night (Hunter and Jeffrey, 1997).

Blame as a tool of crime prevention can be used legitimately not just against these business victims, but also against those who produce criminogenic products. Many cities in the United States are currently engaged in suing gun manufacturers for the irresponsible overproduction of weapons, which has led to enormous criminal justice and healthcare costs. Under the Tories, the government in Britain tried to shame car manufacturers into improving vehicle security by publishing league tables of the most stolen cars (Houghton, 1992). Under New Labour, this approach is being broadened as outlined by Pease (1998) to include a wider range of criminogenic products.

'CONSERVATIVE' VALUES AND POLITICS?

It has been argued above that the harmful consequences of situational prevention are often overstated. These can often be anticipated and averted and, where this is not possible, more acceptable alternative measures can usually be found. This is particularly the case for the narrower form of situational prevention discussed here, which is specifically located within the value system of a liberal democratic society (Felson and Clarke, 1997; Seve, 1997). It is carefully targeted to specific problems, which facilitates an assessment of the costs and benefits of intervention. It is focused on criminogenic situations and not on 'criminal' people. It includes a wide repertoire of alternative ways to reduce opportunities that can be selected to minimise harmful consequences in any particular setting. Finally, its action-research methodology includes (1) pre-implementation assessments of the costs and harms of proposed measures, (2) post-implementation evaluations of the actual costs, and (3) a subsequent phase of corrective action where this is needed.

Despite all this, it seems unlikely that situational prevention will be given more than a peripheral role in official policy. This is because much informed opinion believes that the only truly effective way to reduce crime in society is by attacking its 'root causes' – discrimination, disadvantage, poor parenting, unemployment, etc. Many criminologists certainly see the mission of their discipline as being to improve society through exposing the deep-rooted causes of crime. This goal is not assisted by the thesis that crime results from choosing to take advantage of tempting opportunities. Nor does it sit well with situational prevention, which seems in danger of turning criminology into a technical discourse, more compatible with the security industry than with academia. Moreover, by delivering 'quick fixes', situational prevention diverts society's attention from the need to remedy the inequalities and discriminations thought to be at the heart of the problem.

The existing evidence of its effectiveness has therefore done little to garner support for situational prevention from substantial numbers of criminologists. Many continue to criticise its focus on the situational aspects of causation. Others are suspicious of its origins in 'administrative criminology', which they believe is aligned with conservative values and politics. They find evidence for this in situational prevention's neglect of crimes against women and of white-collar and corporate crimes. In fact, not just situational prevention, but criminology in general is focused on predatory crime, perhaps for the reasons given by the Left Realists – this kind of crime causes such direct hardship and fear to so many ordinary people. It can also be difficult to obtain data about the less familiar forms of crime. As Gilling (1997) has noted, however, the pertinent question is not what crimes *have been*, but what crimes *could* be the focus of situational prevention. The answer is that all forms of crime are open to situational prevention since all are dependent on opportunity.

Anyway, there is little evidence that situational prevention appeals to conservative values. True, there is a superficial fit between situational prevention and conservative ideas of 'small government', value for money, individual responsibility and so forth. Many conservatives might also agree that crime is a choice, but for them it is a *moral* choice not an economic or instrumental one. Consequently, conservatives generally have little sympathy for the opportunity-reducing goals of situational prevention. Instead, they regard it as a fundamentally irrelevant response to crime because it neglects the need for punishment or incapacitation of those responsible for the harms caused.

CONCLUSIONS

Despite its improved theory and its growing record of success, situational prevention still meets with indifference from many criminologists. Why should this lack of a criminological constituency matter? After all, situational prevention has already achieved a place in crime policy in Britain and elsewhere. David Garland (1996) has shown that it has been widely applied as a consequence of the devolution of crime control to local agencies and private institutions. It has been implemented by a broad range of public and private agencies and has attracted the interest of the security industry and the police. Some commentators have even described it as the fastest growing method of crime control in the world. Surely these facts demonstrate that situational prevention can prosper without the support of academic criminologists?

This argument ignores some other equally telling facts. Situational prevention and other forms of environmental crime prevention have made little headway in the United States since 'defensible space' and 'crime prevention through environmental design' (CPTED) concepts fell into disfavour at the end of the 1970s. In Britain, where situational prevention originated, it is regularly de-emphasised when a new set of politicians comes into power. In government-supported projects, it is subordinated to other preventive approaches such as multi-agency partnerships, safer city initiatives, community safety action, crime reduction strategies, and now risk management.

Situational prevention, at least in its narrower form discussed in this paper, is therefore a somewhat fragile enterprise. Without the support of criminologists, it will lack the scientific and research basis so vital to its successful application and its future development. Equally important, it will lack the kind of philosophical and ethical scrutiny that the papers of this volume have begun to provide. Absent such efforts, it could easily degenerate into a set of techniques applied without much thought, and therefore with increasing ineffectiveness and insensitivity, by agencies unacquainted with its rationale and origins. This seems already to have happened to problem-oriented policing, a closely related approach. Because so few researchers have been involved in the latter strategy's recent applications, most of the work undertaken in its name is inferior to the pioneering efforts in Newport News, Virginia (Eck and Spelman, 1988). In particular, the problem-oriented focus has often been lost in misguided efforts to combine it with underdeveloped notions of strengthening community ties and improving police-community relations (Clarke, 1998).

Situational prevention may need criminology, but there are reasons for thinking the need is reciprocal. First, situational prevention's focus on opportunity and situational variables is helping to improve criminological theorising, which has neglected these important determinants of crime. Second, its emphasis on specificity has encouraged research into particular forms of crime, which has extended the range of criminological knowledge. Third, concepts associated with situational prevention, such as crime hot spots, crime displacement, diffusion of benefits and repeat victimisation, have led to new directions in research. Fourth, situational prevention has helped to stimulate the development of newer research techniques such as victim surveys, crime audits, crime mapping and Geographical Information Systems (GIS) applications. Fifth, it provides a natural link with other disciplines, such as economics and social geography, which have an important contribution to make to criminology.

Finally, and most important, situational prevention gives criminology a direct and practical role in crime control, which substantial numbers of students entering the discipline would find attractive. Properly trained, they could enjoy absorbing and rewarding careers helping to deal with crime problems, and improving both the lives of ordinary people and the functionality of many social institutions. At the same time, they would be helping to provide a credible alternative to the extremely expensive and intrusive deterrence afforded by the criminal justice system – the centre-piece of current crime policy.

REFERENCES

Ayres, I. and Levitt, S.D. (1998) 'Measuring positive externalities from unobservable victim precaution: an empirical analysis', *Quarterly Journal of Economics*, February: 43–77.

Barr, R. and Pease, K. (1990) 'Crime placement, displacement and deflection', in M. Tonry and N. Morris (eds.), *Crime and Justice: A Review of Research* 12: 277–318, Chicago: University of Chicago Press.

Blakely, E. J. and Snyder, M.G. (1998) 'Separate places: crime and security in gated communities', in M. Felson and R. Peiser (eds.), *Reducing Crime through Real Estate Development and Management*, Washington D.C.: Urban Land Institute.

Brown, B. (1996) *CCTV in Town Centres: Three Case Studies*, Police Research Group Crime Detection and Prevention Series Paper 68, London: Home Office.

Clarke, R. V. (1995) 'Situational crime prevention', in M. Tonry and D. Farrington (eds.), *Building a Safer Society: Strategic Approaches to Crime Prevention. Crime and Justice: A Review of Research* 19: 91–150, Chicago: University of Chicago Press.

—— (ed.) (1997) *Situational Crime Prevention: Successful Case Studies.* (2nd ed.), Albany, N.Y.: Harrow and Heston.

—— (1998) 'Defining police strategies: problem-solving, problem-oriented policing and community-oriented policing', in T. O'Connor Shelley and A.C. Grant (eds.), *Problem-Oriented Policing: Crime-specific Problems, Critical Issues and Making POP Work*, Washington, DC: Police Executive Research Forum.

—— and Bichler-Robertson, G. (1998) 'Place managers, slumlords and crime in low rent apartment buildings', *Security Journal* 11: 11–19

—— and Mayhew, P. (1998) 'Preventing crime in parking lots: What we know and what we need to know', in M. Felson and R. Peiser (eds.), *Reducing Crime through Real Estate Development and Management*, Washington D.C.: Urban Land Institute.

—— and Weisburd, D. (1994) 'Diffusion of crime control benefits: observations on the reverse of displacement', in R.V. Clarke (ed.), *Crime Prevention Studies* 2: 165–183, Monsey, N.Y.: Criminal Justice Press.

Crawford, A. (1998) *Crime Prevention and Community Safety*, Harlow, UK: Addison Wesley Longman.

Duff, R.A. and Marshall, S.E. (2000) 'Benefits, burdens and responsibilities: some ethical dimensions of situational crime prevention', this volume.

Dwyer, J. (1991) *Subway Lives*, New York: Crown.

Eck, J. E. and Spelman, W. (1988) *Problem–Solving: Problem-Oriented Policing in Newport News*, Police Executive Research Forum/National Institute of Justice, Washington, DC: Police Executive Research Forum.

Ekblom, P. (1998) 'Situational crime prevention: effectiveness of local initiatives', in C.P. Nuttall, P. Goldblatt and C. Lewis (eds.), *Reducing Offending: An Assessment of Research Evidence on Ways of Dealing with Offending Behaviour*, Research Study 187, London: Home Office.

Felson, M. and R.V. Clarke. (1997) 'The ethics of situational crime prevention', in G. Newman, R. V. Clarke and S.G. Shoham (eds.), *Rational Choice and Situational Crime Prevention: Theoretical Foundations*, 197–217, Aldershot: Ashgate.

—— (1998) *Opportunity Makes the Thief: Practical Theory for Crime Prevention*, Police Research Series, Paper 98, London: Home Office.

Garland, D. (1996) 'The limits of the sovereign state: strategies of crime control in contemporary society', *British Journal of Criminology*: 36: 445–71.

Gilling, D. (1997) *Crime Prevention: Theory, Policy and Politics*, London: UCL Press.

Hesseling, R. B. P. (1994) 'Displacement: A review of the empirical literature', *Crime Prevention Studies* 3:197–230, Monsey, NY: Criminal Justice Press.

Homel, R., Hauritz, M., McIlwain, G., Wortley, R. and Carvolth, R. (1997) 'Preventing drunkenness and violence around nightclubs in a tourist resort', in R.V. Clarke (ed.), *Situational Crime Prevention: Successful Case Studies* (2nd ed.), Albany NY: Harrow and Heston.

Houghton, G. (1992) *Car Theft in England and Wales: The Home Office Car Theft Index*, Crime Prevention Unit Paper 33, London: Home Office.

Hughes, G. (1998) *Understanding Crime Prevention*, Buckingham: Open University Press.

Hunter, R. and Jeffrey, C.R. (1997), 'Preventing convenience store robbery through environmental design', in R.V. Clarke (ed.), *Situational Crime Prevention: Successful Case Studies* (2nd ed.), 194–204 Albany NY: Harrow and Heston.

Lasley, J. (1998) *Designing-Out Gang Homicides and Street Assaults*, Research in Brief, National Institute of Justice, Washington DC: US Department of Justice.

Matthews, R. (1986) *Policing Prostitution: A Multi-Agency Approach*, Centre for Criminology Paper No.1, London: Middlesex Polytechnic.

—— (1993) *Prostitution and Multi-Agency Policing*, Crime Prevention Unit Paper 43, London: Home Office.

Newman, O. (1972) *Defensible Space: Crime Prevention Through Urban Design*, New York: MacMillan.

O'Malley, P. (1997) 'The politics of crime prevention', in P. O' Malley and A. Sutton (eds.), *Crime Prevention in Australia*, Sydney: The Federation Press.

—— and A. Sutton (eds.) (1997) 'Introduction', *Crime Prevention in Australia*. Sydney: The Federation Press.

Painter, K and Farrington, D. (1997) 'The crime reducing effect of improved street lighting: the Dudley project', in R.V. Clarke (ed.), *Situational Crime Prevention: Successful Case Studies* (2nd. ed.), Albany NY: Harrow and Heston.

—— and Tilley, N. (eds.) (1999) 'Surveillance of public space: CCTV, street lighting and crime prevention', *Crime Prevention Studies*, vol. 10, Monsey, NY: Criminal Justice Press.

Pease, K. (1998) 'Changing the context of crime prevention', in C.P. Nuttall, P. Goldblatt and C. Lewis (eds.), *Reducing Offending: An Assessment Of Research Evidence On Ways Of Dealing With Offending Behaviour*, Research Study 187, London: Home Office.

Poyner, B. (1988), 'Video cameras and bus vandalism', *Journal of Security Administration* 11: 44–51

Seve, R. (1997), 'Philosophical justifications of situational crime prevention', in G. Newman, R. V. Clarke and S.G. Shoham (eds.), *Rational Choice and Situational Crime Prevention: Theoretical Foundations*, Aldershot, England: Dartmouth Publishing Company.

Sherman, L.W. *et al.* (1997), *Preventing Crime: What Works, What Doesn't, What's Promising*, Office of Justice Programs Research Report, Washington DC: US Department of Justice.

7

Situational Prevention: Social Values and Social Viewpoints

Joanna Shapland

Ronald Clarke starts his paper in this volume by indicating firmly that the heart of situational crime prevention is the claim that 'the systematic reduction of opportunities for crime would lead to substantial reductions in a society's crime rate'[1]. I entirely agree with Ron Clarke that situational crime prevention (SCP), meaning the 'systematic reduction of opportunities for crime', can have substantial effects in reducing crime in particular situations – provided, of course, that the opportunity reduction measures are properly targeted to real crime problems and reviewed regularly.

The evidence for such substantial reductions has been seen not only in North America, but in Great Britain and in Europe more widely[2]. It is obvious that if opportunities for crime are removed (such as replacing cash in gas or electricity meters with tokens) or made far less visible (locking property left in cars away out of sight), offending of that kind will decrease. If offending opportunities start being perceived as being more difficult to undertake, those offenders with less skills or less need are likely to be induced to desist. It has been argued that crime will not be reduced, but displaced. However, any idea of complete displacement presumes a perfect hydraulic model of crime – that if you squeeze at one point, exactly the same amount of crime (or in the hydraulic analogy, water) will pop out at another. Complete displacement ignores 'wastage' (leaks in changing from one offending locus to another, or one offence to another) and 'friction' (the effort in moving the crime to another point). The findings of environmental criminology – that most crime is localised to the areas where offenders live, work and undertake their leisure

---

[1] Clarke (2000), p. 97.

[2] Clarke (2000) refers to the standard reviews of such evaluations, notably Clarke (1997) and Sherman et al, (1997), but further examples can be found within the Home Office Crime Prevention Unit Papers and Reducing Crime series for England and Wales. Our own experience of such reductions is illustrated by measures taken against theft from cars and burglary in a London police division (Johnston et al, 1993).

pursuits and the areas they find familiar and feel at home[3] – tend to suggest that frictional effects will be large. Displacement, as Clarke (2000) argues, is unlikely to be anywhere near complete displacement, or even a major factor, for bulk crime.

Whether the effects of SCP techniques on crime are sufficiently large so as substantially to reduce a society's crime rate, however, depends not only on the effectiveness of SCP itself, but also very much on the extent to which the techniques are used, whether the crimes at which they are directed are volume (bulk) crimes, how well actual crime patterns are targeted, and whether initiatives are regularly reviewed and renewed to fit crime patterns as they change. The effectiveness of SCP in practice depends upon the extent to which people are prepared to use it, as well as upon its theoretical integrity and practical vigour.

In this commentary, I shall explore both the theoretical basis of SCP and its acceptability in use. Ron Clarke has set out, in his paper, a number of criticisms of SCP which he attempts to answer. One of these concerns is the potential effect of displacement. As indicated above, I would agree with him that the evidence and, indeed, the theoretical basis for displacement is that, though a real phenomenon, it is likely to be far less extensive than many have feared. The other criticisms of SCP, which he attempts to answer, however, essentially relate to societal perceptions of the likely effects of SCP and of the mechanisms which some would use in implementing SCP initiatives. Essentially, the critics say that some SCP practice and some SCP effects are normatively unacceptable. Hence, the second criticism is that SCP will reinforce (or even produce) a harsh, uncaring fortress society. The third is that SCP will result in the exclusion of people labelled 'undesirable'. The fourth is that SCP measures include CCTV, speed cameras and Caller-ID and these are a threat to civil liberties. The fifth is that SCP measures are inconvenient in use for the law-abiding. The sixth, and final, criticism is that SCP promotes 'victim blaming'.

The difficulty I have is not with the validity or otherwise of the criticisms, but that, in responding to these criticisms, Clarke has introduced balancing considerations which do not themselves flow from the original SCP theoretical considerations, but from entirely different theoretical sources. Moreover, I will suggest that these balancing mechanisms, which stem from human rights and ideas of equity, reflect the different perspectives of those involved in SCP, and that the lack of such mechanisms within SCP explains the reluctance of criminologists to take SCP into their bosoms and promote it vigorously, which Clarke bemoans. The failure of SCP by itself to provide answers to these social criticisms, more importantly, may also explain the diffidence of policy makers and of ordinary people in their everyday lives in implementing SCP

---

[3] See Bottoms and Wiles (1997) for a review of this literature, also Brantingham and Brantingham (1984).

measures to the extent that they can have a significant effect on the crime rate of a society. I shall start by discussing the theoretical basis of SCP and why I think it does not contain the social and ethical elements needed to counter the criticisms, and then turn to look at the relationship between the theory of SCP and the likelihood of its effective implementation.

DIFFERENT PERSPECTIVES ON SCP

Ron Clarke (2000) explains that SCP has come to mean many things to many people. It has been used to imply any attempt at opportunity reduction, through whatever mechanisms. He, however, focuses on a narrower definition and problem solving approach, which emphasises careful examination of the actual crime problem and selection of the appropriate technique for opportunity reduction (and, he argues in his paper, further observation of the consequences of the implementation of the techniques and preparedness to act to counter any unexpected crime-reinforcing outcomes). I am adopting this narrower viewpoint in this discussion.

Antony Duff (2000), in his paper in this volume, has provided a very clear and, to my mind, convincing, exposition of the major philosophical and ethical issues concerning SCP. I would, however, wish to suggest a further complexity. If the burdens and benefits of a particular technique for preventing or controlling crime (such as SCP) fall on different parts of society, then I think we need to examine what SCP looks like from each perspective.

Ron Clarke's perspective seems to be a 'top-down' one, though it is not problematised in his paper. He is looking down on a whole society from what seems to me the perspective of government. He looks at particular neighbourhoods from the position of an outsider, considering one neighbourhood in relation to another.

If we consider SCP from such a top-down, governmental perspective, then SCP offers the benefit of lower crime rates, and lower levels, possibly, of some government expenditure. However, government, at least in Western countries, has been trying to encourage others to bear most of the cost burden. Hence potential individual victims are exhorted through publicity campaigns and advice from official agencies (such as police crime prevention visits to householders) to purchase stronger locks and bolts and to watch out for suspicious strangers in their neighbourhood[4]. Potential corporate victims are enjoined continuously to re-evaluate their security precautions and to install security devices such as CCTV and monitored alarms. Manufacturers (as well as consumers) are being urged to improve security alarms for more valuable

---

[4] Neighbourhood Watch is perhaps the most organised form of such increased surveillance by private individuals, but television programmes (such as Crimestoppers) and moves by governments (such as the Dutch government) to restore or create the use and acceptability of guardians (doormen, concierges) in residential premises reinforce these trends.

products such as cars. If this privatisation of security expenditure occurrs and if the SCP measures are well targeted and effective, governments could reap the rewards in lower criminal justice expenditure and so SCP could result in a net benefit.

If we consider SCP now from the perspective of a gated community, then the benefits and the burdens will fall on that community's residents and landlord – and presumably they will only take on the burden of cost and restrictions if it is outweighed by the benefits of less crime. However, if we consider poor neighbourhoods near that gated community, it is clear that the burdens/benefits equation does not work to their advantage. Ron Clarke has himself, in his paper, indicated that it has been necessary in the US to take government action to prevent the affluent from protecting their cars from theft and directing thieves' attention, by implication, onto the poor. He shows on p. 102 that many municipalities in America make it a condition of police co-operation with tracking devices on cars that the cars fitted with the tracking device do not advertise this fact. Of course, such lack of advertisement probably adversely affects the SCP effectiveness of the tracking device as preventing the car being stolen initially (though its potential effectiveness as a car recovery or thief catching mechanism will remain).

My point is that SCP theory by itself does not explain how to prevent the creation of an increasingly unequal society. This must stem from the ethical standards of implementing SCP measures in a liberal democracy. Clarke (2000) refers to the general principles which Felson and Clarke (1997) have proposed to govern crime prevention policy, which include that crime prevention should be provided equally to all social strata and that responsibility for crime prevention should be shared with all sections of society. However, it is the ethical standards of liberal democracies, rather than the ethical standards of SCP, which directly prescribe these limits to crime prevention action. Another example is that of gated communities. Clarke argues that gated communities (or in UK terms traffic calming measures and town planning to create the appearance of neighbourhoods which keep strangers out) are even more effective in poorer areas. My point is that it will require differential government investment in poorer areas to institute this.

The more general conclusion from this rapid discussion is that we need to consider theories not only from what they will necessarily produce, but from the way in which they are likely to be used. It is not intrinsic to SCP that it will create displacement from the rich to the poor (an inverse Robin Hood world) or lead to fortress societies where those that have barricaded themselves from those who have not. But if one applies SCP in a democratic society with disparities of resources and offence rates between communities, then benefits and burdens will not be distributed equally either. It will require positive action from outside the communities which are suffering excess burdens (i.e. government action, from either national government or local government) to redress the exacerbating effects of pure SCP application. Any such positive government action will need to be based on principles other than utilitarianism seen from top-down. It is possible to imagine such action being based on a bottom-up form of utilitarianism, which states that action must lead to benefits outweighing burdens for each and every strata of society, or, at least, those sections of society which have fewer resources to mitigate injurious consequences. Alternatively, it might be based on equity principles stemming from human rights, which abjure the benefits/burdens equation for a more universalistic view – about the least injurious ways in which we can treat all sections of the population and all individuals.

EXCLUSION SEEN FROM COMMUNITIES

Secondly, I want to look briefly at exclusion when seen from different perspectives. From top down, one can possibly justify the amount of the overall burden of exclusion from, say, shopping malls, on the basis of the benefit it brings in reduced crime and disorder to the larger number of people happily shopping in the malls, compared to the small number of excluded persons. From a top down government view and certainly from a shopping centre management view, the burden/benefit equation may come out as positive for benefit.

But if one looks at the burden/benefit balance from the point of view of local communities near the mall, I think the balance changes. Here is this huge emporium of possible delight (as advertised) on their doorstep. But are they welcome in it? It is, as Andrew Costello's research is suggesting[5], the local young people that are being excluded. The local population gazes in envy at the shopping mall, but is barred from it and disconsonantly has to trek miles to what are proclaimed to be inferior facilities in the city centre.

Clarke (2000) argues that widespread use of exclusion is not SCP in the narrow sense at all, but involves 'order-maintenance' functions which are not part of SCP. He also says that properly targeted SCP would only lead to the use of access control for private facilities, to keep people out who have no right to be there (p. 104). There would be no point in using access control against specific groups of 'undesirables', he argues, because SCP theory would suggest that, in such public or semi-public space, anyone, not just a particular group of people, would have an equal likelihood of committing offences. Hence targeted SCP would not use exclusion as a means of crime control – though, he agrees, 'order maintenance' policing might.

However, it is contradictory to argue that targeted SCP is not suitable for public pedestrian areas, but entirely suitable for the public roads to prevent car theft (as discussed above). Moreover, an effective, targeted SCP strategy

---

[5] Ongoing PhD research. Contact Andrew Costello at the Department of Law, University of Sheffield. See also Shapland (1999a).

for semi-public space, such as shopping centres, is one which will act against the most common offences in that centre. The most common crimes, as shown by Alison Wakefield's (2000) research reported in this volume, and my own study of two shopping centres (Shapland 1999a), are shop theft and theft from and of cars – though the latter offences are not always acknowledged by management as crime linked to the shopping centre. So an effective, targeted SCP strategy might well aim at these offences. Another problem in semi-public space is minor disorder by youths – jostling others, scuffles, loud calls. Targeted action against this is surely a form of SCP, not just order maintenance by the police.

What type of SCP action would be most effective against these forms of offending? The most effective utilitarian-based SCP in terms of reducing opportunities in shopping centres is not to make the goods inaccessible (since this might stop crime, but also drive the centre out of business), but to keep offenders from goods. The most likely culprits, from centres' own statistics and police statistics, quantitatively speaking, are young people. The easiest/economically most effective technique is hence to keep out all such young people there on their own (as Shearing and Stenning (1987) and Shapland (1995a) have pointed out). Young people by themselves have low purchasing power. Targeting known offending individuals is very difficult because of the potentially large number of people visiting shopping centres and because of the large number of known offenders from some distance away – because shopping centres draw from a wide regional population (and that is necessary for their economic success). It is much easier to bar those who look wrong. Unfortunately, that is likely to be the local young people, who, in England and Wales, often come from the poorer areas next to the shopping centres — that have been built on the previously industrial, brownfield sites which originally provided the workplaces for members of poorer neighbourhoods.

Again, SCP needs limiting in its likely practical application in order to satisfy equity considerations. If we do not want profile-based exclusion, as Andrew von Hirsch and Clifford Shearing (2000) term it in their paper in this volume, then we will have to introduce equity considerations (to create rights for all social strata to shop or enter mass private space) into SCP. SCP has no equity concerns built in.

SCP SEEN FROM CRIMINOLOGISTS' VIEWPOINT

Finally, on this tour of perspectives, I want to turn to criminologists. I have argued previously that it is the ethical duty of criminologists to create an ethics of criminology (Shapland 1999b). I discussed some of the ethical implications of crime reduction and crime prevention programmes, such as the current Crime Reduction Programme of the Home Office for England and

Wales[6]. These ethical concerns can be summed up as a series of questions to those criminologists undertaking crime prevention activity. They are all premised on the idea that criminologists should not be undertaking crime prevention evaluation or crime prevention activity if they do not think the activity has a chance of reducing crime (analogous to the medical ethic which says that experimentation on human beings or animals should not be undertaken unless there is a theoretical basis or, preferably, evidence from previous work which shows that the likely benefits to the patient or animal will outweigh the disadvantages). Clearly, SCP has shown it has the potential to reduce crime if SCP activity is properly targeted and evaluated. However, I argue that there are further questions we need, as criminologists, to ask ourselves before undertaking such activity. They are:

- if we think we can reduce crime, what is likely to be the overall impact of our current crime prevention efforts? So, first, what crimes are we concentrating on and whom do they affect?
- hence, who primarily is going to benefit from those efforts and who may be affected adversely? Does this equation, given the resources of those affected adversely to cope with the consequences, suggest that the initiative will have a net positive effect?
- what kinds of pressures, controls and strains are we putting on people and neighbourhoods whose crime we are reducing, to create that reduction? Can the extent and nature of these pressures, controls and strains be justified, both absolutely, in human rights terms, and relatively, in relation to the potential crime reduction benefit?
- have we developed a suitable idea of informed consent to be given by individuals, businesses and communities who will be affected, before we intervene?

Ron Clarke laments the lack of interest from criminologists in SCP. Some of this may stem from the 'fashion' effect. SCP was originally put forward some years ago, and is clearly not the latest theoretical offering. However, given its potential effectiveness in reducing crime rates and given the increasing emphasis in governmental research spending and in government policy on evaluation and effective ways of reducing crime, longevity cannot be the main reason for its lack of popularity.

So what is the problem with SCP from the point of view of criminologists – given its attraction from a governmental, top-down perspective and hence from a research funding perspective? My provisional answer is that SCP may pose more burdens on criminologists than more fuzzy, 'making it better' crime prevention initiatives, which promise a better life for community participants

---

[6] Details of which may be found on the Home Office website, at
http://www.homeoffice.gov.uk/crimeprev/cr_index.htm

and which do not spell out clearly potential downsides. Better education and social conditions are 'motherhood and apple pie' initiatives, which often do not spell out the implications of the prioritisation of resources to certain communities on others. Of course, there are other crime reduction initiatives which do have clear (sometimes negative) effects, and which are different from SCP initiatives. Early intervention initiatives are one such example[7]. They also pose substantial ethical constraints, but different ones from SCP. They similarly have a limited band of criminological adherents. I wonder whether this is because, as a discipline, criminologists are not very good at sorting out our ethical duties and working out how to carry them out. But criminologists are becoming increasingly aware (on the back, possibly, of increasing awareness of human rights generally) that we might have such duties. Criminology, and particularly the evaluation of crime reduction initiatives, is beginning to 'grow up' as a discipline and to think about how to create the kinds of mechanisms to deliver ethical duties which are already commonplace for other professionals[8].

If criminologists can say that an initiative will make things 'better' all round for everyone, then sorting out what we mean by informed consent, making it happen in practice, feeding back evaluation results to communities and individuals (not just research funders), and all the other ethical constraints, can be seen as less necessary. But if we suspect that it won't be better for everyone concerned – if we're applying differential burdens and benefits, as I've argued – then we become uneasy.

Criminologists, like all other researchers and scholars, choose their particular aspect of their field of study for ideological and personal reasons (as well as instrumental ones). Choosing SCP means, to my mind, confronting the ethical demands of SCP. That means, I suspect, that SCP won't recruit many criminologists until it undertakes the practical work of sorting out the ethical questions, techniques and instruments criminologists need to employ to do SCP action research. As I've argued, some of those ethical considerations involve considering how questions of equity and rights may need to constrain the application of pure SCP.

---

[7] The ethical implications of early intervention crime reduction initiatives are not the same as those of SCP ones. They may include the potential stigmatisation of those children who are selected to take part in the initiative (and possible labelling effects thereafter). Efforts to combat such effects have often included relaxing selection criteria so that only volunteers or, alternatively, whole communities take part. As the community taking part widens, so such initiatives become more like the more fuzzy, 'social benefits for everyone' type of initiative (and, often, less cost effective). If volunteers only take part, then it is difficult to evaluate the initiative (because of self-selection effects) and its impact may be lessened. This tension between ethical considerations and potential theoretical effectiveness is similar to the tension with SCP measures.

[8] See, for example, the ethical codes required of clinicians, such as doctors and psychologists, in relation to informed consent, thinking about consequences, and feeding back effects.

THE DIFFICULTIES OF IMPLEMENTATION AND THE
ACCEPTABILITY OF SCP

Criminologists, like other researchers and professionals, do not operate in an ethical or societal vacuum; they are influenced by the society in which they live and work. The ethical constraints, safeguards and quandaries which they need to consider are also those which participants in SCP initiatives need to consider – at least if they are to give informed consent to such an initiative. Hence, if SCP is to be undertaken within a particular community, then that community needs to consider what the consequences of SCP action will be and how they fit within the community's ethical framework.

The difficulty in undertaking this is, I have argued, that SCP does not itself contain the ethical boundaries and constraints necessary to set acceptable limits to the choice of techniques to apply. SCP merely provides a palette of techniques, which vary in their implications for different parts of the community. It also provides tools for analysing the crime problems of the community and some indications of what technique may be most effective in which kind of community, as well as how to assess effects and consequences. The sheer range of the palette, however, is both its strength and its weakness. The strength, emphasised by Clarke (2000) is that choice allows a good fit to that community's circumstances. If CCTV is resisted on privacy grounds, then human guardians (police, civilian street patrols) or alarm-activated sound or video recording may be acceptable, without loss of surveillance potential (though the economic cost may be higher). The weakness of a full palette is the difficulty of making the choice. It may require technical skills (including professional criminological skills) to be able to work through the potential effectiveness of each option, assessing it against both past evaluation results and the current crime and community profile. Given that different parts of the community may have different benefit/burden profiles (and even different ethical views), it may be difficult to obtain agreement on the final choice – important in a democratic society.

SCP is peculiarly susceptible to these weaknesses. Particularly in its narrow form, it requires close attention to the precise crime profile of the specific area in which it is to be implemented. We know that crime profiles vary considerably from area to area, with each small neighbourhood having its own pattern of offending, attractions for offenders and community crime reputation (Bottoms and Wiles, 1997). SCP is not the kind of crime reduction initiative that can be delivered top-down in a uniform manner by government or business headquarters. Indeed, in corporate security, an initial emphasis on uniform solutions throughout the company has had to be replaced by far more responsibility being given to local managers to create crime reduction packages suitable for that outlet and the area in which it is situated (Shapland, 1995b). Environmental analyses have become of vital importance to companies planning to open a new store or new factory.

This means that SCP has to be usable for those implementing it locally. It is they who need to understand the palette and its applicability to their situation. It is also they who will need to work through the ethical implications of their chosen SCP activity. The problem is that SCP, by itself, gives them very little help in doing this. Local crime reduction decision makers are put in the same position as criminologists. Is it then surprising that localities can come to different conclusions, even conclusions that appear to be ineffective in SCP terms, as Clarke (2000) illustrates in his paper? I would argue that SCP, without an accompanying discussion of its ethics and practical guidance to answering the ethical questions it raises, is very difficult to use both for criminologists and for the governments, communities and businesses who will decide whether or not to implement it. If this is correct, then the prognosis for SCP is grave – but it is not terminal. Ethical guides can be produced, as they have been for other techniques in other areas. However, that work needs to be done before SCP will become easily usable for criminologists or communities.

REFERENCES

Bottoms, A.E. and Wiles, P. (1997) 'Environmental criminology', in M. Maguire, R. Morgan and R. Reiner (eds.), *The Oxford Handbook of Criminology*, (2nd ed.), 305-359, Oxford: Oxford University Press.

Brantingham, P.L. and Brantingham, P.J. (1984) *Patterns in Crime*, New York: Macmillan.

Clarke, R.V. (ed.) (1997) *Situational crime prevention: Successful Case Studies*, (2nd ed.), Albany, NY: Harrow and Heston.

Clarke, R.V.G. (2000) 'Situational prevention, criminology and social values', this volume.

Duff, R.A. (2000) 'Benefits, burdens and responsibilities: some ethical dimensions of situational crime prevention', this volume.

Felson, M. and Clarke, R.V. (1997) 'The ethics of situational crime prevention', in G. Newman, R.V.G. Clarke and S. Shoham (eds.), *Rational Choice and Situational Crime Prevention*, Aldershot: Dartmouth.

Johnston, V., Shapland, J. and Wiles, P. (1993) *Developing Police Crime Prevention Management And Organisational Change*, Crime Prevention Unit Paper No. 41, London: Home Office.

Shapland, J. (1995a) 'Views on crime: public and private problems', in R. Light (ed.), *Public And Private Provisions In Criminal Justice. Proceedings of the British Criminology Conference 1989*, Bristol: Bristol Centre for Criminal Justice, University of the West of England.

—— (1995b) 'Preventing retail-sector crimes', in D. Farrington and M. Tonry (eds.), *Building a Safer Society: Strategic Approaches to Crime Prevention, Crime and Justice: a Review of Research* 19: 263-342, Chicago: University of Chicago Press.

—— (1999a) 'Private worlds: social control and security in Britain' in J. Shapland and

L. van Outrive (eds.), *Police et Sécurité: Contrôle Social et Interaction Public/Privé (Policing and Security: Social Control and the Public/Private Divide)*, Paris: L'Harmattan.

—— (1999b) 'Reducing crime: implications for criminology present and criminology's futures', Paper for the 1999 British Criminology Conference, Liverpool.

Shearing, C. and Stenning, P. (eds.), (1987) *Private Policing*, Newbury Park, CA: Sage.

Sherman, L.W., Gottfredson, D., MacKenzie, D., Eck, J., Reuter, P. and Bushway, S. (1997) *Preventing Crime: What Works, What Doesn't, What's Promising*, Report to the United States Congress, Washington, D.C.: National Institute of Justice.

von Hirsch, A. and Shearing, C. (2000) 'Exclusion from public space', this volume.

Wakefield, A. (2000) 'Situational crime prevention in mass private property', this volume.

8

*Situational Crime Prevention in Mass Private Property**

Alison Wakefield

INTRODUCTION

Private security guards are now a prominent feature of British shopping centres, leisure complexes, transportation terminals and other territories of 'mass private property'[1] which form sites for public life. Their presence in mass private property' environments is indicative of the enduring appeal of situational crime prevention (SCP) to the commercial sector for securing environments and as an aid to profit-making. Few criminologists, however, have explored the functions of security guards in detail. This paper draws on case studies of three publicly-accessible territories of mass private property to discuss what security guards do within these territories and the roles they fulfil in performing these functions.

RESEARCH METHODS

My research explored the role of private security teams in a range of public settings, through case studies of three publicly-accessible commercial facilities. The first was the *Arts Plaza*[2], an arts centre in a major English city, with visual and performing arts and licensed refreshment facilities. The second was a large shopping centre situated in a northern coastal town, referred to as the *Quayside Centre*; and the third was the *City Mall*, a retail and leisure complex located in a northern urban centre, with retail outlets for daytime shopping, as well as pubs, restaurants and nightclubs.

The data collection included 20 days of observation at each site, carried out through accompanying security guards in the course of their daily routines. The observations were followed by interviews with security guards, contract

---

* In this paper I draw on findings from my doctoral research, 'The Private Policing of Public Space', currently in progress at the Institute of Criminology, University of Cambridge.
[1] A term coined by Shearing and Stenning (1981) to describe large, privately-controlled tracts of property.
[2] The names of the research sites have been changed to preserve anonymity.*f*

security managers, local police officers and managers from the three centres. Documents such as duty sheets and daily log books maintained during the course of the observation periods were also examined.

The sites were different types of leisure environment, chosen to reflect the increasing development and use by the British public in their leisure time of large, privately-owned, mixed-use centres. Today, most sectors of the population will have used facilities such as these, and together the three sites presented a range of customer groups, a range of facilities and a range of crime risks and problems.

THE FUNCTIONS OF PRIVATE SECURITY

A study of the variety of duties performed by private security guards at the three sites revealed the multi-faceted nature of their work. The objectives for policing the centres were manifested in six core functions, which may be termed 'housekeeping', 'customer care', the 'prevention of crime and 'nuisance' behaviour', 'rule enforcement and the use of sanctions', 'response to emergencies and crimes in progress' and the 'gathering and sharing of information'.

Housekeeping

The security guards at each of the centres were closely involved in their day-to-day upkeep, in order to maintain the fabric of the buildings, to ensure the centres operated safely and smoothly, and in so doing, to promote a pleasant and well-kept environment which people would be encouraged to visit. Such a function seems best described as 'housekeeping'. It was enabled by means of foot patrol and CCTV monitoring, and involved ensuring that the sites were properly maintained by identifying and reporting breakages and spillages; making sure that the legal and insurance obligations of the property owners, such as adherance to fire or health and safety regulations, were fulfilled; and carrying out ancillary duties which fell outside the natural remit of other staff members, and were assigned to the security personnel on account of their continuous presence and impression of being 'available'. These included setting up displays at the Quayside Centre, and controlling background music in all three centres.

It was evident that the housekeeping function formed a major aspect of the security guards' role. It was central to profit-making in the centres in two ways: in reducing the direct costs of high insurance premiums, fines or lawsuits associated with the poor upkeep of the buildings or damage to property; and in encouraging the custom of visitors who would be attracted by a well-maintained environment.

Customer care

A second function of the security guards at all three sites was one of customer care. This was carried out in the interests of public relations, and the guards usually acted as the first port of call for customers needing assistance. At the Arts Plaza customer care duties were afforded a particularly high priority, as visitors were regularly in need of directions around the large complex, or of information about the daily events and exhibitions. All of the guards had been required to participate in customer care training led by an external training consultant.

The account of a manager at the Quayside Centre reflected the value placed on customer care within the Centre. He reported: '. . .What they say to this potential customer of ours is either dynamite or they've put oil on . . . choppy waters, so they're very important to us'. At all three centres the security guards were often the focus for customer queries or complaints, and on a number of occasions members of the public were observed behaving in a rude or even abusive manner as they made complaints which usually related to non-security matters. The guards were required to respond with courtesy.

Information-giving was the most common reason for guards' contact with members of the public. As a patrol guard at the Quayside Centre described: 'Basically you're an information centre . . . You're dealing out everything you can think of and help [the customers] out to the best of your abilities . . .' The guards who staffed the CCTV control rooms were placed in a similar role, responding to telephone queries and, in the case of the two retail centres, using the public address system to make announcements throughout the buildings. Dealing with lost and found property was another major aspect of the customer care function.

The guards responded to an assortment of other requests, which included relaying telephone messages to customers, and stepping in to assist when staff members from other departments were unavailable (on one occasion at the Arts Plaza, for example, releasing a customer's car from the car park when the car park staff had left their post unattended). Some customer care duties were, as with many of their housekeeping duties, assigned to the guards on account of their ready presence. The guards were involved in such tasks as providing wheelchairs for disabled customers; acting as stewards for special events or exhibitions; and in the case of the Quayside Centre, even being asked to wear the padded bear costume of the Centre mascot and entertain visiting children!

At two of the centres the guards' uniforms were used to emphasise their customer care function. The uniform at the Arts Plaza consisted of blazers and slacks, whereas at the City Mall the guards conveyed a different image in police-style uniforms, including flat caps and tunics. The management at the Quayside Centre had recently changed the guards' uniforms to the more casual style, and a manager explained the reason for the change of image:

. . . The customers we were aware didn't like the official 'I'm nearly a policeman' look, so we actually changed image totally at the beginning of this year into blazers and slacks. Up until then that look was ideal because the Centre was quite wild . . . and now it's all calmed down . . . you can bring the image down into the softer look . . . people come up and talk to them quite happily when they didn't before . . .

His account showed how the two uniform styles were used for very different purposes, with the police-style uniforms seen to have a more effective deterrent impact, and the more casual uniforms used to create the impression that there was no problem of disorder within the centres, as well as portraying increased responsiveness to customers. As the crime level in the Centre fell, the priority afforded by the management to each of these objectives changed. According to a director from the security firm which supplied guards to the Quayside Centre, the lower visibility or 'soft option' uniform, as it was known in the industry, had become the standard uniform style for the 14 shopping centre security teams which were employed by the company. It seemed, therefore, that the police-style image presented by the guards at the City Mall was seen within the retail sector as old-fashioned in style.

The function of customer care was, like the housekeeping function, central to the objective of creating and maintaining a pleasant environment, but in this case the guards were required to attend to the customers directly rather than to the general upkeep of the buildings. The association of the guards with profit-making was apparent once again. Their continuous and ready presence placed them in a similar role to that of 'the bobby on the beat', and reflected an aim to capitalise on the popularity of the patrol officer with the public (see Skogan, 1996). The requirement to be responsive to customers *in the interests of encouraging their regular custom* was, however, a key difference to public policing and took the public relations aspect of this policing role a significant step further.

Prevention of crime and 'nuisance' behaviour

A third function of private security personnel was the prevention of crime and 'nuisance' behaviour. In carrying out this function the guards were placed in a different type of relationship with the customers, as they were required to prevent criminal behaviour as well as 'anti-social' behaviour seen to discourage the custom of other visitors. The prevention of crime and 'nuisance' was facilitated through the extensive surveillance of visitors, by means of foot patrol and CCTV monitoring. The CCTV systems at all three centres were powerful surveillance tools, equipped with cameras with pan, tilt and zoom facilities, colour monitors and 'multiplex' facilities allowing footage from numerous cameras to be viewed and recorded simultaneously. Foot patrol duties included target-hardening measures such as locking and unlocking areas of the centres and escorting employees who were carrying cash. The guards' surveillance capabilities were aided by shared radio systems which ensured that intelligence was readily passed on, and at the Quayside Centre a secondary system connected the control room operators with security and sales staff in the stores.

Terrorism prevention was a central aspect of the guards' responsibilities, particularly at the Arts Plaza, where abandoned vehicles or unattended baggage provoked immediate suspicion. At all of the sites the centre managers were responsive to directives from the police in relation to changing terrorism prevention policies. At the Arts Plaza, the guards also provided protection for special events when VIPs were present, or when corporations had booked areas of the Plaza for annual general meetings. On such occasions the security concerns included terrorist risks brought by certain VIP guests such as ambassadors or royalty, the potential nuisance behaviour of fans of celebrity visitors, or disruption of corporate meetings by protestors. At the Quayside Centre, late-night shopping during the Christmas period also posed potential public order problems, and extra guards were drafted in to manage these busy evenings.

The guards' surveillance practices involved monitoring the centres for potential criminal and 'nuisance' behaviour, and the types of people selected for surveillance divided into three categories: those seen to be behaving in an anti-social manner, those who fitted risk profiles, and 'known offenders'[3]. Norris and Armstrong (1999), who conducted a study of the surveillance practices of operators of local authority-controlled town centre CCTV systems, identified a number of working rules which were used by the operators for determining who and what to watch, and there is considerable overlap with their classification in the analysis presented here.

1. Anti-social behaviour

The guards at all three centres were often observed searching for and monitoring behaviour by visitors seen to pose a potential nuisance to other patrons within the centres, and in many cases it was the activities of children and young people whose actions were viewed in this way. The three centres were all used as meeting places by groups of young people, and their presence was invited by the provision of seating, the warmth, and the background music that together produced a comfortable setting and a congenial atmosphere. Each centre had come to serve as a communal gathering place for local people of all ages. At all three sites, a number of regular visitors were observed who visited the centres on a daily basis to meet with friends or sit and observe the day-to-day occurrences within, rather than purchase the goods and services on offer.

This usage of the centres by many adult visitors appeared to be accepted by the security staff and management, who in many cases had established a

---

[3] See von Hirsch (2000) for a discussion of the actual and potential uses of CCTV from an ethical perspective.

friendly rapport with the regular patrons. Shapland (1999), described this type of visitor as the 'social order welcome customer', whose quiet presence and similarity of nature to those who are likely to purchase goods were seen as complementary to the familiar and welcoming social orders of these commercial environments. In contrast, gatherings of young people were often less welcome, for reasons which included the size of the gatherings, complaints from other visitors or tenants, noise or perceived misbehaviour. Young people in groups often attracted observation immediately upon their arrival at the sites, in anticipation of future misbehaviour.

Behaviours that were generally prohibited inside the centres included actions seen as risks to the health and safety of other centre users, such as entering with a bicycle or dog; and boisterous behaviour by visitors of any age which might cause distress or irritation to other customers, including anything from 'horseplay' to various forms of drunken behaviour. Other types of 'anti-social' behaviour included in the guards' log book entries included illegal trading, urinating in a public area or begging.

The monitoring of 'nuisance' behaviour (which would normally be followed by the deployment of security personnel to ask perpetrators to desist or to leave, as described in the next section) mirrored Norris and Armstrong's (1999) observations of local authority CCTV operators, that behaviours which were themselves criminal or disorderly would unquestionably warrant surveillance, and non-criminal 'anti-social' conduct was perceived to indicate potential for breaches of the criminal law. At the case study sites, however, the guards searched for and monitored such behaviour because it was actually seen to breach the standards of behavioural conduct laid down by the management. The target populations for surveillance therefore exceeded in breadth those which traditionally concerned the public police, as Shearing and Stenning (1981) have noted.

2. Risk profiles

A second category of surveillance involved the use of risk profiles of visitors deemed *likely* to behave in a criminal (or 'anti-social') manner. Body language or behaviour considered out of the ordinary attracted attention. This approach was used to the greatest extent during the hours of retail at the City Mall, where opportunities to commit theft were great, and the security staff tended not to be familiar with 'known offenders', because of the size of the city. Profiling activities tended to fall into three sub-categories, and the first was the surveillance of persons whose behaviour or body language was perceived as suspicious. Behaviour which often invited suspicion included loitering, looking around, appearing lost, or seeming to take what was considered to be an unnatural interest in the observers themselves.

The second category involved the identification of types of person who were seen as likely to commit crime or nuisance behaviour on the basis of the guards' prior understanding of which persons were likely to be troublesome (however accurate that understanding might be). Target populations included young people, the homeless, and other groups who were seen as potentially disruptive or criminal, as a security guard at the Arts Plaza described:

> If I saw a gang of 17 or 18 year old blacks coming through, say six or seven of them walking through, not belonging to a school or, you know, obviously just off the street, then I would watch them, yeah, because you don't get many come in like that. Youths in that number not belonging to a school party or something. If I saw a lot of white skinheads walking in, obviously liquored up, I'd be watching them. Any kid under the age of 16 or 17 that isn't accompanied by adult, you look at them. Then you look at the people who are mentally retarded.

The guards' understanding of who was likely to behave in an 'anti-social' or criminal manner could, evidently, incorporate their personal prejudices against certain types of person.

A third type of risk profiling focused on persons who seemed to be out of place in relation to the area or time of day. The interviews with security guards provided some examples of such people, for example those dressed in a scruffy or casual manner at evening times when it was more usual for visitors to be dressed smartly, those who appeared at odd times of day, or those who by their race or culture were, as shown above, considered out of the ordinary for the location. These types of surveillance activity were all consistent with Norris and Armstrong's (1999) descriptions of the working procedures of CCTV operators.

3. 'Known offenders'

At all three centres, there were a number of regular visitors who were known to the security staff in virtue of their previous behaviour, and they automatically provoked observation. Norris and Armstrong (1999) also observed surveillance of this nature. This was particularly apparent at the Quayside Centre, located in a fairly isolated geographic area with a static population, where the guards were familiar with a large number of 'known offenders': up to 90 individuals who they knew by sight if not by name for their previous convictions for offences in the centre, on suspicion of prior offending, or for associating with known or alleged offenders. The majority of these persons were seen as being involved in shoplifting. They frequented the Centre on such a regular basis that the guards' surveillance activities were primarily dedicated to the observation of those known to them, as opposed to unknown individuals acting 'suspiciously'.

Decision-making by security staff about who to observe reflected the requirements of a variety of interest groups. Behaviours deemed 'anti-social' were often targeted as they were seen to threaten the congenial atmosphere which centre managers aimed to create. The perspectives of members of other staff departments or tenant companies in the centre as to what constituted a nuisance were also taken into account; as were the viewpoints of visitors to the centres, reflected in guards' responsiveness to complaints and comments presented directly to them or offered in customer feedback forms. Behavioural standards in the privately-controlled centres were thus more stringent than those applying to public spaces.

The guards also selected visitors for surveillance on the basis of knowledge or suspicion of their prior offending behaviour, or because they possessed personal or behavioural characteristics which the guards saw as potential predictors of criminal or nuisance behaviour. A danger of this type of risk management is that it is self-reinforcing, and that any misbehaviour by such persons comes to be used to justify greater scrutiny and a perception of them as 'other'. The subjective perceptions (and prejudices) of the guards influenced their choices about who to monitor, and their association with private interests rather than a requirement to act according to 'the public interest' did not place a priority on fairness in policing.

Rule Enforcement and the Use of Sanctions

Although general access to each of the centres by the public was uncontrolled, the security guards were required to enforce rules of conduct in each centre to which customers were expected to adhere. A control room operator at the Quayside Centre justified the existence of these rules on the following grounds:

> People who behave improperly, you wouldn't like them to be in your own home. If you've got standards in your own home, and somebody's behaving badly in your own home, you'd get them out and you'd chastise them, even your own kids. So basically that's what happens with the Centre, because it's somebody's home, isn't it? Somebody's business.

Guards often asked individuals or groups found to be causing a nuisance to desist from their behaviour, and if those persons refused, to leave the centres. Those seen to be seeking opportunities to offend were often asked to leave the sites immediately, particularly the 'known offenders' described earlier. The threat or use of exclusion has been grounded in English common law, which has traditionally afforded a right to owners of property to decide who may enter and remain on their land, so that they may exclude any visitor at will[4] and employ security guards to exclude persons on their behalf.

[4] Such a ruling emerged from the English Court of Appeal in 1995 in *CIN Properties Ltd* v. *Rawlins* (1995, 2 EGLR 130) in which a group of youths were permanently denied access to all the facilities in a town's major shopping centre. In the more recent case of *Porter* v. *Commissioner of Police for the Metropolis*, decided by the Court of Appeal on 20 October 1999 and as yet unreported, however, comments were made by Sedley LJ which suggested that the right of property owners arbitrarily to exclude persons from facilities of this nature may be open to

On Saturdays at the Quayside Centre the guards were often involved in enforcing behavioural rules, when groups of children and teenagers congregated in areas of the site. The favourite meeting place was a seating area outside a cluster of shops popular with the young, including a record store and clothing chain stores, and the group gathered there could number as many as 50 young people. An extra guard was employed at weekends to patrol that area of the Centre and prevent the young people from gathering in large groups, partly in response to frequent complaints from staff within the nearby stores that the young people's presence discouraged entry to the shops. The strategy adopted by the guards was to ask the young people not to congregate and to keep moving whilst in the Centre, and the extra guard remained present to prevent them regrouping in the same place. They were regularly threatened that failure to comply with these instructions would lead to their exclusion from the Centre. This was usually sufficient to gain the young people's compliance. Other behaviours which guards regularly asked visitors to desist from in the three centres included sitting in groups on the floor, riding on bannisters and playing on escalators.

The daily log books maintained by the security teams indicated the occasions on which exclusions were made, the reasons for the exclusion, and the numbers of people excluded on each occasion[5]. Figures were therefore available on the number of times that exclusions were used at each centre, as well as the total number of persons excluded in the course of these actions. During the observation periods[6] at each site, one or more people were excluded on 12 occasions at the Arts Plaza, and the total number of excludees was 34 (allowing for the multiple counting of persons repeatedly excluded). At the Quayside Centre exclusions were made on 234 occasions, and a total of 578 persons were excluded. At the City Mall exclusion was used 45 times, and the total number of excludees was 63. Table 1 indicates the reasons given for each exclusion.

successful challenge in future cases. The case was a claim for damages against the Commissioner of the Metropolitan Police for assault, battery, wrongful arrest, false imprisonment and malicious prosecution, following a request by London Electricity for the police to remove the plaintiff from the electricity showroom when she refused to leave. Sedley LJ observed: 'Both because London Electricity is a statutory undertaker providing a service essential to most people's lives, and because its shop premises, when open, constitute an invitation to the public to enter and remain there for proper purposes, it is arguable that it cannot arbitrarily or improperly exclude or expel members of the public.' The action failed, however, and Sedley's observations were technically *obiter dicta* (that is, of no binding effect).

   [5] Occasionally the security guards did not record precise numbers of people excluded at any one time. When this occurred, references to excludees in the plural were taken to mean two persons, and references to 'a number of' persons or 'a group of' persons was taken to mean three persons.

   [6] Although the observations at each site were conducted over 20 days of a five week period, exclusions logged during the full five weeks were included in the analysis.

Table 1.: Reasons for exclusion

Reason for exclusion	Arts Plaza	Quayside Centre	City Mall	Total
Named regular offender(s)	1	194		195
Drunk/drinking/vagrancy		3	33	36
Children/youths playing or loitering	3	11	2	16
Undisclosed	5	12	1	18
Associates of 'known offender'		11		11
Argumentative or threatening behaviour/fighting	2	4	2	8
Begging			4	4
Bringing a bicycle into the Centre		4		4
Bringing a dog into the Centre		3		3
Suspected of theft/attempted theft		1	1	2
Trespass on service areas			2	2
Smoking cannabis		1		1
Indecent behaviour	1			1
Total	12	244	45	301

There was clearly a vast difference between the three centres in the use of exclusion. Recorded exclusions were highest at the Quayside Centre, where so-called 'known offenders' were the main targets. In view of the geographic location of the Centre (in an isolated area with a static population), it was easy for the guards to familiarise themselves with visitors who were deemed to be persistent offenders. 194 out of the 244 exclusions were of persons known to the Centre staff, often along with their companions, who were seen to be continually seeking opportunities to steal from the stores. Most were reported to be 'banned' from the Centre, although bans tended to be invoked on a verbal basis for indefinite periods rather than by serving banning notices. One injunction had been served on a shoplifter by the management of the Quayside Centre, although the guards' accounts indicated that it had not been rigorously enforced and had since been forgotten. People who were known to keep company with 'known offenders' were often seen as guilty by association and excluded from the Centre, and as shown in Table 1, 11 of the exclusions were made on these grounds.

Most of these persons were asked to leave so frequently that a routine had emerged whereby the guards followed them and they would usually depart immediately (often then entering the Centre by another door). Even if no words were exchanged (as was usually the case), these instances were logged as exclusions by the security guards. The offenders referred to by name in the log book numbered 41, and they accounted for 207 of the 578 persons excluded from the Quayside Centre (again, allowing for the multiple counting

Table 2: Individuals[7] excluded most frequently from the Quayside Centre

Name of 'known offender'	Exclusions during one month
1. Andrew Piggott	35
2. Simon Turner	21
3. James Foreman	12
4. Gillian McGyver	11
5. Darren Jensen	10
6. Jason Davies	10
7. Carol Hanson	10
8. Graham, David and Louis Dawson*	24
Total	133

* Log book data often failed to distinguish between these three brothers, referring only to their surname.

of individuals repeatedly excluded). A large proportion of the remaining 371 persons were associates of the 'known offenders' who were excluded simultaneously. Table 2 shows the frequency of recorded exclusions of the small group of 'known offenders' excluded most regularly. These eleven individuals accounted for a quarter of the 578 exclusions, and the most frequently excluded person was excluded once a day on average.

The other forms of exclusion tended to be temporary in nature, so that the 'offenders' were able to return on subsequent days. The second most common category of exclusion, as shown in Table 1 and which was most prevalent at the City Mall, included people found to be drinking alcohol in public, those who were excessively drunk and some homeless people or alcoholics. It was impossible to differentiate between these three types of behaviour where they were recorded in the log books due to a lack of systematic distinction between them in the guards' recording practices, with the terms 'dosser', 'drunk', 'drinker' or 'vagrant' used interchangeably. This suggested that in some cases people were being excluded simply for their unkempt appearance. Homeless people and alcoholics often frequented the Mall, which housed the only off-licence in the locality, and the manager considered the prevalence of alcoholics in the area to be a particular problem. The guards were regularly required to challenge homeless people or people drinking alcohol inside the Mall and to exclude them from the premises, and thus their daily routines tended to include more direct confrontation of visitors than was apparent at the other two sites. The police-style uniforms which they were required to wear reflected this authoritarian role.

The third largest category of recorded exclusions, as shown in Table 1, was that of groups of children or teenagers seen to be causing a nuisance. This was particularly the case at the Arts Plaza. Other reasons for exclusion which were

[7] The names have been changed to preserve anonymity.

provided in the security guards' own accounts included rowdiness, abusiveness to other members of the public, spitting, gathering in large groups, drunkeness, soliciting and behaving indecently (which had occurred for a period in the toilets provided for visitors to the Arts Plaza), and on occasions, environmental protest.

A formal banning letter had been served in only one case around the time of the research period, by the manager at the Arts Plaza in charge of security matters. The recipients of the three-month ban were three teenagers who had threatened members of a visiting school party with a knife. The school authorities did not wish to press charges, yet the Plaza management were able to use the ban as an alternative sanction when they were precluded from recourse to the criminal law.

Exclusion and banning policies varied between the three centres, as did the decision-making processes about who to exclude or ban. At the Arts Plaza exclusion decisions were made by the security manager, senior contract security staff, and the house managers whose role was to manage the site during its hours of opening, while decisions to ban any individuals from the Plaza were made by the security manager. The guards reported that they initiated exclusions themselves only when the individuals had been excluded before on the authority of senior staff. There was no consistent policy in place at the Arts Plaza concerning the exclusion of children or homeless people, as the seven house managers worked in rotation and operated their own policies. At the Quayside Centre and City Mall the guards were afforded greater autonomy and made decisions themselves as to the types of behaviour which were deserving of exclusion, except on occasions when they were acting on a manager's behalf. At the Quayside Centre banning decisions were made by the centre manager or on-site manager of the contract security team; but formal bans were not used at the City Mall as the manager felt that they were impractical and overly confrontational, partly because he did not feel that he could rely on the local police to provide back-up when necessary.

In sum, it was evident that the rights of property facilitated rule enforcement within the centres more extensive than that usually applicable to public spaces. The use or threat of exclusion could be used both to pre-empt offending by visitors who, on account of their prior behaviour, were seen to be seeking opportunities to offend (in contrast with public policing, which is generally based on responding to misdemeanors which have already occurred or are in progress); and to curb non-criminal behaviours seen as anti-social (such as gathering in groups or drinking alcohol in public).

Response to emergencies and crimes in progress

At all of the sites the guards were required to respond to various emergencies. Crime-related and other incidents were identified by means of surveillance by the security staff or through reports from visitors, other centre employees or staff from the tenant companies.

During the observation periods the non-crime incidents at the three centres included four (false) fire alarms, a small fire, a number of water leaks and the rescue of a man trapped in a stairwell. The guards at each centre also frequently administered first aid to patrons taken ill on the premises, or called for an ambulance in more serious cases. Many of the guards had been sent on first aid courses and held basic first aid qualifications. At the Arts Plaza there was a paramedic on duty at all times during opening hours, but the guards sometimes gave support by communicating with the emergency services or clearing the area of people. The guards at the other centres were called upon to administer first aid more frequently, particularly at the Quayside Centre when fourteen incidents of illness were recorded during the observation period.

As reported above, the threat of terrorism at the Arts Plaza was a particular concern to the security staff. During the observation period at the Arts Plaza five abandoned bags or packages provoked concern. The guards described how, at a time when the terrorist threat from the IRA was at its peak, they had used mirrors to check underneath vehicles for explosives, and they still used vapour detecting equipment occasionally on the discovery of abandoned baggage or suspicious packages. In each of the five cases, however, the owners returned to their items before further action was taken.

At the Quayside Centre a considerable proportion of the guards' time during busy periods was spent responding to reports from retailers and retail security staff of shoplifting in their stores. The Centre was a particularly attractive target for shoplifters because most of the high street brands operating within the town had located their stores within the Centre rather than the retail premises in the nearby public streets. The retailers' radio network ensured that suspicions were readily passed on to the control room operators, who often deployed the Centre security staff to assist the retailers.

It was impossible to estimate the number of thefts which occurred in the centres because the retailers did not record or report thefts systematically. Incidents of retail theft usually came to the attention of the security staff only when the retailers called for assistance. During the observation periods at the three sites, the daily log books documented six incidents of theft at the Arts Plaza, four at the City Mall, and 28 at the Quayside Centre. Fourteen of the shoplifters involved in the incidents at the Quayside Centre were known by name to the security staff, many of whom were excluded immediately if seen within the Centre. Three of the shoplifters were juveniles who were not known to have offended previously, and the names of the other shoplifters at the two shopping centres were unknown. Where possible the offenders were apprehended pending the arrival of the police, although in nine cases the offenders escaped or were not seen.

The guards at the three centres were also required to respond to public order problems, which were sometimes alcohol-related. 14 of the incidents recorded during the observation periods involved threatening behaviour or fighting. This occurred with particular frequency at the Quayside Centre where ten such incidents took place. At the City Mall, however, the public order problems were often more serious, involving larger groups of people, often under the influence of alcohol, visiting the pubs or nightclubs. Potential for conflict regularly arose as visitors were denied access to the nightclubs, or were ejected for their behaviour inside. Other recorded incidents during the month included drunk and disorderly behaviour, criminal damage, and a suspected burglary in progress at the City Mall.

The guards' response to crimes in progress placed them in frequent contact with the police. They often drew on the police for assistance with public order problems, or to hand over persons they had arrested. During the observation periods, one offender was arrested at the Arts Plaza for drunk and disorderly behaviour, 13 arrests for retail theft were made at the Quayside Centre, there were 11 arrests for theft or fighting at the City Mall.

At the Quayside Centre, the security team sometimes provided back-up to the police when they arrested offenders, on request from the local home beat officer with whom they had established a close working relationship. This usually occurred in relation to dealing with a shoplifter or a person charged with theft from the Centre who was wanted for failing to appear at court or sign in at the police station on bail. The home beat officer reported:

> I know in the past if I've ever been in sticky situations they've always been there . . . and that, that really is my first call for back-up. If I was to call for [police] assistance from [the Quayside Centre], I could wait 10 minutes, 15 minutes. The other day I was asking for a marked vehicle to come down [and] it took 50 minutes . . .

The guards at all three sites aided the police by reporting incidents beyond the boundaries of the centres which they discovered through perimeter patrols or CCTV surveillance. They were not observed becoming directly involved in such incidents, although they occasionally fulfilled an auxiliary role, as indicated in the following extract from the observations documented at the Quayside Centre:

> As Warren and I passed gate four on our patrol of the centre, we witnessed an altercation beginning outside the Centre by the bank. Two male street traders were selling . . . flags outside the bank in advance of the forthcoming cup final. Two men tried to snatch the flags from them and a fight ensued. Warren immediately radioed a request to the control room to contact the police. The police arrived quickly and broke up the fight, and the two street traders joined Warren and me inside the Centre while the police dealt with the aggressors outside. The traders reported that the two aggressors were drunk and had tried to seize the flags to sell themselves. After sending the aggressors away in a police van, two police officers entered the Centre to ask the men if they wished to press charges. (17 April 1998)

Occasionally the guards were notified by the police about serious incidents in the locality, and on one occasion in which a man armed with a knife who had threatened a shop worker was reported to be in the town centre, it was a guard from the Quayside Centre whose actions led to the detention of the man:

> . . . We was contacted by the control room . . . 'Look out for this guy. If you see him, notify control' . . . and this guy was, sort of, what, 15, 20 foot in front of me. And I radioed through. I knew he was armed. Didn't really think much of it. Kept him talking. Till the police arrived and I was assisted by my supervisor. Basically we got him out the Centre as quick as we could.

The guards' function of responding to emergencies in the centres mirrored the role of the police in providing an emergency service within the territories they control, although the security guards dealt with a wider range of non-crime emergencies. While many of the problems they responded to were incidents of crime or potential terrorist threats, others related to the health and safety of customers or the upkeep of the buildings so were more closely linked to their functions of housekeeping and customer care. The security staff were able to carry out this emergency service role very effectively due to their surveillance capabilities.

The gathering and sharing of information

The sixth function of the security guards may be described as the gathering and sharing of information, and these practices took several forms: CCTV monitoring, form-filling, participating in security networks, engaging in informal liaison with the police and providing information to police investigations. These are described in more detail below.

1. *CCTV monitoring*

The continuous twenty-four hour recording of CCTV footage was a form of information-gathering, providing a record of events in the centres which could be drawn on for evidence on a later occasion. Von Hirsch's (2000) paper in this volume notes that the systems are able to record the activity of anyone present in the location, whether or not they have violated the behavioural standards prevailing there. When behaviour regarded as a nuisance, as criminal or as suspicious was observed, images were documented in stills taken from the CCTV systems or in live recordings. 'Rogues' galleries' showing images of persons regarded as suspicious or criminal were maintained privately at the two shopping centres, and pictures of recent wrongdoers were often displayed on security noticeboards for particular attention. Live recordings were saved and tapes reviewed for evidence if it was known that offences had occurred. At the Arts Plaza, for example, the security staff were seen to review videotapes following incidents such as the theft of a laptop, and a driver's breakout from the car park without paying.

2. Form-filling

Security staff at the centres were required to document daily events using an assortment of forms. These forms were required to satisfy the bureaucratic requirements of their clients, their security companies, and sometimes the police, so that information about incidents was readily available as evidence if needed, or in case officers were challenged in the future about their actions in dealing with an incident. This included the completion of pocket note books, log books, accident registers, record books for the signing in and out of keys, lost and found property forms, incident reports and police statements.

3. *Security networks within the centres*

At the two shopping centres where retail security staff operated in parallel with the centre guards, the two groups frequently engaged in information-sharing concerning shoplifting, even though the centre guards were employed to police the common areas of the centres and not the stores. At the Quayside Centre the dual radio system allowed continuous communication between the two groups via the control room operators. In addition, monthly meetings were held at the Centre between representatives from the participating stores, the manager of the Centre security team and the police, providing a forum for the exchange of information and circulation of CCTV stills. Information was provided by the police about alleged shoplifters whose bail conditions excluded them from the centre, and persons wanted on warrants for failing to appear at court.

4. *Informal liaison with the police*

While the retailers' security network at the Quayside Centre had been instigated by the retailers themselves, during the observation period at the City Mall the local police contacted the manager to seek his involvement in an inter-agency scheme they were hoping to set up. It was to involve the establishment of radio communication between the police and security staff in shopping centres and stores throughout the city, as well as the targeting of 20 persistent shoplifters, and participants were to receive copies of 20 police photographs of the offenders and their accompanying personal details. The proposed scheme was a police response to the requirements in the Crime and Disorder Act 1998 for community safety partnerships, and therefore reflected a potential new role for private security in formal partnership with the police[8].

Police visits to the research sites in the course of patrols provided further opportunities for information exchange, whether carried out on an informal, social basis or in relation to specific incidents. Neighbourhood beat officers

---

[8] The Act also permits the police and local authorities to share information previously restricted under the Data Protection Act 1984, as amended by the Data Protection Act 1998, with other agencies in community safety partnerships, and this legislation allowed for the proposed circulation of police photographs. It states that personal data processed for the prevention or detection of crime, and/or the apprehension or prosecution of offenders, may now be exchanged in the course of partnership work associated with the Act's requirements.

called periodically at the Arts Plaza and the Quayside Centre, and at all three sites divisional patrol officers occasionally visited for informal discussion or in connection with an offence that had occurred. Security staff at the centres were themselves a useful source of information for the police, regularly reporting incidents which they observed occurring outside the centres, and providing information gained through their day-to-day patrols:

> . . . They do get to know the [regulars] who come and hang around there. They do get onto them, they do know who they are . . . If they've got a group of kids in there that they've stopped and maybe talked to – yeah, they do act like police officers in there, they do stop kids, and at this moment in time the kids do give their names and addresses over to them which is quite good. (Police officer, Arts Plaza)

> I've got a lot of information and intelligence and also . . . some good friends from the town centre. But anyway it helps now because, certainly at least on a weekly basis, I liaise with somebody from that centre. And because they're there day-in, day-out, [they] see a lot of our regular shoplifters that are usually involved with drugs and burglaries and things as well, they can pass on quite a lot on information and names that, you know, we just haven't got the time to get, really, so . . . It's a good source of information . . . (Police officer, Quayside Centre)

At the Quayside Centre, the local home beat officer made regular use of the security staff and control room operators by passing on details of people who were wanted for failing to sign in at the police station whilst on bail or failing to appear at court,[9] and found their assistance to be extremely valuable:

> Every day that I work in there, I always go in and I see them. After all, they are my eyes and ears. My success in there is down to them. My arrest rate in there is, I should say, mostly down to them. I've got a good rapport with them, I've got a good rapport with the people in the CCTV room. They know how they can get in touch with me immediately . . . And they ring up and they've got the list of people that I'm interested in, which was the case the other day, 'So-and-so's in.' 'Fine, where is he?' 'He's at such-and-such at the minute.' My radio is tuned into one of their radio channels, and they can more or less talk me to where they are.

The police also made occasional use of the surveillance capabilities of the Quayside Centre security by passing on information about more serious incidents with which the security staff were in a position to offer assistance. As mentioned in the previous section, in one case the police had notified the control room operators at the Centre that an armed man was at large in the area, and the security guards responded by looking out for him, identifying him and reporting his presence to the police.

[9] Other disclosures of information by the police to non-police agencies were already permitted in the data protection legislation, for the purpose of the prevention and detection of crime, or the apprehension of offenders, in circumstances where failure to disclose would be likely to prejudice those objectives. It is questionable whether the circulation of this information could be justified on the grounds that failure to disclose would be likely to prejudice those objectives.

5. Providing information to police investigations

The guards at the three centres were occasionally called upon to assist in police investigations, and this was found to occur most frequently at the City Mall, located in a busy urban area. During the observation period the Mall guards were able to assist the police in an investigation of the rape one afternoon of a female shopper, identifying him from police descriptions as a regular visitor to the Mall, and notifying the police when he appeared in the Mall two days after the incident. A second example was provided by the control room operators at the Quayside Centre, who described an occasion when they gathered information to aid an ongoing police investigation, as reported in this extract from the observation notes:

> Carl described how the control room operators had assisted the local criminal investigation department (CID) in connection with their observations of a local drug dealer. This occurred from Sept 1995 to Jan/Feb 1996 when a convicted drug dealer was thought to be dealing from the food court in the Centre, using associates to deliver the drugs but sitting there apparently taking orders on his mobile phone. The food court staff were instructed to bring everything from his table into the control room, and they were able to collect slips of paper with phone numbers scrawled on them. They reported that eventually he had been arrested and received a four and a half year sentence. (18 April 1998)

More frequently the guards' assistance in police investigations involved supplying CCTV footage or reviewing videotapes themselves for evidence. During the period of research at the City Mall, a boy was raped in the toilets of a department store on the other side of the city centre. A suspect was identified in footage recorded within the shopping centre in which the store was located, and a police officer brought a copy of the videotape into the City Mall so that the security team could reproduce images of the suspect. Following this, the guards began looking back through CCTV footage recorded on the day of the offence, in case the attacker had travelled through the Mall at any time[10]. CCTV footage from the Mall was instrumental in the indentification of a suspect in solving a third rape case, which occurred after a woman was dragged down a side street by a man whom she had met in one of the nightclubs in the Mall. The alleged offender was arrested by police following the publication in the media of CCTV images from a videotape obtained from the City Mall.

The security guards' function of gathering and sharing information considerably widened their role in policing. Their collaboration with retailers against shoplifters was supplementary to their core role of policing the main communal areas of the centres, but it greatly extended their general control

---

[10] In fact the original footage from the other shopping centre was instrumental in the arrest of the alleged perpetrator when it was shown in the local news.

of the territories. Through co-operation with the police they contributed to local policing beyond the territorial boundaries of the centres, and therefore formed a part of wider policing networks. In the gathering and sharing of information the guards gave assistance to the police far more than they received such assistance from them, although police support was reciprocated in many of the emergency situations described in the previous section. Information was shared with the police through day-to-day communication as well as the lending of CCTV footage, and at the Quayside Centre the police regularly furnished the security staff in the centre with information on local offenders, mobilising the support of the guards to extend their own surveillance capabilities.

The guards' 'unremitting watch' of the territories they controlled, as well as the area immediately beyond the boundaries of the centres, meant that they were a rich source of information about the areas and those who visited. They were able to aid the police in many ways, and therefore formed an inportant role in local policing networks.

DISCUSSION

Through the privatisation of urban space, many areas that are privately-controlled now serve as sites for public life. The arts centre, shopping centre and retail and leisure complex described in this paper are examples of this contemporary phenomenon.

The private security guards in each of the centres maintained extensive territorial controls, with their continuous and ready presence having similarities in role to that of a warden or caretaker, as well as to that of 'the bobby on the beat'. Through their 'unremitting watch' of the centres, the guards could carry out considerable supervision of the territories they policed. They were able to identify and deal with criminal and 'nuisance' behaviour, and to monitor closely visitors viewed as a potential threat by nature of their personal characteristics or prior misbehaviour in the centres. Exclusion strategies were used when recourse to the criminal law was not available or, in their view, not appropriate. Visitors could be asked to desist from behaviour seen as a nuisance, with exclusion from the centre available as a sanction, and sometimes invoked if they refused to comply. The types of behaviour for which persons were excluded included drunkenness, vagrancy, rowdiness or horseplay, begging, fighting or arguing loudly, and entering with a bicycle or dog. Young people and vagrants were the main subjects of exclusions for behaviour deemed anti-social. In addition, at the Quayside Centre those who were known to have offended previously were regularly excluded in order to restrict their opportunities to reoffend, and the use of exclusion here far exceeded that at the other two centres.

The policies of exclusion in the centres fell short of discouraging poor consumers to use the centres. Most of the non-criminal behaviours for which visitors were excluded were at least somewhat disruptive in nature, although the exclusion of vagrants raises ethical problems[11]. By driving these behaviours from the centres and displacing them outside, however, the centre authorities were to a certain extent choosing their visitors and leaving the outside world to deal with the social problems that non-conformers sometimes displayed.

The exclusion of potential offenders (as the so-called 'known offenders' at the Quayside Centre were perceived) raises further cause for concern as it is based on predictions of future offending. The danger is that through this form of policing, individuals may be prevented from using important communal spaces in their localities (see von Hirsch and Shearing, 2000). The centres in the study were able to gain commercially from their status as sites for public life, yet to impose controls so that not everyone was welcome.

The relationship of the guards with the local police at all three centres showed evidence of an increasingly collaborative approach, involving them in the policing of the wider areas in which the centres were located. The informal liaison practices between the security teams and the police showed evidence of shared goals, although strategies for dealing jointly with the social problems of homelessness or disaffected youth, for example, were noticeably absent in the collaborations between the two sectors.

The use of security guards appeared to be effective in the maintenance of order in the facilities described here, and for the most part, the guards policed the centres in a manner which was low key and helped to promote a pleasant environment. Its association with private interests, however, gave priority to the exclusion of 'undesirables' over the accessibility to all and the inclusionary character of public spaces. For privately-controlled territories to operate as sites for public life, there is a need to strike a balance in the controls that are adopted, so that they may serve their local communities effectively as truly communal spaces.

REFERENCES

Clarke, R.V. (2000) 'Situational crime prevention, criminology and social values', this volume.

Norris, C. and Armstrong, G. (1999) *The Maximum Surveillance Society: The Rise of CCTV*, Oxford: Berg.

---

[11] See von Hirsch and Shearing (2000) for a more detailed discussion of the ethics of exclusion from public space.

Radzinowicz. L. (1968) *A History of English Criminal Law and its Administration from 1750, Vol.4: Grappling for Control*, London: Stevens and Sons.

Shapland, J. (1999) 'Selling safety: policing and social control over the public-private divide', in J. Shapland and L. van Outrive (eds.), *Police et Sécurité: Contrôle Social et l'Interaction Publique-Privé* (Policing and Security: Social Control and the Public-Private Divide), Paris: L'Harmattan.

Shearing, C. and Stenning, P. (1981) 'Modern private security: its growth and implications', in M. Tonry and N. Morris (eds.), *Crime and Justice: An Annual Review of Research* 3, Chicago: University of Chicago Press, 193–245.

Skogan, W. (1996) 'Public opinion and the police', in W. Saulsbury, J. Mott and Newburn, T. (eds.), *Themes in Contemporary Policing*, London: Police Foundation/Policy Studies Institute.

von Hirsch, A. (2000) 'The ethics of public television surveillance', this volume.

—— and Shearing, C. (2000) 'Exclusion from public space', this volume.

9

Changing Situations and Changing People

David J. Smith

In his first full account of situational crime prevention (SCP), Ron Clarke (1982) started by making the distinction between the offender's long-term 'dispositions' and features of the immediate situation that make offending more or less likely. He wrote that most current criminological theories:

> ...are seeking to explain why some individuals or groups are born with, or come to acquire, a 'disposition' to offend. The explanation may be sought in genetic differences of physiological functioning (e.g. slow autonomic[1] reactivity and low cortical arousal), in psychological factors of personality and upbringing (e.g. faulty conditioning of extroverted neurotics), or in sociological influences (e.g. 'anomie', 'subcultural', and 'labelling' theories). Whatever the source of criminal dispositions, they are presumed to express themselves over a diverse range of conditions and circumstances. This being so, there is little to be gained by action that reduces opportunities for crime only at particular times and places. The mainstream of criminological thought would therefore prescribe measures that attempt to prevent the disposition from developing in the first place, or, once developed, to eradicate it or compensate for it (Clarke, 1982: 228).

SCP was presented as a reaction against these mainstream 'dispositional' theories. There had to be a motivated offender, but in most cases the motivations would be the ordinary needs and desires shared by the rest of humanity. Offending was not the expression of a special or persisting underlying urge or disposition. Instead, a crime was the outcome of a choice between a constellation of competing risks and rewards, and firmly rooted in a particular, concrete situation. Hence, SCP emphasised specific situations, as opposed to the stable dispositions of individuals, as the interesting determinants of whether a criminal act would occur. In starting, thus, from an apparently simple contrast, and in shifting the spotlight from one pole of this contrast to the other, SCP proceeds like much other criminological theorising. However, my purpose in this article is to show that theory can progress only by going beyond such simple contrasts, and by exploring the links between these apparently opposed terms.

---

[1] The word printed in the original is 'automatic', but presumably 'autonomic' was meant.

A person does not, of course, exist in the abstract, withdrawn from the world. An organism can only become a person by interacting with others in immediate, concrete situations. At the same time, a bundle of contingencies only becomes a situation when some person perceives and assesses the facts and acts in the light of them. Persons come into existence through acting and being acted upon in situations, and situations arise out of interactions between persons. So persons are partly constituted by situations, and situations by persons.

Given that persons and situations are closely inter-dependent, it is unlikely that theory can advance by shifting the spotlight from one to the other. The central problem, instead, must be to understand how persons and situations mutually influence one another. If that is accepted, then it turns out that SCP is not radical enough. Certainly the particular, concrete situation has an important influence on whether a specific crime will occur. But the influence of situations extends beyond the patch of space and time that they occupy, because persons are shaped by the situations through which they move. There are, of course, personal characteristics (skills, habits, knowledge, ways of perceiving the social world, moral codes) that have an important influence on how people behave, and these are influenced by the individual's lifetime of experiences in a multitude of situations. By manipulating these situations, therefore, it should be possible not only to influence the immediate opportunities for crime, but also to change longer-lasting propensities to conform or deviate.

Driving on the motorway can be used to illustrate the interplay between propensities and situations. The skills, habits, and aggressiveness of the driver have a strong influence on whether the car will crash. Equally, the driver's habits and expectations will be strongly influenced by experiences on the road. Those whose entire driving experience has been in Weston-super-Mare will negotiate the streets of Cairo very differently from a local taxi driver. It is plausible that the introduction of new road design and traffic management measures in Cairo would eventually change the expectations and habits of Egyptian drivers. Equally, Egyptian drivers on coming to Sweden soon learn that in Stockholm it is not customary to drive straight through a red traffic light.

A central task for criminology is to find out how expectations, habits, social controls, and self-controls are influenced beyond the immediate moment by the situations that people encounter. At present, discussion of the topic has to be largely speculative, because most of the relevant research has not yet been done. The most appropriate theoretical perspective for such a discussion is the social cognitive theory of Albert Bandura. Before spelling out this argument in more detail, and speculating on the longer-term effects of situations, it will be helpful to reflect on the origins of SCP, which led to the narrow focus on the immediate effects of situations.

Besides the contrast between propensities and situations, SCP has been developed, substantiated, and justified by reference to further pairs of contrasting concepts, for example: crime events versus criminality; causal explanation versus choice; policy analysis versus understanding causes; changing people versus preventing crime; shaping morals versus reducing opportunity; treating potential offenders versus manipulating the risks and rewards of crime. Although these contrasts have been rhetorically effective, they obstruct analysis and limit our vision. Instead of oscillating between each pair of terms, criminological theory needs to reach beyond the apparent opposition between them. Just as situations and persons are inter-dependent, not opposed, so SCP exists in a symbiotic relationship with law enforcement, criminal justice, and punishment. A more integrated criminological theory re-emphasises the importance of SCP. Instead of a technical fix, which operates mechanistically on depersonalised situations, SCP emerges as a potential method of moralising individuals and society. The most challenging problem is to understand what are the conditions in which SCP can have a moralising or alternatively a demoralising effect.

BEYOND CONVENTIONAL CONTRASTS

In his book *Thinking About Crime*, J.Q. Wilson (1975) developed an argument about how to tackle crime that was built on apparently simple contrasts. He judged that criminologists such as Sheldon and Eleanor Glueck (1950), Walter B. Miller (1958), and Albert K. Cohen (1955) had developed plausible accounts of the causes of delinquency, which they located in family conditions, such as instability and conflict, lack of affection, and harsh or inconsistent discipline, in working class values of toughness, smartness, and masculinity, and in a striving to achieve a form of status and success through repudiating middle class values. But he argued that these explanations of the causes of delinquent behaviour provided no basis for choosing policies to reduce crime. That was because the 'root causes' of crime are beyond the reach of any arm of public policy. It is easy to see that happy families tend not to produce criminals. It is hard to see how public policy can decree that family relationships be constructive and positive. Quoting McCord and McCord (1959) on family factors as the causes of delinquency, he elaborated: 'They are quite possibly correct; indeed, if I may speak on the basis of my own wholly unscientific observation, I am quite confident they are correct. But what of it? What agency do we create, what budget do we allocate that will supply the missing 'parental affection' and restore to the child consistent discipline supported by a stable and loving family?' (Wilson, 1975: 52).

He expanded on this contrast between causes and remedies by developing a metaphysical account of different causal categories that is reminiscent of St Thomas Aquinas. He distinguished between ultimate causes ('those factors that are not themselves caused') and intervening variables (which are caused by other factors). An explanation in terms of intervening variables would be unsatisfactory, and would not be a causal explanation. Sociologists are therefore concerned with ultimate causes: 'But ultimate causes cannot be the object of policy efforts precisely because, being ultimate, they cannot be changed' (ibid.46). On this model, sociologists or criminologists are concerned with the uncaused cause, the first cause (God in Thomist philosophy), whereas policy analysts have a purely pragmatic concern with what can be done to reduce crime. In deciding what can be done, it is more important to study what is pragmatic – what it is possible for state and private institutions to do – than to understand the causes of criminal conduct.

Wilson's robust pragmatism[2], and his contrast between causal explanation and policy prescription, were one of the influences on the early development of SCP, as can be seen, for example, from Clarke's references (1982: 228; 1995: 104) to Wilson's aphorism about making parents love their children. Wilson developed a number of further contrasts, which were also influential. The most important of these was the contrast between the view that there are causes of criminality, which determine that the criminal acts the way he does, and the model of the potential criminal as someone making choices, who is influenced by the likelihood of being caught, and by the severity of prospective punishment. Having set up this apparent contrast, which is an interpretation of the historic debate between classicism and positivism, Wilson was driven to advocate a rational choice perspective, again for entirely pragmatic reasons. If criminal acts are to be explained by the causes of criminal dispositions, then the remedy must be some form of treatment to reform those dispositions; but Wilson argued on the basis of the evidence then available, just a year after the publication of Martinson's (1974) famous article, that treatment does not work. It is necessary instead to manipulate punishments and rewards, 'because the only instruments society has by which to alter behavior in the short run require it to assume that people act in response to the costs and benefits of alternative courses of action' (Wilson, 1975: 56).

Table 1 sets out in a schematic form the related sets of contrasts on which Wilson's argument and later, SCP, were built. It would be too neat to represent them as contrasts between exactly opposing terms, although there are a few neat oppositions of this kind (such as criminality versus crime, or treatment versus punishment). Instead, the table illustrates three broad contrasts by listing distinct but overlapping terms. The first group contrasts backward-looking causal explanations (which appear to deny human choice) with forward-looking decisions by free individuals, and also with forward-looking analysis of policy options and remedies. Of course, there are two distinct oppositions here, with causal explanation on one side, and on the other side either individual choice, or choice of policy. However, Wilson did present

---

[2] I have taken the phrase 'robust pragmatism' from David Garland, who used it in commenting on a paper by J.Q. Wilson at the first Scottish Criminology Conference in Edinburgh, 1996.

Table 1: Three related sets of contrasting terms

(a) Terms related to positivism	(b) Contrasting terms related to classicism
1(a) causes and explanations causes (sometimes 'root' causes) explanation causal explanation causally determined	*1(b) choice and policy prescription* choice autonomy policy analysis policy prescription, remedies
2(a) changing people treatment reform rehabilitation	*2(b) manipulating choices* punishment rewards risks
3(a) dispositions or propensities criminality morals attitudes	*3(b) events and situations* crime events situations

these two contrasts as closely linked with one another. On his view, forward-looking policy prescriptions are about influencing the forward-looking choices of individuals, and neither has anything to do with understanding the past causes of conduct.

The second group of terms opposes changing people (by means of treatment or reform programmes) with manipulating punishment, risks, and rewards, so as to influence the choices they freely make. The third group of contrasts are those brought out by Clarke rather than Wilson. They set up criminal dispositions in opposition to crime events and the situations that give rise to them. This whole structure of contrasts was already largely present in Wilson (1975), but Wilson was mostly interested in reducing crime by increasing the certainty or severity of punishment, hence he emphasised the second group of oppositions. The originality of Clarke's approach lay in shifting the emphasis to the third group of contrasts, and especially in emphasising the importance of the concrete situation, and the potential for manipulating situational factors.

Each of these three sets of contrasts obscures more than it illuminates, and tends to hold back the development of theory.

(a) Causes versus choice and policy prescription

Sociologists and criminologists have tended to get stuck in profound and possibly intractable philosophical debates concerning free will and determinism. David Matza (1964) went to the lengths of proposing 'soft determinism' as a kind of low-alcohol version for half-hearted positivists, in an attempt to resolve the apparent conflict between causal explanation and free choice. In parallel with academics, politicians regularly set up understanding the causes of crime in opposition to placing moral responsibility on the criminal as a free agent, as when John Major, then Prime Minister, tried to make a populist appeal to punitiveness by asserting that we should 'understand a little less and blame a little more'. Sociologists and politicians agree on very few things, but they do seem to agree that free choice along with moral responsibility, on the one hand, are opposed to understanding the causes of behaviour along with predicting it, on the other. Yet without going deep into the philosophical issues, it is sufficiently obvious that this supposed opposition is a nonsense.

It is only by virtue of living in a structured society with defined institutions and dependable relationships that people have the capacity to choose. Social practices and institutions depend on the predictability of much behaviour. Indeed, it is that predictability that constitutes the fabric of those practices and institutions. When relationships become highly unpredictable (as with economic relations in present-day Russia) we speak of society breaking down. People then have less capacity to choose, because the consequences of acting in one way or another have become difficult to predict. It follows that structure and predictability are a condition of free choice, and not opposed to it.

In everyday dealings, providing explanations for people's behaviour, and predicting it, are by no means opposed to ascribing free choice and moral responsibility. For example, I can predict with a very high level of confidence that anyone approaching the closed door of my office will knock before coming in. I could also construct a convincing causal explanation of their behaviour.[3] Nobody will be tempted to conclude from this that my colleagues and students are robots who have been deprived of freedom of choice. People who know each other very well – husbands and wives, for example – can often predict what the other will do or say, for example: 'If you suggest a game of squash, he will jump at it'. We are not tempted to conclude from this that the husband is driven to play squash by ineluctable forces which deprive him of any choice in the matter.

We are perfectly happy to say that the student performed badly in the examination because he was hung over, which implies that the hangover was the cause of his bad performance; but even nowadays this would not count as grounds for appeal against the result, because it would not be interpreted as meaning that he had no choice in the matter. He could have chosen not to drink the night before. Of course, further causes might be uncovered to explain why the student drank (say isolation and despair arising from a failed love affair) and why he didn't take enough paracetemol to allow him to concentrate on the exam (not being in the habit of drinking, he had no supply

---

[3] In detail, the explanation would be rather lengthy: it would cover the perception of my office as private space, the meaning of the closed door, the universal acceptance of certain conventions within the faculty, the severe informal sanctions for breaking them.

of tablets to hand). That might lead us to say that he had a weakened capacity for self-control, and limited ability to deal with the consequences of his drinking. This example shows that some causal explanations have no relevance at all to the capacity to choose (for example 'he performed badly because he had been drinking the night before'); whereas others are relevant (for example, 'he had lost his self-control because of a failed love affair'). In other words, providing a causal explanation in itself is not opposed to free choice and moral responsibility: the crucial question is whether the student retained his capacity for self-control.

Wilson's (1975) attempt to distinguish between intermediate causes and root causes steers us into the furthest reaches of confusion. Every cause is from another point of view an effect, so that the search for a first, uncaused cause has nothing to do with science. If sociologists or criminologists speak of the 'basic' or 'root' causes of crime, they do not refer to states of affairs that are uncaused and therefore cannot be changed. Instead, they mean to propose a model of the processes leading to criminal behaviour in which certain causal factors (such as poverty or family conflict) have a more fundamental status than others (such as criminal opportunities). For example, poverty and family conflict would be more fundamental than criminal opportunities if these pressures cause young people to seek out opportunities for crime, whereas criminal opportunities are rarely the cause of poverty and family conflict. Whether poverty and family conflict actually are more fundamental in this sense than criminal opportunities is a matter to be settled by empirical research. It is possible that enticing criminal opportunities may often divert the course of life into a path that leads to poverty, unemployment, and conflict with close associates.

There are occasions when we want to say that someone had no choice because of an irresistible inner compulsion (say to steal, to light fires, or to have sexual relations with children); or because of psychosis, amounting to detachment from human sympathies and moral worlds; or because of physical deprivation or exhaustion. Yet if there is indeed something distinctive about these conditions, it is not that they exceptionally provide a causal explanation of people's behaviour. The crucial point, again, is that this particular kind of explanation implies that a person has lost the capacity for self-control. What is thrown into high relief by the examples of pyromania, kleptomania, paedophilia, and schizophrenia, is that the capacity for self-control lies at the heart of what it is to be human. Those who completely lack this capacity, even if only within a small compartment of their lives, are regarded as gravely abnormal. The capacity for self-control, or what Bandura (1997) calls self-efficacy, is closely related to the capacity to make choices. We rightly regard people who completely lack self-control as incapable of taking responsibility for their actions: by stating that they lack self-control, we are asserting that the usual methods of encouraging them to assume moral responsibility will not work.

Hence, it is not true that the difference between the pyromaniac and the responsible citizen is that a causal explanation can be given for the pyromaniac's behaviour, but not for the responsible citizen's. On the contrary, Bandura's (1997) research and writings have shown that it is possible to furnish powerful causal explanations for the different levels of self-efficacy in different individuals. Since self-efficacy is the capacity for self-control, which gives people the power to choose, it follows that there are causes (perhaps even 'root causes'!) of an individual's strong or weak capacity to exercise choice.

Consequently, rational choice theories of crime are not opposed in principle to dispositional theories. Causal explanation and the ability to predict behaviour are wholly compatible with the idea that people choose to commit crimes, and that these choices sometimes or often emerge out of a process of rational calculation. This contrast only has relevance if it is re-interpreted as a contrast between substantive explanations of behaviour. In that perspective, rational choice theories are akin to cognitive theories in psychology, which emphasise the way people perceive, order, and think about the social world as influences on their behaviour. These can be contrasted with psychological theories that emphasise personality or distinctive inner drives. However, both cognitive and personality theories are attempts to provide causal explanations.

In making the contrast between root causes and policy prescriptions, Wilson (1975) was carried away with his own rhetoric in making a useful and important point. It is true that the focus of interest of the policy analyst is different from that of the sociologist. The policy analyst is concerned with what can be done, whereas the sociologist is interested in every kind of causal explanation. What Wilson wrote was that evaluating policy options has little to do with understanding causes, and that pragmatic considerations lead policy analysts to adopt some kind of rational choice theory of crime. What he might more convincingly have written is that many different causes come together to bring about criminal offending. Some of these, such as family functioning (he argued) are largely out of the reach of public policy or the private institutions that government can directly influence. Others, such as the design of cars, the organisation of shopping, or the checks built into credit card systems (he held) are much easier to change, although they are not directly controlled by government. Policy analysts are not necessarily interested in which are the most powerful or fundamental[4] causes of criminal offending. They focus instead on the most effective, economic, and efficient methods of reducing offending (in the official terminology of the Thatcher years). This may involve concentrating on causes of crime that are not the most powerful or fundamental, but ones that can be most easily and cheaply manipulated.

---

[4] Although Wilson's interpretation of what is meant by a 'fundamental cause' does not make sense, it can be re-interpreted in a coherent way, as argued above.

On this re-stated version of Wilson's argument, the policy analyst must be concerned with the causes of crime: for example, unless opportunity forms part of a good causal account of criminal offending, there can be no point in manipulating risks and rewards. Also, depending on whether opportunity is a strong or weak causal factor, the yield of crimes prevented by reducing it will be greater or smaller. However, Wilson's point was that feasibility and cost will often be more important factors determining policy than the relative importance of different causes. This is an important point in principle, and remains the central impetus behind SCP, which is explicitly an attempt to concentrate on changing what can be changed. It is interesting that the leading writers on SCP have now equally explicitly dropped Wilson's metaphysical baggage, and now routinely describe opportunity as a *cause* of crime.[5]

Wilson was right to point out that policy makers inevitably concentrate on what they think governments can change, but judgements about what can and cannot be changed are highly contestable. It is also interesting that these judgements are rather loosely related to political ideologies. Wilson thought it was obvious that governments could not influence family functioning, whereas they could influence, for example, anti-theft measures taken by credit card companies or shops. On the other hand, the idea that governments can influence the family remains popular both on the Right and on the Left. A recurrent theme on the Right is that state social security systems have caused the breakdown of the traditional family (Morgan, 1995; Murray, 1994, 1996). A recurrent theme on the Left is that conflict and lack of care in many families is caused by a shortage of material resources, which can be remedied by redistribution or economic growth (Walker, 1996). Furthermore, the history of SCP shows that governments have great difficulty in getting public and private sector institutions to adopt opportunity-reduction measures, even when they recognise that these could help to reduce crime. One reason is that the losses (for example, through theft from the HMV record shop in Oxford Street) are less consequential to the specific organisation than to the public interest, particularly bearing in mind the cost of policing and prosecution. In principle the argument that we should concentrate on changing what can be changed may be sound, but in practice hasty and superficial judgements have often been made about what can be changed most easily. Judgements about what can be changed may too easily emerge from cultural biases, rather than analysis. For most British people, gun control would 'obviously' be the most effective and efficient method of reducing homicides in the United States, but for most Americans it is equally 'obvious' that such a policy could not be implemented. This example starkly illustrates the limits of Wilson's robust pragmatism.

A further difficulty in forming judgements about what can most effectively be done is that policies may have either a broad or a narrow focus.

---

[5] Marcus Felson and Ron Clarke wrote a booklet for the Home Office in London with the working title *Opportunities Cause Crime*, although this was changed to *Opportunity Makes the Thief* when the report was actually published (Felson and Clarke, 1999).

SCP is clearly focused on preventing specific kinds of crime, whereas pre-school education in poor neighbourhoods may produce a wide range of benefits, including improved educational achievement, lower rates of unemployment, and higher earnings, as well as a lower rate of crime among those who earlier attended the pre-school programmes compared with those who did not.[6] As Wilson (1975) pointed out, broadly-based and expensive social programmes such as pre-school education cannot be justified by refer-ence to their crime prevention benefits alone. They may, however, be justi-fied by reference to a range of benefits, but there is no way of deciding what proportion of expenditure on pre-school education should be attributed to crime prevention, so whether pre-school education or SCP is the most efficient (pragmatic?) way for governments to reduce crime must always remain imponderable.

Despite the rhetorical appeal of these contrasts, therefore, there is no conflict between causal explanations and choice or moral responsibility, and a general appeal to pragmatism does not help to decide on priorities between crime prevention policies.

(b) Changing people versus influencing choices

Thinking About Crime was first published at a time when the pendulum was swinging against reform and rehabilitation, and the book reflected the prevailing mood. In contrast to the failed policy of changing known offenders, it offered the prospect of influencing choices to prevent future offending by manipulating the risks and rewards of crime. This is another contrast that does not withstand closer analysis. Reducing offending opportunities is, of course, perfectly compatible with programmes of education, reform and treat-ment for known offenders: the two policies are not opposed in any way. But arguments against posing reform and opportunity reduction in opposition to one another run much deeper than that.

Not only are these two types of policy compatible, but they are complemen-tary, because they are aimed at different targets. Treatment, reform, or rehabilitation is an attempt to change people who have been captured by the criminal justice system, whereas opportunity reduction is an attempt to manipulate the risks and rewards of offending for the general population who are mostly not captured by the system at any one time. As well as being aimed at different population groups, these policies target different points in the life course, and have fundamentally different objectives. Opportunity reduction is an attempt to reduce the number of crimes of specific types that are success-fully committed. Reform, rehabilitation, or treatment are attempts to give people who are in trouble the option to change. People captured by the system

---

[6] See Schweinhart and Weikart (1980); Berrueta-Clement et al. (1984); Schweinhart et al. (1993); Consortium for Longitudinal Studies (1983).

are usually damaged in various ways, even before being caught, and entanglement in criminal justice process and punishment is likely to damage them further. Hence, there is a moral obligation as far as possible to give people who are punished the opportunity to learn, grow, and develop, whether or not they take advantage of it. Of course, to the extent that they do, there are likely to be benefits in terms of crime reduction, and more recent reviews of the evidence (McGuire, 1995) tend to refute the too-sweeping view that treatment never works. Nevertheless, it is inappropriate to evaluate reform, rehabilitation, and treatment as primarily methods of reducing crime, and to see them, therefore, as alternatives to opportunity reduction.

Not only are reform and opportunity reduction complementary rather than opposed, but they are also closely intertwined, because reducing offending opportunities may be an important way of helping offenders to change. Wilson (1975) argued that it is easier to change behaviour than attitudes, and in doing so he seemed to identify attitudes with the inner core of the self, unchanging and unchangeable, and behaviour with the contingent manifestations of the self, malleable and responsive to circumstances. Even if we stick with this attitudes versus behaviour model, it is important to recognise that if people's behaviour and experience change, then their attitudes may change as a consequence.[7] But in any case, there is no reason to assume that attitudes are the inner core of the stable self. Probably more important are habits, patterns of perception, and cognitive processes. All of these are strongly influenced by learning and experience. Persistent and frequent offenders get into the habit of offending; they acquire other habits (such as drinking alcohol and taking drugs) which draw them into offending; and they acquire habits (such as not getting up in the morning) which are inconsistent with going straight. Even if their attitudes towards crime are disapproving, they may continue to offend out of habit. If their offending opportunities are reduced, their offending habits will tend to be weakened. Since our notion of personhood is defined in part by the person's habits, changing behaviour (by manipulating risks and rewards) can change the person.

(c) Propensities versus situations

It was Clarke (1982) who particularly emphasised the third set of contrasts (Table 1) between situations and events on the one hand and dispositions or propensities on the other. One response to this is simply to point out that any coherent account of thought and action must be interactionist: it must explain how persons and the environment mutually act upon each other, rather than shifting the spotlight from one to the other. Behaviour is the product of a

---

[7] Perhaps the best illustration is the vast body of research exploring the 'contact hypothesis' (for a summary, see Brown, 1995). This evidence shows that people who are prejudiced against another group become less prejudiced against them as a result of co-operative contacts on an equal footing, especially when they view the others as representatives of the whole group.

sequence of interactions between the person and the environment, such that the person selects and changes the environment, and the environment shapes and teaches the person. But at any given time, either the situation or the person may be the main determining factor. To use an example suggested by Bandura (1986), if someone is thrown into water, the situation is absolutely determinative: he or she will immediately swim, or try to do so, regardless of personal characteristics. On the other hand, if a girl is given a range of dolls to play with, the one that she chooses will reflect the way she sees herself and the social world.

To state in a completely general way that dispositions or propensities do not help much in predicting behaviour, as Clarke (1982) appears to do in the passage quoted at the beginning of this article, is obviously nonsense. For example, from a knowledge of the tennis-playing skills of Pete Sampras and Ron Clarke, I can predict with a very high degree of certainty that Sampras will win any tennis match between them.[8] However, the interesting questions are which kinds of characteristics of persons are influential, and at what level of generality to theorise them. Clarke shoots at three more specific 'dispositional targets': slow autonomic reactivity and low cortical arousal; psychological factors of personality and upbringing; and sociological influences such as anomie, subculture, and labelling. With regard to the first of these, there is in fact strong evidence that a high proportion of life-course persistent and frequent offenders have abnormally low autonomic reactivity, and that this is associated with low adrenaline secretion (Magnusson, 1987, 1988; White et al., 1990). The significance of this finding for crime prevention seems obscure, but attention deficit syndrome or hyperactivity diagnosed before the age of five does seem to predict a substantial criminal career. With regard to the third group of 'sociological influences', these are a mixed bag of theories which are not primarily concerned with the influence of individual 'dispositions'. With regard to the second group of 'psychological factors of personality and upbringing', the important questions are which psychological factors, and at what level of generality.

It seems fairly clear that in seeking to shift the spotlight from 'psychological factors of personality and upbringing' to situations, Clarke had in mind first and foremost theories of personality traits such as Eysenck's neuroticism and extraversion. These theories try to identify multi-purpose personality dimensions which are supposed to have an influence on behaviour across all situations. Theories of this kind have been generally rather unsuccessful. Bandura (1986: 6) puts the matter as follows:

Over the years numerous studies have been published showing that measures of

---

[8] Nor is this example irrelevant to crime. In many fields, the people who commit crimes are those who have acquired the relevant skills, including physical and intellectual techniques (e.g. for breaking into the car or computer) and techniques for overcoming fear and neutralising moral condemnation.

personality traits usually correlate weakly with social behavior in different settings. [Bandura's references omitted] When they show significant relationships, such measures usually account for about 10 percent of the variance in performance. Past behavior predicts future behavior in similar situations with moderate success, but conduct varies across situations differing in properties that affect the functional value of a particular form of behavior. Thus, for example, a measure of an aggressive trait does not help much in predicting whether or not a person will behave aggressively in dissimilar situations.

The tradition in psychology that Clarke was reacting against was one that tried to find completely general traits that are manifested across all situations. There is no reason to doubt Bandura's conclusion about the lack of success of this general approach. On the other hand, at a more specific level, people do differ very markedly in self-efficacy (a grounded belief in their ability to perform specific tasks), skills, knowledge, habits, and perceptions (of risks and rewards, for example), and these factors predict their behaviour much more powerfully than generalised personality traits. These are not completely general dispositions, but they are, of course, propensities that go well beyond any specific situation. It is obvious, for example, that competencies (such as the ability to read) are highly persistent and irreversible, and have a predictable influence across a wide range of situations, although there are some situations in which they have no influence at all. Once we focus on these more specific propensities, it is equally obvious that they are formed and re-formed out of continuous interaction with the social environment.

This analysis suggests that we should move beyond the opposition between situations and dispositions to consider how habits, skills, and perceptions are shaped by crime opportunities and offending experience, and how moral concepts through which people regulate their own behaviour are formed, and engaged or disengaged in particular situations.

IMPLICATIONS OF SOCIAL COGNITIVE THEORY

The usual criticism of SCP is that it changes situations without changing people, and is therefore superficial and amoral. It is said to be like hiding the tin of sweets from the children, as opposed to teaching them not to eat more sweets than is good for them (Bottoms, 1990). On any interactive account of situations and dispositions, this kind of criticism and example must be much too simple. Situations have a lasting as well as an immediate influence on people, and people on situations. What needs to be examined is whether changing situations in the ways that SCP seeks to change them will lead to the lasting changes in behavioural norms that policy makers desire. It is possible to imagine that opportunity reduction could make people less inclined to break the law when the opportunity does arise: for example, if design changes make car theft very difficult, then people may no longer notice the rather infrequent opportunities for car theft that still do arise, and people will no longer have the necessary knowledge and skills to carry out the offence, or the distribution networks to dispose of the vehicle. However, it is also possible to imagine that opportunity reduction could erode self-controls and community controls on criminal behaviour: for example, if there are systems that make it physically impossible to avoid paying the fare on a public transport system, or to drive a vehicle faster than the speed limit, then people might become less inclined to pay the proper fare or stay within the speed limit in situations outside the control of these systems, because automatic external regulation had, over time, led to the erosion of internal self-regulation.

Bandura's social cognitive theory provides a general framework within which these interactions could be examined. Social cognitive theory can be described as a modern version of social learning theory that takes account of the cognitive revolution in psychology. The foundational account is given in *Social Foundations of Thought and Action* (Bandura, 1986). The part of the theory that deals with the self-system is developed further in *Self-efficacy: The Exercise of Control* (Bandura, 1997). In its origins, social cognitive theory is a reaction against the radical behaviourism of Skinner. In the social cognitive view, behaviour is generated, not automatically evoked or reproduced: this is similar to Chomsky's account of the way that speech is creatively generated, so that young children utter many sentences they have never heard. At the same time, behaviour emerges out of learning, but learning is essentially cognitive: it involves classifying, contrasting, forming expectations, formulating rules, making inferences, not just forming associations between stimulus and response. There are three main categories in Bandura's system: persons, behaviour, and the environment (with the emphasis on the social rather than the physical environment). We can make up three pairs out of these categories (persons and behaviour, persons and the environment, behaviour and the environment). Within each pair, there is mutual reciprocal causation between the two terms, so that, for example, the person has a causal influence on his own behaviour, but his behaviour also has a causal influence on the person; similarly, the person influences the environment, but the environment also influences the person.

Current research and theorising in developmental psychology fits very well into this framework of mutual, reciprocal causal influence. For example, continuity of an individual's pattern of behaviour over time can be explained as emerging from a pattern of progressively intensifying interactions between the individual and the social environment, in which the person selects environments that tend to reinforce his original pattern of behaviour. An initially aggressive boy may find only other aggressive boys to play with, so that subsequent interactions reinforce the original tendency towards aggression. That is an example of reciprocal causation between the person and the environment. Equally, aggressive or sexual behaviour may change the hormonal balance, so that these kinds of behaviour become more likely in the future. This is an example of reciprocal causation between the person and his behaviour.

In the social cognitive view, we learn more from observing others ('modelling') than from our own direct experience. The information gathered about the social world is symbolically transformed so as to provide rules or guides for action. Social learning provides us with competencies, but also with motivations which help to determine whether and when these competencies will be put to use. Behaviour (like physiological processes) is functional, hence it is regulated to some extent by external outcomes, either observed or experienced first hand. However, humans (unlike lower animals) have the capacity to persist with immediately unproductive behaviour for very long periods of time. They can do this because they exercise control over their own thoughts, feelings, and actions by rewarding and punishing themselves. Performance and persistence in difficult tasks are strongly influenced by self-efficacy beliefs: faith in one's own competence and ability to control. These beliefs are unlike a generalised self-esteem, because they are beliefs in one's ability to perform specific tasks or control particular situations. They are influenced by actual performance, by the way this is observed and perceived, and by the responses, reports, and evaluations of other people.

People observe their own behaviour, assess it on a number of dimensions, including morality and deviancy, judge it against personal and social standards, then react to it accordingly, either in a positive or negative, a punishing or a rewarding, way. However, although everyone has (to a greater or lesser degree) the capacity to regulate their own behaviour, this capacity is not continuously and invariantly exercised. Here Bandura's account of self-control differs crucially from socialisation theories, all of them ultimately derived from Freud, which assume that commands and rules externally derived from parents and wider social contacts are internalised in early childhood, and become a constant presence within the self. On Freud's account, and others derived from it, the superego is always present and active (even if its commands can be blocked). In the social cognitive view, by contrast, the self-system is selectively activated and disengaged. Moral disengagement can be achieved, for example, by techniques of neutralisation similar to those discussed in a much earlier article by Sykes and Matza (1957), such as minimising, ignoring, or misconstruing the consequences of an action. It is not clear whether Bandura thinks it would be logically or psychologically impossible for someone to say 'I am now about to do something which is wrong and inexcusable', then do it. In any case, he argues that people seldom, or possibly never, intentionally do things which they believe at the time to be wrong. Instead, they disengage the self-system in order to do things they would judge to be wrong, if the system were engaged.

Both Bandura and Sykes and Matza ignored the complexities that arise in applying rules or principles to particular cases or situations. They tended to assume that the question of what principle should be applied is unproblematic, and that any justification for not applying a principle (such as a justification for not telling the truth) is a dishonest evasion of moral responsibility. In fact, because cases are unique and rules often conflict, the decision to apply a rule is often contestable, but that only strengthens the argument that how people make these decisions is just as important as what principles they hold and how strongly they believe in them.

In seeking to understand the effects of SCP, it may be particularly important to make this distinction between morals and moral engagement, between principles and their application to particular cases. One way in which SCP might work is to engage people's moral awareness in the specific situation; alternatively (or in addition) it might strengthen people's belief in the underlying principle. For example, specific measures may be used to encourage people to keep particular areas clean. These should make people feel guilty about dropping litter in those areas, that is, activate their moral sense in those environments. There is a separate question as to whether experience of these situational measures across a number of environments will eventually change general beliefs about the importance of keeping public areas clean. This change in moral beliefs, as a result of their activation in particular situations, is a possible mechanism producing a diffusion of benefits of SCP beyond the immediate situation (Clarke and Weisburd, 1994).

ANALYSIS OF EXAMPLES

SCP was initially developed as a rational choice model, with the emphasis on features of the immediate situation that influence the calculation of costs and benefits. In recent years, the conception of SCP has broadened considerably to include mechanisms that do not fit within a rational choice model, unless that is very broadly interpreted. Clarke's early schema of SCP techniques included three main categories: increasing the effort, increasing the risks, and reducing the rewards. Various techniques that are directly concerned with moral engagement or moral beliefs were included within this schema, but did not really fit. Later, Clarke (1997) added 'removing excuses' as a fourth main category; while in an alternative schema, Clarke and Homel (1997) added 'inducing guilt or shame' instead. Wortley (1996) has argued that 'inducing guilt and shame' confuses social controls by others with self controls; instead of Clarke and Homel's fourth category, he proposed two additional categories: increasing social controls, and activating self-controls (which he described as 'inducing guilt'). These attempts to broaden the SCP model are not entirely coherent, because they burst the bounds of the original rational choice framework, without establishing a new theoretical framework that embraces all SCP methods.

Social cognitive theory may in future be used to provide a sounder theoretical underpinning for SCP. A broad assumption underlying social cognitive theory is that behaviour is adaptive and functional, but it does not follow that the dominant influences are always the risks and rewards perceived in the immediate situation. In fact, this was early recognised by Clarke (1982: 231) who wrote: 'In addition, people adopt rules of thumb or 'standing decisions' that eliminate the need to analyse every decision'. The consequences of what Clarke called 'standing decisions' are far-reaching, and make it necessary to adopt a much broader theoretical approach like Bandura's.

The best way forward, therefore, will be to develop a detailed theory of crime prevention based on social cognitive principles. As a preparation for that work, the rest of this article uses a few examples of SCP to analyse mechanisms through which situational changes may have an effect beyond the immediate situation.

Speed cameras

The control of driving speed provides an interesting example of crime prevention, because this is a clear case where moral beliefs and legal rules have differing influences on behaviour. Presumably, most people believe it is wrong to drive dangerously fast; and probably believe that it tends to be dangerous to exceed speed limits. Yet most drivers exceed speed limits by considerable margins at least some of the time. Bourne and Cooke (1993) have evaluated a programme in Victoria, Australia, starting in 1989, which aimed to reduce speeding by enforcement of speed limits through speed cameras, backed up by 'a high-level advertising/public education campaign to inform drivers of the risks of speeding and of the risks of getting caught'.[9] The 60 new speed cameras are fitted in vehicles or on tripods and can be moved to any site quickly, so presumably they are not normally visible to drivers. The human and technological resources devoted to the programme made it possible to carry out a very large number of checks: 8.2 million during 1990–91, growing to more than 2 million per month in 1992. 'A total of 374,050 speeding penalty notices were issued during 1990–91, with A$23.6 million paid in fines that year. A further 607,165 notices were issued in 1991–92, with an additional A$55.8 million collected from fines.'

Immediately following the introduction of the new speed cameras and advertising campaign, there was a sharp reduction in the percentage of vehicles exceeding the speed limit, in collisions, in fatalities, and in injuries. The authors claim that the most important factor in this change is the threat of loss of driving licence that can result from accumulated penalty points. Other jurisdictions (such as South Australia) which have similar speed camera enforcement levels, but without the deterrent of license loss, have not reduced speeding to the same extent.

[9] No information about the advertising campaign is given in the article. The speed cameras, red light cameras, and advertising campaign were accompanied by a range of other initiatives, but were probably much the most important measures in the package.

No research was carried out on the attitudes, beliefs, or cognitive processes of drivers in Victoria before and after the programme. There was clearly a massive increase in the actual likelihood of detection, and the scale of enforcement was such that the perceived risk of a penalty for speeding must presumably have increased substantially. However, Bourne and Cooke's interpretation goes beyond the rational choice model, narrowly defined. They pointed out:

> There has been no social stigma attached to being a speedster. The flashy executive or sporty youth with a racy car can be a fashionable role model. Moreover, no one believes that he or she is a bad driver.

This alludes to moral beliefs, informal social controls, and moral disengagement. The objective was to change moral beliefs, strengthen informal social controls, and discourage moral disengagement, primarily through enforcement of speed limits backed up by advertising: 'The challenge was to make speeding socially unacceptable.' The authors also recognised that driving depends on habits and skills which persist beyond the immediate situation. They argued that increasing the level of detection would increase the time before which bad habits could reassert themselves, and that a change in habits should lead to a change in attitudes, which would in turn tend to sustain the changed habits: 'This suggests that resources need to be 'ramped up' initially to maintain the detection rate, but, after a period of time, the effect will, to a large extent, sustain itself and require decreased resource input.' However, they did not provide data to show that reduced speeds were in fact maintained with a reduced number of detections after the first couple of years.

It may be said that this is an example of targeted law enforcement rather than SCP. However, SCP is much more closely related to law enforcement than is commonly recognised, especially when it concentrates on increasing the risks of offending. As Ekblom (1994) has argued, crime prevention normally relies on increasing the risk of being caught and punished by the criminal justice system, and the criminal justice system itself performs many preventive functions. The dividing line becomes still more blurred if we consider speed camera programmes in Britain, where warning signs announce the presence of cameras, which are clearly visible, but many of which are actually replicas, or contain no film. Presumably a real speed camera with film in it is an instance of law enforcement, whereas a replica speed camera is an instance of crime prevention, but in reality the whole speed camera programme uses enforcement along with a mix of other methods to prevent drivers from exceeding speed limits.

There are a number of distinct mechanisms through which speed camera programmes may bring about a reduction in speeding:

1. Situational cues, in the context of general awareness of the enforcement programme, increase perceptions of the risk of being caught and punished on particular roads at particular times.

2. Actual experience of being caught and punished increases perceptions of risk on particular roads at particular times. (Because of the vast number of penalty notices issued in Victoria, actual experience of sanctions was probably an important factor.)
3. Situational cues or actual experience of sanctions change driving habits, so that the effect can extend beyond situations that now appear to involve increased detection risk. This is akin to Clarke's (1982) 'standing decisions'. Instead of deciding from one moment to the next whether to speed depending on an assessment of the risk in the current situation, the driver gets into the habit of staying within the speed limit.
4. Situational cues or actual experience of sanctions activate moral engagement: they remind the driver that in speeding he may be doing something wrong, and hence re-engage his self-regulatory system. This moral re-engagement might be highly situation-dependent, or it might be more persistent.
5. Advertising, backed by increased perceived risks or actual experience of sanctions, may change the driver's moral beliefs so that he becomes more fully convinced that speeding is wrong.
6. The various elements of the programme activate informal social control mechanisms: for example, children in the back of the car now complain that the driver is going too fast, his mother remonstrates with him when he gets points on his driving license.
7. The driver is now less likely to learn from observing other drivers that one can exceed the speed limit with impunity: fewer drivers are seen to exceed the limit, drivers are seen to have been stopped and given penalty notices, and friends give accounts of their experiences of being caught. Hence vicarious learning conveys information about increased risks.
8. Moral principles and strategies for disengaging moral rules are also acquired vicariously, from modelling. If mechanisms (4) and (5) work, then a further, knock-on effect is an increased likelihood that people will learn from their friends and admired associates that it is wrong to break speed limits or to avoid applying these rules to one's own driving.

The mechanisms that go beyond the immediate situation are potentially very powerful, but not much is known about when they do and do not come into play. This could be investigated by more detailed research on the implementation and outcomes of speed control programmes. For example, in Britain, where visible cameras along with warning signs are put up on certain roads, it would be interesting to find out whether there are speed reductions on those roads only, or on all roads. Survey research among drivers and others would help to establish which mechanisms are actually at work. It seems obvious that moral beliefs will be much easier to activate for some kinds of offence than for others. For example, it would be extraordinarily difficult to convince people that illegal parking is wrong.

Breath testing

Breath testing as a method of reducing drink driving is a technique fairly similar to speed cameras for reducing speeding. An important difference in the context is that there is now considerably more moral disapproval of drink driving than speeding, and the proportion of drivers who sometimes exceed speed limits is much higher than the proportion who sometimes drive when over the legal alcohol limit. This may mean that mechanisms involving moral engagement are easier to deploy in the case of drink driving than speeding. There is also a difference in the specific techniques of enforcement. Cameras monitor the speed of all vehicles passing them, whereas drivers can only be breath-tested if they have committed a moving traffic offence or have been involved in an accident, or if there are reasonable grounds for suspicion that they have been drinking. In practice this gives the police wide scope for requiring a breath test, but presumably drivers may believe that if they are skilful enough, they will be able to drive after drinking but avoid detection. It seems less likely that drivers in Victoria think they can avoid detection by a speed camera.

In the case of drink driving, there is a study by Riley (1991) which provides survey-based evidence on the attitudes, beliefs, and cognitive processes of drivers in areas with high and low levels of enforcement through breath testing. Drivers in the high-enforcement area were significantly less likely to drink and drive (according to their own reports) than those in low-enforce-ment area, yet there was no difference between the areas in perceptions of the risk of being caught. However, drivers in the high-enforcement area were much more likely than those in the low-enforcement area to expect family and friends to disapprove if they were to drink and drive. Also, they were less likely to say that drinking alcohol made them feel relaxed or act impulsively:

> In addition, drivers in the high-enforcement area were less likely to regard themselves as able to handle more alcohol than the average drinker and were less likely to regard limiting alcohol consumption as affecting their enjoyment of social occasions or to see alcohol as a necessary part of their social lives. Finally, in the high-enforcement area drivers were more aware of the general dangers of mixing alcohol and driving and of the increased risk of a road accident. They were also less likely to believe they could avoid detection when over the limit by careful driving. (Riley, 1991: 27)

From these findings and others, Riley concluded that higher enforcement levels had their effect not through changing perceptions of the risk of being caught and punished in a specific situation, but through reinforcing social pressures and increasing awareness of accident risks. If confirmed, this supports the argument that changes in situations can, through a variety of mechanisms, bring about changes that extend well beyond the immediate situation both in time and in space. To give one example, family and friends may hear about people who have been caught driving over the limit, then consequently exert pressure on a driver in their circle. On that model, the function of breath testing could be to set in train a process of social diffusion rather than influence the risk calculations of drivers in specific situations. Here is an example where 'fundamental' and 'immediate', or 'distal' and 'proximal' causes appear to change place, because manipulation of risk in the driving situation sets in train social processes that create different norms.

Reducing fare evasion

The analysis of efforts to reduce fare evasion on public transport systems has particularly important implications for an understanding of the wider signifi-cance of situational crime prevention. The weakness and ambiguity of norms concerning paying fares is one reason why the example is an important one. Another reason is that design and technological solutions in this field can be pushed very far: to the point where new questions are raised about the relationship between effective external control, and internalised rules that depend on a sense of personal autonomy.

There are a number of reasons for weakness, uncertainty, or ambiguity of the principle that one should pay the correct fare for a journey on public transport. To some extent, this is probably connected with very general features of moral and political reasoning. It is easy to think of trains and buses, like the air we breathe, as a common resource that should be available to be used as needed, because they are always there, and they are provided by an impersonal and remote authority. Nothing tangible is being stolen. It is difficult to identify or visualise anyone who loses if I do not pay the proper fare, and the train will run anyway, incurring the same costs, whether I pay my fare or not. Also, the train is usually not completely full, so I am not using up a resource, or inconveniencing any other passenger, by travelling on it. These background factors make it easy to achieve moral disengagement. Every case is different in detail, but some of these factors are also at work in making it easy to avoid a sense of obligation to pay parking charges; and shoplifters find it easier to bring themselves to steal from large chain stores than from small local businesses.

However, it also seems likely that a sense of ambiguity about the obligation to pay fares arises from inconsistent and lax enforcement. Some twenty years ago in London it was common for suburban tube stations to be open with the ticket office closed at certain hours, and with no automatic ticket machines working. Passengers would travel then pay voluntarily at the other end, saying they had come from such-and-such a station. This was a common practice that was fully accepted (at least in practice) by the staff of London Transport. Naturally, passengers often mis-stated the station where they had started in order to minimise the fare paid. Furthermore, if there was a queue at the ticket office, passengers in a hurry would get on the train without paying and 'pay at the other end' perhaps claiming that the ticket office had been closed. From time to time there would be crack-downs, when inspectors would find passengers without tickets on trains and exact penalties; this would often be seen as grossly unfair, in the context of generally lax enforcement, and a practice of trusting passengers to 'pay at the other end'.

This example illustrates the interplay between the formal rule (the law in the books) and the informally accepted practice (the law in action). It might be said that belief in the norm of paying the correct fare was weakened by lax and inconsistent enforcement; or that weak enforcement made it easy for people to disengage their self-control mechanisms from this norm. However, it may be that enforcement practice played a more fundamental role in conveying information about what the norm actually was. If laws are never, or hardly ever, enforced, they eventually cease to operate as laws at all. Hence lax or inconsistent enforcement might eventually change the norm from 'everyone must always pay the correct fare' to 'people should pay the fare if the machines are working, they are not in too much of a hurry, they have the right change'. An interesting example of changing and clashing norms has arisen recently from the creation of separate private companies running different train services in Britain. Practice on many services in the days of British Rail was that ticket collectors were equipped with ticket-issuing machines, and accepted fares from passengers on trains during the journey. There was some ambiguity about whether they could take advantage of special fares or would always have to pay the full fare if they had not bought a ticket before boarding the train. After privatisation, some rail companies continued the British Rail practice, others allowed passengers to buy tickets on the train, but only at the full fare (often much more than what they would otherwise have paid), and others required them to pay a penalty in addition to the full fare. Hence, passengers had to acquire a complex structure of new norms through experience of travelling on different train lines.

At the end of 1989, a new system for the issue and collection of tickets was introduced on the London underground. This included automatic ticket gates and new ticket issuing machines at 63 central stations. When travelling from these stations, it became easier to buy a ticket than before. The automatic turnstiles would not let a person through until a valid ticket had been fed into the slot, and the electronic system ensured that only a valid ticket would work. (The system can distinguish between single-use tickets, daily and weekly 'travelcards', and season tickets valid for longer periods.) In the stations with the automatic facilities, the passenger exits by feeding the ticket into a turnstile slot. If the turnstile will not allow him to exit, he then has to go to another point to explain the problem to a member of staff and, if required, pay an excess fare.

The results of annual surveys by teams of inspectors show a sharp decline in the proportion of passengers found without valid tickets from 6.0 % in 1989 to 1.9 % in 1990, after the introduction of the automatic ticket system (Clarke, 1993). When automatic ticket gates were later introduced (in December 1991) at Brixton and Stockwell stations, there was a substantial increase in the number of ordinary and excess tickets sold.

Although this has not been established from more detailed research, it seems likely that the automatic ticket system works in a number of different ways. The system makes it more difficult for a passenger to travel without purchasing any ticket, and to exit without having paid the correct fare. These are constraints on passengers' ability to avoid full payment in the immediate situation. At the same time, the system conveys the expectation that passengers should always pay the full fare in advance – an expectation that was markedly absent at various earlier periods. Probably it also conveys the information that fare evasion carries the risk of paying a penalty fare, or being prosecuted, although in practice penalties are rare, and most people found without valid tickets are merely required to pay the normal fare. Hence stricter and more consistent enforcement may re-establish the norm itself, strengthen belief in the norm, and make it more difficult for people to disengage from it.

It is important to recognise, however, that the London system does not by any means make it physically impossible for someone to avoid paying the correct fare. The barriers are about three feet high, so that even an unfit person can easily jump over them both at the entrances and at the exits. At many stations for much of the time, there are few staff on duty outside the ticket offices, so that if someone does jump over the barrier, often nothing is done. In the terms of SCP, the barriers increase the risk and effort involved in evading the fare; but on many particular occasions, the risk and effort involved remains fairly small. The barriers create the impression that the risk is greater than it really is. On some occasions, jumping over the barrier would be extremely risky (for example, if there were many police officers about on the day of a football match) so the most prudent course is to take a 'standing decision' (Clarke, 1982) not to jump the barriers, rather than assessing the level of risk on this particular occasion. More important, the turnstile forms a symbolic barrier. Passing through it with a valid ticket is a ritual of lawful acceptance, whereas jumping over it is a flagrant transgression. Under the old system, fare evasion merged imperceptibly into informal fare transactions in a succession of half-tones and ambiguities. Under the new system, the automatic gate forms a symbolic barrier which dramatises the choice between morality and deviance.

As an alternative to the low-level barriers, it is possible to build floor-to-ceiling turnstiles with accompanying railings which make it physically impossible for someone to enter without presenting a token or valid ticket. Weidner (1996) reports an evaluation of the effects of introducing such high-wheel turnstiles at one station (110th and Lexington) in the New York subway. Unfortunately, the evidence is weaker than in Clarke's (1993) study, because there were no sample surveys providing a general measure of the level of fare evasion. Instead, the evaluation relies on the statistics of the numbers of summonses and arrests for fare evasion. These appear to show some reduction at the experimental station compared with two control stations, but the results are somewhat inconclusive. In combination, the findings of these two studies might be consistent with the theory that the effect of setting clear boundaries to behaviour through low-level automatic gates are greater than the effects of moving from clear boundaries to physical exclusion.

For many years, the Paris métro has used high turnstiles (at the entrances to platforms rather than stations) and in recent years it has used automated ticketing systems that make it extremely difficult to enter without having paid the fare. Myhre and Rosso (1996) report that the new Météor line in Paris will be designed to make fare evasion and other crimes physically impossible, but also to increase natural surveillance, and to create an exciting, bright, and comfortable environment. Lianos (1997) has argued that the existing Paris métro amounts to a system that strips people of their personal autonomy and destabilises moral principles founded on personal choice. On this view, a system that forces compliance tends to weaken self-controls, since these are no longer needed.

This leads to the intriguing possibility that consistent enforcement, for example through automatic ticketing systems, may have a moralising or alternatively a demoralising effect, depending on exactly how it is achieved. A system which delivers a strong and consistent symbolic message (that the fare must always be paid before crossing this barrier) may have the effect of creating or reinforcing norms, strengthening belief in them, and making it harder for people to disengage their self-controls from these norms. By contrast, a system which removes all personal choice may tend to weaken self-controls, for a variety of reasons. If people are denied any autonomy, then they perceive that the moral responsibility lies entirely with the system, and they no longer retain any obligations themselves. In addition, there are bound to be occasions when the outcome is unjust (I have paid my fare but the machine refuses to accept my ticket). Unless there is the possibility of discussion and redress, people will perceive the system as a mindless brute, so they will have no shame in outwitting it, whenever the opportunity happens to arise. For example, automatic exit gates at French motorways let a car through on payment of a set fee. If they do not open on payment of the correct fee, attendants will not countenance any discussion of the matter. After experience of failing to get a hearing, no motorist will have any compunction about driving through if, perchance, the machine should open the gate after payment of only one franc. By contrast, the same person might well point out that he had been under-charged in a shop.

The evidence on methods of reducing fare evasion is limited, but it leaves open the possibility that the interaction between situational and self controls is crucial, and that it is finally the self controls that do most of the work, although situational factors play a crucial role in strengthening or weakening, activating or de-activating, personal controls.

Inhibiting graffiti

In the 1970s and early 1980s, most subway cars in New York City were covered in graffiti. Most commentators (e.g. Glazer, 1979) thought that these graffiti made people feel that the subway was a dangerous, disordered, and violent place, and that the authorities were not in control of it. From 1985, there started a determined programme to clean the graffiti. The general principle was that no car would remain in service once it was vandalised. If that could be achieved, it would mean that in time no graffiti artist would ever see his work on display. Sloan-Howitt and Kelling (1997 [1990]) reported that the objective was achieved, so that in time very few graffiti were seen on the subway – a dramatic change. The number of arrests for vandalising subway cars plummeted, and the number of cars that had to be cleaned before being returned to service also declined substantially.

Within the tradition of SCP, this method of prevention can be construed as 'reducing the reward' (Clarke, 1992): the graffiti artist is deprived of the satisfaction of seeing his work and knowing that others can see it. However, a more satisfactory explanation can be provided within the broader framework of social cognitive theory. The practice of tagging subway cars was one that had spread by a process of social diffusion within certain groups. The graffiti artists themselves had developed specific skills connected with gaining access to the subway cars, and doing the decorative work itself. Various tagging idioms had developed, with more or less precise symbolic significance for the groups involved, and the artists had developed a range of satisfactions connected with tagging. Thus habits, skills, symbolic meaning, and cultural forms are all involved in a practice transmitted by a process of social diffusion. On this account, the result of the intervention was that the social practice was eroded. After the turning point had been reached, it was not merely that the reward for tagging cars was removed, but that there were now many fewer people about who knew how to gain access to the cars to tag them, who remembered the shapes and symbols involved, or who thought of this as a suitable method of protest, entertainment, or self-expression. The cultural form itself was dying, along with the associated habits, practices, and meanings.

CONCLUSION

Examples like these show that proponents of SCP have, curiously, tended to understate the importance of situations. They have tended to emphasise the immediate and direct effects of changing concrete circumstances, yet increasingly the practice of SCP has tended to burst the bounds of such a limited model. Instead of emphasising the contrast between changing situations and changing people, it is necessary to study how persons, behaviour, and the social and physical environment interact. When this broad, interactive perspective is adopted, it becomes clear that persons develop and change in response to their experience in particular situations, so that changes in situations can produce more persistent changes in people. Also, social practices (such as the tagging of subway cars) arise out of a configuration of situations, so that intervening in situations can help to foster or destroy particular practices. Hence crime prevention that targets situations may be just as fundamental as that which targets structural inequality or family functioning.

Although SCP is just as fundamental as other methods of prevention, and although it addresses causes just as much as any other method, it does not follow that it is necessarily the best method, or the most practicable. The streak of robust pragmatism in SCP, which ultimately derives from J.Q. Wilson (1975), is rhetoric that does not stand up to close analysis. Changing the social security system to help poor families in Britain is far more practicable than strengthening gun control in the United States. SCP is fundamental, and is practicable and good value for money in some cases (though not in others). That is enough. It is not necessary to argue that SCP is generally superior to the wide variety of other methods of crime prevention, especially since many of these other methods have different, often wider, objectives, and are aimed at different target groups.

REFERENCES

Bandura, A. (1986) *Social Foundations of Thought and Action: A Social Cognitive Theory*, Englewood Cliffs: Prentice Hall.

—— (1997) *Self-efficacy: The Exercise of Control*, New York: W. H. Freeman.

Berrueta-Clement, J.R., Schweinhart, L.J., Barnett, W.S., Epstein, A.S. and Weikart, D.P. (1984), *Changed Lives: The Effects of the Perry Preschool Program on Youths Through Age 19*, Ypsilanti, Michigan: High/Scope Foundation.

Bottoms, A.E. (1990) 'Crime prevention facing the 1990s', *Policing and Society* 1: 3–22.

Bourne, M.G. and Cooke, R.C. (1993) 'Victoria's speed camera program', in R.V. Clarke (ed.), *Crime Prevention Studies* 1: 177–94, Monsey, NY: Criminal Justice Press.

Brown, R. (1995) *Prejudice: Its Social Psychology*, Oxford: Blackwell.

Clarke, R.V. (1982) 'Situational crime prevention: Its theoretical basis and practical scope', in N. Morris and M. Tonry (eds.), *Crime and Justice: An Annual Review of Research* 4: 225–56, Chicago: University of Chicago Press.

—— (1992) 'Introduction', in R.V.Clarke, (ed.), *Situational Crime Prevention: Successful Case Studies* 3–38, New York: Harrow and Heston.

—— (1993) 'Fare evasion and automatic ticket collection on the London underground', in R.V.Clarke (ed.), *Crime Prevention Studies* 1: 135–46, Monsey, NY: Criminal Justice Press.

—— (1995) 'Situational crime prevention,' in M. Tonry and D.P. Farrington (eds.), *Building a Safer Society: Strategic Approaches to Crime Prevention. Crime and Justice: A Review of Research* 19: 91–150, Chicago: University of Chicago Press.

—— (1997) 'Introduction', in R.V.Clarke (ed.), *Situational Crime Prevention: Successful Case Studies, (*2nd ed.*),* 2–43, New York: Harrow and Heston.

—— and Homel, R. (1997) 'A revised classification of situational crime prevention techniques', in S.P. Lab (ed.), *Crime Prevention at the Crossroads,* Cincinnati, OH: Anderson.

—— and Weisburd, D. (1994) 'Diffusion of crime control benefits: observations on the reverse of displacement', in R.V.Clarke (ed.), *Crime Prevention Studies* 2: 165–184, Monsey, NY: Criminal Justice Press.

Cohen, A. K. (1955) *Delinquent Boys: The Culture of the Gang,* New York: Free Press.

Consortium for Longitudinal Studies (1983) *As the Twig is Bent. . . Lasting Effects of Pre-School Programs,* Hillsdale, NJ: Erlbaum.

Ekblom, P. (1994) 'Proximal circumstances: a mechanism-based classification of crime prevention', in R.V. Clarke (ed.), *Crime Prevention Studies* 2: 185–232, Monsey, NY: Criminal Justice Press.

Felson, M. and Clarke, R.V. (1998) *Opportunity Makes the Thief: Practical Theory for Crime Prevention,* Police Research Series 98. London: Home Office Research, Development and Statistics Directorate.

Glazer, N. (1979) 'On subway graffiti in New York', *Public Interest* (Winter).

Glueck, S. and Glueck, E. (1950) *Unravelling Juvenile Delinquency,* Cambridge, Mass.: Harvard University Press.

Lianos, M. (1997) *La Poétique de la Peur: Le Sujet Hyper-Régulier,* Paris: Doctoral thesis, Université Paris VII Diderot.

Magnusson, D. (1987) 'Adult delinquency in the light of conduct and physiology at an early age: a longitudinal study', in D. Magnusson and A. Öhman (eds.), *Psychopathology,* 221–234, Orlando, FL: Academic Press.

—— (1988) 'Antisocial behaviour of boys and autonomic activity/reactivity', in T.E. Moffitt and S.A. Mednick (eds.), *Biological Contributions To Crime Causation* 135–146, Dordrecht: Martinus Nijhoff.

Martinson, R. (1974) 'What Works? Questions And Answers About Penal Reform', *The Public Interest* (Spring): 22–54.

Matza, D. (1964) *Delinquency and Drift,* New York: Wiley.

McCord, W. and McCord, J. (1959) *Origins of Crime,* New York: Columbia Press.

McGuire, J. (1995) *What Works: Reducing Re-offending,* Chichester: Wiley.

Miller, W.B. (1958) 'Lower class culture as a generating milieu of gang delinquency', *Journal of Social Issues* 14: 15–19.

Moffitt, T.E. (1993) 'Adolescence-limited and life-course persistent antisocial behavior: A developmental taxonomy', *Psychological Review* 100: 674–701.

Morgan, P. (1995) *Farewell to the Family? Public Policy and Family Breakdown in Britain and the USA,* London: IEA Health and Welfare Unit, Choice in Welfare Series No. 21.

Murray, C. (1994) *Underclass: the Crisis Deepens,* London: IEA Health and Welfare Unit, Choice in Welfare Series No. 20.

—— (1996) 'The Emerging British Underclass', in C. Murray *et al.* (eds.), *Charles Murray and the Underclass,* 23–52, London: IEA Health and Welfare Unit, Choice in Welfare No. 33.

Myhre, M. L. and Rosso, F. (1996) 'Designing for security in météor: A projected new métro line in Paris', in R.V. Clarke (ed.), *Crime Prevention Studies* 6: 199–216, Monsey, NY: Criminal Justice Press.

Riley, D. (1991) *Drink Driving: The Effects of Enforcement*, Home Office Research Study 121, London: HMSO.

Schweinhart, L.J. and Weikart, D.P. (1980) *Young People Grow Up*, Ypsilanti, Michigan: High/Scope.

——, Barnes, H.V. and Weikart, D.P (1993) *Significant Benefits: The High/Scope Perry Preschool Study Through Age 27*, Ypsilanti, Michigan: High/Scope.

Sloan-Howitt, M. and Kelling, G. (1997) 'Subway graffiti in New York City "Gettin' Up" vs. "Meanin' It and Cleanin' It",' in R.V. Clarke (ed.), *Situational Crime Prevention: Successful Case Studies* (2nd ed.), 242–49, New York: Harrow and Heston.

Sykes, G.M. and Matza, D. (1957) 'Techniques of Neutralization: a Theory of Delinquency,' *American Sociological Review* 22: 664–70.

Walker, A. (1996) 'Blaming the victims', in C. Murray *et al.* (eds.), *Charles Murray and the Underclass* 66–74, London: IEA Health and Welfare Unit, Choice in Welfare No. 33.

Weidner, R. R. (1996) 'Target hardening at a New York city subway station: decreased fare evasion—at what price?', in R.V. Clarke (ed.), *Crime Prevention Studies* 6: 117–32, Monsey, NY: Criminal Justice Press.

White, J.L., Moffitt, T.E., Earls, F., Robins, L. and de Silva, P.A. (1990) 'How early can we tell? Predictors of childhood conduct disorder and adolescent delinquency', *Criminology* 28: 507–533.

Wilson, J. Q. (1975) *Thinking About Crime*, New York: Basic Books.

Wortley, R. (1996) 'Guilt, shame and situational crime prevention', in R. Homel (ed.), *Crime Prevention Studies* 5: 115–132, Monsey, NY: Criminal Justice Press.

10

For a Sociological Theory of Situations (or How Useful is Pragmatic Criminology?)

Tim Hope and Richard Sparks[1]

In this essay we explore certain problems and limitations of situational crime prevention (SCP) and its partner in crime reduction routine activities theory (RAT)[2]. The problems that we identify include both practical and theoretical dimensions, and given the pragmatic and applied character of SCP/RAT it is none too surprising to discover that these are closely connected. We at no point suggest that the concerns of SCP are either trivial or disposable, and we are to this extent moderately friendly critics. However, we will argue that the highly pragmatic emphasis of SCP/RAT (its self-denying ordinances against speculation and its distaste for all things political) is inhibiting, both from the point of view of usefulness and that of theoretical development.

What is the distinction between pragmatism and usefulness on which this argument depends? We suggest that SCP/RAT is marked by a certain lack of curiosity towards and of systematic enquiry into the conditions of adoption of crime-prevention technique. In the absence of any well-developed enquiry into these conditions SCP proponents tend to reduce their role to that of purveyors of a certain set of purely technical prescriptions. What is entailed in plumping for this consultative, expert role? Must it, for example, go with an inattentiveness to the institutional and political contexts of preventive activities (Which

[1] We are grateful to David Garland, Ronald Clarke, Paul Rock, and Alison Wakefield for their comments on earlier drafts of this paper.

[2] For the purposes of this essay we follow Clarke (1997: 4–6) in defining SCP as the conscious design or manipulation of immediate environments in 'as systematic and permanent way as possible so as to make crime more difficult, more risky and/or less rewarding...to potential offenders' (see also Cornish and Clarke, 1986; Crawford, 1998: 66-68; Hughes, 1998: 18-23). We understand RAT to be an approach to the aetiology of crime which focuses on the manifold ways in which modern living generates criminal opportunities and temptations by bringing together likely offenders and suitable targets in the absence of 'capable guardians' (Felson, 1998: 53); Crawford, 1998. 78–80). In using the shorthand SCP/RAT we indicate the high degree of common ground between these positions, with SCP primarily providing the micro-level theory of *interventions* and RAT a macro-level *explanatory* thesis about the crime-producing characteristics of mundane aspects of contemporary social organization.

strategies are chosen? At whose behest? With what collateral consequences and for whom?)? Does this produce a temptation to settle for what appears to be a 'good-enough' theory, even though the questions that are potentially broached by the notions of 'situations' and 'routine activities' are very much more theoretically fertile and expansive? We will suggest that among the consequences of their pragmatism is that SCP/RAT criminologists manifest a degree of parochialism – an insensitivity with regard to the diverse cultural and political circumstances within which SCP-type initiatives may be taken up (or not). Amongst the variable features of those circumstances are the mix of preventive styles that may be adopted in different times and places (the prevention of what, by what combination of means?), the relations between the actors involved (at a minimum these could include central states, local public bodies, corporations and private individuals) and, in consequence, the dynamics involved in locating responsibility and accountability for the initiation and implementation of such measures. In place of the prevailing situational positivism[3], therefore, we propose attempting something a little more ambitious, namely the development of a sociological theory of situations.

In beginning to sketch the outlines of a sociological theory of situations (and hence to argue for a broader and more reflexive understanding of what 'situations' comprise) we deal briefly with the following issues. We begin by considering some aspects of the relationship between the practical, interventionist focus of SCP and the rather larger claims about the criminogenic (and, equally importantly, crime-preventive) properties of routine activity made by RAT. If these two, SCP and RAT, are coming to represent a common position (or at least are in very close alliance) how well and how comprehensively do the two levels of explanation relate to one another? This is a question of cross-level adequacy of the kind often summarised by sociologists as the 'micro-macro link' (Alexander *et al.*, 1987; Mouzelis, 1995). We argue that one of the main open and as yet insufficiently explored areas here is that of *institutional practices* in the control of crime (i.e. the contributions of 'macro-actors' such as states and corporations). One good (perhaps primary) way of exploring the latter issue would be through comparative empirical enquiry – though this remains to be undertaken. Here, we can do no more than suggest a prospectus for what such work might look like. We go on to examine what kind of theory of practices SCP/RAT expounds or implies. What conceptions of *interests* and *costs* are mobilised, for example, and are these sociologically plausible?

---

[3] We are indebted to David Garland (personal communication) for this expression. It may seem odd to invoke the notion of positivism given that SCP/RAT consciously eschews many of the mentalistic and correctionalist claims traditionally associated with criminological positivism. What we intend by 'situational positivism' is a tendency to accept the givenness of situations (albeit that they may be alterable to reduce their criminogenic aspects). SCP/RAT is marked by a preference for the tangible and immediate rather than the structural, historical, cultural or ideological. We explain below why we think this makes for a somewhat sociologically thin notion of situations (see also Garland, 1999).

Finally we draw some connections and comparisons with notions of *situations* and *routines* that arise in some other areas of sociological enquiry and suggest that certain of these may be helpful in extending the scope of discussion.

CROSS-LEVEL ADEQUACY AND INSTITUTIONAL PRACTICE

We take 'situational crime prevention' (SCP) to be a 'practical theory' – one whose aim is to guide the analysis, implementation and evaluation of measures intended to prevent crime as it occurs *in situ*. Many varieties of social theory accept that in order to be useful – that is, in order to be able to guide enquiry and, where relevant, intervention – they need to offer explanation at both the macro-level (i.e. the collective or structural level of society) and at the micro-level (i.e. the level of individual social action) in ways that are coherently related. Perhaps rather haphazardly, SCP has acquired both a macro-level theory – what has become known as *'routine activity theory'* (RAT) (Felson, 1998) – and an individual-level 'rational choice' theory – that is, a theoretical framework for explaining the occurrence of crime events. One main way in which SCP/RAT can vindicate its claims to practicality and utility is by showing its capacity to influence crime-control practices at either individual or institutional levels, or both. In principle, therefore, SCP/RAT is a position with a highly *reflexive* component: it depends for its influence on 'knowledge-work' and recursive feedback. Unless people (whether they be 'lay' individuals or 'experts' of various kinds) amend their behaviour in some fashion its effects will be neutralised. There must be some form of security or precautionary consciousness, whether this be embedded almost unnoticed in everyday routine practice or introduced by design. To the extent that such restructuring arises this would seem to provide a text-book instance of Giddens's notion of a 'double hermeneutic', whereby theoretical constructs 'fall back' into everyday life (Giddens, 1984: xxxv).

SCP is thus now not just a theoretical proposition but also a corpus of preventive practices – whether constituted as 'natural' social phenomena (Felson, 1998: 166) or as purposive 'governmental' interventions in the control of crime. Hence, the two spheres of SCP inter-penetrate: SCP 'theorists' make claims to practicality; SCP 'practitioners' use the theory to guide and/or legitimise their activities. Ironically, one obstacle in the way of evaluating the SCP/RAT position *qua* sociological *theory* is precisely its political and institutional success. It has ceased to be merely a set of propositions whose adequacy is open to dispassionate examination and has become instead part of the tool-kit of professional wisdom of diverse professional groups (amongst insurance companies and property developers just as much as for the police and other public bodies, as well as amongst their clients – ranging from store-managers to individual homeowners). It may be the case that two senses of 'reflexivity' are at odds with one another here. One is the supple movement between theoretical prescription and everyday practice (in which sense SCP/RAT is highly reflexive). The other is intellectual self-interrogation either with regard to the approach's internal logic or about the institutional and political conditions in which these effects are produced (in which respect it tends to shun reflexivity – its interest lies in cultivating a practical *savoir-faire* rather than 'vague', 'general' or 'fancy' ideas (Felson, 1998: 166-7)).

The institutional 'success' of SCP – both as an academic discourse and as a progenitor of a general movement towards crime prevention in public policy and commercial activity – has also captured the attention of social theorists and critics. For them, SCP is an important phenomenon precisely *because of* its ability to restructure crime control practices. It is notable for its increasing embeddedness in the ways in which late modern societies are governed and regulated. The focus here falls upon the consumption of security goods and services, the spread of CCTV and other surveillance technologies, 'dataveillance', credit-rating and the telematic control of opportunities for fraud and theft and so on (O'Malley, 1992; Ericson and Haggerty, 1997; Rose, 2000). For these reasons Garland (1996) numbers such largely unobtrusive yet somewhat pervasive techniques, and the varieties of criminological knowledge on which they depend, among the 'adaptations' that contemporary societies make to the normality of criminal opportunity. This critical literature signals a number of concerns that are muted in the SCP/RAT literature itself, especially the divergent fates of those who are the beneficiaries of such security practices (the respectable, the legitimate shopper, the creditworthy) and those who are excluded, surveilled and targeted by them (see in particular Rose, 2000).

Yet both SCP/RAT's proponents, especially Felson, and some more critical commentators (for examples, Garland, 1996; Rose, 2000) have a tendency to make claims of historical inevitability – that implicitly or explicitly SCP is the method of crime control most characteristic of late modernity. What has not therefore been much discussed – for reasons we also need to discover – is the apparent *disparity* in the degree to which SCP has penetrated the language and practice of crime prevention in distinct national settings across the advanced economies of the 'western' world. What then explains the apparent enthusiasm – or at least preparedness – of actors in some settings to follow the situational route as compared, say, with the hesitancy, lack of interest, scepticism or outright hostility of others? If SCP is the characteristic crime control apparatus of late modernity, why has it taken root more deeply in certain (political, institutional) contexts and not others? Why also does it seem to sit alongside other crime control approaches, in more and less coherent *mixes* of governmental styles and interventions?

Such institutional disparities require us to look at SCP in two, related, ways. In the first place, we need to address the reasons for the varying take-up of SCP ideas and practices by different institutions in different settings, including nation-states (perhaps most notably among the member states of the

European Union). In such an enquiry, one would be taking SCP's impact itself as a 'variable' and seeking to explain the variation in its adoption across different settings, even amongst those whose societal and economic trajectories are ostensibly similar and representative of the general tendencies noted in some main currents of recent social theory. In pursuing such a programme of research, it would be necessary to adopt, as O'Malley puts it 'a more substantively political frame' (O'Malley, 1999), or as we prefer a *comparative-institutional framework* for analysis. We need to ask, of particular polities, whether SCP has been or is being entertained as a crime control strategy. In what contexts, directed towards what settings, offences and populations, and at whose behest have its diagnoses and practical proposals taken root? Conversely what forms, if any, of resistance or adaptation has it encountered in the course of its *political* progress in different settings? Such an enquiry would direct us, as it has other writers on contemporary crime control, to classic issues of comparative political and legal study – for example, of disparities in legal and political *culture* or of the *structural* location of strategic and political decision-making, or of the varying formations of democratic deliberation. To what degree, moreover, do different contemporary nation-states rely on public or private initiative for crime control and risk management, and what difference does this make to the particular mix of preventive strategies that they adopt? In what contexts, then, is 'crime' coming to be viewed as the kind of problem to which SCP is seen as the solution and, conversely, what other kinds of crime-problem/preventive-solution patterns also emerge?

Second, it is also necessary, in order to guide such enquiry, to find a way of asking questions about the political resonances or attractions of SCP which would reveal the sources of variation in take-up and hence, through comparison, in its political nature. In particular, we need to ask whether there is a *necessary* homology between certain preventive practices and certain forms of politics and modes of urban governance. Such questions thus lead towards an unravelling of the practical and political characteristics of SCP. In highlighting these dimensions of SCP as a focus of study, we anticipate that one difference which might emerge between the varying polities and settings would be the extent to which practices of crime prevention are openly acknowledged as *political responses.*

By this we mean two things: first, that proposals and measures for reducing crime are understood by their participants as constituting part of the various practices, ideologies and discourses of government, here understood to include the actions of businesses and corporations and not only of 'the Government'. That is, how much are crime prevention practitioners aware, or how far do they acknowledge, that they are engaged in political acts or that a political rationality informs their actions? There is, then, the issue of whether, and how much, the application of preventive measures (including those derived from SCP) in the implementation of practices within various polities is *politically reflexive.* Theorists of SCP/RAT (especially Felson, 1998) deny or, at best, play down political reflexivity in the development and promulgation of SCP measures. One device for doing this is their disavowal of theoretical curiosity (at least outside a fairly narrow range of specifically criminological theories). This appears in some part to be a deliberate attempt to de-dramatise many traditionally 'hot' criminological (and associated public) debates and to remove them from the realms not only of speculative social theory but also of political rhetoric (cf. Felson's 'agenda fallacy'), rendering them instead the subject of 'naturalistic' observation, 'common-sense' appraisal and pragmatic intervention (Felson, 1998).

The originality of this move lies in its displacement of aetiological, normative and structural questions (i.e. things mostly to do with offenders and the problems of their motivation), to be replaced by a focus on *situations* and their propensity to generate or inhibit risk (Garland, 1999). While this effort at de-politicisation is itself, of course, a political act, the concomitant shift away from a concern with offender-motivation constitutes, in practice, not so much a denial of aetiological and political issues as an implicit *displacement* of them to the realm of 'situations'. Hence our reference above to the notion of 'situational positivism': situations are treated in SCP/RAT as given. They arise *naturally* (which tends to imply that they are beneficial) or *accidentally* and unintendedly (which tends to suggest that they are unfortunate). In the former case they need to be mimicked or replicated; in the latter to be modified and secured. What they cannot do is indicate that there is anything abidingly or fundamentally faulty about our social organisation: the connection between criminology and critique is thereby severed.

Our second point, then, about the (lack of) political reflexivity in SCP, is best illustrated by posing an aetiological question: if certain 'situations' cause crime, what causes criminogenic situations? By addressing this question to the present corpus of SCP theory we may be able to facilitate examination of the theory's assumptions. More than that, though, the question directs attention back toward the *utility* of SCP itself, as presently constituted, as a practical theory. Unless we address aetiological questions about situations how are we to acquire the knowledge which would allow us to select locales of intervention and measures which would alter them? In our view SCP – or any theory of crime prevention – requires a *theory of practice* to accompany its basic theory. That is to say, the corpus of theory of SCP ought to contain ideas and prescriptions about how to go about selecting problems for intervention, engineering strategies for intervention, and implementing corrective measures. And it ought also to be able to *anticipate* the consequences of such practices. Further, we ought to be able to ask such questions of SCP and make assessments of its practicality, and to compare this with the practicality of other proposals for crime control. So, what are the practical and political consequences of SCP's current premises about the occurrence of criminogenic situations? We will seek to address these issues in the remainder of our paper.

SCP: THE THEORY OF PRACTICE

Felson's macro-level routine activity theories of crime have come to comprise the preferred account for the aetiology of criminal situations underpinning SCP (Felson, 1998; Clarke 2000, this volume). Although he shares some preoccupations with other theorists of late modernity, unlike them, Felson seems remarkably un-reflexive and uncritical – faux-naif perhaps – about the circumstances of 'everyday life' which give rise to crime. Implicitly in his writings, crime is seen as the unintended consequence of mundane, routine and essentially *normal* practices of social life (see further Garland, 1999). This diagnosis has a number of advantages (or so it must seem to its proponents): it extracts crime from issues of politics and morality (Felson, 1998, Ch. 1); the normality of crime at the macro-level provides an homology with the normality of crime at the individual-level (normal in the sense of the offender employing an understandable, everyday, calculus of decision-making); and it establishes a role for technical-scientific intervention – providing corrective remedies for the adverse by-products and side-effects of otherwise socially-acceptable and desirable practices. It also allows Felson to dispose of what he calls the 'pestilence' and 'agenda' fallacies – that crime is related to, or a consequence of, other unacceptable social practices and conditions, including disadvantage and deprivation (Felson, 1998: 18-19). Felson thereby empirically fulfils James Q. Wilson's (1975) critique of positivist criminology's failure to account for the simultaneous growth of crime and affluence during the 1960s and 1970s (Cohen and Felson, 1979)[4].

Nevertheless, whatever theoretical advantages the issue of unintended consequences has for SCP, it also entails political liabilities which, paradoxically, undermine its theory of practice. Essentially, the problem is one of being unable to provide, from within its own theoretical framework, a convincing set of mechanisms promoting implementation of measures to address the harm arising from criminogenic situations. We must assume for SCP, in the absence of evidence to the contrary (or by virtue of the same standards which it applies to offenders), that other parties to putative criminal events – including putative victims – are also rational actors. They too are likely to maximise their personal utility. Now, if criminogenic outcomes of particular situations are unintended, then it may remain unclear and contested which actors carry the *responsibility* to take the action necessary to produce the desired outcome. The only alternatives to persuade relevant actors to act would be appeals to altruism or compulsion from a third party – that is, the

---

[4] Of course in order to deal seriously with crime trends, RAT would need to return to the macro-level concerns acknowledged by Cohen and Felson (1979) and take proper account of the comparative disparities they disclose (e.g. between the United States and Japan, between the United States and England and Wales since 1975, or between England and Wales and other European countries).

state or another macro-actor with sufficient leverage such as perhaps an insurance company. Of course, SCP seeks to overcome this problem by appeals to individual or corporate self-interest. It assumes that persons (or firms? or local authorities?) who are responsible for – or have some stake in – criminogenic situations will act rationally, in their own self-interest, to reduce the harms and losses which they would otherwise suffer. In other words, they will be prepared to invest sufficient amounts of their resources in actions which will reduce the costs of the crimes directly incurred by them. The overall social cost of crime will likewise reduce in proportion to the reduction in the sum of individual costs in society. The logic implies that the social cost of crime is the sum of particular costs.

Nevertheless, a harm like crime is not just an individual cost but also a *social cost*. The cost of crime not only includes the direct costs incurred by victims but also a range of additional social costs – the latter are not just financial (represented by the costs of the criminal justice system maintained by the State) but are also generally regarded in most polities as *moral costs* to society at large, representing the putative consequences of lawlessness, unpunished crime and impunity. Like most 'public goods' (or 'bads' in this case), these social costs are non-rival and non-excludable – a person suffering more of such moral costs does not mean that another suffers less; and people cannot be exempted from sharing these moral costs as long as they remain citizens, even if they do not suffer them directly. It follows that security from crime – the 'product' of crime prevention activity – is also a public good in this sense as well as a private good for individuals[5]. However, if we assume (as SCP does) that would-be crime preventers will act in their rational self-interest then, as students of welfare economics will know, they are only likely to be persuaded to invest in actions which will address their direct costs, leaving the social costs of crime unmet. In this respect, the social costs of crime are an *externality* to those responsible for criminogenic situations. And such persons, acting only in their rational self-interest, have no responsibility or direct incentive to take actions to reduce these social costs. On these grounds, the logic of reliance upon individual or indeed corporate self-interest implies that the level of prevention in society as a whole will be less than optimum, since investment to cover the social costs of crime will be under-provided voluntarily (Field and Hope, 1990).

There are numerous cases where appeals solely to rational self-interest as a basis for eliciting individual and corporate actors' contributions to crime prevention as a public good will produce sub-optimum or even 'perverse' outcomes. For example:

- Where individuals who invest in their own protection consequently adopt

---

[5] In other words, amongst the things that Felson wishes to discount amongst his other 'fallacies' is a large proportion of the Western tradition on the structure, functions and justifications of criminal law and its relationship to the political legitimacy of the State.

fewer security precautions than they would if they had to cover the full costs of their crime risks (as is acknowledged institutionally by excess (deductible) clauses and 'moral hazard' provisions in insurance contracts).

- Where the full direct costs of crime do not fall to those who have the capacity to adopt preventive measures. This is the case with regard to auto-theft, where neither manufacturers nor owners have direct incentives to take preventive measures: the former because the costs of motor crime fall mainly to consumers after the point of sale, in which manufacturers have little direct interest (Field, 1993; Clarke and Harris, 1992); the latter because most costs are defrayed within highly competitive insurance markets (Field, 1993).
- Where the benefits which producers and retailers gain from 'fast-moving' consumer goods and services – including credit cards and motor vehicles – outweigh those actors' direct crime costs, by virtue of high-volume transactions, the impairment of which by security measures will reduce turnover below profitability in a competitive market (Levi *et al.*, 1991).
- Where public crime prevention goods are being generated on the basis of voluntary participation – as in the provision of natural surveillance through 'neighbourhood watch' – there is a built-in incentive to *free-ride* for any individual (and an absence of penalties) to the extent that the good becomes under-provided (Field and Hope, 1990; Hope, 1999).
- Where the 'displacement' of crime to other locales, victims, etc. is an *externality* which those responsible for the target situation have little direct incentive to forestall (Barr and Pease, 1990).
- Where the 'diffusion of benefits' – whereby others than those who provided the prevention gain benefits from the measures, without incurring costs (Clarke and Weisburd, 1994) – constitutes *fortuitous free-riding*, serving as a disincentive (a negative externality) to those who are obliged to bear the costs of prevention.

In sum, the argument which we wish to advance here is not that SCP cannot provide *technical* crime prevention solutions to some or all of these problems, but that its inherent implementation strategy – implicitly relying upon voluntary participation and individual self-interest – contains few if any incentives for actors to meet all the relevant direct *and* indirect (i.e. social) costs of crime and that as a consequence the public good of safety is likely to be under-provided, or at any rate to be patchily provided in ways that are arbitrary from the point of view of equity or distributive fairness.

Thus, the deficiency *vis-à-vis* political theory is that SCP does not contain a mechanism for adequate provision of public goods of safety and security. So long as this deficiency is not addressed, SCP will remain the hand-maiden of the private market and will respond to, and reinforce, inequalities in the means of private protection, leaving the public good of security under-provided. Additionally, by default, sectional interest groups – including the better-off — will be able to provide for themselves *exclusive club goods*. For example:

- Retailers may club together in shopping centres and malls to share in the common infrastructure of security (and other infrastructural benefits besides) and, by virtue of the private nature of the locale, be able to exclude certain members of the public from sharing in, or prejudicing, such security (Shearing and Stenning, 1983; Wakefield, 2000, and von Hirsch and Shearing, 2000, this volume).
- Residents of 'exclusive' suburbs are able to take advantage of the low crime rates which their communities bestow by virtue of the capacity of the private housing market to protect and distance them from other members of society (Hope, 1999).

In other words they get public good benefits for themselves which are denied to others, thus exacerbating inequality in the distribution of security (Hope, in press). In short, in order to address these deficiencies, SCP requires a better *theory of situations*, one which contains within it an *account of the public interest* in the reduction of crime. We struggle to detect any account of these issues in SCP's current macro-level travelling companion RAT.

TOWARDS A SOCIOLOGICAL THEORY OF SITUATIONS?

A sociological theory of criminogenic situations would address the aetiological question posed earlier. Constructively, we suggest that there is something that SCP could learn from some varieties of social theory in which it presently disavows interest. For example, its predeliction for *rational choice* has certain obvious affinities with Coleman's Rational Action Theory, though we would suggest that it might benefit from the 'collective action' aspect of Rational Action Theory (see Coleman, 1990), if only to remedy its deficiencies in handling the public goods problem.[6] Additionally, there are also less apparent affinities with contemporary social theory which would help in the development of a *social* theory of situations.

---

[6] Rational action theories, such as those of Coleman (1990), are concerned not just with explaining individual action in terms of rational choice and utility maximisation but also in accounting for the social systematic and collective consequences of individual rational choice, which in turn frame and shape the exercise of individual choice. A central conern of such theories is to account for seemingly 'irrational' or counter-intuitive collective outcomes of individuals acting rationally (see also Hargreaves Heap, et al., 1992; Barry and Hardin, 1982). One classic problem addressed by such theories is the apparent voluntary under-provision of *public (or collective) goods* by groupings of individuals notwithstanding that it would be in each individual member's rational self-interest to have such goods provided. Some of the examples described in the previous section are illustrations of public goods problems and of ways of (partially) overcoming them, e.g. through the creation of *club goods*. Needless to say, there are also moral and normative ways of conceptualising public good problems (see Loader and Walker, forthcoming).

Several important contemporary accounts are concerned with the interlacing of everyday 'situated' conduct with the larger patterns of stability and change in social life. For example SCP/RAT's interest in how criminal opportunities are built into everyday life in late modern settings (and the prospects that therefore arise for 'designing out crime') opens out (at least potentially) into a wider consideration of the properties of the *systems* in which they arise, for example *vis-à-vis* the intersections between their physical or spatial and their social dimensions. This would appear in principle to have something in common with Giddens's concern for the 'patterning of social relations across time-space' (his definition of 'system') and the examination of the 'reproduced practices' which make such *'system-ness'* possible. In Giddens's view, the proper domain of study for the social sciences is the investigation of 'social practices ordered across space and time' (Giddens, 1984: 2); and RAT would seem to be one specialised version of such inquiry. But Giddens goes on to insist that the analytic next step is to consider how the reproduction of situated practice becomes co-ordinated in the form of institutions and organisations. Routines necessarily enjoy a prominent position in any such account, Giddens argues, since routinisation is implicit in the very notion of practice.

But routinisation is also a specific feature of *organisations*. For Giddens, the 'modern period is the era *par excellence* of organisations' (1987: 149). Organisations (offices, factories, schools, hospitals, prisons) direct the activities of their members via the precise control of time; their hierarchies are reflected and sustained in their 'zoning' of space; they monitor their own activities through *surveillance* considered both as the collation and storage of information (files, records, inventories, accounts) and through 'direct supervision' especially of subordinate members, and all organisations use 'specifically designed locales' (1987: 157). In other words, routine activity theory's signature concept (routine activity obviously) is not one that it can readily corral, copyright, restrict or patent so that it refers purely or principally to the production of criminal opportunities or crime preventive interventions. Rather the reverse – the notion of routine activity is the point of connection between crime prevention studies and the wider concerns of social analysis with system, organisation, agency, constraint and power (see Giddens, 1984; Sparks et al., 1996: Ch. 2).

For example, Bottoms et al., 1995 (see also Bottoms and Sparks, 1998) have demonstrated in a prison setting that even in this most highly situationally controlled of environments, SCP-style interventions are neither self-evidently and automatically effective nor clearly separable from the stew of routines, social relations and motivations on which they are imposed (and which they also tend to restructure). 'Situations' may be unintended, and often indeed perverse, outcomes of institutional arrangements, but this does not make them any the less institutionally produced. Such concerns led Bottoms et al. to conclude that one could not ignore either the dimension of power in the implementation of control measures nor indeed (even in so unlikely a setting as a prison) the contribution of normative reasons for compliance (*cf.* Bottoms, 1998) (which also entails that situational measures can have perverse outcomes of their own)[7].

We have argued that SCP's current macro-level theory (i.e. RAT) provides insufficient grounds for genuinely *public* action because it does not adequately provide a mechanism for implementing change and compliance. A precursor for identifying such mechanisms would be to identify the particular *interests* which sustain criminogenic situations in their present state. In other words, to problematise the 'unintendedness' of the consequences of social action. Felson's descriptive naturalism (Garland, 1999) tends to act as a set of blinkers to posing aetiological questions about crime situations which, paradoxically, might actually allow greater scope for intervention, or at least the saving of wasted or futile effort on ineffectual measures. To give two practical examples:

- Felson cites Hope's (1982) study of burglary of schools which showed, *inter alia*, that 'large, modern and sprawling' schools faced greater risks than 'small, old and compact' schools and, in combination with Barker's 'under-manning' theory and small-town nostalgia, recommends that schools should be small or moderate in size (Felson, 1998: 116). Nevertheless, Felson ignores the general conclusion to this work (Hope, 1985) that: (a) the observed dichotomy in size between schools was an *historical* product; (b) that the well-protected small schools were, on other defensible educational grounds, obsolescent, deteriorated, under-utilised and inefficient; and (c) because of this, the architectural design of schools inevitably constituted a compromise between conflicting and equally desirable curricular and educational needs which an insistence on smallness for security purposes alone might disrupt at some perhaps even greater social cost. Thus although the criminogenic potential of school building size was an 'unintended' consequence of social change, addressing one of its *unintended* consequences might in itself produce other, not necessarily beneficial, *unintended* social consequences.
- An analysis of the contributory factors which sustained the situational pattern of violence associated with city centre pubs and clubs – which went beyond the immediate characteristics of the bar-room settings in which the violence occurred – to include issues of drinking culture and practice, the

---

[7] Another properly sociological attempt to come to terms with the significance of routine activity for societal reproduction and change is Bourdieu's theory of practice (Bourdieu, 1977, 1990; Bourdieu and Wacquant, 1992). Bourdieu conceives this in terms of the relationship between *habitus* (roughly the actor's acquired set of dispositions understood as a 'generative principle' for new actions and improvisations) and *field* (the 'game space' of possibilities, opportunities and constraints characteristic of particular domains of activity). If a certain kind of criminal activity constitutes a field then both committing and preventing it are embedded practices that 'make sense' in terms of the *habitus* of the actors concerned (i.e. from the angle of the *prise de position* that each assumes *vis-à-vis* the field).

character of city centres and transport systems, the commercial dynamics of the drinks and leisure trades, and the impact of the existing regulatory system itself (Hope, 1985), provided not only a more adequate explanation of the phenomenon of violence in bars (Bottoms, 1994) but also a more comprehensive assessment of the possible range of practices and actions which would have a bearing on the control of crime in city centres (Wikström, 1995).

CONCLUSION

For reasons of this sort, a sociological theory of criminogenic situations (and its counterpart a sociological theory of routine criminal and preventive practices) would look somewhat different from SCP/RAT, as currently consti-tuted. It would still be an account designed with practical intent – indeed, as we have argued above, it should aim to develop a *theory of interventions* which is part of what we think is currently lacking. It would not, however, share the view that the aims of clarity or practicality in crime prevention studies were best served by bracketing-out institutional, comparative, aetio-logical or normative questions. Rather it would find itself required to subject those dimensions of discussion to lucid and dispassionate examination as well (rather than consigning them to the 'sea of vagueness' that RAT takes itself to be surrounded by). In this sense it would unquestionably learn from and build upon the increasingly impressive record of examples and case studies that SCP/RAT generates in order to situate them in a larger field, namely the reflexive study of a certain set of practices in which contemporary western societies increasingly engage but which are in turn conditioned by the partic-ular administrative and political cultures in which they find their application.

Let us then briefly return by way of conclusion to the questions we raised at the outset (even if these remain, in the absence of the research that we see as necessary, questions rather than conclusions):

1. We remain to be convinced that SCP/RAT has yet properly addressed the question of cross-level adequacy (the nature of the micro-macro link that it suggests or proposes). The question of the generation of criminal oppor-tunties in late modern settings demands something which RAT deals with only sketchily and informally – namely an account of the societal and technological changes that have delivered them. Similarly, we have suggested that the propensity of offenders to take advantage of those opportunities – and of other actors to react to their doing so – looks like something that stands in need of *a theory of practices and situations* which, as Giddens argues, cannot be restricted to the 'micro' level of analysis. Moreover, since we are concerned not only with transactions between individuals but with the contexts in which those transactions take place, we

also require an account of the behaviour and interests of the macro-actors (*cf.* Mouzelis, 1995) who are also intrinsically involved (states, municipal authorities, police, insurance companies, transport systems etc).

2. Since in our view this topic necessarily has *institutional* dimensions (and this is where we came in), we cannot indefinitely disregard the comparative issues involved in the selection of distinct strategies and methods of prevention in different places. Even strong versions of 'convergence' and 'globalization' perspectives are increasingly having to take account of the fact that different western societies have followed distinct trajectories through modernity (Therborn, 1995), with persistent implications for their legal, political and administrative cultures (*cf.* Nelken, 1994). RAT unfits itself from commenting on this by construing its menu of solutions as given by technical necessity rather than flowing from political judgement. Since it largely escapes RAT's attention that the construction (in the sense both of setting priorities and providing explanation) placed upon crime problems can differ from place to place, it has little or nothing to say about the political and organizational contexts within which the relevant choices are made. Having decided already that political commitment on this matter belongs in the category of fallacies it has nothing interesting to say about politics. By contrast, the project of developing a reflexive theory of criminogenic situations and preventive practices would (almost by definition) take the existence of points of diversity and convergence as its theoretical point of departure.

3. By extension, the technicism of the SCP/RAT outlook has surprisingly little to say about how to *scale* the harms that it seeks to prevent or about their actual impacts on the daily lives of the individuals and communities in which they arise (i.e. their capacity to arouse fear, anger and other powerful feelings). This blandness and normative disengagement occupies a peculiar position in the instabilities of the contemporary politics of criminal justice (*cf.* Garland, 1996). Garland identifies a tendency for discussion of these issues to shift gear abruptly – to move from unemotive discussion of loss reduction to vivid expressions of rage, pity and enmity. For now, we would merely wish to point to the discovery of such disparities in many arenas of current thinking about risk (such as nuclear safety, industrial accidents, pharmaceuticals etc. as well as crime – *cf.* Krimsky and Golding, 1992). It seems increasingly apparent, in many such domains, that the attempt to purge discussions of risk of their moral and emotive associations rarely prove entirely successful, but it can also be the case that the sophistication and subtlety of such discussion can be damaged in the attempt (*cf.* Douglas, 1992). Douglas castigates those who contend that risk can be discussed in purely unemotive and technical terms for their 'innocence' and misrepresentation of its social meanings and political force. By extension, then, we would argue that in failing to address the cultural and political location of criminogenic situations (and hence their necessary

relation to questions of equity, accountability and legitimacy), SCP/RAT may actually undermine its own claim to practicality.

Here, we have only begun to set out an agenda for enquiry; and we recognise, necessarily, that such an approach may frustrate those who are impatient to get on with the business of crime prevention and for whom a 'good enough' theory will suffice. Our argument, however, is that eschewing the wider domains of social and political theory may turn out not to be good enough in the longer run for an approach which self-consciously makes a claim to practicality. 'Politics' – by which we mean the realm of moral judgement and collective choice – is not something to be bracketed-off from practice without itself producing political consequences, some of which indeed may be 'unintended'. In particular, the reluctance of SCP/RAT proponents to address problems in the application of SCP itself, particularly concerning the questions of *distribution* (i.e. who *gets* what security?) and *compliance* (i.e. who *does* what prevention?) is a severe self-imposed limitation. There is not merely one politics of SCP. But to inform political choice, we need a theory of politics and of interests applicable to 'situations' – whether we like it or not.

REFERENCES

Alexander, J., Giesen, B., Munch., R. and Smelser, N. (1987) *The Micro-Macro Link*, Berkeley CA: University of California Press.

Barr, R. and K. Pease (1990) 'Crime placement, displacement and deflection', in M. Tonry and N. Morris (eds.), *Crime and Justice: A Review of Research* 12:277–310, Chicago: University of Chicago Press.

Barry, B. and Hardin, R. (eds.), (1982) *Rational Man and Irrational Society?*, Beverly Hills: Sage.

Bottoms, A. (1998) 'Five puzzles in von Hirsch's theory of punishment', in A. Ashworth and M. Wasik (eds.), *Fundamentals of Sentencing Theory*, Oxford: Oxford University Press.

—— (1994) 'Environmental criminology', in Maguire, M, Morgan, R. and Reiner, R. (eds.), *The Oxford Handbook of Criminology*, Oxford: Clarendon Press.

—— and Sparks, R. (1998) 'How is order in prisons maintained?', in A. Liebling (ed.), *Security, Justice and Order in Prison*, University of Cambridge, Cropwood Conference Series.

—— Hay, W. and Sparks, R. (1995) 'Situational and social approaches to the prevention of disorder in long-term prisons', in T. Flanagan (ed.), *Long-Term Imprisonment: Policy, Science and Correctional Practice*, London: Sage.

Bourdieu, P. (1977) *Outline of Theory of Practice*, Cambridge: Cambridge University Press.

—— (1990) *The Logic of Practice*, Cambridge: Polity Press.

—— and Wacquant, L. (1992) *An Invitation to Reflexive Sociology*, Cambridge: Polity Press.

Clarke, R.V. (1997) 'Introduction', in R.V. Clarke (ed.), *Situational Crime Prevention: Successful Case Studies* (2nd ed.), Albany, NY: Harrow and Heston.

—— and P.M. Harris (1992) 'Auto theft and its prevention', in M. Tonry (ed.), *Crime and Justice: A Review of Research* 16: 1–54, Chicago: University of Chicago Press.

—— and Weisburd, D. (1994) 'Diffusion of crime control benefits: observations on the reverse of displacement', in R.V. Clarke (ed.), *Crime Prevention Studies*, Monsey, NY: Criminal Justice Press.

Cohen, L.E. and Felson, M. (1979) 'Social change and crime rate trends: a routine activities approach', *American Sociological Review* 44: 588–608.

Coleman, J. (1990) *Foundations of Social Theory*. Cambridge, MA.: Belknap Press.

Crawford, A. (1998) *Crime Prevention and Community Safety*, London: Routledge.

Douglas, M. (1992) *Risk and Blame*, London: Routledge.

Ericson, R. and Haggerty, K. (1997) *Policing the Risk Society*, Toronto: University of Toronto Press.

Felson, M. (1998) *Crime and Everyday Life* (2nd ed.), Thousand Oaks, CA: Pine Forge Press.

Field, S. (1993) 'Crime prevention and the costs of auto theft: an economic analysis', in R.V. Clarke (ed.), *Crime Prevention Studies* 1: 69–91, Monsey, NY: Criminal Justice Press.

Field, S. and Hope, T. (1990) 'Economics, the consumer and under-provision in crime prevention', in Morgan, R. (ed.), *Policing Organised Crime and Crime Prevention*, British Criminology Conference 1989, vol. 4, Bristol: Bristol Centre for Criminal Justice.

Garland, D. (1996) 'The limits of the sovereign state', *British Journal of Criminology* 36: 445–71.

—— (1999) 'The commonplace and the catastrophic: interpretations of crime in late modernity', *Theoretical Criminology* 3: 353–64.

Giddens, A. (1984) *The Constitution of Society*, Cambridge: Polity Press.

—— (1987) *Social Theory and Modern Sociology*, Cambridge: Polity Press.

Hargreaves Heap, Hollis, S.M., Lyons, B., Sugden, R. and Weale, A. (1992) *The Theory of Choice: A Critical Guide*, Oxford: Blackwells.

Hope, T. (1985) *Implementing Crime Prevention Measures*, Home Office Research Study No. 86, London: HMSO.

—— (1999) 'Privatopia on trial? Property guardianship in the suburbs', in K. Painter and N. Tilley (eds.), *Surveillance: Lighting, CCTV and Crime Prevention*, Monsey, NY: Criminal Justice Press.

—— (in press) 'Inequality and the clubbing of private security', in Hope, T. and R. Sparks (eds.), *Crime, Risk and Insecurity,* London: Routledge.

Hughes, G. (1998) *Understanding Crime Prevention,* Buckingham: Open University Press.

Krimsky, S. and Golding, D. (eds.), (1992) *Social Theories of Risk,* New York: Praeger.

Levi, M., Bissell, P. and Richardson, T. (1991) 'The prevention of cheque and credit card fraud', *Crime Prevention Unit Paper No. 26,* London: Home Office.

Loader, I. And Walker, N. (forthcoming) 'Policing as a public good: reconstituting the connection between policing and the state', *Theoretical Criminology* v. 5.

Mouzelis, N. (1995) *Sociological Theory: What Went Wrong?,* London: Routledge.

Nelken, D. (1994) 'Whom can you trust?: the future of comparative criminology', in D. Nelken (ed.), *The Futures of Criminology,* London: Sage.

O'Malley, P. (1992) 'Risk, power and crime prevention', *Economy and Society* 21: 252–75.

—— (1999) 'Volatile and contradictory punishment', *Theoretical Criminology* 3: 175–196.

Rose, N. (2000) 'Government and control', *British Journal of Criminology* 40: 321–339.

Shearing, C. and Stenning, P. (1983) 'Private security: implications for social control', *Social Problems* 30: 493–506.

Sparks, R., Bottoms, A. and Hay, W. (1996) *Prisons and the Problem of Order,* Oxford: Oxford University Press.

Therborn, G. (1995) *European Modernity and Beyond,* London: Sage.

Von Hirsch, A. and Shearing, C. (2000) 'Exclusion from public space', this volume.

Wakefield, A. (2000) 'Situational crime prevention in mass private property', this volume.

Wikstrom, P-O. (1995) 'Preventing city-centre street crimes', in M. Tonry and D.P. Farrington (eds.), *Building a Safer Society: Strategic Approaches to Crime Prevention. Crime and Justice* 19: 429–468, Chicago: University of Chicago Press.

Wilson, J. Q. (1975), *Thinking About Crime,* New York: Basic Books.

11

*Situational Crime Prevention, Urban Governance and Trust Relations**

Adam Crawford

INTRODUCTION

In this chapter I want to locate situational crime prevention (SCP) within a broad canvas stretched across two frames: first, the vertical relations between government and the governed, and secondly, the horizontal social relations and interactions between people bound together in close proximate spaces or localities. In so doing, I want to connect SCP to a much broader set of shifts in the terrain and form of socio-political governance. What I hope to do here is to sketch tentatively some of the wider social conditions that have facilitated the rise of SCP (notably in Britain) and to explore some of the social and cultural implications that this may have, with particular regard to trust relations. In extending David Smith's (2000) line of argument, I wish to contend that situations and persons, traditionally juxtaposed against each other in SCP literature, need to be connected together in terms of their inter-dependent cultural contexts and social relationships, as well as in relation to the political programmes which have facilitated the appeal of given SCP strategies. The reception of specific modifications to situations and the environment, the form they take and their implications for social behaviour, are likely to be infused with cultural and political inflexions and reflect changes in social ecology and urban governance.

Academic and policy debates have largely ignored the cultural and social implications of the dramatic rise of SCP, and the massive investment in forms of technology and design which it has inspired. I wish to argue that SCP connects with, and is a visible representation of, a much wider restructuring of modes of governance which reconfigure the nature, form and basis of trust relations – with implications for crime and its control. It is my contention that SCP constructs symbolic representations of 'orderly environments': through

* This chapter has benefited from comments by David Garland, Robert Reiner and Tony Bottoms, as well as other participants at the workshop on 'Situational Crime Prevention – Ethics and Social Contexts', Fitzwilliam College, Cambridge, 14–16 October 1999. Any inadequacies of the arguments presented, however, are all mine.

notions of territoriality, exclusivity, surveillance, protection and defensiveness. At the same time, SCP inscribes *distrust* into the physical environment through the modification, design and manipulation of situational attributes. These interventions result in a reconfiguration of what can be trusted, by producing new abstract systems and symbolic tokens. I shall argue that they encourage new forms of 'thin trust', which are simultaneously reflexive (in that they elicit awareness of the bases of trust relations) but brittle (in that they are easily shattered). In this context, however, the demand for trust, rather like the demand for security, may become insatiable.

SITUATIONAL CRIME PREVENTION: THE CRIMINOLOGIES OF PLACE AND EVERYDAY LIFE

At the heart of SCP, as Clarke and Felson argue, is an:

> Image of the criminal in which temptation and opportunity are central to the explanation of crime. All persons have some probability of committing crime and can be criminal one moment and noncriminal the next. Legal behaviour is malleable and displacement of illegal to legal behaviour may be complete (1993: 10).

What is notable about the 'criminologies of place' which infuse SCP – namely 'routine activity' theory, crime pattern analysis and 'rational choice' theory – is that they proceed from the premise that crime is an usual and normal aspect of modern life and that criminals are essentially 'like us': no different from other rational actors (Clarke, 1983). 'The reality', as Marcus Felson notes, 'is that ordinary people can do ordinary crime – young and old. Everybody could do at least some crime some of the time' (1998: 11).

Hence, in contrast to earlier criminology, crime is understood as a series of events which require no particular motivation or pathology, but rather, is seen as inscribed within the routines of contemporary social existence. Crime is viewed as a risk to be calculated, and hence, avoided or managed rather than a moral abnormality in need of explanation. These criminologies construct crime as 'risk' alongside other 'harms'. Crime is normalised as 'routine activity' (Cohen and Felson, 1979). As Garland aptly terms them, these are 'the new criminologies of everyday life' (1996: 450),[1] whereby the 'rational choice actor' is identified as an enterprising or autonomous subject.[2]

The theories that underpin SCP not only give up on, but are also not interested in, questions of aetiology. They do not seek to *know* – let alone under-

---

[1] As Garland (1996) notes, this normalisation of crime should be understood as an adaptation to a context in which high recorded rates of crime have become a normal social fact. Such an adaptation may serve to limit the level of demand placed upon criminal justice systems.

[2] This analogy is extended beyond the avoidance, prevention and management of risk by potential victims, to include the 'enterprising prisoner', who is enlisted by regimes of choice with incentives and disincentives, as an entrepreneur of his own personal development (Bottoms et al., 1990; Garland, 1997: 191).

stand – the criminal or his predispositions. Offenders are constructed as 'abiographical individuals' (O'Malley, 1992) abstracted from their social or structural context and personal history. In this sense, SCP significantly shifts the focus of study away from criminal personalities or disorganised sub-cultures to the criminal event and the immediate situational context in which crimes (are allowed to) occur. As such, SCP strategies are uninterested in differentiating the 'criminal' or 'deviant' from the 'normal'. Offending, on this account, is a normal and routine social fact. Moreover, this emphasis on normalcy is inscribed into SCP mechanisms of control. In some senses, as Garland (1999: 360) suggests, this represents a radical departure in crimi-nology as it marks a process of 'de-dramatisation' and 'de-differentiation'. In this sense, SCP is both generalised and universal in that its gaze falls upon, and is directed at, us all: either as potential victims or as potential offenders. As Marcus Felson states:

> This is why we should avoid thinking of people with either stigmas or halos. Perhaps, the best policy is to regard most strangers and even neighbours with a moderate dose of benign suspicion (1998: 43).

As such, the 'de-differentiation' that SCP heralds etches a generalised distrust into its environs.

In an important early statement Hough and colleagues defined SCP as constituting:

  (i) measures directed at highly specific forms of crime;
 (ii) which involve the management, design or manipulation of the immediate environment in which these crimes occur;
(iii) in as systematic and permanent a way as possible;
 (iv) so as to reduce the opportunities for these crimes;
  (v) as perceived by a broad range of potential offenders (1980: 1).

SCP encompasses a vast range of interventions into, and modifications of, the environment. Clarke (1992) highlights three principal (and often interrelated) ways in which opportunity reduction through SCP occurs:

- *increasing the perceived effort* involved in crime by making the targets of crime harder to get at or otherwise hindering the commission of crime;
- *increasing the perceived risks* of detection and apprehension; and
- *reducing the anticipated rewards* of crime.

Hence, in diverse forms SCP seeks to block crime in practical and simple ways. In so doing, it places an emphasis upon alterations to the *physical* environment, the aim being to routinise opportunity reduction into the design and fabric of everyday life.

And yet, this raises two often-ignored specific issues. First, given the breadth of possible interventions, the interesting question is: why have certain forms of opportunity reduction been emphasised over others? A subsidiary, but no less crucial question, then, is: in what ways is this emphasis influenced by the nature of given political and cultural contexts? Secondly, as Clarke and other proponents recognise, SCP operates at a symbolic, as well as a real, level. It references *perceived* or *anticipated* consequences. This, of course, is one of the primary flaws of rational choice theory in that 'rational choice actors' are never in a position of full knowledge about the limitations of interventions upon which to premise their decisions. Let us consider some of the practical implications of these two issues.

First, some SCP interventions have met a much more favourable reception than have others. In Britain, at least, the practical expression of SCP often takes a highly visible, technological and physical form. Indeed, the most heavily promoted and financed SCP intervention has undoubtedly been the CCTV camera (see Wakefield, 2000, and von Hirsch, 2000, in this volume), the widespread proliferation of which began in the mid-1990s, when the Conservative government made it a central feature of its law and order policy. Towards the end of 1995 the government announced the establishment of a special fund, known as the 'CCTV Challenge Competition' to encourage local authorities to set up and part fund surveillance schemes.[3] In the three years to the end of 1997 the Home Office and local authorities collectively invested £120 million in CCTV systems (*Guardian*, 9.1.1998). More recently, the Labour government announced that it intends to invest a further £150 million in CCTV in order to extend surveillance coverage to new locations, most notably social housing complexes and other quasi-private spaces.[4] This expansion has not been restricted to governmental facilities but is also reflected in the commercial sector.[5]

There has also been a favourable reception of 'defensible space' ideas, intellectually championed in Britain by Alice Coleman (1985; 1989), particularly at the levels of government as witnessed, for example, by the Department of the Environment's circular on planning and crime (DoE, 1994). These ideas have also been well received within British policing in the 1990s, with the establishment of 'secured by design' programmes and the appointment of Police Architectural Liaison Officers. The question, therefore, is why have these forms of SCP been so well received, whilst others have largely been ignored?[6]

Secondly, the physical form that favoured SCP strategies often take may also, importantly, be symbolic. Rational choice theory does not presuppose that interventions are effective on their own terms, merely that they are

---

[3] As part of this programme £15 million was to be made available in the financial year 1996/7, with the intention to help provide up to 10,000 more CCTV cameras in high streets and other places over the ensuing three years (Home Office, 1995).

[4] By 1999 the number of town centres and business districts estimated to be subject to the gaze of the video surveillance camera stood at 530 in England and Wales.

[5] For example, in 1995 Marks and Spencer announced that it was committing most of its £30 million budget for security improvements towards CCTV (*Guardian*, 21.9.1995).

[6] For a good list of the variety of diverse SCP interventions and techniques available see Clarke and Homel (1997).

perceived as such by potential offenders. Hence, SCP mechanisms can 'work' without being effective – such as the CCTV cameras which unbeknown to passers-by have no film (or poor quality film) in them, or are not switched on – they may nevertheless affect the perception of risks of detection and the effort of crime, or the anticipated rewards of crime. Moreover, the 'diffusion of benefits' which are claimed to arise from SCP interventions will often be explained by rational choice theories in precisely these terms: namely, by offenders not knowing the limitations of the SCP intervention (see Felson and Clarke, 1998: 23; Clarke and Weisburd, 1994). In some senses, the technical efficacy of SCP is less important than their role in the production of organised legitimate symbols of 'orderly environments'.

In order to understand the reception of certain forms of SCP we need to relate this not only to political programmes, but also to the manner in which given favoured SCP interventions seek to evoke certain types of environments, in which representations of orderliness – through territoriality, exclusivity, surveillance, protection and defensiveness – are held out to assuage feelings of insecurity. It is my contention that the reception of SCP, in Britain at least, both reflects changes in social ecology and connects with the rise of new forms of political governance, which in turn have cultural effects for relations of trust in the new environments generated by SCP interventions.

However, the political reception and cultural effects of SCP have largely been ignored. In some senses, the technicist and rationalistic discourse of SCP and routine activity theory deliberately avoids and marginalises such questions and concerns. SCP and routine activity theory are presented, by proponents, as providing universal, technical solutions divorced from political questions and normative judgements. Consequently, there has been little understanding of, or concern for, the specific attractiveness of given SCP interventions in divergent organisational and social contexts, and the way in which forms of SCP resonate with, or affect, aspects of legal and political culture within different societies. As Hope and Sparks (2000) suggest, there is now a need for a comparative enquiry into SCP's 'political message' and social effects. Such an enquiry should seek to reveal the culture-bound qualities of crime control (Crawford, 2000; Nelken, 2000). For, as David Nelken warns, many claims about 'crime control which purport to be universal in fact take their sense and limits of applicability from such cultural connections' (1994: 221). Moreover, lessons from comparative enquiries may alert us to the implications which forms of crime prevention have for aspects of our culture which we may take for granted, or to which we may have been blind (see Crawford, 1998a: Ch. 7).

Hence, Clarke appears unable to answer his own very pertinent question (posed in this volume): why is it that SCP has apparently achieved such a prominent place in crime policy in Britain but not in the USA? We could go on to ask: why it is that, unlike some of our European counterparts, in Britain we have tended to opt for technologically driven SCP – most notably as 'capable guardians' (to use the language of routine activity theory) – while preferring to ignore what Bottoms and Wiles (1992) call a more 'people dynamic' focus to crime prevention? Notions of 'order' and 'orderliness' to which SCP interventions appeal are intrinsically bounded by ideological, cultural and normative assumptions of appropriateness and 'social fit'. For example, 'order' in a British rural community is very different from that experienced in a suburb and different again from that of a cosmopolitan city centre (Young, 1999). Moreover, the sense of orderliness and disorderliness of adult residents in 'middle England' (Loader et al., 1998) will undoubtedly differ significantly from that in Northern Italy or the expanding commuter belt of American cities. The 'gated communities' outside Los Angeles and elsewhere in the USA (Blakely and Snyder, 1997) occupy a very different cultural place from similarly 'defensible spaces' inhabited, for example, by residents in apartment buildings in the centre of Paris. They may conform in similar ways to 'defensible space' ideas – concerning limited access, use of concierges or security guards, and so on – but they have a fundamentally different cultural salience, moral place and social meaning.

THE SALIENCE OF PLACE

It is my contention that the rise of SCP connects with new modes of urban governance, which are both fragmented and highly territorialised. In contrast to earlier modern forms of territorialisation which have expressed a 'social' or 'societal' dimension, these new forms are remarkably localised. Whereas before the territorialisation of governmental programmes and thought has been tied to the nation-state and the government of populations within its territories, localised forms of territorialisation have now taken on a new salience. The community or neighbourhood has become the affective field expressing these forms of territorialisation. To some degree, the ideas which inform SCP – notably rational choice theory – have encouraged a micro-social focus to the level of community or neighbourhood.

Interestingly, these localising pressures coincide with globalising tendencies. Just at the moment in which global trends appear to be displacing the primacy of place by stretching social relations across time and space, new forms of localised relations organised in terms of place are emerging. Hence, under contemporary conditions of late (or high) modernity there is an enduring significance of symbols of place and location. As Giddens suggests, alongside the disembedding processes of late modernity is a process of re-embedding (1990: 79). Here, disembedded social relations are recast within local conditions of time and place. Foremost amongst these are trust relations, recast through interactions, encounters, experiences and the very nature of the physical environment.[7] Spatial relations have become saturated with, rather

[7] In this regard, Giddens refers to the significance of 'locales' which constitutes 'A physical region involved as part of the setting of interaction, having definite boundaries which help to concentrate interaction in one way or another' (1984: 375).

than vacated of, meaning (Lash and Urry, 1994). Local relations provide the context in which trust relations can be produced, maintained and fractured. They also provide contexts through which apparently distant systems of technology and expertise can be reflected. Furthermore, localities occasion situations for social interaction which can serve to reinforce relations of trust.

The symbols of 'orderly environments' which SCP heralds through a territorialisation of control (by way of forms of 'defensible space', surveillance, target hardening and other physical protective barriers) are becoming increasingly important bounding mechanisms for social interaction. These spaces and forms of 'community as territoriality' constitute a realm of governance that connects with people's everyday experiences of locality under contemporary conditions. They afford the potential to retrieve control over territory. As such, they are essentially defensive in that they seek to reduce opportunities for crime, target-harden potential objects of criminality and limit access by outsiders (Clarke, 1995). This is precisely what Oscar Newman means by 'territoriality', as people's sense of ownership over a demarcated space. For, according to Newman:

> "Defensible space" is a surrogate term for the range of mechanisms – real and symbolic barriers, strongly defined areas of influence, and improved opportunities for surveillance – that combine to bring an environment under the control of its residents (1972: 3).

This defensiveness also operates at a psychic level as it allows people to evoke nostalgic 'imagined communities' of tradition (Lacey, 1996). The territorialisation of control to the community level has profound emotional overtones, in that it holds out the ideal of genuine human identity, connectedness and reciprocity, precisely at a time in which these appear most absent. Yet these symbolic representations of order are forced to meet everyday experiences of safety which reflect both the fact that SCP can produce feelings of security and actual security, and failures to secure them. This has significant implications for future trust relations. For example, having invested in 'security'—technologies or people – failures of such schemes may deal a severe blow to any trust relations which that person had sought through expert systems or personnel, ones which subsequently may be hard to repair.

The notion of 'security as commodity' which SCP offers provides consumers with real choices, enabling them to confront and manage their sense of insecurity. As such, a sense of security informs tangible decisions that people make regarding where they go, live, shop, the nature of their leisure activities, etc. However, investments in security as a commodity are at best tentative attempts to control an unknowable, unpredictable and risky social world. This requires an investment of trust, one which is always subject to being undermined by new developments or shifts in feelings of (in)security. Consequently, the commodified notion of *private* security may itself be an unachievable goal: 'a new form of "magic" within a system that eschews the invisible and the unknowable'

(Spitzer, 1987: 47). Perversely, the acquisition of more and more 'security as commodity', may serve to undermine feelings of genuine 'security' by institutionalising anxiety. Moreover, the individualistic quest for personal security may undermine the public sphere and people's experience of it, particularly as people withdraw from it. The marketisation of security calls upon individuals and groups to act as 'responsible' rational choice actors in weighing up the risks and security dimensions of social interaction. And yet, these are individual choices which may impact upon others' security and sense of safety. Hence, in a regime in which security is an exalted (but potentially insatiable) commodity, there may be an inherent antagonism between *feeling secure* and *being social*. As Richard Sennett (1970) noted some time ago, the quest for private or communal security is often premised upon stifling introspection which threatens social contact and understanding, and erodes tolerance of diversity.

Unsurprisingly, it is increasingly privately controlled spaces which appear to offer greater symbols of security through their use of technologies, cameras, guards, fences and so on. In everyday ways many of us buy into the commodification of security and, in discernible ways, this may pacify and moderate our fears, albeit that these 'safe havens of territoriality' and private 'zones of governance' are themselves predicated upon, and potentially their appeal lies in, processes of social exclusion. As a consequence, 'security' may be less a 'public good' and more a 'club good' which increasingly derives from wealth and the ability to find sanctuary in secure zones, private guards, new technologies, architectural designs and defended communities. As such, commodification may generate 'security differentials' which increasingly become significant characteristics of wealth, power and status.[8]

In part, this defensiveness reflects changes in social and urban ecology. The contemporary processes of de-urbanisation or counter-urbanisation – through which cities are losing populations to more suburban and rural areas[9] – have tended to highlight the problem of social polarisation and disintegration of urban areas, encouraging new sources of insecurity and anxiety, and producing what Hope refers to as 'the frightened city' (1995).[10] Thus, the new

---

[8] However, private 'zones of governance' which SCP facilitates also offer potentially positive social opportunities for crime control in semi-public spaces. First, they tend to emphasise the instrumental rather than the moral elements of control and policing (Shearing, 1992). Secondly, as a consequence, they tend to place less emphasis on detection and punishment and more on the prevention of future offences. Symbolic and ritualistic punishments are not a moral imperative. However, ensuring that the risk of an offence recurring is reduced is an instrumental and financial imperative. As such, they are inclined to invest in a future-orientation. Thirdly, and partly on the basis of this, they tend to inscribe incentives for conformity and orderly conduct – a 'rewards infrastructure' (Kempa et al., 1999: 206), rather than rely upon punishments. Finally, they tend to operate through apparently consensual forms of control rather than coercive ones, as traditionally associated with state regulation.

[9] The flight from Britain's metropolitan areas between 1981 and 1994 is estimated to be 1.25 million more people leaving than arriving, equivalent to a net migration loss of 90,000 a year (Champion et al., 1996).

[10] In stark contrast to the confident, expanding cities studied by Chicago School sociologists.

symbols of 'orderly environments' also evoke an anxiety borne of social dislocation. Security, or at least a sense of it, may be becoming a predominant characteristic in the map of social relations in urban areas, with insulation from undesirable 'others' as its defining logic. This raises the concern that, in a globalising era that celebrates mobility, cities may be increasingly fragmenting into 'no go areas for some, no exit areas for others' (Social Exclusion Unit, 1998: 9).

A dominant level at which this new territorialisation occurs is the neighbourhood or community. The reconstruction or revival of networks of civic trust is a key theme within crime prevention generally and community-based crime prevention specifically (Wilson and Kelling, 1982; Sampson et al., 1997). For communitarians, 'community' is the focus for a remoralisation of social relations, which holds interdependency and mutal trust as central concerns. Appeals to community represent the territorialisation of political thought and the manner in which conduct is collectivised (Crawford, 1997; Rose, 1999a). 'Defensible space' embodies this form of territorialisation:

> Defensible space is a model for residential environments which inhibits crime by creating the physical expression of a social fabric that defends itself. All the different elements which combine to make a defensible space have a common goal – an environment in which latent territoriality and sense of community in the inhabitants can be translated into responsibility for ensuring a safe, productive, and well maintained living space (Newman, 1972: 3).

The decline of governmental strategies of social solidarity and the rise of private and communal governments constitute a disaggregating force, which fractures and pluralises.[11]

Hence, SCP practice exhibits an incongruity, namely that its social reality of differentiation and dislocation runs in contrast to its de-differentiating ethos. As a consequence, territoriality – through access and exclusion – becomes a means of 'differentiating' persons: they are strangers and outsiders who do not belong or have rights of access to disaggregated 'zones of governance' and 'gated communities'. Trust, in this context, is generated through the processes of exclusion, in which undesirables are filtered out. Trust becomes context and place specific. Increasingly, towns, districts and city centres vie for new positions of influence and wealth through their capacity to attract investors, both capital and people, by the attractiveness of a city as a 'safe place'. This has encouraged 'safe havens of territoriality' and offers of 'orderly environments',

---

[11] This is often exacerbated by a central paradox in crime prevention, the existence of an often inverse relationship between activity and need with regard to SCP. Despite limited attempts by local governments to redress the balance, years of research have shown that community responses to crime are easiest to generate in exactly those areas where they are least needed, and hardest to establish where the need is greatest. Moreover, performance-led and output-driven priorities for local government can encourage concentration upon easy or 'soft' targets, most likely to yield positive results. This paradox is compounded by any problems of spatial (or other forms of) displacement.

where symbols of security and safety are inscribed into the architecture and surroundings.

GOVERNING AT A DISTANCE

SCP surveillance connects with new modes of 'governing at a distance' encouraged by managerialist reforms of the public sector.[12] The new governance manifests a novel relationship between the state and civil society: it straddles and, to some extent, fractures the public-private divide. The new regulatory style is captured in the new-found phraseology of 'a partnership' between government and the community. It is a relationship of 'less government but more governance' (Osborne and Gaebler, 1992: 32).[13] Here, we see the state as facilitator and 'animator' (Donzelot and Estèbe, 1994). This combines the activation of the public (civil society) and the market to take on board traditional state functions, as well as the transformation of the state itself. In this 'reinvention of government', future modes of governance should be market-based, outcome-oriented, future-focused, prevention-concerned, mission-driven and customer-focused (Osborne and Gaebler, 1992: 20). These modes of governance simultaneously embody strategies of responsibilisation, pluralisation, autonomisation and commodification, all of which connect with, and inform the favourable reception of, SCP.

Responsibilisation is a central element in the new forms of governance (Garland, 1996). The relationship between government and the governed is now one in which we are all reconfigured as 'partners'. The language of 'partnership' has become an important element in this new governance. More specifically, crime prevention was one of the earlier sites for the articulation of a partnership approach by the British government (see Interdepartmental Circular 8/1984). We are now all cast as 'partners against crime' in a new corporate approach (Crawford, 1994), involving a fundamental rearticulation of individual and group responsibilities and professional 'expertise', as well as state paternalism and monopoly of control. Where once we were told to 'leave it to the professionals', now we are enjoined to active participation in a 'self-policing society'.

[12] Managerialist reforms have emphasised transferring certain traditional aspects of public service delivery to the private sector or rendering bureaucracies subject to market disciplines by disaggregating separable functions into quasi-contractual forms, particularly by introducing purchaser/provider distinctions, and opening up provider roles to competition between agencies or between public, private and voluntary sector bodies. They advocate a responsiveness to 'consumers' and 'customers'. Efficiency, economy and value for money are the totems of these neo-liberal inspired reforms. Bottoms (1995) highlights three distinct aspects of managerialism within criminal justice – namely its systemic, consumerist and actuarial dimensions.

[13] As I have argued elsewhere (Crawford, 1997: 210–12), we should not assume, unproblematically, the effectiveness of such strategies. In practice, strategies of 'governance at a distance' often result in more complex and confused relations – what Taylor (1997) illustratively refers to as 'arm's length but hands on'.

Pluralisation includes the fragmentation and dispersal of policing and control. Fragmentation itself has been encouraged by the introduction of privatisation and quasi-markets through purchaser-provider splits, where services could not easily be privatised. We can no longer speak (if we ever could) of a state monopoly in crime control and policing (Jones and Newburn, 1998). Policing in its broadest sense – as the process of governing or the condition of ordered regulation aimed at the promotion and maintenance of security – has become dispersed among a plethora of actors, with implications for the locus of power and the nature or absence of sovereign authority. It has become parcelled-up and shared, as diverse agencies, organisations, groups and individuals are implicated in these tasks. SCP, with its appeal to local order and the retrieval of control over territory, plays a central role in this pluralisation. This has produced a complex array of interlaced alliances of organisations and active citizenry which transcend the 'public' and 'private' spheres, constituting hybrid mixes of plural agencies, places and functions. It has also seen the expansion of 'private government' and the policing *by* communities rather than *of* communities. As a result, this process of fragmentation itself has generated a demand for greater co-ordination, and ripened the conditions for the emergence of networks and partnerships which attempt to draw together the diverse services in new, and ever more complex, 'tangled webs' (Charlesworth et al., 1996).

Autonomisation occurs in that these strategies of governance set individuals free as 'calculating selves' (Rose, 1999*b*). The neo-classical 'rational choice actor' at the heart of SCP theory holds aloft the abstract individual stripped from his personal biography as well as social and economic constraints, and capable of self-actualisation and of constructing himself anew, both in identity and destiny. In a neo-liberal political climate which celebrates autonomy and responsibility, choice becomes the operative language in which individuals are constructed as the architects of their own social position and personal security.

Consumerisation also occurs in that choice operates within a marketplace of consumption in which, as already noted, security has become commodified. The private sector has been quick to exploit the opportunities presented by the expanding 'market' in crime prevention. In everyday ways many of us buy into the commodification of security. It offers real choices and, in tangible ways, this may pacify and assuage our fears. As a commodity, crime prevention holds out the promise that 'security' is attainable through purchase, by buying 'expert' preventive technology and security hardware; employing 'trustworthy' intermediary services; moving to 'safe' areas, and so on.

Managerialist shifts in regulatory style demand that new flows of information be generated by the redrawing of state functions, necessitating processes of control and verification which allow those that 'steer' – setting norms and agendas – to monitor and correct the activities of those that 'row' – the doing of things (Osborne and Gaebler, 1992: 32). Contracts, performance indicators, audits and inspections are some of the practical tools used to deliver this relationship of 'governing at a distance'. The audit, as Michael Power (1997) has shown, has been a central instrument in the transformation of modes of governance and control. As the state has redrawn its functions and become increasingly committed to a supervisory role, audit and accounting practices have assumed a more prominent place. Despite its technical discourse, the audit – rather like SCP – is also a system of values and goals which are inscribed in the official programmes which demand and encourage it (Power, 1997: 7). It helps shape public conceptions of the problems for which it is the perceived solution: 'It is constitutive of a certain regulatory or control style which reflects deeply held commitments to checking and trust' (*ibid.*) Audit, like SCP, is not merely a technical solution to a problem: 'It also makes possible ways of redesigning the practice of government' (*ibid.*: 11). As such, it has become a central mechanism in delivering strategies of 'rule at a distance'.

I suggest that SCP is a complementary element to the 'audit explosion'. The audit, like SCP, encourages a society organised to observe itself through mechanisms of control. They both encourage the self-inspecting and self-monitoring capacity of society. Audit, like SCP, is a paradoxical and complex combination of surveillance and trust (ibid.: 134). Whereas SCP mechanisms – notably forms of surveillance – act through environments upon individuals, audits have as their primary object organisations and their sub-systems of control. SCP and audits constitute complementary, but different levels of control. SCP is a form of 'first order control', whereas audit is the control of control (*ibid.*: 128). Moreover, SCP interventions lend themselves to constituting the subject of audit.[14]

In reciprocal ways, SCP mechanisms and audits are technologies of apparent mistrust contrived, in part, in reaction to trust deficits and in the hope of restoring trust between people in given social settings and trust in organisational competence. As such, they are also concerned with the production of comfort, order and security. And yet, rather than resolving trust deficits, they may multiply and disperse these into the fabric of the physical and organisational environment. Moreover, they presuppose and necessitate trust in themselves as instruments of verification and control. We are required to trust in the CCTV camera, controlled access, surveillance, security technology, the audit and the audit process itself.

TRUST

Social theorists and political commentators are increasingly coming to realise the importance of trust as the mainstay of inter-personal and inter-organisational relations (see Gambetta, 1988*a*; Fukuyama 1995; Leadbeater, 1999). In a

---

[14] This has interesting implications for the community safety partnerships established under the Crime and Disorder Act 1998 and the requirements upon them to audit community safety (see Crawford, 1998*b*).

criminological context, the concepts of risk, security and trust are not only closely bound up with one another, but also have significant implications for crime prevention mechanisms of security and the social and cultural place that they occupy. Trust is a means of coping with the 'freedom of others' and connects with the idea of the possibility of co-operation (Gambetta, 1988*b*: 217). Trust affords and facilitates a sense of security and acts as a generalised means of exchange. Trust releases people from the need for checking. Hence, it is a foundational prerequisite for security and serves to restrain uncertainty. Trust, by its nature, necessitates taking risks. As such, trust presupposes an awareness of circumstances of risks. Hence, risk-taking in relation to one's security, as far as it involves others, requires trust. As Giddens notes: 'The experience of security usually rests upon a balance of trust and acceptable risk' (1990: 36). As such, trust and risk are complementary concepts. Yet despite the considerable criminological attention given to the analysis of risk (see Ericson and Haggerty, 1997; O'Malley, 1998), questions of trust have largely been ignored within the criminological literature.

Trust acts as a lubricant to informal social control: it forms the basis of social exchange. Trust fosters co-operation, inter-dependence and risk-sharing which facilitate social interaction and innovation. Moreover, trust is both active and interactive. It cannot merely be called upon but must be generated and reproduced. Trusting is linked to social contexts. Forms of trust are not universal but rooted in cultural understandings and assumptions. The salience and place of trust relations within different cultures and social settings and explorations in the type, manner and level of trust, as Nelken (1994) has illustrated, constitute a rich lever for comparative analysis.[15] For our purposes, we can identify a number of forms of trust:

- trust in people;
- trust in expertise, on the basis of claims to knowledge;
- trust in abstract systems (procedures and rules); and
- trust in symbolic tokens.

These are not disaggregated but inter-related aspects of trust, often one implies or relates to another.[16]

Many traditional bases for trust and forms of acquaintance – class, community, family, religion and so on – have been eroded by social, economic and

[15] For example, as some Japanese commentators have noted, the cultural importance of interpersonal trust relations in Japanese society has produced forms of cultural resistance to some SCP mechanisms, particularly of a target hardening variety (Moriyama, 1995). In Japan, localised social relations organised in terms of place form the premise of trust (Komiya, 1999: 373). In this context, specific SCP interventions which fracture or interfere with the social structure of face-to-face interactions present problems for trust and the encounters which sustain it. As a consequence, despite Japan's propensity toward technological advancements, there has been some reluctance to adopt certain Anglo-American developments in SCP.

[16] As I have argued elsewhere (Crawford 1997; 1998*b*), new modes of governance have significant implications for inter-organisational trust relations.

technological change. As a result, we must increasingly rely upon abstract and expert systems which are premised upon novel forms of trusting. Trust in late modernity has become harder to sustain but is also increasingly in demand. In an anonymous and individualised consumer age we are increasingly asked to trust products, services, organisations and people all of which we know little about. Factors which make trust more valuable also render it more difficult to nurture. The demand for trust springs from the very conditions which produce its deficit. The uncertainty, volatility and innovation of contemporary life encourage the thirst for security and safety but also erode the conditions which allow strong relations of trust to flourish.

Despite the importance of trust, *more* trust is not a self-evident good. Just as it is possible to have too little trust, it is also possible to have too much trust. Uncritical or blind trust is itself problematic, whilst the 'decline of deference to authority' has been an element in the construction of a more critical and reflexive modern public polity. Too much trust, particularly within the criminal justice context, can equally be the source of organisational ineffectiveness, abuses of power and corruption (Nelken, 1994: 237). Distrust is itself an important social commodity, as trust is not always mutual, reciprocal, interdependent or deserved and can lubricate relationships of dependency and power.

Investments of trust involve giving up a moral hostage to fortune, which if breached may have significant implications for future social relations and trusting. Trust is inevitably easier to destroy than it is to generate. As Baier suggests, 'trust comes in webs, not in single strands, and disrupting one strand often rips apart whole webs' (cited in Power, 1997: 135). Rather like 'community', trust is more likely to be noticed by its absence.

TRANSFORMATIONS IN TRUST

As a number of commentators have noted, the nature of trust in organisations is being transformed by managerialist reforms seeking to construct forms of 'governance at a distance' (see Kramer and Tyler, 1996). The rise of contracting expresses a loss of faith in the 'binding power of obligations' (Tyler and Kramer, 1996: 3). In the private security context, the contract of membership becomes a fundamental way in which to access privately controlled public spaces. Here, exclusion and access control encourage 'environments of trust' which are contractualised through the terms of entry or membership. The expansion of 'private residential associations' and planned residential developments regulated by a complex of land-use servitudes (Alexander, 1997) are testimony to this contractualisation of everyday life, as is the growth of 'mass private property' (Shearing, 1992). These 'zones of governance', 'contractual communities' and 'clubs' are governed by contracts enlisting powers of removal, dismissal, exclusion or termination of membership, all of which constitute potent administrative instruments.

Some commentators have suggested that the 'irony of contracting' is that whilst efficient contracting requires environments of trust, the introduction of contract in such an environment may result in the breakdown of trust (Neu, 1991: 247). It has long been recognised that the strict adherence to contractual specification is often antithetical to ongoing trust relations, both in business and social interactions which are sustained over time (Macaulay, 1963; Macneil, 1980). The new-found emphasis upon contracts and audits involves the formalisation and fixing of fluid social relationships. As a consequence, there is a shift in the fundamental character of trust, whereby trust is invested in the formal procedures of surveillance, recording and monitoring. This shift also vests power in the auditor or regulator of breaches of contractual terms.

Managerialism, like SCP, disrupts trust relations by replacing traditional forms of trust in professional use of discretion with forms of audit, inspection and surveillance. Relations of trust in and between functionaries which have traditionally allowed large scope for policy discretion have been curtailed by managerialism. It has encircled trust, by reducing the boundaries of discretion and rendering it subject to inspection and budgetary constraint.

Whilst trust in abstract systems has become increasingly mediated by expertise, expertise itself is being reconfigured. SCP theory and practice question notions of professional expertise. Rather like wider neo-liberal and managerialist critiques of welfarism, advocates of SCP claim to speak on behalf of 'consumers', residents and taxpayers, feeding off critiques of 'self-serving professional élites'. As such, they claim to represent a challenge to the 'cosy cultures of professional self-regulation' (Power, 1997: 44) and claims to expertise. Felson illustrates this in his critique of the 'naive ideologies' of criminology:

> The issue is not how good or bad government is to people but whether public places are designed and organised to allow people to control their own environments informally (1998: 145).

Here lies an appeal to open up a new circuit of power between the demands of communities and individuals as against those of criminal justice agencies. As such, SCP replaces the trust that welfarist governments have placed in professional wisdom and the decisions and actions of criminal justice specialists. SCP embodies an implicit critique of the edifice of criminal justice and its practices. Moreover, the internal logics and technical requirements of SCP displace the logics of expertise. In its place, individuals and communities are enjoined to be suspicious, to participate in communal control, to engage in observation and surveillance and to be vigilant.

As such, managerialism, like SCP, institutionalises *distrust*. However, recourse to audits, contracts and SCP interventions does not necessarily *destroy* trust – as some have argued (Broadbent et al., 1996) – but rather reconfigures it. Hence, we need to distinguish clearly between two forms that 'difficulties of trust' take (Sennett, 1998: 141): in the first, trust is simply absent or emptied out, in the second by contrast, there is an active suspicion of institutions, organisations and others. It is this second form which is encouraged and fostered by new modes of governance and SCP. The active institutionalisation of distrust is different from the empty absence of trust. The former may have implications for the weakening of trust relations but this is not a zero sum game. Distrust and trust can co-exist, precisely because trust is a reflexive act which occurs within given social and cultural contexts. Trust is fostered and reproduced through situations and processes in which it is actively tested.

Trust and the contractualisation of relations are not mutually exclusive. In many senses, contracts presuppose a certain degree of trust. The new governance does not obliterate trust altogether, in fact it necessitates that trust is placed in new 'guardians of trust', auditors, inspectors and security systems. But this is a different form of trust, involving a 'second order' relationship. Ultimately, however, these systems of control are themselves the subject of questions as to their competence.[17] The trust that new technologies demand must itself be the subject of 'verification'. The 'audit' is the managerial mechanism for delivering this.

Interestingly, 'trust in abstract systems' may increase the importance of 'trust in persons'. Thus, relations may become increasingly characterised by both more and less trust: more interpersonal trust and less impersonal trust. At another level, trust in people has become highly localised. Paradoxically, in an era of growing globalisation people's *Umwelt* – the area in which one feels secure and the area in which one is aware of dangers and opportunities (see Young, 1999: 71–73) – may be shrinking.

Consequently, we are required increasingly to place trust in 'symbolic tokens' (Giddens, 1990). For example, as consumers we place trust in brand names and 'labels', or what Sennett calls 'hollow signs' (1998: 56). In many senses, the symbols of trust in crime control and security increasingly take less the human form of the blue-coated police officer and more the form of the physical representations of SCP: the CCTV camera, security fixtures and the tracks of territoriality: arguably less intrusive, often visible but tangible nevertheless. These are 'the physical expressions of a social fabric that defends itself', in Newman's terms.

Yet SCP does not reconfigure trust in a unidirectional manner in the sense of less trust, its effects are more complex than that. Some SCP practices, particularly those informed by 'defensible space' theory, seek to increase trust among the internal community of residents (the 'insiders'), whilst they simultaneously attempt to keep out non-residents and hence increase distrust of such

---

[17] It is interesting in this light to note the manner in which the originally unsceptical public reception of CCTV cameras in public places in Britain has recently become more ambiguous, less so for ethical or legal reasons, but more because of their failure to secure: because the images are poor, the technology does not work, controllers are poorly trained, and so on.

'outsiders' and 'strangers'. They seek to demarcate and differentiate who can be trusted on the bases of shared territoriality. Trust is bifurcated as communities of interests are formed: the shared interest being communal security. Distrust in those unknown people (and things) can increase the salience of the bonds of trust amongst people who know each other whether due to kinship relations or through living in close proximity. The localism of SCP – often taken to a highly specific, almost micro-local, level – may heighten the salience of local experience in structuring a sense of security. As such, trust in other people simply because they are 'locals' may be an important means of managing security (Evans *et al.*, 1996: 377). In some senses, SCP can also be characterised by both more and less trust: more impersonal trust and less inter-personal trust. For example, heightened trust placed in the surveillance camera on a lonely train station platform co-exists with, and may encourage, increased suspicion and distrust in fellow passengers.

However, encouraged by new modes of governance, trust relations themselves are becoming more contingent. They involve a greater degree of reflexive monitoring of the conditions and contexts which sustain trust. This affords the potential for the development of new forms of trust which are open and subject to revision (Leadbeater, 1999: 162–66). This we may refer to as 'thin trust': which is potentially more transparent and accessible (in contrast to exclusive, closed systems of trust) but also more fragile. Moreover, this form of 'thin trust' can breed the seeds of its own fracturing, in that new systems of trust – such as those heralded by SCP – remind us of our own insecurity, the root of many of our collective demands for, and conditions of, trust. As such, SCP can produce a form of 'over-deterrence', based upon forms of surveillance, which may achieve their goal at the expense of exerting a 'chilling effect on public spontaneity' (Grabosky, 1996: 33) with its own implications for people's sense of security.

CONCLUSION

Whilst highlighting the connections between SCP and broader shifts in governance, it is important to stress that these do not represent an inevitable unfolding of conditions of late modernity in which the quest for 'ontological security' is fuelled by processes of 'de-traditionalisation' and 'globalisation', as some commentators imply (Giddens, 1998). Certainly, the rise of SCP has been facilitated by, and expresses, conditions of late modernity combined with technological advancements. However, it is also aligned with a specific political programme heralding a restructuring of relations between the state and civil society (O'Malley, 1992). In this regard, as I have argued, there is much to be learnt from comparative research focused on the salience of SCP both within different cultures and in response to different political agendas.

In this chapter, I have not intended to suggest that the transformation of trust outlined here necessarily constitutes an intrinsically 'bad thing'. Nor have I outlined a clear or unambiguous understanding of the full implications of the changes identified. I would suggest that not only is the reception of certain SCP strategies a product of its time, in that these strategies resonate with a particular kind of social organisation (one in which high rates of crime have become a normal social fact, as Garland has argued (1996), but also that it reflects and echoes a wider political transformation in modes of governance. This transformation in relations within and between the state and civil society has serious implications for feelings of security and relations of trust. This social restructuring of the field of political governance simultaneously institutionalises new forms of suspicion and distrust and yet is designed, at least in part, in the hope of restoring trust in the competence of governments, organisations, groups and individuals – through their power to 'make a difference' in crime control. However, the danger is that the very technologies of distrust – from CCTV cameras through houses kite-marked as 'secured by design', to crime prevention audits – may only serve to dissolve further the bases of social interaction and informal control whilst failing to reassure the public against anxieties over personal safety. Just as the quest for security may be insatiable, so too trust may become caught up in a similar spiralling dynamic, where demands for more trust fail to be met as we search for novel forms of trust, and institutionalise ever newer forms of distrust.

REFERENCES

Alexander, G.S. (1997) 'Civic property', *Social and Legal Studies*, 6(2): 217–34.

Blakely, E.J. and Snyder, M.G. (1997) *Fortress America: Gated Communities in the United States*, Washington, DC: Brookings Institution Press.

Bottoms, A.E. (1995) 'The philosophy and politics of punishment and sentencing', in C. Clarkson and R. Morgan (eds.), *The Politics of Sentencing Reform*, 17–49, Oxford: Clarendon.

——, Hay, W. and Sparks, R. (1990) 'Situational and social approaches to the prevention of disorder in long-term prisons', *The Prison Journal*, 70: 83–95.

—— and Wiles, P. (1992) 'Explanations of Crime and Place', in D.J. Evans, N.R. Fyfe and D.T. Herbert (eds.), *Crime, Policing and Place: Essays in Environmental Criminology*, 11–35, London: Routledge.

Broadbent, J., Dietrich, M. and Laughlin, R. (1996) 'The development of principal-agent, contracting and accountability relationships in the public sector: conceptual and cultural problems', *Critical Perspectives in Accounting*, 7: 259–84.

Champion, T., Wong, C., Rooke, A., Dorling, D., Coombes, M. and Brundson, C. (1996) *The Population of Britain in the 1990s*, Oxford: Clarendon.

Charlesworth, J., Clarke, J. and Cochrane, A. (1996) 'Tangled webs? Managing local mixed economies of care', *Public Administration*, 74: 67–88.

Clarke, R.V. (1983) 'Situational crime prevention: its theoretical basis and practical scope', in M. Tonry and N. Morris (eds.), *Crime and Justice: An Annual Review of Research* 4: 225–56, Chicago: University of Chicago Press,.

—— (ed.) (1992), *Situational Crime Prevention: Successful Case Studies*, Albany, NY: Harrow and Heston.

—— (1995) 'Situational crime prevention', in M. Tonry and D. Farrington (eds.), *Building a Safer Society: Strategic Approaches to Crime Prevention Crime and Justice: A Review of Research* 19: 91–150, Chicago: University of Chicago Press.

—— and Felson, M. (1993) 'Introduction: criminology, routine activity, and rational choice', in R.V. Clarke and M. Felson (eds.), *Routine Activity and Rational Choice. Advances in Criminological Theory* 5: 1–14, New Brunswick, NJ: Transaction.

—— and Homel, R. (1997) 'A revised classification of situational crime prevention techniques', in S.P. Lab (ed.), *Crime Prevention at a Crossroads*, 17–27, Cincinnati, OH: Anderson Publishing.

—— and Weisburd, D. (1994) 'Diffusion of crime control benefits: observations on the reverse of displacement', *Crime Prevention Studies*, 2: 165–83, Monsey, N.Y.: Criminal Justice Press.

Cohen, L. and Felson, M. (1979) 'Social change and crime rate trends: a routine activity approach', *American Sociological Review*, 44: 588–608.

Coleman, A. (1985) *Utopia on Trial*, London: Hilary Shipman.

—— (1989) 'Disposition and situation: two sides of the same crime', in D.J. Evans, and D.T. Herbert, (eds.), *The Geography of Crime*, 108–34, London: Routledge.

Crawford, A. (1994) 'The partnership approach: corporatism at the local level?', *Social and Legal Studies*, 3: 497–519.

—— (1997) *The Local Governance of Crime: Appeals to Community and Partnerships*, Oxford: Clarendon.

—— (1998a) *Crime Prevention and Community Safety: Politics, Policies and Practices*, Harlow: Longman.

—— (1998b) 'Community safety and the quest for security: holding back the dynamics of social exclusion', *Policy Studies*, 19: 237–53.

—— (2000) 'Contrasts in victim/offender mediation and appeals to community in France and England', in D. Nelken (ed.), *Contrasting Criminal Justice*, 207–31, Aldershot: Ashgate.

Department of the Environment (1994) *Planning Out Crime*, Circular 5/94, London: DoE.

Donzelot, J. and Estèbe, P. (1994) *L'État Animateur: Essai sur la Politique de la Ville*, Paris: Éditions Esprit.

Ericson, R. and Haggerty, K. (1997) *Policing the Risk Society*, Oxford: Clarendon.

Evans, K., Fraser, P. and Walklate, S. (1996) 'Whom can you trust? The politics of 'grassing' on an inner city housing estate', *Sociological Review*, 44: 361–80.

Felson, M. (1998) *Crime and Everyday Life* (2nd ed.), Thousand Oaks, CA: Pine Forge Press.

—— and Clarke, R.V. (1998) *Opportunity Makes the Thief: Practical Theory for Crime Prevention*, Police Research Series Paper 98, London: Home Office.

Fukuyama, F. (1995) *Trust: The Social Virtues*, London: Hamish Hamilton.

Gambetta, D. (1988a) (ed.), *Trust: Making and Breaking Cooperative Relations*, Oxford: Basil Blackwell.

—— (1988b) 'Can we trust trust?', in D. Gambetta (ed.), *Trust: Making and Breaking Cooperative Relations*, Oxford: Basil Blackwell.

Garland, D. (1996) 'The limits of the sovereign state: strategies of crime control in contemporary society', *British Journal of Criminology*, 36: 445–71.

—— (1997) '"Governmentality" and the problem of crime', *Theoretical Criminology*, 1: 173–214.

—— (1999) 'The commonplace and the catastrophic: interpretations of crime in late modernity', *Theoretical Criminology* 3: 353–64.

Guardian (1995) 21 September.

—— (1998) 9 January.

Giddens, A. (1984) *The Constitution of Society*, Cambridge: Polity Press.

—— (1990) *The Consequences of Modernity*, Cambridge: Polity Press.

—— (1998) *The Third Way: The Renewal of Social Democracy*, Cambridge: Polity Press.

Grabosky, P.N. (1996) 'Unintended consequences of crime prevention', *Crime Prevention Studies*, 5: 25–56.

Home Office (1995) *Closed Circuit Television Challenge Competition 1996/97*, London: Home Office.

Hope, T. (1995) 'Community crime prevention', in M. Tonry and D. Farrington (eds.), *Building a Safer Society. Crime and Justice: A Review of Research* 19: 21–89, Chicago: University of Chicago Press.

—— and Sparks, R. (2000) 'For a Sociological Theory of Situations', (Or How useful is Pragmatic Criminology), this volume.

Hough, M., Clarke, R.V. and Mayhew, P. (1980) 'Introduction', in R.V. Clarke and P. Mayhew (eds.), *Designing Out Crime*, 1–17, London: HMSO.

Jones, T. and Newburn, T. (1998) *Private Security and Public Policing*, Oxford: Clarendon Press.

Kempa, M., Carrier, R., Wood, J. and Shearing, C. (1999) 'Reflections on the evolving concept of "private policing"', *European Journal on Criminal Policy and Research* 7: 197–223.

Komiya, N. (1999) 'A cultural study of the low crime rate in Japan', *British Journal of Criminology* 39: 369–90.

Kramer, R.M. and Tyler, T.R. (1996) (eds.), *Trust in Organisations: Frontiers of Theory and Research*, London: Sage.

Lacey, N. (1996) 'Community in legal theory: idea, ideal or ideology?', *Studies in Law, Politics and Society*, 15: 105–46.

Lash, S. and Urry, J. (1994) *Economies of Signs and Space*, London: Sage.

Leadbeater, C. (1999) *Living on Thin Air*, London: Viking.

Loader, I., Girling, E. and Sparks, R. (1998) 'Narratives of decline: youth, dis/order and community in an English "middletown"', *British Journal of Criminology*, 38: 388–403.

Macaulay, S. (1963) 'Non-contractual relations in business: a preliminary study', *American Sociological Review* 28: 55–67.

Macneil, I.R. (1980) *The New Social Contract: An Inquiry into Modern Contractual Relations*, New Haven: Yale University Press.

Moriyama, T. (1995) 'The possibilities of situational crime prevention in Japan', Paper presented to the British Criminology Conference, University of Loughborough, 18–21 July.

Nelken, D. (1994) 'The future of comparative criminology', in D. Nelken (ed.), *The Futures in Criminology*, 220–43, London: Sage.

—— (ed.) (2000), *Contrasting Criminal Justice*, Aldershot: Ashgate.

Neu, D. (1991) 'Trust, contracting and the prospectus process', *Accounting, Organizations and Society* 16: 243–56.

Newman, O. (1972) *Defensible Space: People and Design in the Violent City*, London: Architectural Press.

O'Malley, P. (1992) 'Risk, power and crime prevention', *Economy and Society* 21: 252–75.

—— (ed.) (1998) *Crime and the Risk Society*, Aldershot: Ashgate.

Osborne, D. and Gaebler, T. (1992) *Re-inventing Government*, Reading, Massachusetts: Addison-Wesley.

Power, M. (1997) *The Audit Society*, Oxford: Oxford University Press.

Rhodes, R.A.W. (1996) 'The new governance: governing without government', *Political Studies* 44: 652–67.

Rose, N. (1999a) 'Inventiveness in politics', *Economy and Society* 28: 467–93.

—— (1999b) *Powers of Freedom: Reframing Political Thought*, Cambridge: Cambridge University Press.

Sampson, R.J., Raudenbush, S.W. and Earls, F. (1997) 'Neighborhoods and violent crime: a multi-level study of collective efficacy', *Science*, 277: 918–923.

Sennett, R. (1970) *The Uses of Disorder: Personal Identity and City Life*, New York: Norton.

—— (1998) *The Corrosion of Character*, New York: Norton.

Shearing, C. (1992) 'The relation between public and private policing', in M. Tonry and N. Morris (eds.), *Crime and Justice: A Review of Research* 15: 399–434, Chicago: University of Chicago Press.

Smith, D. (2000) 'Changing Situations, and Changing People', this volume.

Social Exclusion Unit (1998) *Bringing Britain Together: A National Strategy for Neighbourhood Renewal*, London: Cabinet Office.

Spitzer, S. (1987) 'Security and Control in capitalist societies: the fetishism of security and the secret thereof', in J. Lowman, R. Menzies and T. S. Palys (eds.), *Transcarceration: Essays in the Sociology of Social Control*, 43–58, Aldershot: Gower.

Taylor, A. (1997) '"Arm's length but hands on". Mapping the new governance: the department of national heritage and cultural politics in Britain', *Public Administration*, 75: 441–66.

Tyler, T.R. and Kramer, R.M. (1996) 'Whither Trust?', in R.M. Kramer, and T.R. Tyler (eds.), 1–15, *Trust in Organisations: Frontiers of Theory and Research* London: Sage.

von Hirsch, A. (2000) 'The ethics of public television surveillance', this volume.

Wakefield, A. (2000) 'Situational crime prevention in mass private property', this volume.

Wilson, J. Q. and Kelling, G. (1982) 'Broken windows', *The Atlantic Monthly*, March: 29–37.

Young, J. (1999) *The Exclusive Society: Social Exclusion, Crime and Difference in Late Modernity*, London: Sage.

12

The New Criminologies of Everyday Life: Routine Activity Theory in Historical and Social Context[1]

David Garland

Criminological theory has adapted in interesting ways to the structural conditions of late modernity – conditions in which high crime rates are a normal social fact and the limited effectiveness of criminal justice is widely acknowledged. The most fundamental aspect of this development has been the shift in the discipline's focus away from theories of social deprivation (or relative deprivation) towards explanations couched in terms of social control and its deficits. 'Control' is the defining term of the new problematic – social control, self-control, situational control – and criminologies that are otherwise quite opposed nowadays share this common problem-space. We can see this clearly if we consider 'the new criminologies of everyday life'.[2]

The appearance of a revised edition of Marcus Felson's text *Crime and Everyday Life* (1998), originally published in 1994, offers an opportunity to consider the characteristics of this new criminological genre in a little more detail. Felson's book is particularly apposite for this purpose because in this new edition Felson has expanded his account to merge routine activity theory with the themes and insights of the other criminologies of everyday life, most notably situational crime prevention, lifestyle analysis, and rational choice theory. If there is a text that exemplifies this new genre, then this is undoubtedly it.

The acknowledged background to the new criminologies of everyday life – like their contrasting counterpart, the 'criminology of the other' – is the emergence, since the 1960s, of comparatively high levels of crime and violence as stable features of the social structure and culture of late modernity – levels that remain high despite the significant declines of recent years (see Garland,

---

[1] This discussion of Marcus Felson (1998) first appeared as part of a review essay (Garland 1999). It has been revised for publication in this collection.

[2] In Garland (1996) I discuss these 'criminologies of everyday life' together with their contradictory counterpart, the 'criminology of the other'.

1996). Felson's response to this, which I take to be typical of his genre, is adaptive, pragmatic and focused upon everyday social practices: we need to understand the ways in which our daily activities produce criminal opportunities and we need to invent routine precautions that will minimize these.

This, of course, is by no means the only possible response to the normality of high rates of crime. William Bennett's and his co-authors' recent book *Body Count: Moral Poverty and How to Win America's War Against Crime and Drugs* (1986) responds in a strikingly contrary manner by identifying an immoral culture as the 'root cause' of the 'crime epidemic' and calling for a concerted moralising effort, a renewal of religious faith, and drastic enhancements of penal and welfare controls. In rhetorical, political and criminological terms these two positions could not be more different. One response presents a 'criminology of the self', refusing to draw lines between offenders and the rest of us, characterizing criminals as rational individuals who respond to temptations and controls in much the same way as anyone else. The other revives the ancient 'criminology of the other', of the threatening outcast – Bennett and his colleagues talk of the 'superpredator' – who is deeply marked by moral deprivation and a profound lack of empathy and impulse control. One criminology de-dramatizes crime, seeks to allay disproportionate fears and promotes routine preventative action. The other demonizes the criminal, works to arouse popular fears and hostilities, and strives to excite popular support for drastic measures of control.[3] But both share a common situation (as responses to the pervasive crime problem and the limits of the criminal justice state), both share the new emphasis upon the enhancement of control (situational controls in one case, social and moral controls in other), and both represent significant shifts away from the liberal and conservative positions that characterized the earlier period of correctionalism.

Felson's criminology emphasizes the ways in which criminal opportunities are structured by, and arise out of, the recurring transactions and routines that characterize daily life. In his account, the 'chemistry of crime' can be reduced to the interaction of three vital elements – a likely offender, a suitable target, and the absence of a capable guardian against the offence (p. 53). The ways in which these elements are made to coincide in time and space is a function of our social arrangements and everyday routines. The commute to work, our leisure time activities; the flow of customers through a shopping mall; the daily passage of teenagers as they go to and from school or home; the rapid circulation of goods and cash – these are the patterned activities that make crime a built-in feature of our social organization.

In this account, offenders are no different from other individuals. Crime 'is very human' and 'ordinary people' do 'ordinary crimes' (p. 11). Offenders typically display no special motivation and no abnormal or deviant disposition: they merely respond, with the standard-issue degree of rationality, to the

---

[3] For a more detailed discussion of the Bennett volume, see Garland (1999).

mix of temptations and controls involved in specific situations. The key variable in explaining crime rates is therefore the extent to which the basic arrangements of social life do or do not facilitate crime events by regularly placing individuals in criminogenic situations. To borrow the language of economics, crime is a supply-side phenomenon – a consequence of the production and delivery of opportunities to commit offences. The massive increase in crime and violence that occurred in the 1960s and 70s – in the USA and elsewhere – was a direct consequence of post-war changes in the social ecology and recurring routines of everyday life. The new levels of mobility made possible by the automobile, the new temptations offered by masses of consumer goods, the diminishing presence of guardians as dense urban neighborhoods gave way to sprawling suburbs and married women moved into the workplace – these are the changes that brought about modern crime rates. And, to bring the story up to date, Felson in his second edition adds that it has been the development of technology and defensive measures (such as the use of electronic transfers instead of cash) and the growth of situational crime prevention (place managers, improved surveillance arrangements, etc.) that lie behind the recent successes in the effort to contain and reduce criminal events.

What would the sociology of knowledge say about this kind of text and the theoretical position that it develops? How are we to understand its emergence in the space and time of criminological discourse? I will argue that, whatever the strength of its truth claims – many of which are quite forceful – the criminology of everyday life should be understood as an adaptation to a social field in which high rates of crime have become a normal social fact. This is true in two respects. First of all, this style of analysis emerged in the wake of a dramatic historical transformation that made the relation between social ecology and crime rates stand out in bold relief. The production of criminal opportunities by routine activities could, in principle, have been identified on the basis of comparative study between different social areas (and, indeed, the social disorganization theory of the Chicago School did something of this kind). But it was the tremendous increase in crime levels, occurring between the mid-1960s and the mid-1970s, that made the importance of routine activities stand out in stark contrast. Secondly, as I will argue at greater length below, both the substance and the form of Felson's routine activity theory express an adaptation to a society in which high rates of crime have become part of the normal scheme of things. This adaptation is apparent in the theory's explanatory claims and practical prescriptions, but it is also, and perhaps most tellingly, revealed in the rhetorical style that it adopts – a style that Marcus Felson develops in its purest form.

I can best bring out these characteristics of routine activity by subjecting Felson's work to a stylistic comparison with the work of David Matza (1964;1969), which dates from a different historical period (prior to the crime boom) and espouses a very different relation to crime and deviance, but which adopts a style of inquiry that is actually very close to that of Felson. The use of

David Matza to think about Felson may seem a surprising choice. Matza's work doesn't feature at all in Felson's text or bibliography, and whatever memories and associations David Matza's name might trigger in the criminological consciousness – drift, existential mood, culture, identity – the concerns of routine activity and crime prevention are not prominent among them. Moreover Matza writes in a different criminological context, where the object of study is the offender and his relation to the law (and beyond that, to the culture) while Felson's concern is with crime events, criminogenic situations and ways in which social and economic life routinely supply criminal opportunities to those who choose to use them. But despite the unlikely nature of the pairing, I believe that Matza's work can throw light on Felson and his genre, revealing what it is that Felson is (and is not) doing, and pointing up how much has changed in the 30 years that lies between Matza's classic texts and the appearance of Felson's new approach.

Once the connection is made, one finds a whole series of themes and arguments that link Matza's work quite closely with that of Felson, so much so that Matza can be reinvented as an unacknowledged (and unwitting) forerunner. Both writers focus upon what Matza calls the 'the mundane delinquent', who is neither 'compulsive' nor 'committed' but instead a normal character who, on occasion, chooses to break the law. In the work of each, we find pathology replaced by pathos and differentiation replaced by a more nuanced and all-embracing account of normalcy. There is, in each, an emphasis upon the situational character of crime and delinquency, and upon the specific inducements and controls of the particular locale or mode of interaction. Both writers stress the generalized nature of deviance. Both point to the interdependencies that link 'mainstream' and 'deviant' culture, or legal and illegal activities, and both enjoy revealing the irony involved where our most cherished arrangements – freedom, mobility, affluence – give rise to the most unwanted results in the shape of crime and delinquency.

Matza and Felson share other traits too – a scepticism about correctionalism, a classical emphasis upon choice, a sense of the subtleties of the relationship between action and moral belief – but the most important continuity that links these two writers, and the most revealing, is their shared commitment to *naturalism* as a philosophy of science and a mode of inquiry. What is meant here by 'naturalism'? Matza (1969) defines naturalism as the commitment 'to remain true to the nature of the phenomenon under study or scrutiny'. It is a style of inquiry that prefers naturalistic observation to more abstracted modes of knowing – a philosophy that, however paradoxically, 'stands against all forms of philosophical generalization'. As Matza puts it, 'its loyalty is to the world with whatever measure of variety or universality happens to adhere' (p. 5) Naturalism's 'preference for concrete detail', its 'appreciation of density and variability', its 'dislike of the formal, the abstract, the artificial' (p. 9) make this a decidedly 'anti-philosophical philosophy' (p. 8). And, as Matza comments with evident approval, 'the fidelity of for matter-of-fact interventions and routine precautions. We need to build it into our habits and routines in the same undemonstrative way that preventative medicine has us wash our hands, brush our teeth, and clean the bathroom.

Frank Tannenbaum coined the phrase 'the dramatization of evil' to describe how we, as society, react to offending. Marcus Felson's project is the de-dramatization of crime. His goal is naturalistic understanding, as a basis for calm, routinized counter-measures. And if the book's style and substance epitomize the criminology of everyday life, so too do its practical proposals, which reproduce all the standard prescriptions of that genre (see generally Garland, 1996). The usual preference for situational adjustment over social engineering is clearly stated here: 'do not try to improve human character. You are certain to fail' and: 'Try to block crime in a practical, natural, and simple way, at low social and economic cost' (p. 166). So too is the irrelevance of the criminal justice state to the control of much criminal offending: we need to 'put criminal justice into smaller perspective' (p. 7). Crime control ought to become a generalized, de-differentiated activity, built into the routines and consciousness of all citizens: 'The best policy is to regard most strangers and even neighbors with a moderate dose of benign suspicion' (p. 43). Above all, it would no longer be monopolized by the state with its misguided political agendas and its lack of local knowledge:

Crime prevention strategies have been foolish and ineffective. Leadership fell into the hands of naive ideologies, first liberal and then conservative. The first proposed to reduce crime by trying to make government good to people, assuming they would be good in return. The pendulum then moved toward the equally naive position that a government bad to people will get them to be good in return. The issue is not how good or bad government is to people but whether public places are designed and organized to allow people to control their own environments informally' (p. 145).

book's explanations and practical proposals are often persuasive, and nt to a forceful restatement of social structure's role in the distribution me. But they will surely not pass uncriticized into the criminological Felson's rather monomaniacal focus on 'supply-side' issues of opportu-d control has the effect of silencing questions of motivation which have central focus for much criminological research and which are especially nt where offense-behavior appears unusually cruel or inhumane. who believe that cultural norms play an independent role in shaping and that these norms have changed with the coming of late moder-l be dismayed by Felson's resolute avoidance of such questions: 'The portant method is not teaching or building character, but rather oung people under some degree of supervision' (p. 24)... 'The United not psychologically or culturally more violent than other countries: just deliver worse injuries' (p. 34), and by his implicit assumption eralized propensity to criminal conduct is something of a constant in tory. Radicals will object that the theory represents an uncritical

naturalism to the empirical world has created a certain stress on the mundane, the matter-of-fact – even the vulgar' (p. 8).

It seems to me that Felson's work falls squarely within this tradition. His theoretical claims and his investigative method insist upon attention to detail and naturalistic description. Density and variability are key elements of his account of criminal events and criminological categories. In his account, 'all crime is local' (p. 75) and no two situations are ever altogether alike. His dislike of abstraction is registered on virtually every page, with his insistence upon being 'down to earth' (p. xii), on developing an analysis that doesn't 'move towards the clouds', treating crime as a 'tangible phenom-enon' (p. xii) and avoiding what he calls 'vague terms' such as 'social disor-ganization, anomie or social strain' (p. 27) in favor of 'precise and tangible concepts'. Even theoretical arguments with the immediacy of Wilson and Kelling's 'broken windows' or Skogan's 'spiral of decline' are to be accepted only 'so long as we do not let them draw us back into a sea of vagueness' (p. 133). As for more general theories, Felson is simply allergic to them. His slogan is, 'don't get fancy' (p. 167) and his advice to students (credited to his colleague and fellow naturalist Ronald Clarke) is 'do not worry about academic theories. Just go out and gather facts about crime from nature herself' (p. 166).

So Felson is writing in the naturalist mode, and that, as I will argue, has a certain social significance today. In contrast to David Matza's *poetic* naturalism – which was written in elegant prose, rich with intellectual allusion, and motivated by an existentialist concern to restore meaning to deviant conduct and celebrate the human freedom that deviance entailed – Felson offers what I would describe as a *prosaic* naturalism. He adopts an authorial style reminiscent of the Italian neo-realist cinema and films like De Sica's *The Bicycle Thief,* or perhaps the black and white, kitchen-sink naturalism of Sillitoe's *Saturday Night and Sunday Morning* – both of which portray crime and deviance with the same ordinariness and pathos that Felson seeks to evoke. Without drawing attention to itself, Felson's style of writing and his recurring rhetorical tropes perfectly mimic his substantive view of the world. His style is avowedly matter-of-fact, workaday, mundane, down to earth – indeed it is *artfully* so. Many of Felson's observations are so droll and humdrum as to be highly amusing. One suspects that behind the dead-pan delivery there lurks a broad indulgent smile, taking pleasure in the banal details of the human barnyard. On every page he stresses the quotidian ordinariness of it all. Time and time again he emphasizes that crime is less dramatic than people think; that offenders are mundane individuals, more to be pitied than feared; that despite our cultural stereotypes, the real world of crime lacks all charm, or daring, or any sustaining narrative interest. A few examples will illustrate what I mean.

On murder: 'Sherlock Holmes would have no interest whatsoever in most of the 22,076 murders reported in the US for 1994'. Murder should be regarded 'not as a crime but as an outcome'. Most murders are the result of a stupid little quarrel'(p. 3). 'Murder has two central features: a lethal weapon too close and a hospital too far' (p. 4).

On violent crime: 'Even violent crime is largely minor'.

On the consequences of offending: 'Offenders ... suffer more from the consequences of their own lifestyles than from the actions of public officials' (p. 10).

On crime and criminals: The criminal is typically 'a drunken fool' (p. 14), organized crime is 'not very businesslike' (p. 17), 'a common fight is rather a bore' (p. 64), juvenile gangs are 'very boring' (p. 17).

On the complexity of criminal causation: 'Opportunity makes the thief' (pp. 38, 48). 'People blunder into fights' (p. 66). 'Reducing the rewards [that offenders seek] is akin to eliminating the root causes of crime' (p. 180). And my personal favorite – borrowed by Felson from his brother Richard and concealing goodness knows what childhood memories – 'Big people hit little people' (p. 57).

The text is traced through with lovingly detailed descriptions of the most mundane preventative practices – the simpler the better. He tells us that 'to learn how to design out crime, it is best to get specific' (p.153) and that, of course, is precisely what he does. He deliberates about how high a fence should be in the back and on the side of a house, and, since the answer depends on the size of the surrounding garden, he discusses this as well. (*Answer*: 'A garden space of about 10 feet in the front, if not too bushy' turns out to be about right. It ' keeps people away from the fence, guiding them to the gate for legitimate business' pp. 153–4). He reports that he and a colleague were able to predict annual burglary rates from the weight of the lightest television set in the Sears catalog each year (p. 61) – a scientific project that is so delightfully and appealingly mundane that it could stand as an emblem of Felson's whole approach. (I have heard Professor Felson recount how he constructed a detailed steal-ability index by going through the Sears catalogue, item by item and calculating the price-to-weight ratio for each of the commodities.)

The *heroes* of Felson's account also share these same qualities of undemonstrative insight and robust common sense. He delights in stories about shopkeepers and security staff who come up with simple but ingenious methods of preventing crime – such as the 'clever merchant who learned to alternate the directions of hangers on the [garment] rack, so they locked when grabbed', or the security staff who solved the problem of unauthorized persons in hospital wards by locking a door and removing its handle (p. 150).

Felson repeatedly celebrates this practical knowledge and inventiveness, this small-scale ingenuity and practical wisdom. It is a human trait close to his

heart in the way that the subject's irrepressible capacity to choose wa centre of Matza's project. So too is the character type of the can-do tioner, whose engagement with the world is somehow more vivid tha the philosophizing professor. As for Felson's relation to the offender the quality of a rather weary tolerance and a mildly-expresse Offenders are low-skilled, low-energy, casually parasitic. They much daring or initiative, don't put in much effort, and they typic upon the carelessness of victims who offer them easy opportuniti naturalism that – unlike Matza's – avoids all trace of the outlaw r

I have emphasized Felson's discursive style and implied evalua they have a function in his work, which is to say they form part get us to think about crime in a particular way. The delibera merely felicitous) use of a prosaic rhetorical style – a style reinforces the theory's substantive claims – is a striking fea work. In its substantive arguments, the routine activity appr crime opportunities and crime events occur 'in the nature of being shocking aberrations or even unusual disruptions of of events, criminal incidents are widespread, constantly prising features of the social landscape. They are written things, as concomitants of the personal freedoms, affluen tarian arrangements that characterize liberal democraci 20th century. His presentational style says precisely message is that crime is nothing to get excited about. Its to it. What we must do is understand crime in disp removed from the drama and political posturing th nature. It is a feature of our way of life and we must w and when we can.

This exhortation to work at crime prevention is e of this story, because it is the one point at which slightest hint of passion. Murder, violence, drug-ga tunistic sex offenders – none of these enrage him to displacement as a reason to doubt the effective singled out for moral outrage. 'It is', he says, 'a as an excuse to hold back creativity in preventi interpret this mild but uncharacteristic outbu defence of his practitioner-heroes in response know-nothing theorists of the academy.

In the recent past, crime was always a s social dislocation or personal maladjustmer nothing more. It is a reality. A normal social terms, for its own sake, and not as a metap The problem of crime is cause for neither it: 'Criminology in the past has swung bet am arguing for something different: a no accommodation to the social structures of late modernity (render them a little less criminogenic, otherwise they're fine), that it too readily separates out questions of crime from questions of social justice, and that it fails to point to the dangers of commodification and mal-distribution of security that are liable to accompany a crime prevention strategy that depends so much upon private initiative rather than state provision.

But my concern here is not with the book's criminological value – rather, the claim I am making here is a claim in the sociology of knowledge. I am arguing that Felson's work – and by extension that of the whole genre I have termed the criminologies of everyday life – can be understood as responses to, and the product of, a particular kind of social organization: one in which high rates of crime have become a normal social fact. The social structure of late modernity 'delivers' crime opportunities in a regular, recurring, widespread manner, and does so in a way that is qualitatively different from the social structure of the first two thirds of the 20th century. In that earlier period, criminological inquiry assumed that crime was an aberrational phenomenon, an interruption to the normal course of events, and sought to understand what was wrong with the individuals responsible. In the late 20th century it is harder to think of crime in this way. Our knowledge of crime's generality makes it clear that there may be nothing special about offenders, and nothing unusual about the occurrence of criminal events.[4] Criminology's usual concern with the question of individual differentiation (and sometimes group differentiation) thus begins to give way to a concern with the structural generation of the mass of criminal events.

My claim, then, is that Felson's work is itself socially structured, or at least located within a social field that has structured its possibility and its reception. It is a criminology made possible, desirable and relevant by identifiable features of late modern social organization. Felson's argument is that today's social structures routinely produce crime events, or at least 'supply opportunities' and 'produce chances' for crime – which, with the addition of a 'likely offender' result in actual offences. I want to make a related claim which is that these same social structures also supply the opportunity and produce the chances for a new form of *criminology* – and Marcus Felson (for whatever biographical, institutional and intellectual reasons) has turned out to be the 'likely offender' who has exploited that opportunity. Not that this 'just happened'. Despite his anti-theoretical posture, Felson didn't 'go out and gather facts about crime from nature herself'. That part of Felson's naturalism is bogus and self-contradictory, as are all philosophical positions that claim to be 'anti-philosophical'. Felson, together with others such as Ronald Clarke – has clearly embarked upon a theoretical reorientation that would shift criminology's object of study from the criminal individual or disorganized group to

---

[4] For a discussion of the evidence of the widespread prevalence of criminal conduct, see Gabor (1994).

the criminal event and the criminogenic situation. My point is not to deny them credit for this intellectual undertaking – merely to point to the social conditions that facilitated it. This, after all, is quite a fitting application of Felson's theory to its own intellectual production. If 'opportunity makes the thief' why wouldn't it also make the theorist?

REFERENCES

Bennett, W.J., DiIulio, J., and Walters, J.P. (1996) *Body Count: Moral Poverty and How to Win America's War Against Crime and Drugs*, New York, Simon and Schuster 1996.

Felson, M. (1998) *Crime and Everyday Life* (2nd ed.), Thousand Oaks CA: Pine Forge.

Gabor, T. (1994) *Everybody Does It: Crime by the Public*, Toronto, Toronto University Press.

Garland, D. (1996) 'The limits of the sovereign state: strategies of crime control in contemporary society', *The British Journal of Criminology* 36:1.

—— (1997) 'Governmentality and the problem of crime', *Theoretical Criminology* 1: 173-214.

—— (1999) 'The commonplace and the catastrophic: interpretations of crime in late modernity', in *Theoretical Criminology* 3: 353-364.

—— (forthcoming) *The Culture of Control: Crime and Social Order in Late Modernity*, Oxford: Oxford University Press.

Matza, D. (1964) *Delinquency and Drift*, New York: Wiley.

—— (1969) *Becoming Deviant*, Englewood Cliffs, NJ: Prentice Hall.

PARTICIPANTS IN
THE CAMBRIDGE COLLOQUIA ON
'SITUATIONAL CRIME PREVENTION – ETHICAL AND SOCIAL ISSUES'

January 3–5, 1997 – Robinson College

Andrew Ashworth
AE Bottoms
Ronald Clarke
Stanley Cohen
Antony Duff
Paul Ekblom
John Gardner
David Garland
Tim Hope
Mike Hough
Richard Jones
John Kleinig
Nicola Lacey
Gloria Laycock
Sandra Marshall
Marina Myhre

Kate Painter
Ken Pease
Paul Rock
Clifford Shearing
Jonathan Simon
ATH Smith
David Smith
Richard Sparks
Nick Tilley
Michael Tonry
Andrew von Hirsch
Martin Wasik
P-O Wikström
Paul Wiles
Lucia Zedner

October 14–16, 1999 – Fitzwilliam College

AE Bottoms
Elizabeth Burney
Ronald Clarke
Adam Crawford
Janet Foster
Loraine Gelsthorpe
Benjamin Goold
Kevin Gray
Tim Hope
Richard Jones
Vicky Kemp
John Kleinig
Amanda Matravers
Jon Olafsson
Kate Painter

Ken Pease
Sandra Marshall
Robert Reiner
Paul Roberts
Paul Rock
Joanna Shapland
Clifford Shearing
David Smith
Richard Sparks
Michael Tonry
Andrew von Hirsch
Beatrice von Silva Tarouca
Alison Wakefield
P-O Wikström

Index

Printed in the United Kingdom
by Lightning Source UK Ltd.
104473UKS00002B/35-38